# Tests and Measurements in Child Development: Handbook II

Volume 2

Orval G. Johnson

# Tests and Measurements in Child Development: Handbook II

## Volume 2

 Jossey-Bass Publishers
San Francisco · Washington · London · 1976

TESTS AND MEASUREMENTS IN CHILD DEVELOPMENT: HANDBOOK II
Volume 2
by Orval G. Johnson

Copyright © 1976 by: Jossey-Bass, Inc., Publishers
615 Montgomery Street
San Francisco, California 94111
&
Jossey-Bass Limited
44 Hatton Garden
London EC1N 8ER

Library of Congress Catalogue Card Number LC 76-11890

International Standard Book Number ISBN 0-87589-279-5

Manufactured in the United States of America


JACKET DESIGN BY WILLI BAUM


FIRST EDITION

Code 7606

The Jossey-Bass
Behavioral Science Series

# Preface

*Tests and Measurements in Child Development: Handbook II* is the second of two collections designed to keep researchers, evaluators, and clinicians up-to-date on the most recent developments in unpublished measures of child behavior. Both the size of the task of compiling the two volumes of *Handbook II* and the length of the final collection itself greatly exceeded our expectations. *Handbook I* and *Handbook II* combined provide access to over twelve hundred unpublished measures. Of these, about nine hundred are contained in *Handbook II*, although it covers a slightly shorter time span than *Handbook I* (nine years as opposed to ten years). The difference in the number of measures included in the two handbooks is attributable to an increase in age coverage (from birth to twelve years, to birth to eighteen years) in *Handbook II*, a search of more journals (148 as opposed to 53), and the greatly expanded activity in child research during the last decade.

Although some measurement procedures, such as "intelligence" testing of children, are being criticized by laymen and professionals, the need for appropriate assessment and evaluation procedures and tools remains. Today more than ever before, focused instruments are needed to assess specific changes in behavior and to diagnose individual characteristics and traits. More broadly, measures are needed to evaluate psychological and educational behavior-change studies, to plan training and educational strategies, and to assess the effects of ameliorative and corrective programs. The research trend toward tighter specification of objectives requires a correspondingly precise definition of measurement options.

ix

I am indebted to my professional colleagues from many disciplines who kindly provided their measures and descriptions, and whose response, interest, and willing participation make me proud to identify myself with them.

The dedicated, energetic, and conscientious staff members of the Child Measurement Project were essential to the production of this book. Burt Dwyre's organization, sense of humor, and willingness to take on any task and carry it out efficiently were extraordinary assets to the project. Nina Johnson's journalistic skills expedited the whole search and editorial process. Mary Lawton's library skills were likewise valuable. Janna Hughes typed reams, kept voluminous records, and, most importantly, organized the office impressively.

I am grateful for the cheerful help provided by the administrators and staffs of the following libraries: Norlin Library, University of Colorado (with special thanks to Marie Campbell); Penrose Library, University of Denver; and Denison Library, University of Colorado School of Medicine.

Finally, I am indebted to James Bommarito for providing numerous leads to much useful material; to Ingrid and Lisa Johnson for contributing their typing skills during the last stages of the project and for helping to tie up the inevitable loose ends; to Laura and Kurt Johnson for valuable clerical help; and to the superintendents of the Weld County (Colorado) Board of Cooperative Educational Services (BOCES) for their enlightened appreciation of the importance of the research process.

The project was made possible by Grant No. 1 R01 MH23875 from the National Institute of Mental Health.

*Boulder, Colorado*                                                          Orval G. Johnson
*July 1976*

# Contents

# Volume 2

# Tests and Measurements in Child Development: Handbook II

### Volume 2

# Category 4

## Self-Concept

These instruments are designed to measure the child's feelings about himself. Some of them are concerned with the general self-concept, while others focus on specific aspects or components of the self-concept, such as body image and capacity for responsibility. Some of these measures deal with the child's self-concept in various roles, such as that of student.

# ABOUT ME

AUTHOR: James Parker

AGE: 8 to 14 years

VARIABLE: Self-concept

TYPE OF MEASURE: Rating scale

SOURCE FROM WHICH MEASURE MAY BE OBTAINED: James Parker, Box 374, Cordele, Georgia 31015. Send self-addressed stamped envelope.

DESCRIPTION OF MEASURE: This scale is designed to appraise the following five areas of the self-concept as inferred from the self-reported behavior of school children: the self, the self in relation to others, the self as achieving, the self in school, and the physical self. The items in the scale are arranged so that those lettered A tap the self in school; B, the self as achieving; C, the self; D, the physical self; and E, the self in relation to others. The scoring system suggested is summing the numerical values of the individual's ratings. In this scheme low scores indicate positive self-concepts, and high scores reveal predominately negative self-concepts. It is also possible to obtain separate scores for each of the five areas of the self-concept.

As examples, the first ten items of the thirty-item scale are given below. They are to be answered on a 5-point response scale from "I'm friendly" to "I'm not so friendly."

| | |
|---|---|
| 1A. I'm good in school work. | I'm not good in school work. |
| 2B. Mostly I have good ideas. | My ideas are poor. |
| 3C. I'm a worthwhile person. | I'm not a worthwhile person. |
| 4D. I'm pretty strong. | I'm not too strong. |
| 5E. Most people trust me. | Most people don't trust me. |
| 6A. Teachers like me pretty well. | Teachers don't like me too much. |
| 7B. I can do most things well. | I do very few things well. |
| 8C. I'm a happy person. | I'm an unhappy person. |
| 9D. I'm healthy. | I'm not too healthy. |
| 10E. I'm popular. | I'm not too popular. |

RELIABILITY AND VALIDITY: This informal device was not rigorously standardized. It was presented to thirty-one sixth graders on a test-retest basis, and an agreement of 64.2 percent between the two administrations was found.

BIBLIOGRAPHY:

Parker, J. "The Relationship of Self-Report to Inferred Self-Concept." *Educational and Psychological Measurement,* 1966, *26,* 691-700.

# ABOUT ME AND MY SCHOOL WORK

AUTHOR: Edward Earl Gotts

AGE: Elementary-school years

VARIABLE: Arithmetic self-concept; academic self-concept

TYPE OF MEASURE: Questionnaire with self-ratings

SOURCE FROM WHICH MEASURE MAY BE OBTAINED: Edward Earl Gotts, Appalachia Educational Laboratory, P.O. Box 1348, Charleston, West Virginia 25325. Cost: $1.00 for postage and handling.

DESCRIPTION OF MEASURE: As the child encounters new challenges and opportunities, he comes to think of himself in relationship to them. School is such an opportunity and challenge. Presumably the child develops a concept of himself in relation to school in general (academic self-concept) and with regard to particular subject context domains (arithmetic self concept). In field studies prior to developing this measure, it was found that children spontaneously conceptualize the self in these areas in terms of (1) amount of accomplishment, (2) ability to perform competitively with peers, (3) liking for the subject, (4) progress as judged by the teacher, (5) how smart the teacher thinks the child is, and (6) whether the child is able to complete correctly particular tasks (e.g., particular kinds of arithmetic problems). The items are written along the lines of these natural self-conceptions of children. The test is individually or group-administered. Directions focus on teaching the child first to use a 7-point scale of happy faces through sad faces as a physical analogy for estimating the feeling response evoked by each item. This format allows testing of nonreaders individually. After two practice items, the scored questions begin. Total score for the first twenty-six items is academic self-concept. Arithmetic self-concept is measured by the next twelve items plus six questions from the first twenty-six. The thirty-eight questions require 10 to 20 minutes for completion. The final twelve items only are for grades 4 to 6; these items are different for grades 1 to 3. A very, very happy response is scored 1, through a very, very unhappy response, scored 7. Thus, a low score indicates a more favorable self-concept. No norms are available; local norms would be advisable in any event. The instrument has been used as an evaluation device in conjunction with a National Science Foundation project designed to improve the child's self-concept through a new approach to mathematics education.

As examples, ten selected items from the thirty-eight are given below. The child answers on a 7-point "faces" scale ranging from "very, very happy" to "very, very unhappy." The first twenty-six items are numbered by single alphabet letters; the last twelve are numbered by double alphabet letters.

A. You have 20 new arithmetic problems to finish before tomorrow. (How feel?)
B. You have to read 20 pages from a story book before tomorrow. (How feel?)
C. You have to learn 20 new spelling words before tomorrow. (How feel?)
D. You have to draw 20 small pictures before tomorrow. (How feel?)
E. You have to learn 20 new science facts before tomorrow. (How feel?)

R. Your teacher compares your daily work in science to the science work that you did earlier this year. (How does this comparison make you feel?)

S. Your teacher compares your daily work in reading to the reading work that you did earlier this year. (How does this comparison make you feel?)

T. Your teacher compares your daily work in art to the art work that you did earlier this year. (How does this comparison make you feel?)

CC. The teacher asks you to show the class how to multiply by 8s and by 9s. (How feel?)

JJ. The teacher asks how many children were out during recess if there are four rooms with 29 children each and one room with 28 children. (How feel?)

RELIABILITY AND VALIDITY: Prototypes of the arithmetic self-concept items were administered orally to the four 7- to 9-year-olds with the lowest arithmetic achievement in their school. Each child's arithmetic self-concept became more favorable ($p <$ .01) as he progressed through a successful remedial program (Dil and Gotts, 1971). Inner-city fourth ($N = 41$) and fifth ($N = 22$) graders, whose achievement lagged behind national norms by about one year, participated in an experimental math curriculum, project SEED. An equal number served as control $S$s from each grade. These children, who attended three different schools, completed the thirty-eight-item instrument (Gotts, 1971). Internal consistency reliability for academic self-concept was *alpha* = .87; for arithmetic self-concept (the twelve items only), *alpha* = .85. Stability coefficients over three months (control $S$s only) were: academic, $r = .78$, twelve-item arithmetic, $r = .66$. Validity coefficients between arithmetic self-concept and six standard ability and achievement measures ranged from .46 to .57 (all $r$s, $p < .01$). Academic self-concept had consistently smaller coefficients, .03 to .29, in relation to the standard measures.

For the experimental $S$s, participation in the program significantly reduced all six correlations between arithmetic self-concept and the standard measures (all six differences exceeded $Z$ values of 2.0). In a third study (Gotts, 1973), 273 different fourth and fifth graders from six inner-city schools participated in project SEED. A comparable control group was selected. The eighteen-item arithmetic self-concept scale was internally consistent—*alpha* = .92, mean = 48.53 for 518 $S$s; reading self-concept—five-item *alpha* = .80, $M = 13.37$; five-item spelling *alpha* = .81, $M = 12.73$; five-item art *alpha* = .78, $M = 11.82$; science *alpha* = .85, $M = 16.44$; all thirty-eight items *alpha* = .96, $M = 102.88$. Mean arithmetic self-concept of control $S$s did not change over the school year; academic self-concept declined slightly. Project SEED $S$s become more favorable in arithmetic self-concept ($p = .0039$) and were unaffected in self-concept areas of reading, spelling, science, and overall, although art self-concept became less favorable ($p = .0042$). Stabilities among control $S$s over an entire school year for the various self-concept components were: arithmetic (.46), reading (.45), spelling (.46), art (.40), science (.43), overall (.46). These are about equivalent to the median intercorrelations of the subscales themselves. This is not simply a measure of general self-concept. Concurrent correlations of the components with the Piers-Harris are low (.04 to .34). Arithmetic self-concept is the most highly related to the Piers-Harris.

BIBLIOGRAPHY:

Dil, N., and Gotts, E. E. "Improvement of Arithmetic Self-Concept Through Combined Positive Reinforcement, Peer Interaction, and Sequential Curriculum." *Journal of School Psychology,* 1971, *9,* 462-472.

Gotts, E. E. "An Arithmetic Competency Measure of Self-Concept for Elementary
    School Children." Mimeographed. Report to National Science Foundation,
    1971.
Gotts, E. E. "Self-Concept Effects of Project SEED upon Low-Achieving Elementary
    School Pupils." Mimeographed. Report to National Science Foundation, 1973.

---

## BLEDSOE SELF-CONCEPT SCALE

AUTHOR: Joseph C. Bledsoe

AGE: 7 to 13 years

VARIABLE: Self-esteem and self-ideal

TYPE OF MEASURE: Adjective checklist

SOURCE FROM WHICH MEASURE MAY BE OBTAINED: Joseph C. Bledsoe, Box
325 Aderhold Hall, University of Georgia, Athens, Georgia 30602.

DESCRIPTION OF MEASURE: The Bledsoe Self-Concept Scale consists of thirty descriptive adjectives; respondents are asked to check on a 3-point scale to each adjective,
"This is the way I am" and "This is the way I would like to be." Eighteen adjectives
are scored positively, twelve negatively. Ten adjectives each are drawn from evaluation,
potency, and activity dimensions (six positive and four negative in each dimension).
The subject checks as characteristic of himself "Nearly always," "About half the
time," or "Just now and then," with positive adjectives scored 3, 2, and 1, respectively, and negative adjectives reversed. The scale was slightly modified from Lipsitt's
adaptation of Bills' Index of Adjustment and Values.
    The adjectives in the scale are as follows (negative ones are asterisked): friendly,
cold*, brave, small*, helpful, honest, cheerful, active, jealous*, quiet*, strong, a good
sport, mean*, lazy*, poor*, smart, popular, useful, clean, kind, selfish*, dull*, healthy,
timid*, slow*, faithful, lonely*, polite, talkative, happy.

RELIABILITY AND VALIDITY: Test-retest reliabilities (two-week interval) ranged
from .66 to .81 for the ages 8 to 14. Correlations with anxiety scales run consistently
negative, ranging from −.30 to −.46. For boys, correlations are positive with intelligence (California IQ) and achievement (CAT) .43 (fourth-grade total battery, $N = 65$),
and .39 (sixth grade, $N = 76$). Correlation with California Tests of Personality Self-
Adjustment Scale is .39 ($N = 56$, fifth-grade pupils).

BIBLIOGRAPHY:

Bills, R. E., Vance, E. L., and McLean, O. S. "An Index of Adjustment and Values."
    *Journal of Consulting Psychology,* 1951, *15,* 257-261.
Bledsoe, J. C. "Self-Concepts of Children and Their Intelligence, Achievement,

Interests, and Anxiety." *Journal of Individual Psychology,* 1964, *20,* 55-58.

Bledsoe, J. C. "Sex Differences in Self-Concept: Fact or Artifact?" *Psychological Reports,* 1973, *32,* 1253-1254.

Lipsitt, L. P. "A Self-Concept Scale for Children and its Relationship to the Children's Form of the Manifest Anxiety Scale." *Child Development,* 1958, *29,* 463-472.

---

# BODY-IMAGE IDENTIFICATION TEST

AUTHOR: Eleanor Bell Gottesman

AGE: Boys 8 to 12 years; boys and girls 13 to 17 years

VARIABLE: Feelings of masculinity-femininity as they relate to body image

TYPE OF MEASURE: A quantitative projective test

SOURCE FROM WHICH MEASURE MAY BE OBTAINED: Eleanor Bell Gottesman, 1 West 72nd Street, New York, New York 10023.

DESCRIPTION OF MEASURE: This test consists of seven outline drawings of the anterior view of the human body, seven drawings of faces, seven of shoulders, and seven of hips (twenty-eight in all), each on a 4 X 7-inch white card and each drawing differing from the next one in the series on a continuum according to an exact scale. The drawings differentiate qualities thought to be feminine and masculine physical attributes: curve of eyebrow, direction of eye glance, amount of eyelash, shape and fullness of lips, width of shoulders, waist size, and hip size. There were no genitalia. The only changes in the figures from most masculine to most feminine are those described above. Questions asked are: "Which is most nearly like you?" "Which would you rather be like?" and others related to the separate body parts using objective methods to evaluate subjective feelings. Additional qualitative material is obtained through observing nonverbal language and spontaneous verbal language. This test is administered to one person at a time but could be administered to a group. It takes only a few minutes to administer and to interpret.

RELIABILITY AND VALIDITY: The test was administered to and validated on four groups or samples: (1) emotionally disturbed males aged 8 to 11 (placed in special schools and in residential centers), (2) normal males aged 8 to 11 (attending regular classes in public schools), (3) slow learners—males aged 13 to 17 (in special classes for slow learners), and (4) slow learners—females aged 13 to 17 (in special classes for slow learners). Differences (*chi*-square) were found between normal males and disturbed males at the .02 and .05 levels. Male slow learners differed from female slow learners on the .05, .02, .01, and .001 levels. There were significant differences on eight criteria measuring body-image feelings unconsciously or consciously but subjectively experienced and on an exact scale.

BIBLIOGRAPHY:

Gottesman, E. B., and Caldwell, W. E. "The Body-Image Identification Test: A Quantitative Projective Technique to Study an Aspect of Body Image." *Journal of Genetic Psychology*, 1966, *108*, 19-33.

---

## BODY-SIZE-CONCEPT TEST AND BODY-IMAGE TEST

AUTHOR: Frederick A. Mulhauser

AGE: 4 to 6 years

VARIABLE: Concept of body size and body image

TYPE OF MEASURE: Test

SOURCE FROM WHICH MEASURE MAY BE OBTAINED: Fred A. Mulhauser, Department of Physical Education, Wayne State University, Detroit, Michigan 48202.

DESCRIPTION OF MEASURE: The Body-Size-Concept Test consists of triads of schematic body parts depicting heads, torsos, arms, and legs. There are sizes for each of the body parts. The sizes are weighted for scoring purposes: 3 points for large, 2 points for medium, and 1 point for small. The sizes correspond to the largest, middle, and smallest size figures used in the Body-Image Test. Scores for each subject range from 6 to 18 and are obtained by adding the score for each body part selected. The Body-Size-Concept testing procedures are patterned after the techniques used by Katcher and Levin (1955). The subjects are presented with the unassembled triads of schematic body parts and asked to "build" a boy (girl) like himself (herself). After the subject has selected and assembled the six body parts to form his (her) "body," the score is calculated by adding the scores for each of the body parts chosen. The materials for the Body-Image Test consist of two sets of ten identical cutout figures, one for males, another for females. The figures are graduated in size, the largest being 12 inches in height with each successive one decreased in size by 5 percent.

The Body-Image testing is completed by the following procedure. The set of ten figures, which are mounted on a piece of poster board, spaced ½ inch apart and arranged according to size, are placed on a table in front of the subject. The largest figure is on the subject's left and the smallest on the right. The largest figure has a value of 10, and there is a decremental value of 1 for each figure in descending order down to the smallest figure, which has a value of 1. The following standard procedure is used for testing each subject. With the subject seated and facing the figures the examiner states: "We are going to play a game. See all these boys (girls). They are all 5 years old. Some are big and some are small and some are in between just like real 5-year-olds. There is no right or wrong answer; just pick out the one which is most like you. Now show me the one you would like to be." The figure values for the subject's selection of his perceived body image (PBI) and desired body image (DBI) are recorded by the examiner. These values do not appear on the figures. The score is the number of positions changed from the PBI to the DBI. The maximum score is 9.

RELIABILITY AND VALIDITY: Subjects for the study were fifty-four boys and girls attending kindergarten classes. The correlation coefficients for the Body-Image Test with the space-utilization measures were not significant ($p = .25$). However, an examination of the frequencies of positions changed between the perceived body image (PBI) and the desired body image (DBI) reveals that 40 percent of the $S$s made only a 30-percent change in position. Further, the mean magnitude of change was 4.5, and this indicates that 54 percent of the $S$s made a 40-percent change in position. Eighteen of the $S$s, or 33 percent, changed only one or two positions. Adams and Caldwell (1963) found that normal children tended to make less change in position than retarded children and that when a change is made between PBI and DBI the disturbed children tend to make a change of greater magnitude. There was no significant difference for the body-image score between boys and girls. The correlation coefficients for the Body-Size Test with the space-utilization variables are not significant. The distribution of the frequencies of the scores for the Body-Size Test indicate that most of the $S$s chose to assemble the larger figures. Of the fifty $S$s, twenty-nine had composite scores above the mean of 13.4, while fifteen $S$s had the highest possible score of 18. These results suggest the functioning of social learning rather than the degree of success the child experiences in his use of space. There was no significant difference between the mean scores of boys and girls on the present Body-Size Test, but the study by Katcher and Levin (1955) showed sex differences.

BIBLIOGRAPHY:

Katcher, A., and Levin, M. M. "Children's Conception of Body Size." *Child Development,* 1955, *26,* 103-110.

Mulhauser, F. A. "An Exploratory Study of Relationships of Space Utilization with Selected Dimensions of Behavior in Children Age Five." Unpublished doctoral dissertation. University of Michigan, Ann Arbor, 1970.

Mulhauser, F. A. "An Exploratory Study of Relationships of Space Utilization with Selected Dimensions of Behavior in Children Age Five." *Research Quarterly,* 1972, *43,* 47-54.

---

# CHILD TASK/SOCIAL RELATIONS COMPETENCE SCALE (TSRCS)

AUTHOR: George Thomas

AGE: Grades 3 to 12

VARIABLE: Task/social-relations competence

TYPE OF MEASURE: Self-rating scale

SOURCE FROM WHICH MEASURE MAY BE OBTAINED: Regional Institute of Social Welfare Research, Tucker Hall, University of Georgia, Athens, Georgia 30602.

DESCRIPTION OF MEASURE: The TSRCS measures child task and social-relations competence and was designed for use with institutionalized children. Modifications are easily made for use with other child populations. The scale is composed of five subscales: Task Subscale (15 items), sample item: "I am better than most kids at playing games." School Mate Subscale (8 items), sample item: "Kids in my class are always picking on me." Cottage Mate Subscale (8 items), sample item: "Most of the kids I live with like me a lot." Teacher Subscale (7 items), sample item: "I get along very well with my teachers." Cottage Parent Subscale (8 items), sample item: "I can always tell my cottage parent(s) my problems." Response categories ("like me" or "not like me") are scored 1 if reflecting high assessment of competence, 0 if not, resulting in a total scale score ranging from 0 to 46. In practice the scale was administered to groups of children and normally took no more than 20 minutes to complete. Items were read aloud (grades 3 to 8 only), and time was permitted for children to ask questions and clear up ambiguities before responding. Less than .5 percent of all tested children failed to score all items satisfactorily.

RELIABILITY AND VALIDITY: The scale has been administered to 2,268 different children in Georgia, grades 3 through 12, including 1,243 institutionalized neglected/dependent children in thirty-two institutions (1972), 1,025 noninstitutionalized children in forty-seven classrooms in seven schools (1973), and, as a retest, 857 institutionalized children in nineteen institutions one year following initial administration. Internal consistency for the total scale using data from 845 institutionalized children is .80 per Kuder-Richardson formula 20. Subscale/total scale product-moment correlations are: Task (.81), School Mates (.75), Cottage Mates (.77), Teacher (.77), and Cottage Parents (.75). A principal components factor analysis with orthogonal rotations confirmed the scale's structure (only three of forty-six items loaded above .30 on more than one factor), reproducing the subscales as originally ordered. ACOVA results for test-retest data for 426 children in eighteen institutions are significant (F = 6.125, $p <$ .05), indicating the scale's ability to discriminate between populations. Difference of means tests performed on total scale scores for such groups of a total sample of 1,753 institutionalized/noninstitutionalized children, controlling for family income level, school grade, and institutional status, all were highly significant, further indicating that the scales discriminate.

Criterion validity was established by product-moment correlations between children's TSRCS Task and School Mate Subscale scores and classroom peer sociometric ratings (using standardized forms) of task/social-relations competency. Correlations were significant beyond the .05 level in all cases for a sample of 457 sociometrically rated children. Correlated tests or test-retest data ($N = 875$) further indicate the sensitivity of the task and school-related subscale's ability to measure change (Task Subscale: t = 1.80, $p <$ .05; School Mate Subscale: t = 5.40, $p <$ .01; Teacher Subscale: t = 2.30, $p <$ .05).

BIBLIOGRAPHY:

Thomas, G. *A Baseline Evaluation of Child Caring Institutions in Georgia.* Athens, Georgia: Regional Institute of Social Welfare Research, 1973.

Thomas, G. *The Effectiveness of Community-Oriented Institutions for Department Dependent/Neglected Children.* Athens, Georgia: Regional Institute of Social Welfare Research, 1975.

---

## COOPERSMITH BEHAVIOR RATING FORM FOR APPRAISING ASSURED AND CONFIDENT BEHAVIORS

AUTHOR: Stanley Coopersmith

AGE: 9 years to adult

VARIABLE: Self-esteem

TYPE OF MEASURE: Rating scale

SOURCE FROM WHICH MEASURE MAY BE OBTAINED: Self-Esteem Institute, 1736 Stockton Street, San Francisco, California 94133. Cost: $27 per 100 copies.

DESCRIPTION OF MEASURE: This rating scale consists of thirteen items in which a child is rated by somebody else on a scale from 1 to 5. The first ten items provide an appraisal of behaviors that are associated with poise, assurance, and self-thrust. They include reactions to new situations and failure reactions to criticism and failure, self-depreciation, and hesitation to express opinions publicly. The last three items provide an index of behaviors that are frequently defensive in nature, such as bragging, domination or bullying, and attention seeking.

As examples, the first two items of the scale are given below.

1. Does this child adapt easily to new situations, feel comfortable in new settings, enter easily into new activities?
   always      usually      sometimes      seldom      never
2. Does this child hesitate to express his opinions, as evidenced by extreme caution, failure to contribute, or subdued manner in speaking situations?
   always      usually      sometimes      seldom      never

RELIABILITY AND VALIDITY: None

BIBLIOGRAPHY:

Lindskold, S., and Tedeschi, J. T. "Self-Esteem and Sex as Factors Affecting Influence-ability." *British Journal of Social and Clinical Psychology,* 1971, *10,* 114-122.

*Prepared by Orval G. Johnson*

## COOPERSMITH SELF-ESTEEM INVENTORY (SEI)

AUTHOR: Stanley Coopersmith

AGE: 9 years to adult

VARIABLE: Self-esteem

TYPE OF MEASURE: Attitude questionnaire

SOURCE FROM WHICH MEASURE MAY BE OBTAINED: Self-Esteem Institute, 1736 Stockton Street, San Francisco, California 94133.

DESCRIPTION OF MEASURE: There are two forms of the Self-Esteem Inventory. Form A consists of fifty-eight items that make up five subscales as follows: General Self (twenty-six items), Social Self-Peers (eight items), Home-Parents (eight items), Lie Scale (eight items), and School-Academic (eight items). The subscales do not have to be scored separately, with the exception of the Lie Scale. Form B is briefer, taking about half of the administration time of Form A, but it is not broken down into sub-scales. The author provides overall norms for male and female adolescents aged 9 to 15, and for young adults.

As examples, the first eight of the fifty-eight items of Form A are given below.

|  | *Like Me* | *Unlike Me* |
|---|---|---|
| 1. I spend a lot of time daydreaming. | | |
| 2. I'm pretty sure of myself. | | |
| 3. I often wish I were someone else. | | |
| 4. I'm easy to like. | | |
| 5. My parents and I have a lot of fun together. | | |
| 6. I never worry about anything. | | |
| 7. I find it very hard to talk in front of the class. | | |
| 8. I wish I were younger. | | |

RELIABILITY AND VALIDITY: The total scores of Forms A and B correlate .86. The author points out that Form B was based on an item analysis of Form A and includes those twenty-five items that show the highest item-total score relationships of scores obtained with Form A. Current reliability and validity data are reported in the monthly Self-Esteem Institute Newsletter.

BIBLIOGRAPHY:

Coopersmith, S. *The Antecedents of Self-Esteem.* San Francisco: Freeman, 1967.

Fishman, C. A. and Fishman, D. B. "Maternal Correlates of Self-Esteem and Overall Adjustment in Children with Birth Defects." *Child Psychiatry and Human Development,* 1970, *1,* 255-265.

Fishman, C. A. and Fishman, D. B. "Emotional, Cognitive, and Interpersonal Confrontation Among Children with Birth Defects." *Child Psychiatry and Human Development,* 1971, *2,* 92-101.

Flammer, D. P. and Matas, L. "An Exploratory Investigation of Three Self-Other Orientation Measures." *Journal of Personality Assessment,* 1972, *36,* 447-450.

Kokenes, B. "Grade-Level Differences in Factors of Self-Esteem." *Developmental Psychology*, 1974, *10*, 954-958.

Larsen, S. C., Parker, R., and Jorjorian, S. "Differences in Self-Concept of Normal and Learning-Disabled Children." *Perceptual and Motor Skills*, 1973, *37*, 510.

Michael, J. J., Plass, A., and Lee, Y. B. "A Comparison of the Self-Report and the Observed Report in the Measurement of the Self-Concept: Implications for Construct Validity." *Educational and Psychological Measurement*, 1973, *33*, 433-439.

Prytula, R. E. and Thompson, N. D. "Analysis of Emotional Indicators in Human Figure Drawings as Related to Self-Esteem." *Perceptual and Motor Skills*, 1973, *37*, 795-802.

Purkey, W. W., Cage, B. N., and Graves, W. "The Florida Key: A Scale to Infer Learner Self-Concept." *Educational and Psychological Measurement*, 1973, *33*, 979-984.

Richmond, B. O. and White, W. F. "Predicting Teachers' Perceptions of Pupil Behavior." *Measurement and Evaluation in Guidance*, 1971, *4*, 71-78.

Simon, W. E. "Some Sociometric Evidence for Validity of Coopersmith's Self-Esteem Inventory." *Perceptual and Motor Skills*, 1972, *34*, 93-94.

Spatz, K. C. and Johnston, J. O. "Internal Consistency of the Coopersmith Self-Esteem Inventory." *Educational and Psychological Measurement*, 1973, *33*, 875-876.

Weinstein, L. "The Zoomer Class: Initial Results." *Exceptional Children*, 1971, *38*, 58-63.

White, W. F. and Richmond, B. O. "Perceptions of Self and of Peers by Economically Deprived Black and Advantaged White Fifth Graders." *Perceptual and Motor Skills*, 1970, *30*, 533-534.

*Prepared by Orval G. Johnson*

---

# ELEMENTARY SELF-RATING SCALE

AUTHORS: Bert P. Cundick and Michael C. Rose

AGE: 7 to 12 years

VARIABLE: Self- and ideal self-perceptions

TYPE OF MEASURE: Rating scale

SOURCE FROM WHICH MEASURE MAY BE OBTAINED: Bert P. Cundick, Department of Psychology, Brigham Young University, Provo, Utah 84601.

DESCRIPTION OF MEASURE: The Elementary Self-Rating Scale consists of twenty descriptions of children. There are some differences between the girl and boy forms. The children are read each item and then presented a card inscribed with the adjectives *tiny*, *little*, *medium*, *large*, and *gigantic*. The adjectives are printed with letter sizes that correspond to their descriptions. *Tiny* is in very small print and *gigantic* is in very large print. The child is asked to place his finger on the adjective that best corresponds to how similar the child sees him or herself to the description. He is then asked to indicate how much like the description he would like to be. The twenty items were constructed after asking over four hundred children the personality characteristics of children that they admired the most and those that they admired the least. The items reflected the most commonly mentioned traits. Ten of the descriptions are generally perceived as positive traits and ten as negative traits. The negative item scores are totaled and subtracted from the totaled positive item scores, for both the self- and ideal self-ratings.

As examples, the first nine of the twenty items of both the girls' and boys' scales are given below. Except for item nine, the two are the same.

1. This girl (boy) is friendly and smiling and is nice to be around.
2. This girl (boy) likes to tease others.
3. This girl (boy) is funny and is always making you laugh.
4. This girl (boy) likes to tell others what to do.
5. This girl (boy) is generous. She shares what she has.
6. This girl (boy) has trouble with her reading.
7. This girl (boy) does her arithmetic very well.
8. This girl (boy) is sad a lot of the time.
9. This girl is pretty and is careful to dress nicely.
9. This boy is a good runner and does well at other sports.

RELIABILITY AND VALIDITY: Test-retest reliabilities were computed for thirty-two children after two weeks. The *r* of the self-rating score was .82; the *r* of the ideal self-rating was .71. The self-ratings for thirty-two children were correlated with the peer ratings on a sociometric choice form. The *r* was .71.

BIBLIOGRAPHY:

Rose, M. C. "Self, Peer, and Teacher Perceptions of Child Sociometric Status." Unpublished master's thesis. Brigham Young University, Provo, Utah, 1975.

---

# EXPRESSED ACCEPTANCE OF SELF AND EXPRESSED ACCEPTANCE OF OTHERS

AUTHOR: Emanuel M. Berger

AGE: 14 years and up

VARIABLE: Expressed acceptance of self and others

TYPE OF MEASURE: Likert-type scales

SOURCE FROM WHICH MEASURE MAY BE OBTAINED: See Shaw and Wright (1967, p. 432) or Robinson and Shaver (1969) or write Emanual M. Berger, Student Counseling Bureau, 101 Eddy Hall, University of Minnesota, Minneapolis, Minnesota 55455.

DESCRIPTION OF MEASURE: The Expressed Acceptance of Self Scale consists of thirty-six items, with four items selected to accord with each of nine elements of the definition of the self-accepting person. Similarly, the Expressed Acceptance of Others Scale consists of twenty-eight items, with four items selected to accord with seven elements of the definition of the person who is accepting of others. Items for both scales are largely statements about self and others taken verbatim from recorded counseling interviews. The definitions essentially came from Sheerer (1949).

As examples, eight of the sixty-four items on the two scales are given below. The respondent answers on a 5-point scale ranging from "not at all true of myself" to "true of myself."

1. I'd like it if I could find someone who would tell me how to solve my personal problems.
4. I can become so absorbed in the work I'm doing that it doesn't bother me not to have any intimate friends.
6. When people say nice things about me, I find it difficult to believe they really mean it. I think maybe they're kidding me or just aren't being sincere.
14. I'm afraid for people that I like to find out what I'm really like for fear they'd be disappointed in me.
16. Because of other people, I haven't been able to achieve as much as I should have.
20. I seem to have a real inner strength in handling things. I'm on a pretty solid foundation and it makes me pretty sure of myself.
22. The person you marry may not be perfect, but I believe in trying to get him (or her) to change along desirable lines.
30. Sometimes people misunderstand me when I try to keep them from making mistakes that could have an important effect on their lives.

RELIABILITY AND VALIDITY: Matched-half reliabilities were computed, and the Spearman-Brown formula was then used to estimate whole-test reliability. These estimates of whole-test reliability were all .89 or greater for the Self-Acceptance Scale except for one group, for which it was .75. For the Acceptance-of-Others Scale the estimated whole-test reliabilities ranged from .78 to .88. One approach to the validity of the scales consisted in having one group of subjects ($N = 20$) write freely about their attitudes toward themselves, and a second group ($N = 20$) write freely about their attitudes toward others. Both groups used the elements of the definitions as a guide for each written paragraph. The paragraphs were then rated by four judges and the mean ratings for each individual were correlated with their scores on the corresponding scale. The Pearson product-moment correlation between scores and ratings was .90 for self-acceptance and .73 for acceptance of others. Both these correlations were significantly greater than zero. The average of the intercorrelations among judges' ratings was .87 for self-acceptance, .77 for acceptance of others. A second approach to validity compared the means of groups of stutterers and prisoners to the means of college students matched for age and sex. Significant differences in the expected direction were found for prisoners on Expressed Acceptance of Self ($p < .01$) and Expressed Acceptance of Others ($p < .02$). The difference for stutterers was in the expected direction on Expressed Acceptance of Self, although the obtained *t* was .06 lower than that required for the 5-percent level of significance. The differences were expected on empirical as well as a priori grounds.

BIBLIOGRAPHY:

Berger, E. M. "The Relation Between Expressed Acceptance of Self and Expressed Acceptance of Others." *Journal of Abnormal and Social Psychology,* 1952, *47,* 778-782.
Berger, E. M. "Relationships Among Acceptance of Self, Acceptance of Others, and MMPI Scores." *Journal of Counseling Psychology,* 1955, *4,* 279-284.
Cummings, S. T., Bayley, H. C., and Rie, H. E. "Effects of the Child's Deficiency on the Mother: A Study of Mothers of Mentally Retarded, Chronically Ill, and Neurotic Children." *American Journal of Orthopsychiatry,* 1966, *36,* 595-608.
Gonzales-Temayo, E. "Dogmatism, Self-Acceptance, and Acceptance of Others Among Spanish and American Students." *Journal of Social Psychology,* 1974, *94,* 15-25.
Havener, P. H., and Izard, C. E. "Unrealistic Self-Enhancement in Paranoid Schizophrenics." *Journal of Consulting Psychology,* 1962, *26,* 65-68.
Jandt, F. E. "An Experimental Study of Self-Concept and Satisfactions from Consummatory Communication." Unpublished doctoral dissertation. Bowling Green State University, Bowling Green, Ohio, 1970.
Omwake, D. T. "The Relation Between Acceptance of Self and Acceptance of Others Shown by Three Personality Inventories." *Journal of Consulting Psychology,* 1954, *18,* 443-446.
Robinson, J. P., and Shaver, P. R. *Measures of Social Psychological Attitudes.* Ann Arbor, Michigan: Survey Research Center, Institute for Social Research, University of Michigan, 1969.
Shaw, M., and Wright, J. *Scales for the Measurement of Attitudes.* New York: McGraw-Hill, 1967.
Sheerer, E. "An Analysis of the Relationship Between Acceptance of and Respect for the Self and Acceptance of and Respect for Others in Ten Counseling Cases." *Journal of Consulting Psychology,* 1949, *13,* 169-175.
Streitfeld, J. W. "Expressed Acceptance of Self and Others by Psychotherapists." *Journal of Consulting Psychology,* 1959, *23,* 435-441.

---

## FLORIDA KEY: A SCALE TO
## INFER LEARNER SELF-CONCEPT

AUTHORS: William W. Purkey, Bob N. Cage, and William Graves

AGE: Preschool to high school

VARIABLE: Student self-image as learner

TYPE OF MEASURE: Rating scale

SOURCE FROM WHICH MEASURE MAY BE OBTAINED: William W. Purkey, College of Education, University of Florida, Gainesville, Florida 32601; or see Purkey, Cage, and Graves (1973).

DESCRIPTION OF MEASURE: The Florida Key is a scale (two forms) that teachers and others may use to infer pupils' self-concept as learner without relying on self-report. It may be quickly and easily scored by a classroom teacher with prior training. It does not require the cooperation of the subject (as do self-report instruments) nor involve the subject's awareness of being measured. Two procedures were involved in the development of the test. The first was item identification and pilot testing. A group of elementary teachers were asked to evaluate student behaviors in terms of their worth in inferring pupil self-concepts as learners. From these activities eighteen behavioral acts were isolated, described in written form, and juxtaposed within a rating scale to measure perceived frequency of occurrence. The items were then clustered into factors as determined by factor analysis. Four factors were identified, accounting for 92 percent of the common factor variance. They are relating, asserting, investing, and coping. In the second procedure, pupil populations of two elementary schools were evaluated by teachers, followed by six other schools (approximately one thousand students).

As examples, the first five (relating) items from the elementary form of the eighteen-item scale are given below. The subject responds on a 6-point scale from "never" to "very often."

Compared with other students his age, does this student
1. get along with other students?
2. get along with the teachers?
3. keep calm when things go wrong?
4. say good things about his school?
5. tell the truth about his school work?

RELIABILITY AND VALIDITY: When three teachers rated the same eleven students, an index of reliability of .84 was obtained through using an analysis-of-variance procedure. Coefficients of reliability employing the split-half procedure were determined for all teachers. These coefficients ranged from .62 to .96. A split-half estimate of reliability of total score across all teachers was found to be .93. Teacher ratings were compared with Florida Key scores. In separate analyses for each teacher, of sixteen correlation coefficients produced, ranging from .40 to .79, only two were not significant at the .01 level (one was significant at the .02 level, the other at the .10 level). The average correlation (using Fisher's transformation) was .62. In another validation study, twenty-seven teachers chose five students as "feeling best about themselves as learners" and five who "felt badly about themselves as learners." The mean factor score in the four Florida Key factors for each of the two groups was used to determine a point-biserial correlation coefficient. The mean total score was also calculated for each of the two groups, and a point-biserial coefficient of correlation was obtained. These coefficients ranged from .57 (relating) to .71 (coping) with the correlation for total score being .68, all of which were significant at the .01 level.

BIBLIOGRAPHY:

Purkey, W. W. *Self-Concept and School Achievement.* Englewood Cliffs, New Jersey: Prentice-Hall, 1970.

Purkey, W. W., Cage, B. N., and Graves, W. "The Florida Key: A Scale to Infer Learner Self-Concept." *Educational and Psychological Measurement,* 1973, *33,* 979-984.

---

## GELLERT BODY DRAWING TEST

AUTHOR: Elizabeth Gellert

AGE: 4½ or 5 years to old age

VARIABLE: Conception of bodily appearance of self and of other persons

TYPE OF MEASURE: Scores of human figure drawings

SOURCE FROM WHICH MEASURE MAY BE OBTAINED: The supplement on file with the ADI Auxiliary Publications Project, Photoduplication Service, Library of Congress, Washington, D.C. 20540, contains instructions, scoring criteria for all but the *Additional Measures*, and a transcription of raw data. Order Document No. 9796. Cost: $4.25 for 35 mm microfilm, $12.50 for photocopies. Instructions for deriving the *Additional Measures* appear in Gellert (1968) and may also be obtained from Elizabeth Gellert, Department of Psychology, Hunter College of the City University of New York, 695 Park Avenue, New York, New York 10021.

DESCRIPTION OF MEASURE: To obtain the drawings to be scored the subject is seated at a table in a room devoid of any pictures of human beings. On an 8½ X 11-inch white sheet of paper he is instructed, "Draw a picture of yourself wearing a bathing suit. Draw it standing up and facing frontwards. Tell me when you are finished." This drawing, henceforth called the DYS (draw yourself) drawing, is removed when completed. A new sheet of paper is offered and the subject is told, "Now make a picture of a *girl* (or *boy, man, woman,* whichever is a different sex peer of the subject's) wearing a bathing suit, who is just as old as you are. Draw it standing up and facing frontwards." This drawing is called the DOSP (draw opposite sex peer) test. The complete scoring system consists of 110 items, which can be subclassified under a variety of categories to suit the purposes of particular studies. Categories derived thus far are: Number of Body Parts Represented, Appearance and Orientation of Parts, Attachment and Location of Parts, Symmetry (raw score and quotient), Proportion (Raw score and quotient), Sex Differentiation, Emphasis upon Mouth, Emphasis upon Eyes, Height of Figure, Placement on Page, and Line Quality. Scoring instructions are provided in the materials entitled *DYS Diagram Instructions, DYS Measurement and Proportion Form,* and *Description of Additional Measures.* These materials are used interchangeably for drawings of the self (DYS) and for drawings of opposite-sexed peers (DOSP). The author has used the measure to study the development of children's body images from kindergarten age to adolescence, and to compare children's conceptions of their own bodies to their conceptions of opposite-sexed peers.

   As examples, the first ten of twenty-one items from subsection E, Proportion, are given below.

1. Proportion of head length to total height of figure ranges between .10 and .33.
2. Proportion of head length to total height of figure ranges between .10 and .25.
3. Proportion of trunk length to leg length (average) ranges between .75 and 1.40.
4. Proportion of trunk length to leg length (average) ranges between .80 and 1.20.
5. Average arm length exceeds trunk length, but not by more than .33 of trunk length.
6. Proportion of neck length to trunk length not greater than .13.
7. Proportion of trunk length to total height ranges between .25 and .75.
8. Proportion of trunk length to total height ranges between .33 and .50.
9. Trunk length greater than trunk width (measured at greatest point).
10. Proportion of trunk width to trunk length ranges between .33 and .67.

RELIABILITY AND VALIDITY: No assessment of validity was made. Reliability: total-item score = 95 percent; Depiction of Hair = 100 percent; Emphasis upon Mouth = 74 percent; Emphasis upon Eyes = 86 percent; Pubescence = 90 percent; Symmetry = 89 percent; Proportion = 93 percent; Height of Figure = 100 percent; Placement = 100 percent; Line Quality = 80 percent. For further details, see Gellert (1968). Wherever scores were based upon sums of credited points, percent-agreement protocol was stated as (number of points agreed upon)/(maximum attainable points). Indices of interscorer agreement are based upon a minimum of thirty doubly scored drawings (the first of each ten protocols processed), which were scored independently by any two of nine assistants.

BIBLIOGRAPHY:

Gellert, E. "Comparison of Children's Self-Drawings with Their Drawings of Other Persons." *Perceptual and Motor Skills,* 1968, *26,* 123-138.
Goodenough, F. L. *Measurement of Intelligence by Drawings.* New York: Harcourt Brace Jovanovich, 1926.
Harris, D. B. *Children's Drawings as Measures of Intellectual Maturity.* New York: Harcourt Brace Jovanovich, 1963.

---

# HOW I PERCEIVE MYSELF (HIPM)

AUTHOR: Eui-Do Rim

AGE: Kindergarten to grade 3

VARIABLE: Self-concept

TYPE OF MEASURE: Questionnaire

SOURCE FROM WHICH MEASURE MAY BE OBTAINED: Eui-Do Rim, Research for Better Schools, Inc., 1700 Market Street, Philadelphia, Pennsylvania 19103.

DESCRIPTION OF MEASURE: How I Perceive Myself consists of ten items and is designed to measure the students' self-concept in respect to what the student thinks about himself/herself and what the student thinks his/her classmates think about him/her. Samples of two types of questions are as follows: "Do you think you are friendly? Do the kids in your class think you know a lot?" The test can be administered to small groups or to intact classes of twenty to thirty-five students. Instructions for each item are designed to be read by the administrator so that nonreaders can respond to it. Students are instructed to respond to each item by marking one of "yes," "?," "no" options that are printed on a thirteen-page color-coded answer booklet. There is no time limit for administering the test, but 20 minutes is the approximate time needed.

RELIABILITY AND VALIDITY: The HIPM was administered on a pretest-posttest basis in the 1974-1975 school year to about two hundred second- and third-grade children who were enrolled in six Philadelphia Checkpoint Centers for basic skills remedial work. Internal consistency coefficients computed on the posttest data ranged from .42 to .57. The *alpha* coefficient based on the total data ($N = 206$) was .48. The content validity of the instrument was checked by the Peer Review Panel of Research for Better Schools, Inc. An empirical validation study has not yet been undertaken.

BIBLIOGRAPHY: None reported.

---

# I AM A PERSON WHO

AUTHOR: Don Dinkmeyer

AGE: 8 to 12 years

VARIABLE: Self-concept

TYPE OF MEASURE: Checklist test

SOURCE FROM WHICH MEASURE MAY BE OBTAINED: See Dinkmeyer (1965).

DESCRIPTION OF MEASURE: The I Am A Person Who Test consists of forty items clustered in several areas involving such variables as sociability, achievement, and dependence. The test is designed to have the child respond to statements by indicating this description is "very much like me," "a little like me," or "not like me." The preferred answer ("very much like me" on positive items or "not like me" on negative items) is given a score of 5 points, the intermediate answer is given 3 points, and the undesirable answer is given 1 point. Presumably the child with the highest numerical rating is the best-adjusted in the group.

As examples, the first ten of the forty items of the test are given below.

I am a person who
1. has many friends.
2. needs a lot of help.
3. has trouble going to sleep at night.
4. usually does well in school.
5. likes to play alone rather than with other children.
6. shows I am bothered when I lose a game.
7. is sick a lot.
8. always gets my way.
9. feels I have to figure out my own problems.
10. is often tired during the day.

RELIABILITY AND VALIDITY: None reported.

BIBLIOGRAPHY:

Dinkmeyer, D. C. *Child Development: The Emerging Self.* Englewood Cliffs, New Jersey: Prentice-Hall, 1965.

---

## INDEX OF SELF-CONCEPT (ISC)

AUTHOR: Walter W. Hudson

AGE: 12 years and up

VARIABLE: Self-esteem

TYPE OF MEASURE: Rating scale

SOURCE FROM WHICH MEASURE MAY BE OBTAINED: Walter W. Hudson, George Warren Brown School of Social Work, Washington University, St. Louis, Missouri 63130.

DESCRIPTION OF MEASURE: This scale was designed for use in repeated administrations to monitor and evaluate client responses to treatment over time. Positively worded items are reverse scored, all item scores are then summed, and a constant of 25 is subtracted from the total to produce a possible range from 0 to 100. Scores below 30 give little evidence of a problem with self-esteem, while those above 30 indicate the client is having problems with self-esteem. A history of scores exceeding 30 over several time periods is much more indicative of a clinically relevant self-esteem problem than is a single score at one point in time. The scale is sensitive to transient or temporary shocks to self-esteem, and it is this sensitivity that makes the scale useful in monitoring client's response to treatment. Age and sex differences appear thus far to be second-order disturbances, but the scale has not yet been normed on a sufficiently large sample to disregard second-order effects. The scale was not designed as a classification tool and should not be used for that purpose. Rather it was intended as a means of measuring the magnitude of a problem with self-esteem over time. The scale should not be factored into subscales, as it was not designed as a multidimensional measure of self-esteem.

As examples, the first ten of the twenty-five items on the index are given below. The respondent answers on a 5-point frequency scale ranging from "rarely or none of the time" to "most or all of the time."

1. I feel that people would not like me if they really know me well.
2. I feel that others get along much better than I do.
3. I feel that I am a beautiful person.
4. When I am with other people I feel they are glad I am with them.
5. I feel that people really like to talk with me.
6. I feel that I am a very competent person.
7. I think I make a good impression on others.
8. I feel that I need more self-confidence.
9. When I am with strangers I am very nervous.
10. I think that I am a dull person.

RELIABILITY AND VALIDITY: Based on a sample of 281 persons, seven estimates of split-half and test-retest reliabilities ranged from .87 to .97 with a mean of .93. The scale has been shown to have high face, discriminant, and construct validity, with a discriminant validity coefficient of .68. Additional statistical details are reported in Hudson and Proctor (in press).

BIBLIOGRAPHY:

Hudson, W. W., and Proctor, E. K. *Assessing Self-Esteem Problems in Social Work Practice.* George Warren Brown School of Social Work, Washington University. St. Louis, Missouri (in press).

---

# JUNIOR HIGH SCHOOL INDEX OF ADJUSTMENT AND VALUES (JHSIAV)

AUTHOR: Robert E. Bills

AGE: Grades 6 to 9

VARIABLE: Self-concept, acceptance of self, ideal self, self-discrepancy, and comparable measures of other people

TYPE OF MEASURE: Rating scale

SOURCE FROM WHICH MEASURE MAY BE OBTAINED: See Bills (1975).

DESCRIPTION OF MEASURE: The JHSIAV consists of thirty-five trait-words that have been selected from responses of junior high school students in free and controlled association. Children respond on a 3-point scale to say how often the trait is characteristic of them, how they feel about being this sort of person, and how often they would like the trait to be characteristic of them. In addition, they complete the instrument as they think the average person in their peer group would complete it for himself.

As examples, the first ten items of the thirty-five item "Self" form are given below.

| | I | | | | II | | | III | |
| | *I Am Like This* | | | | *The Way I Feel About Being as I Am* | | | | *I Wish I Were* | |
| | Most of the Time | About Half the Time | Hardly Ever | I Like It | I Neither Like Nor Dislike | I Dis- like | Most of the Time | About Half the Time | Hardly Ever |
| Agreeable | | | | | | | | | |
| Alert | | | | | | | | | |
| Brave | | | | | | | | | |
| Busy | | | | | | | | | |
| Careful | | | | | | | | | |
| Cheerful | | | | | | | | | |
| Considerate | | | | | | | | | |
| Cooperative | | | | | | | | | |
| Dependable | | | | | | | | | |
| Fair | | | | | | | | | |

RELIABILITY AND VALIDITY: Item and scale reliabilities have been studied based on a sample of several thousand junior high school children. These reliabilities ranged from .87 to .95. Intercorrelations of the scale, based on 1,544 cases, are available, as are normative data based on grade. Examples of variations among schools, grade, and sex are reported. Item reliabilities for all scales are available from the author.

BIBLIOGRAPHY:

Bills, R. E. *A System for Assessing Affectivity.* University, Alabama: University of Alabama Press, 1975.

# LAURELTON SELF-ATTITUDE SCALE

AUTHORS: George M. Guthrie, Alfred Bennett, and Leon Gorlow

AGE: Developed on female subjects, 14 to 22 years

VARIABLE: Self-attitudes of mildly retarded individuals

TYPE OF MEASURE: A self-rating scale, written or oral

SOURCE FROM WHICH MEASURE MAY BE OBTAINED: George M. Guthrie, Department of Psychology, Pennsylvania State University, University Park, Pennsylvania 16802.

DESCRIPTION OF MEASURE: The Laurelton Self-Attitude Scale consists of 150 statements with which an individual is asked to agree or disagree. A shorter scale consisting of fifty representative and most reliable items has been developed from the longer 150-item form. The longer form consists of items calculated to assess the individual's attitudes toward her (his) own physical appearance, physical health, interpersonal relationships with peers, interpersonal relationships with others, personal worth, and mental health. In these six categories there are items that express positive attitudes and negative attitudes toward the respondent. Finally, there is a lie scale patterned after the scale on the MMPI but made up of different items. The scale was developed within an approach that emphasized the phenomenology of the retardate. The authors felt that the failures of the mildly retarded are frequently attributed to their feeling of low self-worth and expectation of failure.

As examples, the first twenty of the 150 items of the experimental form of the scale are given below.

1. I always do what I am told.
2. The teacher thinks I'm sort of jittery.
3. People think I get upset too easily at work.
4. Others think I have trouble getting along with older people.
5. I feel at ease playing games with older people.
6. New jobs scare me to death.
7. It is easy for me to read aloud in class.
8. People think I get into more trouble than most girls my age.
9. I am as smart as most girls.
10. I tell the truth every single time.
11. Other girls can sew better than I can.
12. People think I am pretty good at games and sports.
13. It's my fault when something goes wrong.
14. At school, the girls think I am as good looking as the others.
15. I am better than others.
16. I like to stick up for people.
17. Sometimes other people think I am a pest.
18. I feel left out of things.
19. It takes me a long time to make up my mind.
20. I seem to get into a lot of fights.

RELIABILITY AND VALIDITY: Test-retest reliabilities for the various subscales are all in the .80s.

BIBLIOGRAPHY:

Gorlow, L., Butler, A. J., Einig, K. G., and Smith, J. A. "An Appraisal of Self-Attitudes
    and Behavior Following Group Psychotherapy with Retarded Young Adults."
    *American Journal of Mental Deficiency,* 1963, *67,* 893-898.
Gorlow, L., Butler, A. J., and Guthrie, G. M. "Correlates of Self-Attitudes in Retardates."
    *American Journal of Mental Deficiency,* 1963, *67,* 549-555.
Guthrie, G. M., Butler, A. J., and Gorlow, L. "Patterns of Self-Attitudes of Retardates."
    *American Journal of Mental Deficiency,* 1961, *66,* 222-229.
Guthrie, G. M., Butler, A. J., and Gorlow, L. "Personality Differences Between Institu-
    tionalized and Noninstitutionalized Retardates." *American Journal of Mental De-
    ficiency,* 1963, *67,* 543-548.
Guthrie, G. M., Gorlow, L., and Butler, A. J. "The Attitude of the Retardate Toward
    Herself: A Summary of Research at Laurelton State School and Hospital." *Penn-
    sylvania Psychiatric Quarterly,* 1967 (Spring), 24-34.
Harrison, R. H., and Budoff, M. "Demographic, Historical, and Ability Correlates of
    the Laurelton Self-Concept Scale in an EMR Sample." *American Journal of Mental
    Deficiency,* 1972, *76,* 460-480.
Harrison, R. H., and Budoff, M. "A Factor Analysis of the Laurelton Self-Concept Scale."
    *American Journal of Mental Deficiency,* 1972, *76,* 446-459.
Kniss, J. T., Butler, A. J., Gorlow, L., and Guthrie, G. M. "Ideal Self-Patterns of Female
    Retardates." *American Journal of Mental Deficiency,* 1962, *67,* 245-249.
Shulman, L. S. *The Vocational Development of Mentally Handicapped Adolescents: An
    Experimental and Longitudinal Study.* Washington, D.C.: Bureau of Education for
    the Handicapped, U.S. Department of Health, Education and Welfare, 1967. ERIC
    document no. ED 025 095.
Shulman, L. S. "Negro-White Differences in Employability, Self-Concept, and Related
    Measures Among Adolescents Classified as Mentally Handicapped." *Journal of
    Negro Education,* 1968, *37,* 227-240.
Smith, J. A. "The Relationship of Self-Attitudes to Goal-Setting Behavior in Two Groups
    of Female Retardates." Unpublished master's thesis. Pennsylvania State Univer-
    sity, University Park, 1959.
Wink, C. F. "Learning of Retardates Under Symbolic Reinforcement in View of Self-
    Acceptance." Unpublished doctoral dissertation. Pennsylvania State University,
    University Park, 1962.

---

## McDANIEL-PIERS YOUNG CHILDREN'S SELF-CONCEPT SCALE

AUTHORS: Ernest D. McDaniel and Ellen V. Piers

AGE: 6 to 9 years

VARIABLE: Self-concept

TYPE OF MEASURE: Questionnaire

SOURCE FROM WHICH MEASURE MAY BE OBTAINED: Purdue Educational Research Center, Purdue University, West Lafayette, Indiana 47907.

DESCRIPTION OF MEASURE: This questionnaire is a downward extension of the Piers-Harris Children's Self-Concept Scale. Items that seemed particularly appropriate for young children were selected from the parent instrument and the wording simplified. Preliminary tryouts with first-grade children and subsequent item-analysis procedures were used to select items for the final edition. The scale contains forty items to be read aloud by the test administrator. Children respond "yes" or "no" on a special answer sheet. The scale provides a total score and three part scores: Feeling Self, School Self, and Behaving Self. Norms for the total score are based on over two thousand children from eight metropolitan school systems.

RELIABILITY AND VALIDITY: The scale has been used in a longitudinal study examining the stability of self-concept during the first three years of school. Results of factor analysis are reported by Denner (1975). No validity is reported.

| Grade | N | Feeling Self | | | School Self | | | Behaving Self | | | Total | | |
|---|---|---|---|---|---|---|---|---|---|---|---|---|---|
| | | $\overline{X}$ | KR-20 | SE | $\overline{X}$ | KR-20 | SE | $\overline{X}$ | KR-20 | SE | $\overline{X}$ | KR-20 | SE |
| 1 | 143 | 7.64 | .48 | – | 8.81 | .67 | – | 6.40 | .53 | – | 22.85 | .73 | – |
| 2 | 444 | 9.13 | .60 | 1.86 | 9.8 | .67 | 1.64 | 6.91 | .60 | 1.4 | 25.87 | .80 | 2.77 |
| 3 | 367 | – | – | – | – | – | – | – | – | – | 26.46 | .86 | 2.68 |

BIBLIOGRAPHY:

McDaniel, E. D., and others. *Longitudinal Study of Elementary School Effects: Design, Instruments, and Specifications for a Field Test.* Final report, Purdue Educational Research Center. Purdue University, West Lafayette, Indiana, 1973.

Denner, P. R. "The Relationship of Self-Concept Factors to Peer-Evaluation Factors and Factors of Attitude Toward School for Second and Fifth Grade Elementary School Children." Unpublished master's thesis. Purdue University, West Lafayette, Indiana, 1975.

---

## MEASURE OF SELF-CONFIDENCE AND INDEPENDENT THINKING IN ELEMENTARY SCHOOL STUDENTS

AUTHORS: Howard Groveman and Nancy Kuntz

AGE: Approximately 6 to 10 years

VARIABLE: Self-confidence and independent thinking

TYPE OF MEASURE: Multiple-choice test

SOURCE FROM WHICH MEASURE MAY BE OBTAINED: Nancy Kuntz, BUSM Box 311, 80 E. Concord St., Boston, Massachusetts 02118.

DESCRIPTION OF MEASURE: This measure is a thirty-five-question multiple-choice test consisting of general information questions at the first- to fourth-grade levels. Answers (mostly incorrect, but with a few introductory correct ones) are penciled in on the test sheet, as in the example that follows:

7. Marie Antoinette was (1) a queen of France, ((2)) a movie star, (3) a famous witch, (4) Snow White's friend.

The subjects are given the test with the instructions to answer each question and then indicate whether it was a "hard" or an "easy" question—ignoring answers that might have been written on the test sheet by a class who had taken the test previously and had not followed instructions. By correlating compliance with the suggested answers to "hard" questions between two different groups of students, one obtains a comparison of yielding to influence. Students who have learned self-confidence and are independent in their thinking due to a positive self-concept will have a lower compliance than students who have not.

RELIABILITY AND VALIDITY: The measure was administered to a group of thirty-six third-grade students who were randomly divided into "open" and "traditional" classrooms at the beginning of a school year. They were matched in terms of achievement test scores and socioeconomic backgrounds. The results have been reported (Bleier and others, 1972).

BIBLIOGRAPHY:

Bleier, M., and others. "A Comparison of Yielding to Influence in Open and Traditional Classrooms." *Childhood Education,* 1972, *49,* 45-50.
Patel, A., and Gordon, J. "Some Personal and Situational Determinants of Yielding to Influence." *Journal of Abnormal and Social Psychology,* 1960, *61,* 411-418.

*Prepared by Nancy L. Kuntz*

---

## MOVEMENT SATISFACTION SCALE

AUTHORS: Barbara Nelson and Dorothy Allen

AGE: 9 years to college

VARIABLE: Degree of satisfaction or dissatisfaction with movement ability

TYPE OF MEASURE: Rating scale

SOURCE FROM WHICH MEASURE MAY BE OBTAINED: See Rohaly (1971) or write to Barbara A. Nelson, Physical Education Division for Women, Ohio State University, Columbus, Ohio, 43210.

DESCRIPTION OF MEASURE: From a pool of 129 items, eight professionals in psychology and physical education with expertise in movement theory selected the highest seventy-five based on relevance of content, clarity of meaning, and appropriateness of vocabulary and content. These items were administered to 176 men and women aged 18 to 21, and on the basis of variance and reliability scores for each item, the number of items was reduced to fifty.

As examples, ten selected items of the fifty are given below. They are scored on a 5-point scale from "have strong negative feelings" to "have strong positive feelings."

1. Pride in physical ability.
2. Ability to learn physical skills easily.
3. Ability to participate in sport activity on a varsity level.
4. Ability to jump for height.
5. Ability to run with speed.
6. Ability to do cartwheels and gymnastic stunts.
7. Ability to learn new movements without becoming discouraged.
8. Ability to throw overarm for distance.
9. Ability to walk with poise.
10. Ability to balance on one leg.

RELIABILITY AND VALIDITY: The seventy-five-item version (Form B) given to students aged 18 to 21 ($N = 176$) yielded a reliability coefficient of .96. Form A administered to 877 students aged 14 to 18 yielded a reliability coefficient of .95. There were significant differences in movement satisfaction between age levels, even within the relatively restricted (14 to 21) range, and significant differences were found between the sexes. The younger students and the males manifested greater movement satisfaction.

BIBLIOGRAPHY:

Beveridge, S. K. "Self-Expressed Movement Satisfaction and Reading Achievement in Elementary Grade Children." Unpublished master's thesis. Ohio State University, Columbus, 1971.

Beveridge, S. K. "The Relationship Among Motor Creativity, Movement Satisfaction, and the Utilization of Certain Movement Factors of Second Grade Children." Unpublished doctoral dissertation. Ohio State University, Columbus, 1973.

Nelson, B. A., and Allen, D. J. "Scale for the Appraisal of Movement Satisfaction." *Perceptual and Motor Skill,* 1970, *31,* 795-800.

Rohaly, K. "The Relationship Between Movement Participation, Movement Satisfaction, Self-Actualization, and Trait Anxiety in Selected College Freshman Women." Unpublished doctoral dissertation. Ohio State University, Columbus, 1971.

Tanner, P. "The Relationship of Selected Measures of Body Image and Movement Concept to Two Types of Programs of Physical Education in the Primary Grades." Unpublished doctoral dissertation. Ohio State University, Columbus, 1969.

*Prepared by Barbara Nelson and Orval G. Johnson*

## MSW SELF-ESTEEM INVENTORY

AUTHORS: Phelon J. Malouf, Cecil O. Samuelson, and Y. T. Witherspoon

AGE: Adolescents (secondary-school students)

VARIABLE: Self-esteem as a component of the self-concept

TYPE OF MEASURE: Self-report inventory

SOURCE FROM WHICH MEASURE MAY BE OBTAINED: Pehlon J. Malouf, 319 MBH, University of Utah, Salt Lake City, Utah 84112.

DESCRIPTION OF MEASURE: Defining self-esteem as the extent to which the person respects himself, feels worthy, feels that he compares favorably with others, accepts himself, recognizes his limitations and expects to deal with them, feels that others view him favorably, and believes that he will be able to cope with life, the measure includes fifty statements that require "true" or "false" responses and twenty-two adjective pairs that follow semantic differential procedures. Three scores reflecting aspects of self-esteem are identified: (1) student competency (based upon an item-analysis testing of the degree to which each item differentiates between students rated by their teachers as being high in self-esteem and those rated low); (2) personal adequacy (based upon the pooled judgments of psychologists as to feelings of worth and adequacy in personal and interpersonal matters reflected in the items); and (3) personal satisfaction (based upon responses to the paired adjectives in the semantic differential portion). The inventory is hand-scorable in about 5 minutes.

As examples, eight selected items from the fifty statements requiring a "true" or "false" response are given below, followed by the first three of the twenty-two adjective pairs.

1. I usually feel quite good about myself.
5. I would rather write a theme or story than give a speech in class.
9. I am a leader more than a follower.
12. I view myself as a capable person.
15. I attend school regularly.
18. It is difficult for me to get started on the things I'm supposed to do.
21. I believe that I will be successful financially as I go through life.
24. I wish I could get more recognition for the things I do.

| | | |
|---|---|---|
| *Happy* | _____ | *Unhappy* |
| *Ambitious* | _____ | *Lazy* |
| *Dependable* | _____ | *Undependable* |

RELIABILITY AND VALIDITY: Although much more work needs to be done to establish the reliability and validity of the measure, preliminary data are favorable. Test-retest coefficients for fifty-eight tenth-grade students were .90 and for thirty-five college students, .91. Face or content validity is reflected in the direct nature of the items included. Support for construct validity is evident in the coefficient of .70 between student competency scores and teacher ratings for seventy-six tenth-grade students, and the coefficient of .73 between personal adequacy scores and self-ratings for thirty-five college students. Constancy of the self-esteem measure is supported by the more than 75-percent agreement in responses for fifty-five boys and fifty-five girls who took the measure as tenth graders and again as twelfth graders. Also, increased self-esteem as individuals progress in school is supported by data that indicate higher means at successive stages. More work needs to be done in determining the impact of "social desirability" on the responses, but it is felt that the construction of the measure keeps this effect at a minimum.

BIBLIOGRAPHY:

Fullmer, M. L. "The Effects of a Volunteer Tutorial Experience on High School Students." Unpublished master's thesis. University of Utah, Salt Lake City, 1971.

Hiett, W. R. "The Individual Self-Esteem of High School Students with Minority Group Background." Unpublished master's thesis. University of Utah, Salt Lake City, 1969.

Malouf, P. J. "Self-Esteem: What Is It and Can We Measure It?" Paper presented at the National Convention of the American Personnel and Guidance Association. Dallas, Texas, April 1967.

Malouf, P. J. "Self-Esteem of the Entering College Student." Paper presented at the National Convention of the American Personnel and Guidance Association. Detroit, Michigan, April 1968.

Malouf, P. J. "The Measurement of Self-Esteem." Presidential address. Utah Psychological Association. Salt Lake City, December 1968.

---

## NOBLE'S IDENTIFICATION MEASURE
## VIA REPERTORY GRID

AUTHOR: Grant Noble

AGE: 6 years and up

VARIABLE: Salient identification choices, integration of self-concept

TYPE OF MEASURE: Interview rating scale

SOURCE FROM WHICH MEASURE MAY BE OBTAINED: Grant Noble, Department of Psychology, Trinity, Dublin 2, Ireland. Cost: $1.00 for postage and packaging.

DESCRIPTION OF MEASURE: Identification is defined as the perceived images of self and significant others experienced in terms of personal constructs. It is assessed as a relationship rather than a process and as a perceived rather than an actual similarity. The measure is infinitely flexible and has the distinct advantage that any perceived relationship is construed in the subject's own words. Using standard repertory grid procedures, the interviewer elicits similarities and differences between any three significant others. Similarities are recorded on the right-hand side and differences on the left-hand side of the squared paper that constitutes the repertory grid. The subject is then asked which pole of the construct applies to each significant other person and each aspect of self assessed. This assessment may be binary or scaled. Relative identification is scored by counting the number of common similarities perceived between self and significant others. When used as a measure of personal adjustment, the degree of consistency between various aspects of self is calculated.

RELIABILITY AND VALIDITY: By definition identification with significant others changes in the long term. In the short term the measure gives consistent results ($r$ = .83). Kagan (1958) maintains that the boy's identification with the father will decrease with age. The data support this view, since matching scores between ideal self and father were at 12 years, 79 percent; at 13 years, 67 percent; at 14 years, 62 percent; and at 15 years, 59 percent.

BIBLIOGRAPHY:

Jones, R. E. "Identification in Terms of Personal Constructs: Reconciling a Paradox in Theory." *Journal of Consulting Psychology,* 1961, *25,* 276.
Kagan, J. "The Concept of Identification." *Psychological Review,* 1958, *65,* 296-305.
Noble, G. "Some Comments on the Nature of Delinquents' Identification with Television Heroes, Fathers and Best Friends." *British Journal of Social and Clinical Psychology,* 1971, *10,* 172-180.

---

## PHYSICAL ESTIMATION AND ATTRACTION SCALE (PEAS)

AUTHOR: Robert J. Sonstroem

AGE: Males, 12 to 18 years; others with small modifications

VARIABLE: (1) Self-perception of physical ability; (2) attraction to physical activity

TYPE OF MEASURE: Questionnaire, true/false responses

SOURCE FROM WHICH MEASURE MAY BE OBTAINED: Robert J. Sonstroem, Department of Physical Education, University of Rhode Island, Kingston, Rhode Island 02881.

DESCRIPTION OF MEASURE: The Estimation Scale of the PEAS consists of thirty-three items assessing self-perception of physical ability at sports activities. Respondents affirm or deny the possession of physical characteristics, physical fitness, and athletic ability or potential. The Attraction Scale consisting of fifty-four items asks respondents to affirm or to deny desires for participation in specific and vigorous sports activities. Other items assess attraction to more general aspects of physical activity.

As examples, ten of the one hundred items on the scale are given below. The respondent answers "true" or "false."

2. I prefer exercising to reading.
6. My body is strong and muscular compared to other boys my age.
8. Most sports require too much time and energy to be worthwhile.
16. I prefer team sports to individual sports because of the experience of playing with different people.
27. I would enjoy difficult mountain climbing.
31. I would rather watch a good movie than a hockey match.
35. Compared to other people I am somewhat clumsy.
53. When tensions are high, I prefer to lie down and rest rather than to absorb myself in physical activity.
58. After a day at school, I prefer to take it easy instead of participating in vigorous sports activities.
89. I would rather play touch football than go to an amusement park.

RELIABILITY AND VALIDITY: Internal consistency values (Kuder-Richardson formula 20) are .87 for the Estimation Scale and .89 for the Attraction Scale. One-week test-retest reliability coefficients (grades 10 to 12) are .92 for estimation and .94 for attraction. Factor analysis of PEAS items has shown a differentiation between estimation and attraction items within factor structures. In repeated testing estimation scores have produced coefficients of .41, .48, and .53 with composite physical fitness indices. Coefficients obtained between estimation scores and global self-esteem (Tennessee Self-Concept Scale, 1965) have been of a similar magnitude.

BIBLIOGRAPHY:

Sonstroem, R. J. "Attitude Testing Involving Certain Psychological Correlates of Physical Activity." *Research Quarterly*, 1974, *45*, 93-103.
Sonstroem, R. J. "Assessment of Attitude Toward Physical Activity and Estimation of Physical Ability: Theoretical and Applied Considerations." Paper presented at the annual meeting of the American College of Sports Medicine. New Orleans, Louisiana, May 1975.
*Tennessee Self-Concept Scale.* Nashville, Tennessee: Counselor Recordings and Tests, 1965.

---

# PHYSICAL SELF TEST

AUTHORS: Martin L. Maehr and Harold I. Haas

AGE: 12 to 14 years

VARIABLE: Concepts of physical self

TYPE OF MEASURE: Rating scale

SOURCE FROM WHICH MEASURE MAY BE OBTAINED: Martin L. Maehr, College of Education, University of Illinois, Urbana, Illinois 61801; or Harold I. Haas, Concordia Senior College, Fort Wayne, Indiana 46825.

DESCRIPTION OF MEASURE: This is a thirty-item rating scale designed to explore the subject's feelings about his physical abilities. The instrument contains three subtests of ten items each. The Criticized Scale contains body-coordination and motor-skill items directly related to the tasks the subjects perform for the "experts" (experimenters). The approval and disapproval evaluations given by the "experts" are directly related to these items. The Related Scale items concern general athletic skill, and the Unrelated Scale items concern general physical fitness. These items are *not* directly related to the tasks the subjects perform and are *not* referred to directly by the "experts." A separate score is calculated for each subscale; this score is the sum of the ratings a subject circles divided by ten. However, seven items are stated in negative form, and these items must be transposed to their opposite value when totaling a subject's score.

As examples, the first eight of the thirty-item test, to be answered on a 9-point scale from "extreme disagreement" to "extreme agreement," are given below. To the left of each item is the subscale to which the item belongs. (R) indicates a reversed-scoring item.

C    1. I demonstrate good coordination in my walking.
C    2. For my size and body build I run smoothly and quickly.
U    3. In an emergency I could defend myself well against physical attack.
R    4. I have the ability to play most sports well.
U    5. A doctor would most likely consider me to be in excellent physical condition.
(R)  6. I have always shied away from playing on an athletic team.
R    7. I have the physical ability to make an interscholastic team.
U    8. I have the physical ability to work consistently at a heavy construction job.

RELIABILITY AND VALIDITY: As predicted (Ludwig, 1970) ratings on a shortened twenty-item version of the Physical Self Test were negatively correlated with the extrapunitive (−.22) and extragression (−.21) scores on the Rosenzweig Picture-Frustration Study. Ludwig also predicted a relationship between the Physical Self Test and the feedback received in an interpersonal situation. The $F$ ratio for the difference between the Physical Self Test given before and after the feedback was significant at the .001 level, with a significant increase in the mean rating following positive feedback and a significant decrease following negative feedback (all at the .01 level or better). A control group, which received no feedback, showed no significant change. He further predicted that the feedback would cause a change in perception of the specialist giving the feedback. An analysis of variance between the three groups (given positive feedback, negative feedback, and control) was computed to test the hypothesis, and the difference between the individual means was tested for significance. The $F$ ratio was significant at the .05 level or better (with the exception of the negative and control groups of one school) and in the predicted direction.

BIBLIOGRAPHY:

Haas, H. I., and Maehr, M. L. "Two Experiments on the Concept of Self and the Reaction of Others." *Journal of Personality and Social Psychology*, 1965, *1*, 100-105.
Ludwig, D. J. "Evidence of Construct and Criterion-Related Validity for the Self-Concept." *Journal of Social Psychology*, 1970, *80*, 213-223.

Ludwig, D. J., and Maehr, M. L. "Changes in Self-Concept and Stated Preferences." *Child Development*, 1967, *38*, 453-467.

Maehr, M. L., Mensing, J., and Nefzger, S. "Concept of Self and the Reaction of Others." *Sociometry*, 1962, *25*, 353-357.

---

# PICTURE GAME

AUTHORS: Nadine M. Lambert and Eli M. Bower

AGE: Kindergarten to grade 3

VARIABLE: Self-rating

TYPE OF MEASURE: Picture-choice test

SOURCE FROM WHICH MEASURE MAY BE OBTAINED: Nadine M. Lambert, School of Education, University of California, Berkeley, California 94720.

DESCRIPTION OF MEASURE: The Picture Game is designed to give a measure of young children's perception of self. It is used to identify pupils who are vulnerable to or handicapped by emotional problems. The measure consists of seventy-two pictures, including two sample pictures. Each picture is illustrative of normal home and school relationships and events. With the exception of the two sample pictures and the first ten pictures, each picture is emotionally neutral in the portrayal of the relationship or event. The child is asked to classify each picture into one of two categories: "This is a happy picture" or "This is a sad picture." The first ten pictures the child judges are stereotypes—obviously happy or obviously sad situations. The purpose of including them in the test items is to check on each pupil's understanding of the task. If a child judges the first ten pictures correctly, it is fairly certain that he has understood the process well enough for his score to be used in screening. There are separate forms of the test for boys and for girls. The boys' form is printed on gold paper and the girls' form on green. Administration time is about half an hour including time for distribution and collection of the materials.

RELIABILITY AND VALIDITY: When the Picture Game scores (the number of happy pictures) for the second-grade sample of boys and girls were correlated with a summary clinical criterion, the result was significant at the .05 level for boys, but not for girls. When clinical factors were used as criteria and the samples combined, a significant multiple $R$ was obtained. The correlation between the Picture Game scores and the original teacher rating of adjustment was significant for boys but not for girls.

BIBLIOGRAPHY:

Hartsough, C. S. *Classroom Adaptation of Elementary School Children Varying with Respect to Age, Sex, and Ethnic Status.* Berkeley: University of California, 1973.

Lambert, N. M. *The Prediction of School Adjustment.* U.S. Office of Education,

Cooperative Research Project No. 1980. Sacramento: California State Department of Education, 1964.

Lambert, N. M. "Intellectual and Nonintellectual Predictors of High School Status." *Journal of Special Education,* 1972, *6* (3), 247-259.

Lambert, N. M. *Technical Report Supplement: The Development of Instruments for the Nonintellectual Assessment of Effective School Behavior.* Berkeley: University of California, 1974.

Lambert, N. M., and Bower, E. M. *A Picture Game Manual.* Berkeley: University of California, 1974.

Lambert, N. M., and Bower, E. M. *A Process for In-School Screening of Emotionally Handicapped Children.* Atlanta: Educational Testing Service, 1961, 1974.

Lambert, N. M., Hartsough, C. S., and Zimmerman, I. L. "The Comparative Predictive Efficiency of Intellectual and Nonintellectual Components of High School Functioning." *American Journal of Orthopsychiatry,* 1976, *46* (1), 109-122.

---

## PRESCHOOL SELF-CONCEPT PICTURE TEST (PS-CPT)

AUTHOR: Rosestelle B. Woolner

AGE: Early childhood (approximately 3 to 7 years)

VARIABLE: Self-concept

TYPE OF MEASURE: Nonverbal interview, forced choice

SOURCE FROM WHICH MEASURE MAY BE OBTAINED: Rosestelle B. Woolner, 3551 Aurora Circle, Memphis, Tennessee 38111.

DESCRIPTION OF MEASURE: The Preschool Self-Concept Picture Test (PS-CPT) is a nonverbal picture-type measure composed of four separate but comparable forms. Appropriate sets may be administered to black and white boys and girls. Each set consists of ten plates with paired pictures on characteristics that preschool children commonly attribute to themselves. Pictured characteristics included, for example, dirty-clean, strong-weak, sharing-not sharing, and so forth. As the examiner shows the pictures to the child, he asks, "Which are you? Is this me or that me?" Then the examiner asks, "Which boy would you like to be?" A discrepancy score is obtained and reflects incongruence between self- and ideal self-concept, that is, dissatisfaction with self. Response-type frequency counts are provided for each item by sex.

RELIABILITY AND VALIDITY: Content validity was achieved by asking children to describe the pictures. Their descriptions agreed with what the test designer intended the pictures to represent. A correlation calculated between the PS-CPT and the Draw-a-Man Self-Concept Test ($N = 21$) approached significance. Coefficients of stability calculated for the self- and ideal self-measures were, respectively, $r = .94$ and $r = .80$.

BIBLIOGRAPHY:

Diggs, A. T. "A Validity Study of the Woolner Preschool Self-Concept Picture Test." Unpublished master's thesis. Memphis State University, Memphis, Tennessee, 1974.
Ehlers, B. R. "The Relationship of Articulation Defects and Self-Concept." Unpublished master's thesis. California State University, Sacramento, 1975.
Marcotte, E. L. "Self-Concept and Personal Space in Preschool Children." Unpublished master's thesis. Iowa State University, Ames, 1975.

---

## PRIMARY SELF-CONCEPT INVENTORY (PSCI)

AUTHORS: Douglas G. Muller and Robert Leonetti

AGE: 4 to 12 years

VARIABLE: Self-concept factors relevant to school success

TYPE OF MEASURE: Dichotomous pictorial stimuli

SOURCE FROM WHICH MEASURE MAY BE OBTAINED: Learning Concepts, 2501 North Lamar, Austin, Texas 78705. Cost: Test manual, $2.95; male test booklet (not reusable), $.60; female test booklet (not reusable), $.60; technical report, $4.95; specimen set (manual, 1 male and 1 female booklet), $4.15.

DESCRIPTION OF MEASURE: The Primary Self-Concept Inventory is designed to provide an economical procedure for evaluating several aspects of self-concept relevant to school success. While this test was initially constructed for use with the child of Spanish or Mexican descent in the Southwest, field-testing has shown it can be used successfully with Anglo-American and Indian children. The PSCI is composed of twenty items: two warm-up items and eighteen scored items. Each item depicts at least one child in a positive role and at least one child in a negative role. There are separate male and female forms of the test, so that the sex of the principal character in the test items may be matched with that of the examinee. The examinee is told a simple descriptive story about each illustration and is instructed to draw a circle around the person that is most like himself. The stories are printed in both Spanish and English in the test manual. The test is designed to measure six aspects or factors of self-concept, with three items measuring each factor. These factors can be clustered into the three major domains of: personal self, social self, and intellectual self. Norms are available.

As an example, the first of the twenty items is given below.

Turn to picture one with the square next to the number. (The administrators should hold up a copy of the test open to the correct illustration each time to allow children to confirm every page selection.) Look very carefully at the pictures. One picture on this page shows children who are fighting. The other picture shows some boys who are sharing a ball and some girls who are sharing a doll. Draw a circle around the child you think is most like you.

Do not worry about what anyone else thinks. Please do not look at anyone else's booklet. Go ahead and draw a circle around the boy or girl you feel is "truly" most like you. (The following directions are to be added for grades 3 and 4 only.) I am interested only in how *you* feel. Be honest. Remember, draw a circle around the boy or girl that you feel is most like you.

RELIABILITY AND VALIDITY: Pearson product-moment correlation coefficients were computed between test and retest scores of the PSCI for two samples ($N = 372; N = 100$). These coefficients were $r = .91$ and $r = .57$, respectively. Both coefficients were significantly different from zero ($p \leqslant .01$). The first of these values suggests very high reliability, the second only moderate reliability. The moderate reliability of the second sample may be due to the relatively small sample size. Test validity appears to be high. Repeated factor analyses yield highly consistent results, indicating that the test is measuring two factors of each domain mentioned above. The content validity of the test was supported by the opinions of five specialists who have done postgraduate study in measurement and evaluation. They felt that the PSCI is an easily administered and scored instrument for assessment of self-concept. For current information on validity and reliability, contact the authors.

BIBLIOGRAPHY:

Leonetti, R. "A Primary Self-Concept Scale for Spanish-Surnamed Children, Grades K-4." Unpublished doctoral dissertation. New Mexico State University, Las Cruces, 1973. ERIC document no. ED 071 813.
Muller, D. G., and Leonetti, R. "Self-Concepts of Primary-Level Chicano and Anglo Students." *California Journal of Educational Research*, 1974, *25*, 57-60.

*Prepared by Robert Leonetti*

---

# PRIMARY SELF-CONCEPT INVENTORY (PSCI)

AUTHORS: Kay Pomerance Torshen, Leonard Kroeker, and Rolf Peterson

AGE: 5 to 8 years

VARIABLE: Self-reported self-concept

TYPE OF MEASURE: Paper-and-pencil, group-administered questionnaire

SOURCE FROM WHICH MEASURE MAY BE OBTAINED: Kay Torshen, Department of Psychology, University of Illinois at Chicago Circle, Box 4348, Chicago, Illinois 60680.

DESCRIPTION OF MEASURE: The PSCI consists of two scales. Each scale contains twenty-four items measuring the child's self-evaluation in seven areas: learning-work habits, athletics, personal appearance, relationship to teachers, relationship to boys, relationship to girls, and relationship to others in general. The item content and response modes were adapted from the Self-Concept Inventory (Sears, 1963), which is appropriate for ages 9 to 13. The PSCI employs two forced-choice response formats, one for each of the two inventory scales. On scale I, the respondent rates himself in relation to his classmates on all twenty-four items on a 3-choice format. A sample learning-work habits item is given below.

"If you learn things faster than most of your classmates, put an X in the box with the circle. If you learn things at the same rate as most of your classmates, put an X in the box with the square. If you learn things slower than your classmates, put an X in the box with the triangle."

On Scale II, the respondent reports positive and negative feelings about himself on all twenty-four items in the 2-choice format. A sample athletics item is given below.

"If you think you are good at games at recess time, put an X in the box with the circle. If you are not good at games at recess time, put an X in the box with the square."

Administration of the inventory requires one group session of about 15 minutes for each scale. Respondent reading skill is not required.

RELIABILITY AND VALIDITY: A version of the PSCI, containing forty-five items and two response formats, was administered three times during one school year to 120 middle-class urban and suburban first-grade students. Application of factor analysis to the data (ninety responses) from the first administration of the PSCI yielded two strong factors, one corresponding to each of the two response formats. On the basis of this first analysis, the data from each rating were analyzed separately. Principal components decompositions of the intercorrelation matrix obtained from each set of forty-five items were obtained. Seven principal components were extracted from each of the two sets of forty-five items. The remaining principal components were not considered since their corresponding eigenvalues were less than one. Within each set of items the seven principal components were rotated according to a normalized varimax criterion. Highly similar component structures were obtained within each set. The resulting components were interpreted in terms of the content and function of the items that were maximally correlated with the respective components. Multidimensional items were eliminated, and twenty-four items remained to form the seven subscales (components) of the two scales of the PSCI. The entire principal-components analysis was repeated on the data obtained in the third administration of the PSCI. There was a six-month interval between administrations. This analysis replicated the results of the prior analysis.

Test-retest reliability estimates were obtained for the seven PSCI subscales of Scale I on another sample of seventy-seven first graders. The administrations of the PSCI used for these estimates were separated by a time interval of six months. The following test-retest reliability estimates were obtained: learning-work habits, .53; athletics, .70; personal appearance, .38; relationship to teachers, .46; relationship to boys, .73; relationship to girls, .63; relationship to others in general, .45. Reliability estimates have not been obtained for Scale II.

BIBLIOGRAPHY:

Sears, P. S. *The Effect of Classroom Conditions on the Strength of Achievement Motive and Work Output of Elementary School Children.* Cooperative Research Project no. OE 873. Stanford University, Stanford, California, 1963.

Torshen, K. P., Peterson, R. A., and Kroeker, L. P. "A Self-Concept Inventory for the Primary Grades." Paper presented to the annual meeting of the American Educational Research Association. Chicago, April 1974.

---

## PRIMARY SELF-CONCEPTS TEST

AUTHOR: R. J. Andrews

AGE: 10 to 13+ years

VARIABLE: Self-concepts

TYPE OF MEASURE: Pencil-and-paper Q-sort

SOURCE FROM WHICH MEASURE MAY BE OBTAINED: R. J. Andrews, Schonell Educational Research Center, University of Queensland, St. Lucia, 4067, Australia.

DESCRIPTION OF MEASURE: The test consists of seventy-six items grouped into two parts. Fifty-one adjectives make up the first part of the test, while the second part consists of twenty-five descriptive statements. Responses to the items are weighted on the basis of four response categories, "very much like me," "like me," "not like me," and "not at all like me." Each item contributes to one of six subscales: self as striving for success, sufficient, confident; self as tense, apprehensive; self as socially adequate; self as hostile, aggressive; physical and psychological self-worth; and self as conforming, conscientious, dependent. Tentative norms are given for each subscale in the form of percentiles or stanines.

As examples, the first eight of the twenty-five items in Part 2 of the test are given below.

52. Wants to do things successfully.
53. Has an interesting hobby.
54. Feels secure and safe.
55. Is cheerful.
56. Is not accepted by his class.
57. Is confident.
58. Is rarely trusted by other people.
59. Often has success in the things he does.

RELIABILITY AND VALIDITY: Preliminary try-out testing and analyses of test items were undertaken with data obtained from 10-year-old children enrolled in Brisbane schools. A subsequent validity study to establish construct validity of the test using a multitrait-multimethod matrix (Campbell and Fiske, 1959) indicated construct validity adequate for further development of the test. Results obtained from administration to 389 boys and girls aged 10 to 13 years provided data for a principal-axis factor analysis and oblique-rotation procedure to establish subscales within the test items. The present experimental version of the test is based on these subscales. Test-retest reliability on preliminary adjective checklist and pencil-and-paper Q-sort combined yielded a product-moment coefficient of .86, with six weeks intervening.

BIBLIOGRAPHY:

Andrews, R. J. "The Relationship Among Self-Concepts, Motivations, and Pupil Achievements in School." Unpublished doctoral dissertation. University of Queensland, Australia, 1970.
Andrews, R. J. "The Self-Concepts of Good and Poor Readers." *The Slow Learning Child,* 1971, *18,* 160-167.
Campbell, D. T., and Fiske, D. W. "Convergent and Discriminant Validation by the Multitrait-Multimethod Matrix." *Psychological Bulletin,* 1959, *56,* 81-105.
Miles, J., and others. "The Long- and Short-Term Predictive Efficiency of Two Tests of Grading Potential." *The Slow Learning Child,* 1973, *20,* 131-141.

---

# RESPONSE-TO-CONSTRUCTS TEST

AUTHOR: Arthur D. Wooster

AGE: 10 years and up

VARIABLE: Conceptions of self and others

TYPE OF MEASURE: Sorting test

SOURCE FROM WHICH MEASURE MAY BE OBTAINED: Arthur D. Wooster, School of Education, University of Nottingham, University Park, Nottingham, England NG7 2RD.

DESCRIPTION OF MEASURE: This technique, highly adaptable in its application, is a sorting test. Test materials are variable but dictated by the constructs being examined. A set of questions, formulated by the investigator to clarify an area, or areas, of the subject's phenomenal field, make up the test content. These are presented as sorting categories, for example: "Which boy is most like you?" "Which boy is most like you as you would like to be?" "Which boy is most likely to feel shy when meeting strangers?" The subject is required to order the test material repeatedly, each individual ranking being a demonstration of the meaning of the question to the subject. In Wooster and Harris (1972) the test material was eight photographs of boys with whom the subject could identify. Comparison between rankings yields an estimate of association that is assumed to reflect the degree of psychological relationship between the constructs embodied in the questions.

RELIABILITY AND VALIDITY: The reliability of an individual's protocol is higher for constructs that are meaningful to him. Constructs central to his phenomenal world show less change over time. Low reliability of some constructs for such populations as the subnormal, the very young, and the highly mobile is to be expected. Conventionally opposed constructs may be introduced as a check on validity. Test protocols are examined in practice for conventional responses, for example, negative associations between orderings made in response to constructs embodying notions of aggression and kindness. Subjects for whom the construct presented has no meaning will show this by making random choices and forming weak associations; idiosyncratic interpretations or lying would yield unusual but systematic choices. Indications of the reliability and validity of this form of testing are provided in the references.

BIBLIOGRAPHY:

Wooster, A. D. "Testing the Ability to Respond to Verbal Instructions." *British Journal of Disorders of Communication,* 1968, *3,* 156-160.
Wooster, A. D. "Assessment of the Ability to Respond to Verbally Labeled Concepts." *British Journal of Disorders of Communication,* 1969, *4,* 127-133.
Wooster, A. D. "Social and Ethnic Differences in Understanding the Spoken Word." *British Journal of Disorders of Communication,* 1970, *5,* 118-125.
Wooster, A. D. and Harris, G. "Concepts of Self and Others in Highly Mobile Service Boys." *Educational Research,* 1972, *14,* 195-199.

---

# SELF-APPRAISAL INVENTORY (SAI), PRIMARY FORM

AUTHORS: Instructional Objectives Exchange—UCLA Center for the Study of Evaluation

AGE: 7 to 10 years

VARIABLE: Self-concept

TYPE OF MEASURE: Self-report

SOURCE FROM WHICH MEASURE MAY BE OBTAINED: Instructional Objectives Exchange, UCLA Center for the Study of Evaluation, Box 24095, Los Angeles, California 90024. The SAI is contained in an objectives collection entitled *Measures of Self Concept.* Cost: $8.00 for total collection.

DESCRIPTION OF MEASURE: The SAI is a direct self-report test designed to measure positive self-concept. The test is available in three levels: primary, intermediate, and secondary. This description will be concerned with the primary form. The primary level SAI is a forty-item test requiring yes/no responses to a series of questions dealing with self-concept along four dimensions or subscales: peer, family, scholastic, and general. The following are sample practice items for the primary form: (1) Are you a child? (2) Are you a train? (3) Do you have a brother? (4) Do birds fly? The composite score can also be used to provide a more global estimate of self concept. Although the SAI was originally designed as a criterion-referenced instrument, Edeburn and other writers (see Popham, 1972) have established its use in general research situations.

RELIABILITY AND VALIDITY: Popham (1972) reported test-retest stability of .73 for the composite score. Edeburn (1973) reported internal consistency coefficients (Cronbach's *alpha*) of .78, .83, and .86 for three groups on the composite score.

BIBLIOGRAPHY:

Edeburn, C. E. "An Analysis of Self-Concept in Two Elementary Schools in Relationship to Sex, Grade Level, and Teacher." Unpublished doctoral dissertation. University of North Dakota, Grand Forks, 1973.

Edeburn, C. E., and Landry, R. G. "Self-Concepts of Students and a Significant Other, the Teacher." *Psychological Reports,* 1974, *35,* 505-506.

Edeburn, C. E., and Landry, R. G. "Teacher Self-Concept and Student Self-Concept." Paper presented at the annual meeting of the American Educational Research Association. Chicago, April 1974. ERIC document no. 088 892.

Instructional Objectives Exchange. *Measures of Self-Concept.* Los Angeles: Instructional Objectives Exchange, 1970.

Popham, W. J. "Empirical Based Revision of Affecting Measuring Instruments." Paper presented at the annual meeting of the California Educational Research Association. San Jose, November 1972.

*Prepared by Carl E. Edeburn*

---

# SELF-APPRAISAL SCALE

AUTHORS: Helen H. Davidson and Judith W. Greenberg

AGE: 8 to 14 years

VARIABLE: Self-concept

TYPE OF MEASURE: Rating scale

SOURCE FROM WHICH MEASURE MAY BE OBTAINED: Judith W. Greenberg, City College of the City University of New York, Convent Avenue and 138th Street, New York, New York 10031.

DESCRIPTION OF MEASURE: The Self-Appraisal Scale is designed to measure personal and academic self-concepts. Each of the twenty-four items presents a word or short phrase, and the child is instructed to check one of three columns describing the frequency with which the concept fits. (For example, "I think I try my best—most of the time—about half of the time—hardly ever.") The items cover learning behaviors and personal and interpersonal qualities. Positive words and phrases are scored 3 if checked "most of the time," 2 if "half the time," and 1 if "hardly ever." Scoring is reversed for negative items. Response-set controls consist of an intermixture of positive and negative items. Factor analysis yielded four factors: personal competence, social competence, academic competence, and nonintellectual competence. The first three factors differentiated significantly between high and low achievers in a fifth-grade ghetto sample.

As examples, the first ten of the twenty-four items on the scale, answered "most of the time," "about half the time," or "hardly ever," are given below.

1. Near.
2. A big help at home.
3. Smart in school.
4. Shy.
5. A pest.
6. Very good in art.
7. Scared to take chances.
8. Full of fun.
9. A hard worker.
10. Polite.

RELIABILITY AND VALIDITY: The split-half reliability of the scale is .77.

BIBLIOGRAPHY:

Davidson, H. H., and Greenberg, J. W. *School Achievers from a Deprived Background.* New York: Associated Educational Services, 1967.
Strauss, S. "The Effects of Social Integration on the Self-Concept of Negro and Puerto Rican Children." *Graduate Research in Education and Related Disciplines,* 1966, *2,* 63-76.

*Prepared by Judith W. Greenberg*

---

# SELF-AS-PUPIL Q-SORT

AUTHORS: Edward A. Wicas and Thomas W. Mahan, Jr.

AGE: 9 to 15 years

VARIABLE: Self-concept and ideal self-concept as a pupil

TYPE OF MEASURE: Self-description rating scale

SOURCE FROM WHICH MEASURE MAY BE OBTAINED: Edward A. Wicas, School of Education, University of Connecticut, Storrs, Connecticut 06268.

DESCRIPTION OF MEASURE: The instrument is designed to measure the concept of self-in-role and concept of ideal self-in-role as a tool in exploring adequacy of performance in a specific setting: the school classroom. The Q-sort procedure follows that suggested by Stephenson (1953) and used by Rogers (1954) and others. The Self-as-Pupil Q-Sort consists of fifty descriptive statements of personal functioning permitting clinical inferences about children's behavior in school, personal feelings, attitudes toward teachers and classmates, abilities, achievement, marks, and social life. Respondents are requested to force-sort the fifty items over a 9-point scale on a continuum from "describes me best" to "describes me least," first to describe the present view of self, then a second sort describing how the individual would like to be. The paper-and-pencil format permits group administration. Most pupils can complete the two sorts in approximately 50 minutes.

Examples of the descriptive statements from the Q-Sort are given below.

1. I like to be the boss or leader.
2. I give in to others easily even when I don't want to.
3. I like to be different.
4. I like to annoy the teacher.
5. I am smart.
6. I am afraid others will laugh at me when I have to recite.
7. I do only enough school work to get by.
8. I don't like other people to help me with my school work.
9. I feel like I never have all my work done.

RELIABILITY AND VALIDITY: One hundred and six ninth-grade pupils wrote autobiographical essays describing the way they presently saw themselves and the way they would like themselves to be. Content and language analysis of the essays produced the pool of meaningful and appropriate descriptive statements that form the basis for content validity of the final fifty items extracted for inclusion in the instrument. The Q-sort was administered to 221 eighth-grade pupils divided into an adequate (adjusted) group, $N = 155$, and an inadequate (maladjusted) group, $N = 66$, along the dimensions of underachievement, overachievement, disciplinary difficulties, and social isolation. Findings substantiated the hypothesis that adequacy of behavior in a specific role is related to the size of descrepancy between the individual's perception of self in that role and one's perception of how one ought to be in that role. Wicas and Mahan (1965) provide the ranges, means, standard deviations, and $Z$s for the total sample and the adjusted and maladjusted halves.

BIBLIOGRAPHY:

Rogers, C. R. "An Overview of the Research and Some Questions for the Future." In C. R. Rogers and R. F. Dymond (Eds.), *Psychotherapy and Personality Change.* Chicago: University of Chicago Press, 1954.

Stephenson, W. *The Study of Behavior: Q Technique and Its Methodology.* Chicago: University of Chicago Press, 1953.

Wicas, E. A., and Mahan, T. W., Jr. "Phenomenological Constructs, Social Standards, and School Performance." *Journal of School Psychology,* 1965, *4,* 29-36.

# SELF-CONCEPT OF ABILITY AS A WORKER SCALE

AUTHORS: Donald Burke and Donald Sellin

AGE: Adolescent and older

VARIABLE: Self-concept

TYPE OF MEASURE: Interview

SOURCE FROM WHICH MEASURE MAY BE OBTAINED: See Burke (1972).

DESCRIPTION OF MEASURE: The Self-Concept of Ability as a Worker Scale consists of six sections of questions (a total of thirty-seven items) designed to be used as a research instrument or to identify persons who might require special counseling and/or program alternatives to improve self-concept. The first six items (Section I) are warm-up questions. In Section II the respondent is asked about Significant Others (three items). Section III deals with Self-Concept of Ability as a Worker: General (thirteen items). The remaining fifteen items concern Perceived Self-Concept of Ability as a Worker by Parents, Friend, and Teacher. Most of the items of the measure are scored on a 5-point scale. The scale should be used as a formative rather than a summative measure; that is, the results should *not* be used to screen a person out of a program because of a "low" self-concept.

As examples, three of the thirteen items from Section III, Self Concept of Ability as a Worker: General, together with possible answers, are given below.

4. How do you rate yourself in *job ability* compared with your close friends?
   (5) I am the best.
   (4) I am above average.
   (3) I am average.
   (2) I am below average.
   (1) I am the poorest.
6. Where do you think you will rank in *job ability* when you leave this school?
   (5) Among the best.
   (4) Above average.
   (3) Average.
   (2) Below average.
   (1) Among the poorest.
9. In order to become a more skilled worker (nurse, secretary, tool and dye worker, TV repairman), more training beyond this school is necessary. Do you think that you could complete such training?
   (5) I'm sure I can.
   (4) I think I might.
   (3) I am not sure.
   (2) I think I might not.
   (1) I'm sure I can't.

RELIABILITY AND VALIDITY: Test-retest reliability and internal consistency have been found to be acceptable. The question of validity remains open to investigation, especially in the area of predictive validity. However, based upon two studies, it is felt that the scale is highly appropriate for research studies concerning comparisons of normal populations with exceptional populations.

BIBLIOGRAPHY:

Burke, D. A. "Measuring the Self-Concept of Ability as a Worker." *Exceptional Children,* 1972, *39,* 126-132.

*Prepared by Donald Sellin*

---

# SELF-CONCEPT AS A LEARNER (SCAL)

AUTHOR: Walter B. Waetjen

AGE: 10 to 18 years

VARIABLE: Student's view of self as a learner

TYPE OF MEASURE: Likert-type scale

SOURCE FROM WHICH MEASURE MAY BE OBTAINED: Walter B. Waetjen, Office of the President, Cleveland State University, Cleveland, Ohio 44114. Cost: $.12 per copy.

DESCRIPTION OF MEASURE: The instrument is a rating scale containing fifty items arranged into four subsections dealing with the following areas: problem-solving ability, motivation, task orientation, and class membership. A sample test item reads as follows: "I solve problems quite easily." The instrument was developed by obtaining a universe of 400 self-referential items that were given to a large sample population. Ultimately, factor analysis and item analysis yielded the subtests as well as the fifty stems included in the present form of the instrument. The test is designed to be given to groups of students by a teacher, counselor, or principal. Approximately 20 minutes is required to take the test, which employs the Likert scaling technique with answers on a 5-point scale ranging from "completely true" to "completely false." The scoring takes approximately 5 minutes following instructions, which are available. Five scores are obtainable, one for each subsection and a composite score.

RELIABILITY AND VALIDITY: Three studies of reliability of SCAL have been conducted with normal subjects. Two of the studies investigated overall reliability of the instrument as well as reliability of each of the component parts. The third study yielded a reliability figure only for the total test. Results are as follows:

|          | Motivation | Task Orientation | Intellectual Ability | Class Membership | Total |
|----------|-----------|------------------|---------------------|------------------|-------|
| Study A  | .61       | .73              | .80                 | .66              | .80   |
|          | (test-retest after seven days) | | | | |
| Study B  | .61       | .81              | .73                 | .75              | .90   |
|          | (test-retest after eight days) | | | | |
| Study C  | (test-retest after thirty-five days) | | | | .90 |

Content validity was indicated by judges who were able to agree on the responses of students with high SCAL and low SCAL.

BIBLIOGRAPHY:

Beehrman, H. D. "The Effects of a Change from an Older School Building to a Newly Constructed School Building on the Self-Concept as a Learner of High School Students." Unpublished doctoral dissertation. Pennsylvania State University, University Park, 1971.

Bouchard, R. P. "An Experiment in Student Self-Concept Change Through Teacher Interaction." Unpublished doctoral dissertation. St. Louis University, Missouri, 1970.

Fisher, J. K. "An Investigation of the Relationship Between Separation by Sex of Eighth Grade Students and English Achievement and Self-Concept." Unpublished doctoral dissertation. University of Maryland, College Park, 1964.

Flynn, R. V., and Stone, R. W. "A Comparison of Students' Self-Concepts and Teachers' Perceptions of the Individual's Self-Concept with Rate of Adjustment in a Changed Learning Environment." Unpublished doctoral dissertation. University of Pittsburgh, Pennsylvania, 1972.

Kolodner, F. K. "The Self-Concept of Nonachieving Readers." Unpublished master's thesis. University of Maryland, College Park, 1964.

Lovin, J. C., Jr. "The Effect of the School's Physical Environment on the Self-Concepts of Elementary School Students." Unpublished doctoral dissertation. University of Georgia, Athens, 1972.

Miller, S. D. "Personalized Learning in a High School Psychology Course: An Experimental Investigation." Unpublished doctoral dissertation. University of Akron, Ohio, 1973.

Olavarri, M. C. "Some Relationships of Ability Grouping and Student Self-Concept." Unpublished doctoral dissertation. University of California, Berkeley, 1967.

Owen, E. H., Jr. "A Comparison of Disadvantaged and Nondisadvantaged Elementary School Pupils on Two Measures of Self-Concept as Learner." Unpublished doctoral dissertation. University of Florida, Gainesville, 1972.

Pankratz, S. M. "The Effect of an Evaluation Procedure on a Student Nurse's Self-Perceptions." Unpublished master's thesis. University of Saskatchewan, Regina, Canada, 1972.

Pumphrey, R. "Relationship Between Teachers' Perceptions of Organizational Climate in Elementary Schools and Selected Variables Associated with Pupils." Unpublished doctoral dissertation. University of Maryland, College Park, 1968.

Ross, J. D. "A Study of the Effect of the Learning Environment on Selected Factors Related to the Self-Concept of School Children." Unpublished doctoral dissertation. University of Massachusetts, Amherst, 1972.

Wiesen, H. H. "An Investigation of Relationships Among Intelligence, Organizational Climate in the Classroom and Self-Concept as a Learner Among Ten and Eleven Year Olds." Unpublished doctoral dissertation. University of Maryland, College Park, 1965.

---

## SELF-CONCEPT AS A MEASURE OF DIRECTIONALITY TOWARD AND AWAY FROM DELINQUENCY

AUTHORS: Walter C. Reckless, Simon Dinitz, and others

AGE: 12 to 14 years

VARIABLE: Directionality toward or away from delinquency

TYPE OF MEASURE: Checklist

SOURCE FROM WHICH MEASURE MAY BE OBTAINED: Walter C. Reckless, Department of Sociology, Ohio State University, 112 Hagerty Hall, 1175 South College Road, Columbus, Ohio 43210.

DESCRIPTION OF MEASURE: This self-concept instrument reflects directionality— toward or away from delinquency. Low scores are in the delinquent direction; high scores represent tendencies to stay out of trouble. The instrument is best administered to sixth-grade classes in public schools. The low scorers can receive special attention from special school services and from teachers. There is a long form of thirty-two items and a short form of fourteen items. Of the thirty-two items, sixteen are scored. High scores reflect poor self-concepts and tendencies toward delinquency. Of the fourteen items in the short form, seven are scored in the unfavorable direction.

As examples, the first ten of the thirty-two items of the long form of the instrument are given below. The respondent answers "yes," "no," or "don't know" to each item.

1. Do you think that things are pretty well stacked against you?
2. Will you probably be taken to juvenile court sometime?
3. Did anyone ever tell you that you have a problem?
4. Will you probably have to go to jail sometime?
5. If you could start all over again, would you choose the same friends?
6. If you found that a friend was leading you into trouble, would you continue to run around with him or her?
7. Do you consider yourself to be a wise guy?
8. Do you plan to finish high school?
9. Do your parents punish you when you don't deserve it?
10. Do you think you'll stay out of trouble in the future?

RELIABILITY AND VALIDITY: Reckless and his associates made certain that the wording used in the self-concept instrument was understandable by 12-year-old boys in slum areas. They administered the instrument by having qualified graduate research assistants make a satisfying statement in front of each class and then proceed to hand out the schedule. The assistants would then read the directions and follow by reading each question aloud and indicating the directionality of the three possible answers. The wording of the questions was checked against a fourth-grade word list. The researchers also obtained ratings of directionality of each subject's behavior from the teachers of the various classrooms. They also checked the ratings of directionality given by mothers of the subjects. They cleared the cases through the police files (delinquency section) and through the juvenile court for previous, present, and future delinquency involvement. They also correlated the scores on the self-concept instrument with other pertinent tests of the directionality of behavior.

BIBLIOGRAPHY:

Dinitz, S., Scarpitti, F. R., and Reckless, W. C. "Delinquency Vulnerability: A Cross-Group and Longitudinal Analysis." *American Sociological Review*, 1962, *27*, 515-517.

Reckless, W. C., Dinitz, S., and Kay, B. "The Self-Component in Potential Delinquency." *American Sociological Review*, 1957, *22*, 566-570.

Reckless, W. C., Dinitz, S., and Murray, E. "Self-Concept as an Insulator Against Delinquency." *American Sociological Review*, 1956, *21*, 744-746.

Scarpitti, F. R., Murray, E., Dinitz, S., and Reckless, W. C. "The 'Good' Boy in a High Delinquency Area: Four Years Later." *American Sociological Review*, 1960, *25*, 555-558.

---

# SELF-CONCEPT AND MOTIVATION INVENTORY (SCAMIN)

AUTHORS: George A. Farrah, Norman J. Milchus, and William Reitz

AGE: Junior high and secondary school

VARIABLE: Self-concept and motivation

TYPE OF MEASURE: Pictorial rating scale

SOURCE FROM WHICH MEASURE MAY BE OBTAINED: Person-O-Metrics, 20504 Williamsburg, Dearborn Heights, Michigan 48127. Cost: Complete specimen set (secondary form keys excluded), $5.00; response sheets, $8.00 per 50 (minimum order $10.00). Postage charges will be added to invoice.

DESCRIPTION OF MEASURE: The Self-Concept and Motivation Inventory was developed on a theoretical, factorial model that attempts to control the vagueness and multidimensionality of item content (Farrah, Milchus, and Reitz, 1967). Theoretical constructs for this academic (junior high and secondary-school forms) model divides self-concept into scores for role expectations and self-adequacy (Mead, 1934). Motivation is composed of academic and social goal/achievement needs and personal investment. Items that are typical of the total sixty-four are given below.

1. What face would you wear if your parents were openly pleased with your grades?
2. —if your favorite teacher was warning the class about the dangers of being a drop-out, and she or he looked straight at you?

RELIABILITY AND VALIDITY: By 1966, SCAMIN was extended to include higher levels and was field-tested on stratified, randomized, proportionate samples of over one thousand public school youth in and near Detroit and Wayne and Oakland Counties, Michigan. The Spearman-Brown split-half method, utilizing a correction formula for the odd-even items, revealed reliability coefficients for the subparts ranging from .73 to .92 and a total inventory reliability of .93. All coefficients were significant at the 5-percent level. In addition to concurrent validity (teacher judgment and SCAMIN scores), multiple-group methodology of factor analysis with both oblique and orthogonal solutions was performed. Validity coefficients, with $p < .05$, ranged from .54 to .91.

BIBLIOGRAPHY:

Farrah, G. A., Milchus, N. J., and Reitz, W. "The Treatise on Methodology: Estimating Reliability and Validity for the Self-Concept and Motivation Inventory." Unpublished document. 1967.

Farrah, G. A., Milchus, N. J., and Reitz, W. "The Construct Validity of a Self-Concept and Motivation Inventory Which Controls Item Content Through Factorial Structure." Paper presented at the annual meeting of the National Council on Measurements in Education. Chicago, February 1968.

Mead, G. H. *Mind, Self, and Society.* Chicago: University of Chicago Press, 1934.

---

## SELF-CONCEPT TARGET GAME (SCTG)

AUTHOR: Ann M. Fitzgibbon

AGE: Grades 2 to 3

VARIABLE: Level of aspiration

TYPE OF MEASURE: Test of dexterity utilizing feedback

SOURCE FROM WHICH MEASURE MAY BE OBTAINED: Ann M. Fitzgibbon, Far West Laboratory for Educational Research and Development, 1855 Folsom Street, San Francisco, California 94103. For research purposes at no cost, providing data are made available to author.

DESCRIPTION OF MEASURE: The game is played by throwing or passing a bean bag along a plastic board while attempting to hit a target with a particular value. The large box nearest the starting circle has a value of 1, the middle box a value of 3, and the box farthest from the target a value of 5. Within each large box are smaller targets, each with more points to earn. Since the smaller targets are harder to hit, they are worth more points. The subject decides which target to try for, calls his target, and the bean bag must land there in order to earn the value of the target. If he misses, the subject earns no points on that trial. The game consists of eleven trials, and after each trial the subject is advised of his last call and success or failure and is asked to pick his next target. While the object of the game as explained to the subject is to earn as many points as possible, interest is chiefly in how choices are revised based on feedback. For this reason, a total score on the game is determined by subtracting the value of the guess on any one trial from the actual performance on the previous trial and summing the discrepancies ignoring the signs. Since smaller discrepancies are more desirable, the lower the total score, the more realistic the level of aspiration. The SCTG may be administered individually or to groups of up to five subjects.

RELIABILITY AND VALIDITY: The Self-Concept Target Game has undergone three field-tests with second and third graders throughout the country. In the first field-test, a simple procedure of sorting the test protocols into those who made realistic choices of targets (up after success and down after failure) indicated that the game has some validity since the results correlated with teachers' choices of children high and low in self-concept. In scoring the results of the second and third field-test, a simple discrepancy score was used as a measure of performance; that is, the differences between the hit on one trial and the choice on the next trial were summed, ignoring the differences. Results of the second field test indicated that Responsive Model Follow-Through children performed better (had lower discrepancy scores) than children not exposed to the special program, and that the most realistic performance was given by children whose teachers scored highest on the Responsive Observation Schedule for teachers and who were black. While white children out-performed blacks, black children in integrated classrooms did better than black children in segregated classrooms. In general, girls did better than boys. Reliability for the test was found to be .87. The third and largest field-test included 553 second and third graders in five school districts throughout the country. The large sample allowed for determining various characteristics of the Target Game. The number of trials on the game was increased from six to eleven in the hope of increasing the reliability. Results indicated that of the ten possible comparisons between each school district with every other one, nine were significantly different. In general, second graders did better than third graders, blacks were less realistic than whites, boys less than girls, and enrollment in the Responsive Model Follow-Through program did not seem to make a difference in score. While these differences appeared for the total group and each school as well, when school boundaries are ignored, differences between grades are reduced, and differences between races disappear. Schools in the same district differed more from one another than did one district from another. Reliability for the total test in five school districts ranged from .46 to .54.

BIBLIOGRAPHY:

Fitzgibbon, A. Self-Concept Target Game: A Revised Report. Berkeley, California: Far West Laboratory for Educational Research and Development, 1971.

Fitzgibbon, A. *Self-Concept Target Game: A Comprehensive Report.* San Francisco: Far West Laboratory for Educational Research and Development, 1973.

---

## SELF-DESCRIPTION SELF-RATING SCALE

AUTHORS: Edward Clifford and Miriam Clifford

VARIABLE: Self-concept

AGE: 10 to 17 years

TYPE OF MEASURE: Rating scale, checklist

SOURCE FROM WHICH MEASURE MAY BE OBTAINED: Edward Clifford, Box 3894, Duke University Medical Center, Durham, North Carolina 27710.

DESCRIPTION OF MEASURE: This dual scale was used originally on a group of adolescent boys in an Outward-Bound School summer camp in Colorado to measure change in self-concept. The scale was subsequently modified for use with adolescents aged 11 to 17 in a research program comparing self-concept among groups of cleft-palate, asthmatic, obese, and normal adolescents. Response categories were reduced from seven to four, and some items were more appropriately reworded. The number of items on the Self-Description Scale was reduced from thirty-four to twenty. The fifteen items of the Self-Rating Scale remained the same. Direction of scoring was reversed so that higher scores indicate positive self-concept. See Clifford and Clifford (1967).

As examples, the first ten of the twenty items on the Self-Description Scale are given below. They are answered on a 4-point scale ranging from "exactly like me" to "exactly unlike me."

1. Able to get along with everybody.
2. Accomplish things.
3. A good leader of others.
4. Ambitious.
5. Athletic.
6. Confident.
7. Fearful.
8. Friendly.
9. Healthy.
10. Look good.

The first seven of the fifteen items on the Self-Rating Scale are given below. They are answered on a 4-point scale ranging from "all of the time" to "none of the time."

1. I believe in myself.
2. I expect to succeed in things I do.
3. Life is a strain for me.
4. I think very little of my abilities.
5. I am satisfied with the way I am.
6. I am a good mixer.
7. I can't do anything right.

RELIABILITY AND VALIDITY: Test-retest reliability was measured using twenty-nine normal adolescents. The test-retest interval ranged from two to nineteen months with an average of 10.5 months. The reliability coefficient for the Self-Description Scale was .54 and for the Self-Rating Scale, .57. In the Outward Bound-School study (Clifford and Clifford, 1967) the test did measure change in self-concept in the predicted direction after survival training.

BIBLIOGRAPHY:

Clifford, E. "Connotative Meanings of Self- and Asthma-Related Concepts for Subgroups of Asthmatic Children." *Journal of Psychosomatic Research*, 1965, *8*, 457-475.
Clifford, E., and Clifford, M. "Self-Concepts Before and After Survival Training." *British Journal of Social and Clinical Psychology*, 1967, *6*, 241-248.
Dickey, B. A. "Attitudes Toward Sex Roles and Feelings of Adequacy in Homosexual Males." *Journal of Consulting Psychology*, 1961, *25*, 116-122.

# SELF-ESTEEM SCALE

AUTHOR: Morris Rosenberg

AGE: Adolescent

VARIABLE: Self-esteem

TYPE OF MEASURE: Questionnaire, structured interview

SOURCE FROM WHICH MEASURE MAY BE OBTAINED: Morris Rosenberg, Laboratory of Socioenvironmental Studies, National Institute of Mental Health, 9000 Rockville Pike, Building 10, Room 3D-45, Bethesda, Maryland 20014.

DESCRIPTION OF MEASURE: The Self-Esteem Scale is a ten-item Guttman scale designed to measure global positive or negative attitudes toward the self. The ten items are of the Likert type allowing one of four responses: "strongly agree," "agree," "disagree," and "strongly disagree." Positively and negatively worded items are presented alternatively in order to reduce response set. Through the use of contrived items, the ten items are scored to yield a 7-point scale. Items are of the following type: "I feel that I have a number of good qualities. All in all, I am inclined to feel that I am a failure. I am able to do things as well as most other people. I feel I do not have much to be proud of. I take a positive attitude toward myself. I wish I could have more respect for myself." High self-esteem signifies that the individual respects himself and considers himself worthy; it does not indicate that he believes himself to be superior to others. Low self-esteem reflects both lack of self-respect and feelings of inadequacy.

RELIABILITY AND VALIDITY: The scale was originally administered to 5,024 high school juniors and seniors from ten randomly selected public high schools in New York state. Using the Guttman procedure, the reproducibility was 92 percent and the scalability 72 percent. The items thus have internal reliability. Test-retest reliability for forty college students studied by Silber and Tippett (1965) was .85. Evidence of construct validity appears in the high correlation between the Self-Esteem Scale and a scale of depressive affect on the one hand and a measure of psychophysiological indicators of anxiety on the other. In addition, ward nurses observing fifty young adult normal volunteers at the National Institute of Mental Health described those who had scored low on the Self-Esteem Scale as being often gloomy and frequently disappointed. An additional study found adolescents with low self-esteem to have lower sociometric scores.

BIBLIOGRAPHY:

Rosenberg, M. "The Association Between Self-Esteem and Anxiety." *Journal of Psychiatric Research*, 1962, *1*, 135-152.

Rosenberg, M. "The Dissonant Religious Context and Emotional Disturbance." *American Journal of Sociology*, 1962, *68*, 1-10.

Rosenberg, M. "Self-Esteem and Concern with Public Affairs." *Public Opinion Quarterly*, 1962, *26*, 201-211.

Rosenberg, M. "Parental Interest and Children's Self-Conceptions." *Sociometry*, 1963, *26*, 35-49.

Rosenberg, M. *Society and the Adolescent Self-Image.* Princeton, New Jersey: Princeton University Press, 1965.

Silber, E., and Tippett, J. S. "Self-Esteem: Clinical Assessment and Measurement Validation." *Psychological Reports*, 1965, *16*, 1017-1071.

---

# SELF-EVALUATION OF PERSONAL ACTION

AUTHOR: Barbara J. Brandes

AGE: 10 to 18 years

VARIABLE: Self-concept

TYPE OF MEASURE: Self-rating; dichotomous response

SOURCE FROM WHICH MEASURE MAY BE OBTAINED: Research for Better Schools, Inc., Public Information Office, 1700 Market Street, Philadelphia, Pennsylvania 19103. Will be provided at cost.

DESCRIPTION OF MEASURE: Self-Evaluation of Personal Action is a twenty-item scale that is useful in obtaining a quick assessment of self-concept in a group setting, particularly for purposes of program evaluation. It yields an index for evaluations of one's own actions. Emphasis is on aspects of the self-concept pertaining to personal actions and behaviors. Specifically excluded are those aspects of the self-concept, such as feelings about personal appearance and family relationships, that are unlikely to be changed in a school context.

As examples, the first five of the twenty items on the scale are given below. The respondent answers "yes" or "no."

1. There are lots of things I've done that make me feel good.
2. I have a hard time thinking of things to do with my free time.
3. Other kids seem to have much more fun than I do.
4. I feel that I have as much to be proud of as most people.
5. I feel OK about the way I do in sports.

RELIABILITY AND VALIDITY: An estimate of the reliability of the instrument is based on a sample of 1,359 10- to 12-year-old children representing primarily the middle and upper-middle economic classes in a large metropolitan area. An internal consistency reliability of .77 was computed for the scale using Kuder-Richardson formula 20. Empirical validity for the scale has been determined primarily through its relationship to other variables. A correlation of $-.49$ was obtained with a measure of test anxiety, and a correlation coefficient of .35 was obtained with a measure of internal locus of control.

BIBLIOGRAPHY:

Brandes, B. J. *Achievement Competence Training: Field Test and Evaluation.* Philadelphia, Pennsylvania: Research for Better Schools, 1974.

---

## SELF-FATHER RATING SCALE (SFRS)

AUTHOR: Darryl E. Matter

AGE: 9 years and older

VARIABLE: Perception of self-competence compared with father

TYPE OF MEASURE: Rating scale

SOURCE FROM WHICH MEASURE MAY BE OBTAINED: See Matter (1964). A limited number of copies are also available at no cost from Darryl E. Matter, Department of Child Development and Family Relations, South Dakota State University, Brookings, South Dakota 57006.

DESCRIPTION OF MEASURE: The SFRS consists of fifteen areas in which the respondent can rate himself in comparison with his father on a 3-point scale: "I am better than my father," "I am equal with my father," or "My father is better than I am." Scoring is simple and the measure would be easily quantifiable for research purposes. Area scores as well as overall scores for each subject on his perception of his own competence compared with his father are easily derived. Additional subscales can be added by the researcher in areas not included in the original SFRS.

As examples, five of the fifteen areas of comparison are given below.

1. Common sense (good judgment).
2. Friendliness
3. Saving money.
4. Courage.
5. Health.

RELIABILITY AND VALIDITY: None reported.

BIBLIOGRAPHY:

Matter, D. E. "The Development of Selected Aspects of the Self-Concept in Children, From the Third Grade Through High School." Unpublished master's thesis. Kansas State University, Manhattan, 1964.

Matter, D. E. "Children's Comparison of Selves with Father." *Mental Hygiene,* 1967, *51,* 193-196.

Matter, D. E., and Matter, S. L. "College Student's Comparison of Selves with Fathers." Unpublished paper, 1972.

---

## SELF-PERCEPTION INVENTORY (STUDENT FORMS)

AUTHORS: Anthony T. Soares and Louise M. Soares

AGE: Elementary and secondary school

VARIABLE: Self-concept, ideal concept, various reflected selves

TYPE OF MEASURE: Semantic differential

SOURCE FROM WHICH MEASURE MAY BE OBTAINED: Anthony T. Soares and Louise M. Soares, University of Bridgeport, Bridgeport, Connecticut 06602. Cost: $1.00 per specimen set, plus $.25 postage and handling per specimen set; each test copy, $.10.

DESCRIPTION OF MEASURE: The student forms of the Self-Perception Inventory, utilizing forty traits as dichotomous pairs expressed in sentences, measures various dimensions of self-perceptions: Self-Concept (SC), Ideal Concept (IC), Reflected Self (as the respondent thinks others look at him/her—classmates, teachers, parents—$RS_c'$, $RS_t'$, $RS_p'$), and Student Self-Concept ($SC_s$). The Student Self-Concept uses school-oriented traits in the same format but having fifty traits measured. There is also a Per-ceptions-of-Others form to be used by the groups mentioned above—classmates, teach-ers, parents—in conjunction with the forty traits of the first set and also with the fifty traits of the Student Self-Concept. Each of the SPI forms is scored the same way. With four spaces of distance between the ends of the continuum, the "very" positive posi-tion receives a score of +2 when checked; the "more" positive position, a score of +1; "more" negative, −1; "very" negative, −2. The algebraic sum yields an index score.

As examples, the first items from four of the forms of the inventory are given below.

| | | |
|---|---|---|
| *Self-Concept:* | I am happy, most of the time. | I am not happy, most of the time. |
| *Ideal Concept:* | I would like to be a happy person. | I would not want to be a happy person. |
| *Reflected Self:* (*Classmates*) | My friends think I am a happy person. | My friends think I am not a happy person. |
| Student Self-Concept: | I do well in school. | I do poorly in school. |

RELIABILITY AND VALIDITY: A test-retest reliability coefficient was .88. The correlation of Coopersmith's Self-Esteem Inventory with the SPI scores was .68. Self-scores also have been validated against the scores on the same traits as given by the three groups mentioned above. See Soares and Soares (1974).

BIBLIOGRAPHY:

Soares, A. T., and Soares, L. M. "Self-Perceptions of Culturally Disadvantaged Children." *American Educational Research Journal,* 1969, *6,* 31-45.

Soares, A. T., and Soares, L. M. "Self-Concepts of Disadvantaged Students." *Child Study Journal,* Winter 1970-1971, *1,* 69-73.

Soares, A. T., and Soares, L. M. "Comparative Differences in the Self-Perceptions of Disadvantaged and Advantaged Students." *Journal of School Psychology,* 1971, *9,* 424-429.

Soares, A. T., and Soares, L. M. "Self-Perceptions of Middle School Students." In *Education U.S.A.* Washington, D.C.: National School Public Relations Association, 1971.

Soares, A. T., and Soares, L. M. "A Comparative Study of the Self-Perceptions of Middle-School Pupils." *Elementary School Journal,* 1973, *73,* 381-389.

Soares, A. T., and Soares, L. M. "Significant Others and Self-Perceptions of Disadvantaged Students." Paper presented at annual meeting of the American Educational Research Association. Chicago, April 1974.

*Prepared by Louise M. Soares*

---

# SOMATIC APPERCEPTION TEST (SAT)

AUTHORS: Allen S. Rowe and Willard E. Caldwell

AGE: Males 12½ to 15½ years

VARIABLE: Perception of own body

TYPE OF MEASURE: Quantitative projective technique

SOURCE FROM WHICH MEASURE MAY BE OBTAINED: This test was designed as a research instrument. The test drawings can be made by following the procedures outlined in Rowe and Caldwell (1963). The test is not sold and if duplicated and used in research, proper credit must be given to authors (including name of test).

DESCRIPTION OF MEASURE: The test consists of seven body outline drawings. A model body type was copied from each of the seven major classes and somatypes described by Sheldon (1954). The anthroposcopic photographs of 18- and 20-year-old males were used for the drawings. These were utilized because they could serve as a frame of reference for adolescent as well as adult male *S*s for making judgments of their own body sizes. There was also an actual height-weight ratio for each photograph. In order to duplicate the actual physical limits of each figure, the drawings were carefully outlined along the boundary of each physique. The head and feet were proportioned according to the general characteristics of the somatotype. All the figures were drawn to a $3\frac{1}{8}$-inch scale and centered on 6 X 6-inch squares of illustrator board. The SAT cards were presented randomly to each $S$ and placed in front of each $S$ in a horizontal array. All $S$s were given the following instructions: "Look these drawings over. Select one you think looks the most like yourself." After the selection the $S$ is told, "Now select another drawing that you think looks the least like yourself."

The height divided by the cube root of weight, which Sheldon used in classifying somatotypes, served as one of the basic measures in this test. For each of the seven somatotypes there was a corresponding height-weight ratio. In order to compare the $S$s SAT selections with actual body size, the actual height-weight ratios were computed for each $S$. All $S$s were measured on standard physician scales either ten to thirty days before testing or immediately after the administration of the SAT. The $S$s actual height-weight ratio and the actual height-weight ratio of the SAT figures are the basic measures of the study, and a discrimination ratio is derived from these two. The DR score is derived from the following formula: $DR = M - A/M - L$. The $M$ stands for the SAT figure the $S$ considers "most like himself"; $L$, the SAT drawing he judges "least like himself"; and $A$, the $S$'s actual body size (as indicated by $S$'s actual height-weight ratio). The numerator ($M - A$) denotes an accuracy index of the $S$'s judgment of his own body size. The algebraic sign of this index indicates a tendency to either overevaluate or underevaluate body size. The denominator ($M - L$) indicates the range of discrimination of the $S$'s judgment of his body size. This absolute range reflects how well the $S$ differentiates his own body size. The DR score indicates the relative accuracy of judgments of body size.

RELIABILITY AND VALIDITY: The test was administered to fifty-eight male black adolescent delinquents, ranging from 12½ years to 15½ years, with a mean age of 14 years. These $S$s were divided into three groups: twenty $S$s with a mean age of 11.2 years, eighteen $S$s with a mean age of 13.1 years, and twenty $S$s with a mean age of 14.2 years. The combined data of the three age groups indicated that these black adolescent delinquents tended to underestimate their actual body size, and of the 14-year-old group 70 percent underestimated their actual body size. Three theoretical interpretations were proposed to account for these findings.

BIBLIOGRAPHY:

Adams, N. M., and Caldwell, W. E. "The Children's Somatic Apperception Test: A Technique for Quantifying Body Image." *Journal of General Psychology*, 1963, *68*, 43-57.

Caldwell, W. E., and Matoon, C. U. "The Somato-Chroma Apperception Test: A Quantitative Projective Technique." *Journal of General Psychology*, 1966, *74*, 253-272.

Rowe, A. S., and Caldwell, W. E. "The Somatic Apperception Test." *Journal of General Psychology*, 1963, *68*, 59-69.

Sheldon, W. H. *Atlas of Men.* New York: Harper & Row, 1954.

*Prepared by Willard E. Caldwell*

# WHAT I AM LIKE

AUTHOR: Cincinnati Public Schools: Psychological Services, Program, Research, and Design

AGE: 9 to 15 years

VARIABLE: Self-concept

TYPE OF MEASURE: Rating scale

SOURCE FROM WHICH MEASURE MAY BE OBTAINED: Charles B. Miller, Psychological Services, Cincinnati Public Schools, 230 East Ninth Street, Cincinnati, Ohio 45202. Sample copy on request.

DESCRIPTION OF MEASURE: This is an instrument to measure self-concept by having young people rate themselves on a 5-point, bipolar adjective scale. This technique is based on Osgood's concept of the semantic differential. The first subtest, *What I Look Like,* consists of adjectives characterizing physical attributes. The second, *What I Am,* attempts to measure self-image from a psychological point of view. The third, *What I Am Like When I Am With My Friends,* concerns social attributes. For each item on the rating scale, a score of 5 represents the positive pole of the trait and a score of 1 the negative pole. A rating of 3 may be viewed as neutral. In a few cases it is difficult to assign positive and negative polarity. The position of positive and negative poles is randomized to avoid a psychological set in rating the items.

RELIABILITY AND VALIDITY: None reported.

BIBLIOGRAPHY:

Jacobs, J. N. "A Description of the 'What I Am Like' Test." *Journal of Instructional Research and Program Development,* 1967, *3,* 29-35.

*Prepared by Charles B. Miller*

# Category 5

# Qualities of Caregiving and Home Environment

*Most of the measures in this category concern characteristics of parents, including their attitudes toward their children and child rearing. Measures of family characteristics such as communication patterns and integration are included here, as well as socioeconomic status and home stimulation and deprivation.*

# ADAPTIVE STRATEGIES INTERVIEW

AUTHOR: Daniel R. Scheinfeld

AGE: Parents

VARIABLE: Parents' ideas regarding children, child rearing, and the child's relationship to the world

TYPE OF MEASURE: Interview

SOURCE FROM WHICH MEASURE MAY BE OBTAINED: Manual of scoring dimensions and procedures available from D. Scheinfeld, Institute for Juvenile Research, 1140 S. Pauline, Chicago, Illinois 60612. See also Scheinfeld (1973).

DESCRIPTION OF MEASURE: Scoring dimensions and procedures have been developed for the following areas: purposeful agent (degree to which child is endorsed as an agent with his/her own purposes); social connectedness outside the family; active exchange with the environment beyond the home; dominance vs. exchange in relationships with parents and other adults; trust-selectivity (trust in the child's judgment); process of growth of competence (recognition and emphasis upon this process); the meaning of being adapted (appetitive vs. aversive); and adaptation to threat (the degree to which the adaptive model is oriented toward avoidance of threat in the here and now).

RELIABILITY AND VALIDITY: The interview was administered to thirty-three black mothers by black interviewers. Interviews were conducted with regard to mothers' ideas about raising *boys*. All correlations are on these data and data for boys' academic achievements. Coding was done by three coders, and their ratings were averaged. Correlations with an "achievement" factor composed of grades, achievement test scores, and IQ of the two boys in the family closest to age 13 were as follows: purposeful agent, .48; social connectedness, .48; active exchange with the environment, .48; dominance vs. exchange in relationships with parents and other adults, −.41; trust-selectivity, .49; and process of growth of competence (.66). Correlation between a factor made up of the above six dimensions with the achievement factor yielded .59. Correlations of the two remaining dimensions with the achievement factor were as follows: the meaning of being adapted, .51 and adaptation to threat, −.45. Correlation between a factor made up of all eight dimensions with the achievement factor was .59. Significance levels for all the above correlations are .40 = .01 level and .44 = .005 level.

BIBLIOGRAPHY:

Scheinfeld, Daniel R. "Dominance, Exchange and Achievement in a Lower Income Black Neighborhood." Unpublished doctoral dissertation. University of Chicago, 1973.

# ANDERS' CHILD-REARING ATTITUDE SURVEY

AUTHOR: Sarah Frances Anders

AGE: Adults working with dependents

VARIABLE: Permissiveness in socialization (infancy through adolescence)

TYPE OF MEASURE: Likert-type scale

SOURCE FROM WHICH MEASURE MAY BE OBTAINED: Sarah Frances Anders, Box 817, Louisiana College, Pineville, Louisiana 71360.

DESCRIPTION OF MEASURE: This scale was developed as a part of two research projects involving institutional personnel who worked with dependents (mentally retarded and mentally ill). It includes forty-seven items, of which forty-two are weighted to form a total CA score. The weightings for the various responses to items were established by a panel of experts, all department heads from one of the institutions involved in the study and from a local college. Possible score range was +84 to −83, the positive score representing the more permissive or child-oriented attitude and the negative score a more restrictive or adult-oriented attitude.

As examples, the first four items from each of the three subscales are given below.

*Infancy and Early Childhood*

1. The feeding of an infant or small child should be
   a. at the convenience of mother.
   b. at a definite and regular time.
   c. according to when he/she wants it.
2. If a baby cries when he is neither hurt, "wet," nor hungry, I believe
   a. he should be left to cry.
   b. he should be picked up.
3. A child should be weaned
   a. before 9 months.
   b. between 9 and 18 months.
   c. before 2 years.
   d. anytime he/she seems ready.
4. A child should be bowel/toilet trained
   a. as soon as possible.
   b. before 12 months.
   c. 12-24 months.
   d. anytime he/she seems ready.

*Childhood and Prepuberty*

1. I believe that correction of children should be the responsibility of
   a. mother.
   b. father.
   c. About equal between M and F.
   d. mother more than father.
   e. father more than mother.

2. I believe that physical punishment is necessary (spanking, whipping, etc.).
   a. Strongly agree.
   b. Agree somewhat.
   c. Disagree somewhat.
   d. Strongly disagree.
3. I approve of the following types of punishments (more than one may be checked):
   a. Earlier bedtime.
   b. To bed without supper.
   c. Sit in the corner.
   d. Withholding privileges.
   e. Cutting allowance.
   f. Lectured.
   g. Locked in room.
4. If a child masturbates, I believe he should be
   a. punished severely.
   b. told it's dirty.
   c. told not to do it in public.
   d. ignored.
   e. allowed to do it.

*Adolescence*

1. A child should be taught all the "facts of life" before he reaches his teens.
   a. Strongly agree.
   b. Somewhat agree.
   c. Disagree somewhat.
   d. Strongly disagree.
2. As soon as a person reaches his teens, he is ready to date.
   a. Strongly agree.
   b. Somewhat agree.
   c. Disagree somewhat.
   d. Strongly disagree.
3. Girls ought to start dating younger than boys.
   a. Strongly agree.
   b. Somewhat agree.
   c. Disagree somewhat.
   d. Strongly disagree.
4. A teenager should be allowed a considerable amount of freedom in making decisions.
   a. Strongly agree.
   b. Somewhat agree.
   c. Disagree somewhat.
   d. Strongly disagree.

RELIABILITY AND VALIDITY: The attitudinal scale was pretested on a group of married students for clarity and consistency. It was used with slight modifications in two different research projects: the first sample included forty-three married couples who were both employed as attendants in direct patient care at a state institution for the mentally deficient; the second sample included 284 attendants in direct patient care at a state hospital for the mentally ill. The first sample involved only white married couples, while the second included individuals of mixed racial and marital status.

BIBLIOGRAPHY:

Anders, S. F. "New Dimensions in Ethnicity and Childrearing Attitudes." *American Journal of Mental Deficiency*, 1968, *73*, 505-508.

Anders, S. F. and Dayan, M. "Variables Related to Childrearing Attitudes Among Attendants in an Institutional Setting." *American Journal of Mental Deficiency*, 1967, *71*, 848-851.

## ASSESSING BEHAVIORS OF CAREGIVERS
## (ABC-I, ABC-II, AND ABC-III)

AUTHORS: Alice S. Honig and J. Ronald Lally

AGE: Birth to 6 years

VARIABLE: Caregiver behavior

TYPE OF MEASURE: Checklist

SOURCE FROM WHICH MEASURE MAY BE OBTAINED: See Honig and Lally (1973a), or write Journal Supplement Abstract Service, American Psychological Association, 1200 Seventeenth Street N.W., Washington, D.C. 20036. Cost: $2.00.

DESCRIPTION OF MEASURE: ABC-I is a forty-item checklist developed to focus on seven behavioral areas. These areas reflect the following goals for teachers of infants under 18 months: (1) facilitation of early language in infants; (2) positive social-emotional behaviors toward and with infants; (3) adult negative social-emotional behaviors with infants (hopefully frequencies in this category will be found to be minimal); (4) presentation of Piagetian games and opportunities for sensorimotor learning; (5) provision of caregiving routines (such as feeding and diapering) to infants; (6) performance of necessary housekeeping tasks; and (7) provision of motoric and kinesthetic experiences for infants.

ABC-II and ABC-III are forty-four-item checklists (with five optional additional items) that reflect the following additional teacher behaviors with older infants and with preschoolers: (1) (a) facilitation of social personal skills, (b) facilitation of physical skills; (2) facilitation of concept development; and (3) optional items: qualitative categories reflecting teacher attention to the problem of the match, child creativity, and so forth. The checklists have an additional "do nothing" category.

As examples, the first nine of the forty items of ABC-I are given below. They are the complete section on language facilitation.

I. *Language Facilitation*
  1. Elicits vocalization.

2. Converses with child.
3. Praises, encourages verbally.
4. Offers help or solicitous remarks.
5. Inquires of child or makes requests.
6. Gives information or culture rules.
7. Provides and labels sensory experience.
8. Reads or shows pictures to child.
9. Sings to or plays music for child.

The six items that comprise the second section of ABC-II are given below.

II. *Facilitates Development of Skills: Social and Personal*
   1. Promotes child-child play (cog. and sensori.).
   2. Gets social games going.
   3. Promotes self-help and social responsibility.
   4. Helps child recognize his own needs.
   5. Helps child delay gratification.
   6. Promotes persistence, attention span.

The eight items that comprise the second section of ABC-III (for teachers of preschoolers) are given below.

II. *Facilitates Development of Skills: Social and Physical*
   1. Promotes child-child play (cog. and sensori.).
   2. Gets social games going.
   3. Promotes self-help and social responsibility.
   4. Helps child recognize his own needs.
   5. Helps child delay gratification.
   6. Promotes persistence, attention span.
   7. Small muscle, perceptual motor.
   8. Large muscle, kinethesis.

RELIABILITY AND VALIDITY: Nineteen half-hours of interobserver ratings have been analyzed for ABC-I for two pairs of raters. The agreement between observers for ABC-I was 84 percent. Reliabilities have ranged between 50 and 100 percent for the different categories. The three categories with consistently higher reliability scores are language inputs, positive social-emotional inputs, and caregiving inputs.

BIBLIOGRAPHY:

Honig, A. S., and Lally, J. R. *Assessing the Behaviors of Caregivers, ABC-I and ABC-II.* Washington, D.C.: American Psychological Association Journal Supplement Abstract Service. Abstracted in *Catalog No. 109 of Selected Documents in Psychology,* 1973a, *3,* 79-80.

Honig, A. S., and Lally, J. R. *Behavior Profiles of Experienced Teachers of Infants.* Syracuse, New York: Syracuse University Children's Center, 1973b. ERIC document no. ED 093 444.

Honig, A. S., and Lally, J. R. "Assessing Teacher Behaviors with Infants in Day Care." In B. Friedlander, G. Kirk, and G. Sterritt (Eds.), *Infant Assessment and Intervention.* New York: Brunner/Mazel, 1975.

# ATTITUDE SURVEY ABOUT KIDS (ASK)

AUTHORS: A. Alpern, Ruth F. Deich, and E. G. Lu

AGE: Part A: parents of school-age children; Part B: 3 to 12 years

VARIABLE: Part A: perception by parents of themselves and offspring; Part B: child's perception of self and parents

TYPE OF MEASURE: Part A: checklist plus rating scale; Part B: structured interview

SOURCE FROM WHICH MEASURE MAY BE OBTAINED: Institute for Research in Human Growth, 1737 Finecroft Drive, Claremont, California 91711.

DESCRIPTION OF MEASURE: Part B of the ASK, which is administered to children, is to be used in a clinical setting by a clinician and must be interpreted by an expert. Part A of the ASK is an objective measure designed to obtain demographic characteristics of different groups, and to assess parental views toward child rearing, parents' self-perceptions, and parents' perceptions of their children. Results can be used for group comparison as well as for individual clinical counseling. Thus, parents differing sharply in their child-rearing attitudes and/or their views of their children might benefit from counseling. Attitudes are scaled on a 5-point scoring system ranging from "never" to "always." Analyses include such variables as acceptance of parental role, sensitivity to child's needs, succorance, and dominance.

As examples, items from Part A are given below.

*Child Rearing*
1. Do you follow books on child rearing?
2. Do you follow your mother's approach on child rearing?
3. Do you follow your father's approach on child rearing?
4. Are you consistent in your child-rearing practices?
5. Are you confident that your child-rearing practices are best for you and your child?
6. Do you and your spouse agree on child-rearing practices and rules?
*If you have only one child,* please skip questions 7-12.
7. Do you feel more anxiety about handling your first-born?
8. Do you ask one child to follow the good examples of another?
9. Do you ask one child to avoid the bad examples of another?
10. Do you find you expect more of the oldest?
11. Do you find you expect more of the middle one?
12. Do you find you expect more of the youngest one?
*The following questions apply to young children.*
1. If you are busy and your child interrupts you,
   a. do you stop work in order to talk?
   b. do you stop work in order to play?
   c. do you stop work in order to help?
   d. do you scold him?
   e. do you spank him?
   f. do you ignore him?

RELIABILITY AND VALIDITY: None reported.

BIBLIOGRAPHY: None reported.

*Prepared by Ruth F. Deich*

---

## AUTHORITARIAN FAMILY IDEOLOGY
## ("RAISING CHILDREN" TO THE RESPONDENT)

AUTHORS: Claire B. Ernhart and Jane Loevinger

AGE: Late adolescence and adulthood

VARIABLE: Authoritarianism in family problems

TYPE OF MEASURE: Attitude scale of two-choice items

SOURCE FROM WHICH MEASURE MAY BE OBTAINED: Claire B. Ernhart, Psychology Department, Hofstra University, Hempstead, New York 11550.

DESCRIPTION OF MEASURE: The Authoritarian Family Ideology Scale consists of forty-one items reflecting belief in hierarchical family organization, demand for respect from children, the right of parents to intrude in the lives of their children, and a tendency to stereotypy and banality.

As examples, the first five of the forty-one items on the scale are given below. The respondent checks A or B. Direction of scoring each item is indicated by italics.

1. (*A*) You can spoil a tiny baby by picking him up every time he cries.
   (B) You cannot spoil a tiny baby by picking him up every time he cries.
2. (A) Parents should not pay any attention when small children use naughty words.
   (*B*) Parents should punish small children when they use naughty words.
3. (*A*) A father should be his son's best pal.
   (B) A father should not try to be his son's best pal.
4. (A) Overalls are often the most practical thing for a little girl to wear.
   (*B*) A little girl should wear dresses instead of overalls.
5. (*A*) If a mother trains her baby properly, he will not need diapers after he is one year old.
   (B) It is better not to start toilet training a baby until he is at least one year old.

RELIABILITY AND VALIDITY: The scale was standardized by homogeneous keying of the responses to 939 racially mixed and educationally heterogeneous women. Kuder-Richardson formula 20 values over several studies range between .85 and .90. In several studies scores are negatively related to education, to intelligence, to intelligence of one's children, and to parity. Blacks score higher than whites. In several studies (not yet published) the scale is found acceptable to males, and sex differences are not significant. Correlations ranging from .50 to .75 are found with the Manifest Rejection, Achievement Pressure, and Overprotection Scales of the Child Behavior Inventory (Hurley and Hohn, 1971). Evidence from all studies is consistent with the construct of authoritarianism.

BIBLIOGRAPHY:

Ernhart, C. B. "Changes in Authoritarian Family Ideology with Child-Rearing Experience." *Psychological Reports,* 1975, *37,* 567-570.

Ernhart, C. B., Jordan, T. E., and Spanier, S. D. "Maternal Quick Test (QT) Scores in Child Development Research." *Psychological Reports,* 1971, *28,* 669-670.

Ernhart, C. B., and Loevinger, J. "Authoritarian Family Ideology: A Measure, Its Correlates, and Its Robustness." *Multivariate Behavioral Research Monographs,* 1969 (69-1), 3-82.

Hurley, J. R., and Hohn, R. L. "Shifts in Child-Rearing Attitudes Linked with Parenthood and Occupation." *Developmental Psychology,* 1971, *4,* 324-328.

Johns, B. L. "Maternal Childrearing Attitudes: Identification, Measurement, and Relation to Parity and Other Variables." Unpublished doctoral dissertation. Hofstra University, Hempstead, New York, 1975.

Loevinger, J. "Measuring Personality Patterns of Women." *Genetic Psychology Monographs,* 1962, *65,* 53-136.

---

# BARON'S REINFORCEMENT HISTORY
## QUESTIONNAIRE (RHQ)

AUTHOR: Reuben M. Baron

AGE: Grade 3 to junior high (approximately 8 to 14 years)

VARIABLE: Self-perceptions of reinforcement history

TYPE OF MEASURE: Nominal scale using fixed-alternative multiple choice

SOURCE FROM WHICH MEASURE MAY BE OBTAINED: Reuben M. Baron, Department of Psychology, University of Connecticut, Storrs, Connecticut 06268.

DESCRIPTION OF MEASURE: The Baron Reinforcement History Questionnaire consists of forty items that assess children's recollections of type of evaluative reaction elicited from parents, peers, and school teachers when certain behaviors are performed in school, home, and play settings. The evaluative categories are equally weighted, and separate frequency distributions for the four types of evaluative responses (positive, negative, neutral, does not apply) are obtained within sources to yield subscale scores and across sources for a total score (simple summation scores are used, for example, total number of positive evaluations received).

As examples, the first two items of the forty-item questionnaire are given below. Every sentence stem has four possible responses.

1. When there are friends of the family visiting your house, your mother usually
    a. compliments you on your good manners.
    b. scolds you on your poor manners.
    c. doesn't care much how you act.
    d. Does not apply.
2. When you tell your father something new you learned in school, your father usually
    a. seems pleased with how much you learned.
    b. makes you feel that you really have not learned much.
    c. doesn't care much one way or the other.
    d. Does not apply.

RELIABILITY AND VALIDITY: In a pilot study the scale was administered to thirty-six fifth- and sixth-grade black elementary children in an urban area in the Midwest. In this preliminary study (Katz, 1967; Baron, 1970) strong evidence was found for the construct and predictive validity of the RHQ. Specifically, the RHQ significantly differentiates between high and low academic achievers, and is significantly positively correlated with task self-evaluation (persons with high perceived history of positive reinforcement evaluated their task performance more favorably than did persons with past history of a low level of positive reinforcement). Further, positivity of past reinforcement history significantly negatively correlated with Sarason's Test Anxiety Scale for Children (Sarason and others, 1960). The above results were found for boys; the RHQ failed to differentiate for females.

The scale was also administered in a subsequent study involving black and white male pupils in grades 4 through 6 at two racially integrated small city public schools in Michigan. All the boys in these grades were used, a total of sixty-eight black and eighty-eight white pupils. In this study items involving teachers as sources of reinforcement were added for the first time. For black students, (1) amount of perceived past positive reinforcement from teachers was significantly negatively correlated with the number of poor self-evaluations on task performance and positively correlated with the number of "very good" task self-evaluations; and (2) total perceived negative reinforcement (fathers, mothers, teachers, and peers combined) was significantly positively correlated with the number of present self-evaluations of one's performance as poor. For white subjects, total perceived positive reinforcement history was significantly positively correlated with use of "very good" as a task self-evaluation, as were teachers' positive reinforcement scores. Test-retest reliability for the RHQ typically runs in the low .70s, while internal consistency measures based on coefficient *alpha* yield correlations averaging .60.

BIBLIOGRAPHY:

Baron, R. M. "The SRS Model as a Predictor of Negro Responsiveness to Reinforcement." *Journal of Social Issues,* 1970, *26,* 61-81.
Katz, I. "The Socialization of Academic Motivation in Minority Group Children." Paper presented at Nebraska Symposium on Motivation. University of Nebraska, Lincoln, 1967.
Katz, I., Cole, J. O., and Baron, R. M. "Self-Evaluation, Social Reinforcement, and Academic Achievement of Black and White School Children." *Child Development* (in press).

Mehrabian A., and Ksionsky, S. *A Theory of Affiliation.* Lexington, Massachusetts: Lexington Books, 1974.

Sarason, S. B. and others. *Anxiety in Elementary School Children.* New York: Wiley, 1960.

---

# BROUSSARD NEONATAL PERCEPTION INVENTORY (BNPI)

AUTHOR: Elsie R. Broussard

AGE: Mothers of infants 1 or 2 days old and 4 to 6 weeks old

VARIABLE: Maternal perception of the neonate

TYPE OF MEASURE: Rating scale

SOURCE FROM WHICH MEASURE MAY BE OBTAINED: Elsie R. Broussard, 201 Lytton Avenue, Pittsburgh, Pennsylvania 15213.

DESCRIPTION OF MEASURE: The Broussard Neonatal Perception Inventory consists of the "Average Baby" and "Your Baby" perception inventories. These represent a measure of the mother's perception of her neonate as compared to the average infant. The following behavioral items are included in each of the inventories: crying, spitting, feeding, elimination, sleeping, and predictability. Using a 5-point scale, the categories to be marked are signified "a great deal," "a good bit," "a moderate amount," "very little," and "none." Values of 1 to 5 are assigned to each of the six single-item scales comprising each of the perception inventories. Total scores are then obtained for each perception inventory completed. Lower scores represent the more desirable infant behavior. By obtaining a discrepancy score between the total scores for the "Your Baby" and "Average Baby" perception inventories, an indicator of infants at high or low risk for subsequent emotional disorder is obtained. Those infants not rated better than average by their mothers are categorized as high-risk; those rated better than average are considered as low-risk.

RELIABILITY AND VALIDITY: The inventory has shown both construct and criterion validity. The BNPI was first administered to 318 primiparae all delivering single, full-term, healthy, first-born infants without recognized congenital abnormalities. These were administered on the first or second postpartum day (Time I) and again when infants were 1 month old (Time II). Infants were categorized into high- or low-risk groups on the basis of the BNPI score at Time II. One hundred and twenty of these children were evaluated at age 4½ by two child psychiatrists who had no knowledge of the children's predictive risk ratings. A statistically significant association was evident between prediction and outcome ($p < .001$). Of those at high-risk, 66 percent had psychopathology compared with 20.4 percent among those at low-risk. In order to determine if the predictive value of the BNPI was maintained over time, 104 of the children were evaluated at age 10 to 11 years by three psychiatrists having no knowledge of the risk ratings of the children or of the previous psychiatric evaluations. These were not the same psychiatrists who evaluated at age 4½. Of those at high-risk, 78.3 percent were found to have psychopathology, compared with 48.7 percent of those at low-risk (significant at $p < .04$).

When the ratings obtained at both Time I and Time II are combined and used as a predictor, the instrument is somewhat more discriminating. This method categorized infants into four relative risk groups. At age 10 to 11 years, the percentages of mental disorder are as follows: low-low, 36.8 percent; high-low, 60 percent; low-high, 66.6 percent; and high-high, 85.7 percent (significant at $p < .04$). The BNPI was administered in 1973 to a second population of 281 primiparae whose infants met the same criteria as the 1963 population. Of these, 27 percent were categorized as high-risk and 73 percent were at low-risk. At 1 year of age, eighty-five of these infants were evaluated. Preliminary inspection of the data suggests that it is possible to distinguish between the high- and low-risk infants by measuring age-appropriate attachment to mother and the infant's development of aggression at 1 year of age.

BIBLIOGRAPHY:

Broussard, E. R. "Longitudinal Study of First-Borns Aged 10/11 Years." Paper presented at American Psychiatric Association meeting. Anaheim, California, May 1975.

Broussard, E. R. *Evaluation of Televised Anticipatory Guidance to Primiparae.* Manuscript in preparation.

Broussard, E. R., and Hartner, M. S. "Maternal Perception of the Neonate as Related to Development." *Child Psychiatry and Human Development,* 1970, *1*, 16-25.

Broussard, E. R., and Hartner, M. S. "Further Considerations Regarding Maternal Perception of the First-Born." In J. Hellmuth (Ed.), *Exceptional Infant, Volume 2, Studies in Abnormalities.* New York: Brunner/Mazel, 1971.

---

# CAREGIVER LANGUAGE OBSERVATION INSTRUMENT

AUTHOR: Mary Knox Weir

AGE: 16 years and up

VARIABLE: Caregiver language

TYPE OF MEASURE: Observation framework

SOURCE FROM WHICH MEASURE MAY BE OBTAINED: Mary Knox Weir, Division of Child Development and Family Relationships, School of Human Resources and Family Studies, 1105 West Nevada, University of Illinois, Champaign-Urbana, Illinois 61801.

DESCRIPTION OF MEASURE: The Caregiver Language Observation Instrument provides a scheme for observing the language behavior of caregivers in infant day-care settings within eleven categories. The categories are: approves; disapproves; cautions; soothes; talks to; questions; labels; imitates; elaborates; sings, reads, shows pictures; and directs. In addition to language observations the instrument provides for the collection of data on the state of the child (distress or nondistress) and the situation in which the child is functioning when the language is observed. The situations are: feeding, dressing, diapering, entering/leaving, waking/sleeping, and playing. To the right of the categories are vertical columns in which the frequency of language per 10 seconds of time, the nature of the language, and an identifying number for the child to whom the language is addressed are recorded. Each completed vertical column is a 10-second interval. Twelve 10-second intervals can be recorded on each sheet, or a total of 2 minutes.

RELIABILITY AND VALIDITY: Coding agreement among observers is .95.

BIBLIOGRAPHY:

Weir, M. K. *Caregiver Language Observation Instrument: Manual of Instructions and Definitions*. Unpublished document, n.d.

---

# CHILD BEHAVIOR TOWARD THE PARENT INVENTORY

AUTHORS: Earl S. Schaefer and Neil W. Finkelstein

AGE: 10 to 18 years

VARIABLE: Child behavior toward the parent

TYPE OF MEASURE: Inventory

SOURCE FROM WHICH MEASURE MAY BE OBTAINED: Earl S. Schaefer, Department of Maternal and Child Health, School of Public Health, University of North Carolina, Chapel Hill, North Carolina 27514.

DESCRIPTION OF MEASURE: The Child Behavior Toward the Parent Inventory was designed to complement the Children's Reports of Parental Behavior Inventory (Schaefer, 1965) as a tool for the investigation of the parent-child relationship. The method may contribute to research on child effects upon parent behavior, on parent-child interaction, and on reciprocity in dydadic relationships. The child's behavior toward the parent may be as important as the parent's behavior toward the child for the understanding of family relationships and child development. Recent research suggests that the parent's perception of the child may be related to parent behavior and child behavior, just as the Children's Reports of Parental Behavior has shown significant correlations with parent behavior and child behavior. The inventory form includes thirty-one five-item scales. The high internal consistency reliabilities and factor analysis suggest the feasibility of developing short forms for efficient data collection in future research.

As examples, the first ten of the 155 items on the inventory are given below. The parent answers on a 4-point scale ranging from "very much like" to "not at all like."

1. Tells me about his/her friends or activities.
2. Tries to do things for himself/herself.
3. Says I'm stricter than other parents when he/she doesn't like a rule.
4. Pushes me away when I get close.
5. Tries to show me his/her skills.
6. Likes to sit close to me.
7. Makes his/her decisions without my advice.
8. Always has something else to do when I suggest we do something together.
9. Does what I ask even though he/she doesn't like it.
10. Smiles at me when I show him/her affection.

RELIABILITY AND VALIDITY: Internal consistency reliability for the thirty-one five-item scales varied from .68 to .95 with a median of .88. Construct validity was supported by a factor analysis that revealed major dimensions of acceptance vs. rejection, control, and independence vs. dependence that parallel major factors in children's reports of parent behavior. Extraction and rotation of additional factors differentiated minor factors of affection, helpfulness, and considerateness among scales that had loadings on the major dimension of acceptance vs. rejection.

BIBLIOGRAPHY:

Schaefer, E. S. "Children's Reports of Parental Behavior: An Inventory." *Child Development,* 1965, *36,* 413-424.
Schaefer, E. S. "Development of Hierarchical, Configurational Models for Parent Behavior and Child Behavior." In J. P. Hill (Ed.), *Minnesota Symposia on Child Psychology.* Vol. 5. Minneapolis: University of Minnesota Press, 1971.
Schaefer, E. F., and Finkelstein, N. W. "Child Behavior Toward the Parent: An Inventory and Factor Analysis." Paper presented at the American Psychological Association annual meeting. Chicago, Illinois, August 1975.

---

# CHILD-REARING PRACTICES QUESTIONNAIRE

AUTHORS: T. E. Dielman and Keith Barton

AGE: Potential or actual mothers and fathers

VARIABLE: Sixteen factors of child-rearing practices

TYPE OF MEASURE: Factor-analytic questionnaire

SOURCE FROM WHICH MEASURE MAY BE OBTAINED: The Institute for Personality and Ability Testing, 1602 Coronado Drive, Champaign, Illinois 61820. Cost not yet determined.

DESCRIPTION OF MEASURE: The questionnaire is the result of research initiated with the factor analysis of a child-rearing practices questionnaire adapted from the Sears, Maccoby, and Levin (1957) interview schedules. The replicated factors emerging from the analysis of the father's data are: high use of reward in child rearing, high use of physical punishment, promotion of independence, preference for younger children, strict discipline, low use of reasoning, wife responsible for child rearing, and dissatisfaction with home life. The replicated factors appearing in the analysis of the mother's data are patriarchial family structure, high use of physical punishment, mother's lack of self-confidence, promotion of independence, high use of reward in child rearing, preference for older children, and low use of discipline. Second-order solutions were also obtained resembling the earlier seven-factor solutions of Milton (1958) and Minturn and others (1964).

RELIABILITY AND VALIDITY: The initial study (Dielman and others, 1971) included 156 fathers and 133 mothers, and the cross-validation study (Dielman and others, 1973) included 307 fathers and 331 mothers. The mean education of the fathers was 14.5 years with a standard deviation of 3.2 years, and the mean education of the mothers was 13.5 years with a standard deviation of 2.3 years. Eighty-two percent of the children were white and 18 percent were black. In the cross-validation, the initial rotation was to the oblimax criterion (Saunders, 1961) followed by nine Rotoplat-assisted (Cattell and Foster, 1963) graphic rotations in the case of the mothers' data and seven in the case of the fathers' data to unimprovable $\pm.15$ hyperplane percentages of 80 and 76, respectively. Congruence coefficients were then computed among the final rotated factor pattern matrices. All factor matches were significant at least at the $p < .05$ level. Additional validation research completed on the questionnaire includes the relation of child-rearing practices to achievement in school (Barton and others, 1974); prediction of behavior problems in 6- to 8-year-old children (Dielman and Cattel, 1972); early school child personality factors (Dielman, Cattell, and Rhoades, 1972); and family relationships (Dielman, Barton, and Cattell, 1973).

BIBLIOGRAPHY:

Barton, K., Dielman, T. E., and Cattell, R. B. "Child-Rearing Practices and Achievement in School." *Journal of Genetic Psychology,* 1974, *124,* 155-164.

Cattell, R. B., and Foster, M. J. "The Rotoplot Program for Multiple Single-Plane, Visually-Guided Rotation." *Behavioral Science,* 1963, *8,* 156-165.

Dielman, T. E., Barton, K., and Cattell, R. B. "Cross-Validation Evidence on the Structure of Parental Reports of Child-Rearing Practices." *Journal of Social Psychology,* 1973, *90,* 243-250.

Dielman, T. E., and Cattell, R. B. "The Prediction of Behavior Problems in 6-to-8-Year-Old Children from Mothers' Reports of Child-Rearing Practices." *Journal of Clinical Psychology,* 1972, *28,* 13-17.

Dielman, T. E., Cattell, R. B., Lepper, C., and Rhoades, P. A. "A Check on the Structure of Parental Reports of Child-Rearing Practices." *Child Development,* 1971, *42,* 893-903.

Dielman, T. E., Cattell, R. B., and Rhoades, P. A. "Child-Rearing Antecedents of Early School Child Personality Factors." *Journal of Marriage and the Family*, 1972, *34*, 431-436.

Milton, G. A. "A Factor-Analytic Study of Child-Rearing Behavior." *Child Development*, 1958, *29*, 381-392.

Minturn, L., Lambert, W. W., Fischer, J., Fisher, A., Romney, R., Nydegger, W., Nydegger, C., Martetzki, H., Levine, R., and Levine, B. *Mothers of Six Cultures: Antecedents of Child Rearing.* New York: Wiley, 1964.

Saunders, D. R. "The Rationale for an 'Oblimax' Method of Transformation in Factor Analysis." *Psychometrika*, 1961, *26*, 317-324.

Sears, R. R., Maccoby, E., and Levin, H. *Patterns of Child Rearing.* New York: Harper & Row, 1957.

*Prepared by David G. Watterson*

---

# CHILD-REARING PRACTICES REPORT (CRPR)

AUTHOR: Jeanne H. Block

AGE: Form 1, parents; Form II, 16+ years

VARIABLE: Child-rearing attitudes and practices

TYPE OF MEASURE: Q-sort

SOURCE FROM WHICH MEASURE MAY BE OBTAINED: Jeanne H. Block, Institute of Human Development, Tolman Hall, University of California, Berkeley, California 94720.

DESCRIPTION OF MEASURE: The Child-Rearing Practices Report is a ninety-one-item Q-sort by which mothers and fathers describe their socialization attitudes and orientations (Form I). The items are also available in a second form (Form II) permitting adolescents and young adults to describe their perceptions of parental child-rearing behaviors and attitudes. The item pool was derived from empirical observations of mothers interacting with their children in different structured experimental situations. The Q-sort format for administrations, using a 7-point rectangular distribution of responses, was selected in order to control for response sets. Intensive field-testing of instructions for completing a self-descriptive Q-sort were conducted, making it possible to administer the test in group situations or to use the mails for data collection. The CRPR has been administered to more than three thousand respondents including high school and college students (Form II) and to parents representing different socio-economic levels, educational achievements, and ethnic groups. The item pool is suitable for cross-cultural studies, and the test has been translated and given to subject samples in Denmark, Sweden, Norway, Finland, the Netherlands, Yugoslavia, Egypt, and Hong Kong.

As examples, ten of the ninety-one items on Form I of the Q-sort are given below. The respondent is asked to sort the items into seven equal piles corresponding to a 7-point scale ranging from "most descriptive" to "most undescriptive."

8. I watch closely what my child eats and when he/she eats.
11. I feel a child should be given comfort and understanding when he/she is scared or upset.
12. I try to keep my child away from children or families who have different ideas or values from our own.
13. I try to stop my child from playing rough games or doing things where he/she might get hurt.
21. I encourage my child to wonder and think about life.
24. I feel a child should have time to think, daydream, and even loaf sometimes.
27. I do not allow my child to say bad things about his/her teachers.
33. I expect a great deal of my child.
38. I talk it over and reason with my child when he/she misbehaves.
40. I joke and play with my child.

RELIABILITY AND VALIDITY: Test-retest reliabilities were as follows: one-year interval: $r = .71$, Form I (first-person form), $N = 90$; three-year interval: $r = .64$ (mothers) and .65 (fathers), Form II (third-person form), $N = 66$. Validity studies have been completed comparing the self-described parental child-rearing attitudes to observational measures obtained during several mother-child interaction situations, and considerable correspondence was found between self-reported attitudes and observed behaviors.

BIBLIOGRAPHY:

Arnell, N. "A Study of Factors Which Affect Maternal Teaching Styles." Unpublished master's thesis. San Francisco State College, California, 1968.
Block, J. H. "Generational Continuity and Discontinuity in the Understanding of Societal Rejection." *Journal of Personality and Social Psychology,* 1972, *22,* 333-345.
Block, J. H. "Conceptions of Sex-Role: Some Cross-Cultural and Longitudinal Perspectives." *American Psychologist,* 1973, *28,* 512-526.
Block, J., and Block, J. H. "Ego Development and the Provenance of Thought: A Longitudinal Study of Ego and Cognitive Development in Young Children." Progress report for National Institute of Mental Health. Mimeographed. Department of Psychology, University of California, Berkeley, 1973.
Block, H., and Christiansen, B. "A Test of Hendin's Hypotheses Relating Suicide in Scandinavia to Child-Rearing Orientations." *Scandinavian Journal of Psychology,* 1966, *7,* 267-288.
Block, J. H., Haan, N., and Smith, M. B. "Socialization Correlates of Student Activism." *Journal of Social Issues,* 1969, *25,* 143-177.
Block, J. H., Jennings, P. H., Harvey, E., and Simpson, E. "Interaction Between Allergic Potential and Psychopathology in Childhood Asthma." *Psychosomatic Medicine,* 1964, *26,* 307-320.
Feshbach, N. "Cross-Cultural Studies of Teaching Styles in Four-Year-Olds and Their Mothers." In A. D. Pick (Ed.), *Minnesota Symposia on Child Psychology.* Minneapolis: University of Minnesota Press, 1973.

Haan, N., Smith, M. B., and Block, J. H. "The Moral Reasoning of Young Adults: Political-Social Behavior, Family Background, and Personality Correlates." *Journal of Personality and Social Psychology,* 1968, *10,* 183-201.

Haley, M. E. "Sex Differences in Internal and External Adolescents' Perceptions of Their Child Rearing." Unpublished master's thesis. Purdue University, West Lafayette, Indiana, 1974.

Hesselbart, S. L. "Self-Concepts, Achievement Patterns, and Perceived Parental Rearing Practices in Honors College Women." Unpublished honors thesis. University of Michigan, Ann Arbor, 1968.

Mussen, P., Rutherford, E., Harris, S., and Keasey, C. B. "Honesty and Altruism Among Preadolescents." *Developmental Psychology,* 1970, *3,* 169-194.

Smith, M. B., Haan, N., and Block, J. H. "Social-Psychological Aspects of Student Activism." *Youth and Society,* 1970, *1,* 261-288.

---

## CHILD STUDY INVENTORY

AUTHORS: Albert I. Rabin and Robert J. Greene

AGE: Adults

VARIABLE: Motivation for parenthood

TYPE OF MEASURE: Ranking questionnaire

SOURCE FROM WHICH MEASURE MAY BE OBTAINED: A. I. Rabin, Department of Psychology, 114 Olds Hall, Michigan State University, East Lansing, Michigan 48224.

DESCRIPTION OF MEASURE: This is an experimental instrument originally devised to test some specific hypotheses regarding motivation for parenthood. It consists of eighteen incomplete sentences. Each sentence stem is supplied with four endings to be rated from 1 to 4—from most to least preferred. Four of the sentences are "filler" items and are disregarded in the scoring. The completions of the remaining items to be rated represent four motivational categories: altruistic, fatalistic, instrumental, and narcissistic. The final profile consists of the total score in each category (minimum, 14; maximum, 56).

     As examples, five items from the inventory are given below. Letters preceding the options designate the motivational category of the option but are not included on the form given to *S.*

    Indicate the answer you feel is the best by placing a 1 in front of it. Rank the remaining answers 2, 3, and 4 to show order of preference.

1. Parents expect their children

   *F*  to fulfill the purpose of life.

    *I*  to strengthen the family.
    *A*  to be healthy and happy.
    *N*  to follow in their footsteps.
2. Men want children because
    *N*  they would like to prove their sexual adequacy.
    *F*  it is a natural instinct.
    *I*  they need them to enhance their social status.
    *A*  they like children.
3. Mother expects her daughter
    *I*  to give her companionship and affection.
    *F*  to take the place in the world for which she is destined.
    *N*  to be like herself.
    *A*  to be happy and well.
5. Men want children because
    *I*  children hold the marriage together.
    *A*  they like to care and provide for children.
    *F*  it is a function of the mature adult.
    *N*  they want to perpetuate themselves.
7. Women want children because
    *A*  they like children.
    *I*  they need them to enhance their social status.
    *N*  they would like to prove their sexual adequacy.
    *F*  it is a natural instinct.

RELIABILITY AND VALIDITY: Thirty-six college students completed the inventory twice with an interval of two-and-a-half weeks between each administration of the test. Coefficients of correlation were .79, .54, .68, and .53 for the altruistic, fatalistic, instrumental, and narcissistic dimensions, respectively. It must be noted, however, that the scores are not entirely independent. Some construct validity was obtained in several studies (see Greene, 1967; Major, 1967; and Rabin and Greene, 1968).

BIBLIOGRAPHY:

Greene, R. J. "Motivation for Parenthood in Mothers of Disturbed and Mothers of Normal Children: An Exploratory Study." Unpublished master's thesis. Michigan State University, East Lansing, 1967.

Major, M. A. "Assessment of Motivation for Parenthood in Parents of Disturbed and Normal Children." Unpublished doctoral dissertation. Michigan State University, East Lansing, 1967.

Rabin, A. I. "Motivation for Parenthood." *Journal of Projective Techniques and Personality Assessment,* 1965, *29,* 405-411.

Rabin, A. I., and Greene, R. J. "Assessing Motivation for Parenthood." *Journal of Psychology,* 1968, *69,* 39-46.

# CHILDHOOD LEVEL OF LIVING SCALE (CLL)

AUTHORS: Norman A. Polansky and staff

AGE: 4 to 6 years

VARIABLE: Quality of home environment

TYPE OF MEASURE: Questionnaire and observation framework

SOURCE FROM WHICH MEASURE MAY BE OBTAINED: See Polansky, Borgman, and DeSaix (1972) or Polansky, DeSaix, and Sharlin (1972).

DESCRIPTION OF MEASURE: The Childhood Level of Living (CLL) Scale was developed by the University of Georgia Child Research Field Station staff to be used as one indicator of the conditions of care under which children are reared—in fact, to measure the child's "level of living." The scale follows the approach used by Sears, Maccoby, and Levin (1957) but was focused to get at conditions at a lower level than the Sears material. There were 316 items in the original CLL scale used by the project social workers in scoring sixty-five homes of 5-year-olds attending a year-round Head Start program in a rural county of western North Carolina. Subsequently many items were dropped because they were nondiscriminating or because scoring reliability was low. The 136 items now in the scale are those actually used in analysis of data and reports stemming from the study. Persons using the CLL scale should be thoroughly familiar with the entire content and overall purpose of the scale prior to attempting to use it. To decrease the possible loss of items due to differences in interpretation and/or application, it is imperative that adequate training be made available to the persons who are to complete the schedule.

Although designed for "yes" and "no" answers, this basically is not a question-answer scale. Many of the questions are best answered through the observation of the researcher, while others ask for information best obtained from collateral sources such as teachers, welfare workers, and public health workers. In the same manner, it is not necessary to begin with item one and continue consecutively through the remaining items. There are, however, certain groupings of items that lend themselves to completion during one interview.

The instrument is designed to be flexible. Items can be rephrased or expanded for clarity, if necessary, as long as the meaning remains unchanged. A high score indicates problematic or actual low level of living. For scoring purposes items were grouped to make composite scores or indices. Composite or index scores are unweighted in this scale. The score is the number of pluses. Normative data are provided on sixty-five mother-child pairs living in a rural county of western North Carolina. Norms are provided for the areas of physical care and emotional-cognitive care.

As examples, two sections of the measure are given below.

Part A. *Physical Care*
        IX. Clothing

*YES*   *NO*      50. Child has both play clothes and good clothes.

               51. Clothing usually appears to be hand-me-downs.

               52. Buttons and snaps of child's clothing are frequently missing and not replaced.

53. Shoes are in reasonably good repair.
54. Child is usually dressed appropriately for weather conditions.
55. Child is usually dressed appropriately for activity.
56. Clothing is clean when child is picked up for DCC.
57. Evidence that underwear is changed as needed.
58. Items requiring ironing have been ironed.
59. Child sleeps in pajamas or gown.

Part B. *Emotional/Cognitive Care*

XVII. Promoting Curiosity

YES    NO
100. Family has been to a town outside the county.
101. Planned vacation trip has been taken by the family.
102. Child has been taken by parents to see different animals.
103. Child has been taken by parents to a county fair.
104. Child has been taken by parents to a carnival.
105. Child has been taken by parents to watch construction.
106. Child has been taken by parents to see some well-known natural attraction.
107. Mother mentions child asks questions showing curiosity about how things work.
108. Mother mentions that she answers child's questions about how things work.

RELIABILITY AND VALIDITY: None reported.

BIBLIOGRAPHY:

Polansky, N. A. *Childhood Level of Living Scale.* Athens, Georgia: University of Georgia School of Social Work, 1968.

Polansky, N. A., Borgman, R. D., and DeSaix, C. *Roots of Futility.* San Francisco: Jossey-Bass, 1972.

Polansky, N. A., DeSaix, C., and Sharlin, S. *Child Neglect: Understanding and Reading the Parents.* New York: Child Welfare League of America, 1972.

Polansky, N. A., and Pollane, L. "Measuring Adequacy of Child Caring." *Child Welfare,* 1975, *54,* 354-359.

Sears, R. R., Maccoby, E. E., and Levin, H. *Patterns of Child Rearing.* New York: Harper & Row, 1957.

*Prepared by Orval G. Johnson*

## CHILDREN'S REINFORCEMENT SURVEY

AUTHORS: Paul W. Clement and Robert C. Richard

AGE: Parents of preschool through junior high school children

VARIABLE: Major reinforcing events in a child's life

TYPE OF MEASURE: Questionnaire

SOURCE FROM WHICH MEASURE MAY BE OBTAINED: Child Development Center, 190 North Oakland Avenue, Pasadena, California 91101. Cost: $.05 per copy.

DESCRIPTION OF MEASURE: The Children's Reinforcement Survey is normally given to parents as part of a package of materials they fill in prior to the development of a treatment plan. Older children may be asked to fill in the Reinforcement Survey alone or in collaboration with a parent. The survey is used primarily to help the parents and psychological consultant identify reinforcing events to be used in contingency management programs.

As examples, sections A and C are given below. Sections B and D follow the same format as Section A and are concerned with Places (where child spends the most time) and Activities (on which the child spends the most time).

A. *People*

List below the 10 people with whom your child spends the most time each week. Put the person with whom he spends the most time after "1." Put the person with whom he spends the second most time after "2," and so on. In making the list, consider brothers, sisters, parents, relatives, playmates, etc. (Ten spaces follow)

There may be other people (children or adults) with whom you think he would like to spend more time each week, but doesn't get to. List below any such persons with whom you feel your child would like to spend more time than he presently gets to. (Six spaces follow)

C. *Things*

List below the 10 things with which your child spends the most time each week. Put them in order beginning with the thing with which he spends the most time. In making the list consider such things as specific toys (identify each kind), pets, books, puzzles, mechanical objects, musical instruments, bicycle, etc. (Ten spaces follow)

List below the things your child does not own or to which he does not have ready access which he would most like to have. (Six spaces follow)

List below your child's 10 best liked foods and drinks. Include candy, desserts, and other treats in the list. Record the items according to preference beginning with the most preferred first. Include items which you may not allow your child to have very often, but which fall high on his list of preferences. (Ten spaces follow)

RELIABILITY AND VALIDITY: None reported

BIBLIOGRAPHY: None reported.

# COGNITIVE HOME ENVIRONMENT SCALE (CHES)

AUTHOR: Norma Radin

AGE: Parents of preschool and kindergarten children

VARIABLE: Parental attitudes, home activities, and possessions

TYPE OF MEASURE: Semistructured questionnaire

SOURCE FROM WHICH MEASURE MAY BE OBTAINED: Norma Radin, School of Social Work, University of Michigan, Ann Arbor, Michigan 48104.

DESCRIPTION OF MEASURE: The Cognitive Home Environment Scale (CHES), based on Wolf's (1964) Environmental Process Scale, is a semistructured questionnaire designed to measure the degree of cognitive stimulation in the home. It contains twenty-five items whose answers are scored with a 7-point rating scale, from a low to a high level of cognitive stimulation. The questions cover such areas as the availability of educational and craft items to the child, the grades the responding parent wants and expects the child to receive in school, the kinds of activities the child shares with the respondent and the rest of the family, the respondent's plans for the child's future education, and so forth. The instrument has been used in a number of intervention programs, as well as in research examining the relationship between maternal or paternal behavior and preschoolers' cognitive functioning. The responses of 115 low-income mothers of 4- and 5-year-old children were factor analyzed through a principal-component solution and varimax rotation (Radin and Sonquist, 1968). Five factors emerged, which were labeled: Educational Materials in the Home (items 4, 7, 9, and 10); Grades Expected (items 1 and 2); Future Expectations (items 20, 21, 22, and 23); Educationally-Oriented Activities (items 13, 15, 24, and 25); and Direct Teaching (items 11, 14, 16, and 18). In another investigation (Epstein and Radin, 1974), the responses of 180 fathers of 4-year-old boys and girls from middle-, working-, and lower-class families were factor analyzed through the same procedure. Of the five factors emerging, two were labeled Future Expectations (items 20, 21, 22, and 25) and Grades Expected (items 1 and 2). The other three factors were left unnamed because the items did not constitute a logical grouping. Many of the items on these unnamed factors contained questions to which fathers did not know the answers. It is probably because many fathers guessed at the answers that these items did not appear to be logically grouped as they had been for mothers. Research with the CHES has primarily involved analyses of both factor scores and total CHES scores. In addition, analyses using scores on individual items would constitute an appropriate use of this instrument.

As examples, the first ten items of the scale, plus the scoring criteria for the first three items, are given below.

1. (When _____ starts to school.) What grades do you expect _____ to receive in most subjects? (Circle one) A    B+    B    C+    C    D+    F
2. What grade would satisfy you? (Circle one) A    B+    B    C+    C    D+    F
3. a. What towns has _____ visited outside of Ypsilanti?
   b. Why was one of the recent trips not connected with school taken?

   c. Who went with him?
   d. What did he do there?
4. a. What newspapers and/or magazines do you have in your home at present?
   b. Who reads them?
   c. Does _____ usually look at them? (Circle one) Y    N
   d. If so, which ones?
5. What did you get _____ on (his) last birthday?
6. b. For Christmas?
   c. What would you like to get (him) for (his) next birthday or Christmas?
7. a. Does any member of your family have a public library card? (Circle one)
     Y   N
   b. How often is the card used? Once a week—once a month—less often than once a
     month?
   c. When was it used the last time?
8. Are any of these things available for _____ to use at home at present? (Check if
   yes)

   a. _____ paste              g. _____ ruler
   b. _____ paper              h. _____ crayons
   c. _____ paints              i. _____ playdough
   d. _____ coloring books    j. _____ scissors
   e. _____ paper cut-outs    k. _____ pencils
   f. _____ books             l. _____ other (specific)
9. Do you have a dictionary in your home? (Circle one) Y    N
   b. Who uses it?
   c. How often? Once a week—once a month—less often than once a month? (Circle
     one)
10. Do you have an encyclopedia in your home? (Circle one) Y    N
   b. Who uses it?
   c. How often? Once a week—once a month—less often than once a month? (Circle
     one)

*Scoring Criteria*
1. 7 = A; 6 = B+/A−; 5 = B; 4 = B−/C+; 3 = C; 2 = C−; 1 = below C−. 2. 7 = A; 6 =
A−/B+; 5 = B; 4 = B−/C+; 3 = C; 2 = C−; 1 = below C−. 3. 7 = many opportunities
exist through conscious efforts on parent's part (e.g., to Greenfield Village, museum,
etc.); 5 = many opportunities exist with no conscious effort on parent's part (4 or
more towns); 3 = some opportunities exist (2-3 towns); 1 = few or no opportunities
exist (1 or no towns). Use even numbers to reflect distance and variety of experience.

RELIABILITY AND VALIDITY: A reliability test of the scoring of the CHES, used
with mothers of children in a preschool intervention program (Radin and Sonquist,
1968), yielded agreement between two independent scorers on 91 percent of the items.
In addition, interobserver reliability on the CHES scores of 180 fathers was 94.9
percent (Epstein and Radin, 1974). None of the CHES factors showed a significant
change when used as a pre- and posttest with a control group of mothers in a compensatory preschool program (Radin, 1972). No other tests on the reliability of the instrument have been performed to date. The construct validity of the CHES has been suggested by a number of studies. Significant changes in the total CHES scores and factor
scores of mothers after various intervention programs (Radin and Sonquist, 1968;

Radin 1969b, 1972) indicate that the CHES does appear to be sensitive to home activities and materials that are conducive to cognitive growth. The sensitivity of the CHES to the home environments of different social classes has also been demonstrated (Radin, 1973; Epstein and Radin, 1974), and sex differences have been assessed in paternal expectations for preschool boys and girls (Epstein and Radin, 1974). In addition, total and/or factor scores on the CHES have been significantly correlated with mothers' authoritarianism on the Parent Attitude Research Instrument (Radin and Glasser, 1972), with observed maternal behavior (Radin, 1969a), observed paternal behavior (Radin, 1973; Epstein and Radin, 1974), and children's cognitive functioning on such measures as the Peabody Picture Vocabulary Test, Binet IQ, and Piagetian tasks (Radin, 1969a, 1969b, 1973; Epstein and Radin, 1974).

## BIBLIOGRAPHY

Dave, R. H. "The Identification and Measurement of Environmental Process Variables that are Related to Educational Achievement." Unpublished doctoral dissertation. University of Chicago, 1963.

Epstein, A. S., and Radin, N. *Paternal Expectations, Paternal Behavior, and Child Performance.* Unpublished manuscript. University of Michigan, Ann Arbor, 1974.

Radin, N. "Childrearing Antecedents of Cognitive Development in Lower-Class Preschool Children." Doctoral dissertation. University of Michigan, 1969a. (University Microfilms, 1970, no. 70-4170.)

Radin, N. "The Impact of a Kindergarten Home Counseling Program." *Exceptional Children,* 1969b, *36,* 251-256.

Radin, N. "Three Degrees of Maternal Involvement in a Preschool Program: Impact on Mothers and Children." *Child Development,* 1972, *43,* 1355-1364.

Radin, N. "Observed Paternal Behaviors as Antecedents of Intellectual Functioning in Young Boys." *Developmental Psychology,* 1973, *8,* 369-376.

Radin, N., and Glasser, P. "The Utility of the Parent Attitude Research Instrument for Intervention Programs with Low-Income Families." *Journal of Marriage and the Family,* 1972, *34,* 448-458.

Radin, N., and Sonquist, H. *The Gale Preschool Program: Final Report.* Ypsilanti, Michigan: Ypsilanti Public Schools, 1968.

Wittes, G., and Radin, N. "Two Approaches to Parent Work in a Compensatory Preschool Program." *Social Work,* 1971, *16,* 42-50.

Wolf, R. D. "The Identification and Measurement of Environmental Process Variables." Unpublished doctoral dissertation. University of Chicago, 1964.

*Prepared by Ann S. Epstein*

## COMMUNICATION CHECKLISTS

AUTHORS: Daniel Ling and Agnes H. Ling

AGE: 1 month to 3 years, and adults

VARIABLE: Frequency of communication behaviors

TYPE OF MEASURE: Checklist for time sampling

SOURCE FROM WHICH MEASURE MAY BE OBTAINED: See Ling and Ling (1974).

DESCRIPTION OF MEASURE: There are two checklists: one to record the types of communication used by the mother (adult or older child), the other to record those used by the child, 1 month to 3 years old. Items are classified as pertaining to one of eight communication modes: vocal behavior, verbal behavior, eye contact, facial expression, body posture, action, demonstration, and gesture. The particular items were selected to suit the populations studied (normal-hearing infants and their mothers, and hearing-impaired children), but alternative items could be substituted. These checklists, perhaps with minor modifications, would be suitable for studying communication development of normal infants raised in different social milieux, or infants and young children with autism, mental retardation, or other communication disorders. They could be used to measure the effect of rehabilitation treatment on the child and his parents. The checklists have been used to study communication in forty-eight children and their mothers. A first-born boy, a first-born girl, a last-born boy, and a last-born girl were studied at each of the following age levels: 1, 3, 5, 7, 9, 11, 14, 18, 24, 28, 32, and 36 months. All subjects were of middle-class background. The same checklists were used with a few young hearing-impaired children and their mothers. Markedly different communication styles were observed prior to a rehabilitation program. More normal patterns of communication were observed following parent guidance in the use of residual hearing.

As examples, the items for vocal behavior are given below. Items marked (m) are used in observing the mothers, those marked (c) used in observing the children, and those marked (b) used for both.

| | | |
|---|---|---|
| Whimpering | (c) | |
| Crying | (c) | |
| Screaming | (c) | |
| Whispering | (m) | |
| Laughing | (b) | |
| Vocalization | (b) | Noncrying vowel or vowel-like sounds with only occasional consonants. |
| Syllabic babble | (b) | Syllables, usually repetitive, consisting of both vowels and consonants, for example, "agaga." |
| Word approximation | (b) | Incomplete words, for example, "nana" for "banana." |
| Jargon | (c) | Nonmeaningful flow of syllables with speechlike rhythm and intonation. |

RELIABILITY AND VALIDITY: None reported.

BIBLIOGRAPHY:

Ling, A. H., and Ling, D. *Communication Development of Normal and Hearing-Impaired Infants and Their Mothers.* Proceedings of the Conference on the Effects of Blindness and Other Impairments on Early Development. Ann Arbor, Michigan, April 1972.

Ling, D., and Ling, A. H. "Communication Development in the First Three Years of Life." *Journal of Speech and Hearing Research,* 1974, *17,* 146-159.

*Prepared by Agnes H. Ling*

---

## CONSCIOUS AFFECTION-HOSTILITY SCALE

AUTHOR: Richard A. Gardner

AGE: Parents

VARIABLE: Parental affection and hostility toward a child

TYPE OF MEASURE: Structured interview

SOURCE FROM WHICH MEASURE MAY BE OBTAINED: Richard A. Gardner, 155 County Road, Cresskill, New Jersey 07626.

DESCRIPTION OF MEASURE: The questions in the scale are in part derived from Levy's (1958) criteria for the determination of maternal feeling through observation and questioning, but additions and elaborations were made by the author. There are separate scales for each parent, and each one attempts to evaluate the relative degree of affection and hostility a parent feels toward a child. The information elicited is primarily that which is in the parent's conscious awareness and that which can be directly observed by the examiner. A parent whose feelings of affection markedly predominate over those of hostility would obtain a high score. The parent whose hostile feelings predominate over the loving feelings would obtain a low score. Each parent's score falls at some point on a continuum between marked affection and marked hostility. The scale was designed as part of a study of the psychodynamics of the inappropriate parental guilt reaction to a child's illness (Gardner, 1969). A score of +21 or above in that study was considered high, a score of +10 to +20 was considered normal, and a score of below +9 was considered low.

As examples, selected items from the female and male forms are given below, the first three from the female form, the last three from the male form.

5. When you were a young girl, what were your feelings about helping care for the younger children and/or baby sitting?
   (+) Enjoyed it; voluntarily did it; often baby-sat without pay.
   (0) Did it on occasion; take it or leave it.

(−) Hated it; never did it; did it with bitter resentment.
19. What do you like doing most with him (her)?
     (+) Parent exhibits genuine pleasure in doing things that give child pleasure.
     (0) Things done with the child done perfunctorily or out of a sense of duty, with limited or occasional pleasure.
     (−) Parent unable to provide an answer; much resentment exhibited in describing activities with child.
24. Have you ever been continually worried by thoughts that he might get harmed, injured, or sicker?
     (+) Worries appropriate to the child's illness, present or past.
     (0) No worries when no worrying is appropriate.
     (−) No worries when no worrying is inappropriate; obsessive fears unrelated to, or exaggerated with respect to, illness.
 9. When your wife was pregnant with (*patient*), did you want a boy or a girl? How did you feel about his (her) sex later on? Now?
14. Going from the oldest to the youngest, describe each of your children to me. For each, tell me both their good and bad points.
17. Have you ever been continually worried by thoughts that she (he) might be harmed or injured? If so, under what circumstances?

RELIABILITY AND VALIDITY: Face validity only is claimed.

BIBLIOGRAPHY:

Levy, D. M. *Behavioral Analysis.* Springfield, Illinois: C. C Thomas, 1958.
Gardner, R. A. "The Guilt Reaction of Parents of Children with Severe Physical Disease." *American Journal of Psychiatry,* 1969, *126,* 636-644.
Gardner, R. A. "A Proposed Scale for the Determination of Maternal Feeling." *Psychiatric Quarterly,* 1971, *45,* 23-34.

---

# CORNELL SOCIALIZATION INVENTORY (PPT)

AUTHORS: Urie Bronfenbrenner, Ed C. Devereux, Jr., and R. R. Rodgers

AGE: 10 to 14 years

VARIABLE: Parent, peer, and teacher socialization practices

TYPE OF MEASURE: Questionnaire

SOURCE FROM WHICH MEASURE MAY BE OBTAINED: See Devereux and others (1974).

DESCRIPTION OF MEASURE: The PPT instrument measures specific behaviors of socialization agents (parents, teachers, peers, and so forth) that appear to be significant in influencing the behavior and development of children. It was derived from the longer Cornell Parent Behavior Inventory (previously titled the Bronfenbrenner Parent Behavior Questionnaire; see Johnson and Bommarito, 1971) and uses eleven items representing different dimensions of behavior such as expression of affection, modes of discipline, and expectations and demands. The group-administered questionnaire asks the child to report how often during the past year the agent being evaluated engaged in the particular kind of behavior described by the item. The instrument permits a comparison of the extent to which various types of socialization behaviors are practiced by mother, father, teacher, peer group, or other agents of socialization. In general, two factors have emerged from analysis of the inventory of eleven items: support and discipline. In some cultures control emerges as a third, separate factor. The support factor is comprised of items representing variables such as nurturance, achievement demands, and instrumental companionship. The discipline factor is comprised of variables such as physical punishment, rejection, and strictness. Examples of items representing specific variables for each of the two factors are: Nurturance—"I can count on her to help me out if I have some kind of problem." Rejection—"She acts cold and unfriendly when I do something she doesn't like."

As examples, three items are given below. The items are identical for "mother," "father," "teacher," and "the kids I go around with" except for the appropriate pronouns. The respondent answers on a 5-point scale from "never" to "very often," and the order is reversed on alternate items.

2. She says she will hit or smack me, if I do something she doesn't like.
3. She keeps pushing me to do my best in whatever I do.
4. She lets me off easy when I do something she doesn't like.

RELIABILITY AND VALIDITY: The Cornell Socialization Inventory has been administered in the United States, Canada, Switzerland, Israel, Japan, Brazil, and Holland. Samples were drawn from the fifth through the seventh grades from middle- and working-class settings. For analysis, separate scales were constructed, one for support items and one for discipline. For some countries one or more of the eleven items were dropped during scale construction. The range of reliabilities by agent for the eleven items derived from separate analyses for *each* country were: mother: .58 to .72; father: .68 to .77; peer: .58 to .73; and teacher: .66 to .82. The range of reliabilities by agent for the support and discipline factors *across* countries, were: mother: support, .56 to .69, discipline, .45 to .68; father: support, .62 to .76, discipline, .63 to .78; peer: support, .46 to .67; discipline, .49 to .77; and teacher: support, .57 to .77, discipline, .62 to .84. In those societies where control was a separate factor, the reliabilities ranged from .43 to .49 for mother and .43 to .72 for father. The control factor does not appear for peer and teacher.

BIBLIOGRAPHY:

Devereux, E. C., Jr., Shouval, R., Bronfenbrenner, U., Rodgers, R. R., Kav-Venaki, S., Kiely, E., and Karson, E. "Socialization Practices of Parents, Teachers, and Peers in Israel: The Kibbutz vs. the City." *Child Development,* 1974, *45,* 269-281.

Johnson, O. G., and Bommarito, J. *Tests and Measurements in Child Development: A Handbook.* San Francisco: Jossey-Bass, 1971.

Smart, R., and Smart, M. "New Zealand Preadolescents' Parent-Peer Orientation:

Parent Perceptions Compared with English and American." *Journal of Marriage and the Family*, 1973, *35*, 142-149.

*Prepared by Elizabeth Kiely*

---

# DEPRIVATION INDEX

AUTHORS: Martin Deutsch, Martin Whiteman, and Estelle Peisach

AGE: 6 to 12 years

VARIABLE: Environmental conditions

TYPE OF MEASURE: Structured interview

SOURCE FROM WHICH MEASURE MAY BE OBTAINED: Martin Deutsch, School of Education, New York University, Washington Square, New York, New York.

DESCRIPTION OF MEASURE: The Deprivation Index was designed to assess specific environmental factors that were both socially patterned and related to scholastic performance. From a broader array of background factors, six variables were found to be significantly correlated both with lower SES (socioeconomic status) and lower Gates Reading scores among fifth-grade children. These variables, whose summated score comprises the Deprivation Index, related to economic conditions (poor housing), parental motivational factors (less schooling desired for the child), familial setting (greater number of children under 18 years), parental interaction with child (less reported conversation during dinner), activities with adults (lesser number of anticipated cultural activities), and previous schooling opportunity (no kindergarten experience).

RELIABILITY AND VALIDITY: The Deprivation Index was utilized in a study of the language development of 163 fifth-grade and 127 first-grade children. A factor analysis of thirty-three background variables revealed that the items of the Deprivation Index loaded mainly on two factors: interactive experience with adults and aspiration level. For grades 1 and 5, scores on the index denoting less deprivation correlated with higher Lorge-Thorndike IQ and with WISC Vocabulary independently of both SES and race (black vs. white). Among the fifth graders, SES differences on a number of verbal tests were significant among children showing more rather than less deprivation. More deprivation was associated with a lower self-concept score. Among the advantaged first graders (higher SES and low deprivation score), black-white differences were not significant.

BIBLIOGRAPHY:

Deutsch, M., Katz, I., and Jensen, A. R. *Social Class, Race, and Psychological Development.* New York: Holt, Rinehart and Winston, 1968.

Peisach, E., Whiteman, M., Brook, J., and Deutsch, M. "Interrelationships Among Children's Environmental Variables as Related to Age, Sex, Race, and Socioeconomic Status." *Genetic Psychology Monographs,* 1975, *92,* 3-17.

Whiteman, M., Brown, B. R., and Deutsch, M. "Some Effects of Social Class and Race on Children's Language and Intellectual Abilities." In Martin Deutsch and Associates (Eds.), *The Disadvantaged Child.* New York: Basic Books, 1967.

Whiteman, M., and Deutsch, M. "Social Disadvantage as Related to Intellective and Language Development." In Martin Deutsch and Associates (Eds.), *The Disadvantaged Child.* New York: Basic Books, 1963.

*Prepared by Martin Whiteman*

---

# DIFFERENTIAL ENVIRONMENTAL PROCESS VARIABLES (DEPVAR) SCALE

AUTHOR: Harry Mosychuk

AGE: 8 to 12 years

VARIABLE: Dynamic characteristics of the home environment

TYPE OF MEASURE: Structured interview

SOURCE FROM WHICH MEASURE MAY BE OBTAINED: Harry Mosychuk, 5715-114 A Street, Edmonton, Alberta, Canada T6H 3M8.

DESCRIPTION OF MEASURE: The theoretical framework for the development of the DEPVAR Scale is primarily based on the research conducted by Wolf (1964) in the area of examining home environments in terms of process variables. The scale is intended to examine the home environments in terms of dynamic processes or presses as identified by the following ten variables: (1) academic and vocational aspirations and expectations of parents; (2) knowledge of, and interest in, child's academic and intellectual development; (3) material and organizational opportunities for the use and development of language; (4) quality of language in the home; (5) female dominance in child rearing; (6) planfulness, purposefulness, and harmony in the home; (7) dependency fostering—overprotection; (8) authoritarian home; (9) interaction with physical environment (visual and kinesthetic experiences); and (10) opportunity for, and emphasis on, initiating and carrying through tasks. These ten variables are specifically defined in the rating scales section of the instrument. Factor-analysis procedures using the data from the ten variables produced four distinct constructs or factors (Mosychuk, 1969). These were interpreted as (1) aspiration—planfulness-harmony, (2) authoritarian—overprotective, (3) activity—environmental interaction, and (4) female—language.

The DEPVAR Scale is a structured interview schedule designed to be used with boys 4 to 12 years of age from families with both parents living at home. The scale is administered through a personal interview procedure with the boy's *mother* and requires, together with the introduction, approximately 1 to 1½ hours. The interviews are taped. Additional visual observations relating to the responses (smiles, gestures, and so forth) are recorded on the interview schedule form. The tapes are then transcribed and the responses are combined with the comments recorded by the interviewer on the schedule. The complete protocols are scored using the rating scales and the subitem scoring key. All items (fifty-nine) and subitems are scored on the basis of a 7-point Likert-type scale. The subitems are averaged, with equal weight, to obtain item scores. The items related to the variables are similarly averaged to obtain variable scores. Scores for the fourth variable (quality of language in the home) are obtained by using Loban's (1963) length of communication units (T-units). Samples of the mother's speech during the interview are used to arrive at a measure of quality of language.

As examples, five of the fifty-nine multifaceted items on the scale are given below.

5. a. What type of work would you like your boy to do when he grows up? Generally? Specifically?
   b. What type of work would you not like him to do? Generally? Specifically?
   c. How would you feel about your boy getting a permanent job immediately after completion of grade 9? Might it be possible to make a successful career out of the job that he would get with a grade 9 education?
7. a. What *specific questions* do you ask your boy about his school work?
   b. How many times have you asked him about his school performance during the last two weeks?
16. a. Does your child have a public library card?
    b. How often did he go to the library during the last two months? During an average two months?
26. a. Do you feel that, to a certain extent, the situation at home may be one where you "handle the kids" while the husband attends to the other affairs?
    b. If not, then who usually has the final word with respect to the children's privileges and activities?
    c. Do you feel that you would like your husband to be more involved in bringing up the children? In what ways?
35. a. Are there any parts on your appliances that have not been working for a long time and have not been repaired? Why have they (it) not been repaired?
    b. How many times in the last year has your car broken down to the point where you could not use it?

RELIABILITY AND VALIDITY: Theoretical and empirical work done in areas of child development and educational psychology was considered in identifying specific behaviors that represented dynamic developmental presses in the home. Prior to piloting the instrument, three experts in the field reviewed the scale for theoretical consistency and content validity. A similar procedure was conducted prior to the formal study (Mosychuk, 1969) administration. A factor-analysis procedure on the data from the fifty-nine items indicated, on the basis of factor loading, fairly distinct groupings of items into clusters corresponding to the initial assignment of items to variables during the development of the scale. Using the rating scales and the subitem scoring key, interrater reliability coefficients in the order of .85 were obtained.

BIBLIOGRAPHY:

Jones, P. A. "Home Environment and the Developments of Verbal Ability." *Child Development*, 1972, *43*, 1081-1086.

Loban, W. D. "The Language of Elementary School Children." National Council of Teachers of English Research Report no. 1. Champaign, Illinois: National Council of Teachers of English, 1963.

Mosychuk, H. "Differential Home Environments and Mental Ability Patterns." Unpublished doctoral dissertation. University of Alberta, Canada, 1969.

Wolf, R. M. "The Identification and Measurement of Environmental Process Variables Related to Intelligence." Unpublished doctoral dissertation. University of Chicago, Illinois, 1964.

---

# EIGHT-BLOCK SORTING TASK

AUTHOR: Irving E. Siegel, as revised and adapted by Jon C. Jacobs

AGE: Parents of preschool to third-grade children

VARIABLE: Parental teaching cognitive style

TYPE OF MEASURE: Structured block-sorting teaching task

SOURCE FROM WHICH MEASURE MAY BE OBTAINED: A kit including blocks, board, coding forms, descriptive manual, and cassette including samples of differing parent styles is available from J. C. Jacobs, Special Services Department, Plymouth Community Schools, Plymouth, Michigan 48170. Cost: $45.00.

DESCRIPTION OF MEASURE: The pattern of family communication interaction, which is important in a child's cognitive development, is here measured by a block-sorting task by Siegel (reported in Hess, Shipman, and others, 1966). While focused on the cognitive environment that the parent provides for the child in the child's development of problem-solving ability, this task defines the level and mode of abstraction displayed by the parent, which is useful in classifying the parental teaching style as expansive or restrictive. The task is valuable in providing counseling or therapy guides and clues when the parent-to-child interaction is viewed as showing the tone, style, and method of parent relating to child. This task gives a fresh vantage point from which one might view difficult therapy cases. In this technique, eight blocks are arranged in pairs on a board divided into four parts, with each of the pairs sharing some common characteristics (shape or size or markings). The parent is taught to do the task, which is to place an additional block in one of the four areas so that the new block shares the most common characteristics with the other two. Teaching is done by a standardized, nondirective method. Following the parent's mastery of the task, the examiner instructs the parent to teach the task to the child in any way. The parent is told that the adult-child interactions will be tape recorded. The parent teaches the task to the child, after which the child is presented with two additional blocks with the child's correct or incorrect placements and explanations being scored to determine task-teaching success or failure for the parent. The major scoring, however, is a breakdown of the parent's instructions to the child into three basic categories (information, motivation, and feedback requests) and seven subcategories (giving general information, giving specific information, positive reinforcement, negative reinforcement, general feedback request, specific feedback request, and physical feedback request), which results in a description of the parental teaching/cognitive style. Additionally, the tape provides specific clues to the tone, the style, and the method used by the parent in interaction with the child.

RELIABILITY AND VALIDITY: None reported.

BIBLIOGRAPHY:

Hess, R. D., Shipman, V., and others. *The Cognitive Environments of Urban Preschool Children.* Final Report. University of Chicago Graduate School of Education, 1968. ERIC document no. ED 045 179.
Jacobs, J. C. "Evaluation of Mother Teaching Style in High-Ability Families." *Gifted Child Quarterly,* 1971, *15,* 32-35.
Jacobs, J. C. "A View of Parental Cognitive Style as a Therapy Aid in Families with Autistic Children." Paper presented at regional meeting of the National Society for Autistic Children. Honolulu, Hawaii, 1974.
Wiegerink, R., and Weikart, D. "Measurement of Mother Teaching Styles." Paper presented at meeting of the American Psychological Association, 1967.

*Prepared by Jon C. Jacobs*

---

# EMPATHIC BEHAVIOR SCALE

AUTHORS: Bernard G. Guerney, Jr. and Lillian Stover

AGE: Teens through adulthood

VARIABLE: Empathic behavior

TYPE OF MEASURE: Rating scale

SOURCE FROM WHICH MEASURE MAY BE OBTAINED: The measure may be constructed for noncommercial research purposes from the information contained in Stover, Guerney, and O'Connell (1971).

DESCRIPTION OF MEASURE: Five-point scales are used to rate behavior showing communication, allowance of self-direction, and involvement. These are regarded as the three major components of adult empathic behavior in relation to children. The instrument was originally developed to assess the efficacy of adults' learning Rogerian play therapy and represents a refinement of an earlier 7-point scale designed to measure empathy. Intercorrelations suggest that it would not be unreasonable to either use the scales separately or sum them to provide an overall measure of empathy defined so as to incorporate their dimensions. It is recommended, however, that the most advantageous way to use these scales to analyze adult-child interaction is to employ multiple and partial correlations between the scales and the other variables of interest to the investigator. The behaviors that define each of the five parts of each scale, and detailed scoring procedures, may be found in Stover, Guerney, and O'Connell (1971).

RELIABILITY AND VALIDITY: In a study by Stover, Guerney, and O'Connell (1971), intercoder reliability in any six pairs of coders was found to be high for each of the three scales. Some evidence of concurrent and construct validity is also presented in the same study. The overall empathy score from this tripartite measure correlated .85 ($p < .005$) with the single 7-point empathy scale from which it was derived (Guerney, Stover, and DeMeritt, 1968). Evidence for construct validity is shown by the finding that all the scales were successful in demonstrating pre-post change for mothers who were trained to be more accepting, to allow more self-direction, and to show more involvement with their children.

BIBLIOGRAPHY:

Guerney, B. G., Jr., and Stover, L. *Filial Therapy.* Final Report on MH 18264-01, December 1971.

Guerney, B. G., Jr., Stover, L., and DeMeritt, S. "A Measure of Empathy in Parent-Child Interaction." *Journal of Genetic Psychology,* 1968, *112,* 49-55.

Stover, L., and Guerney, B. G., Jr. "The Efficacy of Training Procedures for Mothers in Filial Therapy." *Psychotherapy Theory Research and Practice,* 1967, *4* (3), 110-115.

Stover, L., Guerney, B. G., Jr., and O'Connell, M. "Measurements of Acceptance, Allowing Self-Direction, Involvement and Empathy in Adult-Child Interaction." *Journal of Psychology,* 1971, *77,* 261-269.

---

# ENVIRONMENTAL PARTICIPATION INDEX (EPI)

AUTHOR: Harold I. Mathis

AGE: 15 years and up

VARIABLE: Cultural exposure

TYPE OF MEASURE: Questionnaire-inventory

SOURCE FROM WHICH MEASURE MAY BE OBTAINED: Harold I. Mathis, 803

Northland Towers West, 15565 Northland Drive, Southfield, Michigan 48075. Cost: Manual, $1.00; fifty forms, $3.00; handling charge for nonprepaid orders, $1.00.

DESCRIPTION OF MEASURE: This checklist of possessions and activities is designed to estimate the relative participation an individual has had in the mainstream of American cultural life. In the first section the respondent is asked to answer whether or not a list of twenty possessions were in his home when he was 15 years old. In the second section he is asked about forty-eight activities he did or did not do by the time he was 18. In one study of mothers of Head Start children (Goldstein, 1971), the instructions for the first section were modified to measure possessions the family owned, while the instructions for the second section asked about activities the mother expected her child would do by the time he was 18.

As examples, the first ten of the twenty items in the first section of the checklist are given below.

1. A radio.                                6. A Bible.
2. A telephone.                            7. A dictionary.
3. A television.                           8. A set of encyclopedias.
4. A bicycle.                              9. 30 other books or more.
5. A phonograph.                          10. A family car.

The first ten of the forty-eight items in the second section of the checklist are given below.

1. Dance.                                  6. Drive a car.
2. Smoke.                                  7. Take a taxi.
3. Swim.                                   8. Buy a book.
4. Ice skate.                              9. Visit a zoo.
5. Make a long distance phone call.       10. Cash a check.

RELIABILITY AND VALIDITY: Construct validity is based upon correlations as high as .67 with the General Aptitude Test Battery (GATB).

BIBLIOGRAPHY:

Goldstein, K. M. *Mental Health Consultation with Low-SES Parents.* Staten Island, New York: Wakoff Research Center, 1971.
Mathis, H. *Environment Participation Index. Manual.* Washington, D.C.: Psychometric Studies, 1967.
Mathis, H. "Relating Environmental Factors to Aptitude and Race." *Journal of Consulting Psychology,* 1968, *15,* 563-568.

# ENVIRONMENTAL STANDARDS PROFILE: METHOD OF ASSESSING QUALITY GROUP CARE AND EDUCATION OF YOUNG CHILDREN

AUTHORS: William Fowler and Karen Ogston

AGE: Birth to 6 years

VARIABLE: Quality of infant/preschool group-care environments

TYPE OF MEASURE: Five rating scales in a profile format with scale description guides.

SOURCE FROM WHICH MEASURE MAY BE OBTAINED: William Fowler, Department of Applied Psychology, Ontario Institute for Studies in Education, 252 Bloor Street West, Toronto, Ontario, Canada.

DESCRIPTION OF MEASURE: The Environmental Standards Profile consists of a series of five profile grids for the assessment of environmental quality in preschool environments such as day-care centers or nursery schools. It may be used by centers for self-assessment, by administrators of programs for assessment of a number of centers, by research units, by those setting up programs, or by others. The profiles examine physical environment, adult social structure and socioemotional environment, structure of children's socioemotional environment, cognitive stimulation program, and toys and equipment. Each profile is composed of a series of items examining a thorough range of components of group-care environments on 7-point scales, the points being defined by scale descriptions provided with the profile. The 7 points are divided into high (6-7), average (3-5), and low (1-2) areas, based on existing research data and standards for preschool environments that encourage optimum conditions for child development in all areas. The resulting profiles indicate the comparative position of the assessed center with these standards in all areas. They can be averaged to yield an overall quality score, or clusters of items may be looked at as units of analysis. One or any number of the profiles may be used depending on the purposes of the assessment.

As an example, a section of Form 4 is given below.

### Quality of Cognitive Stimulation Program

|  |  | Low | Adequate | Excellent |  |
|---|---|---|---|---|---|
|  |  | 1  2  3  4  5  6  7 |  |  |  |
| *Frequency* | Infrequent, irregular with large groups. | _____ | | | Regular daily brief and extended sessions with small groups. |
| *Quality and variety* | Didactic, narrow or inappropriate methods of little scope. | _____ | | | Comprehensive, with imaginative developmentally based methods. |

|  | | Low | Adequate | Excellent | |
|---|---|---|---|---|---|
|  | | 1  2  3  4  5  6  7 | | | |
| *Concreteness* | Too abstract with few opportunities for manipulation. | _____ | | | Concrete with active exploration. |
| *Language stimulation* | Language stimulation poor in all situations, either lacking or inappropriate. | _____ | | | Language stimulation appropriate and rich in all situations. |
| *Inquiry orientation* | No encouragement of inquiry. | _____ | | | Active program to elicit inquiry. |
| *Imagination* | Unimaginative stereotyped and structured set of activities and play. | _____ | | | Rich repertoire of learning, play and games used inventively. |
| *Play oriented* | Learning is formalized without the involvement of play. | _____ | | | Learning is often play-oriented. |

RELIABILITY AND VALIDITY: Interrater reliability for two raters at one center did not depart significantly from expected perfect agreement as measured by chi-square statistics calculated on each form of the test with the expected value = sum of the items for 0 departure and the expected value of 0 for all departures. The results are summarized as follows:

| *Form* | $X^2$ | *df* | *p* |
|---|---|---|---|
| 1 | 2.200 | 10 | ns |
| 2 | 9.600 | 10 | ns |
| 3 | 11.825 | 10 | ns |
| 4 | 13.825 | 10 | ns |
| 5 | 15.718 | 10 | ns |

Further reliability data are currently being gathered. Validity of each scale item has been derived from existing data and regulations for standards of preschool and day-care environments to yield low, average, and high ratings.

BIBLIOGRAPHY:

Fowler, W., and Ogston, K. *Environmental Standards Profile: Method for Assessing Quality Group-Care and Education of Young Children.* Unpublished manuscript. Toronto, Canada: Ontario Institute for Studies in Education, 1975.

*Prepared by William Fowler and Karen Ogston*

# FAMILY ADJECTIVE RATING SCALE

AUTHORS: Jacques W. Kaswan and Leonore R. Love

AGE: Families of children 8 years or older

VARIABLE: Interpersonal assessment of family members

TYPE OF MEASURE: Rating scale

SOURCE FROM WHICH MEASURE MAY BE OBTAINED: Leonore R. Love, Professor of Psychology in Residence, Department of Psychology, University of California, Los Angeles, California 90024. Mailing charges only.

DESCRIPTION OF MEASURE: The scale contains ten adjectives representing interpersonal attributes and behavior. First, each rater judges the extent to which each adjective characterizes himself ("never" to "always"). In sequential sets of ratings, he rates others in the family and then makes his estimate of how each of the others will rate him. For example, in a family containing one child, each parent rates each of the ten adjectives on six concepts in turn: myself, my spouse, my child, how my spouse will rate me, how my child will rate me, and the average person of my age and sex. The child rates himself, each parent, his teacher, and his expectation of how each adult will rate him. To ensure understanding of word meaning for children as young as 8 and for adults with minimal education, each adjective is presented along with a standard definition. The adjectives are: *bored, patient, afraid, controlling, clear, angry, rude, active, phony,* and *friendly*. Different numbers and arrangements of concepts can be used to fit an individual family, and ratings can be obtained from the teacher when this seems appropriate. As part of an "information feedback" technique to heighten awareness of interpersonal perceptions and behavior within families, each person's ratings can be graphed on transparent paper, to facilitate the family members' comparisons of themselves and one another.

RELIABILITY AND VALIDITY: The scale was developed with pilot testing of over 350 individuals, including college students and sets of parents and their elementary-school-age children. Test-retest reliability (two-week interval) for college-age adults ranged from .53 to .83, with a median of .67. For children 8 years and older, the median reliability was only .45. This low reliability emphasized the necessity of using careful individual instructions and caution in the interpretation of children's ratings. Ten factor analyses were made on adjective ratings of children viewed in different contexts (playground, classroom, clinic, home) by a variety of raters (teachers, independent raters, parents). Samples used in the factor analyses included ratings of random, referred, and normal control children with sample sizes ranging from 79 to 118. These analyses resulted in the consistent emergence of two factors, negative and positive social impact. Any adjective retained in a factor had to have a factor loading of .40 or higher in at least two out of the three settings (home, school, clinic) in which these independent ratings were made. The two factors were seen as referring to the individual's perceived social impact on others and were used to compare the interpersonal evaluations made in families of children referred for psychological treatment with families of a matched group of children in the same classrooms who were seen by school children personnel as manifesting no major personal or social problems. Similar analyses were made for families at different socioeconomic levels and, within the families of disturbed children, for differences between families of children showing different kinds of problems (aggression, hyperactivity, social withdrawal, or poor attention control).

BIBLIOGRAPHY:

Kaswan, J. W., Love, L. R., and Rodnick, E. H. "Information Feedback as a Method of Clinical Intervention and Consultation." In C. Spielberger (Ed.), *Current Topics in Clinical and Community Psychology.* Vol. 3. New York: Academic Press, 1971.
Love, L. R., and Kaswan, J. W. *Troubled Children: Their Families, Schools, and Treatments.* New York: Wiley-Interscience, 1974.
Love, L. R., Kaswan, J. W., and Bugental, D. E. "Differential Effectiveness of Three Clinical Interventions for Different Socioeconomic Groupings." *Journal of Consulting and Clinical Psychology,* 1972, *39,* 347-360.

*Prepared by Leonore R. Love*

---

# FAMILY COMMUNICATION PATTERNS

AUTHOR: Joseph C. LaVoie

AGE: Parents of children and adolescents

VARIABLE: Parent communicativeness

TYPE OF MEASURE: Rating scale applied to a structured interview

SOURCE FROM WHICH MEASURE MAY BE OBTAINED: Joseph C. LaVoie, Department of Psychology, University of Nebraska at Omaha, Omaha, Nebraska 68101.

DESCRIPTION OF MEASURE: This scale measures parent communicativeness, that is, the degree to which parents request information from their child and use this information in determining a course of action in a conflict or discipline situation. The scale assesses the extent to which the parent actively interacts with the child for the purpose of seeking out details concerning the sequence of events leading to the child's behavior(s) in a particular situation and the child's rationale for the behavior(s) in question, and the use of this information by the parent in reasoning with the child and determining a course of action. The extent to which the parent uses reasoning or explanation as a control measure is incorporated in each rating. This measure of parent communicativeness was constructed to assess parent communication in a family-interaction task where each parent is presented a series of situations involving potential conflicts with a child/adolescent that could arise in a family. The parent individually responds to each conflict situation by writing a statement indicating what he or she would do, or describes his or her actions. This description is then tape recorded. The conflict situations are modifications of problems used by Farina (1960) and Ridberg (1967).

The parent response to each of the situations is given a score, ranging from 1 to 5, using the following scale: (1) No evidence of parent discussion of the situation with the child. The parent makes a judgment of the situation based solely on his perceptions. Use of reasoning or explanation based on these perceptions is absent as a control method. (2) No evidence of actual parent discussion of the situation with the child. The parent makes a judgment of the situation based on his perceptions but incorporates his perceptions in the reasoning or explanation used as a control measure. (3) Some evidence of parent discussion of the situation with the child. The parent makes a judgment of the situation based on his understanding and incorporates this understanding in the reasoning or explanation used as a control measure. (4) The parent discusses the situation with the child, but there is little indication that the parent requests the child's explanation for his behavior or that the parent actively attempts to determine the circumstances surrounding the situation. The parent makes a judgment based on his understanding and incorporates this understanding in the reasoning and explanation used as a control measure. (5) The parent discusses the situation with the child and attempts to ascertain the sequence of events leading up to the situation. The child is asked to explain his behavior and suggest what should be done. The parent uses this information to make a judgment of the situation, which is then referred to the child for verification. This information is then incorporated in the reasoning or explanation used as a control measure. The parent score for each situation is summed, and a mean score is derived reflecting the degree of parent communicativeness. Two rating scales developed by Rohrbaugh (1966) also can be applied to the same conflict situations used to assess family communication patterns.

RELIABILITY AND VALIDITY: The rating scale was used to score responses of eighty fathers and mothers of adolescent boys to eight conflict situations. Validation of this scale is based only on face validity. Reliability of scoring has been assessed in one study (LaVoie and Looft, 1973). Interrater reliability in this study was .71 (Pearson correlation).

BIBLIOGRAPHY:

Farina, A. "Patterns of Role Dominance and Conflict in Parents of Schizophrenic Patients." *Journal of Abnormal and Social Psychology,* 1960, *61,* 31-38.

LaVoie, J. C. and Looft, W. R. "Parental Antecedents of Resistance-to-Temptation Behavior in Adolescent Males." *Merrill-Palmer Quarterly,* 1973, *19,* 107-116.

Ridberg, E. H. "Family Interaction Patterns in Families Containing a Neurotic-Delinquent or Normal Adolescent Boy." Unpublished master's thesis. University of Wisconsin, Madison, 1967.

Rohrbaugh, P. J. "Family Interaction Patterns in Normal Families Containing an Aggressive, Withdrawn, or Sociable Boy." Unpublished doctoral dissertation. University of Wisconsin, Madison, 1966.

# FAMILY CONCEPT TEST

AUTHOR: Ferdinand van der Veen

AGE: 12 years and up

VARIABLE: Family effectiveness, satisfaction, congruence, and eleven family-concept factors

TYPE OF MEASURE: Q-sort and multiple-choice test forms

SOURCE FROM WHICH MEASURE MAY BE OBTAINED: Ferdinand van der Veen, Institute for Juvenile Research, 1140 South Paulina Street, Chicago, Illinois 60612.

DESCRIPTION OF MEASURE: The Family Concept Test consists of eighty carefully selected items that describe social-emotional aspects of the family. Each item is descriptive of the entire family unit, not the individual relationships within the family. An example is: "We just cannot tell each other our real feelings." The test can be used to characterize different family structures, such as the family as it is now (real family concept), the family as it would be ideally (ideal family concept), the family of origin, and so forth. The Family Concept Test exists in two forms: a Q-sort format and a multiple-choice format. The Q-sort presents the eighty items describing families on separate small cards in random order. The respondent arranges the cards into nine piles corresponding to a 9-point scale ranging from "least like my family" to "most like my family," with a specified number of cards permitted in each pile. The multiple-choice version consists of the eighty items listed in a test booklet, with each item rated from 0 (least like) to 8 (most like) the family (or the ideal family), and the respondent circles the appropriate rating. Several global scores have been derived from the item scores. These include the family effectiveness score, which is a summary score of family adjustment based upon forty-eight of the eighty items selected according to an expert ideal key; a family satisfaction score, which is the agreement (correlation) between a person's real and ideal item scores; and family congruence scores, which indicate the degree of agreement between family concepts of two family members. The real family congruence score is the correlation between the real family concepts of two members, and the ideal family congruence score is the correlation between their ideal family concepts.

RELIABILITY AND VALIDITY: The Family Concept Test has been found to be reliable over long and short time intervals. For a wait-list group of fifty parents, the test-retest correlations over a three-and-one-half-month time span were .56 for the real and .66 for the ideal family Q-sort forms of the test. The family concepts of a group of nonclinic parents ($N = 74$) were found to have test-retest correlations of .67 for the real family concept Q-sort, and .71 for the ideal, over a period of seventeen months. The multiple-choice format was found to have high reliability for college students over a four-week retest period. The correlations were .80 for the real test and .87 for the ideal test. The Q-sort format had retest correlations of .69 and .74 for this population. Social desirability effects were negligible for the Q-sort format and mild ($rs$ of .40 to .35 with test scores) for the multiple-choice format in a student group. There was also high correlation between the Q-sort and multiple-choice formats on the family effectiveness and family satisfaction scores (.95 and .90, respectively).

With regard to validity, the family-concept measures have consistently been found to be higher for parents of nondisturbed than for disturbed children, and for normal adolescents than for their disturbed siblings. They have been shown to be positively related to marital adjustment and negatively to child density (number of children per years married). Both real and ideal family congruence between father and child are positively related to the child's socialization as measured by the California Personality Inventory. The family concepts of parents of withdrawn children have been found to be more positive than for parents of aggressive children in both clinic and nonclinic populations. In a study of family perceptions of adolescent runaways and non-runaways, the correlation between a parent's real and ideal family concepts was higher for parents of nonrunaway adolescents than it was for parents of runaways ($r$ = .73 and .30, respectively). Family-concept variables did not show a significant relationship to variables of fourth, fifth, and sixth graders' school adjustment (reading and arithmetic achievement) and teacher ratings of pupil behavior; however, ratings of social acceptance by peer groups were positively related to family adjustment. The family concepts of three-person family groups have also been found to be systematically and meaningfully related to objective family-interaction measures obtained on these families. Abstracts of completed research on the family concept are available upon request. A large factor analysis of the eight test items yielded two main second-order factors: adaptive coping and family integration. These underlying dimensions of the test closely resemble the major instrumental and expressive dimensions of small-group research and thereby support the adequacy of the test for the assessment of basic family processes.

BIBLIOGRAPHY:

van der Veen, F. "Dimensions of the Family Concept and Their Relation to Gender, Generation, and Disturbance." Mimeographed. Chicago: Institute for Juvenile Research, 1975.

van der Veen, F., Howard, K. I., and Austria, A. M. *Stability and Equivalence of Scores Based on Three Different Response Formats.* Proceedings of the Seventy-eighth annual meeting, American Psychological Association. Washington, D.C.: APA, 1970.

van der Veen, F., Huebner, B., Jorgens, B., and Neja, P., Jr. "Relationships Between the Parent's Concept of the Family and Family Adjustment." *American Journal of Orthopsychiatry,* 1964, *34,* 45-55.

van der Veen, F., and Novak, A. L. "Perceived Parental Attitudes and Family Concepts of Disturbed Adolescents, Normal Siblings, and Normal Controls." *Family Process,* 1971, *10,* 327-343.

van der Veen, F., and Novak, A. L. "The Family Concept of the Disturbed Child: A Replication Study." *American Journal of Orthopsychiatry,* 1974, *44,* 763-772.

# FAMILY FUNCTIONING INSTRUMENT (FFI)

AUTHOR: Walter W. Hudson

AGE: No restriction

VARIABLE: Social and familial functioning of a family unit

TYPE OF MEASURE: Likert-type scale

SOURCE FROM WHICH MEASURE MAY BE OBTAINED: Walter W. Hudson, George Warren Brown School of Social Work, Washington University, St. Louis, Missouri 63130.

DESCRIPTION OF MEASURE: The Family Functioning Instrument (FFI) has been designed to measure performance that describes some of the major elements of the overall social and familial functioning of a family unit. The instrument has been divided into two parts. Part I provides a list of performance areas that must be rated by an observer who knows the family quite well. The user completes the instrument by drawing a circle around the rating that best describes the performance of the family. The values to be used in the ratings are as follows: (X) does not apply, (0) qualified judgment cannot be given, (1) inferior, (2) poor, (3) low, (4) average, (5) good, (6) excellent, and (7) superior. Part II of the instrument lists a number of events or activities that measure social, cultural, and educational opportunities for both adults and children. In Part II the user indicates whether the events described have occurred with the family by checking "yes" or "no" on each item. Part I should be scored by first reverse-scoring each item: item 1 = 7, 2 = 6, 3 = 5, 4 = 4, 5 = 3, 6 = 2, and 7 = 1. Then compute the percentage score as PS $(\Sigma X - N/\text{Max})(100)$ where $N$ is the number of items actually rated and Max = $(N)(6)$. Part II should be scored by setting "yes" = 0 and "no" = 1 for every item checked by the user. Compute the percentage score for Part II as PS = $(\Sigma X/N)(100)$ where $N$ is the number of items checked in Part II. With the above scoring procedures, Part I of the FFI provides an estimate of the magnitude of family dysfunction as rendered by a knowledgeable judge of the family situation. Part II represents an estimate of the family's problems in securing for adults and children opportunities for social, cultural, and educational development. A zero or near-zero score indicates the absence of problems in the area of family functioning.

As examples, ten selected items each from Part I and Part II of the eighty-item instrument are given below. Part I items are to be selected for the family being rated on a response scale from 1 to 7, inferior to superior. If a particular item does not apply, (X) is circled; if the item does apply, (0) is circled. Part II items are to be answered "yes" or "no."

*Part I*
1. Cleanliness of rooms and furnishings.
4. Appearance of preschool children's apparel.
7. General health of the family.
10. Use of income to cover clothing.
13. Absence or control of impulse purchases of nonutility items (such as unneeded clothing, jewelry, sweets, colas, etc.).

16. Adults read to or with the children.
19. Adults' participation in community activities.
22. Exposure of the children to large shopping centers.
25. Control of absenteeism from school for children over 6 years old.
28. Rewarding achievement tangibly by giving material rewards.

*Part II*

51. The rent is paid regularly.
54. Adequate space is available for the storage of children's toys.
57. Children promptly return home from school.
60. Do any of the adults have a library card?
63. Does the family have a radio?
66. Have the children ever been to a museum?
69. Have the adults ever been to an aquarium?
72. Have the children ever been to the downtown area of a large city?
75. Have the adults ever been to a large department store?
78. Have the children ever been to the zoo?

RELIABILITY AND VALIDITY: The FFI was administered to 136 families whose children participated in an educational experiment with social-work services. These families were divided into four groups of equal size for purposes of the experiment. The reliability of the FFI was determined separately for each of the four study groups using the split-half method and correcting with the Spearman-Brown formula. The reliability of the FFI equaled or exceeded .96 for all four study groups. No suitable data have been collected to examine the validity of the FFI.

BIBLIOGRAPHY:

Bloom, B. S. "Early Learning in the Home." Paper presented at First B. J. Paley Lecture, University of California at Los Angeles, July 1965. Mimeographed.

Dave, R. H. "The Identification and Measurement of Environmental Process Variables That are Related to Educational Achievement." Unpublished doctoral dissertation. University of Chicago, 1963.

Hudson, W. W. "An Autotelic Teaching Experiment with Ancillary Casework Services." *American Educational Research Journal*, 1971, *8*, 467-483.

# FAMILY INTEGRATION SCALE

AUTHOR: Hans Sebald

AGE: Parents

VARIABLE: Family integration

TYPE OF MEASURE: Rating scale

SOURCE FROM WHICH MEASURE MAY BE OBTAINED: Hans Sebald, Department of Sociology, Arizona State University, Tempe, Arizona 85281; or copy from description below.

DESCRIPTION OF MEASURE: This is an eight-item scale sampling typical family activities. The Family Integration Scale is more specific than the Bardis Scale (1959) from which it was derived. The latter measures familism, which includes both family integration and kinship orientation; the Sebald test more specifically measures family integration and is more applicable to the nuclear family situation.

The items of the scale are given below. Four responses are possible to each question: "often," "sometimes," "seldom," and "never." Numerical values are assigned to the responses.

1. How often do you help your children with their school work and problems?
2. How often do you discuss your children's school situation with the teacher?
3. How often do you participate with the children in vocational activities or hobbies?
4. How often do you attend affairs like fairs, athletic games, picnics, movies, etc. together as a family?
5. How often do you have a family night during the week?
6. How often do you go to church together as a family?
7. How often do you have religious activities together at home as a family?
8. How often do you work around the home or farm together as a family?

RELIABILITY AND VALIDITY: The split-half test for reliability was .89 and was raised to .94 after adjustment by the Spearman-Brown formula. Validity of the scale was tested by correlation with another family integration scale whose reliability and validity was assumed. The test showed an $r$ of .95 (Bardis, 1959). The above tests were run on a sample comprising 303 families.

BIBLIOGRAPHY:

Bardis, P. D. "Attitudes Toward the Family." *Sociology and Social Research*, 1959, *43*, 352-358.
Sebald, H., and Andrews, W. H. "Family Integration and Related Factors in a Rural Fringe Population." *Journal of Marriage and the Family*, 1962, *24*, 347-351.

---

## FAMILY INTERACTION APPERCEPTION TECHNIQUE (FIAT)

AUTHORS: Salvador Minuchin, Braulio Montalvo, Bernard G. Guerney, Bernice L. Rosman, and Florence Schumer

AGE: 7 years to adult

VARIABLE: Internalized view of family interactions

TYPE OF MEASURE: Content analysis of stories to pictures

SOURCE FROM WHICH MEASURE MAY BE OBTAINED: Plates of the pictures and instructions may be obtained from Salvador Minuchin, Philadelphia Child Guidance Clinic, 34th Street and Civic Center Boulevard, Philadelphia, Pennsylvania 19104. Cost: $10.00 to cover reproduction costs. See also Minuchin and others (1967), Appendix D, for the ten pictures.

DESCRIPTION OF MEASURE: The Family Interaction Apperception Technique is a pictorial projective technique modeled after the TAT. It was designed to elicit stories concerning interaction among family members along dimensions such as control, guidance, nurturance, aggression, and so on. The FIAT is composed of ten pictures depicting families in different activities. The pictures are drawn so as to be racially and socioeconomically neutral. The scenes depict family interaction situations primarily; the action in the pictures is more highly specific and structured than in the TAT drawings, and the instructions specifically call for stories about families and family interaction. The testing period takes about 30 minutes. The instrument can be used with children as young as 7 and was found to elicit similar type identifications and productivity from black, Puerto Rican, and white subjects.

RELIABILITY AND VALIDITY: Some research differences were found between responses of families with or without delinquent children (Minuchin and others, 1967). Good reliabilities were established for coding the specific variables for this study—86-percent agreement between coders for rating behavior control, guidance, acceptance of responsibility, nurturance, affection, cooperation, aggression, and family harmony. No other more formal reliability or validity studies have been carried out.

BIBLIOGRAPHY:

Elbert, S., Rosman, B., Minuchin, S., and Guerney, B. G. "A Method for the Clinical Study of Family Interaction." *American Journal of Orthopsychiatry*, 1964, *34*, 885-894.

Minuchin, S. M., Montalvo, B., Guerney, B. G., Rosman, B. L., and Schumer, F. *Families of the Slums*. New York: Basic Books, 1967.

*Prepared by Salvador Minuchin and Bernice L. Rosman*

---

# GREENBERG FIRST-FATHER ENGROSSMENT SURVEY

AUTHOR: Martin Greenberg

AGE: Fathers

VARIABLE: Paternal feelings and involvement with the newborn

TYPE OF MEASURE: Multiple-choice questionnaire

SOURCE FROM WHICH MEASURE MAY BE OBTAINED: See Greenberg and Morris

(1974), or from Martin Greenberg, 2266 Snowden Avenue, Long Beach, California 90815. Cost: $3.00.

DESCRIPTION OF MEASURE: This questionnaire is an attempt to measure evidence of paternal feelings and involvement with the newborn, such as whether the baby was planned or unplanned, the measurement and participation of the father in labor and delivery, how he viewed this experience, and so forth.

As examples, four selected items from the fifty on the questionnaire are given below.

4. Many fathers don't develop a strong feeling toward the baby straight away. This is completely normal. When did you first get the feeling that the baby was all yours?
   a. Immediately after the birth.
   b. After the first three days.
   c. It's coming, but I don't quite have it yet.
10. Are you able to distinguish your baby from other babies by his cry?
   a. All the time.
   b. Some of the time.
   c. Rarely.
   d. Never.
16. How much knowledge did you feel that you had about labor and delivery in general?
   a. Nothing.
   b. A slight amount.
   c. A moderate amount.
   d. A great deal.
24. How did you feel immediately after the delivery?
   a. Very glad.
   b. Glad.
   c. As usual.
   d. A little down.

RELIABILITY AND VALIDITY: None reported.

BIBLIOGRAPHY:

Greenberg, M. *Father's Relationship to His Newborn in the First Week After Birth: A Review.* Unpublished manuscript. 1972.

Greenberg, M., and Morris, N. "Engrossment: The Newborn's Impact Upon the Father." *American Journal of Orthopsychiatry,* 1974, *44,* 520-539.

Greenberg, M., and others. "First Mothers Rooming-in with Their Newborns: Its Impact Upon the Mother." *American Journal of Orthopsychiatry,* 1973, *43,* 783-788.

Levy, P. "Advice and Reassurance." *American Journal of Public Health,* 1954, *44,* 1113-1118.

Morris, N. "Human Relations in Obstetrical Practice." *Lancet,* 1960, *1,* 913-915.

Parson, M., and Morris, N. "The Role of the Father in Pregnancy and Delivery." Paper presented at the International Congress of Obstetrics and Gynecology. London, April 1971.

## HENDERSON ENVIRONMENTAL LEARNING PROCESS SCALE (HELPS)

AUTHOR: Ronald W. Henderson

AGE: Preschool and elementary-school grades

VARIABLE: Home learning environment

TYPE OF MEASURE: Structured interview employing Likert-type scale

SOURCE FROM WHICH MEASURE MAY BE OBTAINED: Office of Child Research, Arizona Center for Educational Research and Development, College of Education, University of Arizona, Tucson, Arizona 85721. Cost: $1.00 for duplication.

DESCRIPTION OF MEASURE: The Henderson Environmental Learning Process Scale (HELPS) is designed to measure characteristics of the home environment that have been found to be related to the intellectual and scholastic performance of young children. It contains items designed to elicit (1) quantifiable information on the aspiration level of the home, (2) range of environmental stimulation available to the child, (3) parental guidance or direct teaching provided in the family, (4) range (variability in occupational and educational status) of adult models available for emulation by the child, and (5) the nature of reinforcement practices used in the home to influence the child's behavior. The instrument yields a subscore for each of these five variables, and a total score. Administration of the scale requires approximately 20 minutes. It can be used successfully by interviewers with limited formal education, but some special training in the use of the scale is required. The administration procedure is designed to make it possible to administer the scale to parents who may have difficulty reading the items. The interviewer and respondent sit side by side at a table. Responses are arranged like a balance scale, with polar descriptions of behavior or circumstances at each end of the scale. The item is read aloud by the interviewer, who points to the reference terms as he or she reads, and the respondent marks 1 of 5 points along the continuum. Local adaptations of some items are advised.

As examples, the first ten of the fifty-five-item instrument are given below. The opposite poles of a 5-point scale are shown in parentheses.

1. Not counting what happens at school, how often does (*child*) go to the library, or a museum, or someplace like that? (Once a week to less than once a year)
2. Not counting things like school field trips, how often does (*child*) go to a zoo, an aquarium, or someplace like that? (Once a week to less than once a year)
3. What chance does your husband have to get ahead in his job? (Good to poor)
4. If (and when) (*child*) graduates from high school, what are his/her chances of getting a good job? (Good to poor)
5. What kind of grades do you expect (*child*) to get in school? (Excellent to failing)
6. When (*child*) has a chance to choose what to do around the house, how often does he/she choose to look at a book or magazine? (Almost every day to very seldom)
7. How often do you attend social gatherings (e.g., parties, dances, church activities, PTA? (Once a week to less than once a year)

8. How often do you take (*child*) on a trip out of town? (Once a week to less than once a year)

9. How often do you take (*child*) along when you go shopping? (Almost weekly to almost never)

10. (*If applicable*) How many organizations does your husband belong to (e.g., PTA, unions, fraternal orders, service clubs, fraternities)? (None to four or more)

RELIABILITY AND VALIDITY: The scale was originally administered to mothers of 126 first-grade children. The sixty-six Mexican-American children in this sample were predominantly from low-income families, while the sixty Anglo-American children were predominantly middle class. Reliability, computed by the Cronbach *alpha* method, was .71 for the Anglo sample and .74 for the Mexican-American sample. In subsequent administrations of the scale Cronbach *alpha* coefficients of .85 for fifty middle-class Mexican-American families, .74 for fifty lower-class Anglo families, and .79 for twenty-seven Papago native American families have been obtained. Predictive validity was determined in one investigation in which the scale provided highly significant predictions of performance of Mexican-American and Anglo first graders on the Stanford Early Achievement Test and the Boehm Test of Basic Concepts. Further evidence of predictive validity was indicated in a study in which the scale predicted achievement of migrant and nonmigrant black and Puerto Rican urban sixth graders.

BIBLIOGRAPHY:

Henderson, R. W., Bergan, J. R., and Hurt, M., Jr. "Development and Validation of the Henderson Environmental Learning Process Scale." *Journal of Social Psychology*, 1972, *88*, 185-196.
Henderson, R. W., and Garcia, A. "Effects of Parent Training Progress on Question-Asking Behavior of Mexican-American Children." *American Educational Research Journal*, 1973, *10*, 193-201.
Prior, D. R. "Inner-City Elementary Pupil Mobility, Reading Achievement, and Environmental Process Variables." Unpublished doctoral dissertation. Fordham University, New York, 1974.

# HOME INDEX

AUTHOR: Harrison G. Gough

AGE: Intermediate and secondary grades

VARIABLE: Social-class status

TYPE OF MEASURE: Questionnaire

SOURCE FROM WHICH MEASURE MAY BE OBTAINED: Harrison G. Gough, Department of Psychology, University of California, Berkeley, California 94720.

DESCRIPTION OF MEASURE: The twenty-two-item Home Index is practically self-administering, can be quickly completed, speedily scored, and preserves to a large extent the precision of the longer, more complex instruments. The scale is based largely on the Sims SCI (1952) and the American Home Scale (Kerr and Remmers, 1942), with the addition of certain original items. The items, to be answered "yes" or "no," relate to material possessions in the home as well as to the activities of the parents and children. The total score is simply the number of "yes" responses. Four part-scores on facets of status may also be obtained. The author cautions that use of the scale probably should be restricted to persons below the age of 18 living at home. Despite the simplicity of the index, the author believes that the scale can yield valid results with school children if care is taken to insure that correct answers are given. The principal advantages that the author perceives this scale to have over the other methods of estimating social status include ease of administration, simplicity in scoring, and specification of subfacets of the status domain.

As examples, the first ten of the twenty-two items are given below.

1. Did your mother go to high school?
2. Did your mother go to a college or university?
3. Did your father go to high school?
4. Did your father go to a college or university?
5. Do you have a fireplace in your home?
6. Does your family have any servants, such as a cook or maid?
7. Does your family leave town every year for a vacation?
8. Does your family have more than 500 books?
9. Is there an electric or gas refrigerator in your home?
10. Is there a telephone in your home?

RELIABILITY AND VALIDITY: The test-retest reliability coefficient based on a sample of fifty-five college students was .99. The Kuder-Richardson coefficient for 252 high school students was .74; this represents a minimum estimate of the scale's internal consistency (Gough, 1949). The intercorrelations of the Home Index with other variables were as follows: .65 with father's occupation, .82 with the Sims SCI, and .88 with the American Home Scale. Gough (1949) found that the Home Index had the heaviest loadings of all three measures on the social-class status factor.

BIBLIOGRAPHY:

Gough, H. G. "A Short Social Status Inventory." *Journal of Educational Psychology,* 1949, *40,* 52-56.

Gough, H. G. "A Cluster Analysis of Home Index Status Items." *Psychological Reports,* 1971, *28,* 923-929.

Gough, H. G. "Socioeconomic Status as Related to High School Graduation and College Attendance." *Psychology in the Schools,* 1971, *7,* 226-231.

Jensen, A. R. "Do Schools Cheat Minority Children?" *Educational Research,* 1971, *14,* 3-28.

Kerr, W. A., and Remmers, H. H. *The American Home Scale.* Munster, Indiana: Psychometric Affiliates, 1942.

Sims, V. M. *Sims SCI Occupational Rating Scale.* Yonkers, New York: World Book, 1952 (out of print).

# HUMAN INTERACTION SCALE (HIS)

AUTHORS: Jean Carew Watts, Itty Chan Barnett, Nancy Apfel, Christine Halfar, and Geraldine Kearse

AGE: 1 to 3 years

VARIABLE: Quantity and quality of interaction

TYPE OF MEASURE: Naturalistic observation

SOURCE FROM WHICH MEASURE MAY BE OBTAINED: Available from authors at Graduate School of Education, Harvard University, Cambridge, Massachusetts 02138. Cost: $1.50 per copy.

DESCRIPTION OF MEASURE: The Human Interaction Scale (HIS) is designed to measure a child's quantity and quality of interaction with people in his environment. The instrument is intended for use with children aged 1 to 3 and is designed primarily to measure the relevance of human interaction experiences to the child's intellectual and social development. The HIS comprises five dimensions: quality of interaction, initiation, encouragement, technique of interaction, and compliance. A sample interaction of verbal and symbolic activity is: "*M* touches eye and says 'eye.' *S* repeats. *M* asks: 'Where is Mommy's eye?' *S* touches *M*'s nose." The HIS was developed through a longitudinal research study involving naturalistic observation of 1-to-3-year-old children. The HIS is rated by a trained observer. Raw data are collected by recording inter-actional units of time for each 10-minute protocol. The HIS has been used for observations of children being raised at home. The major dimensions of the scale differentiate between children who are developing above average vs. those developing below average at age 3.

    The four dimensions and the categories, scoring, and examples (as indicated) from the scale are given below.

*Dimension 1–Activities: Refers to the behavior of the child.*

| | |
|---|---|
| *Cluster I:* | 1 = verbal, symbolic learning |
| (Highly Intellectual) | 2 = spatial, perceptual, fine motor learning |
| | 3 = concrete reasoning |
| | 4 = expressive skills |
| | 5 = executive skills |
| *Cluster II:* | 6 = exploration of and play with household |
| (Moderately Intellectual Activities) |     items |
| | 7 = play with toys |
| | 8 = exploration of nature |
| | 9 = gaining general and routine information |
| *Cluster III:* | 10 = basic care |
| (Nonintellectual activities) | 11 = gross motor activities |
| | 12 = unspecific behavior |
| *Cluster IV:* | 31 = positive social-emotional behavior |
| (Social-Emotional Activities) | 32 = negative social-emotional behavior |
| | 33 = neutral social-emotional behavior |

*Dimension 2—Initiation Index: Keeps track of who initiates an activity.*

1 = mother or the principal caretaker

2 = the subject child

3 = another adult (over 7 years of age)

4 = another child (for age 1 subject = 2-7 years; for age 2 subject = 4-7 years)

5 = peer (for age 1 subject = peer under 2 years; for age 2 subject = peer under 4 years)

0 = doesn't apply or don't know

*Dimension 3—Encouragement Index: Notes the other person's attitude concerning the child's behavior.*

*S* pulls at the cat. *M* says "No, no. Be nice to the kitty." (*M* discourages *S*'s behavior by restriction)

*Dimension 4—Interaction Techniques: An account of the techniques (or types of behavior) used by the other person when he is interacting with the child.*

The fifteen interaction techniques are grouped into the following seven categories:

| | |
|---|---|
| *Category I:* (Teaching) | 21 = didactic teaching<br>25 = justification or statement of a rationale<br>40 = active participation |
| *Category II:* (Informing) | 22 = general information giving |
| *Category III:* (Directive) | 23 = suggestion or command<br>31 = positive reinforcement or affection<br>37 = focusing on a task |
| *Category IV:* (Restrictive) | 24 = restrictive or prohibition<br>32 = negative reinforcement or hostility<br>34 = distraction or ignoring<br>36 = refusal to help or comply |
| *Category V:* (Help) | 35 = providing services or assistance |
| *Category VI:* (Preparatory) | 38 = providing materials<br>39 = changing location |
| *Category VII:* (Neutral) | 33 = observing or interpreting |

*S* points at a balloon on his pajamas and says "red." *M* corrects: "No, *blue*. It is a blue balloon." (Didactic teaching)

*Dimension 5—Compliance Index: The child's response to a directive or restrictive technique noted according to the following codes:*

1 = *S* complies

2 = *S* does not comply

3 = not relevant or unknown

RELIABILITY AND VALIDITY: Interjudge reliability percentages for each dimension are as follows: 86 percent for quality, 78 percent for initiation, 85 percent for encouragement, 78 percent for techniques, and 87 percent for compliance.

BIBLIOGRAPHY:

Watts, J. C. "Environment, Experience, and Excellence in Young Children." In J. P. Kender (Ed.), *Reading: The Tried and the New.* Danville, Illinois: Interstate Printers and Publishers, 1972.

Watts, J. C., Barnett, I. C., and Halfar, C. *Environment, Experience and Development in Early Childhood.* Final report to United States Office of Economic Opportunity, Head Start Division. Washington, D.C., 1973.

White, B., Watts, J. C., Barnett, I., Kaban, B., Marmor, J., and Shapiro, B. *Environment and Experience: Major Influences on the Development of the Young Child.* Englewood Cliffs, New Jersey: Prentice-Hall, 1973.

*Prepared by Christine Halfar*

# HUMAN OR MATERIAL ENVIRONMENT (HOME) SCALE

AUTHORS: Jean Carew Watts, Itty Chan Barnett, and Christine Halfar

AGE: 1 to 3 years

VARIABLE: Experiences of young children and the role of the human and nonhuman environment

TYPE OF MEASURE: Naturalistic observation

SOURCE FROM WHICH MEASURE MAY BE OBTAINED: Jean Carew Watts, Graduate School of Education, Harvard University, Cambridge, Massachusetts 02138. Cost: $5.55 per copy.

DESCRIPTION OF MEASURE: The Human or Material Environment (HOME) Scale is an observational instrument designed for the analysis of the naturally occurring experiences of children 1 to 3 years of age. The aims of the scale are (1) to designate the relevance and value of the child's *experience* for intellectual and social development, and (2) to characterize the role played by the human and nonhuman *environment* in the child's experience. The HOME Scale includes sixteen dimensions that describe simultaneously the child's behavior, the human environment, and the material environment. The focal dimension of the HOME Scale is *Activity*, which is made up of twenty-one categories (see below)—experiences that are highly likely to promote intellectual development, moderately likely to promote intellectual development, or not likely to promote intellectual development; as well as social-emotional experiences. The child may be active or passive in such experiences, and the experiences may or may not involve interaction with another person. The instrument is scored by a trained observer and requires 15-second observation time and 15-second recording of information time per each 10-minute protocol. After the observation is completed the scoring is done for each of the sixteen dimensions. The HOME Scale has been used for children raised at home and for those in day-care centers. The day-care study is not complete at this time, but for the home-care sample the major dimensions of the scale differentiate between children who are developing above average vs. those developing below average at age 3.

The sixteen dimensions are given below.

*Child's Experience*
Dimension 1–Activity
Dimension 2–Type of Experience
Dimension 3–Task Mode
Dimension 4–Task Level
Dimension 5–Task Purpose
Dimension 5s–Success
*The Human Environment*
Dimension 6–Initiation
Dimension 7–Person
Dimension 8–Encouragement Index
Dimension 9–Interaction Technique
Dimension 10–Compliance Index
Dimension 11–Verbal Index
*The Material Environment*
Dimension 12–Room
Dimension 13–Restriction
Dimension 14, 15–Object Quality and Object Size

Below are the twenty-one categories of the Activity dimension. The first thirteen of the categories are considered relevant to intellectual development, and the last eight are considered relevant to social development. The first thirteen are grouped hierarchically according to their presumed value for intellectual development.

*Highly intellectual activities involving:*
Verbal, symbolic learning
Spatial, perceptual, fine motor learning
Concrete reasoning
Expressive skills
Executive skills
*Moderately intellectual activities involving:*
Exploration of and play with household items
Play with toys
Exploration of nature
Gaining general and routine information
*Nonintellectual activities involving:*
Basic care
Large motor learning
Unspecific
Transition behaviors
*Social-emotional activities involving:*
Emotional expression–positive
Emotional expression–negative
Emotional expression–distress
Independence
Social games
Social cooperation
Social contact
Attention/competition

RELIABILITY AND VALIDITY: Rater agreement on each dimension of the HOME Scale ranges between 67 and 95 percent.

BIBLIOGRAPHY:

Watts, J. C. "Understanding Intellectual Experiences in Young Children." Paper delivered at Minnesota Round Table, May 1974.
Watts, J. C., Halfar, C., and Chan, I. "Environment, Experience and Intellectual Development of Young Children in Home Care." *American Journal of Orthopsychiatry*, 1974, *44*, 773-781.

*Prepared by Christine Halfar*

---

# IMPLICIT PARENTAL LEARNING THEORY (IPLET)

AUTHORS: Bettye M. Caldwell and Alice S. Honig (for IPLETs I, II, III, and IV); J. Ronald Lally, J. Wright, Alice S. Honig, and Bettye M. Caldwell (for IPLET V).

AGE: Parents of children from birth to 6 years

VARIABLE: Child-rearing practices

TYPE OF MEASURE: Questionnaire

SOURCE FROM WHICH MEASURE MAY BE OBTAINED: Children's Center, 100 Walnut Place, Syracuse, New York 13210. Cost: $3.50 for five different IPLETs and coding handbook.

DESCRIPTION OF MEASURE: This is a forty-five-item inventory (separate forms available for parents of infants, toddlers, and preschoolers) administered as a structured interview, which assesses via verbal report (1) an array of behaviors likely to appear at least fleetingly in a child's repertoire that a parent would either encourage or discourage, and (2) the type of teaching technique that would be employed to produce either response stabilization or change. Data from (1) give some indication of parental values for developmental achievements and also provide an index of indifference about the child's performance; data from (2) hopefully reflect the type of teaching techniques likely to be used by the parents and thus indirectly the parents' implicit theory about how children learn. The wide range of behavior inquired about includes: "Tries new foods," "Bites or pulls hair when angry," "Likes to play house and pretend he is grown up," and "Goes into the street." The mother is assured of the experimenter's interest in the variety of methods mothers have found useful in bringing up their children.

 Coding of the obtained responses involves a determination of whether a parent tends to rely on (1) direct manipulation of the environment (provision or deprivation of privileges, edibles, or manipulables; utilization of natural consequences; provision of parental positive physical response; physical punishment; provision of behavioral models and of sensory—other than verbal—input); (2) symbolic manipulations (promise or threat of deprivation of privileges, edibles, or manipulables; promise of or provision of parental emotional response; verbal reproach that undermines self-esteem; threat of punishment; verbal input, such as reading; provision of cultural expectations or expected consequences of behaviors; and commands); or (3) absence of response. For any individual the scoring results in a profile of the frequency with which the different types of teaching techniques are employed. IPLET inventories are available for parents of children in five age groups (birth to 6 years).

As examples, the first five of the forty-five items for each of the age groups are given below. The left-hand column states "What child does" and the right-hand column (blank) "What mother does."

*Age 1 year*
1. Climbs out of bed after being put to bed.
2. Turns stove knobs.
3. Shows off when other adults are around.
4. Sucks thumb.
5. Dawdles while eating.

*Age 2 years*
1. Brings you something such as Kleenex or an ashtry, if you ask him.
2. Bites or pulls hair when angry.
3. Tries to dress himself.
4. Likes to play with cars, trucks, guns, etc.
5. Is shy in presence of relatives or friends.

*Age 3 years*
1. Says "please" when he asks for things.
2. Sleeps late in the morning.
3. Gets mad if he can't have his own way.
4. Cries or fusses if he gets dirty while playing.
5. Likes to play with cars, trucks, guns, etc.

*Age 4 years*
1. Says "please" when he asks for things.
2. Sleeps late in the morning.
3. Gets mad if he can't have his own way.
4. Cries or fusses if he gets dirty while playing.
5. Likes to play with cars, trucks, guns, etc.

*Age 5-6 years*
1. Finishes puzzles or games he tries out on his own.
2. Is thoughtful when someone is sleeping or ill.
3. Likes to play only with familiar toys and articles.
4. Chooses his own activities at playtime.
5. Is polite.

RELIABILITY AND VALIDITY: Intercoder reliability quickly reaches the level of .90 or above.

BIBLIOGRAPHY:

Honig, A. S. *Maternal Behaviors in Childrearing Among Poor Urban Mothers in Five Cultures.* Unpublished manuscript. Syracuse University, Syracuse, New York, 1973.

Honig, A. S., Caldwell, B. M., and Tannenbaum, J. "Patterns of Information Processing Used by and with Young Children in a Nursery School Setting." *Child Development,* 1970, *41,* 1045-1065.

Honig, A. S., Tannenbaum, J., and Caldwell, B. M. "Maternal Behavior in Verbal Report and in Laboratory Observation: A Methodological Study." *Child Psychiatry and Human Development,* 1973, *3,* 216-230.

*Prepared by Alice S. Honig*

---

# INDIVIDUAL SELF-REPORT
# SOCIOECONOMIC STATUS MEASURE

AUTHORS: Karl R. White and Kenneth D. Hopkins

AGE: Grades 2 to 8

VARIABLE: Socioeconomic status (SES)

TYPE OF MEASURE: Multiple-choice questionnaire

SOURCE FROM WHICH MEASURE MAY BE OBTAINED: Karl R. White, Laboratory of Educational Research, University of Colorado, Boulder, Colorado 80302.

DESCRIPTION OF MEASURE: The measure consists of a short self-report questionnaire that asks students to indicate the presence or absence in their homes of various objects and experiences as well as the educational level of their parents. Together these items give a measure of socioeconomic status (SES) that is quickly and easily obtainable on individual students. Items are scored 1 or 0 for presence or absence and 2 (yes), 1 (no), and 0 (I don't know) for what levels of education parents have completed. The total score is an indicator of SES with higher scores corresponding to higher SES. The measure can be broken into three logical parts: (1) home characteristics (e.g., telephone, fireplace, dishwasher, lawn mower, and so forth); (2) travel (e.g., Europe, Hawaii, Disneyland, and so forth); and (3) parental education (e.g., "Did your mother finish high school?" and so forth). The measure requires about 15 minutes for completion. Instructions for administration are included.

RELIABILITY AND VALIDITY: In an administration to about twelve hundred students in grades 2, 4, and 6, the Hoyt estimate of reliability was .78. Correlations with academic achievement and IQ were somewhat low, ranging from .12 to .26 (not corrected for attenuation), although these correlations are very similar to the correlations of district academic achievement to average value of home, level of parental education, and yearly income obtained in the 1972 Colorado State Assessment. These correlations ranged from .08 to .24.

BIBLIOGRAPHY:

Hopkins, K. D. *Colorado State Assessment.* Boulder, Colorado: Laboratory of Educational Research, University of Colorado, 1972.

Research Triangle Institute. *Correlates of Socioeconomic Status.* Research Triangle Park, North Carolina: Research Triangle Institute, 1969.

---

# INSTRUMENT FOR ASSESSING CHILD-CARING SKILLS

AUTHOR: Jerome M. Goldsmith

AGE: Adult

VARIABLE: Child-caring skills

TYPE OF MEASURE: Objective paper-and-pencil alternate-choice test

SOURCE FROM WHICH MEASURE MAY BE OBTAINED: See Goldsmith (1965).

DESCRIPTION OF MEASURE: The specific task in the development of this instrument was the construction and evaluation of a test for child-care personnel in residential treatment settings to determine whether persons who manifest differential effectiveness on the job also reveal differential ability in their test performance on an instrument that presents them with problems to solve. The procedures included collection of critical incidents and collection of alternate responses to three questions. Forty-four situations were collected with three alternate responses for each of three questions for each situation: (1) interpreting of the behavior of the child or answering the question, "What is the child trying to do or what does he want?" (2) inferring the affect of the child or answering the question, "What is the child feeling or thinking?" and (3) offering a specific verbal response or answering the question, "What is the most appropriate response in this instance?"

An example is given below of one situation on which three items are based, to be scored "most appropriate," "in between," or "least appropriate."

*Example*

The boys are talking with the cottage parents about the chores in the house. They protest the number of jobs and the need to do some of the community areas not immediately around the cottage. Then the boys add, "Don't push us on these jobs. Just remember what happened to the last cottage parents. We got rid of them."

1. What are the boys trying to do? (What do they want?)
   a. The boys are trying to intimidate the cottage parents and scare them from giving out all the necessary jobs.
   b. The boys are rebelling against doing their chores.

    c. The boys are trying to provoke a fight with the cottage parents.

2. What are the boys feeling or thinking?

    a. The boys wonder if they can scare these new cottage parents.

    b. The boys are probably planning to injure the cottage parents.

    c. The boys are resentful of always being regimented.

3. What is the most appropriate response to the situation?

    a. The jobs have to be done—whether I'm the cottage parent or someone else. If I leave it won't be because you got rid of me but it will be better for everyone if you do your chores without complaining.

    b. We may be fired, but we will not quit. If anyone gets rid of another, we will get rid of one of you.

    c. All right, we will leave. I'm packing now.

RELIABILITY AND VALIDITY: Split-half reliability yielded acceptable results for two of the three areas (inferring child's affect, $r = .74$; inferring verbal response, $r = .60$). Interpretation of the child's behavior showed less reliability ($r = .46$). The correlations between alternate forms yielded similar results. Concurrent validity was assessed by correlating the $S$s' scores on the test with judges' rank-ordering of the child-care workers in their job performances. No evidence for concurrent validity was found. The test was also given to trained social workers judged to be the "best" personnel, and their scores were compared with the scores obtained by the cottage parents. The social workers performed in the first quartile when compared to the child-care staff. The test was also given to a group of teachers working in the school. Twelve of fourteen teachers scored above the midpoint of the cottage parents. These results suggest that trained workers generally agree on the appropriate responses to children in a residential setting. There is evidence of concurrent validity in the comparison of social workers and teachers.

BIBLIOGRAPHY:

Goldsmith, J. M. "The Communication of Clinical Information in a Residential Treatment Setting." *Casework Papers, 1955.* New York: Family Service Association of America, 1955.

Goldsmith, J. M. *The Development and Evaluation of an Instrument for Assessing the Child-Caring Skills of House Parent Personnel in Handling Problem Behavior.* Ann Arbor, Michigan: University Microfilms, 1965.

Goldsmith, J. M., and others. "Integrating Clinical Processes with Planned Living Experiences." *American Journal of Orthopsychiatry,* 1954, *24,* 280-290.

*Prepared by Martin Kohn*

# INTERACTION RATING SCALE
# FOR MOTHERS AND DEAF CHILDREN

AUTHORS: Kathryn P. Meadow and Hilde S. Schlesinger

AGE: 2½ to 9 years

VARIABLE: Mother-child interaction

TYPE OF MEASURE: Rating scale

SOURCE FROM WHICH MEASURE MAY BE OBTAINED: Kathryn Meadow or Hilde Schlesinger, University of California, 1474 Fifth Avenue, San Francisco, California 94143. Cost: $2.00 for manual.

DESCRIPTION OF MEASURE: The scale was developed for the purpose of evaluating videotaped scenarios of semistructured interaction of forty deaf children and their mothers. Twenty children with normal hearing and their mothers were also rated. Ten items of the scale are descriptive of the mother's behavior during the scenario—her approach to the interaction with the child, her response to the situation, her personal behavioral style. Fourteen items are descriptive of the child's behavior during the scenario. Ten of these parallel the items descriptive of the mother's behavior. Four additional items, used for rating the deaf children only, are descriptive of the child's speech and response to auditory cues. Four items describe the quality of the reciprocal interaction between mother and child. Two items indicate the personal response of the coders to the mother and the child. The manual describes each dimension and the procedures for rating.

As examples, three of the ten items descriptive of the mother's behavior, scored on a scale from 1 to 8 (with "?" as an option also), are given below. A scoring guide gives a framework to be used in assigning scores.

M3. Intrusive: inserts self into child's activity field by constant barrage of verbal or nonverbal stimuli. — Nonintrusive but offers appropriate stimuli (fades into background, uninvolved).

M4. Makes frequent use of didactic techniques: uses situation for teaching, never for play. — Makes infrequent use of didactic, teaching techniques: *plays* with child (only).

M5. Unimaginative use of materials, situation. — Creative, imaginative use of materials, situation.

RELIABILITY AND VALIDITY: Interjudge adjusted estimates of reliability (Kuder-Richardson formula 20) ranged from .90 to .65 for the twenty-four dimensions rated, with a mean of .83.

BIBLIOGRAPHY:

Schlesinger, H. S., and Meadow, K. P. *Judges' Manual: Instructions for Rating Mother-Child Interaction from Video-Taped Scenarios.* Unpublished document. University of California, San Francisco, n.d.

Schlesinger, H. S., and Meadow, K. P. *Sound and Sign: Childhood Deafness and Mental Health.* Berkeley: University of California Press, 1972.

---

## INVENTORY OF HOME STIMULATION–I (STIM)

AUTHOR: Bettye M. Caldwell

AGE: Birth to 3 years

VARIABLE: Quality of stimulation found in the early home environment

TYPE OF MEASURE: Observation/interview

SOURCE FROM WHICH MEASURE MAY BE OBTAINED: Bettye M. Caldwell, Center for Early Development and Education, 814 Sherman, Little Rock, Arkansas 72202.

DESCRIPTION OF MEASURE: The Inventory of Home Stimulation–I consists of forty-five binary-choice-type items. It is designed to sample certain aspects of the social, emotional, and cognitive support available to a young child within his home. The selection of items was guided by empirical evidence of the importance of certain types of experience for nourishing the behavioral development of the child. Included are such things as the importance of the opportunity to form a basic attachment to a mother or mother substitute; an emotional climate characterized by mutual pleasure, sensitive need-gratification, and minimization of restriction and punishment; a physical environment that is both stimulating and responsive, offering a variety of modulated sensory experience; freedom to explore and master the environment; a daily schedule that is orderly and predictable; and an opportunity to assimilate and interpret experience within a consistent cultural milieu. These items compose six general aspects of home environment: (1) emotional and verbal responsivity of the mother, (2) avoidance of restriction and punishment, (3) organization of the physical and temporal environment, (4) provision of appropriate play materials, (5) maternal involvement with child, and (6) opportunities for variety in daily stimulation.

As examples, six of the forty-five items on the inventory are given below. They are answered "yes" or "no."

*I. Emotional and Verbal Responsivity of Mother*
   1. Mother spontaneously vocalizes to child at least twice during visit (exclude scolding).
*II. Avoidance of Restriction and Punishment*
   12. Mother does not shout at child during visit.
*III. Organization of Physical and Temporal Environment*
   20. When mother is away, care is provided by one of three regular substitutes.
*IV. Provision of Appropriate Play Materials*
   26. Child has one or more muscle activity toys or pieces.

*V. Maternal Involvement with Child*
    35. Mother tends to keep child within visual range and to look at him often.
*VI. Opportunities for Variety in Daily Stimulation*
    41. Father provides some caregiving every day.

RELIABILITY AND VALIDITY: Internal consistency (Kuder-Richardson formula 20) coefficients based on 176 cases ranged from .44 for subscale no. 6 to .89 for subscale no. 3. The internal consistency coefficient for the total scale was computed at .89. Using data from assessments made at 6, 12, and 24 months on ninety-one families, test-retest correlations were computed for each subscale and the total scale. Results indicate that the inventory has a moderate degree of stability across the 18-month period. With regard to concurrent validity, Inventory of Home Stimulation scores for ninety-one families were correlated with seven socioeconomic-status variables (welfare status, mother education, mother occupation, father presence, father education, father occupation, and crowding in the home). Correlations between subscales and mother education, father presence, father education, father occupation, and crowding in the home were moderate (.25 to .55). Correlations between subscales and welfare status and mother occupation were of smaller magnitude but still positive. Product-moment correlations between STIM scores taken at 6, 12, and 24 months and 36-month Stanford-Binet scores were computed for ninety-one families. Correlations between 6-month STIM subscale scores and 36-month Binet performance ranged from .24 to .33. The multiple correlation between the six subscales and Binet performance was .54. The STIM score taken at 6 months correlated .50 with 36-month Binet performance. Correlations between 12-month STIM subscale scores and 36-month Binet performance ranged from .24 to .56. The multiple correlation was .59, and correlation·between 12-month STIM total score and 36-month Binet performance was .55. Correlations between 24-month STIM subscale scores and 36-month Binet performance ranged from .41 to .64. The multiple correlation was computed at .72, and the correlation between total STIM score at 24 months and Binet score at 36 months was .70.

BIBLIOGRAPHY:

Caldwell, B. M. "On Designing Supplementary Environments for Early Child Development." *BAEYC Reports* (Boston Association for the Education of Young Children), 1968, *10* (1), 1-11.
Caldwell, B. M., Elardo, P., and Elardo, R. "The Longitudinal Observation and Intervention Study: A Preliminary Report." Presented at the meeting of the Southeastern Conference on Research in Child Development. Williamsburg, Virginia, April 1972.
Caldwell, B. M., Heider, J., and Kaplan, B. "The Inventory of Home Stimulation." Paper presented at the meeting of the American Psychological Association. September 1966.
Caldwell, B. M., Wright, C. M., Honig, A. S., and Tannenbaum, J. "Infant Day Care and Attachment." *American Journal of Orthopsychiatry,* 1970, *40,* 397-412.
Cravioto, J., and Delicardie, E. "Environmental Correlates of Severe Clinical Malnutrition and Language Development in Survivors from Dwashiorkor or Marasmus." In *Nutrition, the Nervous System and Behavior.* Washington, D.C.: Pan American Health Organization, Scientific Publication no. 251, 1972.
Elardo, R., and Bradley, R. "The Relation of Infants' Home Environments to Mental

Test Performance from 6 to 36 Months: A Longitudinal Analysis." Paper presented at the southeastern regional meeting of the Society for Research in Child Development. Chapel Hill, North Carolina, March 1974.

---

# INVENTORY OF HOME STIMULATION–II (STIM)

AUTHOR: Bettye M. Caldwell

AGE: 3 to 6 years

VARIABLE: Quality of stimulation found in child's home environment

TYPE OF MEASURE: Observation/interview

SOURCE FROM WHICH MEASURE MAY BE OBTAINED: Bettye M. Caldwell, Center for Early Development and Education, 814 Sherman, Little Rock, Arkansas 72202.

DESCRIPTION OF MEASURE: The Inventory of Home Stimulation–II consists of eighty binary-choice-type items. It is designed to sample certain aspects of the social, emotional, and cognitive support available to a young child within his home. The selection of items was guided by empirical evidence of the importance of certain types of experience for nourishing the behavioral development of the child. Included are such things as the importance of the opportunity to form a basic attachment to a mother or mother substitute; an emotional climate characterized by mutual pleasure, sensitive need-gratification, and minimization of restriction and punishment; a physical environment that is both stimulating and responsive, offering a variety of modulated sensory experience; freedom to explore and master the environment; a daily schedule that is orderly and predictable; and an opportunity to assimilate and interpret experience within a consistent cultural milieu. These items compose seven general aspects of home environment: (1) provision of stimulation through equipment types and experiences; (2) stimulation of mature behavior; (3) provision of a stimulating physical and language environment; (4) avoidance of restriction and punishment; (5) pride, affection, and thoughtfulness; (6) masculine stimulation; and (7) independence from parental control.

As examples, seven of the eighty items on the inventory are given below. They are answered "yes" or "no."

*I. Provision of Stimulation Through Equipment, Toys, and Experiences*
  13. At least ten books are present and visible in the apartment.
*II. Stimulation of Mature Behavior*
  30. Tries to get child to pick up and put away toys after play session without help.
*III. Provision of a Stimulating Physical and Language Environment (Observation items, except no. 45)*
  37. House is not overly noisy (television, shouts of children, radio, and so forth).

*IV. Avoidance of Restriction and Punishment (Observation items, except nos. 51 and 52)*

46. Mother does not scold or derogate child more than once during visit.

*IV. Pride, Affection, and Thoughtfulness (Observation items, except nos. 53, 54, 55, 56, 57, 58, 59)*

59. Child's art work is displayed some place in house (anything that child makes).

*VI. Masculine Stimulation*

69. Child sees and spends some time with father or father figure four days a week.

*VII. Independence from Parental Control*

75. Child is permitted to choose some of his clothing to be worn except on very special occasions.

RELIABILITY AND VALIDITY: None available.

BIBLIOGRAPHY:

Caldwell, B. M. "On Designing Supplementary Environments for Early Child Development." *BAEYC Reports* (Boston Association for the Education of Young Children), 1968, *10* (1), 1-11.

Caldwell, B. M., Elardo, P., and Elardo, R. "The Longitudinal Observation and Intervention Study: A Preliminary Report." Presented at the meeting of the Southeastern Conference on Research in Child Development. Williamsburg, Virginia, April 1972.

Caldwell, B. M., Heider, J., and Kaplan, B. "The Inventory of Home Stimulation." Paper presented at the meeting of the American Psychological Association. September 1966.

Caldwell, B. M., Wright, C. M., Honig, A. S., and Tannenbaum, J. "Infant Day Care and Attachment." *American Journal of Orthopsychiatry,* 1970, *40,* 397-412.

Cravioto, J., and Delicardie, E. "Environmental Correlates of Severe Clinical Malnutrition and Language Development in Survivors from Dwashiorkor or Marasmus." In *Nutrition, the Nervous System and Behavior.* Washington, D.C.: Pan American Health Organization, Scientific Publication no. 251, 1972.

Elardo, R., and Bradley, R. "The Relation of Infants' Home Environments to Mental Test Performance from 6 to 36 Months: A Longitudinal Analysis." Paper presented at the southeastern regional meeting of the Society for Research in Child Development. Chapel Hill, North Carolina, March 1974.

---

# JOHN TRACY CLINIC PARENTS' ATTITUDE SCALE

AUTHOR: Staff of John Tracy Clinic

AGE: Parents

VARIABLE: Parental attitudes toward child rearing

TYPE OF MEASURE: Questionnaire

SOURCE FROM WHICH MEASURE MAY BE OBTAINED: John Tracy Clinic, 806 West Adams Boulevard, Los Angeles, California 90007.

DESCRIPTION OF MEASURE: The scale consists of twenty-three questions about parental attitudes intended to be used with parents of young deaf children, although deafness is not mentioned in the questions. Responses are in the form of a 5-point scale running from "agree strongly" to "disagree strongly."

As examples, five of the twenty-three items on the scale are given below.

1. When a young child is experimenting with new materials like paint or clay, his parents should let him do as he wishes with it and not restrict him in any way.
2. Growing up to be a mature person amounts pretty much to learning to accept the rules and patterns that are given to the person by his parents.
3. When one has serious personal problems to solve which involve other members of the family, it's usually better to think them through completely before openly discussing them.
4. Discipline and punishment should mean about the same thing.
5. Even when a young child has learned to use paints, crayons, and tools, his parents should not teach him what to make with these things.

RELIABILITY AND VALIDITY: For a study that related questionnaire answers to teacher ratings, see Lloyd (1969).

BIBLIOGRAPHY:

Horton, K. B. "Home Demonstration Teaching for Parents of Very Young Children." *Volta Review*, 1968, *70*, 97-101, 104.

Lloyd, A. G. "Preliminary Attitude Scale of Parents of Deaf Children." Unpublished master's thesis. University of Southern California, Los Angeles, 1969.

Lowell, E. L. *Home Teaching for Parents of Young Deaf Children.* Final report. Washington, D.C.: Bureau of Education for the Handicapped, Department of Health, Education and Welfare, 1968. ERIC document no. ED 029 419.

*Prepared by Edgar L. Lowell*

---

# JOHNSEN'S PARENTAL PERMISSIVENESS SCALES

AUTHOR: Kathryn P. Johnsen

AGE: Parents

VARIABLE: Concept of parental role

TYPE OF MEASURE: Questionnaire

SOURCE FROM WHICH MEASURE MAY BE OBTAINED: Institute for the Study of

Social Change, Department of Sociology and Anthropology, Purdue University, West Lafayette, Indiana 47907. Cost: $.50.

DESCRIPTION OF MEASURE: The Johnsen's Parental Permissiveness Scales may be used to measure the subject's concept of her own parental role, or it may be used to compare her responses to the parental role with her perception of her own mother's responses. The three scales together (Concept, Tolerance, and Action) allow comparisons between the generalized concept of what a parent *should* do, the tolerance for types of behaviors representing the general areas, and the usual parental response to *specific* actions depicting the behavioral categories. Response categories for each item move from complete permissiveness (encouragement) to absolute restriction and punishment of the behavior. The instrument has only been used by the author for college-educated mothers; however, there appears no reason for its use to be restricted to this population.

As examples, the first five of the fifteen items in Section A (Concept) are given below. Items measure aggression, obedience, and sex. They are to be answered on a 4-point scale from "strongly agree" to "strongly disagree" with the statement.

1. A  A mother should teach her children that anger *should not be expressed* toward their mother.
2. O  A school-age child should be allowed to question his mother's judgment when he disagrees with her.
3. A  A mother should *encourage* her children to express their angry feelings, even toward herself.
4. S  A mother should teach her children that their curiosity about sex should not be satisfied in play with other children.
5. O  A mother should be able to let her school-age child act on his own judgment, though she may disagree with his decisions.

Below are the first two of the fifteen items in Section C (Tolerance). Numbers in parentheses indicate scoring.

A. 34. Sometimes a child will get angry at his mother and hit her or kick her. How much of this do you allow in your children?
(0)  1. _____As much as they like, I encourage them to express their feelings in this manner, if they are angry at me.
(1)  2. _____Quite a bit, I will not usually stop it, unless it continues for some time.
(2)  3. _____Some, I will allow occasional slaps or kicks, *without comment.*
(3)  4. _____Some, I will allow occasional slaps or kicks, *but discourage it from continuing.*
(4)  5. _____Very little, I will rarely allow this, and only if there is a very good reason.
(5)  6. _____None, I will not allow it.
   35. Until what age do you allow this? _____

Below is the first one of the nine items in Section D (Action).

O. 49. You are ready to serve dinner and your grade-school son has not come in, though you are sure he has heard you call *several* times. When he finally comes, he tells you that he had to finish something he was doing, but he came as soon as he could. What would you be most likely to do?

(0)  1. _____ Smile at him, letting him know you understand.

(1)  2. _____ Say nothing, *even though* this happens quite often.

(2)  3. _____ Say nothing *unless* this has been happening frequently, then express disapproval.

(3)  4. _____ Explain why he shouldn't do this.

(4)  5. _____ Express emphatic disapproval.

(5)  6. _____ Punish or threaten punishment.

RELIABILITY AND VALIDITY: Reliability of the scales was determined by the test-retest method. The correlation coefficients, calculated by the Spearman rank-order formula, using the correction for ties, were as follows:

| Concept scales | Total | Sex | Aggression | Obedience |
|---|---|---|---|---|
| Mothers | .73 | .58 | .77 | .72 |
| Generational change | .78 | .75 | .79 | .74 |
| *Tolerance scales* | | | | |
| Mothers | .82 | .80 | .70 | .81 |
| Generational change | .89 | .87 | .83 | .78 |
| *Action Scales* | | | | |
| Mothers | .55 | .84 | .64 | .51 |
| Generational change | .84 | .60 | .93 | .65 |

The validity of these scales suffers from the same problems as other measures utilizing verbal responses. A detailed discussion of the validity problems can be found in Johnsen (1966).

BIBLIOGRAPHY:

Johnsen, K. P. "An Analysis of Factors Contributing to Within-Class Differences in Maternal Role Change over Two Generations." Unpublished doctoral dissertation. Purdue University, West Lafayette, Indiana, 1966.

Johnsen, K. P., and Leslie, G. R. "Methodological Notes on Research in Child Rearing and Social Class." *Merrill-Palmer Quarterly,* 1965, *11,* 345-58.

Leslie, G. R., and Johnsen, K. P. "Changed Perceptions of the Maternal Role." *American Sociological Review,* 1963, *27,* 919-927.

# KNOWLEDGE OF INFANT DEVELOPMENT SCALE

AUTHOR: Russell A. Dusewicz

AGE: Adults

VARIABLE: Knowledge of concepts and terminology relating to infant and child development

TYPE OF MEASURE: Test

SOURCE FROM WHICH MEASURE MAY BE OBTAINED: Russell A. Dusewicz, Division of Research, Pennsylvania Department of Education, Harrisburg, Pennsylvania 17126.

DESCRIPTION OF MEASURE: The Knowledge of Infant Development Scale was developed as a means for assessing the effectiveness of preservice and inservice training programs upon participants in the child-care services field. Its format incorporates brief statements relating to either concepts or terms associated with infant and child development, to which a standard set of responses may be applied. In this way it allows for relative ease of administration to individuals who are handicapped by reading difficulties or who typically exhibit a high degree of test anxiety in situations and on measures requiring more extensive consideration of test questions and demanding more complex characteristics of item responses. The scale was developed from a battery of over two hundred questions relating to knowledge of concepts and terminology in early childhood development. Fifty-four items were selected by consensus of a committee of professionals in the field, and these were later reduced by item analysis techniques to forty-two. The test was designed for both written and oral administration, with all items of a multiple-choice type consisting of very short statements requiring a response of either "agree," "disagree," or "not sure." In this way the scale assumes the appearance of an opinionaire rather than a test and may be administered under this guise to subjects who present special problems in the formal testing situation.

As examples, four items from the test are given below. The first two involve terminology while the latter two relate to concepts. All of those listed here happen to be incorrect statements requiring the response "disagree" as the correct response.

1. Discipline means punishing a child when he does something wrong.
2. A child's attention span is the time it takes him to solve a problem.
3. The prenatal environment cannot have any effects, either beneficial or harmful, on the unborn child.
4. It is not normal for children two years old and under to be close together but to play separately.

RELIABILITY AND VALIDITY: The original fifty-four-item scale was administered to a sample of seventy-nine individuals participating in their first year at entry, paraprofessional, and teacher-supervisor levels of a State Community Coordinated Child Care (4-C) Manpower Training Program. On the basis of an item analysis of scores on this original version, the test was revised and a reduced scale encompassing forty-two questions remained. This refined and fairly brief Knowledge of Infant Development

Scale was found to have a Kuder-Richardson formula 20 reliability of .81 for the same sample of seventy-nine first-year 4-C participants, with raw scores ranging from 15 to 41. The utility of the scale lies principally in its ability to provide a brief measure of knowledge of concepts and terminology in early childhood development with an adequate range of item difficulty to accommodate quite well those with a background of formal training and experience in the field as well as those who are newcomers lacking in both qualifications. Its rather respectable reliability lends a substantial degree of confidence for oral administration to poor readers or nonreaders and extends its usefulness into areas such as the selection and training of potential early childhood aides from low-income applicants of disadvantaged backgrounds.

BIBLIOGRAPHY:

Dusewicz, R. A. "A Scale for Assessing Knowledge of Infant Development." *Education*, 1973, *93*, 252-253.

---

# LONDON SENTENCE-COMPLETION TEST

AUTHOR: John C. Coleman

AGE: 11 to 18 years; adult form also available

VARIABLE: Perception of interpersonal relationships

TYPE OF MEASURE: Sentence-completion test

SOURCE FROM WHICH MEASURE MAY BE OBTAINED: J. C. Coleman, Department of Psychiatry, The London Hospital Medical College, Turner Street, London E1 2AD, England.

DESCRIPTION OF MEASURE: The measure is useful as a short projective technique, providing the opportunity for adolescents to express feelings and attitudes about a wide range of relationships in which they are likely to be involved. The test can be used in either individual or group settings, and in situations where subjects are unable or unwilling to read or write, it is possible for the tester to read the items aloud and to elicit oral responses. There are slightly different forms for boys and girls. The test contains fourteen items, two for each of the following areas: self-image, person alone, two-person situation (parents), two-person situation (heterosexual), three-person situation (parents), three-person situation (peers), and large-group situation. The test is simple to score, with five basic categories of response: constructive (where the relationship is valued), negative (where the relationship is derogated), neutral (where the evaluation is involved), ambivalent (where both constructive and negative views are expressed), and conditional (where a hoped-for rather than an actual relationship is described).

As examples, the first seven of the fourteen items on the girls' form of the test are given below.

1. Usually when a girl is with her father . . .
2. If someone is not part of the group . . .
3. Often when three people are together . . .
4. For a girl, parents . . .
5. When there is no one else around I . . .
6. A girl and a boy together . . .
7. When someone gives orders to a group . . .

RELIABILITY AND VALIDITY: Interjudge reliability measures, involving three experienced clinical psychologists, were consistently high and provided a mean agreement score of 92 percent. The primary validation for the test has come from comparison between age groups (Coleman, 1974). Eight hundred adolescents covering four age groups were included in the sample, and the results showed highly significant differences between groups. Many important developmental patterns have been delineated, and the interested reader is referred to the full report of the study. In addition, another projective technique of the picture-thematic variety was included, with pictures to match each of the sentence stems. In most areas (particularly parents and peers) there was remarkably high intertest consistency.

BIBLIOGRAPHY:

Coleman, J. C. "The Study of Adolescent Development Using a Sentence-Completion Method." *British Journal of Educational Psychology,* 1970, *40,* 27-34.
Coleman, J. C. *Relationships in Adolescence.* London: Routledge & Kegan Paul, 1974.

---

# MARJORIBANKS FAMILY ENVIRONMENT SCHEDULE

AUTHOR: Kevin Marjoribanks

AGE: Parents

VARIABLE: Learning environment of the family

TYPE OF MEASURE: Semistructured home interview

SOURCE FROM WHICH MEASURE MAY BE OBTAINED: Kevin Marjoribanks, Department of Educational Studies, University of Adelaide, Adelaide, South Australia, Australia.

DESCRIPTION OF MEASURE: The schedule measures eight environmental press variables. These are labeled press for: achievement, activeness, intellectuality, independence, English, second language, dominance (mother), and dominance (father). Each of the press variables is defined in terms of a set of characteristics that provided the framework for the construction of the instrument. Six-point rating scales are provided in order to score 188 items. The schedule is designed to measure both the intensity of the present learning environment of the family and the cumulative nature of the environment.

As examples, three selected items from the scale are given below.

1. What are his *best* subjects in school? What are his *weakest* subjects?
   a. Has definite knowledge of the subjects, and is able to name them.
   b. Has some knowledge of the subjects; is able to name one or two of them and indicates uncertainty about the others.
   c. Indicates uncertainty; names more than one subject (e.g., I think his best is arithmetic and his weakest is spelling).
   d. Indicates uncertainty; names only one subject (e.g., I think his best subject is arithmetic).
   e. No knowledge of the subject.

3. (a) How much time do you think a boy in fifth grade should devote to his studies and homework each day out of schooltime?
   2 or more hours.                          How long? _____hours
   1 to 2 hours.
   1 hour.
   Less than 1 hour.                         How long? _____ minutes
   No time.
   Other answer: _____

   (b) Do you expect *your boy* to spend a regular amount of time each day at his studies or homework outside of schooltime? Yes     No

12. (a) What is the *minimum level* of education that you think he must receive?
    Beyond 4 years of college, graduate school.
    College degree.
    At least some college.
    Graduate from high school plus teachers college or community college.
    Finish high school; or as much as possible.
    Leave school as soon as possible.
    Other answer: _____

    (b) How much schooling do you *want* him to receive?
    Beyond 4 years of college, graduate school.
    College degree.
    At least some college.
    Graduate from high school *plus* teachers college or community college.
    Other answer: _____

RELIABILITY AND VALIDITY: The reliability coefficient of each environmental press scale was estimated by determining coefficient *alpha* ($N$ = 185 families). The coefficients ranged from .66 to .94 with a coefficient of .96 for the whole instrument. The schedule has moderate to high concurrent validities for a set of mental ability scores. The eight measures, when combined, account for 50 percent of the variance in verbal and number scores, 16 percent in reasoning scores, and 7 percent in spatial scores. The measure accounts for significantly more of the variance in the ability scores than social-status variables and family-structure characteristics.

BIBLIOGRAPHY:

Marjoribanks, K. "Achievement Orientation of Canadian Ethnic Groups." *Alberta Journal of Educational Research*, 1972, *18*, 162-173.

Marjoribanks, K. "Environment, Social Class, and Mental Abilities." *Journal of Educational Psychology*, 1972, *63*, 103-109.

Marjoribanks, K. "Ethnic and Environmental Influences on Mental Abilities." *American Journal of Sociology*, 1972, *78*, 323-337.

Marjoribanks, K. "Ethnicity and Learning Patterns: A Replication and an Explanation." *Sociology*, 1972, *6*, 417-431.

Marjoribanks, K. *Environments for Learning*. London: National Foundation for Educational Research, 1974.

Marjoribanks, K., and Walberg, H. J. "Family Environment: Sibling Constellation and Social Class Correlates." *Journal of Biosocial Science*, 1975, *7*, 15-25.

Walberg, H. J., and Marjoribanks, K. "Differential Mental Abilities and Home Environment: A Canonical Analysis." *Developmental Psychology*, 1973, *9*, 363-368.

---

## MARYLAND PARENT ATTITUDE SURVEY (MPAS)

AUTHOR: Donald K. Pumroy

AGE: Approximately 15 years and up

VARIABLE: Attitudes of parents toward child rearing

TYPE OF MEASURE: Forced-choice survey

SOURCE FROM WHICH MEASURE MAY BE OBTAINED: D. K. Pumroy, College of Education, University of Maryland, College Park, Maryland 20742. Cost: $1.00.

DESCRIPTION OF MEASURE: The aim of the Maryland Parent Attitude Survey (MPAS) is to differentiate four types of parents: disciplinarian, indulgent, protective, and rejecting. The MPAS consists of ninety-five pairs of items selected to measure the four types of parents. Only ninety pairs are actually scored; the first five pairs are buffer items and are designed to help the parent establish a set for taking the survey. The items are paired if (1) they represent different types of parents, and (2) they are judged to be approximately equal in social desirability. There are forty-five items representing each type of parent. The task of the parent is to read each item in the pair and to select the one that most represents his or her view. Scoring is done by summing the number of items representing each type of parents chosen by the responder. The scoring can be done on the survey itself or, if the $N$ is large, machine-scoring sheets can be used. Norms and $T$ scores are available for each scale.

As examples, the first ten items, excluding buffer items, of the ninety-five items of the survey are given below.

6. a. Parents should watch their children all the time to keep them from getting hurt.
   b. Children who always obey grow up to be the best adults.
7. a. Children should never be allowed to talk back to their parents.
   b. Parents should accompany their children to the places they want to go.

8. a. Children should learn to keep their place.
   b. Children should be required to consult their parents before making any important decisions.
9. a. Quiet, well-behaved children will develop into the best type of grownup.
   b. Parents should pick up their child's toy if he doesn't want to do it himself.
10. a. Parents should do nothing for their children.
    b. A child's life should be as pleasant as possible.
11. a. Watching television keeps children out of the way.
    b. Children should never be allowed to talk back to their parents.
12. a. Personal untidiness is a revolt against authority, so parents should take the matter in hand.
    b. A good child always asks permission before he does anything so he doesn't get into trouble.
13. a. Sometimes children make a parent so mad they see red.
    b. Parents should do things for their children.
14. a. Children should be taught to follow the rules of the game.
    b. A child's life should be as pleasant as possible.
15. a. Parents should cater to their children's appetites.
    b. Many parents wonder if parenthood is worthwhile.

RELIABILITY AND VALIDITY: Reliability has been established using both the test-retest method and the split-half method. The subjects used were undergraduate college students. The results of the reliabilities for the four scales are as follows:

| | | Split-Half | |
| Scale | Test-Retest ($N = 54$) | Males ($N = 45$) | Females ($N = 45$) |
| --- | --- | --- | --- |
| Disciplinarian | .62 | .74 | .76 |
| Indulgent | .73 | .68 | .84 |
| Protective | .69 | .76 | .73 |
| Rejecting | .65 | .74 | .67 |

The validity of such an instrument is somewhat difficult to establish. Each item has face validity based on the original item-selection process. Since the development of the MPAS, several studies have been completed in which the scales have been related to other instruments of behavior. (1) Males score higher on the D scale than do females, while females score higher on the I scale than do males. (2) Age seems to be related to the D and R scales. The older subjects, both male and female, score lower on the D scale and higher on the R scale than do younger subjects. (3) The relationship between Edwards' SD scale (1954) from the MMPI is not related to the four scales of the MPAS. The correlations range from −.17 to .19, indicating that the scales appear to be relatively free of social desirability. (4) Brody (1964) conducted a study that related mothers' MPAS scores and mothers' ratings of their interacting with their children. She found that mothers high on the D scales showed more directing and restricting behavior than those scoring low. Also, forbidding behavior on the part of the mother was positively related to the mother's score on the R scale. (5) The author found that parents in a parent discussion group who attended fewer meetings scored higher on the R scale than those who attended more meetings. He also found that the more meetings the parents attended, the higher they scored on the D scale.

BIBLIOGRAPHY:

Brody, G. F. "The Relationship Between Maternal Attitudes and Mother-Child Inter-action." Paper presented at the Eastern Psychological Association meeting. Philadelphia, Pennsylvania, April 1964.

Edwards, A. L. *Manual for the Edwards Personal Preference Schedule.* New York: Psychological Corporation, 1954.

Gelso, C. J. "The Transmission of Attitude Toward Child Rearing." *Journal of Genetic Psychology,* 1974, *125,* 285-293.

Pumroy, D. K. "Maryland Parent Attitude Survey: A Research Instrument with Social Desirability Controlled." *Journal of Psychology,* 1966, *64,* 73-78.

Tolor, A. "An Evaluation of the MPAS." *Journal of Psychology,* 1967, *67,* 69-74.

---

# MATERNAL ATTITUDE QUESTIONNAIRE

AUTHOR: Phillida Salmon

AGE: Mothers of junior school children

VARIABLE: Maternal attitudes

TYPE OF MEASURE: Likert-type scale

SOURCE FROM WHICH MEASURE MAY BE OBTAINED: Phillida Salmon, Senior Lecturer in Child Development, Institute of Education, Malet Street, London WC1, England.

DESCRIPTION OF MEASURE: An ad hoc questionnaire, designed to measure acceptance-rejection on the one hand and control-neglect on the other, was administered to a pilot sample of 236 mothers living in the same area as that of the experimental subjects. Principal-component analysis showed two main components. The first, which appeared from its loadings to be a measure of acceptance-rejection, accounted for 13.1 percent of the variance. The second, which seemed from its loadings to be a measure of control-neglect, accounted for 7.3 percent of the variance. By selecting items that were loaded to the extent of at least .20 on either component, a thirty-four-item questionnaire was produced, of which twenty-three items were concerned with acceptance-rejection and twenty items with control-neglect, nine items being shared by the two scales. The fact that nine items were shared did not appear to contaminate the two scales, since these items contributed to acceptance and control as follows: (five items) = acceptance scale: negative score; control scale: negative score; and (four items) = acceptance scale: negative score; control scale: positive score. Calculation of the Pearson product-moment correlation between the scores of the pilot sample on the two scales yielded a value of $r = -.09$, indicating orthogonality between the two scales.

As examples, ten items from the pilot form of the questionnaire, which were retained in the final version of the test, are given below.

3. After the age of 8, children do not need to have a definite bedtime. (*Control* −)
5. Parents ought not to let their children have secrets from them. (*Acceptance* −, *Control* +)
6. It doesn't matter if parents occasionally make mistakes in front of a child. (*Acceptance* +)
7. Children can usually decide for themselves what food they need. (*Control* −)
8. A son should be like his father, and a daughter should be like her mother. (*Acceptance* −)
9. Parents should have rules about what their children watch on TV. (*Control* +)
10. It's sad to see children grow up and need you less. (*Acceptance* −)
11. When a child is unhappy, it's best to leave him alone to sort it out. (*Acceptance* −)
12. Playing too much with a child will spoil him. (*Acceptance* −)
13. It's not the parents' concern what marks their child gets in school. (*Acceptance* −, *Control* −)

RELIABILITY AND VALIDITY: For both scales the Spearman-Brown split-half reliability coefficient was $r = .73$. Scores derived from this questionnaire consisted of the measure of acceptance-rejection, possible scores ranging from 0 to 23, and the measure of control-neglect, possible scores ranging from 0 to 20. The test was administered to sixty mothers. Mothers' acceptance-vs.-rejection scores were associated in the predicted way, although not always at a significant level, with measures of boys' orientation to *either* peers *or* adults. Maternal control vs. neglect, on the other hand, was not associated in any consistent way with the measures of orientation in the boys. The expected positive associations of neglect with *peer*-group orientation and of control with *adult*-group orientation did not emerge. Maternal attitude measured here seemed to account for boys' positive orientation to adults or to peers, but it did not account for choice of the two reference groups for positive orientation by the child.

BIBLIOGRAPHY:

Salmon, P. "Differential Conforming as a Developmental Process." *British Journal of Social and Clinical Psychology*, 1969, *8*, 22-31.

---

# MATERNAL ATTITUDE SCALE (MAS)

AUTHOR: Bertram J. Cohler

AGE: Mothers of children 5 years and younger

VARIABLE: Attitudes toward child care

TYPE OF MEASURE: Likert-type scale

SOURCE FROM WHICH MEASURE MAY BE OBTAINED: For manual, order NAPS document no. 00963 from Microfiche Publications, 440 Park Avenue South, New

York, New York 10016. Cost: Microfiche, $3.00; Photocopy, $6.00. While investigators are free to use the MAS items in any way they wish, those wishing to obtain scores on the five factors described below (and the several other scales listed in the manual) may send the questionnaires to the author to be scored. Typically the data is transcribed on to coding sheets and key-punched. The punched cards are then input to the scoring program. Those wishing to obtain scores on the five factors, at a cost of approximately $.30 per questionnaire, should correspond with the author regarding the details of the format to be followed in punching the item values for further analysis: Bertram J. Cohler, Committee on Human Development, Department of Behavioral Sciences, University of Chicago, 5730 S. Woodlawn Avenue, Chicago, Illinois 60637.

DESCRIPTION OF MEASURE: The MAS is a 233-item instrument that is appropriate for mothers with at least a sixth-grade education. Constructed according to Sander's formulation of the developing mother-child relationship in the first years of life, the test pays particular attention to the assessment of attitudes regarding reciprocity and encouragement of the child's sense of competence and to the assessment of attitudes toward the issue of separation-individuation as described by Mahler (1968). The construction of the instrument is described in greater detail in Cohler, Weiss, and Grunebaum (1970). Developed as a result of extensive pretest studies on more than five hundred working-class and middle-class mothers of young children in an urban New England setting, the instrument yields five second-order orthogonal or independent factors. I. *Appropriate control of the child's aggressive impulses:* Appropriate control reflects the attitude that children's impulses can be channeled into socially appropriate behaviors, rather than inhibited completely. II. *Encouragement vs. discouragement of reciprocity:* Reciprocity reflects the attitude that infants can communicate and seek social interaction with their mothers, and that mothers can understand and respond to the baby's initiation of a demand for reciprocity. III. *Appropriate vs. inappropriate closeness:* Attitudes involving appropriate closeness suggest that a mother does not view her baby as a narcissistic extension of the self and does not seek to attain gratifications through the baby that have been missing in her own life. IV. *Acceptance vs. denial of emotional complexity in child rearing:* Acceptance involves a mother's recognition that motherhood is sometimes more work than pleasure and that mothers do not always know what is best for their children. V. *Comfort vs. discomfort in perceiving and meeting the baby's (physical) needs:* Comfort implies that mothers feel that they can understand what their babies want and provide for these physical needs. Each of these factors refers to a particular developmental issue in the early mother-child relationship. Clearly, both the child's own development and the mother's continued effectiveness and satisfaction in the maternal role are shaped by the extent to which these issues are resolved in an adaptive manner that encourages the further development of the mother's relationship with her child.

As examples, the first twenty-five of the 233 items are given below. They are to be responded to on a 6-point scale from "strongly agree" to "strongly disagree."

1. When the baby is born he (she) already has a personality of his (her) own.
2. Holding and caressing a baby when he (she) cries is good for him (her).
3. A newborn baby doesn't cry unless something is wrong.
4. Snips, snails, and puppy dog tails, that's what little boys are made of.
5. Newborn babies are fragile and delicate and must be handled extremely carefully.
6. A mother just naturally knows when to pick up a crying baby.
7. It is worth a great deal of effort on the mother's part to provide surprises for her child.

8. Taking care of a baby is much more work than pleasure.
9. A mother doesn't really think of her baby as a person until it begins to smile and recognize people.
10. Babies wish that their mothers would stop fussing over them too much.
11. It is a terribly frustrating task to care for a newborn infant, because he (she) can't let you know what he (she) needs.
12. It is upsetting to a mother when her infant leaves half the formula in his (her) bottle.
13. A mother's carelessness, even for a moment, can easily cause an infant to die.
14. A neat, well-ordered home is one of the most important things a parent can provide a child in growing up.
15. Mothers enjoy breast feeding much more than bottle feeding.
16. A mother and her 5-month-old child should be able to understand each other fairly well.
17. Parents often overestimate the importance of encouraging children's curiosity about the world around them.
18. A child never gets angry with his (her) mother.
19. A woman wants her mother nearby when she is giving birth.
20. A 3-month-old baby can't really tell you what he (she) is thinking by a smile.
21. Infants should be kept on a regular feeding schedule and should be fed only at certain times.
22. When a child cries, his (her) parents should comfort him (her).
23. Mothers are better than fathers at raising girls.
24. Infants under 5 months of age are not well able to occupy themselves, and they like frequent adult attention.
25. Bodily changes in pregnancy make a woman feel very unattractive.

RELIABILITY AND VALIDITY: The internal consistency of these five second-order factors is quite high. That is to be expected in deriving scales from factor-analytic procedures. Scales constructed on the basis of items with the highest loadings on these factors show *alpha* coefficients ranging from .81 to .96. Test-retest reliability coefficients for these five factors over a one-month period range from .62 to .78. The validity of these five MAS factors has been demonstrated in a variety of studies, primarily concerning mentally ill mothers of young children as contrasted with nonhospitalized mothers in the community. Cohler, Weiss, and Grunebaum (1970) report that hospitalized mothers believe less in fostering reciprocity (Factor II) and believe more in denying child-care concerns (Factor IV) than nonhospitalized controls. Cohler and others (1974b) have replicated this finding on an independent sample and find that mentally ill mothers also believe less in fostering appropriate closeness (Factor III) than controls. Cohler and others (1971) have demonstrated a relationship between child-care attitudes of mothers and their own mothers, discovering that mothers sharing a common residence with their own mothers believe less in fostering appropriate closeness (Factor III) than mothers who live apart; this finding is also true for the grandmother generation. Tulkin and Cohler (1973) have reported that within a group of middle-class mothers, women who believe to a greater extent in fostering reciprocity (Factor II) spent more time during observation periods in face-to-face interaction with their infants, responded to a greater extent to infant vocalizations, and gave their infants more objects to play with. Cohler and others (1974a) found that, even partialling out maternal IQ, more adaptive attitudes regarding reciprocity (Factor II) were associated with a higher IQ in the children. Within this group of mothers, less adaptive attitudes regarding the encouragement of appropriate closeness (Factor III) were associated with a greater number of birth complications among the children. Finally, Cohler and others (in press) have reported that within a group of mentally ill women, greater field independence was related to more adaptive attitudes regarding the factors of encouragement of reciprocity (II), appropriate closeness (III), and acceptance of emotional complexity (IV). Maternal attitudes were also related to the child's cognitive style.

BIBLIOGRAPHY:

Cohler, B., Gallant, D., Grunebaum, H., Weiss, J., and Gamer, E. "Child-Care Attitudes and Attention Dysfunction among Hospitalized and Nonhospitalized Mothers and Their Young Children." In J. Glidewell (Ed.), *The Social Context of Learning and Development*. New York: Gardner-Wiley (in press).

Cohler, B., Gallant, D., Grunebaum, H., Weiss, J., Gamer, E. "Child-Care Attitudes and the Child's Cognitive Development Among Hospitalized and Nonhospitalized Mothers and Their Young Children." Unpublished paper. Committee on Human Development, University of Chicago, 1974a.

Cohler, B., Grunebaum, H., Weiss, J., Hartman, C., and Gallant, D. "Child-Care Attitudes and Psychopathology Among Formerly Hospitalized and Nonhospitalized Mothers." Unpublished paper. Committee on Human Development, University of Chicago, 1974b.

Cohler, B., Grunebaum, H., Weiss, J., and Moran, D. "The Child-Care Attitudes of Two Generations of Mothers." *Merrill-Palmer Quarterly*, 1971, *17*, 3-17.

Cohler, B., Weiss, J., and Grunebaum, H. "Child-Care Attitudes and Emotional Disturbance Among Mothers of Young Children." *Genetic Psychology Monographs*, 1970, *82*, 3-47.

Cohler, B., Woolsey, S., Weiss, J., and Grunebaum, H. "Childrearing Attitudes Among Mothers Volunteering and Revolunteering for a Psychological Study." *Psychological Reports*, 1968, *23*, 603-612.

Mahler, M. *On Human Symbiosis and the Vicissitudes of Individuation*. New York: International Universities Press, 1968.

Tulkin, S., and Cohler, B. "Childrearing Attitudes and Mother-Child Interaction in the First Year of Life." *Merrill-Palmer Quarterly*, 1973, *19*, 95-106.

---

## MATERNAL CHARACTERISTICS SCALE (MCS)

AUTHORS: Norman A. Polansky, Christine DeSaix, Elizabeth Harkins, and Betty Jane Smith

AGE: Mothers

VARIABLE: Characteristics of the maternal personality

TYPE OF MEASURE: Questionnaire and observation framework

SOURCE FROM WHICH MEASURE MAY BE OBTAINED: See Polansky, Borgman, and DeSaix (1972) or Polansky, DeSaix, and Sharlin (1972).

DESCRIPTION OF MEASURE: The original MCS contained 205 items. These were applied with a sample of sixty-five mothers of 5-year-olds attending a year-round Head Start program in one county of rural southern Appalachia. The original 205 items were subsequently reduced to the present scales. The MCS is designed for use by trained and knowledgeable personnel. Although the items are meant to deal with readily and objectively observable facets of the mother's behavior and personality, this is by no means a self-administering battery. Information from which the worker makes her ratings is to be obtained from direct observation, skilled interviewing, weighing of collateral reports, and opinions of other professionals. Hence, the MCS is simply a device to facilitate quantification and ranking of the mothers along certain parameters of personality. Originally a total of eight scales were composed out of the MCS pool of items. These were modified to the following: (1) the apathy-futility dimension, combining (a) behavioral immobilization and (b) interpersonal detachment; (2) the childlike impulsivity dimension, combining (a) impulsivity and (b) dependency; (3) verbal accessibility—composite scale. For each scale, the total score is simply the algebraic sum of plus and minus scores. Some norms are provided in the manual for the scale.

As examples, the items of the behavioral immobilization scale are given below. Direction for scoring is indicated by pluses and minuses.

1. Claims that she is unable to perform at job or housework or get anything done. +
2. Speaks of herself as healthy, strong, and energetic. −
3. Has volunteered for extra work in day-care center (double credit). − −
4. Face is sometimes dirty, or makeup is smeared despite availability of washing facilities. +
5. Hair is usually unkempt, tangled, or matted. +
6. Clothes are usually dirty or in disarray. +
7. Usually stands or sits erect with concern for posture. −
8. Speech is full of long pauses. +
9. Speaks in a faint voice, or voice fades away at end of sentences. +
10. Sometimes expresses hostility through physical aggression. −
11. Answers questions with single words or phrases only. +
12. Has a sad expression or holds her body in a dejected or despondent posture. +
13. Shows warmth in gestures with interviewer. −
14. Shows enthusiasm. −
15. Is usually aggressive. −
16. When frustrated, flies into rages. −
17. When frustrated, creates a turmoil. −
18. Visits with neighbors. −
19. Has at one time shown capacity to hold a job. −
20. Manages family finances. −
21. Keeps virtually the same posture throughout the interview. +
22. Keeps eyes closed or averted. +
23. Has decorated house in some unexpected way. −

*Notes*
1. Add a constant of +12 to algebraic sum to eliminate minus scores for statistical analysis.
2. Note that item 3 is given two minuses for a "yes" instead of one. The interpersonal detachment scale (31 items), the impulsivity scale (17 items), the dependency scale (18 items), and the verbal accessibility scale (47 items) all have similar formats.

RELIABILITY AND VALIDITY: None reported.

BIBLIOGRAPHY:

Polansky, N. A., Borgman, R. D., and DeSaix, C. *Roots of Futility.* San Francisco: Jossey-Bass, 1972.

Polansky, N. A., DeSaix, C., Harkins, E., and Smith, B. J. *The Maternal Characteristics Scale.* Athens, Georgia: Child Research Field Station, University of Georgia School of Social Work, 1970.

Polansky, N. A., DeSaix, C., and Sharlin, S. *Child Neglect: Understanding and Reaching the Parents.* New York: Child Welfare League of America, 1972.

*Prepared by Orval G. Johnson*

---

# MATERNAL TEACHING STYLE INSTRUMENT (MTSI)

AUTHORS: Howard M. Sandler and Chris R. Barbrack

AGE: 2½ to 5 years

VARIABLE: Components of maternal teaching style

TYPE OF MEASURE: Observation schedule

SOURCE FROM WHICH MEASURE MAY BE OBTAINED: See Sandler, Stewart, and Barbrack (1971) or Benson and Sandler (1973).

DESCRIPTION OF MEASURE: This test was devised as part of a study to determine the feasibility of home-based early childhood intervention, the larger study was conducted by the Demonstration and Research Center for Early Education (DARCEE), and the Maternal Teaching Style Instrument was developed with the partial support of the Appalachian Regional Commission. It was designed to permit direct observation of mothers teaching their children. The original instrument contained ten cards on which there were pictures of geometric forms, varied in color, shape, size, and position on the card. The revised MTSI consists of one practice and four test cards. The mother is instructed to help her child make his card look exactly like hers by getting the child to place blocks varying in size, color, and shape onto his card in the same arrangement as is depicted in drawings on the mother's card. She is told that she may do anything to help the child get the blocks into the proper arrangement except showing the child her card. In this manner, the mother is confined to the class of teaching behaviors but is free to vary within that class, while the child is confined both to and within the class of the behaviors of following instructions. In this kind of situation, the only behavior free to vary is the manner in which the mother teaches.

The essence of the instructions is given below, followed by two categories from verbal responses.

Hand trial card to mother, and say: "(mother's name), you and (child's name) will do this together. You are to help (child's name) fix his card so that it will. match your card. You may help him in any way to fix his card to look like yours so long as you do not show him your card. Make sure he does not see your card."

b. *Questioning* will be counted whenever the mother asks a question of the child. The unit is a sentence.

1. Appropriate Questions are those which focus the child's attention on information which is necessary for the successful completion of the task. These questions must be directed toward information which it is possible for the child to know. Examples are, "Do you know what color that is?" and "Which one is the star?"

2. Inappropriate Questions are those which call upon the child to draw upon information which he cannot reasonably be expected to have, or those which are irrelevant to the successful completion of the task. Inappropriate Questions are of this type: "Is it right?" and "Do you like ice cream?"

f. *Gesture* is coded whenever the mother uses a bodily movement without actually touching the child or the task materials. These movements may impart information to the child or may respond favorably or unfavroably to the child or his performance. The unit is a completed action: from a state of rest to a gesture to a return to a state of rest. One gesture would be a shaking of the head or pointing to a block.

RELIABILITY AND VALIDITY: In a study of eighteen mother-child pairs (Sandler and others, 1973) selected from low-income housing projects in Nashville, Tennessee, each testing session was videotaped and analyzed later by means of a scoring grid onto which the mothers' responses were sequentially coded. Reliabilities ranged from .81 to .99. Sandler, Stewart, and Barbrack (1971) report correlations between raters ranging from .77 to .85. They further report numerous intercorrelations within the sixteen categories of the MTSI and between the sixteen categories and eight other variables (mother's WAIS, child's WPPSI, race, sex, mother's age, mother's education, child's age, and father's presence).

BIBLIOGRAPHY:

Barbrack, C. R. "The Effect of Three Home Visiting Strategies upon Measures of Children's Academic Aptitude and Maternal Teaching Behaviors." *DARCEE Papers and Reports,* 1970, *4* (1).

Bee, H. L., Van Egeren, L. F., Streissguth, A. P., Numan, B. A., and Leckie, M. S. "Social Class Differences in Maternal Teaching Strategies and Speech Patterns." *Developmental Psychology,* 1969, *1,* 726-734.

Benson, A. J., and Sandler, H. *Development of an Alternative Form of the Maternal Teaching Style Instrument.* Contract NE-C-00-3-0261. Washington, D.C.: National Institute of Education, 1973.

Brophy, J. E. "Mothers as Teachers of Their Own Preschool Children: The Influence of SES and Task Structure on Teaching Specificity." *Child Development*, 1970, *41*, 79-94.

Karnes, M. B., Teska, J. A., Hodgins, A. S., and Badger, E. D. "Educational Intervention at Home by Mothers of Disadvantaged Infants." *Child Development*, 1970, *41*, 925-935.

Sandler, H. M., and others. "The Evaluation of a Home-Based Educational Intervention for Preschoolers and Their Mothers." *Journal of Community Psychology*, 1973, *1*, 372-374.

Sandler, H. M., Stewart, L. T., and Barbrack, C. R. "Toward the Development of a Maternal Teaching Style Instrument." *DARCEE Papers and Reports*, 1971, *5* (6).

---

# MEASURE OF DISAPPROVAL OF CROSS-SEX BEHAVIOR

AUTHOR: Saul Feinman

AGE: Adolescent to adult

VARIABLE: Attitude toward cross-sex-role behavior of children

TYPE OF MEASURE: Rating scale

SOURCE FROM WHICH MEASURE MAY BE OBTAINED: Saul Feinman, Department of Sociology, University of Wyoming, University Station, Box 3293, Laramie, Wyoming 82071.

DESCRIPTION OF MEASURE: The Disapproval Measure consists of ten one-sentence descriptions of young children (3 to 8 years) engaging in various behaviors considered to be more appropriate for the opposite sex. Five of the descriptions are of boys and five are of girls. *S*s are asked to rate each behavior on a 7-point approval-disapproval dimension, where extreme approval is 1 and extreme disapproval is 7. A male disapproval score and a female disapproval score can be calculated by summing *S*s' numerical responses to descriptions of the behaviors of boys and girls, respectively. A total disapproval score is the sum of the male disapproval score and the female disapproval score. The measure was given to 107 male and female college students. Male *S*s were more disapproving than female *S*s for both boys' and girls' behavior. Boys' cross-sex-role behavior was more strongly disapproved of by both male and female *S*s than was girls' cross-sex-role behavior.

The ten sentences of the measure are given below.

1. A 4-year-old boy is seen playing with his sister's dolls.
2. A 5-year-old boy is helping his mother bake a cake.
3. A 4-year-old girl is seen wearing jeans and a sweatshirt while playing outside her house.

4. A 5-year-old girl is observed starting fights with her classmates at school.

5. A 6-year-old boy is hit by another boy of about the same size as he is. He does not make an attempt to defend himself and appears helpless.

6. A 5-year-old girl is helping her father repair the car.

7. A 3-year-old boy is very dependent on his mother and does not do anything without looking to her for approval.

8. A 7-year-old girl is playing baseball with some boys.

9. A 4-year-old boy dresses up in his twin sister's clothes and parades up and down the street.

10. A 3-year-old girl is very independent in her behavior.

RELIABILITY AND VALIDITY: The measure was administered to forty male and sixty-seven female college students from three introductory sociology classes at an East Coast state college in 1972. For all subjects combined, Cronbach *alpha* coefficients (homogeneity reliability estimates) were .73, .63, and .67 for the total, male, and female disapproval scores, respectively. The estimates for female $S$s were slightly but not significantly higher than those for male $S$s. Attempts will be made to develop and validate a revised and expanded (longer) version of this measure. The measure in its present state is exploratory and experimental.

BIBLIOGRAPHY:

Feinman, S. "Approval of Cross-Sex-Role Behavior." *Psychological Reports*, 1974, *35*, 643-648.

---

## MEASURING THE CONTENTS OF BOYS' AND GIRLS' ROOMS

AUTHORS: Harriet L. Rheingold and Kaye V. Cook

AGE: 1 to 6 years

VARIABLE: Differences in parental behavior

TYPE OF MEASURE: Checklist

SOURCE FROM WHICH MEASURE MAY BE OBTAINED: Harriet L. Rheingold, Department of Psychology, University of North Carolina, Chapel Hill, North Carolina 27514.

DESCRIPTION OF MEASURE: The furnishings and toys of children's rooms were tallied by the number of items in the following thirteen classes: animal furnishings, books, dolls, educational-art materials, floral furnishings, furniture, musical items, "ruffles" (furnishings with ruffles, fringe, or lace), spatial-temporal objects (toys and objects related to the properties of space, matter, energy, and time), sports equipment, stuffed animals, toy animals, and vehicles. Infrequent classes of items, tallied by the number of children's rooms containing them, were depots, doll houses, domestic objects, fauna, flora, machines, and military toys. The contents of the rooms of ninety-six children, equally divided by sex, revealed that boys' rooms contained more animal furnishings, educational-art materials, spatial-temporal toys, sports equipment, toy animals, and vehicles. The rooms of girls contained more dolls, floral furnishings, and "ruffles." Boys were provided more depots, fauna, machines, and military toys; girls, more doll houses and domestic items. In general, boys were provided objects that encouraged activities directed away from the home, and girls, objects that encouraged activities directed toward the home. These differences were considered to index differences in parental behavior. Furthermore, differences in how parents furnish the rooms of boys and girls, and the toys parents provide them, may well document differences in other classes of their behavior toward their sons and daughters.

RELIABILITY AND VALIDITY: The authors tallied the contents of ninety-six children's rooms (for twenty-one children the major part of their toys were stored elsewhere in the house). The multivariate analysis of variance of the thirteen classes for which the numbers of items were counted yielded a statistically significant sex $\times$ age interaction ($p < .03$), a significant sex effect ($p < .001$), and a significant age effect ($p < .001$).

BIBLIOGRAPHY:

Rheingold, H. L., and Cook, K. V. "The Contents of Boys' and Girls' Rooms as an Index of Parents' Behavior." *Child Development,* 1975, *46,* 459-463.

---

# MOTHER-INFANT OBSERVATION

AUTHORS: Judith L. Rubenstein, Leon J. Yarrow, Frank A. Pederson, Myrna Fivel, Joan Durfee, and Joseph J. Jankowski

AGE: Mothers with infants 3 to 8 months

VARIABLE: Mother-infant interaction

TYPE OF MEASURE: Time sampling observation system

SOURCE FROM WHICH MEASURE MAY BE OBTAINED: Leon J. Yarrow, Social and Behavioral Sciences Branch, National Institute of Child Health and Human Development, Bethesda, Maryland 20014.

DESCRIPTION OF MEASURE: The procedure is a time-sampling system, designed for use in natural environments, that describes mother-infant interaction at a behavioral level. The time-sampling cycle consists of a 30-second observation period and a 60-

second recording period repeated through 120 cycles each day. Selected infant behaviors include positive vocalizations, fussing, or irritable vocalizations, and whether the infant is engaged in focused manipulation of play objects or directing his visual attention to the mother. The infant's interaction with the mother is described in terms of (1) the sensory modalities in which stimulation is given—visual, auditory, tactile, and kinesthetic; (2) the intensity of stimulation—passive touching, active touching, and moving the baby are distinguished from one another; and (3) stimulation contingent on certain infant behavior—contingent vocal responses to the infant's positive vocalization, and social soothing in response to fretting or crying. In addition, the mother's provision of play materials for the infant is described—how often she makes toys available to the infant and the ways in which she directs the infant's attention to play materials or highlights their properties. To measure stimulation from the proximal inanimate environment, all play materials and household objects within reach of the infant are recorded. These objects are then rated in terms of their complexity and responsiveness.

Following are the categories for observation, each of which contains definitions and rules for scoring: Infant Behaviors—proximity and visual accessibility of mother, baby nonnutritive oral behavior, baby's state, infant signals, baby's visual attention; Maternal Behaviors—maternal vocalizations, maternal look, maternal tactile, maternal kinesthetic, affect, encourages attentiveness to the inanimate environment; Maternal Caretaking—(other sections deal with containers and toys).

RELIABILITY AND VALIDITY: The scale was used in observation of forty-one lower and middle socioeconomic black infants and mothers. The median interobserver reliability was .93. Significant relationships were found between a number of environmental variables and infant development at 6 months.

BIBLIOGRAPHY:

Yarrow, L. J., Rubenstein, J. L., and Pederson, F. A. *Infant and Environment: Early Cognitive and Motivational Development.* Washington, D.C.: Winston, 1974.
Yarrow, L. J., Rubenstein, J. L., Pederson, F. A., and Jankowski, J. J. "Dimensions of Early Stimulation and Their Differential Effects on Infant Development." *Merrill-Palmer Quarterly,* 1972, *18,* 205-218.

*Prepared by Leon J. Yarrow*

# PARENT BEHAVIOR INVENTORY

AUTHORS: Jaques W. Kaswan and Leonore R. Love

AGE: Families of children 8 years and up

VARIABLE: Behavior of parents and children in family setting

TYPE OF MEASURE: Questionnaire

SOURCE FROM WHICH MEASURE MAY BE OBTAINED: Leonore R. Love, Department of Psychology, University of California, Los Angeles, California 90024. Cost: Mailing charges.

DESCRIPTION OF MEASURE: The Parent Behavior Inventory covers specific characteristics of the behavior of parents and children in the family setting. Questions include types and frequencies of current behavior, the contexts within which they occur, their antecedents, and their consequences. Items are formulated in terms that are as concrete as possible. They sample mothers' and fathers' separate ratings of their child's behavior and their own actions in relation to him, their activities and relationship with each other, and their involvement and satisfaction with their community. The forms consist of 101 items covering thirty-three pages. Many of the items are multifaceted, however, so that in effect there are many more than 101. They usually take at least an hour to complete and require careful reflection from the parents. A similar inventory of the child's behavior, parallel but briefer, is completed by the teacher (Teacher Behavior Inventory) to determine similarities and differences in perceptions of the child's behavior at home and at school.

As examples, four selected items of the 101 of the inventory, together with the five possible answers for each item, are given below.

| | | | | | |
|---|---|---|---|---|---|
| 2. How much does your child talk? | _____ Usually quiet, inactive. | _____ | _____ | _____ | _____ Almost always talking. |
| 7. When he's working at something he's interested in, how long does he keep at it? | _____ A minute or two. | _____ | _____ | _____ | _____ As long as necessary to finish. |
| 9. How often does your child | _____ At most several times a year. | _____ About once a month. | _____ About once a week. | _____ Almost every day. | _____ Several times a day. |
|   a. play along when other children are around. | | | | | |
|   b. play with brothers and sisters. | | | | | |
|   c. play with other children. | | | | | |
|   d. play with pets. | | | | | |
| 59. When you tell your child you are going to punish him, how often do you carry through with it? | _____ Never. | _____ Occasionally. | _____ About half of the time. | _____ Usually. | _____ Always. |

RELIABILITY AND VALIDITY: Items were developed over two years with approximately two hundred parents of children attending high, middle, and low socioeconomic-level schools. Early effects insured that items were clear and had adequate variance and that substantial portions of them differentiated between parents of children seen as disturbed and nondisturbed by school personnel. Then ninety-five mothers and eighty fathers drawn from the pilot population filled out a version of the inventory very similar to the final form. Results were analyzed using a Kaiser varimax rotation. Items that loaded less than .40 on any factor and factors containing less than three items were eliminated. These factor analyses were later replicated with another equal-size sample. Since about four-fifths of the items appeared in the same factors in both sets of analyses, the factor structure seems quite reliable. Items that showed a radical shift in factor structure from one analysis to the other were eliminated. Factor loading exceeded .30 in all cases and exceeded .40 in 84 percent of all loadings. Between 48 and 70 percent of the cumulative variance was accounted for in each factor analysis. Responses have been analyzed in terms of differences associated with child school-adjustment patterns and family socioeconomic characteristics.

BIBLIOGRAPHY:

Kaswan, J. W., Love, L. R., and Ronick, E. H. "Information Feedback as a Method of Clinical Intervention and Consultation." In C. Spielberger (Ed.), *Current Topics in Clinical and Community Psychology,* Vol. 3. New York: Academic Press, 1971.

Love, L. R., and Kaswan, J. W. *Troubled Children: Their Families, Schools, and Treatments.* New York: Wiley-Interscience, 1974.

Love, L. R., Kaswan, J. W., and Bugental, D. E. "Differential Effectiveness of Three Clinical Interventions for Different Socioeconomic Groupings." *Journal of Consulting and Clinical Psychology,* 1972, *39,* 347-360.

*Prepared by Leonore R. Love*

---

# PARENT-CHILD INTERACTION RATING
# PROCEDURE (P-CIRP)

AUTHORS: Jo Lynn Cunningham and Robert P. Boger

AGE: 3 to 4 years

VARIABLE: Parent-child interaction, parental teaching style

TYPE OF MEASURE: Observation rating procedure

SOURCE FROM WHICH MEASURE MAY BE OBTAINED: Institute for Family and Child Study, Home Management Unit No. 2, Michigan State University, East Lansing, Michigan 48824.

DESCRIPTION OF MEASURE: The Parent-Child Interaction Rating Procedure (P-CIRP) is a combination time and event sampling technique developed to be used with videotapes of parent-child interaction. The setting is an unstructured task-oriented situation where the parent teaches the child a two-dimensional sorting task. The procedure taps both quantitative and qualitative dimensions of interaction while maintaining the sequence of events and context of the activities. The instrument consists of three parts: (1) general information summarizing elements of the total session, (2) a rating form for the parent-child teaching period of the session, and (3) a rating form for the parent-child-examiner testing period. The general behavioral elements encoded for both the parent and the child include dimensions of verbal and nonverbal communication, the interaction process, and the parental teaching style. A variety of analysis strategies can be appropriately applied. Questions dealing with the relative proportion of time individuals spend at various specific and general behaviors can be investigated, as well as questions investigating the dyadic nature of the exchange or the process over time.

The observation categories for the rating procedure and the number of interaction behavior classes under each are: verbalization (14), fantasy (2), voice tone (3), specificity (2), time orientation (3), task orientation (2), nature of interference (8), verbal receiver (4), feedback (3), reward (3), response (6), initiation (6), response object (3), reinforcement (3), affective tone (3), level of involvement (3), anxiety (3), physical behavior (6), concept (7), teaching method (4), dependency (3), inferred motivation (8), cue (2), cue directiveness (3), cue type (3), defensiveness (2), defensiveness target (3), and defensiveness object (7).

RELIABILITY AND VALIDITY: The authors suggest a minimum of 85-percent agreement among observers using the measure. Behavioral constructs are based on theoretical contributions of social and developmental psychology, and many scales have been adapted from previously validated instruments.

BIBLIOGRAPHY:

Boger, R. P., and Cunningham, J. L. *Observation of Socialization Behavior.* Unpublished manuscript. Head Start Research Center, Michigan State University, East Lansing, 1969.

Boger, R. P., and Cunningham, J. L. *Differential Socialization Patterns of Preschool Children.* Interim Report No. 2. East Lansing: Early Childhood Research Center, Michigan State University, 1970.

Cunningham, J. L., and Boger, R. P. *Father-Child Interaction: Nine-Block Sorting Task.* Unpublished manuscript. Head Start Research Center, Michigan State University, East Lansing, 1969.

Cunningham, J. L., and Boger, R. P. *Development of an Observational Procedure for Assessment of Parent-Child Interaction.* East Lansing: Institute for Family and Child Research, Michigan State University, 1972. ERIC document no. ED 064 320.

*Prepared by Robert P. Boger*

# PARENT-INFANT FEEDING OBSERVATION SCALE

AUTHORS: Joy D. Osofsky and Barbara Danzger

AGE: Birth to 4 months

VARIABLE: Parent and infant behaviors during feeding

TYPE OF MEASURE: Observation rating scale

SOURCE FROM WHICH MEASURE MAY BE OBTAINED: Joy D. Osofsky, Department of Psychology, Temple University, Philadelphia, Pennsylvania 19122.

DESCRIPTION OF MEASURE: The Parental-Infant Feeding Observation Scale is useful to evaluate parent-infant interaction during feeding. Items evaluate quality and quantity of auditory, visual, and tactile stimulation by the mothers and auditory, visual, and tactile behaviors and responses of the infants. The scale is used to rate behaviors during the newborn period and at 6 weeks of age. Infant-parent interaction during feeding is observed for about 15 minutes. The neonatal observations are carried out after the mother has fed her infant at least four times, so that they feel reasonably comfortable in the situation. The scoring can be done either during the observation or immediately following the session. The authors have studied only mothers who have been bottle feeding, since in the samples included very few women were breast feeding. At the present time studies are being done to determine the developmental implications of the measured behaviors. The stability and consistency in patterns of mother-infant interaction during feeding at the newborn period and at 6 weeks of age are being studied. The scale is currently being used in several other studies including those evaluating premature and other high-risk infants, as well as parents from different socioeconomic and racial groups.

As examples, the first of the seven items of each scale are given below.

*Infant Rating*
*Initial state (when mother starts to feed)*
1. Deep sleep.
2. Light sleep with eyes closed.
3. Eyes may be open or closed, eyelids fluttering, drowsy, or semidozing.
4. Alert look; doesn't seem to focus attention on source of stimulation.
5. Alert, bright look; seems to focus attention on source of stimulation.
6. Eyes open, considerable motor activity . . . perhaps some fussing.
7. Crying with or without motor activity.
*Maternal Rating*
*Attentiveness and general sensitivity*
1. Inattentive and insensitive to baby's state and sucking response.
2. Forces bottle on baby; no accommodation to baby's state; rough jiggling of nipple in baby's mouth.
3. Attention variable; little accommodation to baby's needs.
4. Intermittent accommodation to state and needs of baby.
5. Frequent accommodation to state and needs of baby.
6. Sensitive to baby's state and needs—always accommodates.
7. Attentive and sensitive to baby's state—stimulates baby at appropriate moments.

RELIABILITY AND VALIDITY: The original scale was administered to fifty-one non-white urban mothers and newborn infants of lower socioeconomic status. Fifty-one percent of the patients were primiparous. The sample included thirty-two boys and nineteen girls. In a later study with a larger sample ($N = 134$), the author replicated the earlier findings (Osofsky, 1975). Reliability on the measure has been reported in Osofsky and Danzger (1974). Interrater reliability was obtained after initial training by having two observers independently rate ten mother-infant pairs. Pearson product-moment correlations ranged from .88 to .99 on the various dimensions, with a mean of .92. After reliability was established observations were done by one observer with periodic checks by a second observer in order to maintain high reliability. The training of observers has been relatively simple, with agreement being reached between the observers after very few observations. Content reliability has been suggested by the agreement by observers of infants that the categories being investigated reflect major behaviors that occur at this time in similar situations.

BIBLIOGRAPHY:

Osofsky, J. D. "Neonatal Characteristics and Directional Effects in Mother-Infant Interaction." Paper presented at biennial meeting of the Society for Research in Child Development. Denver, Colorado, March 1975.

Osofsky, J. D., and Danzger, B. "Relationships Between Neonatal Characteristics and Mother-Infant Interaction." *Developmental Psychology,* 1974, *10,* 124-130.

---

## PARENT REACTION QESTIONNAIRE (PRQ)

AUTHORS: Walter Katkovsky, Vaughn J. Crandall, and Anne Preston

AGE: Parents of school-age children

VARIABLE: Parental reactions to children's achievement behaviors

TYPE OF MEASURE: Forced-choice questionnaire

SOURCE FROM WHICH MEASURE MAY BE OBTAINED: Walter Katkovsky, Psychology Department, Northern Illinois University, DeKalb, Illinois 60115.

DESCRIPTION OF MEASURE: As part of a larger investigation on the role of parents as identification models and reinforcers of their children's achievement development, the Parent Reaction Questionnaire (PRQ) was designed to assess parents' reported reactions to their children's achievement behaviors in four achievement areas: intellectual, physical skills, mechanical, and artistic. The questionnaire consists of forty-eight items each describing a typical situation in which a child exhibits an achievement behavior that is likely to elicit an evaluative response on the part of the parent. Each item is followed by five or six alternatives from which the parent is asked to select his two most typical reactions to his child in situations similar to that described, and to indicate by ranking them which of the two is most typical. The alternatives to each item include reactions of a positive nature (praise, affection, recognition, encouragement, and reassurance); negative reactions (criticism, disappointment, annoyance, and correction); and a neutral reaction (no response). The items describe both successful and unsuccessful achievement behaviors by the child and situations where the parent's attention is directed to the child's performance.

The instructions to parents define the four achievement areas and present examples of each so that the parent can associate his child's specific achievement activities with the items. Two different scoring systems are possible. Weighted scores can be obtained by taking the parents' rankings into consideration, or unweighted scores can be calculated by disregarding the rankings and treating the "1" and "2" responses as equal. Three scores can be calculated for each of the four achievement areas: (1) positive reactivity, referring to the number and/or ranking the parent gave to the positive response alternatives; (2) negative reactivity, referring to the number and/or ranking the parent gave to the negative response alternatives; and (3) total reactivity, which is the sum of the positive and negative reactivity scores in an achievement area and indicates the general parental responsiveness to the child's achievement behavior in that area.

As examples, four selected items, one from each of the four achievement areas, are given below. There are twelve items in each area. *P, N,* and *Neut.* signify whether the alternative is a positive reaction, a negative reaction, or a neutral reaction.

*Intellectual Area*

5. When X was doing school work at home,
P       a. I told him (her) I am very pleased with his (her) progress.
N       b. I showed him (her) some of his (her) mistakes.
N       c. I told him (her) to try to work harder at it than he (she) did before.
Neut. d. I was too busy to pay much attention to what he (she) was doing.
P       e. I told him (her) I am glad he (she) is interested in his (her) school work.

*Mechanical Area*

1. When X began to learn an activity which involved working with his (her) hands (such as carpentry work, repairs, sewing, crocheting, using tools, etc.),
Neut. a. I didn't say anything.
P       b. I watched and told him (her) he (she) was making good progress.
P       c. I told him (her) I was pleased with his (her) work.
P       d. I showed an interest and asked questions about what he (she) was doing.
N       e. I told him (her) he's (she's) not quite capable of doing that yet.
N       f. I showed him (her) what he (she) was doing wrong.

*Artistic Area*

1. When X was pleased with a picture he (she) drew or painted,
P       a. I told him (her) it was nice.
Neut. b. I didn't say much about it.
N       c. I suggested to him (her) how he (she) could improve it.
P       d. I told him (her) I was very pleased and expressed affection to him (her).
P       e. I told him (her) I was proud of him (her) and would show the picture to his (her) father (mother).
N       f. I told him (her) it wasn't as good as some of his (her) other pictures.

*Physical Skills Area*

1. When X started to learn a new physical skill (such as bike riding, skating, swimming, etc.),

N  a. I showed him (her) how he (she) could do it better.

Neut. b. I didn't say anything about it.

P  c. I told him (her) that he's (she's) doing fine.

P  d. I praised him (her) and gave him (her) a hug, kiss, or some other kind of affection.

P  e. I told him (her) I'm pleased he (she) could learn so quickly.

N  f. I told him (her) that he (she) needs to improve and should practice more.

RELIABILITY AND VALIDITY: The questionnaire was administered to the mothers and fathers of twenty girls and twenty boys who were participants in a study on the development of achievement motivation in children. In one set of analyses dealing with the correspondence between parents' achievement attitudes and their reported behavior with their children, a number of the total reactivity scores correlated significantly with the importance parents attached to their own successful achievement. The more mothers valued intellectual achievement for themselves, the more they reported reacting to their daughters' intellectual behaviors. Similarly, the more importance they attached to their own achievement in the physical skills and mechanical areas, the more the mothers reacted to their sons' activities in these areas. The importance fathers placed on their own artistic achievements correlated significantly with their reactivity to their daughters' artistic efforts. Another set of analyses examined the relationships between the PRQ scores and a measure obtained on the parents' children, indicating the children's beliefs in the extent to which they caused the reinforcements they received in intellectual achievement situations (internal vs. external control). A significant correlation was found between fathers' positive reactivity scores and their daughters' beliefs in their control of their intellectual successes. Also, when boys and girls were combined, fathers' positive reactions were found to encourage, and their negative reactions to discourage, the development of beliefs in the internal control of their children. No data are available on reliability and on the consistency between parent self-reports on the PRQ and their actual behavior with their children.

BIBLIOGRAPHY:

Katkovsky, W., Crandall, V. J., and Good, S. "Parental Antecedents of Children's Beliefs in Internal-External Control of Reinforcements in Intellectual Achievement Situations." *Child Development,* 1967, *38,* 766-776.

Katkovsky, W., Preston, A., and Crandall, V. J. "Parent's Achievement Attitudes and Their Behavior with Their Children in Achievement Situations." *Journal of Genetic Psychology,* 1964, *104,* 105-121.

# PARENT AS READER SCALE

AUTHORS: Barry J. Guinagh and R. Emile Jester

AGE: 1½ to 5 years

VARIABLE: Parent-child interaction

TYPE OF MEASURE: Rating scale

SOURCE FROM WHICH MEASURE MAY BE OBTAINED: See Guinagh (1972).

DESCRIPTION OF MEASURE: The instrument rates the parent-child interaction on a 5-point scale as the parent shows the child a story book. The subscales measure (1) parent's introduction of the book, (2) specificity of the parent's language, (3) parent's attempt to get verbal response from child, (4) if parent reads the book, (5) elaboration of pictures, (6) elaboration of sounds, (7) quality of feedback, (8) amount of pointing, (9) emotional climate and (10) sense of humor. The scale takes only a few minutes and can be a useful teaching tool.

As examples, the first three of the ten items of the scale are given below.

1. Does the parent introduce the book to the child?
   a. None.
   b. Vague. "We're going to read this book."
   c. More enthusiastic. "Look at this pretty book."
   d. Two or more sentences of introduction.
   e. Detailed introduction telling child goals. There is an overview of book or child is asked questions about how he wants to use task.
2. How specific is the language of the parents when talking to the child?
   a. Vague language. "Look at that." "What's that?" Absolutely no teaching.
   b. Between 1 and 3.
   c. Some description. "Look at the pretty _____." "Show me the doggie."
   d. Between 3 and 5.
   e. Very detailed. Parent picks out much in the pictures to discuss in detail with the child.
3. Does the parent attempt to get verbal response from child related to the book?
   a. No attempt. "Look at that." Basic type of question.
   b. Attempt to get response but no follow up. "What's that? What's that?" No pause.
   c. Some questions with pause.
   d. Uses questioning style consistently expecting responses.
   e. Parent questions child and follows up question by either asking same question in another manner or asking different question. Follows with answer if child does not know answer.

RELIABILITY AND VALIDITY: None reported.

BIBLIOGRAPHY:

Guinagh, B. J. "How Parents Read to Children." *Theory Into Practice,* 1972, *11,* 171-177.

## PARENT AS A TEACHER INVENTORY (PAAT)

AUTHOR: Robert D. Strom

AGE: Parents and parent-surrogates of preschoolers

VARIABLE: Child-rearing expectations

TYPE OF MEASURE: Likert-type scale

SOURCE FROM WHICH MEASURE MAY BE OBTAINED: Robert D. Strom, Department of Education, Arizona State University, Tempe, Arizona 85281.

DESCRIPTION OF MEASURE: The Parent as a Teacher Inventory (PAAT) is intended as a means for assessing parental strengths and needs in rearing preschool children. Data from the PAAT offer parent educators a relevant basis for diagnosis, guidance, and curriculum planning. A detailed exploration is provided for each of five subsets: (1) parental acceptance of creative functioning in their child and desire to encourage or suppress its development (creativity subset), (2) parent child-rearing frustration and loci of the frustration (frustration subset), (3) parent feelings about control and the extent to which parental control of child behavior is deemed necessary (control subset), (4) parental understanding of play and its influence on child development (play subset), and (5) parental perception of their ability to facilitate the teaching-learning process for their child (teaching-learning subset).

Ten items, designed to assess each of the five variables, make a composite PAAT of fifty items. Items are patterned so that each variable occurs only once in every five items. Each item has four possible answers: "strong yes," "yes," "no," and "strong no." Parents are asked to circle only one answer per item. A numerical value of 4, 3, 2, or 1 is assigned to each of the fifty responses. The most desired responses in terms of what is known from child development research are valued 4. The inventory is constructed with twenty-seven items having "strong no" as the desired response, and the remaining twenty-three are reversed. The total score is obtained by summing all fifty values. Subtotals are derived for creativity, frustration, control, play, and the teaching-learning process. When large populations are used, it is recommended that Veldman's (1967) Testat program be used to score and reduce the scaled data. There is a Spanish-language version of the PAAT.

A profile accompanies the PAAT inventory. The profile divides the items into the five subsets, restating them in an abbreviated and positive form. Each individual respondent's strengths and needs are identified in a form that parent educators can then utilize for planning with parents. In addition, discrepant expectations between mothers-fathers or surrogate-parents can be recognized.

As examples, the first ten of the fifty items of the inventory are given below.

1. I get tired of all the questions my child asks.
2. My child should be able to make noise during play.
3. It is all right for my child to disagree with me.
4. My child needs to play with me.
5. Much of my child's learning will take place before he enters school.
6. I like my child to make up stories.

7. It gets on my nerves when my child keeps asking me to watch him play.

8. I want my child to say more than I do when we talk.

9. Playing with my child makes me feel restless.

10. It is hard for me to tell when my child has learned something.

RELIABILITY AND VALIDITY: The PAAT was also the basis for two doctoral studies involving black mothers (Greathouse, 1972) and white mothers (Sawicki, 1972) and two cross-cultural peer teaching studies involving fourth-grade children who were teaching kindergarten children (Englebrecht, 1973; Kamin, 1974). The most comprehensive field-testing of the PAAT was initiated in the fall of 1973 through the Research Department of the Tucson Public Schools in the ESEA Title I, Parent and Child Education (PACE) Project (a compensatory early childhood education project). At that time the PAAT was administered to 124 participating parent and parent-surrogates whose profiles were used by teachers and instructional aides to implement their family training program. The PACE Project included 69 percent Mexican-American respondents, 20 percent Indian, 6 percent black, 3 percent Anglo, and 2 percent Oriental.

During the Tucson field-tests, recommendations were made for item revisions and rearrangement of some items to different subsets to improve clarity and increase internal reliability. The Tucson 1973 pretest yielded a coefficient *alpha* of .76 for the total instrument. In the spring of 1974 the posttest overall coefficient *alpha* was .81. The posttest included eighty-eight of the original 124 subjects (Slaughter, 1974). In the fall of 1974, following PAAT item revision and subset changes, the instrument was administered to 142 participants of the 1974-1975 PACE project in the Tucson Public Schools. The *alpha* coefficient of internal reliability was .80 for PAAT (form B). In addition, the PAAT-B administered to twenty-seven fathers of intact PACE families yielded an *alpha* coefficient of .81. In her study of thirty intact white families living in Tempe, Arizona, Elmquist (1975) reported an overall reliability of .88 for the PAAT. In another 1975 study the PAAT was administered to 114 parents of preschoolers (including fifty-two Anglos, thirty-one Mexicans, and thirty-one blacks) with an overall reliability of .83.

A validation study was completed by Johnson (1975). The sample consisted of thirty intact Mexican-American families in Phoenix who had a preschool son. Each family was audiotaped and observed at home during play with a Fisher-Price Family Fun Jet. Overall and internal reliability was examined with respect to total (.76) and subset *alpha* coefficients. The validity measure (comparison of expressed feelings with observed behaviors for the thirty-eight observable items) indicated 66-percent consonance between feelings and behaviors.

BIBLIOGRAPHY:

Elmquist, M. "An Assessment of Anglo-American Parent Childrearing Feelings and Behaviors." Unpublished doctoral dissertation. Arizona State University, Tempe, 1975.

Engelbrecht, G. "Formative Research in Peer Teaching Using Toys as a Medium for Instruction." Unpublished doctoral dissertation. Arizona State University, Tempe, 1973.

Greathouse, B. "The Effects of Toy Talk Training and Experiences in Low-Income Black Mothers and Their Preschool Children." Unpublished doctoral dissertation. Arizona State University, Tempe, 1972.

Johnson, A. "An Assessment of Mexican-American Parent Childrearing Feelings and Behaviors." Unpublished doctoral dissertation. Arizona State University, Tempe, 1975.

Kamin, C. "Formative Research in Black-White Peer Teaching Using Toys as a Medium for Instruction." Unpublished doctoral dissertation. Arizona State University, Tempe, 1974.

Sawicki, F. "The Effects of Toy Talk Training and Experiences on Low Income White Mothers and Their Preschool Children." Unpublished doctoral dissertation. Arizona State University, Tempe, 1972.

Slaughter, H. "The Parent as a Teacher Inventory Field Study." Mimeographed report. Research Department of the Tucson, Arizona, Public Schools, 1974.

Strom, R. D. "Observing Parent-Child Fantasy Play." *Theory Into Practice,* 1974, *13,* 287-295.

Strom, R. D. "Play and Family Development." *Elementary School Journal,* 1974, *74,* 359-368.

Strom, R. D. "Education for a Leisure Society." *The Futurist,* 1975, *9,* 93-97.

Strom, R. D. "Parents and Teachers as Play Observers." *Childhood Education,* 1975, *51,* 139-141.

Strom, R. D., and Engelbrecht, G. "Creative Peer Teaching." *Journal of Creative Behavior,* 1974, *8,* 93-100.

Strom, R. D., and Greathouse, B. "Play and Maternal Self-Concept." *Theory into Practice,* 1974, *13,* 296-301.

Strom, R. D., and Johnson, A. "The Parent as a Teacher." *Education,* 1974, *19,* 40-43.

Veldman, D. *Fortran Programming for the Behavioral Sciences.* New York: Holt, Rinehart and Winston, 1967.

---

# PARENT AS A TEACHER PROFILE (PTP)

AUTHOR: Robert D. Strom

AGE: Parents and parent-surrogates of preschoolers

VARIABLE: Child-rearing expectations

TYPE OF MEASURE: Rating scale

SOURCE FROM WHICH MEASURE MAY BE OBTAINED: Robert D. Strom, Department of Education, Arizona State University, Tempe, Arizona 85281.

DESCRIPTION OF MEASURE: The Parent as a Teacher Profile (PTP) was developed to accompany the Parent as a Teacher Inventory (PAAT) as an interpretive guide for feedback and program planning. The profile restates all fifty PAAT items in an abbreviated and positive form for uniformity of interpretation. For example, consider items 16 and 34 on the PAAT and PTP respectively:

PAAT item 16. I want my child to play with toys made for boys and with toys made for girls.

PTP item 16. Toy selection not sexually biased.
PAAT item 34. I try to praise my child a lot when we play.
PTP item 34. Recognizes that the play process is rewarding.

All of the PAAT items are based on a 4-point Likert-type scale. The parent response for each PAAT item is entered on the profile as a score from 1 (low) to 4 (high) depending on the degree to which it is seen as desirable for parent-child interaction, based on principles derived from research on child development. To illustrate, the parent whose PAAT response is "strong yes" for item 16 would receive a score of 4 on the PTP. Conversely, the parent whose PAAT response is "strong no" for item 16 would receive the score of 1. For item 34 it is the parent indicating "strong no" who receives the score of 4, while a "strong yes" response is entered on the PTP as 1.

The most effective analysis of the PAAT is obtained by dividing the inventory results into subsets of conceptually related items. Reducing the framework to manageable size through a subset approach avoids overwhelming a parent with feedback; it also ensures the greater possibility for self-improvement than for self-recrimination. Accordingly the PTP presents a separate focus for five subsets of ten items each, which parent educators can use in planning curriculum and for pre-post evaluation. As an aggregate these five arenas of content provide for detailed exploration concerning (1) parental acceptance of creative functioning in their child and desire to encourage or suppress its development, (2) parent child-rearing frustration and loci of the frustration, (3) parent feelings about control and the extent to which parental control of child behavior is deemed necessary, (4) parental understanding of play and its influence on child development, and (5) parental perceptions of their ability to facilitate the teaching-learning process for their child.

RELIABILITY AND VALIDITY: See Parent as a Teacher Inventory, pp. 829-831.

BIBLIOGRAPHY: See Parent as a Teacher Inventory, pp. 829-831.

---

# PARENTAL AGGRESSION TRAINING SCALE (PAT)

AUTHORS: Knud S. Larsen and Gary Schwendiman

AGE: 16 years and up

VARIABLE: Perceived severity of parent aggression training

TYPE OF MEASURE: Rating scale

SOURCE FROM WHICH MEASURE MAY BE OBTAINED: Knud S. Larsen, Department of Psychology, Oregon State University, Corvallis, Oregon 97330.

DESCRIPTION OF MEASURE: The measure consists of twenty-six items, thirteen items for each parent. The items deal with various forms of aggressive behavior during the subject's childhood and the perceived reactions of mother and father, respectively. The five response categories are: no action, mild reprimand, harsh words, slap, and severe punishment (Larsen and Schwendiman, 1970).

As examples, the first five of the twenty-six items on the scale are given below. The respondent answers on a 5-point scale ranging from "no action" to "severe punishment."

1. If you were to hit another child without provocation, your mother would:
2. If you were to hit your brother or sister, your mother would:
3. If you were to hit your father, your mother would:
4. If you were to hit your mother, your mother would:
5. If you talked back to another adult, your mother would:

RELIABILITY AND VALIDITY: The PAT scale, Levinson's (1957) Internationalism-Nationalism Scale, and Rokeach's (1960) Dogmatism Scale were administered to 305 students selected randomly from the student directory at Brigham Young University. The sample consisted of 157 males and 148 females ranging in age from 17 to 35. Based on the literature (Bandura and Walters, 1959; Dollard and others, 1939; Radke, 1946; and Whiting and Child, 1953), a relationship was predicted between perceived aggression training and chauvinistic nationalism and dogmatism. The results for the total sample show a Pearson product-moment correlation of .48 ($p < .01$) between the PAT and chauvinism, and .17 ($p < .01$) between the PAT and the dogmatism scale. In a second study (Schwendiman, Larsen, and Parks, 1970) the PAT scale correlated .38 ($p < .05$) with dogmatism and .34 ($p < .05$) with the F scale (Adorno and others, 1950). The PAT scale also discriminated between first- and second-born children.

BIBLIOGRAPHY:

Adorno, T. W., Frenkel-Brunswik, E., Levinson, D. J., and Sanford, R. N. *The Authoritarian Personality.* New York: Harper and Row, 1950.

Bandura, A., and Walters, R. H. *Adolescent Aggression.* New York: Ronald Press, 1959.

Dollard, J., Doob, L. W., Miller, N. E., Mowrer, O. H., and Sears, R. R. *Frustration and Aggression.* New Haven: Yale University Press, 1939.

Larsen, K. S. "Aggression—Altruism: A Scale and Some Data on Its Reliability and Validity." *Journal of Personality Assessment,* 1971, *35,* 275-281.

Larsen, K. S., and Schwendiman, G. "Perceived Aggression Training as a Predictor of Two Assessments of Authoritarianism." *Journal of Peace Research,* 1970, *7,* 69-71.

Levinson, D. J. "Authoritarian Personality and Foreign Policy." *Journal of Conflict Resolution,* 1957, *7,* 37-47.

Radke, M. J. "Relation of Parental Authority to Children's Behavior and Attitudes." *University of Minnesota Institute of Child Welfare Monograph,* 1946, No. 22.

Rokeach, M. *The Open and Closed Mind.* New York: Basic Books, 1960.

Schwendiman, G., Larsen, K. S., and Parks, C. "Birth Order, Aggression Training and Authoritarianism." *Psychological Record,* 1970, *20,* 69-71.

Whiting, J. W., and Child, I. L. *Child Training and Personality.* New Haven, Connecticut: Yale University Press, 1953.

# PARENTAL CONTACT SCALE

AUTHOR: John W. Hollender

AGE: 10 years to adult

VARIABLE: Affectionate physical contact with parents

TYPE OF MEASURE: Questionnaire

SOURCE FROM WHICH MEASURE MAY BE OBTAINED: Single copies of the scale, with permission to reproduce, may be obtained without cost from John W. Hollender, Department of Psychology, Emory University, Atlanta, Georgia 30322.

DESCRIPTION OF MEASURE: The Parental Contact Scale consists of seventeen items that briefly describe a variety of types of physical contact parents engage in with children. Response is made to each item separately for each parent on a 5-point frequency scale describing the frequency per unit of time measured by day, week, month, and year. Responses can be requested retrospectively for various time periods or currently according to the needs of the investigator. A simple 3-point frequency scale is used with younger children. The frequency categories are: (1) never or almost never over a year's time, (2) a few times during the year, (3) one or more times per month, (4) one or more times per week, (5) one or more times per 24-hour day.

A sample item is given below, followed by seven additional items.

1. Kissed me good night.                                            *Grades 1-4*          *Now*

                                         Father    ————————    ————————

                                         Mother  ————————    ————————

2. Kissed me goodbye when I left them or when they left me.
3. Kissed me on other occasions.
4. Hugged or embraced me.
5. Held my hand to comfort me.
6. Held my hand for safety reasons (crossing the street, etc.).
7. Held my hand affectionately for reasons other than the above.
8. Stroked or patted my back.

RELIABILITY AND VALIDITY: The scale has been used in several studies. Predicted correlations with other variables have ranged up to .51. Correlations were found between retrospective maternal physical contact and trust in male college students and between maternal and paternal physical contact in third- and fourth-grade children and comfortable interpersonal distance, for male subjects only, however. The only additional validity evidence is of a multimethod type in which a global rating of physical affection received as a child correlated .66 for mothers and .53 for fathers with retrospective recall on the Physical Contact Scale for thirty-four college students. There are no traditional reliability data, although the multimethod study reported above probably gives a good index of the lower limits of reliability for the Parental Contact Scale, especially since the scale has been lengthened from fourteen items to the current seventeen items.

BIBLIOGRAPHY:

Hollender, J. W., Duke, M. P., and Nowicki, S. "Interpersonal Distance: Sibling Structure and Parental Affection Antecedents." *Journal of Genetic Psychology,* 1973, *123,* 35-45.

Martin, W. T. "The Effect of Experimentor's Touch, Perceived Parental Contact, and Perceived Father's Trust on Trusting Behavior in an Experimental Task." Unpublished master's thesis. Emory University, Atlanta, Georgia, 1970.

---

# PARENTAL EXPECTANCY SCALE

AUTHOR: Gerald D. Alpern

AGE: Parents of children age 2 to 13 years

VARIABLE: Beliefs about degree of child's developmental handicap

TYPE OF MEASURE: Structured interview

SOURCE FROM WHICH MEASURE MAY BE OBTAINED: Psychological Development Publications, 7150 Lakeside Drive, Indianapolis, Indiana 46278. Cost: $3.50.

DESCRIPTION OF MEASURE: Parents are interviewed with twenty-six items covering skills in physical, self-help, social, academic, and communication areas. For each item parents are asked whether their child can now perform the skill and whether an imaginary twin of their child (same age, sex, home, and opportunities *but* without any handicap) could now perform the skill. The items cover normative skills ranging from age 2 to adulthood. When parents indicate that their child and/or the imaginary twin could not perform the skill, they are asked to indicate at what age they expect the child and the twin to have the skill. The scoring allows quantitative assessment of the parents' beliefs concerning their child's present and future handicaps.

As an example, one selected item from each of the five skill areas is given below. The number of items in each area is given in parentheses after the name.

*I. Physical Developmental Scale (7)*
Does the child usually walk upstairs and downstairs by placing only one foot on each stair? He may hold railing but it should not be necessary for ordinary support or balance.

*II. Self-help Scale (6)*
Does the child put on his own coat without help? This need not include buttoning the coat.

*III. Social Development Scale (3)*
Can the child do a responsible job of babysitting during the day with a 3-year-old child for at least 3 hours?

*IV. Academic Development Scale (5)*

Could the person carry on political or religious discussions at the level of the average 18-year-old?

*V. Communication Development Scale (5)*

Can the child recognize at least five written words and somehow show he understands what they mean? The child must "read" *the words*, not just name the things like recognizing a cereal box and naming the cereal.

RELIABILITY AND VALIDITY: The validity of the instrument has been investigated through its relationship to a number of other measures of children and their parents in an experimental preschool unit of the Marion County Association for Retarded Children. The Parental Expectancy Scale was administered at the beginning and ending of the 1971-1972, 1972-1973, and 1973-1974 school years along with six other standard measures. The statistical results have consistently documented the usefulness of the Parental Expectancy Scale.

BIBLIOGRAPHY: None reported.

---

# PARENTAL GUILT REACTION

AUTHOR: Richard A. Gardner

AGE: Parents

VARIABLE: Parental guilt reaction to a child's calamity

TYPE OF MEASURE: Structured interview

SOURCE FROM WHICH MEASURE MAY BE OBTAINED: Richard A. Gardner, 155 County Road, Cresskill, New Jersey 07626.

DESCRIPTION OF MEASURE: Many parents exhibit guilty feelings in response to severe illness, accidents, or other calamities that may befall their children. Although they and others may appreciate that the parents could not in fact have brought about the child's difficulties, they often remain preoccupied with their fantasied contributory role. This inquiry enables the examiner to determine whether this type of inappropriate guilt reaction is present and, if so, what its nature is. The initial questions make no specific reference to the guilt reaction but may elicit a description of the reaction. The remaining questions make more specific reference to guilt reactions and, if present, provide information about its nature, intensity, duration, etc. This inquiry was the first in a series designed to study the psychodynamics of this common form of guilt (Gardner, 1969).

As examples, four of the thirteen items from the measure are given below.

5. What were your feelings when you first learned that your child had (name illness)?

6. Many parents of children with this illness feel that they themselves were in some way responsible, and even though the reasons appear far-fetched and even silly, they can't help thinking it. Have you had such feelings? If so, what were they?

7. Some people think it had something to do with something they did around the time of conception, pregnancy, or delivery. Have you had such feelings? If so, what were they?

8. Some people think it had something to do with something they did in earlier life. Have you had such feelings? If so, what were they?

RELIABILITY AND VALIDITY: Face validity only is claimed.

BIBLIOGRAPHY:

Gardner, R. A. "The Guilt Reaction of Parent with Severe Physical Disease." *American Journal of Psychiatry*, 1969, *126*, 636-644.

---

## PARENTAL RESPONSE INVENTORY

AUTHOR: Thomas W. Miller

AGE: Parents and parent-surrogates

VARIABLE: Level of judgment communicated in verbal-response patterns

TYPE OF MEASURE: Likert-type scale

SOURCE FROM WHICH MEASURE MAY BE OBTAINED: Thomas W. Miller, 71 Chestnut Hill Lane South, Buffalo, New York 14221. Cost: $5.00.

DESCRIPTION OF MEASURE: The Parental Response Inventory is a closed-form, structured inventory consisting of twelve prepared situations and a choice of four alternative responses for each situation. Six situations involve behavior of a positive nature, and six situations involve behavior of a negative nature. The extent to which a person is descriptive or evaluative in verbal interaction is assessed. A person is considered to be descriptive when he describes a given situation to another person. It precludes rendering an evaluation, criticism, or censure toward the other person's behavior, verbalization, or his "self." A descriptive response may include how the person feels about the situation as long as the response is, within limits, describing a situation but not rendering an evaluation. A person would be considered to be evaluative in his response pattern if his response involved the rendering of an evaluation, criticism, or censure toward another person's behavior, verbalizations, or his "self."

As examples, the first three of the twelve situations, together with the alternative responses for each, are given below. The respondent chooses the alternative that is most like what he would tell his child in the situation. The category (positive or negative) and the weight assigned to each alternative appear in the left margin.

*Cat./ Wgt.*

Pos.              1. Your child has just polished his shoes and he has done a good job. What
                     would you say to your child?

3.0              a. You really put a lot of effort into shining your shoes.

12.0             b. How much nicer your shoes look now that they are polished.

4.0              c. You've done a great job on your shoes.

10.0             d. Your shoes look nice. You are bigger now and can do a better job.

Neg.             2. Your child had several friends in for a snack. When they left, the kitchen
                     was strewn with pop bottles, potato chips, and games. What would you
                     say to your child?

5.0              a. You must learn to take care of your home. You live here and must help
                     to keep it clean.

3.0              b. You and your friends are very inconsiderate to leave this mess.

12.0             c. The room needs to be cleaned after having your friends over.

8.0              d. Is this the way I've brought you up? This is what a sloppy person does.
                     Clean up your mess.

Pos.             3. Your child has just finished raking the leaves in the yard. What would you
                     say to your child?

7.0              a. From the way you rake leaves, you would make a good gardner.

12.0             b. The yard looks very nice since the leaves have been raked.

5.0              c. Say, that's a great job you've done raking the leaves.

3.0              d. It's good to see that you have decided to help with the chores.

RELIABILITY AND VALIDITY: The split-half (odd-even) reliability coefficient was .70, corrected to .82 by the Spearman-Brown formula. Test-retest reliability for a two-week period on a selected sample was $r = .68$, which is a modest but significant reliability estimate. The Parental Response Inventory is being used with numerous groups to attest to its construct validity. Child psychologists, educators, undergraduate psychology students, policemen, and others selected for both racial differences and demographic differences, have been assessed in a number of studies. For a complete review of validity data, see the references below.

BIBLIOGRAPHY:

Miller, T. W. "An Inquiry into the Differential Response Patterns of Clinicians and Policemen." Unpublished monograph. State University of New York, Buffalo, 1968.

Miller, T. W. "Communicative Dimensions of Mother-Child Interaction as They Affect the Self-Esteem of a Child." *Proceedings of the 79th Annual Convention of the American Psychological Association*, 1971, *6*, 241-242.

Miller, T. W. "Differential Response Patterns of Parents as They Affect the Child's Self-Esteem." Unpublished doctoral dissertation. State University of New York, Buffalo, 1971.

Miller, T. W. "Cultural Dimensions Related to Parental Verbalizations and Self-Concept in the Child." *Journal of Social Psychology*, 1972, *87*, 153-154.

Miller, T. W. "Praise or Criticism: The Art of Being Descriptive with Children." *Journal of Family Counseling*, 1975, *3*, 55-57.

# PARENTAL ROLE QUESTIONNAIRE (PRQ)

AUTHOR: Walter Emmerich

AGE: Parents

VARIABLE: Parental role behavior

TYPE OF MEASURE: Questionnaire

SOURCE FROM WHICH MEASURE MAY BE OBTAINED: See Emmerich (1969).

DESCRIPTION OF MEASURE: The PRQ is a paper-and-pencil instrument consisting of general instructions, a glossary, and separate sections designed to assess parental goal values (Part I), means-ends beliefs (Part II), means-ends capacities (Part III), and goal achievements (Part IV). Ss are instructed to use the glossary, which provides moderately general definitions of each of the ten child behaviors referred to throughout the PRQ. This procedure communicates a designated meaning for each item, thereby serving to reduce intra- and interindividual variability that arises when persons are asked to respond to such global terms as assertiveness, independence, and so forth. Parts I and IV pair each of the ten socialization goals with two "objects" of the child's behavior—the mother and father—resulting in twenty items. This procedure somewhat broadens the sampling of contexts in which the child's behavior occurs. When assessing parents' means-ends beliefs, it is believed useful also to assess the parents' "confidence" in an efficacy judgment. Therefore, in addition to indicating the directionality of means-ends beliefs in Part II, parents are also asked to indicate their degree of confidence in each belief on a 3-point scale, ranging from "very sure" (2) to "unsure" (0). Nine basic component measures were derived as follows: positive and negative goal standards, positive and negative goal achievements, positive and negative means-ends beliefs total, positive and negative goal beliefs-means differentiation, positive and negative goal beliefs-means X goal differentiation, confidence in positive and negative means-ends beliefs, positive and negative means-ends capacities—total, positive and negative goal capacities-means differentiation, and positive and negative goal capacities-means X goal differentiation.

As examples, the first six items of the test are given below. They are to be answered on a 7-point scale. This section concerns how important it is to you that your child acts in certain ways toward his or her parents. Keep in mind that your answers should apply to your child at his or her *present age*. Indicate your response to the left of each item according to the following scale:

+3 if you feel it *essential* that your child act this way.
+2 if you feel it *important* that your child act this way.
+1 if you feel it *desirable* that your child act this way.
 0 if you feel it *doesn't matter* whether or not your child acts this way.
−1 if you feel it *desirable* that your child *not* act this way.
−2 if you feel it *important* that your child *not* act this way.
−3 if you feel it *essential* that your child *not* act this way.

1. Dependency toward mother.
2. Obedience toward mother.
3. Submissiveness toward father.

4. Friendliness toward father.
5. Aggression toward mother.
6. Trustingness toward father.

RELIABILITY AND VALIDITY: Test-retest reliabilities of the eighteen PRQ individual-difference measures are all significant at the .001 level, ranging from .41 to .76 with a mean of .62. In general the correlations are relatively high between the same measures derived from the positive and negative goal sets, ranging from −.18 to .81, median .55. With two exceptions, the positive and negative measures for each component correlate higher with each other than with the positive or negative measures of other components. A factor analysis yielded four factors that are described in detail in Emmerich (1969). A correlation table is provided showing the correlations of the PRQ components (positive and negative separately) with a modified version of the Parental Attitude Research Instrument (1958) and with Cattell's 16 PF Test (1962).

BIBLIOGRAPHY:

Cattell, R. B. *Handbook Supplement for Form C of the Sixteen Personality Factor Test.* Champaign, Illinois: Institute for Personality and Ability Testing, 1962.
Emmerich, W. "Variations in the Parent Role as a Function of the Parent's Sex and the Child's Sex and Age." *Merrill-Palmer Quarterly,* 1962, *8,* 3-11.
Emmerich, W. "Continuity and Stability in Early Social Development, II: Teacher Ratings." *Child Development,* 1966, *37,* 17-27.
Emmerich, W. "The Parental Role: A Functional-Cognitive Approach." *Monographs of the Society for Research in Child Development,* 1969, *34* (8) serial no. 132.
Emmerich, W., and Smoller, F. "The Role Patterning of Parental Norms." *Sociometry,* 1964, *26,* 382-390.
Schaefer, E. S., and Bell, R. Q. "Development of a Parental Attitude Research Instrument." *Child Development,* 1958, *29,* 339-361.

*Prepared by Walter Emmerich and Orval G. Johnson*

---

# PERINATAL RIGIDITY SCALE

AUTHORS: Virginia L. Larsen and others

AGE: Young parents

VARIABLE: Attitudes toward child rearing

TYPE OF MEASURE: Rating scale

SOURCE FROM WHICH MEASURE MAY BE OBTAINED: Virginia L. Larsen, Medical Director, St. Louis Chronic Hospital, 5700 Arsenal Street, St. Louis, Missouri 63139.

DESCRIPTION OF MEASURE: The Perinatal Rigidity Scale is a pencil-and-paper test specifically designed for perinatal research. Statements were taken from the California F-Scale, developed by Adorno and others (1950), and from Rokeach (1960). Subjects are instructed to mark their reaction to each of fifteen dogmatic statements related to child rearing. The fifteen subscores are totaled to provide a perinatal rigidity score with a maximal possible score of 105. Larsen and others (1968) studied couples having their first or third baby from late pregnancy through six weeks postpartum. Home visits were made after delivery to interview and observe the situation and mother-infant interaction. Prenatal scores of first-time mothers correlated negatively with long-term child-care experience and with maternal response to the infant, suggesting that mothers with more child-care experience were less rigid in response to the infant. Likewise, fathers with more experience in child care had low scores. Among third-time mothers, scores correlated positively with the mother's description of the infant. High scores of third-time fathers were associated with good maternal appearance and behavior.

As examples, the first five items of the fifteen-item scale are given below. They are to be answered on a 7-point scale from "strongly agree" to "strongly disagree."

1. Of all the different philosophies of child care which exist there is probably only one which is correct.
2. I am always careful about my manner of dress.
3. When it comes to differences of opinion in religion we must be careful not to compromise with those who believe differently.
4. A family which tolerates too much difference of opinion among its own members cannot exist for long.
5. I find it easy to stick to a schedule, once I have started.

RELIABILITY AND VALIDITY: None reported.

BIBLIOGRAPHY:

Adorno, T. W., Frenkel-Brunswik, E., Levinson, D. J., and Sanford, R. N. *The Authoritarian Personality*. New York: Harper & Row, 1950.

Larsen, V. L., and others. *Attitudes and Stresses Affecting Perinatal Adjustment*. Final report, National Institute of Mental Health. Grant MH-01381-01-02. Washington, D.C.: NIMH, 1966.

Larsen, V. L., and others. *Prediction and Improvement of Postpartum Adjustment*. Final report, Children's Bureau Research, Grant H-66. Fort Steilacoom, Washington: Division of Research, 1968.

Rokeach, M. *The Open and Closed Mind*. New York: Basic Books, 1960.

# QUESTIONNAIRE ON RESOURCES AND STRESS

AUTHOR: Jean Holroyd

AGE: 15 years and up

VARIABLE: Effects of a handicapped or chronically ill person on family members

TYPE OF MEASURE: True-false questionnaire

SOURCE FROM WHICH MEASURE MAY BE OBTAINED: Jean Holroyd, UCLA Neuropsychiatric Institute, 760 Westwood Boulevard, Los Angeles, California 90024.

DESCRIPTION OF MEASURE: This 285-item Questionnaire on Resources and Stress can be applied to a handicapped or chronically ill family member of any age, but research to date has been with children as identified patients. The fifteen face-valid scales fall into three groups: *Personal Problems of the Respondents as Related to the Index Case*–(1) Poor Health/Mood, (2) Excess Time Demands, (3) Negative Attitude Toward Index Case, (4) Overprotection/Dependency, (5) Lack of Social Support, (6) Overcommitment/Martyrdom, and (7) Pessimism; *Family Problems as Related to the Index Case*–(8) Lack of Family Integration, (9) Limits on Family Opportunity, and (10) Financial Problems; *Limitations or Problems of the Handicapped or Chronically Ill Family Member*–(11) Physical Incapacitation, (12) Lack of Activities for Index Case, (13) Occupational Limitations for Index Case, (14) Social Obtrusiveness, and (15) Difficult Personality Characteristics.

As examples, the first items of each of the fifteen scales are given below.

36. Thinking about the future makes me sad. (T)
23. I always watch to make sure _____ does not do physical harm to himself/herself or others. (T)
15. Even if people don't look at _____, I am always wondering what they might think. (T)
65. At times I fear _____ will not be able to function in society if he/she is out of our house. (T)
61. My family argues about how to care for _____. (T)
16. I take on responsibility for _____ because I know how to deal with him/her. (T)
13. I know _____'s condition will improve. (F)
4. _____ is cared for by all members of our family. (F)
6. A member of my family has had to give up education (or a job) because of _____. (T)
5. It will take us three years or more to pay off our debt. (T)
29. Medicine does not have to be given to _____ at a set time. (F)
154. It is hard to think of enough things to keep _____ busy. (T)
24. The special opportunities needed by _____ are available in our community. (F)
34. When others are around I cannot relax; I am always on guard. (T)
1. _____ demands that others do things for him/her more than is necessary. (T)

RELIABILITY AND VALIDITY: None reported.

BIBLIOGRAPHY:

Holroyd, J. C. "The Questionnaire on Resources and Stress: An Instrument to Measure Family Response to a Handicapped Family Member." *Journal of Community Psychology,* 1974, *2,* 92-94.
Holroyd, J. C., Brown, N., Wikler, L., and Simmons, J. Q. "Stress in Families of Institutionalized and Noninstitutionalized Autistic Children." *Journal of Community Psychology,* 1975, *3,* 26-31.

---

# RESPONSE-CLASS MATRIX

AUTHORS: Eric J. Mash, Leif G. Terdal, and Kathryn Anderson

AGE: Parents and children—toddler through primary grades

VARIABLE: Parent-child interaction

TYPE OF MEASURE: Direct behavioral observation

SOURCE FROM WHICH MEASURE MAY BE OBTAINED: See Mash, Terdal, and Anderson (1974).

DESCRIPTION OF MEASURE: The Response-Class Matrix consists of seven behavior categories describing child behavior. The parent categories are command, question-command, question, praise, negative, interaction, and no response. The child categories are compliance, independent play, question, negative, interaction, and no response. Using a time-and-event sampling procedure, frequency counts of dyadic interaction between parent and child are obtained. With two coders it is possible to monitor both child responses to parental behavior and parental responses to child behavior. The instrument is especially useful for obtaining information to be used for a functional analysis of behavior. The matrix may be used both to identify significant features of the parent-child interaction and as an evaluative device to assess the effects of programs designed to modify parent-child interactions.

RELIABILITY AND VALIDITY: Interobserver agreement measures for individual behavior categories have ranged from 78 to 96 percent following four to six hours of training. In general, greater interobserver agreement is obtained with increasing data samples. The measure has been shown to differentiate between interactions in structured and nonstructured situations. Also, differing interaction patterns have emerged for dyads involving mentally retarded children and their parents when compared to interaction involving normal children and their parents (Terdal, Jackson, and Garner, 1974). The measure has also been shown to be sensitive to behavioral intervention strategies.

BIBLIOGRAPHY:

Mash, E. J., Lazere, R., Terdal, L., and Garner, A. "Modification of Mother-Child Inter-
    actions: A Modeling Approach for Groups." *Child Study Journal*, 1973, *3*,
    131-143.
Mash, E. J., and Terdal, L. "Modification of Mother-Child Interactions: Playing with
    Children." *Mental Retardation*, 1973, *11*, 44-49.
Mash, E. J., Terdal, L., and Anderson, K. "The Response-Class Matrix: A Procedure for
    Recording Parent-Child Interactions." *Journal of Consulting and Clinical
    Psychology*, 1973, *40*, 163-164.
Mash, R. J., Terdal, L., and Anderson, K. "Response-Class Matrix." In E. G. Boyer, A.
    Simon, and G. R. Karafin (Eds.), *An Anthology of Early Childhood Observation
    Instruments*. Philadelphia, Pennsylvania: Research for Better Schools, Inc.,
    1974.
Terdal, L., Jackson, R., and Garner, A. M. "Interactions in Families of Mentally Re-
    tarded and Normal Children." Paper presented at the Sixth Banff International
    Conference on Behavior Modification. Banff, Alberta, Canada, 1974.

---

# REVISED OCCUPATIONAL SCALE FOR
# RATING SOCIOECONOMIC STATUS

AUTHOR: Martin Hamburger

AGE: Adult

VARIABLE: Socioeconomic status

TYPE OF MEASURE: Scale

SOURCE FROM WHICH MEASURE MAY BE OBTAINED: Martin Hamburger, School
of Education, New York University, Washington Square, New York, New York 10003.

DESCRIPTION OF MEASURE: This scale is a revision of the Warner Revision of the
Edwards Classification. The scale modifies the Warner and others (1949) framework,
while making extensive use of other researches. Dimensions of income, behavior control, responsibility, and mostly prestige have entered into the revised scale. The scale
may be termed a class-status scale in that economic position and rewards as well as
social prestige are considered the chief links between occupation and socioeconomic
status. Socioeconomic status is rated on a scale from 1 to 7, with 1 being the highest.
There is a two-page manual for use with this revised scale. The manual specifies the
way in which the scale is used, and there is sufficient information to make the scale
readily useful.

RELIABILITY AND VALIDITY: None reported.

BIBLIOGRAPHY:

Hamburger, M. "Realism and Consistency in Early Adolescent Aspirations and Expectations." Unpublished doctoral dissertation. Columbia University, New York, 1958.
Warner, W., Lloyd, M., Meeker, M., and Eels, K. *Social Class in America: A Manual of Procedure for the Measurement of Social Status.* Chicago: Science Research Associates, 1949.

*Prepared by Orval G. Johnson*

---

## REVISED RESIDENT MANAGEMENT PRACTICES SCALE II (RRMP II)

AUTHORS: Norma V. Raynes, M. W. Pratt, and S. Roses

AGE: 16 years and up

VARIABLE: Quality of care provided in residential setting

TYPE OF MEASURE: Questionnaire and ordinal scale

SOURCE: See Raynes, Pratt, and Roses (1974) or write to N. V. Raynes, 3 Highgate Avenue, London, N. 6, England.

DESCRIPTION OF MEASURE: The RRMP II measures the extent to which care practices at the living unit level in residential settings are institutionally or resident oriented. Conceptually, it is an attempt to operationalize the characteristics of staff-resident interaction described by Goffman (1966). Data for the twenty-eight-item scale are collected by administration of an interview schedule: The Residents' Day Interview (an observation schedule), The Residents' Management Practices Observation Schedule, and an Individual Clothing Checklist.

The RRMP II is derived from the measure developed by Raynes and King (1968), which was used in residential settings in England. Two items from this original scale that were found to be age-loaded were excluded in studies carried out in the United States of residential services for the mentally retarded adult. The present scale was constructed using Maxwell's (1971) item-analysis technique, and it correlates .96 with an earlier fifteen-item version. Items are scored on a 3-point rating system: 0 = resident-oriented care, 1 = mixed-care practices, and 2 = institutionally oriented care practices. Possible score range is from 0 to 56, the higher score indicating institutionally oriented caring practices.

Examples of the items used in the scale are: "Do the staff eat with the residents?" "Do residents get up at the same time on weekends as they do during the week?" "Do residents have ten specified items of personal clothing?" Data for the scale have to be obtained from the interview, observation schedule, and the clothing checklist referred to above.

RELIABILITY AND VALIDITY: The mean interviewer and observer reliabilities for the first two data collection procedures were .89 and .85, respectively. All items included in the scale meet the criteria of linearity and discrimination as described by Maxwell (1971). The scale was applied to data obtained in twenty-two living units in three institutions for the mentally retarded in the United States. The data were obtained using the techniques referred to above. Content validity is indicated by the extent to which (1) reported practices were consonant with observed practices, and (2) the scale was consistent with other measures of the quality of care.

BIBLIOGRAPHY:

Goffman, E. *Asylums.* New York: Doubleday, 1966.

Maxwell, A. E. *Analysing Qualitative Data.* London: Methuen, 1971.

Raynes, N. V., and King, R. D. "The Measurement of Child Management in Residential Institutions for the Retarded." In B. W. Richards (Ed.), *Proceedings of the First Congress of the International Association for the Scientific Study of Mental Deficiency.* Surrey, England: Reigate, 1968.

Raynes, N. V., Pratt, M. W., and Roses, S. *Final Report: Organizational Structure and Care in Institutions for the Retarded.* Mimeographed. National Institute of Child Health and Human Development, Department of Health, Education and Welfare, Washington, D.C., 1974.

---

## SEATTLE/KING COUNTY FOUR C'S EVALUATION CHECKLISTS FOR IN-HOME CARE, DAY-CARE HOMES, AND DAY-CARE CENTERS

AUTHORS: Betsey McGuire and Dorothy DeCoster

AGE: Infancy through school age

VARIABLE: Quality and comprehensiveness of service

TYPE OF MEASURE: Checklists and rating scales

SOURCE FROM WHICH MEASURE MAY BE OBTAINED: See King County Child Care Coordinating Committee (1973).

DESCRIPTION OF MEASURE: These three evaluation checklists were developed by the Department of Social and Health Services licensing staff as tools to gauge whether facilities and care meet state and federal day-care requirements. Each checklist is designed for the particular type of locale to be evaluated, but all three contain some common areas, such as health, nutrition, program, and interactions. In addition to these, the checklist for In-Home Care surveys these areas: reasons for in-home care arrangement, safety, guidance and discipline, housekeeping, and personal information about the careworker and the parents. The Day-Care Home Checklist also includes family information, family services, location/transportation, environment, and staffing/ training/career development. The Day-Care Center Checklist also includes identification, environment and physical facility, administration, social services, psychological services, staff, and parents and family involvement. Under each of the categories there are various numbers of items, which are scored in three ways: (1) yes/no, (2) a 4-point frequency scale ranging from "never" to "all of the time," and (3) a 4-point scale ranging from "unsatisfactory, inadequate, very bad" to "excellent, outstanding." The checklists have proved useful in training situations with staff, parents, and early childhood students and have also been used for self-evaluation.

As examples, short sections of the In-Home Checklist and the Family Day-Care Home Checklist are given below.

*In-Home Care Checklist*
II. Children's Health (To be asked of careworker.)
    B. If a child becomes ill,
        10. Is there a telephone?
        11. Is there a list of emergency numbers, including
           a. phone numbers of children's doctors?
             b. phone number where parents can be reached?
             c. Poison Control Center?
             d. Fire Control number?
             e. emergency medical aid (Fire Dept., AID car, ambulance, hospital)?
        12. If there is not a phone, where is the nearest phone available?

*Family Day-Care Home Checklist*
IX. Interactions (This section is to be filled out by observation only, not by asking questions.)
    C. Does the caretaker encourage independence?
        1. Children are allowed to initiate their own activities.
        2. Caretaker allows children a choice in many situations and then abides by the childrens' choice.
        3. Children are praised for specifically independent achievements.
        4. Children are allowed some time alone.
        5. Children are given an opportunity to accept responsibility.
        6. Children are encouraged to complete tasks.
        7. Children are not rushed when washing hands or brushing teeth.
        8. Children are not rushed when eating.
        9. Children finish eating at various times.

RELIABILITY AND VALIDITY: None reported.

BIBLIOGRAPHY:

King County Child Care Coordinating Committee. *In-Home Care Checklist, Family Day-Care Home Checklist, Day-Care Center Checklist.* Washington, D.C.: Day Care and Child Development Council of America, 1973.

*Prepared by Christine Pratt Marston*

## STOLLAK'S SENSITIVITY TO CHILDREN QUESTIONNAIRE

AUTHOR: Gary E. Stollak

AGE: 5 years to adult

VARIABLE: Child caretaking attitudes and behavior

TYPE OF MEASURE: Projective questionnaire

SOURCE FROM WHICH MEASURE MAY BE OBTAINED: Gary E. Stollak, Department of Psychology, Michigan State University, East Lansing, Michigan 48824.

DESCRIPTION OF MEASURE: Sixteen parent-child conflict and need-arousing encounters are described. Respondents are asked to pretend or imagine they are the parent (mother or father) of the 6-year-old child described in each encounter. Respondents are asked to write down (or verbally respond) exactly how they would respond to the child in each of the situations, in a word, sentence, or short paragraph, as if they were writing a script for a play or movie.

As examples, three of the sixteen situations on the questionnaire are given below.

1. You are having a friendly talk with a friend on the phone. Your son Carl rushes in and begins to interrupt your conversation with a story about a friend in school.
2. You and your husband (wife) are going out for the evening. As you are leaving you both say "good night" to your son, Frank. He begins to cry and pleads with you both not to go out and leave him alone even though he doesn't appear sick and the babysitter is one he has previously gotten along well with.
3. After hearing a great deal of giggling coming from your daughter Lisa's bedroom, you go there and find her and her friends, Mary and Tom, under a blanket in her room with their clothes off. It appears that they were touching each other's sexual parts before you arrived.

RELIABILITY AND VALIDITY: Close similarity between maternal and own-child reports of maternal behavior (Kallman and Stollak, 1974) suggests that maternal behavior on the questionnaire is related to social actions of the parent with the child, at least as verified by child perceptions. Child wished-for responses on the questionnaire are significantly different from their perceptions of maternal behavior. There are some indications that college undergraduates whose responses are more "child oriented" and "responsive" are more empathic in their free-play encounters with clinic-referred children than undergraduates whose responses were more "authoritarian" and "adult oriented."

BIBLIOGRAPHY:

Kallman, J. R., and Stollak, G. E. "Maternal Behavior Toward Children in Need-Arousing Situations." Paper presented at the annual meeting of the Midwestern Psychological Association. Chicago, 1974.
Stollak, G. E., Scholom, A., Kallman, J. R., and Saturansky, C. "Insensitivity to Chil-

dren: Responses of Undergraduates to Children in Problem Situations." *Journal of Abnormal Child Psychology,* 1973, *1,* 169-180.

Stollak, G. E., Scholom, A., Schreiber, J., Green, L., and Messe, L. "The Process and Outcome of Play Encounters Between Undergraduates and Clinic-Referred Children: Preliminary Findings." *Psychotherapy: Theory, Research and Practice* (in press).

# Category 6

# Motor Skills and Sensory Perception

*This category includes measures of motor skills, physical fitness, speech production, and sensory perception and discrimination.*

Group 6-a. Motor Skills. *This group includes, in addition to fine and gross motor skills, measures of physical fitness, laterality, speech articulation, rhythm, handwriting, and cerebral dysfunction.*

Group 6-b. Sensory Perception. *This group includes discrimination of visual, auditory, and tactual stimuli, and such related areas as visual memory and oral stereognosis.*

# Group 6-a

## Motor
## Skills

## AMBIDEXTERITY TARGET TEST

AUTHOR: Reuven Kohen-Raz

AGE: 5 to 14 years

VARIABLE: Ambidexterity

TYPE OF MEASURE: Motor test

SOURCE FROM WHICH MEASURE MAY BE OBTAINED: See Kohen-Raz (1965).

DESCRIPTION OF MEASURE: In the Target Test, three round cardboard (or wooden) targets of 25, 15, and 5 centimeters in diameter are fixed on a wall at the height of the child's shoulder. The child stands at a distance of 2 meters from the target and is asked to throw a tennis ball at the target without moving his feet. He is given five trials per left and right hand for each target, to be presented in order of descending size, or a total of thirty trials. If the ball hits the target even marginally, a hit is scored. The ambidexterity score is the absolute difference between right and left hand hits, divided by total of hits and multiplied by 100. The test can be administered by teachers and semiprofessionals.

RELIABILITY AND VALIDITY: None reported.

BIBLIOGRAPHY:

Kohen-Raz, R. "Developmental Increase of Ambidexterity in Target Tests." *Journal of Child Psychology and Psychiatry,* 1965, 6, 43-54.

---

## BASIC MOTOR FITNESS TEST

AUTHOR: Donald Hilsendager

AGE: 4 to 25 years

VARIABLE: Motor performance

TYPE OF MEASURE: Test

SOURCE FROM WHICH MEASURE MAY BE OBTAINED: Donald Hilsendager, Department of Physical Education, Temple University, Philadelphia, Pennsylvania 19122.

DESCRIPTION OF MEASURE: Items were developed that would (1) minimize the effect of mental limitations and lack of comprehension of desired performance on test scores, (2) represent the various factors of physical performance that have been identified in developmental or factor-analysis studies with emphasis on the factors significantly related to the activities of daily living, (3) be meaningful with both normal and handicapped children and thereby provide a ready comparison of the latter with the former without bias induced by mental ability, (4) be objectively scored or at least include a minimum of subjective decisions on the part of the scorers, and (5) provide specific guidelines in respect to the development and evaluation of physical education and activity programs for the emotionally handicapped. The items in Level I measure specific skill achievements important to the successful performance of the everyday activities of normal children through age 5. Level II includes items that are scored on a continuum and that are based upon the assumption of generality of physical performance. Both test levels include a "would not try" and a "not a maximum effort" column. An extensive number of checks in either of these columns indicates the need for a retest, and if the columns again receive numerous checks, it is an indication of the type of cooperation that may be expected from the subject in his physical-activity program. Approximately 20 minutes are required to administer one level of the present test battery to a handicapped child on an individual basis. The more capable child can be tested in 10 to 15 minutes. Norms are provided on some of the items for boys and girls separately, by grade, for kindergarten, second, fourth, and sixth.

The items in the test are given below. The items in Level I are scored "pass," "fail," "would not try," "not a maximum effort." The items in Level II are scored "raw score," "standard score," "would not try," "not a maximum effort."

*Level I*

| | |
|---|---|
| Walk | Hop—left foot |
| Creep | Skip |
| Stand—both feet | March—in place |
| Stand—right foot | Catch |
| Stand—left foot | Throw—right hand |
| Jump—one foot leading | Throw—left hand |
| Jump—both feet simultaneously | Kick—right foot |
| Climb stairs | Kick—left foot |
| Hop—both feet | Ball—bounce and catch |
| Hop—right foot | |

*Level II*

| | |
|---|---|
| Standing broad jump | Push |
| Balance beam | Pull |
| Agility run | 35-yard dash |
| Sit ups (max. 100) | Medicine ball throw |
| Right grip | Flexibility |
| Left grip | 300-yard dash |

RELIABILITY AND VALIDITY: None reported.

BIBLIOGRAPHY:

Mann, L., Hilsendager, D. R., Wright, T., and Jack, H. K. "A Pilot Training Program to Develop Physical Recreation Leaders for Work with Emotionally Disturbed Children." *Community Mental Health Journal,* 1967, *3,* 159-162.

Mann, L., Phillips, W., Hilsendager, D. R., and Jack, H. K. "The Training of Physical

Recreation Leaders to Work with Emotionally Disturbed Children." *Challenge,* 1966, *1,* 3-7.

---

## BERSON INDEX OF LATERAL DEXTERITY (BILD)

AUTHOR: Janet Berson Greenberg

AGE: 5 to 8 years

VARIABLE: Fine motor coordination and differentiation of skill

TYPE OF MEASURE: Test

SOURCE FROM WHICH MEASURE MAY BE OBTAINED: Janet Berson Greenberg or Janet Berson, Department of Psychology, Douglass College, Rutgers University, New Brunswick, New Jersey 08901. Cost: $15.00 per 100 forms, $2.00 for instructions, $8.00 per 100 scoring forms.

DESCRIPTION OF MEASURE: The BILD consists of nine sets of paired lines, five at a primary level, and four at a more advanced level. The child is told to draw a line between the test lines (without touching the sides) first with his preferred hand and then with his nonpreferred hand. This test indicates the relative degree of skill between the two hands as opposed to ordinary measures of laterality that indicate only hand preference rather than differential skill. Test performance is scored according to the time taken and errors made. Six measures are obtained. These are: (1) DDE, difference in number of errors made with preferred and nonpreferred hands; (2) DDT, difference in time scores for preferred and nonpreferred hands; (3) DEP, errors—preferred hand; (4) DEN, errors—nonpreferred hand; (5) DTP, time—preferred hand; and (6) DTN, time—nonpreferred hand. The BILD was administered to eighty-three first-grade students in the original study. It was also given to fifty-nine third graders and sixteen fourth graders in this research. A subsequent project has utilized kindergarten and second-grade students. Means and standard deviations for these grades (temporary norms because of the small numbers as yet tested) are available.

RELIABILITY AND VALIDITY: A significant correlation ($p < .05$) was found for early reading level using a weighted index of IQ and two subscores of the BILD (DDT and DTP). Predictability was greater for girls than for boys. This relationship no longer held in older children in accord with a postulated theory of developmental lag in left-hemisphere functions (Satz and Sparrow, 1970). Reliability data have not yet been obtained.

BIBLIOGRAPHY:

Greenberg, J. B. "Differential Prediction of Reading Ability at the First-Grade Level." Unpublished doctoral dissertation. University of Pennsylvania, Philadelphia, 1972. Abstract in *Dissertation Abstracts International, 33* (7), 1973.

Greenberg, J. B. "Differential Prediction of Reading Failure at the First-Grade Level: The Goal, Prevention." *American Journal of Orthopsychiatry*, 1973, *43*, 223-224.

Satz, P., and Sparrow, S. "Specific Developmental Dyslexia: A Theoretical Formulation." In D. J. Bakker and P. Satz (Eds.), *Specific Reading Disability: Advances in Theory and Method.* Rotterdam, the Netherlands: University of Rotterdam Press, 1970.

---

## COMBINED ARTICULATION SCREENING TEST AND SELF-MONITORING AUDITORY DISCRIMINATION TEST

AUTHOR: Barbara B. Hutchinson

AGE: 5 years and up

VARIABLE: Articulation proficiency and self-monitoring auditory discrimination ability

TYPE OF MEASURE: Test

SOURCE FROM WHICH MEASURE MAY BE OBTAINED: Barbara B. Hutchinson, Speech and Hearing Clinic, Illinois State University, Normal, Illinois 61761.

DESCRIPTION OF MEASURE: The Articulation Test is a picture-word screening test of twenty-three different phonemes. Two scores may be obtained: the number of different phonemes misarticulated and the number total of errors made (this figure can include several misarticulations of the same phoneme occurring in different words). The Self-Monitoring Test of Auditory Discrimination uses the same set of picture cards used for the Articulation Test and is administered at the same time as that test. There are two equivalent forms of both tests. The Self-Monitoring Auditory Discrimination Test is a test of the subject's judgment of his own errors of speech production. In this respect the test differs from traditional tests of auditory discrimination that require the subject's judgment of another person's speech production. The Self-Monitoring Test of Auditory Discrimination has been found to measure differences between children in the first, second, and third grades of elementary school to a finer degree than does the Wepman Auditory Discrimination Test. Its correlation with the total number of defective sounds found on the articulation test has been determined at .88 and above, by three different researchers.

| | | Articulation Errors | | | | | | | | |
|---|---|---|---|---|---|---|---|---|---|---|
| | | No. of Different Phonemes Scored Defective | | | Total No. of Defective Single Sounds | | | Total No. of S-M Aud. Disc. Errors | | |
| Grade | *N* | M | SD | SE | M | SD | SE | M | SD | SE |
| 1 | 150 | 3.20 | 2.38 | .19 | 5.60 | 4.31 | .35 | 5.30 | 3.92 | .32 |
| 2 | 100 | 2.90 | 2.62 | .26 | 5.24 | 4.05 | .41 | 4.64 | 3.16 | .31 |
| 3 | 90 | 2.06 | 1.65 | .17 | 4.94 | 3.71 | .39 | 3.91 | 2.51 | .26 |

RELIABILITY AND VALIDITY: The equivalency of the two forms as determined by reliability coefficients for internal consistency is .94. Interjudge reliability, using four judges and ten subjects, is .99. Test-retest reliability ($N = 32$) is .99.

BIBLIOGRAPHY:

Allison, G. "The Relationship Between Functional Articulation Disorders and Self-Monitoring Auditory Discrimination." Unpublished master's thesis. Central Washington State College, Ellensburg, 1972.

Hutchinson, B. B. "Self-Monitoring of Articulation Responses in Sound Discrimination Tests." *Journal of Communication Disorders,* 1967, *1,* 297-304.

Hutchinson, B. B. "Rationale and Standardization for a Combined Speech Articulation and Auditory Discrimination Test." *Perceptual and Motor Skills,* 1971, *33,* 715-721.

Tobias, C. L. "Auditory Discrimination and Articulation Test Performance in Selected School Children." Unpublished master's thesis. Illinois State University, Normal, 1974.

---

# COMMUNICATION BEHAVIOR SCALE (CBS)

AUTHOR: Nancy Marshall Heisley

AGE: 2 to 6 years

VARIABLE: Quality and quantity of speech, verbal comprehension, verbal expression, intelligibility, and articulation

TYPE OF MEASURE: Questionnaire

SOURCE FROM WHICH MEASURE MAY BE OBTAINED: Nancy Marshall Heisley, University of Oregon Medical School, 3181 South West Sam Jackson Parkway, Portland, Oregon 97201.

DESCRIPTION OF MEASURE: Using the Likert technique, a list of thirty-five behaviorally descriptive items was constructed by the author after the model provided by Adkins and others (1947) and in reference to four communication functioning levels described in the *Manual for Evaluation of Speech, Language and Hearing Development in Children.* This *Manual* is used in the examination of children in the Speech and Hearing Clinic at the University of Oregon Medical School. The *Manual* was developed by the Speech Pathology, Audiology, and Psychology staff at the Crippled Children's Division of the University of Oregon Medical School and was used as the classification basis for the thirty-five-item Communication Behavior Scale (CBS). The CBS was developed to discriminate between amount and type of information that mothers of speech-handicapped or speech-and-hearing-handicapped children possess about their child's problem. The mother's awareness of her child's handicap was determined on the basis of prediagnostic and postdiagnostic responses to items concerning her child's speech and language behavior. It was designed not only to determine maternal awareness of a speech handicap or speech and hearing handicap but also to determine changes in awareness as a result of diagnostic proceedings. The original scale as constructed by the author consisted of eighty-five items administered to sixty mothers in a pilot study to determine which items should be retained when the scale was administered to the three groups of mothers in this investigation.

As examples, the first five of the thirty-five items are given below, to be answered "never," "some of the time," "most of the time," "always," or "don't know."

1. My child uses sounds such as *p, b, m,* and sometimes *t* and *d.*
2. My child uses only one understandable word.
3. My child uses around ten words correctly.
4. I can understand about one-half of what my child says.
5. My child names the objects he/she plays with.

RELIABILITY AND VALIDITY: None reported.

BIBLIOGRAPHY:

Adkins, D., Primoff, M. H., Bridges, C., and Foror, B. *Construction and Analysis of Achievement Tests.* Washington, D.C.: U.S. Government Printing Office, 1947.
Martin, J. G., and Nelson, J. T. "Recognition Tests, Repetition and All-or-None Learning." *American Journal of Psychology,* 1963, *76,* 675-678.

---

# CONCOMITANT STUTTERING BEHAVIOR CHECKLIST

AUTHOR: Eugene B. Cooper

AGE: Unlimited

VARIABLE: Stuttering and related behaviors

TYPE OF MEASURE: Checklist

SOURCE FROM WHICH MEASURE MAY BE OBTAINED: The Speech and Hearing Center, P.O. Box 1965, University, Alabama 35486.

DESCRIPTION OF MEASURE: This is a checklist of thirty-two stuttering-related behaviors that may assist the stutterer and the clinician in identifying stuttering behaviors and to assess any behavioral changes during therapy. They are divided into the following classes: posturing behaviors (six items), respiratory behaviors (four items), facial behaviors (nine items), syntactic and semantic behaviors (five items), and vocal behaviors (eight items). The clinician or other observer notes the dates on which the behavior occurs and records the number of items checked on each observation date.

As examples, the nine items of the facial behaviors section of the checklist are given below.

1. Wrinkling of the forehead.
2. Wrinkling of the nose.
3. Flaring nostrils.
4. Distracting absence of eye contact.
5. Loss of eye contact during stuttering moment.
6. Excessive eyelid movements.
7. Abnormal eyebrow movements.
8. Prolonged eyelid closure.
9. Unusual eye movements during stuttering moment.

RELIABILITY AND VALIDITY: None reported.

BIBLIOGRAPHY: None reported.

---

## COOPER CHRONICITY PREDICTION CHECKLIST FOR SCHOOL-AGE STUTTERERS

AUTHOR: Eugene B. Cooper

AGE: 5 to 18 years

VARIABLE: Probability of spontaneous recovery from stuttering

TYPE OF MEASURE: Questionnaire

SOURCE FROM WHICH MEASURE MAY BE OBTAINED: See Cooper (1973).

DESCRIPTION OF MEASURE: Assuming that as many as two out of three stutterers speech clinicians meet in the schools will recover spontaneously, the value in differentiating between the chronic and the episodic stutterer is obvious. The Cooper Chronicity Prediction Checklist for School-Age Stutterers was developed for research purposes without supporting reliability and validity data. Longitudinal studies will be necessary to produce such information. There are twenty-seven items in three areas, as follows: historical indicators of chronicity (six items), attitudinal indicators of chronicity (five items), and behavioral indicators of chronicity (sixteen items).

As examples, six selected items with their areas are given below.

I. Historical Indicators of Chronicity
   1. Is there a history of stuttering in the child's family?
   5. Is the stuttering now or has it ever been considered by the child to be "severe"?

II. Attitudinal Indicators of Chronicity
    2. Does the child indicate that he or she experiences communicative fear because of stuttering?
    3. Does the child indicate that he or she believes the stuttering to be getting worse?
III. Behavioral Indicators of Chronicity
    2. Is the rapidity of the syllable repetitions faster than normal?
    6. Do prolongations last longer than one second?

RELIABILITY AND VALIDITY: None reported.

BIBLIOGRAPHY:

Cooper, E. B. "The Development of a Stuttering Chronicity Prediction Checklist: A Preliminary Report." *Journal of Speech and Hearing Disorders*, 1973, *38*, 215-223.

---

# DESIGN REPRODUCTION TEST (DRT)

AUTHOR: Edwin E. Wagner

AGE: Unspecified

VARIABLE: Organic brain pathology

TYPE OF MEASURE: Mechanical device for viewing and adjusting visual designs

SOURCE FROM WHICH MEASURE MAY BE OBTAINED: See Schaff (1967). Detailed construction notes are available in Wagner and Schaff (1968). Original production of the DRT in 1967 cost about $150.00 per set and was done by a private graphic arts firm.

DESCRIPTION OF MEASURE: The Design Reproduction Test (DRT) is an objective measure of organic brain pathology and perceptual motor development. Its key advantages are a minimization of motor ability, simplicity of interpretation, brevity in administration and scoring, and objective scoring. The materials for the DRT consists of a 1-foot-square board with a 2-inch-square aperture in the center. Sets of clear plastic strips with opaque geometrical designs are inserted through two side slots, one vertically and the other horizontally. The two strips converge at the center and are viewed through the aperture as a third, more complex design that is alterable by adjusting either the horizontal or the vertical strip. Four sets of plastic slides are used. For each set there are three model designs to be replicated. The subject is instructed to adjust both strips so that the resulting design conforms to the model design that is placed above the aperture window. Scoring consists of recording how many units each slide deviates from the correct position as indicated by calibrated numbers on each slide. A total error score is then derived by summing all deviations.

RELIABILITY AND VALIDITY: Schaff (1967) and Wagner and Schaff (1968) tested four groups of thirty Ss each, fifteen males and fifteen females. Ss were matched by sex, age (all Ss were 22 to 24 years), and race (all white). The four groups were: normal college students, functionally disturbed patients, retardates without organicity, and retardates with organicity. Split-half reliability was .94. The correlation between the DRT and the 4-point diagnostic continuum was .84 ± .03. Wagner and Murray (1969) tested two groups of thirty-two children each, twelve girls and twenty boys with a mean age of 9.6, using the DRT and the Bender-Gestalt. The first group had definite neurological impairment ranging from mild to severe as determined by neurological examinations. The second group served as controls consisting of normal children matched for age and sex. Five diagnosticians who were unfamiliar with the Ss successfully differentiated between pairs of neurological and normal Bender-Gestalt protocols twenty-seven to thirty times out of a possible thirty-two correct ($p < .001$). The DRT also distinguished between pairs of protocols twenty-seven out of thirty-two times.

BIBLIOGRAPHY:

Schaff, J. E. "The Effects of Perceptual Disorganization on Design Reproduction When Motor Performance Is Held Constant." Unpublished master's thesis. University of Akron, Ohio, 1967.

Wagner, E. E., and Murray, A. Y. "Bender-Gestalts of Organic Children: Accuracy of Clinical Judgment." *Journal of Projective Techniques and Personality Assessment,* 1969, *33,* 240-242.

Wagner, E. E., and Schaff, J. E. "Design Reproduction with Motor Performance Held Constant." *Journal of Projective Techniques and Personality Assessment,* 1968, *32,* 395-396.

---

# DEVELOPMENTAL ARTICULATION TEST

AUTHOR: Robert F. Hejna

AGE: 3 to 8 years

VARIABLE: Articulation of consonant sounds

TYPE OF MEASURE: Test

SOURCE FROM WHICH MEASURE MAY BE OBTAINED: Speech Materials, Box 1713, Ann Arbor, Michigan 48106. Cost: Test, complete with picture cards, instruction sheet, and pad of twenty-five scoring blanks, $3.00; extra pads of scoring blanks, 25 blanks per pad, $1.00.

DESCRIPTION OF MEASURE: The test is designed to assess consonant sound usage on a developmental scale, according to the chronological age level by which approximately 90 percent or more children are using the sound correctly. By means of twenty-six picture stimulus cards, consonant sounds are tested in each of the positions within the word, in the initial, medial, and final positions. For example, at developmental age 3, testing for the sound "*p,*" a picture card is presented with illustrations of a *pig,* pu*pp*y, and cu*p.* After testing is completed, a composite picture is obtained of the child's use of the consonant sounds, and a determination can be made as to whether the child is within normal chronological age limits in consonant sound usage.

RELIABILITY AND VALIDITY: The test is based on normative data from Templin (1957).

BIBLIOGRAPHY:

Templin, M. *Certain Language Skills in Children.* Minneapolis: University of Minnesota Press, 1957.

---

# EAU CLAIRE FUNCTIONAL MOTOR ABILITY TEST (ECFMAT)

AUTHORS: James B. House and Margo House

AGE: Functional age from birth to about 2 years

VARIABLE: Basic motor competences

TYPE OF MEASURE: Individually administered ability test

SOURCE FROM WHICH MEASURE MAY BE OBTAINED: See Heal (1972).

DESCRIPTION OF MEASURE: The ECFMAT was designed to be sensitive to fine-grained differences in the motor competences that are required for daily living skills of severely handicapped nonambulatory children. It consists of eleven subscales, each containing nine ordered performance levels. Each level, from 0 to 8, represents a decreasing amount of facilitation (assistance) needed to accomplish a certain motor goal or function. The zero point represents the maximum amount of facilitation needed by a child to achieve a particular goal such as sitting or walking. The ninth point on the scale (a score of 8) represents an ability to achieve the goal in a functional manner with no facilitation at all. The eleven subscales test a broad spectrum of motor ability: prone and supine mat skills, sitting, pulling to and maintaining a stand, sitting from a stand, walking, fine-motor skills, writing, dressing, eating, and drinking.

As an example, subscale 1 of the eleven subscales is given below.

*Mat Tasks*
The child is placed on the mat in a supine position. The child will attempt to perform and complete the entire task sequence. Directions for left and right will be made concrete since this is not a test of the ability to distinguish left and right.
8—The child scores if he completes the following sequence easily. Roll right from su-

pine to prone, continue in that direction rolling prone to supine, turn 180 degrees in supine, roll left from supine to prone, turn 180 degrees in prone, push up to a four-point kneel, back down again to prone, roll left from prone to supine, and come up into a sitting position.

7—The child scores if he completes the above easily, but may have some difficulty in coming to a four-point kneel and/or in sitting up.

6—The child scores if he completes the above sequence but may have some difficulty in performing some or all of the tasks.

5—The child scores if he completes the above sequence but moves awkwardly and/or with great difficulty.

4—The child scores if he completes the above sequence but may need light facilitation in some of the sequence and in coming to a four-point and/or in sitting up.

3—The child scores if he needs light facilitation for some of the sequence and moderate facilitation in coming to a four-point and/or in sitting up.

2—The child scores if he needs moderate facilitation for most of the sequence and heavy facilitation in coming to a four-point and/or in sitting up.

1—The child scores if he needs heavy facilitation for most of the sequence, and must be moved passively to a four-point and to a sit.

0—The child scores if he is able to initiate some of the sequence but must be moved passively to complete most of the sequence.

RELIABILITY AND VALIDITY: The field-testing of fifty-one children ranging in age from 6 to 14 from three orthopedic schools produced an interrater reliability of .997 for the total ECFMAT score. Reliabilities of individual subscales range from .95 to 1.0. The retesting of these subjects sixteen months later produced a test-retest reliability of .96. Intersubscale correlations are available in Heal (1972).

BIBLIOGRAPHY:

Heal, L. W. *Evaluating an Integrated Approach to the Management of Cerebral Palsy.* Volume III. Final report for Grant no. OEG-0-9-592149-4540(032). Bureau of Education for the Handicapped, U.S. Office of Education, Department of Health, Education and Welfare, 1972.

*Prepared by Laird W. Heal*

---

## GLENWOOD AWARENESS, MANIPULATION, AND POSTURE INDEX I (GAMP I)

AUTHOR: Ruth C. Webb

AGE: All ages of profoundly retarded

VARIABLE: Sensorimotor integration

TYPE OF MEASURE: Rating scale

SOURCE FROM WHICH MEASURE MAY BE OBTAINED: Ruth C. Webb, Glenwood
State Hospital School, Glenwood, Iowa, 51534.

DESCRIPTION OF MEASURE: This instrument is comprised of three parts of twenty-
five items each. The awareness scale evaluates functioning of sensory receptors through
approach-avoidance stimuli as well as basic memory processes. The manipulation scale
evaluates fine-motor ability, intentionality, and responses to body and verbal language,
and also has items testing objects and person permanence. It indicates degree of integration of awareness with manual ability. The posture index evaluates the subject's
progress toward independent ambulation. Each item is presented three times and rated
as to the number of times it is performed. Administration procedures are given in a
separate manual. Two persons are required to administer the GAMP I.

As examples, the nine items from the avoidance section of the awareness portion of the measure are given below. Sensory systems are designated by the abbrevia-
tions following each item: T—tactility, (Te—temperature and P—pain), K—kinesthesia,
V—vision, A—audition, G—gustatory, O—olfactory, Me—memory, and At—attention.

1. *Struggles* when held tightly. (T, Pr)
2. *Draws* wrist or knee away from sharp tappings from rubber hammer (underline). (T,
   P)
3. *Draws* cheek away from sandpaper. (T, P)
4. *Draws* right and left hands out of hot (120° F) water and cold (40° F) water
   (underline). (T, Te)
5. *Jumps* or *blinks* eyes when metal basin is dropped 2 feet behind child (underline).
   (K, A)
6. *Turns* away from strong light. (V)
7. *Draws* away from unpleasant odors: (a) potassium sulphate; (b) turpentine. (0)
8. *Draws* away from unpleasant tastes: (a) lemon; (b) salt; (c) alum. (G)
9. *Struggles* to regain upright position (3 to 6 months). (K)

RELIABILITY AND VALIDITY: The awareness and manipulation sections were subjected to a split-half reliability study with forty profoundly retarded adults with the
following results: awareness, $r = .69$; manipulation, $r = .83$. A validity study was made
by correlating the results on the awareness and manipulation sections with scores on
the Binet short-form intelligence scales (and the Cattell downward extension) with the
following correlations respectively: awareness, $r = .37$; manipulation, $r = .72$.

BIBLIOGRAPHY:

Webb, R. C. "Sensory Motor Training of the Profoundly Retarded." *American Journal
of Mental Deficiency,* 1969, *74,* 283-295.
Webb, R. C., and others. *Evaluation of Sensory-Motor Bases of Behavior in the Profoundly Retarded,* 1975. ERIC document no. 073 591.

# GROUP TEST FOR ASSESSING HANDEDNESS

AUTHORS: Herbert F. Crovitz and Karl E. Zener

AGE: Kindergarten and up

VARIABLE: Hand dominance

TYPE OF MEASURE: Questionnaire

SOURCE FROM WHICH MEASURE MAY BE OBTAINED: H. F. Crovitz, Veterans Administration Hospital, Durham, North Carolina 27705.

DESCRIPTION OF MEASURE: This test was designed to give a quantitative measure of hand dominance. It consists of fourteen items that present situations where the respondent would use one or other of the hands in performing an action. He is asked to imagine himself performing the activity described before answering each question and to choose from the following alternatives: (1) right hand always, (2) right hand most of the time, (3) both hands equally often, (4) left hand most of the time, (5) left hand always, and (6) do not know which hand. Five of the items are scored in reverse since the activity described is usually performed by the less-dominant hand.

The fourteen items of the test are given below.

1. Is used to write with.
2. To hold nail when hammering.
3. To throw a ball.
4. To hold bottle when removing top.
5. Is used to draw with.
6. To hold potato when peeling.
7. To hold pitcher when pouring out of it.
8. To hold scissors when cutting.
9. To hold knife when cutting food.
10. To hold needle when threading.
11. To hold drinking glass when drinking.
12. To hold toothbrush when brushing teeth.
13. To hold dish when wiping.
14. Holds tennis racket when playing.

RELIABILITY AND VALIDITY: The questionnaire has been given to over fifteen hundred undergraduates at Duke University and has been used in a number of research studies at other institutions.

BIBLIOGRAPHY:

Crovitz, H. F. "Lateralities and Sex." *Perceptual and Motor Skills,* 1973, *37,* 520.
Crovitz, H. F., and Zener, K. "A Group Test for Assessing Hand and Eye Dominance." *The American Journal of Psychology,* 1962, *75,* 271-276.

# GROUP VISUAL-MOTOR SCREENING FIGURES

AUTHOR: George R. Kelly

AGE: 5 to 7 years

VARIABLE: Paper-and-pencil figure-copying development

TYPE OF MEASURE: Graphic expression

SOURCE FROM WHICH MEASURE MAY BE OBTAINED: Manual and test figure samples from George R. Kelly, 2607 West Walnut, Yakima, Washington 98902. Cost: $1.00. At present all materials may be freely reproduced as long as authorship is properly credited.

DESCRIPTION OF MEASURE: This instrument was designed to select children with possible visual perceptual or motor coordination problems from the general school population. It enables an examiner to screen a classroom in 20 or 30 minutes. It can provide the average classroom teacher with a relatively objective grouping procedure for use without extensive background training in the interpretation of children's graphic expression. It differs from most other figure-copying tests in three aspects. (1) The scoring system is objective and the guidelines were established on relatively large groups of children in public schools. (2) The children are asked to label the figures before they copy them. Initial work suggested that the children labeled them whether they were requested to or not. Advance multiple labeling is used to cut down on mislabeling errors and to keep the child on the stimulus figures. (3) The children watch the examiner make the figures on the chalk board. This tends to eliminate the need for closer evaluation of children who become confused due to lack of familiarity with copying tasks and materials. Since the figures are developmental in nature if the child can copy them adequately after a one-time demonstration, he is not in need of intensive developmental diagnosis or training.

RELIABILITY AND VALIDITY: Sample population numbers are relatively high for the establishment of normative data. They vary from 632 to 3,728. Interscorer reliability on a 300-student first-grade sample was found to be .94 with rank correlation employed as the statistic. On a forty-eight-student sample, 90 percent of the children selected also made low scores in at least one area of the Frostig Test.

BIBLIOGRAPHY:

Kelly, G. R. "Group Perceptual Screening at First Grade Level." *Journal of Learning Disabilities*, 1970, *3*, 640-644.

# HAND EFFICIENCY TESTS

AUTHOR: Robert A. Rigal

AGE: 5 years and up

VARIABLE: Handedness

TYPE OF MEASURE: Tests

SOURCE FROM WHICH MEASURE MAY BE OBTAINED: Robert Rigal, Départment de Kinanthropologie, Université du Québec, Case postale 8888, Montréal 101, Québec, Canada.

DESCRIPTION OF MEASURE: Based on the work of Barnsley and Rabinovitch (1970), a battery of five hand-efficiency tests has been elaborated. These tests evaluating different aspects of hand efficiency are: (1) arm-hand steadiness, in which the subject holds a stylus in a hole $\frac{3}{32}$ inch in diameter for 10 seconds, without touching the edge; (2) aiming, in which the subject is required to make a dot in each of forty circles $\frac{1}{8}$ inch in diameter, regularly spaced at $\frac{3}{8}$ inches; (3) finger tapping, in which the subject is required to tap as fast as possible a mechanical tapper with his forefinger for 15 seconds, his hand firm; (4) finger dexterity, in which the subject takes a block, turns it over, and puts it back in the same hole, using only one hand; and (5) strength, in which the subject grips as hard as possible a hand dynamometer. After all subjects have been tested with both hands, the raw scores of each test are transformed into $z$-scores (multiplying $z$ by $-1$ for tests 1, 2, and 4 so that a positive $z$ always signifies a good performance). For each of the tests, the $z$-scores are then transformed into $T$-scores ($M = 50$; $SD = 10$). The right-hand $T$-scores of each subject for the different tests are added to obtain a right-hand global hand-efficiency score; similarly, the left-hand T-scores are added to obtain a left-hand global score. The handedness of each subject may then be determined by subtracting his left-hand global score from his right-hand global score; the difference is positive for right-handers and negative for left-handers. Another advantage of this procedure is that ambidextrous subjects, who obtain equivalent results with both hands, can be discriminated through ability tests. The difference between their right-hand and left-hand performance is close to 0. The term ambidextrous here denotes any subject whose difference is included between the limits: $\overline{X} - z2$ x $\sigma < D < \overline{X} - z1$ X $\sigma$ where

$$X : \text{mean of all the differences P} - \text{NP}$$
$$\sigma : \text{standard deviation of the distribution of these differences}$$
$$z : \frac{0 - X}{\sigma}$$
$$z1 : \text{the ordinate at the abscissa (z + 0.05)}$$
$$z2 : \text{the ordinate at the abscissa (z} - 0.05)$$

RELIABILITY AND VALIDITY: The reliability coefficients of the different tests used are: arm-hand steadiness, .80; aiming, .93; finger tapping, .84; finger dexterity, .95; and strength, .95. Their validity is well established (Fleishman, 1964).

BIBLIOGRAPHY:

Barnsley, R. H., and Rabinovitch, M. S. "Handedness: Proficiency Versus Stated Preference." *Perceptual and Motor Skills*, 1970, *30*, 343-362.
Fleishman, E. A. *The Structure and Measurement of Physical Fitness.* Englewood Cliffs, New Jersey: Prentice-Hall, 1964.
Rigal, R. A. "Determination of Handedness Using Hand-Efficiency Tests." *Perceptual and Motor Skills*, 1974, *39*, 253-254.

---

# HARTFORD SCALE OF CLINICAL INDICATORS OF CEREBRAL DYSFUNCTION IN CHILD PSYCHIATRIC PATIENTS

AUTHORS: Paul N. Graffagnino, F. G. Bucknam, and M. H. January

AGE: 2 to 17 years

VARIABLE: Cerebral dysfunction

TYPE OF MEASURE: Rating scale

SOURCE FROM WHICH MEASURE MAY BE OBTAINED: See Graffagnino, Boehouwer, and Reznikoff (1968).

DESCRIPTION OF MEASURE: This is a rating scale of thirty clinical items to be rated as "present" or "absent." The data are obtained during the first four to six clinical interviews with parents, child, and family and are supplemented by information from hospital, clinic, or school records. The higher the score (more than seven or eight indicators "present"), the greater the likelihood that cerebral dysfunction is present in the child. The Hartford Scale is divided into three sections: (1) symptoms and signs related to impulsivity of direct aggression, (2) symptoms and signs related to compensatory adjustments against impulsivity or aggression, and (3) items from the early history.

As examples, the first seven items of subsection A are given below.

1. *Hyperactivity:* A history of hyperactivity at home, school, place of worship, clinic, or in other inappropriate situations, that does not respond to routine disciplinary measures and thus indicates that the child has not learned control.
2. *Severe Temper:* Repeated verbal or physical temper outbursts that cannot be quieted down quickly by ordinary means but require such drastic measures as slapping, immersion in a cold tub, etc.
3. *Heedless Self-Injury:* Excessive motion makes the child seem to be fearless or reckless. Repeated (at least three) incidents of so-called "accidental" self-injury or self-mutilation are revealed in a history of cuts requiring stitches, scrapes, broken bones, concussions, etc.
4. *Distractibility:* Short attention span and indiscriminate shifting of attention from object to object, definitely noted by parents or clinic personnel.

5. *Cruelty to Siblings or Peers:* Repetitive physical assault, rock throwing, "poking," pushing, or tripping that inflicts moderately serious injury or mutilation on others.
6. *Pattern of Difficulty with Authority Figures:* A repetitive and ingrained pattern of difficulty with parents, and in older children with teachers and community authorities as well.
7. *Strong Interest in Guns, Explosives, Knives, or Animal Traps.* A strong fascination with these instruments or an inordinate interest in their use manifested in various situations.

RELIABILITY AND VALIDITY: The present scale represents a consolidation and refinement of three lists compiled from clinical experience by the authors. Statistical comparisons with detailed EEG findings in ninety-four consecutive admissions to an outpatients' child psychiatry clinic were published in Graffagnino, Boehouwer, and Reznikoff (1968). In the same study the objectivity of rater scoring was checked by two independent raters with scoring agreements of 92 and 93 percent. Rating scale scores and EEG findings were checked by analysis of variance and *t*-test procedures.

BIBLIOGRAPHY:

Graffagnino, P. N., Boehouwer, C., and Reznikoff, M. "An Organic Factor in Patients of a Child Psychiatric Clinic." *Journal of the American Academy of Child Psychiatry,* 1968, 7, 618-638.

---

# INDEX OF PERCEPTUAL-MOTOR LATERALITY

AUTHOR: Allan Berman

AGE: 6 to 12 years

VARIABLE: Laterality of hand, eye, ear, and foot

TYPE OF MEASURE: Motor tasks

SOURCE FROM WHICH MEASURE MAY BE OBTAINED: A complete explanation of the procedure used to administer the measure and all descriptive material necessary are included in Berman (1971, 1973).

DESCRIPTION OF MEASURE: This index is a means of measuring continuously varying laterality. Whereas most laterality measures are dichotomous, including simply left or right indicators, the current instrument is designed to yield a continuous score ranging from 212 (most highly lateralized) to 0 (most unlateralized or mixed). The score is supplemented by a letter (R or L) indicating direction of laterality. Another feature is that a wide variety of laterality tasks are used, providing a greater sampling of laterality tasks. In addition, there are many tasks where the laterality aspect is very subtle, tasks that discriminate between accuracy of laterality and preference, and tasks that combine the integrated use of several parts of the body to represent more accurately the types of skills children are likely to have to acquire.

As examples, ten selected tasks of the fifty-four that make up the index are given below.

1. "Fold your hands like this." (Demonstration of folding with interlocking fingers. Dominant hand indicated by outermost thumb.)

2. 3. "Draw a circle. . . . Now do it with the other hand. . . . Now do it with both hands at the same time." (Record which hand was used first, and which circle was more accurately drawn.)

4. "Let me see you hop on one leg." (Record which leg was used.)

11. "Stand up. Close your eyes and put your feet together. Now lift up your arms and hold them straight out in front of you." (Record which arm was higher.)

15. "Step up on this chair. Now step down." (Record which foot was used to step down.)

16. "Put your arms on the table with your hands together like this. Now push as hard as you can with both hands." (Record hand opposite direction of tilt.)

25. "Kneel down on one knee." (Record which knee.)

28. 29. "Walk over to the door. Stop facing the door. Now when you come back, walk backward." (Record foot used first walking forward and foot used first walking backward.)

RELIABILITY AND VALIDITY: Both split-half and internal consistency reliability statistics are available (Berman, 1973), as well as correlations between various whole and subscores of the index with intelligence. The index as a whole correlates .81 with measures of nonverbal intelligence.

BIBLIOGRAPHY:

Berman, A. "The Problem of Assessing Cerebral Dominance and Its Relationship to Intelligence." *Cortex,* 1971, *7,* 372-386.

Berman, A. "Reliability of Perceptual-Motor Laterality Tasks." *Perceptual and Motor Skills,* 1973, *36,* 599-605.

# KDK-OSERETSKY TESTS OF MOTOR DEVELOPMENT

AUTHORS: Keith M. Kershner, Russell A. Dusewicz, and John R. Kershner

AGE: Preschool to adult

VARIABLE: Motor development

TYPE OF MEASURE: Test

SOURCE FROM WHICH MEASURE MAY BE OBTAINED: Russell A. Dusewicz, Learning Research Center, West Chester State College, West Chester, Pennsylvania 19380.

DESCRIPTION OF MEASURE: The KDK-Oseretsky Tests are based on the original Oseretsky Tests of Motor Development, which, although revised several times, still remained cumbersome, time-consuming, and in need of standardization of procedure and interpretation. The present instrument was designed to overcome these disadvantages and to provide a viable test for research and clinical use. The KDK tests, developed on a sample of mentally retarded children, measure the following major areas of motor development: general static coordination, general dynamic coordination, dynamic manual coordination, simultaneous voluntary movement, and speed. Each area has been given equal representation and weighting in the design of the test and is measured via a series of physical performance tasks scored on the basis of absolute ability to perform and time required to complete the task. Group administration is possible and permits optimally two testers to work with six Ss. The present version of the tests greatly reduces time required for administration by employing group techniques and by specifying individual dependencies. Where possible items have been ordered in an ascending series of dependence: patterns of prerequisites that must be performed for success on subsequent items in those patterns.

As examples, three representative tasks are given below, from the areas general static coordination, dynamic manual coordination, and simultaneous voluntary movement, respectively.

1. *Task*—Stand on one foot: Stand with full weight of body on one foot only, hands on hips, eyes open. Then repeat using other foot.
14. *Task*—Balancing yardstick horizontally on forefinger: Balance a yardstick on the broad side, horizontally with the side of one forefinger, the forefinger being extended from an otherwise fisted hand whose palm is positioned perpendicular to the floor.
5. *Task*—Tap alternate forefingers with corresponding feet: With hands on knees tap forefingers with corresponding feet as feet are tapped in an alternating manner on floor. Thus, fingers are tapped in the same pattern with corresponding feet.

RELIABILITY AND VALIDITY: None reported.

BIBLIOGRAPHY:

Kershner, K. M., and Dusewicz, R. A. "KDK-Oseretsky Tests of Motor Development." *Perceptual and Motor Skills*, 1970, *30*, 202.

*Prepared by Russell A. Dusewicz*

# LANYON STUTTERING SEVERITY (SS) SCALE

AUTHOR: Richard I. Lanyon

AGE: 14 years and up

VARIABLE: Severity of stuttering

TYPE OF MEASURE: Questionnaire

SOURCE FROM WHICH MEASURE MAY BE OBTAINED: See Lanyon (1967).

DESCRIPTION OF MEASURE: The Lanyon Stuttering Severity (SS) Scale consists of sixty-four true-false items that were selected for their ability to discriminate (1) between fifty stutterers and fifty nonstutterers, and (2) among stutterers rated mild ($N = 14$), average ($N = 19$), or severe ($N = 17$) by speech clinicians who had known them for at least one month. The initial pool of 120 items represented a distillation of a larger number of items that had been prepared by six expert judges to cover comprehensively the total range of behaviors and attitudes that constitute the problem of stuttering. Four of the six judges were speech pathologists and five were stutterers; all had been associated with the University of Iowa Speech Clinic during 1960-1964. The stutterers were mainly college age and came from speech clinics in six states, while the nonstutterers were college undergraduates at Rutgers University. In order to develop a procedure to correct for defensiveness, twenty-eight items from the $K$ (defensiveness) and $L$ (lie) scales of the Minnesota Multiphasic Personality Inventory (MMPI) were also included in the initial item list. Since their use did not improve discrimination, however, they were not included in the final form of the scale. Of the sixty-four items, forty-six refer primarily to behavior and eighteen to attitudes. These categories may be further broken down as follows: for behaviors—general fluency (ten), avoidance (ten), effort (four), associated nonspeech behaviors (five), physical tension (six), lack of control (three), variability in stuttering (three), anxiety (two), and breathing difficulty (three); for attitudes—dissatisfaction (four), feelings of worry and handicap (five), identification as a stutterer (three), sensitivity (four), and feelings of difference (two). The mean SS score for the stutterers was 40.6 (*SD* 11.9), and for the nonstutterers 8.6 (*SD* 6.8). Based on the clinicians' ratings for these subjects, a score of 20-32 would be classified as mild, 33-44 as moderate, and 45-65 as severe.

As examples, the first fifteen items of the stuttering severity (SS) scale, with directions for scoring indicated in parentheses, are given below.

1. When I talk I often become short of breath (T)
2. When I have a hard time talking, I tend to look away from my listener. (T)
3. I am sensitive about my speech problem. (T)
4. I worry about the fact that I stutter. (T)
5. If I want to, I can be very fluent. (F)
6. There is something wrong with my speech. (T)
7. When I can't say a word, there are little tricks I can use to help me. (T)
8. People notice that I talk differently. (T)
9. I avoid meeting some people because I'm afraid I might stutter. (T)
10. If I did not stutter, I would probably speak much more than I do. (T)

11. I stutter more in some situations than in others. (T)

12. I tend to avoid introducing myself. (T)

13. Sometimes my jaws seem to lock together when I talk. (T)

14. Sometimes I avoid talking for fear of being nonfluent. (T)

15. My speech problem is preventing me from following my career. (T)

RELIABILITY AND VALIDITY: Validity of the SS scale was established initially by the rational selection of the item pool, which ensured content validity; and the use of an independent empirical criterion (clinicians' ratings) in selecting the final items. For cross-validation, the SS scale was administered to seventeen new stutterers and thirty-six comparable nonstutterers, all college students. The mean for the stutterers was 39.2 (SD 9.2) and for the nonstutterers 12.0 (SD 7.8). These distributions showed essentially no overlap. The original group of fifty stutterers was used to establish the reliability of the SS scale. Kuder-Richardson reliability was found to be .93. It should be noted that most of the items on the scale are keyed "true," thus presenting the possibility of acquiescence response-set bias. However, since the original item pool contained many "false" items, almost all of which failed to survive validation, it is considered that any acquiescence bias in the surviving items is minor compared with their predictive value.

BIBLIOGRAPHY:

Lanyon, R. I. "The Measurement of Stuttering Severity." *Journal of Speech and Hearing Research*, 1967, *10*, 836-843.

---

# LATERALITY DISCRIMINATION TEST

AUTHOR: Charles M. Culver

AGE: Adults and older children

VARIABLE: Ability to rapidly discriminate right and left body parts

TYPE OF MEASURE: Test

SOURCE FROM WHICH MEASURE MAY BE OBTAINED: Charles M. Culver, Department of Psychiatry, Dartmouth Medical School, Hanover, New Hampshire 03755. Cost: $10.00 per set of thirty-two cards.

DESCRIPTION OF MEASURE: This test of right-left discrimination was developed as one of a battery of instruments designed to measure spatial-perceptual abilities in adults and older children. The stimuli are thirty-two pictures of body parts mounted on unlined 3 X 5-inch index cards. All of the stimuli are body parts that can be assigned to the right or left side of the body; there are sixteen hands, eight feet, four eyes, and four ears. The subject is required to identify each picture verbally as "left" or "right" as quickly as possible. The examiner uses a stopwatch to time the latency of $S$'s responses as he is shown each card. $S$'s score has two components: the sum of his individual latencies for the thirty-two cards and an error score, in which he is penalized five extra seconds for each card on which he gives an incorrect response.

RELIABILITY AND VALIDITY: At an early stage of development of the test a total of fifty-two stimulus cards were employed. For the purpose of testing a group of fifty-one student nurses, these cards were divided into two sets that were administered separately toward the beginning and at the end of a one-hour session containing a variety of spatial-perceptual tests. There were twenty-eight cards in the first set and twenty-four in the second (the subsequent thirty-two-card form of the test included all the cards of the second set and eight from the first). The Spearman rank correlation between these alternate forms of the test was .80. For one freshman class ($N = 81$), the odd-even Spearman rank correlation coefficient was .83; for the other ($N = 76$) it was .86. Culver (1969) presents some evidence for construct validity.

BIBLIOGRAPHY:

Bakan, P., and Putnam, W. "Right-Left Discrimination and Brain Lateralization." *Archives of Neurology,* 1974, *30,* 334-335.

Culver, C. M. "Test of Right-Left Discrimination." *Perceptual and Motor Skills,* 1969, *29,* 863-867.

Culver, C. M., Cohen, S. I., Silverman, A. J., and Shmavonian, B. M. "Cognitive Structuring, Field Dependence-Independence, and the Psychophysiological Response to Perceptual Isolation." In J. Wortis (Ed.), *Recent Advances in Biological Psychiatry.* Vol. 6. New York: Plenum Press, 1963.

Culver, C. M., and Dunham, F. "Birth Order and Spatial-Perceptual Ability: Negative Note." *Perceptual and Motor Skills,* 1969, *28,* 301-302.

Culver, C. M., and King, F. W. "Neuropsychological Assessment of Undergraduate Marihuana and LSD Users." *Archives of General Psychiatry,* 1974, *31,* 707-711.

---

## LEFT-RIGHT DISCRIMINATION TEST (LRDT)

AUTHORS: Daniel R. Boone and Thomas E. Prescott

AGE: 5 to 10 years

VARIABLE: Left-right discrimination

TYPE OF MEASURE: Test

SOURCE FROM WHICH MEASURE MAY BE OBTAINED: For procedure to follow in duplicating test plates and making the recording, see Boone and Prescott (1968).

For test tape, write Daniel R. Boone, Department of Speech and Hearing Sciences, University of Arizona, Tucson, Arizona 85721.

DESCRIPTION OF MEASURE: This forty-item left-right discrimination test is given by auditory tape (takes 2 minutes, 45 seconds) and is standardized on 600 normal school children aged 5 to 10. The child sits before a panel (15 × 28 inches) with colored circles and, following instructions on the recorded tape, points to the circle named. Examples of items are: "left red," "lower green," "red," "right yellow." The child's performance on left-right discrimination is then compared with test norms.

RELIABILITY AND VALIDITY: There appears to be a strong linear trend of increasing chronological age with decreasing left-right errors. Five-year-old children make many errors with only random ability to point to left and right correctly; 10-year-old children are similar to adults in left-right discrimination. A Winer trend analysis found a significant linear $F$ indicating that performance on the LRDT in relationship to chronological age is linear. Test reliability was developed after extensive item analysis. Only left-right items (seventeen) are scored; twenty-three items are retained as foil items. Test-retest and split-half reliability correlations are in excess of .90. The LRDT may be used as a downward extension of the same abilities tested on the Money Road Map Test; the LRDT is more sensitive in finding mild left-right confusions.

BIBLIOGRAPHY:

Boone, D. R., and Landes, B. A. "Left-Right Discrimination in Hemiplegic Patients." *Archives of Physical Medicine and Rehabilitation,* 1968, *49,* 533-537.
Boone, D. R., and Latas, W. F. "Left-Right Discrimination Problems in Neurologically Impaired Children." *University of Kansas Bulletin of Education,* 1966, *21,* 12-18.
Boone, D. R., and Prescott, T. E. "Development of Left-Right Discrimination in Normal Children." *Perceptual and Motor Skills,* 1968, *26,* 267-274.

---

## MIAMI IMITATIVE ABILITY TEST (MIAT)

AUTHORS: Rhoda J. Jacobs, Betty Jane Philips, and Robert J. Harrison

AGE: 30 to 72 months

VARIABLE: Stimulability

TYPE OF MEASURE: Structured interview

SOURCE FROM WHICH MEASURE MAY BE OBTAINED: See Jacobs, Philips, and Harrison (1970).

DESCRIPTION OF MEASURE: The MIAT is a device to evaluate the ability of the child to imitate the acoustic production and the articulatory placement for consonants. Twenty-four consonant sounds are presented in CV (consonant vowel) productions using the neutral vowel /ʌ/. Only the initial position is assessed, because a pilot study involving ten cleft-palate children indicated that production of these sounds remains consistent in the initial, medial, and final positions of syllables. The subject is instructed to "Watch and listen" as the examiner repeats each syllable three times to give the subject adequate opportunity to observe the production. After these stimulations, the subject is instructed, "Now you do it." His ability to imitate the articulatory placement and the acoustic production are scored separately. Responses are assigned 1 point if correct, ½ point if questionable, or 0 if incorrect. Both placement and production scores can range from 0 to 24 points. For visible sounds, placement is scored by direct observation of the articulators. In those instances in which the articulatory placement is not clearly visible, the examiner must judge the articulatory placement on limited visual assessment supplemented by the acoustic production.

The test is scored for articulatory placement and acoustic production separately as: correct (1), questionable (½), and incorrect (0). Criteria for correct articulatory placement are as follows for the first five of the twenty-four consonant sounds:

p, b    Lips approximated, then relaxed.
t, d    Elevate tip of tongue to contact alveolar ridge behind upper incisors.
k, g    Dorsum of tongue elevated to make contact with palate.
f, v    Lower lip contacts upper incisors.
θ, ð    Tongue tip elevated and protruded so that inferior surface rests on lower incisors and tip of dorsal surface contacts upper incisors.

RELIABILITY AND VALIDITY: Cleft-palate children were significantly inferior to the children without cleft palate in ability to imitate both the articulatory placement ($p = .001$) and the acoustic production ($p = .001$) of consonant sounds. Even by 72 months of age, the cleft-palate children did not gain the proficiency in these imitative skills of the 30-month-old children without clefts. The mean scores of the cleft-palate children at 72 months of age were 18.68 for articulatory placement and 16.77 for acoustic production, while those of the other children at 30 months were 20.64 and 19.71, respectively. High correlations were obtained between articulation errors and articulatory placement (.86) and between articulation errors and acoustic production scores (.89). This suggests that a stimulability test that focuses on ability to imitate consonant sounds in CV clusters may have utility as a screening test for articulation skills.

BIBLIOGRAPHY:

Jacobs, R. J., Philips, B. J., and Harrison, R. J. "A Stimulability Test for Cleft-Palate Children." *Journal of Speech and Hearing Disorders,* 1970, *35,* 354-360.

*Prepared by Robert J. Harrison*

# MOTOR DEVELOPMENT TEST

AUTHOR: Napoleon Wolański and Maria Zdańska-Brincken

AGE: 1 month to ambulation (9 to 16 months)

VARIABLE: Motor development

TYPE OF MEASURE: Test

SOURCE FROM WHICH MEASURE MAY BE OBTAINED: See Zdańska-Brincken and Wolański (1969) or Wolański and Zdańska-Brincken (1973)

DESCRIPTION OF MEASURE: The measure comprises thirty-four "tests" or items subdivided into sets that cover: (a) movements of the head and trunk, (b) emergence of the sitting position, (c) emergence of the ability to stand upright, and (d) development of locomotion.

The selection of tests was based on an analysis of scales gleaned from the literature. The thirty-four tests selected correspond to the successive stages of motor development that lead to an infant's assumption of an appropriate body posture as well as to his ability to move through space.

Four grids of motor development were developed by obtaining the age at which successive percentages of children (5, 15, 35, 65, 85, and 95 percents) reached a certain stage.

Each of the percentile grids presented can be used for the single evaluation of a child's motor development at a given age. The basic significance of this method, however, lies in the opportunity it presents to measure motor development in children who are examined more than once—that is, for measuring the *formation* of motor development. The specific developmental stages are shown on horizontal lines corresponding to the state of motor development reached by plotting the points corresponding to the ages at which the child achieves given stages in motor development. When these points are joined, the developmental curve covering the whole group of the child's motor achievements is revealed. These grids permit a ready comparison among children and a longitudinal picture of any one child.

As examples, the first items from each of the four sets are given below.

| Succes-sion | Stage symbol | Stage | Score |
|---|---|---|---|
| | | A. Development of head and trunk movements | |
| 1 | A-1 | The child lies prone on a hard mat, with his upper limbs partly bent at the elbows under his chest. He raises his head about 10 cm. above the base and holds it up for about a minute. He moves his shoulders back, raising the trunk slightly. | 13 |
| | | B. Development of the sitting position | |
| 3 | B-1 | The child lies supine. When he is pulled to a sitting position by his arms his head does not fall forward and does not wobble for a minute. | 20 |

| Succes-<br>sion | Stage<br>symbol | Stage | Score |
|---|---|---|---|
| | | C. Development of the standing position | |
| 10 | C-1 | The child is in a standing position, being held up under his arms with the examiner's thumbs on the child's chest just above the nipple line and his fingers on the child's back at shoulder-blade level. As the soles of the child's feet make contact with a hard surface he straightens his legs and partly supports his weight. | 41 |
| | | D. Development of locomotion | |
| 8 | D-1 | The child lies prone on a hard surface and turns over on his back, while watching a toy which is being shown to him. | 35 |

RELIABILITY AND VALIDITY: None reported.

BIBLIOGRAPHY:

Zdańska-Brincken, M., and Wolański, N. "A Graphic Method for the Evaluation of Motor Development in Infants." *Developmental Medicine and Child Neurology*, 1969, *11*, 228-241.
Wolański, N., and Zdańska-Brincken, M. "A New Method for the Evaluation of Motor Development of Infants." *Polish Psychological Bulletin*, 1973, *4*, 43-53.

*Prepared by Orval G. Johnson*

---

# ORIENTATION AND MOBILITY SCALE FOR YOUNG BLIND CHILDREN—SHORT FORM EXPERIMENTAL EDITION

AUTHOR: F. E. Lord

AGE: 3 to 12 years

VARIABLE: Skills in managing in one's environment

TYPE OF MEASURE: Rating scale

SOURCE FROM WHICH MEASURE MAY BE OBTAINED: See Lord (1967).

DESCRIPTION OF MEASURE: This scale contains twenty-four items relating to directions and turns, movement in space, and self-help. Items have five levels of performance that the examiner checks. Norms expressed in percentage of children at each age level who performed the task are available. All subjects were blind or possessed only light perception and had no other limitations that might interfere with performing the task.

As examples, two of the four items from the directions and turns section are given below.

1. *Responds Correctly to a Command to Turn Left.*
   Procedure: Take child to open doorway. Say, "Let's look at this doorway." Allow him to explore the opening. Examiner stands approximately three feet from opening. Say, "Now come back here where I am. I want you to go out of the door and turn left. Keep walking until I tell you when to stop." Score: Makes left turn correctly. Walks several steps.
4. *Travels a Route with One Turn Described in Terms of Cardinal Directions.*
   Procedure: Use a short hallway in school building or the sidewalk in front of the building. Face the child to the south. Say, "You are now facing south. Walk until I say, 'turn'—then turn to the east." Score: Child makes correct directional turn.

RELIABILITY AND VALIDITY: Reliability coefficient (internal consistency method) for the short form was .91. No validity data are available.

BIBLIOGRAPHY:

Brown, G. D., and Jessen, W. E. "Evaluation of an Orientation, Mobility and Living Skills Workshop for Blind Children." *Exceptional Children,* 1968, *35,* 239-240.

Lord, F. E. *Preliminary Standardization of a Scale of Orientation and Mobility Skills of Young Blind Children.* Project No. 6-2464. Washington, D.C.: U.S. Department of Health, Education and Welfare, Office of Education, Bureau of Research, 1967. ERIC document no. ED 024 198.

Lord, F. E. "Development of Scales for the Measurement of Orientation and Mobility of Young Blind Children." *Exceptional Children,* 1969, *36,* 77-81.

---

# PACIFIC STATE MODIFICATION OF HEAD'S HAND, EYE, EAR TEST

AUTHORS: Thomas S. Ball, Clara Lee Edgar, and Michael Maloney

AGE: Kindergarten and up

VARIABLE: Kephart's concept of laterality

TYPE OF MEASURE: Test

SOURCE FROM WHICH MEASURE MAY BE OBTAINED: See Ball and Edgar (1967) and Maloney, Ball, and Edgar (1970).

DESCRIPTION OF MEASURE: The child is seated opposite the examiner and asked to imitate him in touching an eye or an ear with one or the other hand. The child is instructed simply to watch carefully and to do everything the examiner does. The examiner holds each gesture until the child initiates his response, and he must not look at the correct terminal point of the child's movement. This modified version of Head's (1925) Test retains the original sixteen items. These are divided into parallel halves and their order independently randomized within each half. Eight of the sixteen items involve imitation of ipsilateral movements, for example, touching the right eye with the right hand; and the remaining eight involve cross-lateral movements, for example, touching the left ear with the right hand. The item sequence for the modified version is as follows: 1 and 10, right ear with right hand; 2 and 16, left eye with left hand; 3 and 11, right eye with right hand; 4 and 13, left ear with right hand; 5 and 9, left eye with right hand; 6 and 14, right eye with left hand; 7 and 15, left ear with left hand; 8 and 12, right ear with left hand.

A normal adult is expected to transpose the examiner's right and left in terms of his own body, but we found that the normal kindergarten child gives a *mirror* imitation. For example, if the examiner touches his left ear with his left hand, the adult subject will do the same, whereas the 5-year-old will touch his right ear with his right hand. If credit were given only for an adult response, not a single perfect score of 16 would have been found in either the pre- or posttraining evaluations of our thirty subjects. However, fifteen perfect mirror imitations were encountered (three pre- and twelve posttraining). Since mirror imitations were developmentally normal for our subjects, they were counted as correct. A single transposed response in a series of mirror responses was counted as an error, even though it was technically correct. Rarely was a child's failure on an item limited solely to a confusion of ear and eye, for example, the child touching his right ear when he should have touched his right eye. In the few cases where this occurred, the response was counted as correct. Spontaneous corrections were also counted as correct. In Maloney, Ball, and Edgar (1970) photographs of the test items were used to promote standardization and to decrease training contamination in the testing situation.

RELIABILITY AND VALIDITY: For the Ball and Edgar (1967) version, there was a split-half reliability of .79, and one of .72 for the Maloney, Ball, and Edgar (1970) version. Test-retest reliability estimate based upon a ten-week test-retest interval was .80. Stability coefficient computed for the low-treatment control subjects over a ten-month interval was .76. Regarding construct validity, Ball and Edgar (1967) showed how this measure is operationally related to those deficiencies of integration between the two sides of the body that clinically define the problem of inadequate laterality as conceptualized by Kephart. Midline translation problems measured by this test are associated with organicity in adults and children, and with Benton's right-left discrimination battery. In Maloney, Ball, and Edgar (1970) experimental subjects were still significantly higher on the eye, hand, and ear test seven-and-a-half months after the conclusion of sensorimotor training.

BIBLIOGRAPHY:

Ball, T. S. "Note on 'Effect of Motor Development on Body Image Scores for Institutionalized Mentally Retarded Children.' " *American Journal of Mental Deficiency,* 1974, *79,* 225-226.
Ball, T. S., and Edgar, C. L. "The Effectiveness of Sensory-Motor Training in Promoting Generalized Body Image Development." *Journal of Special Education,* 1967, *1,* 387-395.

Head, H. *Aphasia and Related Disorders of Speech.* Vol. 1. New York: Cambridge University Press, 1925.

Maloney, M. P., Ball, T. S., and Edgar, C. L. "Analysis of the Generalizability of Sensory-Motor Training." *American Journal of Mental Deficiency,* 1970, *74,* 458-69.

---

# PATTERN WALKING TEST

AUTHOR: Barbara K. Keogh

AGE: 5 to 12 years

VARIABLE: Visual-motor spatial organization

TYPE OF MEASURE: Test

SOURCE FROM WHICH MEASURE MAY BE OBTAINED: Barbara K. Keogh, University of California Graduate School of Education, Los Angeles, California 90024.

DESCRIPTION OF MEASURE: This is a research and experimental technique for investigation of visuomotor and spatial organization of children. It is not appropriately used for individual clinical assessment of children. The test consists of ten designs or geometric figures, five simple figures (circle, square, triangle, and so forth) and five complex figures (combinations of the simple figures). Each figure is presented individually in a predetermined order. The child is asked to copy or "draw" the design by walking. Walking conditions are varied to take into account total space available, number of visual cues available on a walking surface, and the like. Each walked pattern is scored 1 to 4, allowing for a single total score and for analyses by individual designs.

RELIABILITY AND VALIDITY: Interrater reliability of scoring for total score ranges from .70 to .90 depending upon the walking condition. Reliabilities for individual figures are more variable, but, with the exception of one design under one condition, are all statistically significant. Relationships between children's walking and drawing of the same figures tend to be moderate to low and nonsignificant. In most cases drawing scores are better than walking scores. Differences across age, by sex, and by IQ have been found consistently.

BIBLIOGRAPHY:

Keogh, B. K. "Pattern Walking Under Three Conditions of Available Visual Cues." *American Journal of Mental Deficiency,* 1969, *74,* 376-381.

Keogh, B. K. "Pattern Copying Under Three Conditions of an Expanded Spatial Field." *Developmental Psychology,* 1971, *4,* 25-31.

Keogh, B. K., and Donlon, M. G. "Field Dependence, Impulsivity, and Learning Disabilities." *Journal of Learning Disabilities,* 1972, *5,* 331-336.

Keogh, B. K., and Keogh, J. F. "Pattern Copying and Pattern Walking Performance of Normal and Educationally Subnormal Boys." *American Journal of Mental Deficiency,* 1967, *71,* 1009-1013.

Keogh, B. K., and Keogh, J. F. "Pattern Walking: A Dimension of Visuomotor Performance." *Exceptional Children,* 1968, *34,* 617-618.

## PERFORMANCE TEST OF SELECTED POSITIONAL CONCEPTS FOR VISUALLY HANDICAPPED CHILDREN

AUTHOR: Everett W. Hill

AGE: 6 to 14 years

VARIABLE: Selected spatial concepts (positional terms)

TYPE OF MEASURE: Performance test

SOURCE FROM WHICH MEASURE MAY BE OBTAINED: Association for Education of the Visually Handicapped, 919 Walnut Street, Philadelphia, Pennsylvania 19107.

DESCRIPTION OF MEASURE: This seventy-five-item performance test is divided into three parts, and selected positional-spatial concepts are tested in different ways in each part. In the first part, the child identifies the location of his various body parts as he follows spoken directions to move and position those parts. In the second part, the child is tested in the same way for "self in relation to environmental objects." The third part consists of manipulating and moving objects in relation to each other. An administration and scoring manual is available. The mean for thirty visually handicapped children aged 7 to 9 was 100; for fifty visually handicapped children aged 9 to 14, the mean was 110. This measure is designed primarily to be used as a basic assessment tool for mobility instructors, classroom teachers, EMR resource teachers, and others working with visually handicapped children.

As examples, the first three items from each of Part I, II, and III, to be scored 0, 1, or 2, are given below.

*Part I*
1. Place your hand on your *face.*
2. Touch the *front* of your leg.
3. Place your hand in *front* of your face.
*Part II*
1. Place yourself *in front* of the chair.
2. Turn yourself, if necessary, so your whole body is *facing* the chair.
3. Put your hands *in front* of the chair.
*Part III*
1. Put the block *in front of* the cup.

2. Put the stick *in back* of the block.
3. Put the block *behind* the cup.

RELIABILITY AND VALIDITY: None reported.

BIBLIOGRAPHY:

Hill, E. W. "The Formation of Concepts Involved in Body Position in Space." *Education for the Visually Handicapped,* 1970, *2,* 112-115.
Hill, E. W. "The Formation of Concepts Involved in Body Position in Space, Part II." *Education for the Visually Handicapped,* 1971, *3,* 21-25.

---

## PPP COPYING TEST

AUTHORS: Eleanor L. Levine, Carol A. Fineman, and Genevieve McG. Donlon

AGE: 6 to 12 years

VARIABLE: Fine motor ability, copying skills

TYPE OF MEASURE: Test

SOURCE FROM WHICH MEASURE MAY BE OBTAINED: Dorothy L. Ozburn, Exceptional Child Education, Dade County Public Schools, Room 104-A Lindsey Hopkins Building, 1410 N.E. 2nd Avenue, Miami, Florida 33132; or Eleanor L. Levine, Project Director, FLRS-South, 47 Zamora Avenue, Coral Gables, Florida 33134.

DESCRIPTION OF MEASURE: The PPP Copying Test was developed in connection with the *Prescriptive Profile Procedure for Children with Learning Disabilities* (Levine, Fineman, and Donlon, 1973). It is intended to assess pure fine motor copying skills in an untimed task involving no memory function. Reversals, orientations, and other indicators of perceptual motor dysfunction may be revealed. This test can be administered individually or to an entire class. Two points are given for each figure that is an accurate replica of the given form. One point is given for slight variation and zero points for complete discrepancies. The PPP Copying Test was standardized on 150 elementary school children aged 5 to 12, including forty-five children with specific learning disabilities.

RELIABILITY AND VALIDITY: None reported.

BIBLIOGRAPHY:

Levine, E. L., Fineman, C. A., and Donlon, G. McG. *Prescriptive Profile Procedure for Children with Learning Disabilities.* ESEA Title VI-B, P. L. 91230. Miami, Florida: Dade County Public Schools, 1973.

*Prepared by Eleanor L. Levine and Carol A. Fineman*

# PPP WRITING TEST

AUTHORS: Eleanor L. Levine, Carol A. Fineman, and Genevieve McG. Donlon

AGE: 6 to 12 years

VARIABLE: Near-point copying ability, fine-motor skills

TYPE OF MEASURE: Test

SOURCE FROM WHICH MEASURE MAY BE OBTAINED: Dorothy L. Ozburn, Exceptional Child Education, Dade County Public Schools, Room 104-A Lindsey Hopkins Building, 1410 N.E. 2nd Avenue, Miami, Florida 33132; or Eleanor L. Levine, Project Director, FLRS-South, 47 Zamora Avenue, Coral Gables, Florida 33134.

DESCRIPTION OF MEASURE: The PPP Writing Test was developed in connection with the *Prescriptive Profile Procedure for Children with Learning Disabilities* (Levine, Fineman, and Donlon, 1973). It enables teachers to pinpoint the level of writing functioning a child has attained based solely on his near-point copying ability. The test progresses developmentally from shapes, to partial letters, to lower and upper manuscript letters, to lower and upper cursive letters, to single and multiple numerals, to single two-letter words up to single six-letter words (manuscript then cursive), to a manuscript sentence, and finally to a cursive sentence. In scoring, 1 point is credited for each figure or group of figures in a given square that is an adequate replica of the sample, taking the child's age into consideration. Five points is given for a correct replication of a total sentence. One point is taken off for each inaccurate letter up to five errors, in a complete sentence. Ten points may be earned for each Section I-VI, for a total possible score of sixty points. Fifty points or above is considered adequate performance, although the most important information for the teacher is the specifics of the child's writing production, which can help her decide on the appropriate writing instruction for the child. The PPP Writing Test was standardized on 150 elementary school children, aged 6 to 12, including forty-five children with specific learning disabilities.

RELIABILITY AND VALIDITY: None reported.

BIBLIOGRAPHY:

Levine, E. L., Fineman, C. A., and Donlon, G. McG. *Prescriptive Profile Procedure for Children with Learning Disabilities.* ESEA Title VI-B, P. L. 91230. Miami, Florida: Dade County Public Schools, 1973.

*Prepared by Eleanor L. Levine and Carol A. Fineman*

# PROVO MULTIPLE-CHOICE TEST OF FIGURE DESIGNS

AUTHORS: Bert P. Cundick, E. Kent Pilling, and David G. Weight

AGE: 5 years to adult

VARIABLE: Perceptual dysfunction associated with brain injury

TYPE OF MEASURE: Test

SOURCE FROM WHICH MEASURE MAY BE OBTAINED: The current sets are all done by hand from templates. Only eight copies have been made. If further development is successful, other copies will be mass-produced. Information can be obtained by writing Bert P. Cundick, Department of Psychology, Brigham Young University, Provo, Utah 84601.

DESCRIPTION OF MEASURE: The test contains ninety-six sets of geometric design cards. Each set is made up of a stimulus and a choice card. Each stimulus card has an inked geometric design drawn upon it. Each choice card displays four possible geometric designs drawn in ink, one of which duplicates the size, shape, and orientation of the choice-card design. The three alternate-choice designs contain other forms, distortions in form size or shape, or rotations or reversals of the original design. Differences also occur in card colors from the stimulus to the choice card, and overlays are used on some of the cards. For each administration the subject is shown the stimulus card for 3 seconds and then given the choice card and asked, "Choose the design that is shaped most like the one that you saw." Three trial cards are given to ensure that the subject can follow the directions.

RELIABILITY AND VALIDITY: This test is still in the development stage. Prior testings with various groups typically yielded reliabilities above .9. Half of the items have been used in a study utilizing twenty-three pairs of matched brain-damaged and normal children. These forty-eight designs were drawn from an original sample of 106 designs and were found to discriminate between the two groups at the < .08 level.

BIBLIOGRAPHY:

Cundick, B. P., and Rovison, L. R. "Performance of Medically Diagnosed Brain-damaged Children and Control Ss." *Perceptual and Motor Skills,* 1972, *34,* 307-310.

Weight, D. G., Pilling, E. K., and Cundick, B. P. "Comparison of Visual-Discrimination Ability of Brain-Injured and Non-Brain-Injured Children of Normal Intelligence." *Perceptual and Motor Skills,* 1975, *40,* 467-470.

# RECOVERY FROM STUTTERING PARENT INTERVIEW FORM

AUTHORS: Sally Davis Lankford and Eugene B. Cooper

AGE: Adult

VARIABLE: Parent knowledge of child's recovery from stuttering

TYPE OF MEASURE: Questionnaire

SOURCE FROM WHICH MEASURE MAY BE OBTAINED: See Lankford and Cooper (1974).

DESCRIPTION OF MEASURE: Recall studies concerning recovery from stuttering suggest that as many as four out of five stutterers recover spontaneously. The data obtained in these studies have been questioned because they are based on the recall of the subjects without validation. This parental questionnaire was developed to attempt to assess the accuracy of the perceptions of junior and senior high school children who had reported that they had recovered from stuttering. There are twenty items with varying response formats. They deal with such variables as age of inception and cessation, family atmosphere, and responses to the child's stuttering behavior.

As examples, eight selected items of the twenty on the interview form are given below.

1. Do you feel that your child stuttered? (yes, no)
2. Do you feel that he has stopped stuttering? (yes, no)
5. What was the level of the stuttering when it began? (mild, moderate, severe)
6. What was the level of the stuttering at its worst? (mild, moderate, severe)
7. At what age was the stuttering at its worst? (3-6, 7-10, 11-14, 15-18)
12. What was the child's emotional reaction to the stuttering? (unaware, fear, aware but unconcerned, embarassment, shame, other)
17. Did you offer suggestions or advice to your child as to how he might overcome his speaking difficulty? (yes, no)
18. What were the suggestions you offered? (slow down, take a breath, think before you speak, start over, other)

RELIABILITY AND VALIDITY: None reported.

BIBLIOGRAPHY:

Lankford, S. D., and Cooper, E. B. "Recovery from Stuttering as Viewed by Parents of Self-Diagnosed Recovered Stutterers." *Journal of Communication Disorders,* 1974, *7,* 171-180.

*Prepared by Eugene B. Cooper*

## RHYTHM PATTERNS: A TEST OF MOVEMENT CLOSURE

AUTHOR: Elizabeth Y. Sharp

AGE: 7 to 9 years, deaf children

VARIABLE: Movement closure

TYPE OF MEASURE: Test

SOURCE FROM WHICH MEASURE MAY BE OBTAINED: Elizabeth Y. Sharp, 5642 Mina Vista, Tucson, Arizona 85718. Cost: $.20 plus postage.

DESCRIPTION OF MEASURE: This test is based on the premise that since speech is movement and has rhythm, the speech reader fills in movements that are either missed or not visible. Therefore, speech reading ability should be related to the ability to complete movement patterns. The test, developed for young deaf children, consists of a demonstration pattern of gestures and six test patterns of gestures of increasing length. The subject is allowed two trials on each pattern. The demonstration pattern, for example, is: clap twice, snap fingers twice, clap twice. Pattern six, the most difficult item, has eight separate movements, as compared with three in the demonstration pattern.

RELIABILITY AND VALIDITY: None reported. Sharp (1970) demonstrated that good speech readers are superior to poor speech readers on this test of movement closure.

BIBLIOGRAPHY:

Moores, D. F. "Application of 'Cloze' Procedures to the Assessment of Psycholinguistic Abilities of the Deaf." Unpublished doctoral dissertation. University of Illinois, Urbana, 1967.

Sharp, E. Y. "The Relationship of Visual Closure to Speechreading Among Deaf Children." Unpublished doctoral dissertation. University of Arizona, Tucson, 1970.

Sharp, E. Y. "The Relationship of Visual Closure to Speechreading." *Exceptional Children,* 1972, *38,* 729-734.

---

## SCORED NEUROLOGICAL EXAM

AUTHOR: Abbott Laboratories

AGE: 6 to 12 years

VARIABLE: Neurological soft signs

TYPE OF MEASURE: Scored rating scale

SOURCE FROM WHICH MEASURE MAY BE OBTAINED: Medical Services Department, Abbott Laboratories, 14th and Sheridan Road, North Chicago, Illinois 60064.

DESCRIPTION OF MEASURE: This Scored Neurological Examination is designed to assist the observer in determining whether neurological soft signs are present in a child. The examiner demonstrates every task to be performed while giving the verbal instructions. The time usually required to perform this test is 15 to 20 minutes. The measure is comprised of forty-three items, most of which are scored on a 4-point scale.

As examples, the first two of the forty-three items on the exam are given below.

1. Finger to Nose. "I want you to touch a finger to your nose. Begin with your arm out here." (Extend the arm laterally with the hand in a loose fist, index finger extended as pointer.) "Now do like this." (Make a wide sweep medially to touch the nose.)
   Score: 1–Smoothly and accurately performed.
          2–Slowly, jerkily, and missing the target, then correcting. (If 10 seconds pass with no attempt, instruct and demonstrate again.)
          3–Same as 2; but correcting only after encouragement or a repeat instruction and demonstration.
          4–Same as 3; but without correcting target error. If the child simply does not do the test, no score is given; instead, a straight line is drawn across the four scoring blanks.
2. Contralateral Finger to Nose. "Now do the other hand." (Demonstrate again.)

RELIABILITY AND VALIDITY: None reported.

BIBLIOGRAPHY:

Close, J. "Scored Neurological Examination." *Psychopharmacology Bulletin,* 1973, Special Issue, 142-150.

*Prepared by John G. Page*

---

## SELECTED DESIGNS

AUTHOR: George Siskind

AGE: 13 years to adult

VARIABLE: Screening device for cerebral dysfunction

TYPE OF MEASURE: Design-copying test

SOURCE FROM WHICH MEASURE MAY BE OBTAINED: George Siskind, Psychology Department, Larue D. Carter Hospital, 1315 West 10 Street, Indianapolis, Indiana

46202; or from the American Documentation Institute Publications Project, Photo Duplication Service, Library of Congress, Washington, D.C., 20540. Request Document no. 9066. Cost: $1.25 for photocopy or 35 mm microfilm of scoring guide.

DESCRIPTION OF MEASURE: The evaluation for possible cerebral dysfunction depends on the quality of performance in copying three geometric designs. One consists of two intersecting planes of a cube, one is an opaque cube, and the third is a transparent cube. Scoring for adequate performance is done by comparison with a scoring guide with particular attention to angles on the right sides of the designs. Administration and scoring of the Selected Designs typically requires 8 to 10 minutes.

RELIABILITY AND VALIDITY: A group of eighty protocols—thirty-five from adult psychiatric patients whose diagnosis included cerebral dysfunction (established by medical, neurological evidence), thirty-five from adult psychiatric patients for whom there was no suspicion of cerebral dysfunction, and ten from college students whose grades indicated they were performing adequately—were scored by two secretaries using the scoring guide. Two of the unsophisticated judges correctly identified thirty-one of thirty-five protocols. False positives were 4, 4, and 2 for an average error of 8 percent. A group of fifty adult patients of Carter Hospital were diagnosed as having at least minimal cerebral dysfunction on the basis of performance on the Selected Designs. For this group of fifty, there was independent confirmation, not involving psychological tests, of forty-four cases (88-percent correct identification). A group of fifty-two adolescent patients, aged 13 to 18, were tested with the Selected Designs. The criteria for cerebral dysfunction (abnormal EEG, or history of injury or insult) were present in thirty-two of the fifty-two patients. Using the scoring guide, two unsophisticated judges correctly identified 77 percent and 79 percent of the protocols with four and five false positives. A study of senior citizens, aged 51 to 84 ($N = 61$), indicated that caution must be used when interpreting the performance of this group on the Selected Designs. From unpublished research and clinical use there is evidence that people who experience difficulty in correctly copying the designs can correctly copy segments of the designs involving three lines and two enclosed angles. They are also able to recognize and indicate the points of difficulty.

BIBLIOGRAPHY:

Siskind, G. "Selected Designs: A Screening Device for the Detection of Cerebral Dysfunction." *Perceptual and Motor Skills*, 1966, *23*, 811-813.
Siskind, G. "Selected Designs: Note on Further Research." *Perceptual and Motor Skills*, 1970, *31*, 317-318.

# STANDARD MANUSCRIPT SCALES FOR GRADES 1, 2, AND 3

AUTHOR: D. R. Bezzi

AGE: 5 to 8 years

VARIABLE: Rate and quality of manuscript writing

TYPE OF MEASURE: Rating scales

SOURCE FROM WHICH MEASURE MAY BE OBTAINED: D. R. Bezzi, College of Education, Box 28, Wichita State University, Wichita, Kansas 67208. Cost: One set of scales, manual, and rate norm table, $3.00.

DESCRIPTION OF MEASURE: These standardized scales afford a means whereby the teacher, pupil, and administrator may evaluate with a high degree of accuracy the manuscript handwriting (both quality and rate) of any pupil or groups of pupils in grades 1, 2, and 3. In scoring for quality, there are three separate scales, one for each grade. There are five standards ranging from low-quality to high-quality scaling for each grade. To measure the quality of any child's samples, compare it with the lowest quality of the scale for the particular grade in which the child is enrolled, move the child's sample up the scale until it reflects the quality of the standard sample, thus arriving at a level of quality. The rate-norm table below shows the number of letters written per minute.

| Grade | Rate Grade F | Rate Grade D | Rate Grade C | Rate Grade B | Rate Grade A |
|-------|-----|------|------|------|------|
| Grade 1 | 0-7 | 8-12 | 13-20 | 21-33 | 34 and up |
| Grade 2 | 8-10 | 11-18 | 19-25 | 26-37 | 38 and up |
| Grade 3 | 11-14 | 15-21 | 22-33 | 34-52 | 53 and up |

The rate norms are also expressed in raw scores, percentiles, and T-scores. The speed score is simply the number of letters written per minute. Directions for administration and quality scales for grades 1, 2, and 3 are provided in the test manual.

RELIABILITY AND VALIDITY: Random stratified sampling was employed to select 130 schools. The scales are constructed from a wide sampling of children in each grade; 7,212 samples were secured, representing a statistical chance sampling by population of schools in all states. The scaling follows the statistical procedure recommended by Thorndike (1910). The only assumption in scaling for quality where there is no objective measure is that normal distribution of quality exists in each grade. Consequently fifty representative samples from each grade were selected. A select group of teachers from each grade rated the fifty samples into five degrees of quality. Five representative specimens were chosen from these ratings. The five representative specimens for each grade appear in the quality scale for that specific grade.

BIBLIOGRAPHY:

Bezzi, D. R. "A Standardized Manuscript Scale for Grades I, II, and III." Unpublished doctoral dissertation. University of Oklahoma, Norman, Oklahoma, 1956.

Bezzi, D. R. "A Standardized Manuscript Scale for Grades 1, 2, and 3." *Journal of Educational Research*, 1962, *55*, 339-340.

Thorndike, E. L. "Handwriting." *Teachers College Record*, 1910, *11*, 78-80.

---

# TEACHING RESEARCH MOTOR-DEVELOPMENT SCALE

AUTHORS: H. D. Bud Fredericks, Victor L. Baldwin, Philip Doughty, and L. James Walter

AGE: Moderately and severely retarded children, preschool to high school

VARIABLE: Motor development

TYPE OF MEASURE: Motor-proficiency tests

SOURCE FROM WHICH MEASURE MAY BE OBTAINED: See Fredericks and others (1972).

DESCRIPTION OF MEASURE: This measure was developed by its authors as a downward extension of the Lincoln-Oseretsky Motor Development Scale. The materials and equipment for administering the test are either standard materials available in most classrooms or materials that are readily procurable, and equipment that can be readily constructed from the descriptions and pictures provided in the manual. According to the authors, the measure is most useful for charting the motor-development progress of retarded children. The authors' position is that norms are not appropriate for this measure. The measure consists of fifty-one activities or items, of which the following are examples: standing on tiptoes with eyes closed, jumping a bar, walking forward on staggered mats, touching fingertips, loosening and opening hands alternately, placing ten match sticks in a box, winding thread, tracing mazes, cutting a circle, bouncing ball and catching with one hand, throwing the ball at a target, hanging from pull-up bars, performing push-ups from knees, and running for a distance of fifty feet. Each activity or item is described with the following format: equipment, number of trials, directions, scoring criteria, and points.

As an example, one of the activities from the test is given below.

C-2 Jumping a Bar: a. Ankle height.
                          b. Between ankle and knee.
                          c. Knee height.
Equipment: A bar 4 feet long and two poles mounted on plywood stands 1 foot square, with 2-inch nails placed on the side of poles at each 6 inches of height with 1¼ inches of the head side of the nail protruding.
Number of Trials: Two per height (if necessary).
Directions: The bar should be mounted on the nails of the two poles to achieve the desired height so that the bar is even with the ankles, between the ankles

and knees, or even with the knees. *S* should jump with both feet together and the knees should flex at the same time as in a standing broad jump. *S* should jump without the feet touching the bar.

Scoring Criteria: Success if *S* completes each jump keeping feet together without touching the bar.

Points for Each of the Three Heights: Success on first or second trial = 3 points. Failure on the first and second trial = 0 points.

RELIABILITY AND VALIDITY: None reported.

BIBLIOGRAPHY:

Fredericks, H. D., Baldwin, V. L., Doughty, P., and Walter, L. J. *The Teaching Research Motor-Development Scale for Moderately and Severely Retarded Children.* Springfield, Illinois: C. C Thomas, 1972.

McGee, J., Fredericks, H. D., and Baldwin, V. L. *Showing Progress: A Systematic Evaluation of Oregon's Program for the Trainable Retarded.* Joint publication (R-139), Mental Health Division/Teaching Research Division, Oregon State System of Higher Education, Corvallis, n.d.

*Prepared by Orval G. Johnson*

---

# TEMPORAL-SPATIAL CONCEPT SCALE (TST)

AUTHOR: Robert R. Hartigan

AGE: 9 to 18 years

VARIABLE: Ability to deal with temporal-spatial problems

TYPE OF MEASURE: Test

SOURCE FROM WHICH MEASURE MAY BE OBTAINED: Robert R. Hartigan, Rural Route 2, Findlay, Ohio 45840.

DESCRIPTION OF MEASURE: The test consists of three parts. Laterality (Part I) contains twenty-six items measuring ability to deal with laterality on a conceptual level. These items involve the egocentric-personal space and the progressive variation of the notion of left and right. Space (Part II), which is divided into two categories, contains twenty-nine items dealing with space on the universal and on the abstract level. The first is made up of items dealing with geographic compass direction and right and left orientation. The second deals with distance and displacement. Time (Part III) contains thirty-one items dealing with temporal concepts and fifteen divided into two general categories. The first category deals with situations involving hours and minutes; the second deals with days, months, and years. There are also items that require a combination of space and time, for example, those dealing with the international date-line and the gaining and losing of time in travel.

RELIABILITY AND VALIDITY: The TST was used with 2,383 parochial school students from diverse socioeconomic backgrounds. Racial distribution was: 23 percent Mexican-American, 6.7 percent Puerto Rican, .3 percent black, and 70 percent white monolingual. Means, ranges, standard deviations, and standard errors for means of part and whole scores are provided, as are item analyses and t-tests of differences between geographic and cultural groups. Some correlations are provided between TST and other tests, and reliability ranges from .75 to .99.

BIBLIOGRAPHY:

Hartigan, R. R., and Fuller, G. B. "A Temporal-Spatial Concept Scale." *Journal of Clinical Psychology,* 1964, *20,* 478-483.
Hartigan, R. R. "A Temporal-Spatial Concept Scale: A Developmental Study." *Journal of Clinical Psychology,* 1971, *27,* 221-223.

---

## WATTS ARTICULATION TEST FOR SCREENING (WATS)

AUTHORS: Shirley Ann Watts and Earlene Tash Paynter

AGE: 5½ to 8½ years

VARIABLE: Articulation

TYPE OF MEASURE: Test

SOURCE FROM WHICH MEASURE MAY BE OBTAINED: Limited copies for research purposes may be obtained from Earlene Tash Paynter, Speech and Hearing Clinic, Texas Tech University, Lubbock, Texas 79409.

DESCRIPTION OF MEASURE: The WATS is designed around a brightly colored picture of a farm scene mounted on a 16 X 20-inch board. The complete test, which includes the board and record charts, is carried in a large portfolio. There are forty-two sound elements elicited from twenty-eight stimulus words. Some of the stimulus words include the names of farm animals, colors, and parts of the body. The examiner presents several stimulus questions or statements to elicit spontaneous speech response and records the incorrect responses. Cutoff scores are provided for white children and for black children.

RELIABILITY AND VALIDITY: The WATS was administered twice to each of 180 white children (thirty males and thirty females at each of three age levels: 6, 7, and 8). The time interval between the two test administrations was one to two weeks. The

Pearson product-moment correlation was .95. One hundred and eighty black children were administered the WATS, and eighty-six of these children were also administered the Arizona Articulation Proficiency Scale (AAPS). To determine the validity of the cutoff scores for the WATS, a comparison was made of the test scores of those who were administered both tests. The AAPS and the WATS test scores were classified as indicative of "adequate" or "inadequate" articulatory performance. The test scores of each of eighty-six children receiving both tests were compared for agreement in classification. There was 87-percent agreement on classification of articulation by the WATS and the AAPS.

BIBLIOGRAPHY:

Hale, Y. M. "Standardization of the Watts Articulation Test for Screening on Anglo Children." Unpublished master's thesis. Texas Tech University, Lubbock, 1973.
Jones, K. E. "Standardization of the Watts Articulation Test for Screening with Black Children." Unpublished master's thesis. Texas Tech University, Lubbock, 1974.
Paynter, E. T., and Watts, S. A. "The Watts Articulation Test for Screening: An Evaluation of a Screening Test." *Perceptual and Motor Skills,* 1973, *36,* 721-722.
Watts, S. A. "The Watts Articulation Test for Screening: An Evaluation of a Screening Test." Unpublished master's thesis. Texas Tech University, Lubbock, 1971.

*Prepared by Earlene Tash Paynter*

---

## WISCONSIN MOTOR STEADINESS BATTERY

AUTHORS: Hallgrim Kløve and Charles G. Matthews

AGE: 5 years to adult

VARIABLE: Various parameters of motor performance

TYPE OF MEASURE: Apparatus

SOURCE FROM WHICH MEASURE MAY BE OBTAINED: Kløve-Matthews Psychological Test Equipment, 2768 Marshall Parkway, Madison, Wisconsin 53713.

DESCRIPTION OF MEASURE: The Wisconsin Motor Steadiness Battery consists of a control unit and various test boards. The control unit has a timer and an impulse counter. The control box also has a feature that permits audio feedback of the patient's motor performance. The control box is connected to the test boards with a wire. The patient operates a stylus. When the patient is off target, the control box will accumulate total time off target and the impulse counter will accumulate the number of times off target. Information about various motor functions will be obtained depending upon the type of test board used. The test board measures static steadiness, resting tremor, and kinetic steadiness parameters. The battery also has a test for fine visuomotor coordination (grooved pegboard) and tests for finger and foot oscillation. Normative data are available in Knights and Moule (1968).

RELIABILITY AND VALIDITY: See bibliography.

BIBLIOGRAPHY:

Daly, R. F., and Matthews, C. G. "Impaired Motor Function in XYY Males." *Neurology*, 1974, *24*, 655-658.

Kløve, H. "Validity of Neuropsychological Inferences in Children." Paper presented to the Children's Bureau Conference. Seattle, Washington, 1962.

Kløve, H. "Clinical Neuropsychology." In F. M. Forster (Ed.), *The Medical Clinics of North America.* New York: Saunders, 1963.

Knights, R., and Moule, A. "Normative and Reliability Data on Finger and Foot Tapping in Children." *Perception and Motor Skills,* 1967, *25,* 717.

Knights, R. M., and Moule, A. "Normative Data on the Motor Steadiness Battery for Children." *Perceptual and Motor Skills,* 1968, *26,* 643-650.

MacAndrew, J., Berkey, B., and Matthews, C. G. "The Effects of Dominant and Non-dominant Unilateral ECT as Compared to Bilateral ECT." *American Journal of Psychiatry,* 1967, *124,* 4.

Matthews, C. G., Cleeland, C. S., and Hopper, C. L. "Neuropsychological Patterns in Multiple Sclerosis." *Diseases of the Nervous System,* 1970, *31,* 161.

Norton, J. C., and Matthews, C. G. "Psychological Test Performance in Patients with Subtentorial Versus Supratentorial CNS Disease." *Diseases of the Nervous System,* 1972, *33,* 312-317.

# Group 6-b
## Sensory
## Perception

# AUDITORY-VISUAL RHYTHM PERCEPTION (AVRP)

AUTHOR: George H. McNinch

AGE: 4 to 8 years

VARIABLE: Oral to visual word correspondence

TYPE OF MEASURE: Performance test

SOURCE FROM WHICH MEASURE MAY BE OBTAINED: See McNinch and Hafner (1971).

DESCRIPTION OF MEASURE: The AVRP is used to evaluate the correspondence between spoken word patterns and visual displays that represent these aural patterns. The test consists of eleven multiple-choice items. Each test item (composed of the correct pattern and two foils) is displayed on a 4 × 6-inch card using ¼ × ½-inch blocks to compose the patterns. There is only one pattern set per card. The oral stimulus is given while S looks at the card. The AVRP is a linguistic modification of the Birch and Belmont Modal Equivalence Test.

Oral stimuli and visual response selections of the test are given below.

1. Help. (pause) Help.          . . / .. . / ..
2. Look at Spot.                . ... / ... / ... .
3. Sally said, (pause) Dick.    .. . / .. . / . . .
4. No, Spot. (pause) No, No.    . .. . / . . . . / ...
5. See Dick run.                .. . / ... / . ..
6. Run. (pause) Run now. (pause) Run.   .... / . .. . / ... ..
7. Come here, (pause) Spot.     ... / . .. / ... .
8. Sally said, (pause) Oh, Jane.   . . . . / ... . / ... . .
9. Dick did not go away.        ... .. / . ... .. / .....
10. Dick said, (pause) Look here Jane.   .. ... / . .... / .....
11. Stop. (pause) Stop now.     ... / . .. / . ..

RELIABILITY AND VALIDITY: Restricted reliability estimates (.79 and .63) for the measure are reported in McNinch and Hafner (1971) and McNinch, Palmatier, and Richmond (1972), respectively.

BIBLIOGRAPHY:

Birch, H. G., and Belmont, L. "Auditory-Visual Integration, Intelligence, and Reading Ability in School Children." *Perceptual and Motor Skills,* 1965, *20,* 295-305.

McNinch, G. H., and Hafner, L. "Systematic Evaluation of an Auditory Perceptual Skill Model in a Prereading Sample." *Perceptual and Motor Skills,* 1971, *33,* 387-394.

McNinch, G. H., Palmatier, R., and Richmond, M. "Auditory Perceptual Testing of Young Children." *Journal of Reading Behavior,* 1972, *4,* 120-128.

McNinch, G. H., and Richmond, M. "Auditory Perceptual Tasks as Predictors of First Grade Reading Successes." *Perceptual and Motor Skills,* 1972, *35,* 7-13.

# AURAL WORD REPRESENTATION TEST

AUTHOR: George H. McNinch

AGE: 3 to 7 years

VARIABLE: Ability to segment aural "words" from speech

TYPE OF MEASURE: Performance task

SOURCE FROM WHICH MEASURE MAY BE OBTAINED: See McNinch and Hafner (1971).

DESCRIPTION OF MEASURE: This instrument requires $S$s to listen to spoken utterances and represent the heard words with small wooden blocks. Words are defined as the units that exist as single entities when transcribed into written form. The stimuli on the instruments range from two-word utterances not separated by open juncture ("black horse") to six-word sentences representing different intonational and junctural patterns ("lightning is flashing in the clouds"). The scores to be used from the instrument are the number of words correctly isolated from the speed stream and the number of words perceived, that is, the number of blocks placed, whether correct or not. As represented by traditional writing patterns, the aural word-boundary task has sixty-one spoken stimuli words. Scoring may vary with the need of the researcher. McNinch and Hafner (1971), Kingston, Weaver, and Figa (1971) and McNinch (1974) offer different scoring possibilities.

The complete test is given below.

| Correct Number | Oral Stimuli |
|:---:|:---|
| 2 | black horse |
| 5 | They went by the truck. |
| 3 | car boat train |
| 3 | asked Dick quietly |
| 6 | They came to a funny house. |
| 4 | by the new building |
| 2 | it is |
| 4 | "No, no," said Dick. |
| 4 | Jim saw the microphone. |
| 5 | The gentleman talked and laughed. |
| 4 | over the quiet school |
| 3 | at the time |
| 5 | School is beginning right now. |
| 5 | Run from the speeding train. |
| 6 | Lightning is flashing in the clouds. |

RELIABILITY AND VALIDITY: Restricted estimates of reliability were computed using the Kuder-Richardson formula 20 technique (.71) and are reported in McNinch (1971).

BIBLIOGRAPHY:

Kingston, A. J., Weaver, W., and Figa, L. "Experiments in Children's Perceptions of Words and Word Boundaries." Paper presented at annual meeting of the National Reading Conference. Tampa, Florida, 1971.

McNinch, G. H. "Auditory Perceptual Factors and Measured First-Grade Reading Achievement." *Reading Research Quarterly*, 1971, *6*, 472-492.

McNinch, G. H. "Awareness of Aural and Visual Word Boundary Within a Sample of First Graders." *Perceptual and Motor Skills*, 1974, *38*, 1127-1134.

McNinch, G. H., and Hafner, L. "Systematic Evaluation of an Auditory Perception Skill Model in a Prereading Sample." *Perceptual and Motor Skills*, 1971, *33*, 387-394.

---

# BUTLER KINDERGARTEN AUDITORY-FIGURE-GROUND TEST (KAFGT), EXPERIMENTAL FORM A

AUTHOR: Katharine G. Butler

AGE: Preschool and kindergarten

VARIABLE: Auditory perception (auditory vigilance and selective listening)

TYPE OF MEASURE: Audiotaped test

SOURCE FROM WHICH MEASURE MAY BE OBTAINED: Katharine G. Butler, Graduate Studies and Research, San Jose State University, San Jose, California 95192.

DESCRIPTION OF MEASURE: The KAFGT is an 8-minute audiotaped test of auditory vigilance and selective listening suitable for screening children, aged 3 to 6, on this parameter of auditory processing. It is composed of the following sections: (1) Training Section; (2) Section I (ten items), directions given against a carefully controlled background ranging from −15 *db.* to +10 *db.*; (3) Section II (six items), directions given against gross sound-controlled background; (4) Section III (ten items), directions given against speech background of meaningful verbal material; and (5) Section IV (eight items), auditory vigilance task requiring intermittent response to signal against speech background. All sections require a motoric, nonverbal response by the child. Since the test is audiotaped, it may be administered by untrained personnel following a short demonstration period in which scoring procedures are identified. This test has been utilized by speech and language pathologists, audiologists, educators, and paraprofessionals in an educational setting. Equipment needed includes a high-quality tape recorder, twelve 1 X 1 X 1-inch blocks of a solid color, a box, a plate, and colored paper, plus a stopwatch. The KAFGT can be used as a criterion-referenced test in conjunction with the KAPP (Kindergarten Auditory Perceptual Program), which is a series of thirty-six audiotaped lessons with response sheets, providing training in such auditory skills as closure, synthesis, analysis, memory, discrimination, and selective listening. Children respond to audiotaped instructions nonverbally; response sheets are for collection of base-ratio data by paraprofessionals. The KAFGT may also be used for diagnostic purposes without the KAPP program and as a norm-referenced test. Experimental Form B is currently being field-tested.

RELIABILITY AND VALIDITY: The KAFGT has been administered to 115 kindergarten children identified as "high risk" for learning difficulties and to eighty-four normal kindergarten children from the same population during the 1974-1975 academic year. Performance scores of children under 5 years of age range from 11 to 33, with a mean of 26.6 among the high-risk sample. Performance scores of children in the normative groups range from 26 to 34, with a mean of 31.1. Analysis reveals that performance of high-risk subjects is significantly reduced for both the total test and for subtests III and IV at the .01 level of significance. Further information on reliability and validity is available from the author.

BIBLIOGRAPHY:

Ballard, M. E., and Butler, K. "An Investigation of Auditory Perceptual Functioning in Relation to Reading Achievement in First Grade." Paper presented at the meeting of the American Speech and Hearing Association. Las Vegas, Nevada, November 1974.

Butler, K. G. "Auditory Perceptual Training." *Acta Symbolica,* 1972, *3,* 123-125.

Butler, K. G. "Current Research in Auditory Perception." *Proceedings: Conference on Auditory Perceptual Problems and Remediation, Ohio Department of Health, Division of Maternal and Child Health,* 1973, 40-54.

Butler, K. G. "Auditory Perceptual Skills as a Function of Oral Language Among Children Entering Kindergarten." Paper presented to the meeting of the American Speech and Hearing Association. Las Vegas, Nevada, November 1974.

Butler, K. G., and Poon, W. R. "Response Patterns of Five-, Six-, and Seven-Year-Olds to the Intraverbal Gesture Subtest of the Parsons Language Sample," *Journal of Speech and Hearing Research,* 1972, *15,* 303-307.

Butler, K. G., and Pratt, J. "The S.I.E.V.E. Approach." In M. V. Jones (Ed.), *Language Development.* Springfield, Illinois: C. C Thomas, 1972.

Butler, K. G., Witkin, B. R., Kedrick, D. L., and Manning, C. "Auditory Processing and Dysfunction: Assessment and Training." Paper presented to the meeting of the Speech and Hearing Association. Detroit, Michigan, October 1973.

## COMPARISON OF SOUND DISCRIMINATION OF CPs and MRs

AUTHORS: Orvis C. Irwin and Don D. Hammill

VARIABLE: Consonantal sound discrimination

AGE: 3 to 16 years

TYPE OF MEASURE: Test

SOURCE FROM WHICH MEASURE MAY BE OBTAINED: See Irwin (1972) or write Institute of Logopedics, Wichita State University, Wichita, Kansas 67208.

DESCRIPTION OF MEASURE: There are two thirty-item forms of this measure. The instructions direct the subject to listen to the examiner say two words and report if they sound alike or different. The different pairs of words vary only in their consonant properties.

The thirty word pairs of Form A are given below.

1. tin-thin
2. late-date
3. pig-big
4. (gun-gun)
5. test-text
6. bud-bug
7. chip-ship
8. habitat-habitant
9. sop-shop
10. conical-comical
11. (hoe-hoe)
12. beats-beads
13. cytology-psychology
14. class-clasp
15. mush-much
16. patriarch-matriarch
17. (peach-peach)
18. were-where
19. biscuit-brisket
20. foal-stole
21. pass-path
22. convergent-conversant
23. falls-false
24. (at-at)
25. refracted-retracted
26. coke-cope
27. carrian-Marion
28. (far-far)
29. frisking-whisking
30. thigh-sigh

RELIABILITY AND VALIDITY: The reliability of Form A was .87; Form B reliability was .88. Parallel-form reliability was .80. A significant age trend affords evidence of the validity of the measure. Correlations with the Templin Sound Discrimination Test were: Form A, .83 ($N$ = 52 mentally retarded children) and Form B, .73 ($N$ = 71 mentally retarded children). A significant $R$ ratio (.01) was found for the difference of extreme age-level means.

BIBLIOGRAPHY:

Irwin, O. C. *Communication Variables of Cerebral Palsied and Mentally Retarded Children*. Springfield, Illinois: C. C Thomas, 1972.

Irwin, O. C., and Hammill, D. D. "A Comparison of Sound Discrimination of Mentally Retarded and Cerebral Palsied Children, Form A." *Cerebral Palsy Review*, 1965, *26* (1), 3-6.

Irwin, O. C., and Hammill, D. D. "An Item Analysis of a Sound Discrimination Test, Form A, for Use with Mentally Retarded Children." *Cerebral Palsy Review,* 1965, *26* (4), 9-11.

Irwin, O. C., and Hammill, D. D. "A Second Comparison of Sound Discrimination of Cerebral Palsied and Mentally Retarded Children, Form B." *Cerebral Palsy Review,* 1965, *26* (2), 3-6.

Irwin, O. C., and Jensen, P. J. "A Test of Sound Discrimination for Use with Cerebral Palsied Children." *Cerebral Palsy Review,* 1963, *24* (3), 3-7.

*Prepared by Don D. Hammill and Orvis C. Irwin*

---

## COMPOSITE AUDITORY PERCEPTUAL TEST (CAPT)

AUTHORS: Belle Ruth Witkin, Katharine G. Butler, Dona Lea Hedrick, and Charlie C. Manning

AGE: Grades 1 to 3

VARIABLE: Auditory perceptual skills

TYPE OF MEASURE: Tape-recorded test

SOURCE FROM WHICH MEASURE MAY BE OBTAINED: Alameda County Education Center, 685 A Street, Hayward, California 94541.

DESCRIPTION OF MEASURE: The CAPT is a 45-minute, audiotaped test suitable for assessing major auditory perceptual processes in primary-grade children. It is targeted for grades 1 to 3 but can be used with older children with suspected learning and/or language disabilities. The CAPT consists of three parts, each approximately 15 minutes long. Children make responses with a crayon or colored pencil in a response booklet, which has pictures in multiple-choice format. Part One consists of forty items testing figure-ground discrimination by presenting simple tasks against a distraction of music and speech. The tasks proceed from easy to difficult by varying the kinds of background distractions, the length and phonemic composition of words, and the signal-to-distraction ratios. Part Two consists of forty items testing temporal sequencing and analysis and discrimination of selected vowels and consonants. Part Three consists of fifty-four items testing phonemic closure, synthesis, memory for number of syllables in real and nonsense words, and discrimination of linguistic forms and verb tenses. The CAPT can be used as a criterion-referenced test in conjunction with the Auditory Perceptual Training Program (Witkin and others, 1973a). It can also be used for diagnostic purposes without the APT program and as a norm-referenced test.

RELIABILITY AND VALIDITY: The test was based on developmental and normative data from the literature on child development and from two factor-analytic studies (Witkin and others, 1973b). Test-retest reliability on the experimental version, derived from normal second graders, was .66. The interval between the two test administrations was seven months. The final version was based on item analyses and on the reliability data. The CAPT items were developed according to specified objectives and criteria in the companion Auditory Perceptual Training Program. Norms were obtained from children in regular classrooms in grades 1 to 3. The norms will yield profiles on individuals or groups. Normative data are included in the *CAPT Examiner's Manual* (Witkin, 1973).

BIBLIOGRAPHY:

Butler, K. G. "Auditory Perceptual Training." *Acta Symbolica,* 1972, *3* (2), 123-125.
Witkin, B. R. "Auditory Perception–Implications for Language Development." *Language, Speech, and Hearing Services in Schools,* 1971, *4,* 31-52.
Witkin, B. R. *CAPT Examiner's Manual.* Hayward, California: Alameda County School Department, 1973.
Witkin, B. R., Butler, K. G., Hedrick, D. L., and Manning, C. C. *Auditory Perceptual Training Program.* Hayward, California: Alameda County School Department, 1973a.
Witkin, B. R., Butler, K. G., Hedrick, D. L., Manning, C. C., and Whalen, T. E. "Parameters of Auditory Processing: Two Factor-Analytic Studies." Paper presented at the meeting of the American Speech and Hearing Association. Detroit, Michigan, October 1973b.

---

# DAYTON SENSORIMOTOR AWARENESS SURVEY

AUTHORS: William Braley, Geraldine Konicki, and Katherine Leedy

AGE: 4 to 5 years

VARIABLE: Aptitude in various sensorimotor areas

TYPE OF MEASURE: Screening test

SOURCE FROM WHICH MEASURE MAY BE OBTAINED: William Braley, Early Childhood Education Program, 3725 Evansville Avenue, Dayton, Ohio 45406.

DESCRIPTION OF MEASURE: This survey was developed for local use in a longitudinal research project in the Dayton, Ohio, Early Childhood Education Project. Originally it was used to screen some nine hundred 4-year-old children. For the last five years it has been used to show gains made by children enrolled in the project. The twelve areas measured by the survey include body image, space and directions, balance, balance and laterality, laterality, rhythm and neuromuscular control, integration of right and left sides of the body, eye-foot coordination, fine muscle control, form perception, hearing discrimination, and eye-hand coordination. Weaknesses in the various areas can be determined by using this survey, and children can then be given additional training where needed.

As examples, three of the twelve areas on the survey, with scoring, are given below.

*Space and Directions:* Score ½ point for each correct direction; 5 points possible.
2. Ask the child to point to the following directions: front     back     up     down
   beside you
   Place two blocks on a table about 1 inch apart. Ask the child to point: under
   over     to the top     to the bottom     between
*Rhythm and Neuromuscular Control:* Score 2 points for each foot if accomplished six
   times; 4 points possible.
6. Have the child hop on one foot. Hop in place.
*Fine Muscle Control:* Score 2 points if paper is completely crumpled. Score 1 point if
   paper is partially crumpled. Score 0 points if child needs assistance or changes hands.
11. Using a half sheet of newspaper, the child picks up the paper with one hand and
    puts the other hand behind his back. He then attempts to crumple the paper in his
    hand. He may not use his other hand, the table, or his body for assistance.

RELIABILITY AND VALIDITY: None reported.

BIBLIOGRAPHY: None reported.

---

# DOWNS' AUDITORY BEHAVIOR INDEX

AUTHOR: Marion P. Downs

AGE: Birth to 2 years

VARIABLE: (1) Approximate hearing thresholds; (2) auditory age

TYPE OF MEASURE: Observations of responses (behavioral)

SOURCE FROM WHICH MEASURE MAY BE OBTAINED: See Northern and Downs
(1974).

DESCRIPTION OF MEASURE: The Auditory Behavior Index was standardized on 200
normal babies from the Well-Baby Clinic of the University of Colorado Medical Center,
from birth to 24 months, divided fairly equally into eight age groupings. The most
consistent results were found in the speech awareness measure, where the *SD*s were so
small as to indicate that even a 10-*db* deviation from the norms should lead to suspicion of a mild hearing loss. The speech tests are done with directional loudspeakers,
placing the voice first in one and then in the other speaker at 45° to each side of the
child. A head turn, with a look of awareness, to the correct side is considered a positive response. The speech signal is increased slowly from −10 *db* in 5 *db* steps, until
the desired localization is seen. The plane-of-localization test is best given by presenting
noisemakers first at a level on the side below the eye level and then above the eye
level, and the path the head goes through to make the localization is charted. The age
levels at which the various types of head turns are seen have corresponded quite
closely to the developmental age level of the child.

As examples, three of the eight items (without the pictures that illustrate the correct response) are given below.

1. *New-born period to 4 months.* Normal infant is aroused from sleep by sound signals of 90 *db* (SPL) in a noisy environment, 50-70 *db* in a quiet one.
2. *Seven to 9 months.* He directly locates a sound source of 30-40 *db* to the side and indirectly below him.
3. *Sixteen to 21 months.* He localizes directly sound signals of 25-30 *db* (SPL) on the side, below, and above.

RELIABILITY AND VALIDITY: The small standard deviations of the infant's responses to speech at each age level indicate that speech produces the most reliable responses of any acoustic signal. Inttratest reliability was obtained by giving the speech tests at the beginning and the end of the battery of tests. The differences between the two tests were insignificant, indicating high test-retest reliability of the speech measure. The level-of-localization tests represent normative data at the various age levels, modeled after the studies of Murphy (1962), whose age levels are slightly lower for each level of response.

BIBLIOGRAPHY:

Downs, M. P. "Testing Hearing in Infancy and Early Childhood." In F. McConnell and P. Ward (Eds.), *Deafness in Childhood.* Nashville, Tennessee: Vanderbilt University Press, 1967.
Downs, M. P. "Identification and Training of the Deaf Child—Birth to One Year." *Volta Review,* 1968, *70,* 154-158.
Murphy, K. P. "Development of Hearing in Babies." *Child Family,* 1962, *1* (British).
Northern, J. L., and Downs, M. P. *Hearing in Children.* Baltimore, Maryland: Williams & Wilkins, 1974.

---

# FOCAL POINT LOCATION TEST

AUTHOR: Harold R. Strang

AGE: Preschool to adult

VARIABLE: Relatedness between the location of focal points in nonrealistic figures and inversion perception

TYPE OF MEASURE: Test

SOURCE FROM WHICH MEASURE MAY BE OBTAINED: Harold R. Strang, Department of Foundations of Education, Ruffner Hall, University of Virginia, Charlottesville, Virginia 22903. Cost: $2.00 handling fee.

DESCRIPTION OF MEASURE: This individually administered test involves presenting an examinee with twelve pairs of identical stimuli, except that the second one of the pair is inverted. The first two pairs (A and B) are realistic stimuli introduced to determine if the examinee understands the meaning of "upside down." The remaining nonrealistic forms (C–L) constitute the test. As each stimulus pair is presented, the examinee is instructed to point to the figure that is inverted. An examinee may change his decision after making a response if he does so before being exposed to the next stimulus pair. No time limits have been set for test administration. A score is derived by tallying the number of inversion responses in the nonrealistic stimulus pairs (C–L) for figures with focal points in the lower position.

RELIABILITY AND VALIDITY: None reported.

BIBLIOGRAPHY:

Barabasz, A. F., Dodd, J. M., Smith, M., and Carter, D. E. "Focal-Point Dependency in Inversion Perception Among Negro, Urban Caucasian, and Rural Caucasian Children." *Perceptual and Motor Skills,* 1970, *31,* 136-138.
Dodd, J., and Barabasz, A. F. "Cross-Cultural Comparison of Inversion Perception at Three Age Levels." *Journal of Educational Research,* 1968, *62,* 34-36.
Strang, H. R. "Relationship Between Focal Point Location and Inversion Perception at Three Age Levels." *The Journal of Genetic Psychology,* 1967, *111,* 3-8.

---

# HOME EYE TEST FOR PRESCHOOLERS

AUTHOR: National Society for the Prevention of Blindness, Inc.

AGE: 3 to 6 years

VARIABLE: Distance visual acuity

TYPE OF MEASURE: Screening test

SOURCE FROM WHICH MEASURE MAY BE OBTAINED: National Society for the Prevention of Blindness, Inc., 79 Madison Avenue, New York, New York 10016. Cost: $4.00 per 100; $30.00 per 1000.

DESCRIPTION OF MEASURE: The Home Eye Test is a self-contained vision screening test that can be administered by parents at home. The test itself consists of a 10-foot Snellen Illiterate "E" Chart with appropriate instructions for use. (The test does not replace a complete professional eye examination, which every child should have before entering school. This point is strongly stressed in the test.) If a child fails the Home Eye Test, parents are advised to take the child for an eye examination. A card for reporting test results to the National Society for the Prevention of Blindness, Inc. is also part of the Home Eye Test. Pediatricians, public-health nurses, eye doctors, nursery-school and day-care center administrators, and others have found the test to be a valuable screening and educational tool.

RELIABILITY AND VALIDITY: The Snellen Illiterate "E" Chart has proven in many studies to be a valid and reliable test for distance visual acuity. However, no specific studies on validity and reliability have been done on the Home Eye Test per se. Two studies were conducted in 1974 on a sample of those ordering the test. These studies proved conclusively that those ordering the test were using it and that when a child failed the test at home, he or she was taken to an eye doctor. Of those children failing the Home Eye Test, 75 percent were confirmed to have a vision problem. This figure compares favorably with that from the Society's regular vision screening program, where trained volunteers annually screen 400,000 preschoolers.

BIBLIOGRAPHY:

Bacharach, J. A., Miller, G. G., Gustafson, V., and others. "Vision Testing by Parents of 3½-Year-Old Children." *Public Health Reports, 85,* 426-432.

Boehm, G. A. W. "Playing the Pointing E." *Reader's Digest,* July 1973, 41-42.

Boyce, V. S. "The Home Eye Test Program." *Sight-Saving Review,* 1973, *43,* 43-48.

"Home Eye Test Roundup." *Sight-Saving Review,* 1974, *44,* 18-19.

Press, E. "New Method for Simplified Screening of Preschool Children for Amblyopia." *Journal of Pediatric Ophthalmology,* November 1968.

Press, E., and Austin, C. "Screening of Preschool Children for Amblyopia." *Journal of American Medical Association,* May 27, 1968.

Teotter, R. R., Phillips, R. M., and Shaffer, K. "Measurement of Visual Acuity of Preschool Children by Their Parents." *Sight-Saving Review,* 1966, *36,* 80-87.

Weisenheimer, F. "Home Vision Screening in the San Francisco Bay Area." *Sight-Saving Review,* 1967, *37,* 157-160.

*Prepared by Dennis Hirschfelder*

---

# INDIANA PERCEPTUAL DEVELOPMENT BATTERY
## (EXPERIMENTAL EDITION)

AUTHORS: Edward Earl Gotts and Richard Reid Zehrbach

AGE: Overall 4 to 10 years; varies by subtest

VARIABLE: Visual perceptual skills

TYPE OF MEASURE: Test

SOURCE FROM WHICH MEASURE MAY BE OBTAINED: Edward Earl Gotts, Preschool Education Program, Appalachia Educational Laboratory, P.O. Box 1348, Charleston, West Virginia 25325. Cost varies depending on what is needed. Author will provide at cost single copies of the manual, videotape, test materials, leaving further duplication to the user. Videotape dubs must be performed by Appalachia Educational Laboratory, to protect the master. *Raven's Coloured Progressive Matrices* is available from Psychological Corporation, 304 East 45th Street, New York, New York 10017.

DESCRIPTION OF MEASURE: Twelve subtests were constructed to measure a six-cell row of the Guilford Structure of Intellect (S.I.) model (that is, the row "figural cognitions") to be administrable to young children. A detailed manual discusses for the subtests the extent to which they appear to be satisfactory early childhood renditions of the Guilford conceptions. Shortcomings of the Guilford model for developmental uses are also explored in detail. Six original subtests of Guilford factors CFU and CFC require use of a standardized videotape presentation. Five-year-olds are testable with these six in small groups, with one adult assisting each four children, and in larger groups at higher age levels. The child marks with crayon or pencil on answer sheets that depict figural items to which the television-presented stimuli are to be matched. Five subtests are much simplified and redrawn revisions of figural tests from the E.T.S. Kit of Reference Tests for Cognitive Factors (Revised), which are entirely of paper-and-pencil design. Finally the Raven's Coloured Progressive Matrices test was the twelfth subtest. This was made simpler by a pretraining procedure. Both formboard and booklet versions of the *Raven's* are used. Scoring is done by scanning of the marked answer forms through acetate overlays. Special scoring procedures are described in the manual. Norms are not available. The authors have used various subtests as control variables of the pertinent skills in other studies, for example, to equate groups on some visual-perceptual skill. The overall battery is designed to allow testing of early childhood visual-perceptual development, including hypothesis testing regarding possible hierarchies of these skills.

RELIABILITY AND VALIDITY: Research to date has been limited to 4- to 10-year-old children of above-average ability and middle-class background. Interpretable developmental trends are evident for eleven of the subtests in this age range. The subtest internal consistency reliabilities (*alphas*) are: .90, .98, .87, .87, .93, .91, .68, .91, .98, .69, .93, and .89. Intercorrelations among the subtests are on the average moderately high, but they do appear to be enough smaller than the subtest reliabilities to suggest that the subtests are measuring different abilities. Nine of the twelve subtests related significantly to Gates Spelling scores and six to Gates Reading scores for 8- to 10-year-olds. Of the nine subtests that could be administered to 5- to 7-year-olds, eight related significantly to a nine-item Piagetian conservation scale. Nine subtests were completed by children 5 to 10 years of age, of which all related significantly to error scores on the Kagan Matching Familiar Figures Test (*Handbook I*, page 107).

BIBLIOGRAPHY:

Gotts, E. E. "A Perceptual Component of Visual Analytic Skill." In J. Pierce-Jones (Ed.), *Final Report on Head Start Evaluation and Research: 1966-67*. Austin: University of Texas, August 1967.

Gotts, E. E., and Zehrbach, R. R. *Manual of Indiana Perceptual Development Battery* (Experimental Edition). Bloomington, Indiana: Institute for Child Study, Indiana University, 1971.

## JUMBLED FIGURES TEST

AUTHOR: Lita Furby

AGE: 7 years to adult

VARIABLE: Linear spatial visualization

TYPE OF MEASURE: Test

SOURCE FROM WHICH MEASURE MAY BE OBTAINED: Lita Furby, Oregon Research Institute, Box 3196, Eugene, Oregon 94701.

DESCRIPTION OF MEASURE: This test was designed to measure linear spatial ability when the stimulus materials are figural in nature. It consists of a string of three to five geometric figures with arrows indicating possible new positions for these figures and thus a new left-to-right order of figures. In addition, there are a number of possible new rearrangements, and the subject's task is to indicate which of these possibilities represent the new order that would result from rearranging the figures as indicated by the arrows. It must be kept in mind that in addition to *visualizing* the indicated rearrangement, it may also be the case that the subject verbalizes it as an aid in remembering the new order. This test is very similar to the better-known Guilford-Zimmerman Spatial Visualization Test, Form B (1953). The major difference between the Guilford-Zimmerman Test and the Jumbled Figures Test is that the latter requires only linear, horizontal (left-to-right) spatial manipulations, while the former also requires vertical and circular manipulations. A 3 X 5-inch card is used with a slot cut out of it. The card covers all of the five possible rearrangements in a column except one, which appears in the slot. The subject is told, "See this row of shapes? Now imagine what it would look like if I moved this one over here." (Experimenter indicates with a pointer the repositioning indicated by the arrow.) "Would it look like this?" (Experimenter positions card so that only the first alternative in the column is visible.) After the subject's response, the experimenter moves the card so that only the second alternative is visible and says, "Would it look like this?" and so forth for all five possibilities in that column. A similar procedure is followed for each of the four rearrangement problems. Each response is recorded and then scored as correct or incorrect. Total score is the total number of correct responses out of thirty.

RELIABILITY AND VALIDITY: None reported.

BIBLIOGRAPHY:

Furby, L. "Children's Perception of Words and Its Relations to Problem-Solving Strategies." Unpublished doctoral dissertation. Stanford University, Stanford, California, 1969.

Furby, L. "The Role of Spatial Visualization in Verbal Problem Solving." *Journal of General Psychology*, 1971, *85*, 149-150.

Guilford, J. P., and Zimmerman, W. S. Guilford-Zimmerman Spatial Visualization Test, Form B. Part VI of the *Guilford-Zimmerman Aptitude Survey*. Orange, California: Sheridan Psychological Services, 1953.

## LANGUAGE-RELATED TESTS OF
## SPEECH-SOUND DISCRIMINATION (LTSD)

AUTHOR: Diane Nelson Bryen

AGE: 6 to 12 years

VARIABLE: Speech-sound discrimination in standard English

TYPE OF MEASURE: Test (A-X paradigm)

SOURCE FROM WHICH MEASURE MAY BE OBTAINED: Diane Nelson Bryen, Department of Special Education, Temple University, Philadelphia, Pennsylvania 19122.

DESCRIPTION OF MEASURE: The LTSD consists of three language forms (one in standard English, one in black English, and one in Spanish), each containing thirty-five items. The development of each language form was built on Jakobson, Fant, and Halle's (1963) distinctive binary features of speech analysis, and the test paradigm was based on Wepman's (1958) A-X paradigm, wherein word A is presented, followed by word X, and where X is either A or another word differing in only one phoneme. The child's task is to make a "same" or "different" judgment in response to these word pairs. Instructions and items were constructed and audiotape recorded first in standard English and then translated and taped in black English by a black male speaker who is bidialectical. This translation is in general conformity with the observed syntax, morphology, and phonology of black English as described by Labov (1967) and Baratz (1969), as well as the experience of the author. Instructions were then translated into Spanish and recorded by a bilingual Puerto Rican male. Minimal word-pairs were chosen and recorded that reflect the phonological structure of Spanish. This test can be used for several purposes. First, when a child is given the LTSD form that most closely approximates the language spoken by that particular child, information can be obtained concerning how the child is developing phonologically within his or her language system. Second, since standard English is the language used in most American schools, the standard English form can be used with *all* children if the information desired is how well the child is developing the phonological features of the language of instruction.

The first ten word-pairs of the thirty-five for the standard English form are:

1. fo*i*l            6. po*u*nd
   fa*ll*            po*n*d
2. mi*ss*           7. ba*r*e
   my*th*           ba*l*e
3. h*i*t            8. goo*s*e
   h*o*t            goo*f*
4. s*i*n            9. roo*f*
   *th*in           Ru*th*
5. west             10. *th*ey've
   west             *sh*ave

The first ten word-pairs of the thirty-five for the black English form are:

1. h*i*t
   h*o*t
2. wes(t)
   wes(t)
3. *dey*'ve
   *sh*ave
4. *l*ord
   *ro*ared
5. trip
   trip

6. *s*in
   *th*in
7. *p*ou*n*(d)
   *p*o*n*d(d)
8. di*n*e
   di*m*e
9. *g*uy
   *b*uy
10. *t*ight
    *k*ite

The first ten word-pairs of the thirty-five on the Spanish form are:

1. d*e*
   d*i*
2. *e*l
   *a*l
3. *r*ata
   *l*ata
4. ho*j*a
   ho*l*a
5. neuve
   neuve

6. ella
   ella
7. ha*d*a
   ha*ch*a
8. m*i*sa
   m*e*sa
9. ma*n*a
   ma*ñ*a
10. *b*año
    *p*año

RELIABILITY AND VALIDITY: Each form of the LTSD was administered in a counterbalanced order to thirty-two white, thirty-two black, and thirty-two Puerto Rican lower-socioeconomic status (SES) children in a large urban area. The three groups were equivalent with respect to chronological age and SES. Each group did significantly better on the LSTD form that reflected the phonological structure of the language spoken; that is, the white group did best on the standard English form, the black group did best on the black English form, and the Puerto Rican group did best on the Spanish form. These findings provide support for the construct validity of the LTSD. Additional evidence of construct validity comes from the findings that on each LTSD form, there were no statistically significant sex differences. These findings are in agreement with those of Templin (1957). In addition, age-related construct validity was partially supported. Content validity was established by ensuring that all major aspects of phonology (specific sound tested, voicing, breath stream, position, and place of articulation) were covered, and in the proper proportion, as evidenced in each language studied. Bryen (1973) provides the means, results of statistical analyses, and tables of content analysis for each of the three language forms.

In order to determine the stability of the three language forms of the LTSD over time, a test-retest product-moment reliability coefficient was computed. Raw scores for thirty-one white subjects on the standard English form, thirty black subjects on the black English form, and thirty Puerto Rican subjects on the Spanish form were used with one to two weeks separating the two testing times. The obtained coefficients were .71 for the standard English form, .67 for the black English form, and .89 for the Spanish form. All coefficients were statistically significant beyond the .01 level of confidence.

BIBLIOGRAPHY:

Baratz, J. C. "Teaching Reading in an Urban Negro School System." In J. C. Baratz and R. Shuy (Eds.), *Teaching Black Children to Read.* Washington, D.C.: Center for Applied Linguistics, 1969.

Bartel, N. R., Grill, J. J., and Bryen, D. N. "Language Characteristics of Black Children: Implications for Assessment." *Journal of School Psychology,* 1973, *11,* 351-364.

Bryen, D. N. "The Construction and Validation of Language Related Tests of Speech-Sound Discrimination for Specific Language Populations in First and Second Grades." Unpublished doctoral dissertation. Temple University, Philadelphia, Pennsylvania, 1973.

Bryen, D. N. "Special Education and the Linguistically Different Child." *Exceptional Children,* 1974, *40,* 589-599.

Jakobson, R., Fant, C. G. M., and Halle, M. *Preliminaries to Speech Analysis.* Cambridge, Massachusetts: MIT Press, 1963.

Labov, W. "Some Sources of Reading Problems for Negro Speakers of Nonstandard English." In A. Frazier (Ed.), *New Directions in Elementary English.* Champaign, Illinois: National Council of Teachers of English, 1967.

Templin, M. C. *Certain Language Skills in Children: Their Development and Interrelationships.* Minneapolis: University of Minnesota Press, 1957.

Wepman, J. P. *Auditory Discrimination Test: Manual of Instructions.* Chicago: Language Research Associates, 1958.

---

## MODIFIED RHYME HEARING TEST (MRHT)

AUTHORS: E. James Kreul, James C. Nixon, Karl D. Kryter, Donald W. Bell, and Janna S. Lang

AGE: Grade 4 reading ability or better; 10 years to adulthood

VARIABLE: Speech discrimination in quiet and in noise

TYPE OF MEASURE: Test

SOURCE FROM WHICH MEASURE MAY BE OBTAINED: MRHT tapes are available on six 7-inch reels of 1.5 mm low-noise tapes. All recordings are of special professional quality meeting rigid requirements. The tapes are full track recordings at 7½ inches per second and can be played on full, half, or quarter track tape units. Cost: $45.00 for six tapes (three talkers), $15.00 for two tapes (one talker), plus $1.50 shipping and handling; $2.20 outside U.S. Available from K-G Recording Service, 4311 Miranda Avenue, Palo Alto, California 94306. Telephone: (415) 948-0972. Sample test forms and unpublished and updated materials can be acquired by writing E. James Kreul, 410 A, Stanford Research Institute, Menlo Park, California 94025.

DESCRIPTION OF MEASURE: The MRHT is a test of speech discrimination useful as a clinical or research tool. The test consists of six tape recordings of four fifty-word lists each, two tapes for each of three talkers. A calibration 1000 Hz tone and 7000 cycle wide band of noise is provided at the beginning of each tape. All necessary instructions for test presentations are recorded on the tapes. The recordings were prepared and evaluated with attention given to insure an appropriate carrier phase, consistent timing sequences, well-controlled recordings, and simplified instructions and test forms. The tests were administered to panels of normal and hard-of-hearing adults and normal fourth- and fifth-grade children. The test results were assessed for possible effects of learning, talker or listener differences, and comparability of test lists. The recordings for all three talkers were selected to yield approximately the same percentage of correct responses for normal listeners of 96, 83, 75, and 96 percent correct. The performance levels were acquired by adding appropriate levels of noise to the recorded word lists. Mean and standard deviation scores are provided for adults and children. In the clinic the tests can be used for purpose of diagnosis, aural rehabilitation, and special-education placement.

RELIABILITY AND VALIDITY: Test-retest reliability was established under carefully controlled laboratory conditions for two homogeneous groups of listeners. The first group consisted of fourteen healthy, young normal-hearing college students. The second group consisted of twelve healthy, middle-aged World War II veterans with a history of noise exposure and with similar audiograms showing a loss of hearing confined primarily to the high frequencies. Mean and standard deviation scores for repeated testing for all lists and all conditions are high. Listeners with similar sensorineural hearing losses are reliably ranked in their ability to discriminate lists of fifty words for most conditions and lists for all three talkers. However, the test does not have sufficient precision to discriminate among healthy young normal college students if such differences really exist for a closed response set.

BIBLIOGRAPHY:

Bell, D. W., Kreul, E. J., and Nixon, J. C. "Reliability of the Modified Rhyme Test for Hearing." *Journal of Speech and Hearing Research,* 1972, *15,* 287-295.

Kreul, E. J., Bell, D. W., and Nixon, J. C. "Factors Affecting Speech Discrimination Test Difficulty." *Journal of Speech and Hearing Research,* 1969, *12,* 281-287.

Kreul, E. J., Nixon, J. C., Kryter, K. D., Bell, D. W., Lang, J. L., and Schubert, E. D. "A Proposed Clinical Test of Speech Discrimination." *Journal of Speech and Hearing Research,* 1968, *11,* 536-552.

# MODIFIED SJØGREN HAND TEST

AUTHOR: Edward Press

AGE: 3 to 5 years

VARIABLE: Visual acuity

TYPE OF MEASURE: Performance test

SOURCE FROM WHICH MEASURE MAY BE OBTAINED: American Academy of Pediatrics, P.O. Box 1034, Evanston, Illinois 60204.

DESCRIPTION OF MEASURE: The Modified Sjøgren Hand Test is a simplified method of screening the vision of 3- and 4-year-old children by a parent-administered test done at home. The test is based on the ability of the child to correctly identify the position in which the image of a human hand (a modified Sjøgren hand test) is rotated. The Sjøgren hand test was modified by changing its shape from round to square and the image recalibrated so that the child's vision can be screened at 12 feet rather than at 20 feet. The stimulus materials and the test materials are markedly simple, and they have been used apparently successfully by parents with their children.

RELIABILITY AND VALIDITY: The 141 pediatricians who used these tests and reported on the results indicated that this parent-administered, modified Sjøgren hand screening test can be performed at home with a minimum of instructions to the parents, and that for most 3- and 4-year-olds this represents a simple, effective, inexpensive method of vision screening for amblyopia ex anopsia. There is an overreferral rate of 4.6 percent. In other words, 7.5 of every 100 children failed to pass the examination by parents, but when they were rechecked only 2.9 still failed to pass the test so that 4.6 of every 100 were "unnecessarily" referred. Children considered normal by their parents were not rescreened by the pediatrician.

BIBLIOGRAPHY:

Press, E., and Austin, C. "Screening of Preschool Children for Amblyopia." *Journal of the American Medical Association,* 1968, *204,* 767-770.

*Prepared by Orval G. Johnson*

# MOVING EMBEDDED FIGURES TEST (MEFT)

AUTHOR: Jacqueline Herkowitz

AGE: 5 to 12 years

VARIABLE: Figure-ground perceptual ability

TYPE OF MEASURE: Filmed, individually administered test

SOURCE FROM WHICH MEASURE MAY BE OBTAINED: Jacqueline Herkowitz, Department of Education, Ohio State University, 309 Pomerene Hall, Columbus, Ohio 43210. For permission to obtain a copy and for wiring diagrams, write Purdue University A-V Center, West Lafayette, Indiana 47902. Cost: $50.00 (approximate).

DESCRIPTION OF MEASURE: The Moving Embedded Figures Test (MEFT) is a 20-minute, 16 mm individually administered filmed test designed for use in movement-behavior research. It assesses elementary-school age children's perceptions of embedded figures that appear to move away from stationary backgrounds. The test is composed of nine sets of items, three test items in each set, each set having a characteristic density in terms of the figures and grounds composing it. The heavy density ground (HDG) contains a great deal of black and little white. The medium density ground (MDG) contains equal amounts of white and black. The light density ground (LDG) contains a predominance of white and little black. The same three characteristic densities were assigned to the four figures utilized in the test. There are four heavy density figures (HDF), four medium density figures (MDF), and four light density figures (LDF). The first three sets are: Set 1. (HDF (rocket, car, ship) and LDG; Set 2. LDF (car, ship, rocket) and HDG; and Set 3. MDF (ship, train, rocket) and LDG.

RELIABILITY AND VALIDITY: Test-retest correlation coefficients estimated on the total scores of a stratified random sample of forty subjects, with test administrations separated by two weeks, were .65, .62, .71, and .79 (for the youngest to oldest age groups examined). Internal analysis of the MEFT for eighty subjects yielded two estimates of reliability. The reliability of the mean or total of all twenty-seven test items was .94. The estimated reliability of a single item was .35. Analysis of variance techniques indicated that the MEFT measured something different than stationary versions of the MEFT, when both tests were administered to the same subjects. On all but five test items, performances on parallel items were significantly different (.05 level).

BIBLIOGRAPHY:

Herkowitz, J. "Filmed Test to Assess Elementary School-Aged Children's Perceptions of Figures Which Appear to Move Away from Stationary Backgrounds." Unpublished master's thesis. Purdue University, West Lafayette, Indiana, 1968.

Herkowitz, J. "Filmed Test to Assess Elementary School-Aged Children's Perceptions of Figures Which Appear to Move Away from Stationary Backgrounds." *Perceptual and Motor Skills,* 1968, *27,* 643-646.

Herkowitz, J. "Filmed Test to Assess the Ability of Elementary School-Aged Children to Divine Figures Which Appear to Move Away from Stationary Backgrounds."

Unpublished doctoral dissertation. Purdue University, West Lafayette, Indiana, 1971.

Herkowitz, J. "Moving Embedded Figures Test." *Research Quarterly*, 1972, *43*, 479-488.

---

# OHIO TESTS OF ARTICULATION AND PERCEPTION OF SOUNDS (OTAPS)

AUTHORS: Ruth Beckey Irwin and Marcia Stevenson Abbate

AGE: 5 to 8 years

VARIABLE: Speech and listening (articulation and sound discrimination)

TYPE OF MEASURE: Test

SOURCE FROM WHICH MEASURE MAY BE OBTAINED: Stanwix House, Inc., 3020 Chartiers Avenue, Pittsburgh, Pennsylvania 15204.

DESCRIPTION OF MEASURE: The OTAPS (eight subtests) were devised to evaluate the articulation and perception of sixty-seven speech sounds in words represented by thirty pictures. All consonants in both initial and final positions, all vowels, diphthongs, and some blends may be tested. Errors in articulation are marked according to type (substitution, omission, distortion). Perceptual items are scored right or wrong.

RELIABILITY AND VALIDITY: The tests were administered to 200 children aged 5 through 8, with equal distribution at each of five age levels. The selection of children was based on distribution of occupations of fathers (U.S. Bureau of the Census, 1964). The test-retest reliability of each of the eight subtests was significant (except for subtest 5): subtest 1, 88 percent; subtest 2, 89 percent; subtest 3, 81 percent; subtest 4, 73 percent; subtest 5, 25 percent; subtest 6, 45 percent; subtest 7, 88 percent; and subtest 8, 70 percent. The examiner had an interpersonal percentage-of-agreement score of 88 percent when compared with fifty experienced clinicians. The examiner's intra-examiner percentage of agreement was 88.7 percent. Concurrent validity coefficients (established for each four articulation subtests with Templin-Darley Screening Test) ranged from .87 to .93.

BIBLIOGRAPHY:

Irwin, R. B. "Evaluating the Perception and Articulation of Phonemes of Children, Ages 5 to 8." *Journal of Communication Disorders*, 1974, *7*, 45-63.

Irwin, R. B., and Musselman, B. W. "A Compact Picture Articulation Test." *Journal of Speech and Hearing Disorders*, 1962, *27*, 36-39.

## ORAL STEREOGNOSTIC DISCRIMINATION TEST

AUTHORS: Charles L. Madison and Donald J. Fucci

AGE: 5 years to adult

VARIABLE: Tactile-kinesthetic three-dimension form perception in the mouth

TYPE OF MEASURE: Test

SOURCE FROM WHICH MEASURE MAY BE OBTAINED: Twenty pairs of forms were randomly selected from the possible paired combinations constructed from the National Institute of Dental Research of Oral Stereognosis. Available from the National Institute of Dental Research, National Institutes of Health, Bethesda, Maryland 20014.

DESCRIPTION OF MEASURE: The Oral Stereognostic Discrimination Test is a twenty-item task that requires subjects to make "same" or "different" judgments about selected pairs of three-dimensional plastic forms. Subjects are instructed that two little plastic forms will be placed in their mouths one at a time by the examiner and are to be retained for 5 seconds, with 5 seconds between forms. Subjects are encouraged to feel the forms all over carefully and upon removal of the second form, indicate whether they were "same" or "different." Subjects are given 2 points per correct response.

RELIABILITY AND VALIDITY: Oral stereognostic testing techniques have been used by several researchers as a means of assessing tactile-kinesthetic discrimination in the oral region. In most instances oral stereognostic testing has been carried out as a specialized research task. No specific reliability data have been developed. The present test was administered to 100 first-grade children screened for intelligence (above 85) and their understanding of "same" and "different." The children ranged in age from 6 years, 4 months to 7 years, 6 months, with a mean age of 6 years, 10 months. Scores for these children ranged from 16 to 38, with a mean of 32 and a standard deviation of 4.3.

BIBLIOGRAPHY:

Bosma, J. (Ed.) *Symposium on Oral Sensation and Perception.* Springfield, Illinois: C. C Thomas, 1967.

Locke, J. L. "Short-Term Auditory Memory, Oral Perception, and Experimental Sound Learning." *Journal of Speech and Hearing Research,* 1969, *12,* 185-192.

Madison, C. L. "The Relationship Between Discrimination Ability in Two Sensory Modalities and Articulation in First Grade Children." Unpublished doctoral dissertation. Ohio University, Athens, 1970.

Madison, C. L., and Fucci, D. J. "Speech-Sound Discrimination and Tactile-Kinesthetic Discrimination in Preference to Speech Production." *Perceptual and Motor Skills,* 1971, *33,* 831-838.

Ringle, R. L., Burk, K. W., and Scott, C. M. "Tactile Perception: Form Discrimination in the Mouth." *British Journal of Disorders of Communication,* 1968, *3,* 150-155.

Ringle, R. L., Housel, A. S., Burke, K. W., Dolinsky, J. P., and Scott, C. M. "Some Relations Between Oral Sensory Discrimination and Articulatory Aspects of Speech Production." *Journal of Speech and Hearing Research*, 1970, *35*, 3-11.

## ORAL VIBROTACTILE STIMULATION FOR THRESHOLD SENSITIVITY MEASUREMENTS

AUTHOR: Donald J. Fucci

AGE: 5 years to adulthood

VARIABLE: Oral tactile sensitivity

TYPE OF MEASURE: Sensitivity threshold test

SOURCE FROM WHICH MEASURE MAY BE OBTAINED: For the apparatus included in the measure, contact Donald Fucci, School of Hearing and Speech Sciences, Ohio University, Athens, Ohio 45701; or Kal Telage, School of Allied Health, Ithaca College, Ithaca, New York 14050.

DESCRIPTION OF MEASURE: To be tested, a subject is seated in a dental chair and asked to extend his tongue or lip between two sterilized plastic disks. The test structure is clamped so that it stays in position yet does not affect normal circulation. The vibrator probe, which produces the tactile stimulus, is lowered until it establishes contact with the oral structure being tested. The extent of vertical displacement of the vibrating probe relates directly to the intensity of the tactile stimulus and can be measured by an accelerometer. Vibrotactile thresholds expressed in decibels can be readily determined for a range of frequencies from 60 Hz to 800 Hz, and considerable data relative to lingual sensitivity are currently available (Telage, Fucci, and Arnst, 1972).

RELIABILITY AND VALIDITY: To date, data have been collected on normal children and adults and on populations with the following problems: functional articulation, deafness, stuttering, and surgical cases in which the tongue has been involved. The bibliography includes these data.

BIBLIOGRAPHY:

Fucci, D. J. "Vibration: A Clinical Tool for Tomorrow." *Ohio Journal of Speech and Hearing*, 1971, *6*, 92-96.

Fucci, D. J. "Oral Vibrotactile Sensation: An Evaluation of Normal and Defective Speakers." *Journal of Speech and Hearing Research*, 1972, *15*, 179-184.

Fucci, D. J., Arnst, D., and Telage, K. "The Effects of Pulsed and Continuous Stimulation on Vibrotactile Thresholds Obtained from the Tongue." *Psychonomic Science*, 1972, *29*, 83-84.

Fucci, D. J., Arnst, D., Telage, K., and McCaffrey, P. "Measurement of Lingual Vibrotactile Sensitivity Using Pulsed and Continuous Stimulation." *Bulletin of the
Psychonomic Society,* 1973, *2,* 85-86.

Fucci, D. J., Blackmon, R., McCaffrey, P., and Lindsey, S. "Oral Vibrotactile Thresholds of an Individual with Oral Facial Anomalies Accompanied by Severe Articulation Defects." *Ohio Speech and Hearing Journal,* Fall 1973.

Fucci, D. J., Hall, D., and Weiner, F. "Normative Study of Oral and Nonoral Structures
Using Vibrotactile Stimuli." *Perceptual and Motor Skills,* 1971, *33,* 1099-1105.

Fucci, D. J., and Kelly, D. "New Instrumentation for Research on Vibrotactile Sensitivity of the Tongue." *Review of Scientific Instrumentation,* 1972, *43,*
1748-1751.

Hall, D., Fucci, D. J., and Arnst, D. "Vibrotactile Stimulation: An Investigation of
Psychophysical Methods for Establishing Threshold." *Perceptual and Motor
Skills,* 1972, *34,* 891-898.

Kelly, D. H. "Oral Vibrotactile Sensation: An Evaluation of Normal Articulating Children and Children with Defective Articulation." Unpublished doctoral dissertation. Ohio University, Athens, 1973.

Telage, K., and Fucci, D. J. "Vibrotactile Stimulation: A Future Clinical Tool for
Speech Pathologists." *Journal of Speech and Hearing Disorders,* 1973, *38,*
442-447.

Telage, K., and Fucci, D. J. "Measurement of Lingual Vibrotactile Sensitivity Using
One Trial and Three Trial Threshold Criteria." *Bulletin of the Psychonomic
Society,* 1974, *3,* 373-374.

Telage, K., Fucci, D. J., and Arnst, D. "Normative Study of Oral Vibrotactile Sensitivity." *Perceptual and Motor Skills,* 1972, *35,* 671-676.

---

## PERCEPTUAL ACUITY TEST (PAT)

AUTHOR: Harrison G. Gough

AGE: 8 to 75 years and up

VARIABLE: Field independence and analytic perceptual ability

TYPE OF MEASURE: Multiple-choice test

SOURCE FROM WHICH MEASURE MAY BE OBTAINED: Harrison G. Gough, Department of Psychology, University of California, Berkeley, California 94720. Cost:
Approximately $2.00 per mounted slide, or $60.00 in all, plus postage and shipping
charges.

DESCRIPTION OF MEASURE: The PAT includes thirty multiple-choice items, presented by means of 35 mm slides. Each item contains geometric forms requiring judgments concerning relative size, length, area, contour, and equivalence. Twenty-five

problems are based on standard optical illusions; five are illusion free. Each slide is exposed for approximately 20 seconds, permitting the entire series to be administered in about 15 minutes (with instructions). Testing should be done in groups of fifty or less, down to the testing of a single individual, as optimum attention and freedom from extraneous noise or interference are important. Three scores may be obtained: number of nonillusion items correct, number of illusion items correct, and a weighted score in which points are given according to the quality of correct and incorrect answers. The last score is most reliable and shows the clearest relationship to age, to Witkin's Rod-and-Frame Test, and to other indices of analytic perceptual ability.

RELIABILITY AND VALIDITY: Odd-even item reliability is usually about .70. Adequate reliability, however, rests on careful administration and the certainty that all Ss understand the task and are prepared to do their best. Validity data include correlations of .41 with accuracy on the Witkin Rod-and-Frame Test, of .30 with Crutchfield's adaptation of the Gottschaldt embedded figures, and of .28 with the Case-Ruch Survey of Space Relations. Cross-cultural study with French, Italian, and Swiss children revealed age-development gradients almost identical to those found for American children.

BIBLIOGRAPHY:

Brothers, W. R. "A Study of Perceptual Differences Between Hippies and College Students." Unpublished doctoral dissertation. University of California, Berkeley, 1972.

Case, H. W., and Ruch, F. *Manual of Directions: Survey of Space Relations Abilities.* Monterey, California: California Test Bureau, 1949.

Chandra, S. "An Assessment of Perceptual Acuity in Fiji: A Cross-Cultural Study with Indians and Fijians." *Journal of Cross-Cultural Psychology,* 1972, *3,* 401-406.

Crutchfield, R. S., Woodworth, D. G., and Albrecht, R. E. *Perceptual Performance and the Effective Person.* Lackland Air Force Base, Texas: Personnel Laboratory, Wright Development Center, 1958. Technical note WADC-TN-58-60, ASTIA no. 151039.

Gough, H. G., and Delcourt, M. J. "Developmental Increments in Perceptual Acuity Among Swiss and American School Children." *Developmental Psychology,* 1969, *1,* 260-264.

Gough, H. G., and Hug, C. "Perception de Formes Géométriques et d'Illusions chez des Enfants Français et Américains." *Journal International de Psychologie,* 1968, *3,* 183-190.

Gough, H. G., and McGurk, E. "A Group Test of Perceptual Acuity." *Perceptual and Motor Skills,* 1967, *24,* 1107-1115.

Gough, H. G., and Meschieri, L. "Cross-Cultural Study of Age-Related Differences in Perceptual Acuity." *Journal of Consulting and Clinical Psychology,* 1971, *37,* 135-140.

Gough, H. G., and Olton, R. M. "Field Independence as Related to Nonverbal Measures of Perceptual Performance and Cognitive Ability." *Journal of Consulting and Clinical Psychology,* 1972, *38,* 338-342.

McGurk, E. "Determinants of Differential Susceptibility to Visual Illusions." Unpublished doctoral dissertation. University of California, Berkeley, 1964.

McGurk, E. "Susceptibility to Visual Illusions." *Journal of Psychology,* 1965, *61,* 127-143.

## PERCEPTUAL SCREENING TEST

AUTHOR: Ernest D. McDaniel

AGE: 9 to 12 years

VARIABLE: Perceptual ability

TYPE OF MEASURE: Motion-picture test

SOURCE FROM WHICH MEASURE MAY BE OBTAINED: Ernest D. McDaniel, Purdue Educational Research Center, Purdue University, West Lafayette, Indiana 47907.

DESCRIPTION OF MEASURE: This test is designed to be used as a group measure in identifying children who may have perceptual disabilities. The test is on a 16 mm sound film, and children mark responses on special answer sheets. The test has two parts. In Part I, a geometric design appears on the screen for 3 seconds. Following the stimulus, four designs appear on the screen, one of which contains the original design in a camouflaging pattern. In Part II, each side of a geometric figure (e.g., a triangle) appears on the screen a single line at a time. The child must form the complete figure in his mind and then recognize the figure from four designs subsequently displayed on the screen. The entire test contains fifty items and requires about 30 minutes to administer. Percentile norms are based on approximately three hundred children at each of the grade levels 4, 5, and 6 drawn from four major cities in the United States.

RELIABILITY AND VALIDITY: The median Kuder-Richardson formula 20 reliability coefficients for children in a standardization study were .84 for the total score—.74 for Part I and .75 for Part II. For validity, see McDaniel (1973, 1974) and Rohr and Ayres (1974).

BIBLIOGRAPHY:

McDaniel, E. D. "Ten Motion Picture Tests of Perceptual Abilities." *Perceptual and Motor Skills,* 1973, *36,* 755-759.
McDaniel, E. D. "Development of a Group Test for Assessing Perceptual Abilities." *Perceptual and Motor Skills,* 1974, *39,* 669-670.
Rohr, M., and Ayers, J. B. "Motion-Picture Screening Device for the Identification of Perceptual Disabilities." *Perceptual and Motor Skills,* 1974, *39,* 347-352.

# PHONETIC ANAGRAMS

AUTHORS: William R. Tiffany and B. R. Witkin

AGE: Upper elementary to college

VARIABLE: Speech sound awareness

TYPE OF MEASURE: Test

SOURCE FROM WHICH MEASURE MAY BE OBTAINED: See Tiffany (1963).

DESCRIPTION OF MEASURE: This measure is composed of fifteen items, each of which is a phonetic anagram. The subject is instructed to write a word composed of the sounds given, rearranging them in any way that makes sense. Each sound is used only once. The item type is exemplified by the following five items:

| Anagram | Answer |
|---|---|
| /ă/-/t/-/l/-/s/ | last, slat, tassle |
| /z/-/p/-/ō/ | pose |
| /o͞o/-/g/-/l/ | glue, ghoul |
| /ă/-/b/-/t/ | bat, tab |
| /ō/-/z/-/t/ | toes |

RELIABILITY AND VALIDITY: A preliminary factor analysis of speech tests has shown this measure to be highly correlated with a phonetic factor. In addition, Phonetic Anagrams correlated .34 with spelling test scores from college entrance examinations, .41 with classroom teachers' judgments of phonetic ability, and .49 with a test of ability to identify stress patterns in speech. Correlations with grade-point average in high school and college were positive but not significant.

BIBLIOGRAPHY:

Tiffany, W. R. "Sound Mindedness: Studies in the Measurement of 'Phonetic Ability.' " *Western Speech,* 1963 (Winter), 5-15.
Witkin, B. R. "An Analysis of Some Dimensions of Phonetic Ability." Unpublished doctoral dissertation. University of Washington, Seattle, 1962.

*Prepared by Orval G. Johnson*

# PICTURE IDENTIFICATION FOR CHILDREN: A STANDARD INDEX (PICSI TEST)

AUTHOR: Susan Johnson Seidel

AGE: 3 to 5 years

VARIABLE: Auditory discrimination

TYPE OF MEASURE: Multiple-choice test

SOURCE FROM WHICH MEASURE MAY BE OBTAINED: The PICSI Test, consisting of the fifty-eight triplet picture sets, test forms, and instructions, may be obtained from Susan Johnson Seidel, 720 Providence, Towson, Maryland 21204. (All rights reserved.) Cost: $45.00, prepaid (includes shipping).

DESCRIPTION OF MEASURE: This is a test of auditory or speech discrimination for young children with insufficient language or speech to respond appropriately to the tests most commonly used in audiology clinics. One hundred and seventy-four monosyllabic nouns were initially chosen on the basis of (1) picturability, (2) supposed familiarity to a normal 3- to 5-year age group, (3) ability to be placed in a triplet with a common medial vowel sound, and (4) a sufficiently wide representation of the phonetic elements of speech. For pictures, simple ink line drawings are utilized, with each picture drawn on a 4 X 4-inch white card. The nouns are systematically divided into three lists, each word in a list representing one word in a designated triplet, termed "like" or "unlike." There are fifty-eight triplets and therefore fifty-eight words in each list. Like triplets have a common initial or terminal consonant and/or consonant cluster. The emphasized consonants, consonant clusters, and vowel sounds are equally represented among the three word lists.

Twenty-two adult judgments of the familiarity of the 174 words for preschool children were made on a continuum of 1 to 5, where 1 means "extremely familiar" and 5 means "unfamiliar." The judgments were subjected to statistical analysis, and comparisons between these results and the sixty preschool children's actual familiarity ratings were made. Maximum familiarity is most desirable in a test of auditory discrimination. Therefore, the nature of the words themselves is the differentiating factor in determining types of hearing losses. Nasca (1964) applied the PICSI to a population of eighty-nine children with sensorineural hearing losses and delayed language to find out whether the items were familiar to them and to determine whether the test will discriminate varying degrees of sensorineural hearing loss.

As examples, the first ten of the fifty-eight triplet word list combinations are given below.

| Triplet Number | List I | List II | List III |
|---|---|---|---|
| 1. | bat | cat | hat |
| 2. | car | jar | star |
| 3. | kite | light | night |
| 4. | hook | cook | book |
| 5. | crown | clown | town |
| 6. | bee | tree | key |

| Triplet Number | List I | List II | List III |
|---|---|---|---|
| 7. | boat | goat | coat |
| 8. | thread | sled | bread |
| 9. | roll | pole | bowl |
| 10. | stairs | bears | pears |

RELIABILITY AND VALIDITY: Adults consistently underestimated the children's familiarity with the individual words. For example, the word "cave" was given an average familiarity rating of 4.00 or "slightly familiar." The children gave the same word an actual familiarity rating of 1.06 or "highly familiar." For this normal population, the individual word familiarity averaged well within the "highly familiar" range. The lists were found to be of equal familiarity so that any of the three lists may be utilized in presenting the triplet test. Nasca (1964) provides an item analysis of all of his subjects' responses. From this the following conclusions can be drawn for his population: (1) The three PICSI lists are equivalent regarding gross error score, (2) the PICSI yields reliable results as a measure of speech discrimination, (3) the words in the PICSI lists are slightly less than "highly familiar" to his population, and (4) a moderately strong correlation of .49 between degree of sensorineural loss and error score on the PICSI was derived from his data.

BIBLIOGRAPHY:

Nasca, L. "An Investigation of the PICSI Test: Picture Identification for Children—A Standard Index—Its Standardization Upon Children with Sensorineural Hearing Loss and Delayed Language Development." Unpublished doctoral dissertation. Indiana University, Bloomington, 1964.

Seidel, S. J. "The PICSI Test: Picture Identification for Children—A Standardized Index." Unpublished master's thesis. Indiana University, Bloomington, 1964.

Shriner, T. H., Beasley, D. S., and Zemlin, W. R. "The Effects of Frequency Division on Speech Identification in Children." *Journal of Speech and Hearing Research*, 1969, *12*, 413-422.

---

# PITTSBURGH AUDITORY TEST BATTERY (PAT)

AUTHORS: Helen B. Craig and William N. Craig

AGE: 3 to 20 years (depending on specific test in battery)

VARIABLE: Auditory discrimination skills

TYPE OF MEASURE: Tests (six multiple-choice, four free-response)

SOURCE FROM WHICH MEASURE MAY BE OBTAINED: Western Pennsylvania School for the Deaf, 300 Swissvale Avenue, Pittsburgh, Pennsylvania 15218.

DESCRIPTION OF MEASURE: The Pittsburgh Auditory Test Battery (PAT) is comprised of ten subtests designed to measure the specific auditory discrimination skills of hearing-impaired children from preschool through high school. It is not intended that all tests be given at once or to one group, but rather that a test or tests be selected appropriate both to the age of the child being evaluated and to the concepts under investigation. Three of the subtests, for example, were designed specifically to measure auditory skills of nursery-school and kindergarten children; these three (nos. 1, 4, and 8) comprise the Preschool Auditory Test. The auditory discrimination factors measured, suggested age range, and sample items from the individual tests include:

| Discrimination Factors | Subtest No. | Age Range | Sample Items |
|---|---|---|---|
| Duration: | | | |
| Gross sounds (beats) | 1 | 3-6 | 3 beats (2 short, 1 long) |
| Words and phrases | 2 | 6-12 | tree/3 bees/3 big trees |
| Vowel Discrimination | 3 | 3-12 | cat/kite/cup/cake |
| Simple Vocabulary | 4 | 3-6 | puppy/pie/bell/mouse |
| Connected Speech | | | |
| Multiple Choice: | | | |
| —Twenty sentences | 5 | 6-20 | A light is over a door. |
| | | | A light is over a table. |
| | | | A picture is over a table. |
| | | | A picture is over a door. |
| —Transition | 6 | 8-20 | The boys rode a boat. |
| | | | The boys wrote a note. |
| | | | The boys found a boat. |
| | | | The boys found a coat. |
| —Conversation | 7 | 8-14 | How are you? |
| | | | How old are you? |
| | | | Are you coming? |
| | | | Come here now. |
| Free Response: | | | |
| —Simple commands | 8 | 3-6 | Find the pencil. |
| —Five-syllable sentences | 9 | 8-20 | Please eat your sandwich. |
| —Ten-syllable sentences | 10 | 12-20 | We went to a party and ate popcorn. |

RELIABILITY AND VALIDITY: Over a five-year span, the various tests of the PAT battery (except for PAT nos. 6 and 7) each have been administered to over one hundred children, ranging in age from 2½ to 18 years and in hearing loss from 70 to 110 *dB*. For each age grouping, the hearing-loss averages were essentially equivalent (approximately 95 *dB*). Data from these evaluations indicate that the PAT subtests do have good validity, as shown by consistent increases in the test scores with increase in age and/or training, and with decrease in hearing loss. As a unit, the Preschool Auditory Test (nos. 1, 4, and 8) was given to 182 verbotonally trained deaf students in three age groupings—nursery I (age 3), nursery II (age 4), and kindergarten (age 5). The percentage of items correct was significantly higher at each age level: 3 years, 34.67 percent; 4 years, 49.17 percent; 5 years, 63.97 percent. The standard deviation per age level averaged 5.87.

PAT no. 5 was given to seventy-four elementary-aged deaf children who were also being educated in the verbotonal (auditory-based) program. Again, a consistently higher percentage of correct responses was shown at each age level tested: 6.3 years, 31.95 percent; 7.9 years, 46.65 percent; 9.3 years, 50.75 percent. Standard deviation averaged 4.5. On this same test, for thirty-six older children (mean age 13.8) who had not received the special training, the percentage correct was 47.38. PAT no. 10 was administered to 138 older deaf children (aged 13 to 14) as a combined lip-reading and auditory-discrimination measure. The mean score here was 44.08 percent, with validity indicated by the correlation between number correct and degree of hearing loss (discussed by Craig, 1975). An item analysis of this instrument showed that differences between the sentences and sentence sets within the test were nonsignificant.

BIBLIOGRAPHY:

Craig, H. B., and Craig, W. N. *Evaluation Manual.* Vol. 2. Pittsburgh: Western Pennsylvania School for the Deaf, 1974.
Craig, H. B. *Verbotonal Instruction for Deaf Children: Report of Verbotonal Demonstration Project, Phase IV.* Pittsburgh: Western Pennsylvania School for the Deaf, 1975.

*Prepared by Helen B. Craig and William N. Craig*

---

# PREPRIMARY AUDITORY SCREENING TEST (PPAST-I)

AUTHORS: Bonnie Ann Plummer, Shelley Harris, Penny Marcus, and Joan Rupert

AGE: Kindergarten

VARIABLE: Four parameters of auditory processing

TYPE OF MEASURE: Tape-recorded test

SOURCE FROM WHICH MEASURE MAY BE OBTAINED: Office of the Solano County Superintendent of Schools, 655 Washington Street, Fairfield, California 94533.

DESCRIPTION OF MEASURE: The Preprimary Auditory Screening Test (PPAST-I) is a nineteen-item screening tool to be used with primary children to assess: (1) auditory discrimination—contrast four minimal pairs in a consonant-vowel-consonant context (six items); (2) auditory figure-ground—respond to stimulus phrase, N Ving, with background of kindergarten babble systematically varying from +5 $dB$ to −10 $dB$ above the signal (five items); (3) auditory memory—recall of two and three monosyllabic words (four items); and (4) auditory sequencing—sequencing of two and three monosyllabic words (four items). This is a 4-minute test to be administered individually. The child is required to point to a visual representation of the auditory stimulus. To facilitate administration of this measurement by paraprofessionals, it is tape recorded on a cassette. Each subtest and total score is converted to a centile with children performing below the first quartile recommended for further assessment and possible remediation.

RELIABILITY AND VALIDITY: The original test battery was administered to 329 kindergarten children. Means, standard deviations, and centile scores are available for each subtest and total test. Test development procedures included measurement of the difficulty level of each item and correlation of each item with every other item and the subtest total. Reliability was estimated by coefficient *alpha*, which for the total test on the total population was .71. Construct validity was determined by intercorrelation of each subtest with every other and with the total test. Intersubtest correlations ranged from .48 for auditory figure-ground to .80 for auditory sequencing.

BIBLIOGRAPHY:

Aten, J. "Auditory Input, the Neglected Behavior." *California Journal of Communicative Disorders,* Summer 1972.

Falck, V. "Auditory Processing for the Child with Language Disorders." *Exceptional Children,* 1973, *39,* 413-416.

Witkin, B. R. "Auditory Perception: Implications for Language Development." *Journal of Research and Development in Education,* 1969, *3,* 53-71.

---

# PRESCHOOL HAND CHART

AUTHOR: Unknown (printed and used in Kansas since 1964)

AGE: 3 to 5 years

VARIABLE: Distance visual acuity

TYPE OF MEASURE: Test (eye chart)

SOURCE FROM WHICH MEASURE MAY BE OBTAINED: A single copy can be obtained from Bureau of Maternal and Child Health, Kansas Department of Health and Environment, Topeka, Kansas 66620.

DESCRIPTION OF MEASURE: This test is used as a screening method for discovering children who need an eye examination. It is administered and scored the same as the Snellen test chart symbol E, which it resembles. Instead of using letters of the alphabet, the chart shows silhouettes of hands decreasing in size from the two largest at the top to the six smallest at the bottom. There are six rows of hands, each representing a degree of visual acuity from $20/100$ (top) to $20/20$ (bottom) when viewed from a distance of 20 feet. The silhouettes show the fingers of the hands pointing left, right, up, or down in a random arrangement so that the child reads the chart by identifying the direction in which the fingers of each hand point. The test has been found to be very useful in preschool screening and in the Early and Periodic Screening, Diagnosis and Treatment Program of the Kansas Department of Health and Environment.

RELIABILITY AND VALIDITY: The validity of the test has been confirmed, since all who have been referred have been accepted as needing further examination.

BIBLIOGRAPHY:

Belleville, M., and Green, P. B. "Preschool Multiphasic Screening Programs in Rural Kansas." Paper presented to the American Public Health Association annual meeting, School Health Section. Minneapolis, Minnesota, October 1971.

*Prepared by Marion Belleville*

---

# PRIMARY AUDITORY SCREENING TEST (PAST)

AUTHORS: Bonnie Ann Plummer, Shelley Harris, Penny Marcus, and Joan Rupert

AGE: 6 to 8 years

VARIABLE: Auditory processing

TYPE OF MEASURE: Tape-recorded test

SOURCE FROM WHICH MEASURE MAY BE OBTAINED: Office of the Solano County Superintendent of Schools, 655 Washington Street, Fairfield, California 94533.

DESCRIPTION OF MEASURE: The PAST is designed as a screening tool for children aged 6, 7, and 8 years old in: (1) nonlinguistic memory—recalling of three, four, and five noisemakers (nine items); (2) linguistic memory—recalling of three, four, and five monosyllabic words (nine items); (3) linguistic sequencing—sequencing of three, four, and five monosyllabic words (nine items); (4) auditory figure-ground—identifying a stimulus phrase (N Ving) in a systematically varying background of kindergarten babble (+2 *dB* to −10 *dB*) (fourteen items); (5) auditory attention—identifying a stimulus phrase within a background of two semantic distractors (eight items); and (6) auditory association—completing incomplete sentences from information presented initially in a short story (six items).

RELIABILITY AND VALIDITY: The standardization of the PAST included 150 students aged 6, 7, and 8 with scores of 85 to 115 on the Peabody Picture Vocabulary Test. To measure the internal consistency, coefficient *alpha* was computed for each subtest and the total test for each age population, and for the total population. Correlation for the total test on the total population was .89. Construct validity was determined by intercorrelations for each subtest with every other subtest and the total test for each age group and the total population. Another measure of construct validity was the correlations of the PAST with the Peabody Picture Vocabulary Test, Northwestern Syntax Screening Test—Receptive, Boehm Test of Basic Concepts, and the Arizona Articulation Proficiency Scale. As a further measure, the test was administered to 155 special-education students in eight categorical areas of handicaps (trainable mentally retarded, aurally handicapped, aphasic, and so forth).

BIBLIOGRAPHY:

Aten, J. "Auditory Memory and Auditory Sequencing." In D. L. Rampp (Ed.), *The Proceedings of the First Annual Memphis State University Symposium on Auditory Processing and Learning Disabilities.* Memphis, Tennessee, 1972.
Chalfant, J. C., and Scheffelin, M. A. *Central Processing Dysfunctions in Children: A Review of Research.* National Institute of Neurological Diseases and Stroke. Bethesda, Maryland, 1969.
Witkin, B. R. "Auditory Perception—Implications for Language Development." *Language, Speech, and Hearing—Services in Schools,* 1971, *2,* 31-52.

---

# ROSNER-RICHMAN PERCEPTUAL SURVEY (RRPS)

AUTHORS: Vivien C. Richman, Jerome Rosner, and Russell H. Scott

AGE: 5 to 12 years

VARIABLE: Perceptual development—auditory, visual, fine and gross motor, and integration

TYPE OF MEASURE: Screening test

SOURCE FROM WHICH MEASURE MAY BE OBTAINED: Learning Research and Development Center, University of Pittsburgh, Pittsburgh, Pennsylvania 15213. Cost: $1.00.

DESCRIPTION OF MEASURE: The RRPS was designed for large urban school districts as an economical method of identifying children with inadequate perceptual-motor development. It can be administered by a teacher or a trained volunteer. It is an individual test that can be administered and scored in about 20 minutes. The instrument yields information about the child's ability to process information visually, auditorially, and so forth, and indicates those areas in which help is needed. It has been used in regular elementary classes and in classes for the emotionally disturbed and the educable retarded.

As examples, the first two of the nine items on the survey, with the scoring, are given below.

1. *General Adjustment Responses*
    The following questions are to be directed to the child. His responses are to be recorded.
    a. "How old are you?"

b. "When is your birthday?"

c. "Are you right or left handed?"

  1) Record his verbal response in space marked "Says."

d. "Show me that hand . . ."

  1) Record his motor response in space marked "Shows."

e. "Touch my right hand with your right hand."

  1) Examiner stands facing the child. Record child's ability to properly manipulate space under such conditions, i.e., *can* or *cannot* reverse space.

*Score:*

  Below age 8.0 years:

    Four (4) correct responses or more = 3.

    Three (3) correct responses = 2.

    Two (2) correct responses or less = 1.

  For age 8.0 and older:

    Five (5) correct responses = 3.

    Four (4) correct responses = 2.

    Three (3) correct responses or less = 1.

2. *Word Repetition*

  Examiner states: "I am going to say some words. You listen and repeat them." (or "Say what I say.") Words are to be presented and responded to singly. "Animal—breakfast—spaghetti—philosophy—elephant"

*Score:*

  Through age 6.0 years:

    Five (5) correct responses = 3.

    Four (4) correct responses = 2.

    Three (3) correct responses or less = 1.

  Beyond age 6.0 years:

    Five (5) correct responses = 3.

    Four (4) correct responses with error committed on "philosophy" = 2.

    All else = 1.

RELIABILITY AND VALIDITY: All subtests but one correlated significantly with the total score at the .005 level. Correlations of the Rosner Perceptual Survey (RPS) with the RRPS were found significant at the .005 level. In order to secure an index of external validity, a summated rating scale was constructed based on the behavioral correlates of learning disabilities described in the literature. Correlation between the rating scale and the RPS was .52, significant at the .001 level. An item analysis was performed. Half the items discriminated between the groups (regular, disturbed, retarded) at the .01 level, and the remainder of the items at the .05 level. The validity is demonstrated by the fact that the items efficiently distinguish between individuals who are high and low in perceptual ability. The validity of the items is further supported by the intercorrelation matrix. Data obtained from a cross-validation sample add support to the validity.

BIBLIOGRAPHY:

Richman, V. C., Rosner, J., and Scott, R. H. *The Identification of Children with Perceptual-Motor Dysfunction.* Pittsburgh, Pennsylvania: Pittsburgh Public Schools, 1968.

Richman, V. C., Rosner, J., Scott, R. H., and Stickney, S. B. "Differential Diagnosis of Children with Perceptual-Motor Dysfunction and Learning Disabilities." *American Journal of Orthopsychiatry,* 1969, *39,* 274-275.

Richman, V. C., Stickney, S. B., and Wilson, G. J. "Mental Health Services in the Pittsburgh Public Schools." *Journal of the International Association of Pupil Personnel Workers,* 1967, *2,* 91-95.

Rosner, J. "Visual Perceptual Survey, an Evaluation Designed for the Oakmont Public School District, Oakmont, Pennsylvania." Mimeographed report. Washington, D.C.: ESEA, Title I, 1966.

---

## SCREENING TEST OF AUDITORY PERCEPTUAL ABILITIES

AUTHOR: R. Ramon Kohler

AGE: Kindergarten to 12 years

VARIABLE: Auditory perception

TYPE OF MEASURE: Screening test

SOURCE FROM WHICH MEASURE MAY BE OBTAINED: R. Ramon Kohler, Department of Speech Pathology-Audiology, Box 3311, University Station, Laramie, Wyoming 82071.

DESCRIPTION OF MEASURE: Speech discrimination has been the primary measure of auditory perception. This test assumes that auditory perceptual abilities consist of many different but related factors that are measurable. The underlying concept for this test came from Karlin (1942), who developed thirty-three subtests under eleven major headings. The present test examines six auditory abilities (loudness, pitch, word synthesis, rhythm, discrimination, and word analysis) and is divided into six subtests. The subtest scores yield a total possible score of 231 points. Portions of the test are recorded and available on cassette tapes. Administration time is approximately 35 minutes, and the test is given individually.

As examples, the directions and the items for the first ten of the twenty-item auditory word analysis subtest are given below. Other subtests contain from nine to twenty-five items each.

*Section A. Front*
*Directions:* I am going to say some words. As I say the first word, listen for the sound that starts the word (comes at the front of the word). Then I will say three additional words. Listen and tell me which of the three words has the same sound at the *start* (front) of it. Be sure to think only of how the word sounds—not how it is spelled.
Example I. *dog*      run      *dish*      time
1. ball          pie          *balloon*          man

|   |   |   |   |
|---|---|---|---|
| 2. hat | cow | toad | *horse* |
| 3. pig | *pie* | big | toy |
| 4. coat | *cat* | chair | rock |
| 5. money | nail | *mother* | Christmas |

*Directions:* We will do the same thing as before, except you are to listen for the ending sound this time and tell me which one of the three following words has the same *ending* sound as the first word.

| Example I: walk | wait | tag | *take* |
|---|---|---|---|
| 6. dog | doll | *frog* | goat |
| 7. car | *chair* | cake | run |
| 8. bath | they | brother | *cloth* |
| 9. boots | *boats* | brown | book |
| 10. watch | children | *witch* | circus |

RELIABILITY AND VALIDITY: In a validation study (Kohler, 1967), children were also tested on the listening portion of the Spache Diagnostic Reading Scales and the Boston University Speech Sound Discrimination Picture Test. To insure that children would not encounter any unfamiliar words, all words were chosen from Murphy's (1957) Spontaneous Speaking Vocabulary of Children in Primary Grades. The test was administered to two boys and two girls on each grade level, grades 1 through 6, in three elementary schools chosen because they were representative of a specific socio-economic level. The total of seventy-two children were screened by their teacher and principal prior to being included. The age range was 80 through 151 months, with a mean age of 115 months. The Screening Test correlated .46 with the Boston University Test and .78 with the Spache Scales, indicating adequate concurrent validity. Test-retest reliability was $r = .93$, and split-half reliability was $r = .96$.

BIBLIOGRAPHY:

*Boston University Speech Sound Discrimination Picture Test.* Boston: Boston University, 1955.

Karlin, J. E. "A Factorial Study of Auditory Function." *Psychometricka,* 1942, *7,* 251-279.

Kohler, R. R. "The Validation of a Screening Test of Auditory Perceptual Abilities of Elementary School Children." Unpublished doctoral dissertation. University of Utah, Salt Lake City, 1967.

Murphy, H. A. "The Spontaneous Speaking Vocabulary of Children in Primary Grades." *Journal of Education,* 1957, *140,* 1-105.

Spache, G. D. *Diagnostic Reading Scales.* Monterey: California Test Bureau, 1963.

# SERIAL INTEGRATION

AUTHOR: Ernest D. McDaniel

AGE: 6 to 7 years

VARIABLE: Perceptual abilities

TYPE OF MEASURE: Motion-picture test

SOURCE FROM WHICH MEASURE MAY BE OBTAINED: Ernest McDaniel, Purdue Educational Research Center, Purdue University, West Lafayette, Indiana 47907.

DESCRIPTION OF MEASURE: This is a research instrument designed to measure serial integration at the first-grade level. Serial integration is defined as the ability to perceive a series of stimuli spaced over time as a single meaningful pattern. This test is a revision and simplification of an earlier motion-picture test designed to identify children with perceptual handicaps, but the Serial Integration Test is seen as having more general application in measuring some of the information processing abilities that may be required in learning school subjects. The twenty-six-item test is on super-8 film (Kodak MFS-8) and is used with a projector, which facilitates stopping the film after a single test item has been exposed. Each item presents lines on the screen one at a time, and children are asked to recognize the pattern that will be formed. Children work with a separate answer booklet presenting three response-pattern options. Testing time is 30 minutes.

RELIABILITY AND VALIDITY: The Kuder-Richardson formula 20 reliability coefficients for kindergarten, first, second, and third grades and for all four grades combined were, respectively, .52, .66, .63, .75 and .72. Validity data collected on the same children are indicated by the following correlation figures between the Serial Integration Test score and subscores on the Primary Mental Abilities Test (SRA): verbal ability, .24; perceptual speed, .29; numerical facility, .43; and spatial relations, .33. Serial integration also correlated .27 with teacher estimates of reading ability.

BIBLIOGRAPHY:

McDaniel, E. D. "Serial Integration and Early Arithmetic Achievement." *Perceptual and Motor Skills,* 1975, *41,* 586.
McDaniel, E. D., Durham, M., and Smith, M. "Relationships Among Serial Integration, Primary Mental Abilities and Initial Reading Success." Paper presented at the Second Scientific Conference of the International Federation of Learning Disabilities. Brussels, Belgium, January 1975.

# SHAPE-O BALL TEST

AUTHORS: Jerry R. Thomas and Brad S. Chissom

AGE: Preschool to grade 2

VARIABLE: Perceptual-motor ability

TYPE OF MEASURE: Performance

SOURCE FROM WHICH MEASURE MAY BE OBTAINED: The Shape-O Ball is a commercial product available from Tupperware, a Division of Dart Industries, Orlando, Florida 32802. Cost: $5.00. Administration and scoring are available from Jerry Thomas, Montgomery Gym, Florida State University, Tallahassee, Florida 32306; or from Brad Chissom, Box 8143, Georgia Southern College, Statesboro, Georgia 30458.

DESCRIPTION OF MEASURE: The test is designed to measure certain perceptual-motor abilities (shape-recognition, perceptual match, and hand-eye coordination) that closely relate to academic readiness. The test is developmental in that it correlates with age but is not influenced by race or sex, provided that subjects are from the same socioeconomic level. The test is to be administered individually and is not designed as a group test. The test administrator places the Shape-O Ball directly in front of the subject on a table of adequate height for the subject's age. The Shape-O Ball consists of a hollow plastic sphere 6 inches in diameter with different geometrically shaped holes in the surface of the sphere. Plastic geometric pieces matching the holes are inserted into the sphere as rapidly as possible by the child, after a practice session. The pieces should be scattered randomly at a point behind the ball and the subject seated comfortably at the table. The examiner explains the task ("Place the pieces in the holes as fast as you can") and lets the subject practice until the child indicates that he understands what is to be done. The subject performs four trials, with each trial timed to the nearest second with a stopwatch. If any trial exceeds 200 seconds, the subject should be stopped and the 200 seconds recorded as the time for that trial. A subject's score on the test is the sum of the four trials. Although norms are not yet available, the authors (Chissom and Thomas, 1973) have indicated that comparisons should not be made between disadvantaged and "normal" subjects. Norms must be provided for both groups in order to make within-group comparisons, and no between-group comparisons should be made.

RELIABILITY AND VALIDITY: The following table summarizes the research findings for the Shape-O Ball test:

| | | | | | *Shape-O Ball Test Data* | |
| Subjects | N | Criterion | r | Reliability | X | S.D. |
| --- | --- | --- | --- | --- | --- | --- |
| Kindergarten | 40 | Otis-Lennon MAT | .54 | .86 | 318.75 | 114.46 |
| Kindergarten | 40 | Teacher Rating | .50 | – | – | – |
| Kindergarten | 38 | Frostig DTVP Total | .70 | .98 | 429.79 | 189.54 |
| Kindergarten | 38 | Teacher Rating | .67 | – | – | – |
| Disadvantaged Preschool | 66 | Otis-Lennon | .23 | .94 | 460.08 | 281.76 |
| Disadvantaged Preschool | 66 | Teacher Rating | .37 | – | – | – |

| Subjects | N | Criterion | r | Shape-O Ball Test Data | | |
|---|---|---|---|---|---|---|
| | | | | Reliability | X | S.D. |
| First Grade | 24 | Otis-Lennon MAT | .24 | .61 | 275.39 | 79.50 |
| First Grade | 24 | Teacher Rating | .58 | – | – | – |
| First Grade | 48 | Otis Lennon MAT | .71 | – | – | – |
| First Grade | 48 | Teacher Rating | .71 | – | – | – |

BIBLIOGRAPHY:

Chissom, B. S., and Thomas, J. R. "Relationship Between Perceptual-Motor and Academic Measures for Disadvantaged Preschool Children." *Perceptual and Motor Skills,* 1973, *36,* 152-154.

Chissom, B. S., Thomas, J. R., and Biasiotto, J. "Canonical Validity of Perceptual-Motor Skills for Predicting an Academic Criterion." *Educational and Psychological Measurement,* 1972, *32,* 1095-1098.

Thomas, J. R., and Chissom, B. S. "Relationships as Assessed by Canonical Correlation Between Perceptual-Motor and Intellectual Abilities for Preschool and Early Elementary-Age Children." *Journal of Motor Behavior,* 1972, *4,* 23-29.

Thomas, J. R., and Chissom, B. S. "An Investigation of the Combination of a Perceptual-Motor Test and a Cognitive Ability Test for Classifying First-Grade Children into Reading Groups." *Psychology in the Schools,* 1973, *10,* 185-189.

Thomas, J. R., Chissom, B. S., and Biasiotto, J. "Investigation of the Shape-O Ball Test as a Perceptual-Motor Task for Preschoolers." *Perceptual and Motor Skills,* 1972, *35,* 447-450.

*Prepared by Brad S. Chissom*

---

## SINGER-BRUNK FIGURE REPRODUCTION TEST

AUTHORS: Robert N. Singer and Jason W. Brunk

AGE: 7 to 12 years

VARIABLE: Perceptual-motor, problem-solving, and spatial-relations abilities

TYPE OF MEASURE: Perceptual-motor performance

SOURCE FROM WHICH MEASURE MAY BE OBTAINED: Robert N. Singer, Division of Human Performance, College of Education, Florida State University, Tallahassee, Florida 32306.

DESCRIPTION OF MEASURE: The test is designed to measure problem-solving ability involving spatial relations as represented by perceptual-motor activity. The task consists of a wooden board, 6½ inches square, on which four rows and four columns of nails, 1½ inches apart, protrude. Subjects attempt to replicate geometrical patterns on the board with the use of rubber bands. The patterns, fourteen in all, range from such simple figures as a square, triangle, and rectangle, to extremely complex patterns. Each pattern, drawn in India ink, can be individually presented on a screen with the use of a slide projector that projects a 5 X 4-foot image. A maximum of 2 minutes is allowed for the completion of each pattern. The students must be spaced in such a way as to discourage glancing at a classmate's work and furthermore should be told to turn their boards over upon completion of each task. After each task the students' efforts are to be evaluated as successful or unsuccessful, with exact replication of the pattern being successful. For individual testing, the patterns can be presented to the subject on a piece of paper. A stopwatch can be used to time performance completions with a maximum of 2 minutes allowed for completion.

RELIABILITY AND VALIDITY: None reported.

BIBLIOGRAPHY:

Singer, R. N. "Interrelationship of Physical, Perceptual-Motor, and Academic Achievement Variables in Elementary School Children." *Perceptual and Motor Skills,* 1968, *27,* 1323-1332.
Singer, R. N. "Physical Characteristic, Perceptual-Motor, and Intelligence Differences Between Third- and Sixth-Grade Children." *Research Quarterly,* 1969, *40,* 803-811.
Singer, R. N., and Brunk, J. W. "Relation of Perceptual-Motor Ability and Intellectual Ability in Elementary School Children." *Perceptual and Motor Skills,* 1967, *24,* 967-970.

---

# SLIDE TEST: A TEST OF MOVEMENT CLOSURE

AUTHOR: Elizabeth Y. Sharp

AGE: Deaf children, 7 to 9 years

VARIABLE: Movement closure

TYPE OF MEASURE: Test

SOURCE FROM WHICH MEASURE MAY BE OBTAINED: Elizabeth Y. Sharp, 5642 Mina Vista, Tucson, Arizona 85718. Cost: $2.25 plus postage.

DESCRIPTION OF MEASURE: The test involves a series of incidents of increasing complexity with the outcome left incomplete, to be filled in by the child. To obtain closure the subject must select the proper outcome. The situations become more complex, yet the number of clues remains the same. The test also assesses speed of perception and short-term visual memory. Each event is on a series of slides presented at the rate of one every 2 seconds. The test consists of two demonstration items and ten slide series. The subject is allowed two trials on each series.

RELIABILITY AND VALIDITY: None reported.

BIBLIOGRAPHY:

Moore, D. F. "Application of 'Cloze' Procedures to the Assessment of Psycholinguistic Abilities of the Deaf." Unpublished doctoral dissertation. University of Illinois, Urbana, 1967.

Sharp, E. Y. "The Relationship of Visual Closure to Speechreading." *Exceptional Children,* 1972, *38,* 729-734.

---

## SLURVIAN TRANSLATION TEST

AUTHOR: William R. Tiffany

AGE: Upper elementary through college

VARIABLE: Speech sound awareness

TYPE OF MEASURE: Test

SOURCE FROM WHICH MEASURE MAY BE OBTAINED: See Tiffany (1963a).

DESCRIPTION OF MEASURE: This test is designed to test awareness of speech sounds *as speech sounds.* In order to be successful on the items in this test, the subject must divorce himself from the tendency to stick to written meanings and instead attend to the "spoken meanings." Thus, he needs to be *sound* rather than *sight* minded. The test comes in two forms that have been administered to high school and college students. The author has found wide individual differences among good students in their ability to succeed on the items. College students varied all the way from one correct to all fifteen correct on Form A, using a 30-second time limit per item. The average score for the college students, with each of the fifteen items counting 1 point, was 6.7, with a standard deviation of 2.8.

As examples, the fifteen items from Form A are given below. The subject is instructed to translate the "nonsense" of each item into familiar sensible sentences, spending no more than 30 seconds on each item.

1. Rocker buy bay bee inner treat hop.
2. Padder keg padder keg peggers mend.
3. Turnip outs fir ply.
4. Roland's tone gadders Nome has.
5. Sinkers honkers sick spent.
6. Lawn tent britches full in town.
7. Diamond died weights fur Nome Ann.
8. But tune toot a gather.
9. My tea hoax farm ladle egg horns crow.

10. Home other rubber winter thick upper.

11. High pled jelly gents two thief lag.

12. A fit furs chewed own suck seed dry egg hen.

13. Want a drain sit bores.

14. Win rum douche a romance stew.

15. Thoroughly Burt gashes swarm.

RELIABILITY AND VALIDITY: Scores on the test correlated essentially 0 with both high school and college grade-point averages. There appears to be some tendency for high school students in slow English classes to find the test difficult, as compared with a normal high school English class. In two samples of college students, the correlations between scores on the test and instructors' independent ratings of the students' speech excellence were .24 and .22. The correlation between test score and the students' own estimates of the amount of their experience as speakers was .20.

BIBLIOGRAPHY:

Tiffany, W. R. "Slurvian Translation as a Speech Research Tool." *Speech Monographs,* 1963a, *30* (1), 23-30.

Tiffany, W. R. "Sound Mindedness: Studies in the Measurement of Phonetic Ability." *Western Speech,* 1963b (Winter), 5-15.

*Prepared by Orval G. Johnson*

---

# SPEECH SOUND DISCRIMINATION TEST (SSDT)

AUTHORS: Jack Victor, Estelle Peisach, and Karen Lombardi

AGE: Disadvantaged preschool children

VARIABLE: Speech sound discrimination

TYPE OF MEASURE: Group test

SOURCE FROM WHICH MEASURE MAY BE OBTAINED: Jack Victor, 82-25 218th Street, Hollis Hills, New York 11427.

DESCRIPTION OF MEASURE: The SSDT is a group-administered test in which paired pictures (e.g., gate/gate and gate/date) are presented in booklets, one item per page, to groups of about ten children. Taped instructions, which were made in a sound studio under carefully controlled conditions so that the intensity level was made constant from item to item, are presented to the children. Three sample items presented by the tester precede the taped instructions in order to ascertain understanding of the task. The child is asked to place an "X" on the picture representing the word pair that is presented aurally. The test was developed to be appropriate for administration to young, low-socio-economic-status, urban black children. It was discovered from previous work (Coller,

Schwartz, and Colemen, 1965) with the Wepman Auditory Discrimination Test (WADT) that errors made by a substantial minority of urban black children are primarily errors in final phoneme discrimination. This instrument was developed to stress final phoneme discriminations and to increase the difficulty level of the discriminations. Primarily, however, the test was developed to provide a group rather than an individual test of speech sound discrimination. The measure was made more difficult by selecting, in addition to the within-family discriminations included in the Wepman test (e.g., voiced stops, d/b: unvoiced fricatives, f/s; and so forth) items that paired voiced phonemes with unvoiced similar phonemes (e.g., t/d). Also added were item pairs that differed only in the absence or presence of certain final sounds (e.g., bow/bowl). Finally, pairs were added that had minimally different consonant clusters (e.g., nk/ng).

RELIABILITY AND VALIDITY: Two samples of black first-grade children in an inner-city school were tested under optimal conditions (soundproof rooms). *Alpha* reliability was .88 for a group of fifty-three children enrolled in an experimental early childhood enrichment program. The control group (forty-six children) showed a reliability coefficient of .82. Where testing conditions were not controlled and, in fact, noisy, reliability was considerably affected (as was shown in testing another group of children of similar background). The test was found to be inappropriate for middle-class first graders. These children scored 93-percent correct on the test. Middle-class kindergarten children were tested and showed a reliability of .70. However, testing conditions involved whole-class testing in regular classrooms. Thirty-three first grade children from an inner-city low-SES area of bilingual background (Chinese and some Spanish-speaking) were also tested. *Alpha* reliability was only .41. These children, however, averaged only 65-percent correct. Since chance is 50 percent, it is evident that the test was not appropriate for these children.

The test scores were correlated with scores on a battery of other cognitive measures presented to the black first grade samples. Seventy-five children received the entire battery. While the correlation between SSDT and the Wepman Test was significant (.46) for the enrichment children, the relationship was virtually zero for the control group. Correlations between the SSDT and two Illinois Test of Psycholinguistic Abilities (Experimental Edition) subtests (Auditory Vocal Automatic and Auditory Vocal Association) were highly significant (.59 and .65, respectively, for the combined groups); WADT correlated .37 and .25, respectively. The SSDT, however, also correlated significantly high (between .46 and .78) with each of fifteen other cognitive measures, including tests of reading and math achievement, reading readiness, general IQ, visual-perceptual skills, and perceptual-motor skills. It is possible, then, that the SSDT may be measuring some general conceptual skill. As noted above, the authors have hypothesized that the skill being tapped is probably not a sensory one but rather an attentional or cognitive skill.

BIBLIOGRAPHY:

Coller, A., Schwartz, S., and Colemen, R. *Auditory Discrimination Tests, I: Analysis of Initial and Final Phoneme Changes in Word-Pairs.* New York: Institute for Developmental Studies, New York University, Research Report, 1965.

Peisach, E., and Victor, J. *The Development of a Group Speech Sound Test for Disadvantaged Children.* Final Report (OEO B89-4612C). Washington, D.C.: Office of Economic Opportunity, 1969.

Peisach, E., Victor, J., and Lombardi, K. *The Development of a Group Speech Sound Test for Disadvantaged Children.* Final Report (OEO BOO-5097C). Washington, D.C.: Office of Economic Opportunity, 1970.

# STAGGERED SPONDAIC WORD TEST (SSW)

AUTHOR: Jack Katz

AGE: 5 years and up

VARIABLE: Central auditory function

TYPE OF MEASURE: Test

SOURCE FROM WHICH MEASURE MAY BE OBTAINED: Auditec of St. Louis, 8613 Rosalie Avenue, Brentwood, Missouri 63144. Cost: SSW (stereo tape), $15.00; tester's manual, $2.00.

DESCRIPTION OF MEASURE: This test was developed as a central auditory test for adults. It is extremely accurate in identifying lesions in various parts of the brain and brainstem. The test can also be used with children. Children with auditory-perception problems, learning-disabled children, and others have been tested. Various applications are described in the literature. The SSW Test is a dichotic competing-message task. Spondaic-type words are presented in a partially overlapped fashion. The words are presented at fifty *dB* above threshold. The test is simple for normal "adults." Adult performance is achieved at about 11 years of age. Below 11 years less stringent criteria are used. Below 5 years there are no standards. Scores would be very poor and standard deviations too wide.

RELIABILITY AND VALIDITY: Validity has been checked and cross-validated with adults who had specific brain lesions confirmed by surgery primarily. A study with 120 adults having conductive, cochlear, VIII nerve-brainstem, cerebral-auditory-reception, and cerebral-nonauditory-reception lesions showed a reliability coefficient ($r$) of .96. A similar study was carried out with sixty learning-disabled children. The split-half reliability was $r$ = .89.

BIBLIOGRAPHY:

Brunt, M. "The Staggered Spondaic Word Test." In J. Katz (Ed.), *Handbook of Clinical Audiology*. Baltimore, Maryland: Williams & Wilkens, 1972.

Katz, J. "The Use of Staggered Spondaic Words for Assessing the Integrity of the Central Auditory Nervous System." *Journal of Auditory Research*, 1962, *2*, 327-337.

Katz, J. "The SSW Test: An Interim Report." *Journal of Speech and Hearing Disorders*, 1968, *33*, 132-146.

Katz, J., Basil, R., and Smith, J. "A Staggered Spondaic Word Test for Detecting Central Auditory Lesions." *Annals of Otology, Rhineology, and Laryngology*, 1963, *72*, 908-918.

Katz, J., and Illmer, R. "Auditory Perceptual Problems in Children with Learning Disabilities." In J. Katz (Ed.), *Handbook of Clinical Audiology*. Baltimore, Maryland: Williams & Wilkens, 1972.

## STERN'S CHILDREN'S AUDITORY DISCRIMINATION
## INVENTORY (CADI)

AUTHOR: Carolyn Stern

AGE: 3 to 6 years

VARIABLE: Simple auditory discrimination

TYPE OF MEASURE: Individually administered test

SOURCE FROM WHICH MEASURE MAY BE OBTAINED: Carolyn Stern, 10323 Lorenzo Drive, Los Angeles, California 90064. Cost: $3.00 plus postage and handling.

DESCRIPTION OF MEASURE: The CADI is part of a battery of tests (ERIC, VDI, and EVI) designed to assess the prereading skills of young children. It is an objective test of auditory discrimination in which the effect of language facility and familiarity is held to a minimum. It consists of thirty-eight pairs of words and thirty-eight pages with two pictures per page. One picture represents a familiar concept and the other a nonsense picture and nonsense word (e.g., "scissors" and "fissors" or "plane" and "plame"). To avoid positional responding, the real and nonsense words are randomly located on the left or right side of the page. All the real words have been pretested and demonstrated to be within the vocabulary of the population for whom the test is intended; the nonsense words and pictures have been selected as being low in association value based on a previous study (Stern, 1962). All the word-pairs have been submitted to linguistic analysis to obtain a hierarchy of phonemic contrasts, ranging from gross discriminations to minimal pairs. The CADI is prepared in two forms. Form A asks for one member of a pair and Form B asks for the second member of the pair. The examiner names both pictures, always naming the real word and pointing to the real picture first. The child is told, for example, "This is a girl and this is a hujuj. Point to the girl." (Form A. For Form B the child would be asked to point to the hujuj.) Only responses to items calling for the nonsense term are used in scoring. The test is easy to administer, requires minimal training, and takes approximately 10 to 12 minutes. The two forms make it an excellent pre-post assessment measure.

RELIABILITY AND VALIDITY: For norming purposes, the test was administered to a total of 476 children, with 234 receiving Form A, 242 receiving Form B, and 153 receiving both A and B in random order. Internal reliabilities for Form A and Form B were .84 and .86, respectively. Interform reliability (Spearman-Brown correction) was .87. The sample included 215 boys and 261 girls; 158 white and 318 black; 124 middle- and 352 low-socioeconomic-status children. There were 140 3-year-olds, 217 4-year-olds, and 119 5-year-olds. All children were from a large metropolitan setting and were in attendance at either a nursery school, children's center, or Head Start class. Norms, in terms of percentiles, are available for three age groups.

BIBLIOGRAPHY:

Stern, C. *The Scaling of Nonsense Materials to be Used in Learning Experiments with Young Children.* Unpublished manuscript. University of California, Los Angeles, 1962.

Stern, C. "Evaluating Language Curricula for Preschool Children." *Monographs of the Society for Research in Child Development,* 1968, *33,* 49-61.

---

## STERN'S VISUAL DISCRIMINATION INVENTORY (VDI)

AUTHOR: Carolyn Stern

AGE: 3 to 6 years

VARIABLE: Visual discrimination

TYPE OF MEASURE: Individually administered test

SOURCE FROM WHICH MEASURE MAY BE OBTAINED: Carolyn Stern, 10323 Lorenzo Drive, Los Angeles, California 90064. Cost: $5.00 plus handling and postage.

DESCRIPTION OF MEASURE: The VDI is part of a battery of tests (ERIC, EVI, and CADI) designed to assess the prereading skills of young children. It is an objective test designed to measure visual discrimination in preschool through primary-age children, without the confounding of motor coordination or intelligence variables. The latter is controlled by an instructional program that teaches the task before test items are administered. If a child does not demonstrate understanding in this introductory sequence, the test itself is not to be given. The test items are 8 X 11-inch pages with black-and-white drawings. There is a model picture in the center of the top half of the page and three alternatives in boxes across the lower half of the page. The task is to select the one of the three alternatives most like the model. The original form of the test (see Stern and Lombard, 1968) consisted of fifty-two items in four subtests: form constancy, figure-ground, closure, and position-in-space. However, more extensive testing and data analyses indicated that the first two subtests were not sufficiently discriminating to warrant inclusion in the total test score. Several items were added so that the current test includes fifteen closure and eighteen position-in-space items, or a total of thirty-three scored responses. Norms, in terms of percentile scores, are available for the two subtests and for the total test. Although middle-class children were included in the norming sample, the test has been used most extensively in pre- and posttest evaluations of Head Start and other disadvantaged populations.

RELIABILITY AND VALIDITY: Three forms were developed to test for position preference. Total-test reliabilities of .90 to .92 (Kuder-Richardson formula 20) were found. Summed over forms, the reliability coefficient was .88. The Spearman-Brown prophecy formula for the same data produced a reliability estimate of .91.

BIBLIOGRAPHY:

Stern, C. "Evaluating Language Curricula for Preschool Children." *Monographs of the Society for Research in Child Development,* 1968, *33,* 49-61.

Stern, C. "A Comparison of Three Intervention Programs with Disadvantaged Preschool Children." *Journal of Special Education,* 1970, *4,* 205-214.

Stern, C., and Lombard, A. "An Instrument to Measure Visual Discrimination in Young Children." *Perceptual and Motor Skills,* 1968, *26,* 1207-1210.

---

## TEMPORAL ORDER PERCEPTION TESTS
### (I. FORERUNNER; II. TEMPORAL ORDER AUDITORY-VISUAL; III. READING PREDICTION TEST)

AUTHOR: Dirk J. Bakker

AGE: 6 to 10 years

VARIABLE: Temporal order perception

TYPE OF MEASURE: Test

SOURCE FROM WHICH MEASURE MAY BE OBTAINED: For Forerunner and the TOAV write Dirk J. Bakker, Paedologisch Instituut, Department of Developmental and Educational Neuropsychology, Koningslann 22, Amsterdam (Z), Netherlands. For the Reading Prediction Test (4PT) write J. J. F. Schroots, Nederlands Instituut voor Preventieve Geneeskunde, Wassenaarseweg 56, Leiden, Netherlands.

DESCRIPTION OF MEASURE: I. *Forerunner:* This consists of ten series of nonsense figures, five of meaningful figures, ten of capital letters, and five of digits. Each series comprises four items to project successively on a white screen. The exposure time for each item is 2 seconds, and the interval between two items is 4 seconds. After presentation of a series the subject is handed a card upon which the same items are presented from left to right in random order. The subject has to indicate which item was seen first, second, third, and last. An answer is considered correct only when reproduction is in the original sequence. II. *Temporal Order Auditory-Visual (TOAV):* Two series of two names, four series of three names, five series of four names, and one series of five names of ordinary objects are mentioned at an approximate rate of one name every 2 seconds. After presentation of a series the subject is handed a card upon which the named objects are visually represented in random order. The subject has to indicate which object was mentioned first and which next. The series are scored either correct (all object names in correct order) or wrong (one or more object names in a wrong serial position). III. *Reading Prediction Test (LPT):* This is an improved and extended version of the TOAV (II). Twelve series of object names are mentioned in temporal succession. After presentation of a series, the subject has to indicate on a card the serial position of each object name mentioned and reproduce vocally and in temporal order the whole series of object names. The authors of the LPT are J. J. F. Schroots and J. H. A. Groenendaal, in collaboration with Dirk J. Bakker.

RELIABILITY AND VALIDITY: I. *Forerunner:* This test was administered to fifty-four boys aged 9 to 15 from a school for learning-disabled children. The series of meaningful figures, letters, and digits discriminates between above-average and below-average readers; the series of meaningless figures does not. No reliability data are available. II. *TOAV:* This was administered to 208 boys and 204 girls aged 6 years, being representative samples of all Dutch kindergarten children of that age. The test was repeated with the same children after one and two years, that is, in the first and second grade of elementary school. At ages 6 and 7, girls perform better than boys. The test-retest reliability was .67 (retest after three months). The correlation coefficients between TOAV at the three ages and reading ability in grades 1 and 2 of the elementary school vary between .38 and .40, and after IQ control between .24 and .27 ($p < .0005$). III. *LPT:* This instrument was administered to about 450 kindergarten children (socioeconomic lower class). Item and factor analyses were applied. Reliability coefficients (test-retest and split-half) up to .81 are reported.

BIBLIOGRAPHY:

Bakker, D. J. "Temporal Order, Meaningfulness, and Reading Ability." *Perceptual and Motor Skills,* 1967, *24,* 1027-1030.
Bakker, D. J. *Temporal Order in Disturbed Reading.* Rotterdam, The Netherlands: Rotterdam University Press, 1972.
Groenendaal, J. A., and Bakker, D. J. "The Part Played by Mediation Processes in the Retention of Temporal Sequences by Two Reading Groups." *Human Development,* 1971, *14,* 62-70.

---

# TEST OF AUDITORY-VISUAL INTEGRATION

AUTHORS: Dale Kahn, Herbert G. Birch, and Lillian Belmont

AGE: 8 to 12 years

VARIABLE: The ability to equate visual and auditory stimuli

TYPE OF MEASURE: Test

SOURCE FROM WHICH MEASURE MAY BE OBTAINED: Mrs. Ida Hafner, Department of Pediatrics, Albert Einstein College of Medicine, Bronx, New York 10461.

DESCRIPTION OF MEASURE: The specific task requires *S*s to identify those visual-dot patterns that correspond to patterns of rhythmic auditory stimuli tapped out by the examiner. The examiner's arm and shoulder movements are hidden by a cardboard screen placed in front of *S* so that no visual cues accompany the auditory presentation. Three visual-dot-pattern choices are available for each item. The total number of correct judgments constitutes *S*'s score, and no correction is made for guessing.
    The entire test is given below.

| AUDITORY TAP PATTERNS | VISUAL STIMULI | | |
|---|---|---|---|
| **EXAMPLES** | | | |
| A ● ● | ●● | ● ● | ●●● |
| B ● ●● | ●●● | ● ●● | ●● ● |
| C ●● ● | ●●● | ● ●● | ●●_● |
| **TEST ITEMS** | | | |
| 1 ●● ●● | ● ●●● | ● ●● ● | ●●_●● |
| 2 ● ●●● | ●●●● | ●_●●● | ●●● ● |
| 3 ●●● ●● | ●●●●● | ●● ●●● | ●●●_●● |
| 4 ● ●● ● | ●_●●_● | ●●●●● | ●● ●● |
| 5 ●●● ●● ● | ●●● ●● ● | ●● ●●● ● | ● ●●● ●● |
| 6 ●● ●●● | ●●● ●● | ●●_●●● | ●●●● ● |
| 7 ●● ●● ●● | ●● ●● ●● | ●●●● ●● | ●●● ● ●● |
| 8 ●●● ●●● ● | ●● ●●● ●● | ●●● ●● ●● | ●●● ●●● ● |
| 9 ●● ● ●●● | ●● ●● ●● | ●●_●_●●● | ●● ●●● ● |
| 10 ● ●●● ●● | ● ●● ●●● | ●_●●●_●● | ●● ● ●●● |
| 11 ● ●●●●● ● | ●● ●●●● ● | ● ●●●● ●● | ●_●●●●●_● |
| 12 ●●● ●●● ●● | ●● ●●● ●● | ●●●● ●● ● | ●●● ●●● ●● |
| 13 ● ●●● ●●● | ●_●●●_●●● | ● ●● ●●●● | ● ●●●● ●● |
| 14 ●● ●●● ●● | ● ●●●● ●● | ●● ●●● ●● | ●● ●● ●●● |
| 15 ●●●● ● ●●● | ●●●● ● ●●● | ●●●● ●● ●● | ●●●●● ● ●● |
| 16 ●●●● ●● ●● | ●● ●●●● ●● | ●●● ●●● ●● | ●●●● ●● ●● |
| 17 ●●● ●● ●●● | ●●● ●● ●●● | ●●● ●●● ●● | ●● ●●● ●●● |
| 18 ● ●●● ●●●● | ● ●●●● ●●● | ● ●● ●●●●● | ●_●●●_●●●● |
| 19 ●●● ●●●● ● | ●●● ●●● ●● | ●●● ●●●● ● | ●●●● ●●● ● |
| 20 ●●●● ●●● ●● | ●●●● ●●● ●● | ●● ●●●●● ●● | ●●● ●●●● ●● |

RELIABILITY AND VALIDITY: The reliability of the measure was assessed by its repeated administration in small groups to thirty-three third-grade boys and thirty-seven fifth-grade boys. Test-retest results, obtained approximately ten days apart, yielded reliability coefficients of .76 for the third-grade group and .90 for the fifth-grade group.

BIBLIOGRAPHY:

Birch, H. G., and Belmont, L. "Auditory-Visual Integration in Normal and Retarded Readers." *American Journal of Orthopsychiatry*, 1964, *34*, 852-861.

Birch, H. G., and Belmont, L. "Auditory-Visual Integration, Intelligence and Reading Achievement." *Perceptual and Motor Skills*, 1965, *20*, 295-305.

Blank, M., and Bridger, W. H. "Deficiencies in Verbal Labeling in Retarded Readers." *American Journal of Orthopsychiatry*, 1966, *36*, 840-847.

Camp, B. N. "Psychometric Tests and Learning in Severely Disabled Readers." *Journal of Learning Disability*, 1973, *6*, 512-517.

Kahn, D., and Birch, H. G. "Development of Auditory-Visual Integration and Reading Achievement." *Perceptual and Motor Skills*, 1968, *27*, 459-468.

# TEST OF DIRECTIONAL SKILLS

AUTHOR: Graham M. Sterritt

AGE: Normals, 3 to 7 years; mentally retarded, any age

VARIABLE: Left-right and top-to-bottom sentence tracking

TYPE OF MEASURE: Test

SOURCE FROM WHICH MEASURE MAY BE OBTAINED: Graham M. Sterritt, 560 South Corona, Denver, Colorado 80209.

DESCRIPTION OF MEASURE: The child is shown twelve cards one at a time and asked, "Where does this sentence begin?" (or "Where do these sentences begin?" for cards with more than one sentence), and "Use your finger to show me how this sentence (these sentences) goes, from the beginning to the end." The score is based upon the number of correct responses (maximum = 27 correct) for pointing to the first word and tracking correctly left to right, without skipping lines.

   As examples, two selected stimulus items of the twelve-item test, with directions for each, are given below.

| *Stimulus* | *Directions (Scoring)* |
|---|---|
| 1. I like my teddy bear. | Point to where the sentence begins. (Beg. _____) |
| 9. Do you like cake? Let me give you a big slice of cake. | Use your finger to show how the sentences go from the beginning of the first sentence to the end of the last one. (Beg. _____, L to R _____, Top to Bot. _____) |

RELIABILITY AND VALIDITY: None reported.

BIBLIOGRAPHY:

Sterritt, G. M., Konty, P., and Padia, W. "Teaching Directional Skills to Preschool and Kindergarten Children" (in press).

## TEST OF NONVERBAL AUDITORY
## DISCRIMINATION (TENVAD)

AUTHOR: Norman A. Buktenica

AGE: 5 to 8 years

VARIABLE: Auditory discrimination

TYPE OF MEASURE: Test

SOURCE FROM WHICH MEASURE MAY BE OBTAINED: Follett Publishing Company, 1010 West Washington Boulevard, Chicago, Illinois 60607. Cost: Less than $20.00 (estimate).

DESCRIPTION OF MEASURE: The TENVAD was constructed for the purpose of assessing auditory discrimination in young children. The stimulus materials are on magnetic tape and are essentially nonverbal. It is comprised of fifty pairs of tones in five subtests: (1) pitch—tone pairs of same or different frequency; (2) loudness—constant frequency, pairs of the same or different decibel value; (3) rhythm—rhythm pairs are either the same or different; (4) duration—at a constant frequency, pairs of the same or different length in duration; and (5) timbre—tone pairs of the same or different quality. The administration of the test is relatively simple and designed to be given to groups as large as a full classroom. It is recommended that kindergarten children be tested in small groups of five to ten. The instructions for administration of the TENVAD are on tape. The child is presented with the task of listening to fifty pairs of tones and asked to indicate if the pairs are the same or different.

RELIABILITY AND VALIDITY: The standardization sample was comprised of children from three school districts that included middle-class white children and lower-class black children. Performance has been fairly stable across socioeconomic and racial lines. Reliability for ages 5½ to 8½ ranges from .75 to .78 based on Kuder-Richardson formula 20. External validity derived from several sources including comparison of performance of TENVAD with the Wepman Auditory Discrimination Test and comparison of TENVAD scores with Metropolitan Achievement Test scores. Both reliability- and validity-derived indices are significant at the .01 level or greater. The findings lend support to the use of TENVAD as an early screening device and as an instrument for developing instructional procedures.

BIBLIOGRAPHY:

Buktenica, N. A. "Auditory Discrimination: A New Assessment Procedure." *Exceptional Children,* 1971, *38,* 237-242.

## TWO-ALTERNATIVE PERCEPTION TEST (APT)

AUTHOR: Lisl M. Goodman

AGE: 3 years and up

VARIABLE: Perceptual whole or part preferences

TYPE OF MEASURE: Projective technique

SOURCE FROM WHICH MEASURE MAY BE OBTAINED: Lisl Goodman, Psychology Department, Jersey City State College, 2039 Kennedy Memorial Boulevard, Jersey City, New Jersey 07305.

DESCRIPTION OF MEASURE: The APT consists of three parallel sets of nine drawings. Each drawing can be seen as a representation of one whole object or as a collection of separate objects. Structures of wholes and subwholes are equally strong and simple, resulting in an equal probability of whole or part perceptions to occur within a set. In the scoring system, Ss are classified into one of three categories: (1) whole-dominant (W-dominant), 0-3 drawings perceived as consisting of parts (6-9 as wholes); (2) part-dominant (D-dominant), 6-9 drawings perceived as consisting of parts (0-3 as wholes); (3) neutral: 4-5 drawings perceived as consisting of parts (or wholes). A normative study of sixty nursery-school to first-grade children (3.5 to 7.2 years old) indicated a gradual decrease in W-dominance and an increase in D-dominance with age: nursery age, 65 percent W-dominant, 0 percent D-dominant, 35 percent neutral; kindergarten, 25 percent W-dominant, 55 percent D-dominant, 20 percent neutral; first grade, 10 percent W-dominant, 75 percent D-dominant, 15 percent neutral. W-dominance was found to be related to ego-boundary permeability (less ego-nonego segregation) and to an integrative cognitive attitude, while D-dominance was found to be related to ego-boundary impermeability (greater ego-nonego segregation) and to an analytic-cognitive attitude.

RELIABILITY AND VALIDITY: Preliminary investigations with 195 teenage Ss established (1) that the APT is evenly balanced within each set and that the three sets are parallel (part and whole perception have equal probability of occurring), (2) Ss are predominantly consistent in perceiving either parts or wholes in a set of nine drawings, and (3) preference for whole or part perception is consistent over time. The strength of association between two testing sessions (using parallel APTs) with an interval of one month is 32 percent, which is significant at the .01 level. However, consistency in part-whole preference over time is not to be expected with preteenage Ss.

BIBLIOGRAPHY:

Goodman, L. M. "Perceptual Preferences in Relation to Aspects of Personality." Unpublished doctoral dissertation. New School for Social Research, New York, 1969.

Goodman, L. M. "The Influence of Success and Failure Experiences on Perceptual Whole-Part Preferences." *Psychologische Forschung,* 1973, *36,* 163-175.

Goodman, L. M. "Perceptual Preferences in Relation to Aspects of Personality." *Genetic Psychology Monographs,* 1973, *88,* 111-132.

## VISUAL DISCRIMINATION TEST

AUTHORS: Joseph M. Wepman, Anne Morency, and Marva Seidl

AGE: 5 to 8 years

VARIABLE: Visual form discrimination

TYPE OF MEASURE: Test

SOURCE FROM WHICH MEASURE MAY BE OBTAINED: Language Research Associates, Inc., 175 E. Delaware Place, Chicago, Illinois 60611.

DESCRIPTION OF MEASURE: This is a test designed to assess the subject's ability to judge relatively gross differences in visually presented forms. Reading requires the ability to distinguish relatively fine differences in orthographic form prior to its application in reading; however, there appears to be a developing capacity to detect form differences that relate to the task of reading at a later time. While for most children this prelinguistic form distinction is well developed by school age, when it has not yet developed, it may lie at the very root of a reading disability. In the development of visual form discrimination there appears to be a process of stabilization of the visual processing of data; when stabilization has not been achieved the error patterns selected indicate the type of instability a child may have, which may be more instructive than a simple count of errors.

The test consists of twenty items with a "target" in the center and the responses in the four corners of the same page. Error types are based on Gibson's transformations, with perspective and size errors not represented, but addition and deletion of features, topological, rotation, and reflection errors available in balanced subsets. The child's task is to point to the figure "just like the one in the middle," and the training items give examples of each kind of error. The task tends to be easy, but the item format avoids the usual way of "making it harder" by right to left arrangement of distractors, with an attractive alternative to the left of the correct response. This common arrangement wreaks total havoc with error analysis because of the common occurrence of response sets among young children. Analysis of the pilot data suggests little patterning of responses with the four-corner arrangement.

RELIABILITY AND VALIDITY: None reported.

BIBLIOGRAPHY:

Gibson, E. J., Gibson, J. J., Pick, A. D., and Osser, H. "A Developmental Study of the Discrimination of the Letter-like Forms." *Journal of Comparative and Physiological Psychology*, 1962, *55*, 897-906.

Wepman, J. "A Perceptual Test Battery: Development and Standardization." *Elementary School Journal*, 1972, *72*, 351-361.

Wepman, J. M., Morency, A., and Seidl, M. *Manual for Administration, Scoring, and Interpretation: Visual Discrimination Test.* Chicago: Language Research Associates, 1975.

*Prepared by Orval G. Johnson*

## VISUAL EFFICIENCY SCALE

AUTHOR: Natalie C. Barraga

AGE: Preschool to adult

VARIABLE: Visual discrimination and visual perception

TYPE OF MEASURE: Rating scale

SOURCE FROM WHICH MEASURE MAY BE OBTAINED: American Printing House for the Blind, Inc., P.O. Box 6085, Louisville, Kentucky 40206. Cost: Low Vision Kit includes Teacher's Guide and one copy of Visual Efficiency Scale, $2.50; package of 10 copies of the scale plus directions, $6.00.

DESCRIPTION OF MEASURE: The Visual Efficiency Scale consists of forty-eight items divided into four sections of increasingly difficult visual tasks. The purpose is to determine the level of efficiency at which visual stimuli can be discriminated and perceived accurately. Items in each section are increasingly complex and decrease in size from 72-point to 8-point. The scale is a revision of the Visual Discrimination Test published in 1964. A profile sheet provides for charting of items in sequence so as to determine a low, marginal, or satisfactory level of efficiency. The theoretical basis for design is derived from specific developmental aspects of visual behavior and encompasses the range of discriminatory and perceptual tasks related to visual learning up to but not including symbol recognition. The scale was designed primarily for severely visually impaired or low-vision children but has been found to be useful with kindergarten, learning-disabled, retarded, and other children with limited visual learning ability.

Following are the visual skills and behaviors related to the items in the four sections of the scale: Section I—Discrimination of geometric form, object contour, light-dark intensity, size and position; Section II—Discrimination of size: object and abstract figure detail, position in space, image constancy of outlines, pattern details and objects; Section III—visual closure, spatial perspective, discrimination of object and abstract figure details; Section IV—Discrimination of size, position, sequence, and relationship of letter and word symbols, and groups of symbols. Following are the directions for the first of the forty-eight items, which is a ¾-inch square followed by four figures (rectangle, hexagon, square, and a diamond with an inclined vertical axis) from which to choose a matching square: Say: "Put your finger by the first row. Look at the form in the box, then mark the one in the row that looks just like (or exactly like) the one in the box."

RELIABILITY AND VALIDITY: The original measure was administered to kindergarten children, mildly visually handicapped children, and low-vision children. Test-retest reliability was established by analysis of initial test and retest scores of the experimental group. An internal consistency reliability of .96 was computed by the Kuder-Richardson procedure. This indicated that individual items differentiated between high and low scorers in a similar manner to the total test scores. A split-half reliability coefficient of .97 corrected by the Spearman-Brown formula indicated that the items were comparable in progressive difficulty. The validity is based upon the rationale that visual behavior is learned, and the sequence is similar in nature to the development of vision in infants and young children.

BIBLIOGRAPHY:

Barraga, N. C. *Increased Visual Behavior in Low-Vision Children.* New York: American Foundation for the Blind, 1964.
Barraga, N. C. (Ed.) *Teacher's Guide for Development of Visual Learning Abilities and Utilization of Low Vision.* Louisville, Kentucky: American Printing House for the Blind, 1970.
Harley, R., and Spollen, J. "A Study of the Reliability and Validity of the Visual Efficiency Scale with Low-Vision Children." *Education of the Visually Handicapped,* 1973, *5,* 110-114.
Harley, R., and Spollen, J. "A Study of the Reliability and Validity of the Visual Efficiency Scale with First-Grade Children." *Education of the Visually Handicapped,* 1974, *6,* 88-93.
Hull, W. A., and McCarthy, D. G. "Supplementary Program for Preschool Visually Handicapped Children." *Education of the Visually Handicapped,* 1973, *5,* 97-104.

---

# VISUAL MEMORY SCALE (VMS)

AUTHOR: James L. Carroll

AGE: 5 and 6 years

VARIABLE: Short-term visual recognition memory

TYPE OF MEASURE: Individually administered test

SOURCE FROM WHICH MEASURE MAY BE OBTAINED: Carroll Publications, 201 East Grand Avenue, Mt. Pleasant, Michigan 48858. Cost: Complete set containing the test cards, manual, and 25 scoring blanks, $9.50.

DESCRIPTION OF MEASURE: The VMS is a test designed to be used by psychologists, learning-disability specialists, and classroom teachers to assess short-term visual recognition memory in children aged 5 and 6. The test requires the child to look at a stimulus design (one or a group of geometric shapes) for 5 seconds. The stimulus design is then removed, and the child is immediately shown a card with four designs on it (including the one he has just seen) and required to indicate by word or gesture the correct design. The number of errors is recorded and the child's performance is compared with the norms (separate norms for 5- and 6-year-olds) in order to evaluate and interpret the test score. The test materials consist of fifty 6 X 4-inch cards. Twenty-five cards have one design printed in black (referred to as the stimulus designs). The remaining twenty-five cards have retention plate for each stimulus design. The designs range from extremely simple geometric shapes (such as a cross and a triangle) to more complex designs employing two or three different geometric shapes in a single array. Each multiple-choice retention plate consists of the correct design (the original stimulus) and three incorrect designs (variations of the correct stimulus but rotated, inverted, or incomplete).

RELIABILITY AND VALIDITY: The normative group includes 325 children (primarily white, middle-class, with IQs in the average range) from central New Jersey and central Michigan. It was found that 6-year-old children made significantly fewer errors than did 5-year-olds. Sex and IQ differences were not related significantly to the child's visual memory abilities. Split-half reliability was computed for one sample, and test-retest reliability was examined twice. The correlations were .96 ($df$ = 28), .68 ($df$ = 28), and .70 ($df$ = 26), respectively. A comparison of the performance of neurologically impaired retarded children ($N$ = 19) and nonneurologically impaired retardates ($N$ = 13) showed that the former made significantly more errors than the latter. Another study with kindergarten children found significant correlation ($r$ = −.39) between VMS errors and the Harper & Row Readiness Test ($df$ = 92). Other studies have found a moderately high relationship (in the area of .60) between the VMS and reading achievement in kindergarten, first, and second grade.

BIBLIOGRAPHY:

Carroll, J. L. "A Visual Memory Scale Designed to Measure Short-Term Recognition Memory in Five- and Six-Year-Old Children." *Psychology in the Schools,* 1972, *9,* 152-158.
Carroll, J. L. "Assessment of Short-Term Visual Memory and Its Educational Implications." *Perceptual and Motor Skills,* 1974, *38,* 574.
Carroll, J. L. "Short-Term Memory in Five- and Six-Year-Old Children: Some Cognitive and Academic Correlates." Paper presented at the annual meeting of the American Psychological Association. New Orleans, Louisiana, 1974.

# VISUAL MEMORY TEST

AUTHORS: Joseph M. Wepman, Anne Morency, and Marva Seidl

AGE: 5 to 8 years

VARIABLE: Visual form memory

TYPE OF MEASURE: Test

SOURCE FROM WHICH MEASURE MAY BE OBTAINED: Language Research Associates, Inc., 175 E. Delaware Place, Chicago, Illinois 60611.

DESCRIPTION OF MEASURE: The test is designed to measure immediate recall of free forms not easily identifiable by name. The ability to hold forms in mind and recall them on presentation appears to be a perceptual task closely related to reading. As the child reads, his ability to see and hold the alphabetic form in mind while he processes the image for meaning seems fundamental. A poor recall ability points to the need for constant visual restimulation with consequent loss of immediate accurate reaction and the tendency to "guess" as a means of avoiding the slowness restimulation causes, as well as the interruption in fluency it produces. Prelinguistic form recall seems closely related to and predictive of later difficulty in reading. Factorially both discrimination and recall are highly correlated with other visual perceptual factors; they are only slightly related to intelligence. The assessment task used is a target form presented for 5 seconds followed by a multiple-choice presentation of five forms including the target form. The task requirement is simply pointing to the recalled form.

RELIABILITY AND VALIDITY: None reported.

BIBLIOGRAPHY:

Wepman, J. "A Perceptual Test Battery: Development and Standardization." *Elementary School Journal*, 1972, *72*, 351-361.
Wepman, J. M., Morency, A., and Seidl, M. *Manual of Administration, Scoring, and Interpretation: The Visual Memory Test.* Chicago: Language Research Associates, 1975.

---

# VISUAL PERCEPTION TEST

AUTHOR: Marguerite P. Ford

AGE: 8 years to adult

VARIABLE: Visual recognition ability

TYPE OF MEASURE: Test

SOURCE FROM WHICH MEASURE MAY BE OBTAINED: Slides available from Marguerite P. Ford, Central Valley Regional Center, 567 West Shaw, Fresno, California 93704. Cost: Simultaneous series, $32.18 plus postage; successive series, $80.45 plus postage.

DESCRIPTION OF MEASURE: The Visual Perception Test contains forty-six items (forty test and six practice items) consisting of straight-line geometric figures. Each item consists of a standard figure and four-choice figures, one of which is identical with the standard. The alternatives were designed to tap relatively small differences along various dimensions, such as right-left orientation and addition or omission of parts. The test items are available on two sets of slides designed for either simultaneous or successive presentation. In the simultaneous series, the standard figure is shown first for 5 seconds, followed immediately by the four-choice figures on a single slide shown for 8 seconds. A blank interval of 5 seconds follows each item. In the successive series the standard is presented for 5 seconds, followed immediately by the four-choice figures shown one at a time for 5 seconds each, with a blank interval of 5 seconds following each item. *S*s are instructed to look carefully at the standard figure in order to be able to recognize it when seen again. They are told that they will see four different figures, that only one of these will match the standard exactly, and that they are to choose the correct match. The exposure intervals and instructions for responding can be modified to suit the experimenter's purpose.

RELIABILITY AND VALIDITY: No data available.

BIBLIOGRAPHY:

Ford, M. P. "Serial Position Preferences in Children in Simultaneous vs. Successive Matching Tasks." *Perceptual and Motor Skills*, 1971, *32*, 963-968.

---

## VISUAL SYNTHESIS TEST

AUTHOR: Judith W. Greenberg

AGE: Approximately 4 to 7 years

VARIABLE: Visual synthesis of parts of geometric figures

TYPE OF MEASURE: Test (individual, multiple-choice)

SOURCE FROM WHICH MEASURE MAY BE OBTAINED: The sets of cards needed for the test may be constructed from information provided in the appendices of Greenberg (1969). All the geometric figures used are included in exact scale, and the multiple-choice options for each item are specified.

DESCRIPTION OF MEASURE: The Visual Synthesis Test assesses the ability to recognize a whole geometric figure after the parts have been shown and then removed. It consists of two series of twenty-five divided figures each, based on forms such as rectangles, diamonds, pentagons, and hexagons. In one series, figures are bisected vertically; in the other, the same figures are dissected; that is, all component lines are separated while maintaining the orientation and relative position of lines. For each item, the separated parts of the test figure, traced with black felt pen on one 5 X 8-inch card, are shown first. The child is asked to think "how the shape would look" if the parts could be "pushed toward the middle until they touched." (The names of forms, for example, square, triangle, are not used by examiner.) After 3 seconds the card is turned over and another card exposed displaying four options, one being the correct whole figure. *S* is asked to point to the whole form whose parts he had seen. Blank cards are inserted between items so that the next item is not visible immediately. A stand at an angle of thirty degrees to the table top is used to display items. Scoring consists of the number right. In the original study of eighty 5- and 6-year-olds, visual synthesis of bisected figures yielded a mean of 15.7 (*SD* = 3.9); for dissected figures, the mean was 12.9 (*SD* = 4.4). A total-synthesis score, based on the fifty combined bisected and dissected items, was also obtained (*M* = 28.4, *SD* = 7.5).

RELIABILITY AND VALIDITY: The following reliabilities were obtained, using Kuder-Richardson formula 20 with the original eighty 5- and 6-year-old subjects: synthesis of dissected figures, .74; synthesis of bisected figures, .69. Analysis of rates and types of errors gave some support for validity of the measure. Dissected figures, completely broken down, were more difficult than bisected figures (correlated *t* = 7.4). On the other hand, whole figures, which involved only memory, were easier than the divided figures that required synthesis. When the twenty-five whole figures were presented and then removed, the mean number correctly selected from four options was 21.3 (*SD* = 2.5). Relatively gross errors (e.g., confusing a trapezoid and pentagon) were made chiefly by *S*s who scored low in the total test; the errors of the high scorers involved more subtle distinctions (e.g., confusing a trapezoid and a parallelogram).

BIBLIOGRAPHY:

Greenberg, J. W. "Synthesis and Analysis of Visually Perceived Forms by Young Children." *Perceptual and Motor Skills,* 1972, *34,* 735-741.
Greenberg, J. W. "Visual Perception Abilities of Young Children in Synthesis and Analysis Tasks." Unpublished doctoral dissertation. Columbia University, New York, 1969.

---

# WILLS AUDITORY GESTALT TEST

AUTHOR: I. H. Wills

AGE: 6 to 14 years

VARIABLE: Auditory closure

TYPE OF MEASURE: Verbal checklist

SOURCE FROM WHICH MEASURE MAY BE OBTAINED: See Banas and Wills (1969).

DESCRIPTION OF MEASURE: The Wills Auditory Gestalt Test is composed of a controlled spelling list for levels one through eight, with words chosen to include those where transpositions or omissions are crucial to proper identification or where familiarity would make identification by minimal clues possible. It is not a spelling test and is only valid if the child can spell the words from the list for the level at which he is being measured. After administration of the Auditory Gestalt Test, those words that are missed should be given as a regular spelling test. If the child can spell the words but cannot identify them from auditory clues, it must be assumed that the limitation is from the auditory pathway. Three patterns showed up on experimental testing: (1) breakdown in holding sufficient individual symbols or sequence, which resulted in too few pieces to enable students to build gestalt; (2) a reaction to minimal clues with good ability to find gestalt, but lack of accuracy (attention) with details affecting accuracy of the gestalt; and (3) complete inability to visualize gestalt though all symbols were held and could be repeated. A child with this last pattern could not be taught with a phonetic approach. Observations of the approach taken by the child may reveal a need for auditory feedback or for kinesthetic clues, or may reveal anxiety during oral presentation.

RELIABILITY AND VALIDITY: During experimental administration, the results compared favorably with previous diagnostic information on the students.

BIBLIOGRAPHY:

Banas, N., and Wills, I. H. "The Vulnerable Child Listens." *Academic Therapy*, 1969, *4*, 311-312.

---

# WIST-ARNOLD AUDITORY DISCRIMINATION TEST

AUTHORS: Anne H. Wist and Richard D. Arnold

AGE: 5 to 8 years

VARIABLE: Auditory discrimination

TYPE OF MEASURE: Test

SOURCE FROM WHICH MEASURE MAY BE OBTAINED: Purdue University Reading Clinic, Education Building, West Lafayette, Indiana 47907. Cost: Package of 35, $3.00; instructions (manual), $1.00.

DESCRIPTION OF MEASURE: This test is modeled after the Wepman Test of Auditory Discrimination but contains items of particular relevance to children whose native tongue is Spanish. It is individually administered but easy to score and interpret. The forty-item test takes 8 minutes to administer, plus time for directions. This is an experimental edition and is in the process of being normatized.

    As examples, ten of the forty items on the test are given below. The respondent listens to each word-pair (there is a pause of approximately 5 seconds between words) and then tells the examiner whether they are the same or different.

1. skin/sin
2. car/car
3. rogue/road
4. mace/maze
5. chop/shop
11. mark/mar
12. cooed/could
13. get/get
14. fan/than
15. sun/sung

RELIABILITY AND VALIDITY: Reliability (Kuder-Richardson) is .81 for the Mexican-American scale and .70 for the Anglo-American scale.

BIBLIOGRAPHY:

Arnold, R. D., and Wist, A. H. "Auditory Discrimination Abilities of Disadvantaged Anglo- and Mexican-American Children." *Elementary School Journal,* 1970, *70,* 295-299.

*Prepared by Richard D. Arnold*

---

# WORD INTELLIGIBILITY BY PICTURE IDENTIFICATION (WIPI)

AUTHORS: Mark Ross and Jay Lerman

AGE: 5 years and up

VARIABLE: Speech discrimination ability in children

TYPE OF MEASURE: Picture identification

SOURCE FROM WHICH MEASURE MAY BE OBTAINED: Stanwix House, Inc., 3020 Chartiers Avenue, Pittsburgh, Pennsylvania 15204. Cost: WIPI test manual, $12.00; WIPI score sheet, $.65 per 50; WIPI combination, $13.00.

DESCRIPTION OF MEASURE: The WIPI test was developed to provide clinicians and educators with a tool for assessing the speech discrimination ability of young hearing-impaired children. Most of these children cannot be tested by conventional methods because of unintelligible speech, vocabulary deficiencies, and inability to make written responses to the verbal stimuli. In the WIPI test, these problems were considered by devising a picture-pointing format, which precluded the necessity of the children's making an oral or written response, and by carefully selecting the words to be pictorially represented. The test was designed to be used in a fashion similar to conventional speech discrimination tests. Scores can be compared to those obtained by other hearing-impaired children, the relative difference between the ears can be measured, differences between hearing aids can be evaluated, and results of an auditory training program can be assessed on a longitudinal basis.

RELIABILITY AND VALIDITY: Sixty-one subjects were studied in the final evaluation phase of the test. Their ages ranged from 4 years, 7 months to 13 years, 9 months, with a mean age of 10 years, 2 months. The hearing level in the better ear for all subjects exceeded thirty *dB* (1964 ISO Standard) at one or more of the speech frequencies. The test-retest reliability coefficients ranged from .87 to .94, while the errors of measurement ranged from 4.7 to 7.7. These results indicate that all four lists of the test are highly reliable with comparable reliabilities for all four lists. The equivalency of the four lists was evaluated by assessing the mean differences and the correlations between lists. The differences between the A and B presentations indicate that a learning effect took place between the first and second presentation of each list. These differences were evaluated by a standard sign test and, except for List III, found to be significant at the .06 level. Since the order of presentation of the four lists was rotated and all four of the lists show the learning effect, it suggests that this effect would still have been present even if a practice list had been utilized. In any event, the differences are not more than the equivalent of one extra word correct (4 percent per word) during the second presentation of each list and should not be clinically significant. A comparison of the means and standard deviations of the four lists indicates that the average level and range of difficulty are comparable. The only significant mean difference was at the .05 level and occurred between Lists III and IV. However, this difference of 2.8 percent is less than a one-word variation and, as in the learning effect, cannot be considered clinically significant. The Pearson product-moment correlation coefficients of the four lists range from .84 to .95, with five of the six correlations .92 or higher. Taken together with the negligible mean difference in lists, these results indicate the four lists to be highly equivalent.

BIBLIOGRAPHY:

Ross, M., and Lerman, J. "A Picture Identification Test for Hearing Impaired Children." *Journal of Speech and Hearing Research,* 1970, *13,* 44-53.
Ross, M., and Lerman, J. *Word Intelligibility by Picture Identification.* Pittsburgh, Pennsylvania: Stanwix House, 1971.

*Prepared by Jay Lerman*

# Category 7

═══════════════════════════════════════════

# Physical Attributes

═══════════════════════════════════════════

*This category includes only a few measures, but they do not logically fit elsewhere. It includes measures of wake-sleep state, physical condition, motion sickness, and health problems.*

# BEHAVIORAL INVENTORY FOR ASSESSING
# STATE IN HUMAN INFANTS

AUTHORS: James D. Boismier, Patricia F. Chappell, and Gilbert W. Meier

AGE: Birth to 1 month

VARIABLE: Behavioral wake-sleep state in human infants

TYPE OF MEASURE: Categorical rating scale

SOURCE FROM WHICH MEASURE MAY BE OBTAINED: James D. Boismier, Nebraska Psychiatric Institute, 602 South 45th Street, Omaha, Nebraska 68106.

DESCRIPTION OF MEASURE: The Behavioral Inventory for Assessing States in Human Infants consists of seventeen behavioral criteria and a set of rules for determining seven wake-sleep states. The behavioral criteria are grouped into five categories with levels arranged in rank order, and the rules map combinations of levels across categories onto the seven wake-sleep states. Wake-sleep-state determinations are made for each 15-second epoch because longer epochs are insensitive to brief changes of state. Definitions of the seven wake-sleep states are as follows: (1) Regular or quiet sleep: regular respiration, eyes closed, no facial movements, no vocalization, and no movement. (2) Irregular or rapid eye movement (REM) sleep: irregular respiration, rapid eye movements, facial movement, no vocalizations, and peripheral or mild limb movement. (3) Transitional sleep: irregular respiration, eyes closed (REMs possible), facial movement, noncrying vocalization, and gross reflex or mild limb movement. (4) Drowsiness: regular or irregular respiration, eyes open or close slowly at least twice, but only briefly, vocalization possible, and gross reflex or gross limb movement. (5) Alert inactivity: regular respiration, eyes open and moving, facial movement possible, no vocalization, mild limb movement possible. (6) Waking activity: irregular respiration, eyes open and moving, facial movement, noncrying vocalization possible, and gross limb movement. (7) Crying: irregular respiration, eyes closed, facial movement, at least two crying vocalizations during 15-second epoch, and gross limb movement.

RELIABILITY AND VALIDITY: Face validity is indicated by comparison with other scales for measuring wake-sleep states in human infants.

BIBLIOGRAPHY:

Boismier, J. D., Chappel, P. F., and Meier, G. W. "Wakefulness and REM Sleep in Human Neonates." *Developmental Psychobiology,* 1974, *7,* 304.

# EDWARDS NEONATAL OBSERVATIONS AT TWENTY MINUTES AFTER BIRTH

AUTHOR: Nancy Edwards

AGE: Neonates 20 minutes of age

VARIABLE: Neonatal physical condition

TYPE OF MEASURE: Rating scale

SOURCE FROM WHICH MEASURE MAY BE OBTAINED: Appendix B, Document no. 0062, ASIS Documents, Microfiche Publications, 440 Park Avenue South, New York, New York 10016. Cost: $3.00 (microfiche); $6.50 (photocopy).

DESCRIPTION OF MEASURE: This scale involves the observation at age 20 minutes of neonatal physical conditions and behavior that are potentially significant for later development. Respiration, motor activity and tone, tone of neck, molding, forceps mark, umbilical cord, skin, cry, and motor reflex are recorded and arranged in scores. A score of 2 is credited for normal appearance, a score of 1 for moderate or slight deviations, and 0 for abnormal signs. Space is allowed for additional comments and findings. These narrative descriptions are listed, ordered, and progressively rated. Descriptions range from "never well flexed" to "vigorous infant."

RELIABILITY AND VALIDITY: Qualitative aspects of functioning, as represented in this measure, show significant correlations with 4-year development. Correlation coefficients between the 20-minute rating and IQ, concept formation, fine motor, and gross motor were .23, .18, .41, and .40, respectively. For each of these variables, apart from concept formation, coefficients were consistently positive and significant at the .001 level. The coefficient between the 20-minute rating and concept formation was significant at the .05 level.

BIBLIOGRAPHY:

Edwards, N. "The Relationship Between Physical Condition Immediately After Birth and Mental and Motor Performance at Age Four." *Genetic Psychology Monographs,* 1968, *78,* 257-289.

## HEALTH PROBLEMS INVENTORY FOR
## HIGH SCHOOL STUDENTS

AUTHOR: Phyllis Sandidge O'Daniels

AGE: Grades 10 to 12

VARIABLE: Acknowledgement of health problems

TYPE OF MEASURE: Likert-type scale

SOURCE FROM WHICH MEASURE MAY BE OBTAINED: Phyllis S. O'Daniels, 1041 Mulberry, North Bend, Nebraska 68649. Cost: $.20 per copy.

DESCRIPTION OF MEASURE: The instrument consists of 190 items involving possible health problems encountered by high school students. The student form can be used in conjunction with the faculty form to determine the degree of awareness among faculty of the various student health-related problems and can be useful in individual and group counseling sessions. It is also useful as a means of determining possible content for health instruction or discussions. The items are categorized as follows: 1-40, Home Environment; 41-81, Boy-Girl Relationships; 82-125, Psychological; 126-181, Physiological; and 182-190, Occupational.

As examples, the first ten of the 190 items on the inventory are given below. The respondent answers on a 5-point frequency scale ranging from "never" to "always" indicating the degree to which the situation presents him with a problem.

1. I live with only one parent.
2. My parents are divorced.
3. One of my parents is deceased.
4. Both of my parents are deceased.
5. My father is an alcoholic.
6. My mother is an alcoholic.
7. My father is a compulsive drug user.
8. My mother is a compulsive drug user.
9. I live in unsanitary conditions.
10. I live in an area with a great amount of air pollution.

RELIABILITY AND VALIDITY: To insure curricular validity, the problems were identified by using high school health texts and other pertinent health topic listings. The listing was submitted to a jury of health educators and guidance counselors for needed revisions.

BIBLIOGRAPHY:

O'Daniels, P. S. "A Health Problems Inventory for High School Students." *Journal of School Health,* 1971, *41,* 266-269.

# MINOR PHYSICAL ANOMALIES:
# A MANUAL FOR EVALUATING AND SCORING

AUTHOR: Mary F. Waldrop

AGE: Birth to 12 years

VARIABLE: Presence of multiple minor physical anomalies

TYPE OF MEASURE: Symptoms checklist

SOURCE FROM WHICH MEASURE MAY BE OBTAINED: Mary F. Waldrop, Building 15K, Laboratory of Developmental Psychology, National Institute of Mental Health, 9000 Rockville Pike, Bethesda, Maryland 20014.

DESCRIPTION OF MEASURE: A group of eighteen minor physical anomalies has been found by several researchers to be associated with important dimensions of problem behavior. For boys this dimension represents fast moving, impulsive, clumsy behavior at one extreme and attentive, controlled, well-coordinated behavior at the other extreme. For girls this dimension tends to represent inhibited, fearful, and ill-at-ease behavior at one end and spontaneous, outgoing, well-coordinated behavior at the other end. Even though the eighteen minor physical anomalies have been identified with Down's Syndrome, most of the general population possess two or more of these anomalies. The list includes such characteristics as epicanthus, curved fifth finger, and low-set ears. The assessment of anomalies, which requires less than 10 minutes per child, could be of importance as the way of early detection of potential problem behavior. It is likely that the same factors operating in the first weeks of pregnancy influence both the occurrence of the slight morphological aberrations and the predisposition to problem behavior. In other words, there is evidence of a genetic or congenital contributor to several aspects of child behavior that are important in basic psychological research on attention, peer behavior, pace, and impulse control, as well as a contributor to clinical conditions.

   As examples, two anomaly categories, with a weight for each item, are given below. Other categories are of anomalies of the eyes, ears, mouth, and hands. Expanded and detailed descriptions of each of the eighteen items are available from the author.

*Head:* Fine electric hair:

| | |
|---|---|
| Very fine hair that will not comb down. | 2 |
| Fine hair that is soon awry after combing. | 1 |
| Two or more hair whorls. | 0 |
| Head circumference outside normal range: | |
| $> 1.5\sigma$ | 2 |
| $> 1.0 \overline{<} 1.5\sigma$ | 1 |

*Feet:* Third toe longer than second:

| | |
|---|---|
| Definitely longer than second toe. | 2 |
| Appears equal in length to second toe. | 1 |
| Partial syndactylia of two middle toes. | 1 |
| Big gap between first and second toes. | 1 |

RELIABILITY AND VALIDITY: Both the total weighted score for minor physical anomalies and the total count of the anomalies have been found to be stable from newborn to 3 months, from newborn to 2½ years, from 3 months to 2½ years, and from 2½ years to 7½ years of age, *r*s ranging from .66 to .86 in sample sizes of sixty-two or more. This means that a score for the multiple incidence of the anomalies is stable even though some of the anomalies, such as epicanthus and tongue furrows, do vary with age. The total score and the total weighted score consistently have been correlated so highly (*r*s of .90) that only one score—the total weighted score—has been used in analyses. Interobserver reliabilities have ranged from *r*s of .70 to .91 in samples ranging from twenty-four to sixty.

BIBLIOGRAPHY:

Halverson, C. F., and Waldrop, M. F. "Maternal Behavior Toward Own and Other Preschool Children: The Problem of 'Ownness.'" *Child Development,* 1970, *41,* 839-845.

Quinn, P. O., and Rapoport, J. L. "Minor Physical Anomalies and Neurologic Status in Hyperactive Boys." *Pediatrics,* May 1974.

Rapoport, J. L., and Quinn, P. O. "Minor Physical Anomalies (Stigmata) and Early Developmental Deviation: A Major Biologic Subgroup of Hyperactive Children." *International Journal of Mental Health,* September 1974.

Rapoport, J. L., Quinn, P. O., and Lamprecht, F. "Minor Physical Anomalies and Plasma Dopamine-Beta-Hydroxylase Activity in Hyperactive Boys." *American Journal of Psychiatry,* 1974, *131,* 386-390.

Waldrop, M. F., Bell, R. Q., and Goering, J. D. "Minor Physical Anomalies and Inhibited Behavior in Elementary School Girls." *Journal of Child Psychology* (in press).

Waldrop, M. F., and Goering, J. D. "Hyperactivity and Minor Physical Anomalies in Elementary School Children." *American Journal of Orthopsychiatry,* 1971, *41,* 602-607.

Waldrop, M. F., and Halverson, C. F. "Minor Physical Anomalies and Hyperactive Behavior in Young Children." In J. Hellmuth (Ed.), *The Exceptional Infant,* Vol. 2. New York: Brunner/Mazel, 1971.

Waldrop, M. F., and Halverson, C. F. "Minor Physical Anomalies: Their Incidence and Relation to Behavior in a Normal and a Deviant Sample." In M. S. Smart and R. C. Smart (Eds.), *Readings in Development and Relationships.* New York: Macmillan, 1971.

Waldrop, M. F., Pedersen, F. A., and Bell, R. Q. "Minor Physical Anomalies and Behavior in Preschool Children." *Child Development,* 1968, *39,* 381-400.

## MOTION SICKNESS QUESTIONNAIRE

AUTHORS: Ruth F. Deich and Patricia M. Hodges

AGE: 11 years and up

VARIABLE: Motion sickness

TYPE OF MEASURE: Questionnaire

SOURCE FROM WHICH MEASURE MAY BE OBTAINED: Institute for Research in Human Growth, 1737 Finecroft Drive, Claremont, California 91711.

DESCRIPTION OF MEASURE: The questionnaire is based on such factors as vestibular functioning, known aspects of motion sickness, and the relation of perception to motion sickness. The measure asks the subject to assess his or her motion sickness (if any) in terms of degree, present or past incidence, and place and conditions of occurrence. Scoring has been devised for only part of the questionnaire, with the subject's responses for amount of motion sickness scored on a 6-point rating scale as follows: (1) has never suffered from motion sickness, (2) has suffered somewhat in the past but not at present, (3) has suffered very often in the past but not at present, (4) has suffered somewhat in the past and occasionally in the present, (5) has suffered very often in the past and somewhat in the present, (6) suffers most of the time at present.

Sections I and II ask the subject to check (1) type of vehicle in which motion sickness occurs (car, plane, boat, amusement ride, "zoom-in" movie), (2) degree of illness and frequency of experience, and (3) types of physical reaction ("do you feel nauseous?" etc.) for the present time and for the past. Section III consists of eleven items answered on a 4-point scale from "very ill" to "feel okay." As examples, the first four items are given below.

Very winding road, curvy.
Bucking, rough movements of vehicle.
Rapid changes of scenery.
Seeing the view outside.

RELIABILITY AND VALIDITY: None reported.

BIBLIOGRAPHY:

Deich, R. F., and Hodges, P. M. "Motion Sickness, Field Dependence, and Levels of Development." *Perceptual and Motor Skills*, 1973, *36*, 1115-1120.

# Category 8

# Attitudes
# and Interests

*Included here are measures of attitudes toward school and various aspects of school, and other attitudes not related to school.*

Group 8-a. Attitudes Toward School. *This group includes measures of general school attitude, attitude toward school subjects, dropout proneness, cheating, teacher reinforcement, and other school-related areas.*

Group 8-b. Miscellaneous Attitudes and Interests. *This large group includes measures of racial attitudes, attitudes toward the handicapped, political attitudes, value surveys, and a variety of other attitudes.*

# Group 8-a

## Attitudes
## Toward School

# ANTTONEN REVISED HOYT SCALE
# OF ARITHMETIC ATTITUDE

AUTHORS: Cyril J. Hoyt and Ralph G. Anttonen

AGE: 8 to 14 years

VARIABLE: Arithmetic attitude

TYPE OF MEASURE: Questionnaire

SOURCE FROM WHICH MEASURE MAY BE OBTAINED: See Malcolm (1971) or Mastantuono (1970), or write Dr. Ralph G. Anttonen, Director, Educational Research, Stayer Research and Learning Center, Millersville State College, Millersville, Pennsylvania 17551.

DESCRIPTION OF MEASURE: The Anttonen-Hoyt Scale of Arithmetic Attitude consists of twenty-eight items to which an elementary-school child is to respond either "yes" or "no." A weight of 1 is given to a favorable response and 0 to an unfavorable response. The total scores can range from a high of 28 to a low of 0.

As examples, fifteen keyed items of the twenty-eight are given below.

| | |
|---|---|
| 1. Do you think arithmetic class is enjoyable? | *Yes* |
| 2. Do you usually hate arithmetic? | *No* |
| 3. Do you like most of the work in arithmetic? | *Yes* |
| 4. Do you feel sorry when you miss arithmetic class? | *Yes* |
| 5. Do you often wish arithmetic class would be shorter? | *No* |
| 6. Is it hard for you to start doing your arithmetic homework? | *No* |
| 7. Have you always liked arithmetic? | *Yes* |
| 8. Do you like to miss arithmetic class? | *No* |
| 9. Do you sometimes wish you had more hard problems in arithmetic? | *Yes* |
| 10. Do you often wish your arithmetic class would be longer? | *Yes* |
| 11. Do you hate to start doing your arithmetic homework? | *No* |
| 12. Do you like the easy problems best in arithmetic? | *No* |
| 13. Do you think most of your other subjects are easier than arithmetic? | *No* |
| 14. Would you take arithmetic next year if you did not have to? | *Yes* |
| 15. Is arithmetic one of your favorite subjects? | *Yes* |

RELIABILITY AND VALIDITY: An original scale of ninety-four items was administered in 1960 by Cyril J. Hoyt to a group of fifth-grade students in a suburb of Minneapolis, Minnesota. This instrument was readministered six years later to a sample of students who were still in the school district. The test-retest correlation for this six-month period was .30 for the entire sample. The correlation of the elementary attitude scores with the Iowa Test of Basic Skills ranged from a low of .22 to a high of .37 for various subgroupings of fifth- and sixth-grade boys and girls. On the basis of factor analysis, the original ninety-four items were shortened to a twenty-eight-item scale. Recent work by Malcolm (1971) has shown a test-retest reliability of .46 for a group of third-, fourth-, and sixth-grade children. In addition, Malcolm has demonstrated Hoyt internal reliability coefficients of .88 to .92 and split-half reliability coefficients of .92 to .95 for grades 4 through

7. Work by Mastantuono (1970) has again demonstrated correlations ranging from .20 to .40 between the Anttonen Revised Hoyt Attitude Scale and the Iowa Test of Basic Skills.

BIBLIOGRAPHY:

Anttonen, R. G. "A Longitudinal Study in Mathematics Attitude." *Journal of Educational Research,* 1969, *62,* 467-471.
Anttonen, R. G., and Deighan, W. *An Exploration into Teacher and Student Arithmetic Attitudes at Grades 3, 5 and 6.* ERIC document no. 047 983, 1971.
Malcolm, S. "An Examination of the Reliability and Attitudinal Changes for Two Arithmetic Attitude Instruments." Unpublished doctoral dissertation. Case Western Reserve University, Cleveland, Ohio, 1971.
Mastantuono, A. "An Examination of Four Arithmetic Attitude Scales." Unpublished doctoral dissertation. Case Western Reserve University, Cleveland, Ohio, 1970.
Travers, R. M. W. (Ed.) *Second Handbook of Research on Teaching.* Chicago: Rand McNally, 1973.

*Prepared by Ralph G. Anttonen*

---

# ARITHMETIC ATTITUDE SCALE

AUTHOR: Wilbur H. Dutton

AGE: Grade 3 to adult (scale is read to grade 3 pupils)

VARIABLE: Attitude toward arithmetic

TYPE OF MEASURE: Attitude scale

SOURCE FROM WHICH MEASURE MAY BE OBTAINED: For consent to use measure, write Wilbur H. Dutton, 1913 Greenfield Avenue, Los Angeles, California 90025.

DESCRIPTION OF MEASURE: This attitude scale was prepared using techniques developed by Thurstone and Chave (1948). Scale values were determined by a sorting process —a graph plotted from the accumulative proportions and a Q value ascertained. Scale values range from 1.0 (most negative) to 10.5 (most favorable). The measure contains fifteen scale items, three items on general information, and two items soliciting other items liked or disliked about arithmetic.

As examples, the first five of the fifteen scale items of the measure are given below. The respondent checks only the items that express his/her true feelings about arithmetic.

1. I avoid arithmetic because I am not very good with figures.
2. Arithmetic is very interesting.
3. I am afraid of doing word problems.

4. I have always been afraid of arithmetic.

5. Working with numbers is fun.

RELIABILITY AND VALIDITY: The original scale was developed using open-ended questions about arithmetic with 600 prospective elementary school teachers. From this work eighty-three statements were selected and used in the Q-sorting done by 125 randomly selected elementary-school teachers. The test-retest reliability was .94.

BIBLIOGRAPHY:

Dutton, W. H. "Attitudes of Prospective Teachers Toward Arithmetic." *Elementary School Journal,* 1951, *52,* 84-90.

Dutton, W. H. "Attitudes of Junior High School Pupils Toward Arithmetic." *School Review,* 1956, *64,* 18-22.

Thurstone, L. L., and Chave, E. J. *The Measurement of Attitude.* Chicago: University of Chicago Press, 1948.

---

# ARLIN-HILLS ATTITUDE SURVEYS

AUTHORS: Marshall Arlin and David Hills

AGE: Grades 1 to 12

VARIABLE: School-related attitudes

TYPE OF MEASURE: Questionnaire

SOURCE FROM WHICH MEASURE MAY BE OBTAINED: Marshall Arlin, Department of Educational Psychology, University of British Columbia, Vancouver, British Columbia, Canada V6T 1W5.

DESCRIPTION OF MEASURE: The Arlin-Hills Attitude Surveys consist of four cartooned questionnaires: (1) attitude toward teachers, (2) attitude toward learning processes, (3) attitude toward language arts, and (4) attitude toward mathematics. Each questionnaire contains fifteen illustrated statements to which the pupil indicates degree of agreement on a 4-point scale. There are three levels of each instrument, appropriate for the following grades: primary (1 to 3), elementary (4 to 8), and secondary (9 to 12). All three levels are articulated with similar illustrated items, allowing a smooth transition between levels and permitting school system comparisons of pupils across all grade levels.

As examples, a few selected items from the teachers and the mathematics questionnaires, excluding the cartoon illustrations, are given below.

1. My teachers try new and fun ways of teaching.

2. Some of my teachers act like they are tired of teaching.

4. My teachers tell us a lot about the good things we do.

6. My teachers treat us like babies.

8. Hard number problems make you freeze up.

10. Working with numbers is good because it makes you think.

14. It is fun to work with numbers outside the classroom.

15. It's too easy to make a mistake working with numbers.

RELIABILITY AND VALIDITY: Reliabilities from a sample of 6,000 students for grades 1 to 12 were computed by the odd-even method and corrected by the Spearman-Brown formula. These reliabilities were: teachers, .86; learning, .90; language, .83; mathematics, .88; and total of sixty items, .95. Even in the primary grades, reliabilities remained above .80. Validity was examined by a multitrait-multimethod study (Arlin and Hills, 1974). In this study, cartoon and noncartoon versions of the learning, mathematics, and language questionnaires were given to 402 pupils, grades 2 to 6. Pupils were asked which version they preferred, and validity was examined using an adaptation of the multitrait-multimethod procedure. Pupils greatly preferred the cartoon versions to the verbal versions, and both convergent and discriminant validity were supported.

BIBLIOGRAPHY:

Arlin, M. "The Interaction of Locus of Control, Classroom Structure, and Pupil Satisfaction." *Psychology in the Schools,* 1975, *12,* 279-286.

Arlin, M. "The Decline of Mathematics Attitudes Across Twelve Grade Levels." *Journal of Research in Mathematics Teaching* (in press).

Arlin, M. "Open Education and Pupil Attitudes." *Elementary School Journal* (in press).

Arlin, M., and Hills, D. "Comparison of Cartoon and Verbal Methods of School Attitude Assessment Through Multitrait-Multimethod Validation." *Educational and Psychological Measurement,* 1974, *34,* 989-995.

---

# ATTITUDE SCALE TO DETERMINE THE ATTITUDE OF PUBLIC SCHOOL STUDENTS TOWARD SCHOOL

AUTHORS: Mary K. Head, Millie W. Shook, Jesse Clemmons, and H. T. Connor

AGE: Grades 4 to 12

VARIABLE: Student attitudes

TYPE OF MEASURE: Likert-type scale

SOURCE FROM WHICH MEASURE MAY BE OBTAINED: Mary K. Head, Food Science Department, North Carolina State University, Raleigh, North Carolina 27606.

DESCRIPTION OF MEASURE: In this 113-item scale, student attitudes toward six categories of school life are measured by the following subscales: school lunch, administration, facilities, program, sensitivity, and transportation. The school lunch category is emphasized in that it contains thirty-eight items; all other subscales consist of fifteen items. Items from subscales are intermingled and unidentified on the instrument as presented. For each statement, students select one of five alternative responses from "strongly agree" to "strongly disagree." Responses are assigned a numerical value from 1 to 5, with 5 representing the most positive response possible.

As examples, the first ten of the 113 items of the measure are given below.

1. We have too much homework.
2. I spend too much time riding to and from school.
3. The school bus is too slow in getting me home.
4. I would rather bring my lunch from home than eat the school food.
5. I hate to learn.
6. Our cafeteria is bright and cheerful.
7. I like to ride the school bus.
8. Our school is clean.
9. My bus driver is impolite.
10. They treat us like a herd of cows at school.

RELIABILITY AND VALIDITY: This scale was used for three years on a research project concerned with the status of school lunch in North Carolina. Split-half reliabilities computed from third-year data for each subscale with elementary, junior high, and senior high groups yielded reliability coefficients ranging from .57 to .89, as reported in Head and others (1974b). The item selection method was believed to enhance scale validity. Statements were selected from those submitted by a group of first-year high school graduates who were asked to garner students' comments that were expressions of attitude relative to school. After being edited by four jurors, statements were then submitted to a second jury of educational and food service research personnel for content validity determinations. The remaining 255 scale items were administered to 949 students throughout the state. An item analysis was conducted on these data, which resulted in the 113-item scale.

BIBLIOGRAPHY:

Head, M. K., Giesbrecht, F. G., and Weeks, R. J. "Optimizing the Effectiveness of School Food Programs for Feeding and Educating Children in North Carolina—Technical Report: Effects of Nutrition Education on School Children." Unpublished report. D. H. Hill Library, North Carolina State University, Raleigh, 1974.

Head, M. K., Giesbrecht, F. G., Weeks, R. J., and Johnson, G. N. "Documentation of Development of a Scale to Measure Student Attitudes Toward School and Toward School Lunch." Unpublished report. D. H. Hill Library, North Carolina State University, Raleigh, 1974a.

Head, M. K., Giesbrecht, F. G., Weeks, R. J., and Johnson, G. N. "A Scale for Measuring Student Attitudes Toward Selected School Factors." *Educational and Psychological Measurement,* 1974b, *34,* 971-976.

# ATTITUDES TO SCHOOL SUBJECTS GRID

AUTHORS: Derek Duckworth and N. J. Entwistle

AGE: 12 to 16 years

VARIABLE: Interest, ease, freedom, and social benefit

TYPE OF MEASURE: Rating scale

SOURCE FROM WHICH MEASURE MAY BE OBTAINED: See Duckworth and Entwistle (1974).

DESCRIPTION OF MEASURE: This repertory grid has twenty bipolar items (two were not used in the final form) designed to measure student attitudes toward academic courses. The courses (English, physics, history, biology, French, chemistry, Latin, mathematics, and geography) appear at the top of the nine columns of the grid, and the items are to the left and right of the columns. Five items each measure the dimensions of interest (I), difficulty (or ease) (D), and freedom (F); the remaining three items measure social benefit (S). Agreement with the indicated pole is scored 2, neutral responses are 1, and disagreement is scored 0. "0" responses are discouraged in verbal instructions. The measure can be used for subject-choice and educational guidance of individuals in conjunction with results of ability tests and interviews by a counselor. It is also used for comparison between groups following academic courses. The grid can be administered to class groups and takes about 20 minutes to complete, depending on the age and number of the subjects. Norms are not yet available, but since the measure is to some degree ipsative, these may not be particularly useful.

As examples, the first four of the eighteen bipolar items used on the grid are given below. The scale and direction of scoring appear in the right margin.

| *Comment A* | Geography / Mathematics / Latin / Chemistry / French / Biology / History / Physics / English | *Comment B* | *Scale* |
|---|---|---|---|
| 1. Rather dull and monotonous. | | Can be exciting. | (I B) |
| 2. Helps to satisfy my curiosity about life. | | Does not really satisfy my curiosity. | (I A) |
| 3. My own ideas can be used. | | Not much room for my own ideas. | (F A) |
| 4. Most pupils can do it quite well. | | Few seem able to do it well. | (D B) |

RELIABILITY AND VALIDITY: The final form of the grid was administered to thirty-three third-year boys and twenty-eight fourth-year girls in grammar schools. The pupils were also asked to put their school subjects in rank order of their "liking" for them. The rank-order correlations between "liking" and scores on the "interest" subscale were between .31 and .81 with a median value of .68, giving acceptable evidence of concurrent validity. The pupils were again asked to complete the grids after an interval of between two and three weeks. Test-retest reliabilities for "interest" and "difficulty" subscales varied between .31 and .90 with a median value of .68. Values on the other two subscales were rather lower, with a median value of .49.

BIBLIOGRAPHY:

Duckworth, D., and Entwistle, N. J. "Attitudes to School Subjects: A Repertory Grid Technique." *British Journal of Educational Psychology,* 1974, *44,* 76-83.

Duckworth, D., and Entwistle, N. J. "The Swing from Science: A Perspective from Hindsight." *Educational Research,* 1975, *17,* 48-53.

---

# ATTITUDES TO SCIENCE

AUTHOR: Sally Ann Brown

AGE: 12 to 14 years

VARIABLE: Attitudes to science

TYPE OF MEASURE: Likert-type scale

SOURCE FROM WHICH MEASURE MAY BE OBTAINED: Sally A. Brown, Department of Education, University of Stirling, Stirling FK9 4LA, Scotland.

DESCRIPTION OF MEASURE: The questionnaire consists of five subscales each comprising twelve items (six positive and six negative). These scales relate to five curriculum attitude objectives that pupils should acquire: (1) awareness of the interrelationship of the different disciplines of science, (2) awareness of the relationship of science to other aspects of the curriculum, (3) awareness of the contribution of science to the social and economic life of the community, (4) interest and enjoyment in science, and (5) an objectivity in observation and in assessing observations. A factor-analytic examination of the responses to the questionnaire of 2,815 pupils suggested that four of the five scales (1, 2, 4, and 5) constructed for assessment of achievement of attitude objectives were also clearly related to dimensions of attitudes on which pupils appear to differ. The negative items of Scale 3 were also related to a distinct attitude dimension, but the interpretation of this dimension ("alienation from science") was different in nature from the attitude objective.

As examples, six of the sixty items on the questionnaire are given below. The respondent answers on a 5-point scale ranging from "strongly agree" to "strongly disagree."

1. Scientists should criticize each others' work.
2. Chemical reactions are of interest only to those who learn chemistry.

3. A knowledge of acids and alkalis is useful in cooking.
4. I would enjoy doing scientific work when I leave school.
5. Mathematics is a great help to science.
6. If the teacher and I do the same experiment but get different results, the teacher's result is the right one.

RELIABILITY AND VALIDITY: A pilot study of 323 11- to 14-year-old pupils gave Spearman-Brown coefficients for internal consistency of .72, .83, .74, .93, and .62 for the five scales. Test-retest reliabilities for a subgroup ($N$ = 126, aged 12 to 14) of these pupils ranged from .69 to .91. A satisfactory level of content validity was achieved by eliciting "position statements" from the curriculum writers that could be used as definitions of the universe of content for the objectives, collecting items for scales from statements by pupils, and using only those items on which validity "expert judges" were able to agree. Some measure of construct validity was achieved using curriculum-based constructs (the position statements) and hypothesizing relationships between scale scores and ages of pupils, and scale scores and sex. These hypotheses were supported.

BIBLIOGRAPHY:

Brown, S. A. "Affective Objectives in an Integrated Science Curriculum." Unpublished doctoral dissertation. University of Stirling, Scotland, 1975.
Brown, S. A., and Davis, T. N. "Development of an Attitude to Science Scale for 12 to 14 Year Olds." *Scottish Educational Studies,* 1973, *5* (2), 85-94.

---

# ATTITUDES TO SIXTH-FORM EDUCATION

AUTHOR: W. A. Reid

AGE: Teachers and other adults

VARIABLE: Attitudes toward educational provision for sixth-form students

TYPE OF MEASURE: Likert-type test

SOURCE FROM WHICH MEASURE MAY BE OBTAINED: See Reid and Holley (1974) and Taylor, Reid, and Holley (1974).

DESCRIPTION OF MEASURE: The test consists of forty items selected on the basis of pretests from a larger pool derived from discussions with teachers and searchers of relevant literature. Five a priori subscales of eight items each are: attitude to innovation (I-scale), specialization (S-scale), openness (O-scale), elitism (E-scale), and the arts and sciences as curriculum components (A/S-scale). Factor analysis (Reid and Holley, 1974) confirms the independence of the scales in first-order factors, with the exception of the E-scale, which is subsumed in I and O. S and A/S appear as two factors each and not one.

As examples, the first five of the forty items on the test are given below. The respondent answers on a 5-point scale ranging from "strongly agree" to "strongly disagree."

1. Entry to a sixth form should always depend upon the attainment of a specified standard at 0-level.
2. The success of sixth form and higher education is best measured by the number of students who gain honors degrees in their specialisms.
3. The arts sixth former is more likely than the science student to show an understanding of human problems.
4. At the present time the universities need all the help they can get in maintaining traditional standards.
5. Sixth form teachers should always have the opportunity of taking junior classes so that they can spot promising pupils and give them encouragement.

RELIABILITY AND VALIDITY: Separate analyses of male ($N$ = 259) respondents showed high stability of factor structure and no important sex differences. Reliability figures for scales derived from item with scale correlations varied from .70 to .77. Validity is inferred from the significant correlation found with teacher variables, such as the type of schools taught in, and with teacher choices of curriculum patterns (Taylor, Reid, and Holley, 1974, pp. 48-59).

BIBLIOGRAPHY:

Reid, W. A., and Holley, B. J. "The Factor Structure of Teacher Attitudes to Sixth Form Education." *British Journal of Educational Psychology,* 1974, *44,* 65-73.
Taylor, P. H., Reid, W. A., and Holley, B. J. *The English Sixth Form.* London: Routledge & Kegan Paul, 1974.

## ATTITUDES TOWARD ARITHMETIC

AUTHORS: Wilbur H. Dutton and Martha Perkins Blum

AGE: 8 years to adult

VARIABLE: Attitudes toward arithmetic and mathematics

TYPE OF MEASURE: Rating scale

SOURCE FROM WHICH MEASURE MAY BE OBTAINED: See Dutton and Blum (1968). For consent to use measure, write Wilbur H. Dutton, 1913 Greenfield Avenue, Los Angeles, California 90025.

DESCRIPTION OF MEASURE: This Likert-type scale is composed of third-person statements to which a subject may make five responses: "strongly agree," "agree," "have no opinion," "disagree," or "strongly disagree." The weighted statements are averaged, and the score is placed on a continuum from 1 to 5, with 5 being most favorable. Since each score is called a rating and since the ratings are summarized for all the statements, the method may be called summated ratings.

As examples, the first five of the twenty-seven items of the scale are given below.

1. Working with numbers is fun.
2. Arithmetic should be avoided whenever possible.
3. Discovering the solutions to new mathematical problems is exciting.
4. Arithmetic is good because it makes you think.
5. It is fun to think about problems outside of class.

RELIABILITY AND VALIDITY: Reliability determined by the Spearman-Brown test-retest reliability coefficient was .84. Validity was not developed. Items were selected from Dutton's (1954) Thurstone-type scale and reworded.

BIBLIOGRAPHY:

Blum, M. P. "Testing the Attitudes of Elementary School Children Toward Mathematics." Unpublished master's thesis. University of California, Los Angeles, 1966.

Dutton, W. H. "Measuring Attitudes Toward Arithmetic." *Elementary School Journal,* 1954, *55,* 24-31.

Dutton, W. H., and Blum, M. P. "The Measurement of Attitudes Toward Arithmetic with a Likert-type Test." *Elementary School Journal,* 1968, *68,* 259-264.

---

# ATTITUDE TOWARD CHEATING SCALE (ATCS)

AUTHORS: S. Thomas Friedman, Bernard Horowitz, Jerry Salisbury, and David Sherrill

AGE: Upper elementary through college

VARIABLE: Attitude toward cheating on a test

TYPE OF MEASURE: Likert-type attitude scale

SOURCE FROM WHICH MEASURE MAY BE OBTAINED: David Sherrill, Department of Educational Psychology, University of Hawaii-Manoa, Honolulu, Hawaii 96822. Please include stamped, self-addressed return envelope with request.

DESCRIPTION OF MEASURE: Each of the items of the ATCS was written to reflect one of four questions: (1) Is cheating a good, bad, or neutral act? (2) Should cheaters be subjected to stern, mild, or no punishment? (3) Is cheating related to academic success? (4) Is cheating justified under given conditions? Each item is responded to in terms of a forced-choice, 6-point scale (strongly agree, agree, slightly agree, slightly disagree, disagree, strongly disagree; coded +3, +2, +1, −1, −2, and −3, respectively). Item responses are equally weighted and summed to yield a scale score ranging from +45 (positive attitude) to −45 (negative attitude). For scoring, the directionality of items 1, 4, 6, 9, 10 and 13 is reversed. An original pool of twenty-five items was reduced by ten by item analysis. The fifteen items that define the scale are those found to be most highly correlated with total-scale scores.

As examples, the first five of the fifteen items of the test are given below.

1. Any reward I can think of for cheating on a test would not be worth the risk of getting caught.
2. Cheating on a test may sometimes be justifiable when the instructor fails to give students any notice that they are to be tested.
3. Cheating on a test, in the long run, increases a student's chances of success.
4. Students who cheat on a test should be failed in the course.
5. Cheating on a test may sometimes be justifiable when the instructor fails to get his subject across to the students.

RELIABILITY AND VALIDITY: Scale reliability in terms of internal consistency (Cronbach's *alpha*) was found to be .89 for each of two comparable samples of 149 and 193 undergraduate students, most of whom were freshmen or sophomores. Bivariate item-scale correlations ranged from .49 to .83, having a mean value of .63. All such values of *r* were determined to be significantly greater than 0 at the .001 level. Scale validity is reported in terms of differences in responses of students behaviorally identified as cheaters and noncheaters (known-groups method of comparison). Attitudes toward cheating on tests of students who cheated on tests were found to be more positive than those of students who had not cheated (*t* test, one-tailed).

BIBLIOGRAPHY:

Horowitz, B. "Attitude Change and Behavior Change in a Cheating Situation as a Function of Previous Reinforcement." Unpublished doctoral dissertation. University of Texas, Austin, 1968. *Dissertation Abstracts International,* 1968, *29,* 1598-A (University Microfilms no. 68-16, 097).

Sherrill, D., Salisbury, J. L., Horowitz, B., and Friedman, S. T. "Classroom Cheating: Consistent Attitude, Perceptions, and Behavior." *American Educational Research Journal,* 1971, *8,* 503-510.

*Prepared by David Sherrill*

## ATTITUDES TOWARD EDUCATION SCALE

AUTHORS: Manuel Ramirez III, Clark Taylor, Jr., and Barbara Petersen

AGE: High school

VARIABLE: Attitudes toward school and school personnel

TYPE OF MEASURE: Likert-type scale

SOURCE FROM WHICH MEASURE MAY BE OBTAINED: Manuel Ramirez III, Social Science Building, No. 25, University of California, Santa Cruz, California 95064.

DESCRIPTION OF MEASURE: The Attitudes Toward Education Scale consists of forty-four items designed to differentiate between high school students who feel positive about school and school-related achievement and those who do not. The pool of items from which the final set was selected was drawn from items used by Demos (1962) and items developed by the authors.

As examples, the first five of the forty-four items of the measure are given below. The respondent answers on a 6-point scale ranging from "I agree very much" to "I disagree very much."

1. I like teachers who lecture better than those who have us make oral reports.
2. One should have a good time even if there is school work to be done.
3. It is necessary for one to have a high school education.
4. My classmates pick on me because I am different.
5. Finishing the eighth grade should be done by everyone.

RELIABILITY AND VALIDITY: None reported.

BIBLIOGRAPHY:

Demos, G. D. "Attitudes of Mexican-American and Anglo-American Groups Toward Education." *Journal of Social Psychology,* 1962, *57,* 249-256.
Ramirez III, M., Taylor, Jr., C., and Petersen, B. "Mexican-American Cultural Membership and Adjustment to School." *Developmental Psychology,* 1971, *4,* 141-148.

---

## ATTITUDES TOWARD RIDING THE SCHOOL BUS

AUTHOR: Donald G. Barker

AGE: 12 to 18 years

VARIABLE: Attitude toward riding the school bus

TYPE OF MEASURE: Rating scale

SOURCE FROM WHICH MEASURE MAY BE OBTAINED: See Barker (1966).

DESCRIPTION OF MEASURE: This is a measure of the extent to which an individual student or a group of students perceives the experience of commuting to school by bus as pleasant and satisfying, as neutral, or as unpleasant and frustrating.

The twenty-four items are given below. The subject responds on a scale of 1 to 5, "strongly disagree" to "strongly agree." Each item refers to the subject's feelings about riding the school bus.

1. Has more advantages than disadvantages.
2. Is fun because of the friendly atmosphere.
3. Is usually very enjoyable.
4. Is better than walking, but that's about all that can be said for it.
5. Is like riding in a pig pen.
6. Is very boring.
7. Is like riding a terrible yellow monster.
8. Teaches students to respect authority.
9. Is something that students will later look back on with great pleasure.
10. Is physically sickening.
11. Is uncomfortable because the busses are generally overcrowded.
12. Is disgusting because of the way the younger students muss up the shoes and clothing of the others.
13. Makes students feel that they are being treated like cattle.
14. Is an unfortunate waste of time that could otherwise be spent in a more interesting, valuable and informative way.
15. Teaches students wholesome personal habits.
16. Is like riding in a tin can on wheels.
17. Is one of the most satisfying activities of the day for many students.
18. Is an experience that every student should have.
19. Is a good way to start the day.
20. Teaches students how to behave themselves in a group.
21. Is one of the most pleasant parts of the entire school day.
22. Is tiresome.
23. Is a desirable experience for students.
24. Is the most miserable part of the whole school day.

RELIABILITY AND VALIDITY: Corrected split-half reliabilities varied from .90 to .95 for several homogeneous subgroups. There are no validity data.

BIBLIOGRAPHY:

Barker, D. G. "Measurement of Attitudes Toward Riding the School Bus." *Psychology in the Schools,* 1966, *3*, 278-281.

# ATTITUDE TOWARD SCHOOL

AUTHORS: Moy Fook Gum and Grace E. Darrigrand

AGE: 7 years and up

VARIABLE: Attitude toward school

TYPE OF MEASURE: Attitude scale

SOURCE FROM WHICH MEASURE MAY BE OBTAINED: See Darrigrand and Gum (1973).

DESCRIPTION OF MEASURE: This twenty-five-item instrument was devised to assess children's attitudes toward school and was developed to be used with second-grade children. It is based on an instrument developed by Fox, Luszki, and Schmuck (1966). A drastic revision was undertaken and many changes made in items as well as new items added. Although steps were taken to be sure second graders (primarily inner-city children) did understand the vocabulary, anyone administering the scale to second graders should take precautions to be sure all children understand each item by reading it aloud. Presumably this instrument would work well with higher grades, and possibly it could be used with first graders. However, no attempt was made to determine how well the instrument would work with other grade levels. The weight assigned to each response for each item is listed in the order presented in the instrument. Responses for the items are intentionally varied to avoid the possibility of a response set. A high score indicates a more positive attitude.

As examples, the first five of the twenty-five items are given below.

1. My schoolwork
   a. is a lot of fun.
   b. is sometimes fun.
   c. isn't much fun.
   d. is not fun at all.
2. Learning from books is
   a. very interesting.
   b. interesting sometimes.
   c. sometimes dull.
   d. very dull and boring.
3. Studying is
   a. a lot of fun.
   b. sometimes fun.
   c. not much fun.
   d. not fun at all.
4. The best thing about school is
   a. the kids in it.
   b. the things we learn.
   c. recess.
   d. the teachers.
   e. the fun we have in class.

5. My schoolwork is
   a. very hard.
   b. sort of hard.
   c. sort of easy.
   d. very easy for me.

RELIABILITY AND VALIDITY: A test-retest with a second-grade class provided a reliability coefficient of .93. No validity data are currently available.

BIBLIOGRAPHY:

Darrigrand, G. E., and Gum, M. F. "A Comparison of the Effects of Two Methods of Developmental Guidance on the Self-Concept, Peer Relationships, and School Attitudes of Second-Grade Children." In G. D. Miller (Ed.), *Additional Studies in Elementary School Guidance: Psychological Education Activities Evaluated.* St. Paul: Pupil Personnel Services Section, Minnesota Department of Education, 1973.

Fox, R., Luszki, M. B., and Schmuck, R. *Diagnosing Classroom Learning Environments.* Chicago: Science Research Associates, 1966.

---

# ATTITUDE TOWARD SCHOOL INVENTORY (ATSI)

AUTHORS: Robert S. Meier and Ernest McDaniel

AGE: Grades 4 to 6

VARIABLE: Attitudes toward school work, teachers, and school in general

TYPE OF MEASURE: Likert-type scale

SOURCE FROM WHICH MEASURE MAY BE OBTAINED: Robert S. Meier, Purdue Educational Research Center, Purdue University, West Lafayette, Indiana 47907. Cost: $1.00.

DESCRIPTION OF MEASURE: The Attitude Toward School Inventory (ATSI) consists of forty-five statements about school. Items are weighted on a 5-point scale in accordance with each of these response categories: "strongly agree," "agree," "not sure," "disagree," and "strongly disagree." The three fifteen-item subscales of this instrument include attitudes toward school work, teachers, and school in general. The ATSI can be administered in 30 minutes or less. Students report enjoying responding to items on this instrument.

As examples, eight of the forty-five items on the inventory are given below, keyed for a positive response and with the subscale (teacher, schoolwork, general) indicated.

4. I am happy when the school day begins. (G+)
5. I tell my friends that I like school. (G+)
6. There is too much work in school. (S−)
7. I look forward to going to school. (G+)
8. Teachers are fair. (T+)
9. Most teachers here are friendly. (T+)
10. I see no use for what we study in school. (S−)
11. It is hard to pay attention in class. (S−)

RELIABILITY AND VALIDITY: Over one thousand fourth-, fifth-, and sixth-grade students were involved in the development of the Attitude Toward School Inventory. The 524 students who participated in five pilot studies were from eleven schools in Indiana and Louisiana. These schools included subjects from both urban and rural school districts. Items with high item-subscale and high item-total correlations in the pilot studies were selected for use on the ATSI. The 509 students who took the ATSI were from four schools in Indiana and Ohio. Self, peer, and teacher ratings served as criterion measures for a multitrait-multimethod matrix. Standards proposed by Campbell and Fiske for criterion-related validity were met in most cases. Construct validity was estimated by item-subscale and item-total correlations. All but two of the forty-five items had item-subscale and item-total correlations of .43 or higher. One-week test-retest reliabilities for student scores were .79, .81, and .83 on the subscales and .85 for total score. *Alpha* reliability coefficients were .83, .88, and .89 on the subscales and .94 for total score.

BIBLIOGRAPHY:

Meier, R. S. "Development and Analysis of an Instrument Designed to Measure Attitude Toward School for Children in Grades 4 to 6." Unpublished master's thesis. Purdue University, West Lafayette, Indiana, 1973.
Meier, R. S., and McDaniel, E. "A Measure of Attitude Toward School." *Educational and Psychological Measurement,* 1974, *34,* 997-998.
Meier, R. S., and McDaniel, E. "Development of the Attitude Toward School Inventory, Grades 4 to 6." Paper presented at the 83rd annual meeting of the American Psychological Association, Chicago, 1975.

---

# BRUNEL PREFERENCE GRID

AUTHOR: M. B. Ormerod

AGE: 14 to 16 years (top 50 percent of class)

VARIABLE: School-related interests and preferences

TYPE OF MEASURE: Rating scale

SOURCE FROM WHICH MEASURE MAY BE OBTAINED: Scientific Educational Aids, 104 Hercies Road, Uxbridge, Middlesex, England, with administration and scoring instructions and computer program for computation of *zeta*. Prices on application.

DESCRIPTION OF MEASURE: The instrument endeavors to get the respondent to make all the paired comparisons needed to produce a perfect ordering of a set of related experiences (e.g., school courses) against some construct such as "overall liking," "perceived difficulty," and "social or personal value." It consists of a triangular matrix of blank cells laid out like a correlation matrix with agreed symbols for the experiences (e.g., art, biology, chemistry = A, B, C) at the edges of the matrix. Respondents first shade out the rows and columns of cells corresponding to experiences inapplicable to them. Then they work through the rest of the grid cell by cell. Each cell corresponds to the comparison of a different pair of experiences on the construct. Respondents put in the cell the symbol for the experience they rate higher on the construct, for example, the one of the two school subjects they prefer. The score for each experience is obtained by summing the symbols for the subject appearing in its row and column. Further rows of cells allow them to indicate preference for teachers on a 3-point scale (+, ?, −) and to state whether they are continuing (or would continue) with the experience for a further period if given the option. Administration takes about 45 minutes, half of which is taken up by careful instruction with a visual aid.

RELIABILITY AND VALIDITY: Reliabilities were as follows: school course preference (test-retest) Spearman's *rho* = .93 ($N$ = 90), teacher liking (test-retest) = .95, and subject choice (test-retest) = .98 in terms of Goodman and Kruskal's *gamma* with $N$ = 159. In completing such grids a respondent can contradict himself; Kendall (1970) introduced the coefficient of consistence, *zeta* (range 1.0 to 0.0), as a measure of this "circularity." With 2,300 pupils the median value of *zeta* was .96 and the first decile was .85. Overall subject ranking for general liking correlated significantly with results obtained by Duckworth and Entwistle (1974) using a repertory grid technique to measure "interest." Ranking subjects for "difficulty" (Keys and Ormerod, in press) also correlates significantly with the same authors' measure of the same phenomenon.

BIBLIOGRAPHY:

Duckworth, D., and Entwistle, N. J. "Attitudes to School Subjects: A Repertory Grid Technique." *British Journal of Educational Psychology,* 1974, *44,* 76-83.

Kendall, M. G. *Rank Correlation Methods.* London: Griffin, 1970.

Keys, W., and Ormerod, M. B. "Some Factors Affecting Pupils' Subject Preferences." *Durham Research Review* (in press).

Ormerod, M. B. "Subject Preference and Choice in Coeducational and Single-Sex Secondary Schools." *British Journal of Educational Psychology,* 1975, *45,* 3.

Ormerod, M. B., and Duckworth, D. *Pupils' Attitudes to Science: A Review of Research.* Slough: National Foundation for Educational Research for England and Wales, 1975; and (USA) Atlantic Highlands, New Jersey: Humanities Press, 1975.

# BRUNEL SOCATT SCALES

AUTHOR: M. B. Ormerod

AGE: 13 to 16 years (top 50 percent)

VARIABLE: Attitudes to school science and social implications of science

TYPE OF MEASURE: Likert-type scale

SOURCE FROM WHICH MEASURE MAY BE OBTAINED: Scientific Educational Aids, 104 Hercies Road, Uxbridge, Middlesex, England. Prices on application.

DESCRIPTION OF MEASURE: This is a forty-four-item scale with five possible responses to each item from "strongly agree" to "strongly disagree." The instrument measures attitude to science as a school subject (SUBATT) and four aspects of attitudes to social implications of science (SOCATT scales). A pool of 200 items was collected from the free expression of pupils of relevant age and ability, and a twenty-item scale was developed from it by a combination of the Thurstone and Likert techniques using sixty judges. Factor analysis yielded a scale of twelve SUBATT and eight SOCATT items (Ormerod, 1973). The potential SOCATT item pool was then increased by the author's own items and other scales to give forty-nine items. Application to 2,300 pupils aged 13 to 15 in thirty-three schools yielded the five factor scales. Similar reliabilities have been obtained with another 400 pupils in Northern Ireland.

Examples of items from the scales are given below. (Number of items appears in parentheses.)

| SUBATT (10) | Science is very exciting. |
| SOCATT | |
| Aesthetic-humanitarian (9) | Science is destroying the beauties of nature. |
| Practical (10) | Without science we would all be living in caves. |
| Money (10) | Money spent on science is well worth spending. |
| Scientists (5) | Scientists do not think of the harm their inventions might cause. |

RELIABILITY AND VALIDITY: Kuder-Richardson formula 20 reliabilities of the scales are: SUBATT, .91; SOCATT: aesthetic-humanitarian, .88; practical, .73; money, .89; and scientists, .74. The basis for the factorial structure of the scales is described above. Significantly different correlations were found between the different attitude scale scores and measures of science subject preferences and choices derived from the Brunel Preference Grid (see pp. 984-985). These statistics vary with the sex and type of schooling of the pupil (coeducational or single sex). Boys' practical scores have higher loadings than other scales on liking for other practical subjects, for example, handicraft and their teachers. Girls' scientist scores have higher loadings than other scales on liking for teachers of academic subjects other than science.

BIBLIOGRAPHY:

Ormerod, M. B. "Social and Subject Factors in Attitudes to Science." *School Science Review,* 1973, *54,* 645-660.

Ormerod, M. B. "Single-Sex and Coeducation: An Analysis of Pupils' Science Preferences and Choices and Their Attitudes to Science Under These Two Systems." Paper presented at a conference, Girls and Science Education—Cause for Concern, March 1975. Published by the ASE, College Lane, Hatfield, Herts, England.

Ormerod, M. B., and Duckworth, D. *Pupils' Attitudes to Science: A Review of Research.* Slough: National Foundation for Educational Research for England and Wales, 1975; and (USA) Atlantic Highlands, New Jersey: Humanities Press, 1975.

# CHILDREN'S PICTORIAL ATTITUDE SCALE

AUTHOR: John W. Lewis

AGE: Grades 1 to 6

VARIABLE: Children's attitude toward school

TYPE OF MEASURE: Attitude scale based on picture presentation

SOURCE FROM WHICH MEASURE MAY BE OBTAINED: John W. Lewis, Winona State College, Winona, Minnesota 55987.

DESCRIPTION OF MEASURE: The Children's Pictorial Attitude Scale was developed to measure the general reaction of children toward school. Seventeen areas of pupil interaction are defined and pictures developed showing students in these situations. The instructions direct pupils to respond to these pictures as though they were in a situation that would make them feel happy, neutral, or unhappy. The situations and pictures are adequately general so that the scale can be used for pupils in most instructional models. Also, the pictures are drawn so as to convey very little, if any, emotion. Thus, the scale is basically projective in nature. Norms and directions for administration and scoring are available from the author on request.

RELIABILITY AND VALIDITY: The original scale was administered to 607 elementary pupils (grades 1 to 6) enrolled in the Winona, Minnesota, public schools. Split-half reliability, corrected with the Spearman-Brown method, was .69. Evidence of validity comes from two sources. First, the scale has face validity from the method by which the scale was developed. Secondly, data have been reported showing that the scale will discriminate among grade levels in school. These data revealed a steady decline in overall attitude with advancement in the grade ladder. However, attitudes toward some school activities remained high during the first six years of schooling.

BIBLIOGRAPHY:

Lewis, J. "The Nature of Stable and Unstable Attitudes Towards School." *Bureau of Educational Research,* Winona State College, Winona, Minnesota, 1973.

Lewis, J. "Do Children Really Learn to Dislike School?" Paper presented at Wisconsin Educational Research Association conference. Madison, Wisconsin, 1974.

Lewis, J. "A Pictorial Attitude Scale for Elementary Pupils." *Educational and Psychological Measurement,* 1974, *34,* 461-462.

---

## COLLEGE ASSESSMENT BY HUMANISTIC
## PSYCHOLOGY QUESTIONNAIRE (CAHP)

AUTHOR: Russell N. Cassel

AGE: Secondary school and college

VARIABLE: Evaluation of school program from student vantage

TYPE OF MEASURE: Rating scale

SOURCE FROM WHICH MEASURE MAY BE OBTAINED: Project Innovation, 1362 Santa Cruz Court, Chula Vista, California 92010.

DESCRIPTION OF MEASURE: The rating scale incorporated in CAHP seeks to take the principles of humanistic psychology and apply them for evaluation of instructional programs at both the high school and college levels of instruction. It is based on the notion that education is a human enterprise with student self-fulfillment as the ultimate end. Under this concept the student becomes the subject, not the object; activity becomes an end, not a means; activity has intrinsic value, not extrinsic value; and so forth. The philosophy underlying CAHP is that the students involved in learning are in a position to provide realistic evaluation of such instruction, and that actual accreditation of academic institutions should be based on such student ratings. Nine part-scores based on twelve items in the form of a rating scale with Likert values each deal with a separate humanistic principle for a school evaluation: student as subject, focus on purpose, adequate faculty present, knowledge of progress, democratic values present, fresh appreciation, competency learning, effective communication, and plant support. A similar instrument developed independently by Hitt (1973) (for elementary schools) employs the same concepts.

As examples, the first six of the 108 items of the questionnaire are given below.

1. Faculty and staff display sincerity and personal respect for students at all times.
2. Full opportunity present for each student to develop in own style to own personal limits.
3. Students encouraged to develop personal self-reliance and independent thinking.
4. Students prepared for the day-by-day demands in the careers of their own choosing.
5. Faculty accept notion typical students capable of perfect mastery and competence in any area.
6. Programs available for effective development of social skills and avocational interests.

RELIABILITY AND VALIDITY: The reliability of the total score on the CAHP by use of the Cronbach *alpha* where each item is correlated with total score yields Pearson *r*s in the middle 90s. Normative data have been obtained for lower-division college students, upper division, and graduate students.

BIBLIOGRAPHY:

Cassel, R. N. "Institution of High Learning Accreditation by Students Based on Principles of Humanistic Psychology." *Psychology,* 1973, *10* (4), 2-13.

Cassel, R. N. "Comparing Classroom Climate with Personal Development for Graduate and Undergraduate College Students." *College Student Journal,* 1974, *8* (2), 38-45.

Cassel, R. N., and Todd, L. W. "Assessing the Organizational Climate of Institutions." In R. Cassel and R. Heichberger (Eds.), *Leadership Development: Theory and Practice.* North Quincy, Massachusetts: Christopher, 1975.

Hitt, W. D. *Education as a Human Enterprise.* Worthington, Ohio: C. A. Jones, 1973.

---

# DULIN-CHESTER READING ATTITUDE SCALE, FORM I

AUTHORS: Kenneth L. Dulin and Robert D. Chester

AGE: Intermediate grades and above

VARIABLE: General attitude toward reading

TYPE OF MEASURE: Forced-choice rating scale

SOURCE FROM WHICH MEASURE MAY BE OBTAINED: Kenneth L. Dulin, University of Wisconsin-Madison, 456F Teacher Education Building, 225 North Mills Street, Madison, Wisconsin 53706.

DESCRIPTION OF MEASURE: Form I of the Dulin-Chester Reading Attitude Scale consists of twenty items, in each of which the subject chooses whether he would rather read a book or engage in some other solitary indoor activity, such as "watch TV" or "listen to records." A third choice is provided in each item for indicating a "tie" or "equally prefer" attitude. Half of the book choices are positioned on the left side of the page and half are on the right, with the "tie" response in every case positioned between the book choice and its alternative. Scoring is done by crediting the subject with 2 points for each book choice and 1 point for each "tie" response, with a range of scores from 0 to 40 possible. Any total score of 20 or more is considered to represent a high attitude toward reading, and any score of 10 or below is considered to represent a low attitude.

As examples, the first five items of the scale are given below.

*Which would you rather do?*

| *This . . .* | *or* | *This . . .* |
|---|---|---|
| Listen to the radio | | read a book. |
| Read a book | | clean up around the house. |
| Play a musical instrument | | read a book. |
| Read a book | | shine your shoes. |
| Write a letter | | read a book. |

RELIABILITY AND VALIDITY: Validity for the Dulin-Chester Scale has been established in three ways. Correlations between subjects' scores on this measure and on the previously validated Estes Attitude Scales (p. 994) have reached .60 and above in studies involving over eight hundred subjects of intermediate, junior high, and senior high age. Scores from this instrument have correlated beyond the $p < .001$ level with teacher-judgment and personal self-judgment attitude-rating scales. Subgroups identified by the above criterion measures have been shown to have stepwise mean scores on the instrument, in most every case each significantly different one from another, throughout a 5-level ("very low" to "very high") series. No test-retest reliabilities have as yet been calculated, but split-half reliability coefficients as high as .90 have been found.

BIBLIOGRAPHY:

Chester, R. D., Dulin, K. L., and Davis, B. "Three Approaches to the Measurement of Secondary-School Students' Attitudes Towards Books and Reading." Paper presented at annual convention of the Wisconsin Educational Research Association, Milwaukee, Wisconsin, January 1975.

---

# DULIN-CHESTER READING ATTITUDE SCALE, FORM II

AUTHORS: Kenneth L. Dulin and Robert D. Chester

AGE: Intermediate grades and above

VARIABLE: General attitude toward reading

TYPE OF MEASURE: Forced-choice rating scale

SOURCE FROM WHICH MEASURE MAY BE OBTAINED: Kenneth L. Dulin, University of Wisconsin-Madison, 456F Teacher Education Building, 225 North Mills Street, Madison, Wisconsin 53706.

DESCRIPTION OF MEASURE: Form II of the Dulin-Chester Reading Attitude Scale is a further adaptation of Form I of the same instrument (see pp. 989-990). Like Form I, it consists of twenty forced-choice items, each of which offers subjects a reading and nonreading choice, but with a 5-step rather than 3-step response scale. Each item is then scored 5, 4, 3, 2, or 1 from the reading-choice to its alternative, thus allowing for a range of summed scores from 20 to 100. Half the reading-choices are on the left and half are on the right. Any score above 65 is considered to represent a high attitude toward reading, and any below 45 is considered to represent a low attitude.

As examples, the first ten of the twenty-item scale are given below.

*Which would you rather do?*

| *This . . .* | *or* | *This . . .* |
|---|---|---|
| Listen to the radio | | read a book. |
| Read a book | | clean up around the house |
| Play a musical instrument | | read a book. |
| Read a book | | shine your shoes. |
| Write a letter | | read a book. |
| Read a book | | watch television. |
| Play with a pet | | read a book. |
| Read a book | | take a nap. |
| Do some work around the house | | read a book. |
| Read a book | | read a magazine. |

RELIABILITY AND VALIDITY: This form has gone through the same validation as has Form I: correlation comparisons with scores attained on various other attitude scales, comparison with criterion measures, and the establishment of stepwise series of mean scores from predetermined attitude groups to attitude groups. Split-half reliability coefficients have been above .90 in several field-studies.

BIBLIOGRAPHY: To date, field-studies only.

---

# EDGINGTON ATTITUDE SCALE FOR
# HIGH SCHOOL FRESHMAN BOYS

AUTHOR: Charles W. Edgington

AGE: 13 to 15 years

VARIABLE: Attitudes toward physical education

TYPE OF MEASURE: Questionnaire

SOURCE FROM WHICH MEASURE MAY BE OBTAINED: Instrument may be used with permission of author without charge. Contact Charles W. Edgington, Bemidji State College, Bemidji, Minnesota 56601.

DESCRIPTION OF MEASURE: The Edgington Attitude Scale for High School Freshman Boys consists of sixty-six statements that differentiate between positive and negative attitudes toward physical education. Items are weighted in accordance with discrimination of each of six response categories. The concepts for the statements were selected from the four general objectives of physical education: physical development, motor development, mental development, and human relations.

As examples, eight of the sixty-six items on the scale are given below. Items are answered on a 6-point scale: "very strongly agree" to "very strongly disagree."

1. Physical education is mainly concerned with muscle building.
2. Physical education should be eliminated from the curriculum.
5. Physical education should develop in students an understanding of the importance of exercise to health.
7. Credit should not be given for physical education.
19. Grades should not be given in physical education.
21. Physical education helps students adapt to group situations.
26. There is a scientific basis for physical education.
30. Physical education is mainly concerned with team games.

RELIABILITY AND VALIDITY: The reliability of the survey, .92, was determined by the split-half method and corrected by the Spearman-Brown formula. Thirty randomly selected ninth-grade boys were chosen to establish construct validity. Using the *chi*-square formula, the results on the test were compared with the subjective judgments of the instructors. The comparison showed a high relationship significant at the 1-percent level of confidence.

BIBLIOGRAPHY:

Edgington, C. W. "Development of an Attitude Scale to Measure Attitudes of High School Freshman Boys Toward Physical Education." *Research Quarterly*, 1968, *39*, 505-512.

---

# EDUCATIONAL VALUES INVENTORY

AUTHORS: Priscilla Pitt Jones and Kenneth J. Jones

AGE: Adults

VARIABLE: Educational values

TYPE OF MEASURE: Ranking; forced-choice questions

SOURCE FROM WHICH MEASURE MAY BE OBTAINED: Multivariate Research Incorporated, Dover, Massachusetts 02030. Single copies available without charge.

DESCRIPTION OF MEASURE: The Educational Values Inventory contains two sections. In the first part, the individual ranks from most important to least important the following five areas of the curriculum noted in Bruner's model: knowledge of the *natural world*, knowledge of the *human condition*, knowledge of the nature and dynamics of *society*, knowledge of the *past*, and knowledge of our *artistic heritage*. In the second section, four concrete examples of each of the five areas are prepared so that there are four items on each of five scales. These items on the five scales are randomly rotated and paired so that an item on one scale is presented with one item from the four remaining scales. In this way, sixteen forced-choice decisions are offered for each of the five scales. This results in forty pairs of items.

As examples, the first ten items of the inventory are given below.

It is extremely important for the elementary school student to understand
1. a. why he enjoys working with his hands.
   b. the feelings of a fellow student.
2. a. The reasons for changing weather patterns.
   b. the use of rhythm in musical expression.
3. a. the functions of the human circulatory system.
   b. the long-term effects of Greek civilization.
4. a. magnetic fields.
   b. the works of Michelangelo.
5. a. what it is like to live in the city.
   b. the use of color in a painting by Van Gogh.
6. a. the values of the people in developing countries in Africa.
   b. some of Robert Frost's poems.
7. a. the reasons for changing weather patterns.
   b. Thomas Jefferson's role in the colonial period.
8. a. the values of the people in developing countries in Africa.
   b. the reasons behind the early Scandinavian explorations.
9. a. the reasons for changing weather patterns.
   b. why he feels happy.
10. a. why he enjoys working with his hands.
    b. the works of Michelangelo.

RELIABILITY AND VALIDITY: Scale reliabilities were computed from coefficient *alpha*, Cronbach's generalization of the Kuder-Richardson formula 20 for continuous scales. These reliability coefficients, which range from .59 to .89, suggest that this instrument has satisfactory internal consistency reliability. The validity coefficients, correlations between rank and scale, range from .25 to .52 and are significant at less than the .01 level, suggesting that the respondents make actual item choices consistent with their stated beliefs. In addition, the results indicate that the Educational Values Inventory is valid with respect to Bruner's goal formulation.

BIBLIOGRAPHY:

Jones, P. P., and Jones, K. J. "The Measurement of Bruner's Philosophy of Curriculum Goals." *Journal of Experimental Education,* 1971, *39* (4), 56-60.

# ESTES ATTITUDE SCALES

AUTHORS: Thomas H. Estes, Julie P. Johnstone, and Herbert C. Richards

AGE: 11 to 17 years

VARIABLE: Attitudes toward English, mathematics, science, social studies, and reading

TYPE OF MEASURE: Likert-type scale

SOURCE FROM WHICH MEASURE MAY BE OBTAINED: Virginia Research Associates, Box 5501, Charlottesville, Virginia 22902. Cost: Specimen kit (manual, one pupil booklet, and one answer sheet), $3.50; reusable pupil booklets, $4.25 for 35; answer sheets, $1.50 for 35; scoring key, $1.50; handling cost, $.50.

DESCRIPTION OF MEASURE: There are five fifteen-item Likert-type scales. Each of the five scales assesses attitude toward one of five content areas: English, mathematics, reading, science, and social studies. The scales are primarily intended for use in evaluating affective aspects of middle-school, junior high school, and senior high school programs. They have readability levels of sixth grade. Each fifteen-item scale may be administered separately and independently, or the entire battery may be given at one sitting. Time of administration for the seventy-five-item scale averages 20 minutes. Attitude toward a content area is here defined as a liking for or dislike of a given subject. Thus favorable attitude is evidenced by verbal statements of that nature, tendency to choose and apply oneself conscientiously in subject-related activities, and belief in the value of the subject. The observant teacher can often identify those students who feel positively or negatively toward his content area, and the Estes Scales will generally confirm these observations. The primary value of the scales is that they provide an indication of degree of favorable or unfavorableness toward a subject area, and they are capable of indicating incremental change over a period of time. On each scale, some items are worded positively ("Reading is a good way to spend spare time.") and some are worded negatively ("Books are a bore."). Positive items are scored on a 1-to-5 scale ("strongly agree" to "strongly disagree") as marked. Students' ratings of negatively worded items are reversed in scoring. Scores for each item of a fifteen-item scale are summed, totaling between 15 and 75.

As examples, the first of the fifteen items for each of the scales are given below.

1. Work in English class helps students do better work in other classes.
16. People who like math are often weird.
31. Reading is for learning but not for enjoyment.
46. Field trips in science are more fun than those in other school subjects.
61. Much of what is taught in social studies is not important.

RELIABILITY AND VALIDITY: An item pool containing several hundred verbal statements was constructed. Items judged both to measure a broad range of content in each subject area and to have high face validity from the point of view of potential respondents were selected for trial administration. On the basis of this informal assessment, a total of 150 items, thirty for each of the five target attitudes, were subsequently used for the preliminary form of the scales. Each thirty-item scale was administered to approximately six hundred secondary-school students attending a rural school in central Virginia. Item analyses were performed on these data, and the twenty items that discriminated most highly between high-scoring and low-scoring subjects on each scale were retained for further refinement and testing. The five twenty-item scales were administered to 629 students, approximately one hundred at each of six grade levels (7 through 12), who were attending two large suburban public schools (one intermediate and one high school). The data were subjected to a principal-components factor analysis in order to examine the overall structure of the instrument. The items tended to cluster according to scale (i.e., school subject area). *Alpha* reliability coefficients for each attitude scale and for two different samples A and B are, respectively, English, .85, .76; mathematics, .86, .84; reading, .93, .87; science, .88, .85; and social studies, .91, .82. Significant relationships were found to exist between Estes Attitude Scales scores and the following six variables: self rating of attitudes, peer judgments of attitudes, course grades, standardized achievement test scores, and extracurricular participation. Other validation data are provided in the manual for the scales.

BIBLIOGRAPHY:

Dulin, K. L., and Chester, R. D. "A Validation Study of the Estes Attitude Scale." *Journal of Reading*, 1974, *1*, 56-59.

Estes, T. H., and Johnstone, J. P. "Assessing Attitudes Toward Reading: A Validation Study." *Twenty-third Yearbook of the National Reading Conference*, 1974, 219-223.

Johnstone, J. P. "Convergent and Discriminant Validity of a Scale to Measure Attitudes Toward School Subjects." Unpublished doctoral dissertation. University of Virginia. Ann Arbor, Michigan: University Microfilms, No. 73-32, 1974.

*Prepared by Herbert C. Richards and Orval G. Johnson*

---

# "FACES" ATTITUDE INVENTORY, FORM M (FAI-M)

AUTHOR: Eui-Do Rim

AGE: Kindergarten to grade 3

VARIABLE: Attitudes toward school and math

TYPE OF MEASURE: Questionnaire

SOURCE FROM WHICH MEASURE MAY BE OBTAINED: Eui-Do Rim, Research for Better Schools, Inc., 1700 Market Street, Philadelphia, Pennsylvania 19103.

DESCRIPTION OF MEASURE: The FAI-M contains twenty items on color-coded pages, ten for each attitude object. It is designed to be administered to small groups in the case of kindergarten and first-grade children and to intact classes in the case of second- and third-grade children. Each item consists of a question about a specific problem situation. For each question there is a corresponding picture that depicts the problem situation. The children indicate their responses to each question by marking one of three faces printed beneath each picture. Instructions for each item are designed to be read by the administrator so that nonreaders as well as readers can respond. There is no time limit for administering the FAI-M, but 30 minutes is probably adequate.

As examples, the instructions for the first five of the twenty test items are given below, to be read by the child or read aloud to nonreaders. Each page contains a large (approximately 5 X 8-inch) picture appropriate to the text. The child responds by making one of three faces (happy, plain, unhappy).

1. Now let's turn to the *pink* page. You are walking down the street. You meet your neighbors. They ask if you like your school. Which is your face?
2. Turn to the *green* page. It is time for math. You get your math materials and start to work. What is your face like?
3. Now turn to the *white* page. Summer vacation is going to be over soon. One of your friends says, "School starts next week." Show how you feel about it.
4. Now turn to the *yellow* page. You are on your way to school in the morning. You get to school. You open the door to go inside. What is your face like?
5. Now turn to the *blue* page. Your teacher says, "We are not going to have math today." How would your face look?

RELIABILITY AND VALIDITY: The FAI-M was administered on a pretest-posttest basis in the 1974-1975 school year to about two hundred second- and third-grade children who were enrolled in six Philadelphia Checkpoint Centers for basic skills remedial work. The internal consistency coefficients of two subscales were .74 and .74 on the posttest data ($N$ = 206). The content validity of the inventory was checked by the Research for Better Schools, Inc. peer review panel. No empirical validation study is reported.

BIBLIOGRAPHY: None reported.

---

# FRENCH LANGUAGE QUESTIONNAIRE

AUTHORS: Bikkar S. Randhawa and Susan M. Korpan

AGE: 10 to 18 years

VARIABLE: Attitudes toward the learning of French as a second language

TYPE OF MEASURE: Likert-type scale

SOURCE FROM WHICH MEASURE MAY BE OBTAINED: Bikkar S. Randhawa, Department of Educational Psychology, University of Saskatchewan, Saskatoon, Canada S7N 0W0. Cost: $.75.

DESCRIPTION OF MEASURE: The French Language Questionnaire consists of twenty-six items designed to measure four kinds of attitudes. These variables are identified as utilitarianism, estheticism, tolerance, and projection. The subjects respond to the statements on a 5-point scale from "disagree very much" to "agree very much." The initial items were administered to sixty-five pupils. On the basis of item-total intercorrelations, the twenty-six most discriminating items comprising the ALFS were selected.

As examples, the first eight of the twenty-six items are given below.

1. All schools should teach French.
2. French is dull.
3. When I leave school I shall give up the study of French entirely because I am not interested in it.
4. French is really great.
5. I find some of the things we learn in French interesting.
6. After the French lesson is over I don't think of French again until the next one.
7. I see no use for French.
8. I intend to work hard at French until I can speak the language fluently.

RELIABILITY AND VALIDITY: The Kuder-Richardson formula 20 estimate of internal consistency was .96. Factor analysis yielded four attitude factors as follows: utilitarian attitude toward learning French, esthetic attitude toward French, tolerance toward the learning of the subject, and projection of the feelings of others about learning French.

BIBLIOGRAPHY:

Randhawa, B. S., and Korpan, S. M. "Assessment of Some Significant Effective Variables and the Prediction of Achievement in French." *Canadian Journal of Behavioral Science*, 1973, *5*, 24-33.

---

# FROST-SAFRAN SCHOOL SITUATIONS TEST (SST)

AUTHORS: Barry P. Frost and Carl Safran

AGE: 7 to 12 years

VARIABLE: Reaction to school situations

TYPE OF MEASURE: Semiprojective test

SOURCE FROM WHICH MEASURE MAY BE OBTAINED: Psychoeducational Clinic, Department of Educational Psychology, University of Calgary, Calgary, Alberta, Canada T2N 1N4. Cost: Specimen set, $15.00.

DESCRIPTION OF MEASURE: The School Situations Test consists of a set of twelve pictures (three male adults, three female adults, three boys, and three girls) and a set of questions. Each of the figures has either a positive, a neutral, or a negative facial expression. For each situation that is presented verbally, the subject is asked for a brief description of a hypothetical child's feelings in that situation (and in some cases he is asked for a possible reason why the situation arose). He is then required to select the two pictures that appear to him to represent best the child's teacher and child's best friend in the same situation. Thus the SST employs the dual approach of an objectively scorable selection method that enables numerical scores to be obtained rapidly, together with a modified association technique that requires relatively little subjective interpretation by the clinician. The response categories are hostility, anxiety, depression, guilt and self-criticism, inadequacy and rejection, happiness, neutral, and indeterminate. Norms are available for eighty 11-year-old boys and 102 11-year-old girls; these were grade 5 children from several Calgary, Alberta elementary schools considered representative of the various socioeconomic classes in the city.

Examples from classroom situations, sports situations, and playground situations are given below.

*In the classroom*
1. A boy has made a mistake in his work.
   a. How does he feel?
   b. Which of these figures is the teacher and which is his best friend?
*On the field*
1. A boy doesn't want to (play) in the game.
   a. Which game are they playing?
   b. How does he feel?
   c. Which of these figures is the teacher and which is his best friend?
*On the playground*
3. The other boys won't let this boy play with them.
   a. Why won't they let him play with them?
   b. How does he feel?
   c. Which of these figures is the teacher and which is his best friend?

RELIABILITY AND VALIDITY: Frost and Adamson (1971) contrast the normative group referred to above with a group referred to the Special Educational Services Division of the Calgary School Board. Qualitative analysis showed that the referred boys and girls gave more depression responses than did the nonreferred children. Several statistically significant results emerged from the quantitative analysis. In particular, the referred children perceived their teachers and friends as more hostile than did the nonreferred children.

BIBLIOGRAPHY:

Frost, R. "The School Situations Test and Its Place in a Psychological Test Battery." *Alberta Psychologist,* 1967, *8*, 8-12.

Frost, B., and Adamson, G. "A Study of the Concurrent Validity of the Frost-Safran School Situations Test." *Personality,* 1971, *2,* 227-237.

---

# HOME AND SCHOOL VALUES INVENTORY

AUTHOR: T. Antoinette Ryan

AGE: Grade 6, parents, and school personnel

VARIABLE: School-related values held by children, parents, and school personnel

TYPE OF MEASURE: Questionnaire

SOURCE FROM WHICH MEASURE MAY BE OBTAINED: T. A. Ryan, University of Hawaii, 1776 University Avenue, Room 126, Honolulu, Hawaii 96822.

DESCRIPTION OF MEASURE: The instrument, which was designed to investigate the home-school values of children, parents, and school personnel across different ethnic, socioeconomic, and occupational groups, consists of an inventory of 168 items with seventeen scales: persistence, competition, success, good grades, manners, status, risks, work, honesty, religion, authority, family, leadership, materialism, altruism, friends, and discipline. The items of the final value inventory were presented as statements with two response categories: "agree" and "disagree."
    Examples of items in seven of the scales are given below.

| | |
|---|---|
| *Persistence* | You should not quit a disagreeable task until it is finished. |
| *Competition* | You should try to be the winner in games and sports. |
| *Success* | Other things may be more important to some people, but being successful is very important to me. |
| *Status* | It feels good when a lot of people know who you are. |
| *Materialism* | I would like to have many fancy and expensive things. |
| *Family* | I feel that I should pay much more attention to my family than to anything else. |
| *Discipline* | All of us need and must have whippings when we are children if we are to grow up healthy and unspoiled. |

RELIABILITY AND VALIDITY: Value statements based on literature analysis and value statements based on informant interviews were edited. A uniform format for value statements was derived. Each value statement included three elements encompassed in the value concept: assertor, locus, and referent. Synthesis of value statements was made to produce a values domain. Each item was put in statement form, providing for response by levels of agreement. Items were sorted independently by judges into value-related and nonvalue-related. *Phi* coefficients computed between each judge and each of his fellow judges for statements defined in common were statistically significant (.05 level) 83 percent of the time. Coefficients of a magnitude greater than .50 were obtained in 32 percent of the comparisons. The total item pool (including those derived from literature and interview protocol analyses and the item writers) consisted of 7,121 items categorized by the fifty-one dimensions of the values domain defined. Duplicate items were eliminated, and a 682-item values inventory was constructed in accordance with five basic principles of item writing so that each item consisted of a statement with three response options: "agree," "disagree," and "?."

The instrument was pilot tested for validity and understandability, revised, and refined. The final set of seventeen scales was selected for the final inventory by applying item-analysis procedures to each of the original fifty-one values dimensions. Each of the seventeen scales contained at least six items, consisted of an equal number of positively and negatively keyed items, and had an *alpha* coefficient greater than or equal to .50 in at least two of the samples consisting of parents, school personnel, and children. Items for each scale were selected on the basis that they had the highest item-scale correlations in two or more subsamples, had the least extreme endorsement percentages, were the lowest in percentage of question marks and blanks, and appeared to be consistent with the substantive construction measured by other items included on the scale. The number of items retained for each scale depended on the *alpha* coefficient for the scale, as well as the number of satisfactory items available to balance the number of positively and negatively keyed items. In the case of several of the scales, one or two new items were written or an old item was rewritten in an attempt to increase scale internal consistency. Consequently, several scales had one or more positively keyed items than negatively keyed items, or vice versa. To isolate random responders, a ten-item "Infrequency Scale" was added. Items were randomly arranged in two different orders to control for serial-order effects, and testees were presented with two response categories: "agree" and "disagree." The average *alpha* coefficients for the three samples was .56, .64, and .69 for children, parents, and school personnel. For the children, six of the seventeen final scales had an *alpha* greater than or equal to an arbitrary criterion of .60 (success, risks, competition, religion, money and materialism, and friends). For parents, ten scales met the criterion in the final inventory. For the school personnel, all but two of the scales, work and discipline, had *alphas* greater than or equal to .60.

BIBLIOGRAPHY:

Ryan, T. A. "Developing Healthy Values for Children and Youth: An Issue Paper." Education Research and Development Center, University of Hawaii, Honolulu, 1971.

Ryan, T. A. *Value Conflict in Elementary Schools in Hawaii.* Final report. Education Research and Development Center, University of Hawaii, Honolulu, 1973.

Ryan, T. A. (Ed.) *Values: A Symposium Report.* Education Research and Development Center, University of Hawaii, Honolulu, 1975.

## HOW I DESCRIBE MY FEELINGS (HIDMF)

AUTHORS: Eui-Do Rim and Thomas Biester

AGE: Grades 6 to 12

VARIABLE: Attitude toward school, mathematics, and self-concept

TYPE OF MEASURE: Semantic differential questionnaire

SOURCE FROM WHICH MEASURE MAY BE OBTAINED: Eui-Do Rim, Research for Better Schools, Inc., 1700 Market Street, Philadelphia, Pennsylvania 19103.

DESCRIPTION OF MEASURE: This is an affective instrument designed to measure student attitude and self-concept by using Osgood's semantic differential technique. "School is," "Mathematics is," "I think that I am," and "People think that I am" are given as concepts. The first two concepts measure attitudes toward school and mathematics, respectively. The remaining concepts are self-concept measures—one for the self-perceived self-concept and the other for the other-perceived self-concept. The researcher may change these concepts to accommodate her/his own interest. Sixteen word-pairs are provided for each of the concepts. These word-pairs appear in different order with their poles being randomly reversed for each concept.

The word-pairs were constructed, selected, or modified based on previous research findings (Yamamoto, Thomas, and Karns, 1969; McCallon and Brown, 1971; Scharf, 1971; Everett, 1973). Word-pairs can be grouped into two categories, perceptive and evaluative, that resemble Osgood's potency and evaluative factors. The perceptive category has two subcategories: likeness (e.g., interesting-boring, pleasant-unpleasant) and descriptive (e.g., easy-hard, simple-complicated). The evaluation category also has two subcategories: value judgment (e.g., useful-useless, important-unimportant) and status evaluation (e.g., popular-unpopular, successful-unsuccessful). Each word-pair is separated on a 7-point scale, of which 1 and 7 represent the extreme description and 4 represents "neither." How I Describe My Feelings is administered to groups. At the present time, a Likert-type rating method is used as the scoring system, and a score is produced for each concept. As research findings accumulate, a partial factor-score system will be developed and two or four factor scores will be produced for each concept.

RELIABILITY AND VALIDITY: This instrument is still under development. The word-pairs were selected and organized on the basis of previous studies and seven in-house evaluators' judgments. It can be said, therefore, that HIDMF has face validity. HIDMF was administered to four classes of students (mostly seventh graders) from an inner-city (Philadelphia) and a suburban (southern New Jersey) school on a pretest-posttest basis in the 1974-1975 school year. A recent factor analysis confirmed four distinct factors that closely resembled the built-in structure for "school is" and "mathematics is" concepts. Although four factors were extracted from each self-concept scale, the factor loadings were a little different from and less distinctive than those that the attitude scales had shown. Cronbach's coefficient *alpha*s calculated for the four concept scales as based on the posttest data were .84, .87, and .88 ($N = 85$). Internal consistencies of factor-score scales will be computed upon completion of a factor-analytic study.

BIBLIOGRAPHY:

Everett, A. V. "Personality Assessment at the Individual Level Using the Semantic Dif-
    ferential." *Educational and Psychological Measurement,* 1973, *33,* 837-844.
McCallon, E. L., and Brown, J. D. "A Semantic Differential Instrument for Measuring
    Attitude Toward Mathematics." *Journal of Experimental Education,* 1971, *39*
    (4), 69-72.
Scarf, E. S. "The Use of the Semantic Differential in Measuring Attitudes of Elemen-
    tary School Children Toward Mathematics." *School Science and Mathematics,*
    1971, *72,* 641-649.
Yamamoto, K., Thomas, E. C., and Karns, E. A. "School-Related Attitudes in Middle-
    School Age Students." *American Educational Research Journal,* 1969, *6,*
    191-206.

---

# HOW I FEEL ABOUT INSTRUCTIONAL TV

AUTHOR: Jerry B. Ayers

AGE: 5 to 8 years

VARIABLE: Young children's interest and attitudes about instructional TV in school

TYPE OF MEASURE: Questionnaire

SOURCE FROM WHICH MEASURE MAY BE OBTAINED: See Payne, Ayers, and
Rowe (1974).

DESCRIPTION OF MEASURE: Few instruments exist to measure the attitudes of
young children toward instructional television. This instrument can be administered in
a group situation to reveal some information about the way children feel toward the
programs and use of instructional television in the classroom. The instrument has been
field-tested in Georgia and Tennessee with a sample of 2,000 children enrolled in
kindergarten through third grade.
    The twenty-item questionnaire is given below. The tester draws four faces—very
happy, rather happy, rather unhappy, very unhappy—and the child draws an "X" on
the appropriate face indicating his or her feeling about each question.

1. How do you feel about school?
2. How do you feel about watching television at home?
3. How do you feel about watching television at school?
4. How do you feel about learning from television in school?
5. How do you feel about the television teachers?
6. How do you think the boys and girls in this class feel about television in school?
7. How do you feel about things the television teacher tells you to do?

8. How do you feel about the way your classroom teacher does things that the television teacher suggests?
9. How do you feel about seeing the same teachers on television each week?
10. How do you think your classroom teacher feels about television in school?
11. How do you feel when the television set is turned off in your classroom?
12. How do you feel about how good your classroom television looks and sounds when it is on?
13. How do you feel about the things that the television teacher uses?
14. How do you feel when you think about television?
15. How do you think your mother and father feel about television in school?
16. How do you feel about the pictures and drawings that the teacher on television uses in talking about the lesson?
17. How do you feel about the things (that I do) (that your classroom teacher does) before you watch television in school?
18. How do you feel about the things (that I do) (that your classroom teacher does) after you watch television in school?
19. How do you feel about the teachers in (your) (our) school?
20. How do you feel about the questions that you have been asked today?

RELIABILITY AND VALIDITY: None reported.

BIBLIOGRAPHY:

Payne, D. A., Ayers, J. B., and Rowe, P. J. "Attitudes of Elementary Students Towards ITV." *Educational Broadcasting,* 1974, 7 (1), 15-19.
Payne, D. A., Ayers, J. B., and Rowe, P. J. "The Development and Field Test of an Evaluation Model for Educational Television." Vol. I. Mimeographed. Atlanta, Georgia Department of Education, 1971.
Payne, D. A., Ayers, J. B., and Rowe, P. J. "Research Studies Conducted as Part of the Development and Field Test of an Evaluation Model for Educational Television." Vol. II. Mimeographed. Atlanta: Georgia Department of Education, 1971.

---

## HOW I FEEL ABOUT SCIENCE (HIF-S)

AUTHOR: Individualizing Learning Program Evaluation Staff, Research for Better Schools, Inc.

AGE: 3 to 8 years

VARIABLE: Six aspects of attitude toward school and science

TYPE OF MEASURE: Questionnaire

SOURCE FROM WHICH MEASURE MAY BE OBTAINED: Eui-Do Rim, Research for Better Schools, Inc., 1700 Market Street, Philadelphia, Pennsylvania 19103.

DESCRIPTION OF MEASURE: How I Feel About Science measures six aspects of children's attitudes toward school and science: attitude toward science class, liking for science in comparison with other school subjects, anxiety about science class, self-direction in science, attitude toward science and science professions, and general attitude toward school. The questionnaire consists of thirty-six items and two examples. It is group-administered and takes approximately 50 minutes. Instructions for administration are designed to be read by the administrator so that nonreaders as well as readers can respond to it.

As examples, the first ten of the thirty-six items are given below, to be answered "yes," "?," or "no."

1. I like school because I learn a lot of interesting things in my classes.
2. I am afraid to make a mistake in my science lesson booklet.
3. Sometimes I do science things at home just for fun.
4. I can't wait for science class to be over.
5. I like to learn about animals.
6. I like the things I do in science class.
7. I like gym class better than science class.
8. I like to work by myself in science class.
9. There are a lot of things I don't like about school.
10. I think science class is boring.

RELIABILITY AND VALIDITY: The HIF-S was administered to two groups of first-, second-, and third-grade children in three schools in a tristate area (Pennsylvania, New Jersey, and Delaware) where Individualized Science was field-tested in the 1971-1972 school year: 655 children in an I.S. group and 236 in a non-I.S. group. Because individualized reading and/or mathematics programs were also used in these schools, the six items from "liking for science in comparison with other school subjects" and two more items were eliminated. From the remaining items, four significant and interpretable factors were ascertained: attitude toward school, attitude toward science, self-direction, and attitude toward science professions. Coefficient *alphas* of these four factor scores resulting from using an unweighted partial factor scoring system were .62, .43, .39, and .43, respectively.

BIBLIOGRAPHY:

Klopfer, L. E., Vous, A. P., and McCall, K. *A Study of How Students Feel About Science.* Pittsburgh, Pennsylvania: Learning Research and Development Center, University of Pittsburgh, 1970.

Unks, N. J., and Stolte, J. B. *How I Feel About Science.* Philadelphia, Pennsylvania: Research for Better Schools, Inc., 1971.

*Prepared by Eui-Do Rim*

# I/D/E/A AFFECTIVE INSTRUMENT PACKAGE

AUTHORS: Irene Frieze, Sol M. Roshal, Antonia Bercovici, Sarale Cohen, Carol Horowitz, Tobie Robinson, and Janet T. Wood

AGE: Upper-grade elementary school

VARIABLE: Attitudes toward school, learning and technology, self-concept, peer relations

TYPE OF MEASURE: Likert-type scale

SOURCE FROM WHICH MEASURE MAY BE OBTAINED: Charles L. Willis, Institute for Development of Educational Activities, Inc., Innovative Programs, 5335 Far Hills Avenue, Suite 300, Dayton, Ohio 45429.

DESCRIPTION OF MEASURE: The I/D/E/A affective instrument package consists of a battery of five student attitude scales developed to provide independent scores of the attitudes of upper-grade elementary school children toward school, learning, technology, self, and peers. Each scale is presented as a paper-and-pencil questionnaire utilizing multiple-choice items, and each is available in two forms. The instruments were designed for group administration and have generally been administered by someone other than a member of the school staff. Some items refer to the teacher and/or a local situation, and it is believed that administration by the local staff might hamper honest responses. The instruments were intended for the assessment of groups, but they have also been used in the assessment of individuals. For most of the instruments the score is the mean rating of the student's response to approximately twenty questions. One scale, peer relations, has differentially weighted items.

As examples, the first five items of the attitude toward technology scale are given below (with permission of the Institute for Development of Educational Activities, Inc., an affiliate of the Charles F. Kettering Foundation). The subject responds on a 5-point scale from "strongly agree" to "strongly disagree."

1. That most new inventions help people live better.
2. That sometimes you can tell that a machine just doesn't like you.
3. That if we don't watch out, machines may be the bosses someday.
4. That I'd have much less fun if there were no machines.
5. That if we had no guns and planes, we wouldn't have any more wars.

RELIABILITY AND VALIDITY: None reported.

BIBLIOGRAPHY:

Roshal, S. M., Frieze, I., and Wood, J. T. "A Multitrait-Multimethod Validation of Measures of Student Attitudes Toward School, Toward Learning, and Toward Technology in Sixth Grade Children." *Educational and Psychological Measurement*, 1971, *31*, 999-1006.

*Prepared by Institute for Development of Educational Activities, Inc.*

## INDEX OF STUDENT PERCEPTION
## OF TEACHER REINFORCEMENT

AUTHOR: Dewitt C. Davison

AGE: Grades 7 to 9

VARIABLE: Student attitude toward teacher reinforcement

TYPE OF MEASURE: Rating scale

SOURCE FROM WHICH MEASURE MAY BE OBTAINED: Dewitt C. Davison, Department of Educational Psychology, University of Toledo, Toledo, Ohio 43606.

DESCRIPTION OF MEASURE: The scale provides a measure of student evaluative reactions to positively and negatively reinforcing behaviors of teachers. Twenty short classroom episodes are presented, each depicting a student behavior and corresponding teacher reinforcement attempt. The respondent examines each of the episodes and indicates how he would feel about the reinforcement following each behavior if he performed that behavior and a given teacher provided the reinforcement. One of five standard choices is made for each item. The choices range from, "I would feel very good if this teacher did this" to "I would feel very bad if this teacher did this." The scale consists of twelve items pertaining to positive reinforcement and eight pertaining to negative reinforcement. The two categories of items are scored separately. The original pool of items was obtained by asking seventy-seven eighth-grade students to list instances of student-behavior-teacher-reinforcement episodes from their own experiences and observations in the classroom. The episodes listed most frequently by students were retained for the questionnaire. See Davison (1967) for a more detailed description of the development of the instrument.

As examples, the first five of the twenty episodes are given below. In addition to answering each item on a 5-point scale of how he feels, the student answers "very often," "sometimes," or "never" to the question, "Has this ever happened (does it ever happen) to you?" following each item.

1. If someone had written in the answers to a test in your book which you knew you would later take, and you told this teacher about it, and she (or he) praised you, saying you were a very honest person, how would you feel?
2. If you were reading a book in class while you were supposed to be studying, and this teacher gave you a mean look and asked angrily: "Don't you know how to follow instructions," how would you feel?
3. If you made a very good project for class, and this teacher liked it very much and showed it to his (or her) other classes, pointing out how good it was, how would you feel?
4. If this teacher had forgotten and left her (or his) book in a room and you found it and returned it to her (or him), and she (or he) gave you some nice fruits for your kindness and honesty, how would you feel?
5. If you passed in your homework poorly done and put together in a shabby manner, and this teacher wrote the word "sloppy" on it, how would you feel?

RELIABILITY AND VALIDITY: Reliability was estimated by the test-retest method using sixty-one eighth graders. The percentage of agreement between testings ranged from a low of 65 to a high of 100, with a median of 80.

BIBLIOGRAPHY:

Davison, D. C. "Some Demographic and Attitudinal Concomitants of the Perceived Reward Value of Classroom Reinforcement: An Application of Newcomb's Balance Theory." Unpublished doctoral dissertation. University of Illinois, Urbana, 1967. Ann Arbor, Michigan: University Microfilms, 1967, no. 68-1739.

Davison, D. C. "Perceived Reward Value of Teacher Reinforcement and Attitude Toward Teacher: An Application of Newcomb's Balance Theory." *Journal of Educational Psychology,* 1972, *63,* 418-422.

---

# INSTRUCTIONAL TV QUESTIONNAIRE

AUTHOR: Jerry B. Ayers

AGE: 9 to 13 years

VARIABLE: Children's attitudes toward instructional TV

TYPE OF MEASURE: Questionnaire

SOURCE FROM WHICH MEASURE MAY BE OBTAINED: Jerry B. Ayers, College of Education, Tennessee Technological University, Cookeville, Tennessee 38501.

DESCRIPTION OF MEASURE: The instrument is designed to measure upper-elementary grade school children's attitudes toward and interest in the use of instructional television in school. It has been field tested with ninety children in Georgia and 787 children in Tennessee in grades 4, 5, and 6. The instrument yields information related to how children feel about the use of television in school.

As examples, five of the first twelve items, to be answered on a 4-point scale from "never" to "always," are given below.

1. Do you like to watch television in school.
2. Do you think that watching television in school helps you with your school work?
3. When you are at home during school hours, do you ever watch the same shows as you see in school?
4. Does your teacher talk about a television show before you see it?
5. Do you do any of the things that the television teacher tells you to do?

Four of the last ten items are below. The student is asked to complete the sentences with the first thought which comes to him.

1. Television in school is _____ .
2. My favorite television program that I see in school is _____ .
3. When it is time for our television lesson _____ .
4. Television lessons are _____ .

RELIABILITY AND VALIDITY: Based on a test-retest situation with sixty children in grades 5 and 6 over a period of forty-five days, the reliability of the instrument was .82. No other reliability or validity data are available.

BIBLIOGRAPHY:

Ayers, J. B. "Elementary School Children's Attitudes Towards Instructional Television." *Elementary English*, 1973, *50*, 137-140.
Payne, D. A., Ayers, J. B., and Rowe, P. J. "The Development and Field Test of an Evaluation Model for Educational Television." Vol. I. Mimeographed. Atlanta: Georgia Department of Education, 1971.
Payne, D. A., Ayers, J. B., and Rowe, P. J. "Research Studies Conducted as Part of the Development and Field Test of an Evaluation Model for Educational Television." Vol. II. Mimeographed. Atlanta: Georgia Department of Education, 1971.

---

# INVENTORY OF STUDENT OPINION

AUTHOR: Harold Brinegar

AGE: 12 to 20 years

VARIABLE: Student attitudes

TYPE OF MEASURE: Checklist

SOURCE FROM WHICH MEASURE MAY BE OBTAINED: See Brinegar (1952).

DESCRIPTION OF MEASURE: The checklist of student attitudes consists of eighty-one items designed to show specific practices, conditions, and other factors associated with student satisfaction-dissatisfaction.

RELIABILITY AND VALIDITY: The original checklist was first administered as a pilot project to two large middle and secondary schools to determine whether any directions or items were in need of clarification. The checklist with refinements was then administered to 9,744 boys and girls in thirty-seven secondary schools representing diverse populations and geographical areas in the state of Indiana. The magnitude of the study was such that checks for validity and reliability were not necessary. Data from the total study were used as standards for subsequent measures for individual schools.

As examples, six of the eighty-one items on the checklist are given below.

16. How do you feel about the way the principal and his assistants manage the school?
    a. The school is very well managed.
    b. The school is well managed.
    c. The school is poorly managed.
    d. The school is very poorly managed.

35. On the average, how much instruction (explanation) do you get when you are assigned new material in classes?
    a. All I need.
    b. Almost as much as I need.
    c. Some, but not as much as I need.
    d. Very little or none.

42. For how many of your teachers do you have a genuine feeling of respect?
    a. All or almost all.
    b. Half or more.
    c. Only a few.
    d. Very few or none.

49. Are your classmates fair in their dealings with you?
    a. Yes, all or almost all.
    b. Yes, half or more.
    c. Less than half.
    d. Very few or none.

57. Do you feel that all the pupils have an opportunity to participate in the activities program of your school?
    a. Yes, all have an opportunity to take part.
    b. All have an opportunity to take part except a few.
    c. Only about one half of the pupils have an opportunity to take part.
    d. Only a few have an opportunity to take part.

66. Should you be learning things in school which are not taught in your school?
    a. Yes.
    b. No.
    c. I have no opinion.

BIBLIOGRAPHY:

Brinegar, H. "The Measurement of Attitudes of High School Students Toward Their Schools." Unpublished doctoral dissertation. Indiana University, Bloomington, 1952.

Brinegar, H. "Pupil Attitudes Toward Extra-Class Activities." *The School Review,* 1955, *63,* 432-437.

Brinegar, H. "What Does the High School Pupil Like Best About His School?" *The Clearing House,* 1958, *33,* 77-79.

Wrightsman, L. S., Nelson, R. H., and Taranto, M. *The Construction and Validation of a Scale to Measure Children's School Morale.* George Peabody College for Teachers, Nashville, Tennessee, 1968. ERIC document no. ED 020 528.

# MARTENS PHYSICAL EDUCATION ATTITUDE SCALE
## (ELEMENTARY LEVEL)

AUTHOR: Fred L. Martens

AGE: 10 to 12 years

VARIABLE: Physical education attitudes

TYPE OF MEASURE: Rating scale

SOURCE FROM WHICH MEASURE MAY BE OBTAINED: Fred L. Martens, P.O. Box 1700, University of Victoria, Victoria, British Columbia, Canada V8W 2Y2.

DESCRIPTION OF MEASURE: This instrument consists of twenty-one items selected by the Thurstone method from a total of 122 statements. Q values for the selected items range from .66 to 3.22, and medians of the judges' placements of items on a 9-point scale range from 1.16 to 8.63. The items are arranged in random order in terms of favorableness and unfavorableness to physical education. Subjects respond with "agree" or "disagree." Scoring is accomplished simply by adding the median scores (available with the scale) for all items checked "agree."

As examples, the first five of the twenty-one items are given below.

1. Skills learned in physical education classes are nonessential to social life.
2. It would be better to study than to spend time in physical education classes.
3. Every school should have good facilities for physical education.
4. Students who are skilled in sports are not popular with the opposite sex.
5. Competitive activities break down emotional self-control.

RELIABILITY AND VALIDITY: In the construction of the scale, subjects were asked to rate themselves on a graphic scale of terms describing a continuum of attitudes. Correlation between the students' self-ratings and their score on the scale resulted in a coefficient of .56 ($N$ = 185). Reliability as determined by the test-retest method was .78 ($N$ = 130).

BIBLIOGRAPHY:

Martens, F. L. "The Relative Effectiveness of Physical Education Programs in Selected Private and Public Elementary Schools in Victoria, British Columbia." Unpublished doctoral dissertation. University of Oregon, Eugene, 1968.
Martens, F. L. "Personality, Attitudes, and Academic Achievement of Athletic and Nonathletic Junior High School Boys." *Perceptual and Motor Skills,* 1974, *39,* 538.

# MINK SCALE

AUTHOR: Oscar G. Mink

AGE: Upper elementary and junior high school

VARIABLE: Dropout proneness

TYPE OF MEASURE: Fixed-alternative questionnaire

SOURCE FROM WHICH MEASURE MAY BE OBTAINED: Information Series 1, Series 68 No. 9-13, 6M.12. Office of Research and Development, Appalachian Center, West Virginia University, Morgantown, West Virginia 26506.

DESCRIPTION OF MEASURE: The Mink Scale is designed to aid in the identification of potential dropouts. The scale, to be completed by school personnel, is divided into four sections: academic ability and performance (eight items), negative identification with education (eleven items), socioeconomic status (fourteen items), and student-personal (twelve items). The sections of the scale roughly represent the social, psychological, and educational forces related to dropout proneness. The items in the scale have been found in previous studies to differentiate dropouts from nondropouts and were selected after an extensive review of the dropout literature. Information for completing the items on the scale is obtained from school records, acquaintance of the rater with the subject, and/or from someone well-acquainted with the subject, such as a teacher.
    As examples, the first two items of each of the four subscales are given below.

1. How many years older or younger is he than other students in his grade?
    0-----1-----2-----3-----or more
2. Has he been retained in grade? No    1 yr.    2 yrs.    3 yrs.    4 or more

1. Is he usually happy in school?                                          Yes    No
2. Does he participate in extracurricular activities such as sports, band,
    clubs?                                                                 Yes    No

1. Is father's occupation unskilled or semiskilled? Please list.          Yes    No
2. Is the parents' attitude apathetic or negative toward completing his
    high school education?                                                Yes    No

1. Does the student appear to lack the basic financial requirements of
    school? Explain.                                                      Yes    No
2. Does the student feel sorry for himself? Seldom    Sometimes    Frequently

RELIABILITY AND VALIDITY: The ability of items on the Mink Scale to differentiate between dropouts and nondropouts was assessed in a pilot study conducted during the 1966-1967 academic year. Subjects for the study consisted of 189 former students (dropouts) who were in the seventh grade in 1961 and 262 high school seniors (nondropouts) who had also attended seventh grade in 1961. The data were analyzed by *chi*-square tests computed for each item for total dropouts and total nondropouts, male dropouts and male nondropouts, and female dropouts and female non-dropouts. Of the forty-five items surveyed, only eight failed to differentiate the total group of dropouts from nondropouts. Of the thirty-seven items that showed a significant difference between the totals, thirty-one also differentiated significantly between male and female subsamples. The profile of the dropout-prone student that emerges is that of a student probably of lower-than-average measured intelligence, performing poorly in academic tasks, somewhat negative about the school situation as shown by little participation in school activities and often becoming a discipline problem, and coming from a family that does not value education highly and has a history of low education attainment. The basic profile seems to fit both males and females.

BIBLIOGRAPHY:

Barker, L. W., and Mink, O. G. *The Mink Scale: An Aid in the Identification of Drop-out-Prone Students in the Appalachian Junior High Schools.* Information Series. Office of Research and Development, West Virginia University, Morgantown, 1968.

Mink, O. G., and Barker, L. W. *Dropout Proneness in Appalachia.* Research Series 3. Office of Research and Development, West Virginia University, Morgantown, 1968.

Smith, J. E., Tseng, M. S., and Mink, O. G. "Prediction of School Dropouts in Appalachia: Validation of a Dropout Scale." *Measurement and Evaluation in Guidance,* 1971, *4,* 31-37.

---

# MOTIVE-ATTITUDE INTENSITY SCALES

AUTHOR: R. Sumner

AGE: 12 to 17 years

VARIABLE: Seven classes of educational attitude; five classes of educational motivation

TYPE OF MEASURE: Questionnaire

SOURCE FROM WHICH MEASURE MAY BE OBTAINED: R. Sumner, Guidance and Assessment Service, N.F.E.R., The Mere, Upton Park, Slough, Berkshire, England SL1 2DQ. Cost: Manual, 54p per copy (provisional); answer sheet, 1p each; scoring stencils, 33p (set of 7 cards); questionnaire, 7p.

DESCRIPTION OF MEASURE: These 150-item scales are designed for use in school guidance and counseling and are, therefore, primarily intended to facilitate informed decisions affecting the individual pupil. A three-way model of educational motivation was developed from theoretical constructs and experimental results to produce a structure incorporating the modalities of motive and attitude and the dimension of intensity. The attitude referents are classified as parents, teachers, friends, self, curriculum, organization, and material, while motives are categorized as reward, self-realization, intellectual stimulation, enjoyment, and social conformity. Items incorporate both motive and attitude referent and are pitched at registering four levels of intensity, designated as receiving, responding, valuing, and commitment. While items may be scored on each of these scales, in practice the motive and attitude profiles are of interest for group evaluation or individual counseling. Correlations and factor analysis of item data confirmed that the items reflected the structural domain operationally and showed also, at the second-order level, that eleven major aspects of educational motivation can be identified. Intercorrelation of the profile scores (which are domain referenced) gave only a single component, implying that the scales each contribute highly to a general school motivation factor. Three experimental versions of the questionnaire were used to examine the stability of items with reference to the concept domain. An amended final version is being used tentatively by psychologists and counselors.

As examples, the first ten of the 140 items are given below. The respondent answers "agree," "disagree," or "uncertain."

1. Teachers always give high marks for good work.
2. My parents expect me to use all my ability at school.
3. My friends want to know their subjects well.
4. Many school subjects give me a great deal of pleasure.
5. Everyone in the school takes care of the apparatus and furniture.
6. There is no need for teachers to give points to the best workers.
7. I work hard so that my parents can be proud of me.
8. Whether or not a lesson is interesting depends on the members of the class.
9. I get little enjoyment from using different shapes and colors in art and craftwork.
10. I should do the same as the others if they were asked to raise money for more library books, camping gear, and so on.

RELIABILITY AND VALIDITY: Retest coefficients for the seven twenty-item attitude scales range from .66 to .81; for the five twenty-eight-item motive scales, from .72 to .81; and for the total score the test-retest coefficient is .91. Sample scale means, differences between first and second administration, were all nonsignificant (for $N = 100$); also, four random groups ($N = 100$) showed only slight sampling fluctuation. There were significant total-score differences between upper and lower streams (tracks) in selective and nonselective schools. A Humanities Curriculum Project evaluation study showed significant gains in motivation of active project groups compared with controls. A reduced version of the model, used for the questionnaire called Your Views on School employed by National Foundation for Educational Research in England and Wales in twelve comprehensive schools, showed significant relationships between total score and social class, home background achievement scores, and (markedly) with future learning and examination intentions. Users have reported its value in case diagnoses.

BIBLIOGRAPHY:

Sumner, R. "An Analysis of the Factors Governing the Motivation of Secondary School Children Aged 13 to 16 Years." Unpublished doctoral dissertation. Manchester University, England, 1970.

Sumner, R., and Warburton, F. W. *Achievement in Secondary School: Attitudes, Personality and School Success.* Slough, Berkshire, England: National Foundation for Educational Research, 1972.

---

# ORAL SCHOOL ATTITUDE TEST

AUTHOR: Juan Rivera

AGE: Kindergarten to grade 3

VARIABLE: Attitude toward school

TYPE OF MEASURE: Test

SOURCE FROM WHICH MEASURE MAY BE OBTAINED: Learning Concepts, Inc., 2501 North Lamar, Austin, Texas 78705.

DESCRIPTION OF MEASURE: The Oral School Attitude Test is composed of twenty-nine items. Each item is designed to elicit a response from the student that will be representative of his attitude toward his school environment and his educational experiences. In response to each of the twenty-nine oral stimuli, the child marks one of a series of faces that represent a range of feelings. These faces are used in various combinations to provide the child with four response options for each stimulus. The following is an example of the examiner's instructions to the child in English (instructions are also provided in Spanish): "Turn the page and put your finger on the bird. Put an "X" on the face which shows how you feel when someone gives you something good." The test can be administered and scored by the classroom teacher in about 20 minutes, and it can be given individually or in groups. A monitor is needed to assist the teacher. The Written School Attitude Test (McCallon, 1973) provided the foundation for the development of the Oral School Attitude Test.

RELIABILITY AND VALIDITY: The Oral School Attitude Test was administered to 200 kindergarten, first-, second-, and third-grade children representing various ethnic and socioeconomic groups. Reliability data were obtained by retesting a 25-percent sample of the original group tested. The test-retest coefficient obtained over a ten-day period was .77.

BIBLIOGRAPHY:

McCallon, E. *School Attitude Test Manual.* Austin, Texas: Learning Concepts, Inc., 1973.

Rivera, J. *Oral School Attitude Test Manual.* Austin, Texas: Learning Concepts, Inc., 1973.

# PARENT OPINION SURVEY

AUTHOR: Fen Rhodes

AGE: Parents of elementary-school pupils, kindergarten to grade 6

VARIABLE: Parental attitude toward child's school experience

TYPE OF MEASURE: Likert-type rating scale

SOURCE FROM WHICH MEASURE MAY BE OBTAINED: Fen Rhodes, Psychology Department, California State University, Long Beach, California 90840.

DESCRIPTION OF MEASURE: The Parent Opinion Survey is a twenty-nine-item questionnaire designed to assess the favorability of parents' attitudes toward the current educational experience of their child. The inventory employs only favorable-appearing statements, all of which correlate positively with total score. A +3 to −3 Likert-type response format with no neutral points is suggested for administration to maximize task understanding by respondents and reduce the magnitude of central-tendency rating bias. The scale has been used as a measure of general parent satisfaction in evaluations of both regular and special programs of instruction.

As examples, the first ten of the twenty-nine items of the survey are given below. The respondent answers on a 6-point scale ranging from "I agree very much" to "I disagree very much."

1. It is clear what the grading policy is and what grades are based on.
2. My child likes his teacher.
3. My child is sufficiently challenged.
4. I feel that the teachers are working with the parents, not sitting in judgment.
5. My child's teacher calls me when problems arise.
6. Other parents at this school seem to be friendly.
7. It is easy to get acquainted with the principal and teachers.
8. There is about the right amount of homework.
9. There is plenty of individual help available to my child.
10. The principal takes a personal interest in my child.

RELIABILITY AND VALIDITY: There is a moderately high degree of internal consistency among statements contained in the scale. The median item-test correlation is .54, based on 293 cases.

BIBLIOGRAPHY:

Rhodes, F. "Team Teaching Compared with Traditional Instruction in Grades Kindergarten Through Six." *Journal of Educational Psychology,* 1971, *62,* 110-116.

## PICTORIAL MEASURE OF SCHOOL-RELATED ATTITUDES

AUTHOR: Sar B. Khan

AGE: 8 years and up

VARIABLE: Attitudes toward school and teacher

TYPE OF MEASURE: Pictorial situations

SOURCE FROM WHICH MEASURE MAY BE OBTAINED: Sar B. Khan, Ontario Institute for Studies in Education, 252 Bloor Street West, Toronto, 181 Ontario, Canada.

DESCRIPTION OF MEASURE: Five pictorial situations were developed to measure attitudes toward school and teacher. Each picture contains a positive and negative instance and the child is asked to put an "X" in the box if he wishes to participate in the activity engaged in by the child in the picture. The instrument is still being developed and should be used for research purposes only.

As an example, instructions to the respondent for the first one of the five pictorial situations are given below.

In the picture on the next page, these are two kids reading a book. The teacher is helping one kid while the other kid is reading the book by himself. Kindly put an X in the box in the picture showing the kid that you would most like to be. Make sure you mark only *one* picture.

RELIABILITY AND VALIDITY: Information on the reliability of the pictorial stimuli is not collected yet. For the purpose of determining validity, responses to the pictures were correlated with subscores in language, work study, and arithmetic of a standardized test of basic skills. These correlations were: language (−.13, .45, .21, .19, .13), work study (−.14, .29, .16, .12, .07), and arithmetic (−.10, .08, .03, .03, −.01). Scores on the five pictures were also correlated to self-report scores. These correlations were: attitudes toward school (−.09, .41, .35, .19, .37), attitudes toward teacher (−.04, .30, .30, .26, .29), attitudes toward self (−.20, .21, .25, .07, −.01), and independence (−.20, .06, .11, −.02, .01).

BIBLIOGRAPHY: None reported.

## PREFERRED STUDENT CHARACTERISTICS SCALE

AUTHOR: Calvin C. Nelson

AGE: Elementary, secondary, and college teachers

VARIABLE: Teacher attitudes toward pupils

TYPE OF MEASURE: Forced-choice questionnaire

SOURCE FROM WHICH MEASURE MAY BE OBTAINED: Calvin C. Nelson, Department of Education, California State University, Fullerton, California 92634.

DESCRIPTION OF MEASURE: This test was derived from the Preferred Instructor Characteristics Scale developed by Krumboltz and Farquhar (1957). Nelson's scale is composed of thirty-six pairs of items that describe affective and cognitive behaviors of students. Each pair of statements consists of one cognitive behavior and one affective behavior. Each cognitive behavior is matched with each affective behavior so that the teacher filling out the questionnaire must make a choice between all listed cognitive and affective behaviors. The total number of cognitive behaviors selected is the score earned on the test. A score of 36 indicates that the teacher has a strong preference for cognitively oriented students. A score of 0 indicates a maximum preference for affectively oriented students. While norms do not exist, various studies have been conducted that are of value and have yielded data that are useful for interpretation. In general, the results of these studies indicate that the more advanced the level of instruction, the more cognitively oriented the teacher. Elementary teachers score approximately 10 to 12, high school teachers score approximately 20 to 25, and college instructors generally score above 30 on this test. When this instrument is used in conjunction with a modification of Krumboltz and Farquhar's Preferred Instructor Characteristics Scale (Nelson, 1964), it is useful in determining the degree of deviation between teacher and student with respect to their preferences for one on a cognitive-affective dimension.

As examples, the first ten of the thirty-six items are given below. The scoring for cognitive responses is indicated by an italic a or b.

I prefer a student
1. *a*. who learns quickly.
   b. who is grown up.
2. a. whose classroom conduct is good.
   *b*. who thinks logically.
3. a. who seems to understand our point of view.
   *b*. who has done well academically.
4. a. who likes the teacher.
   *b*. who does lots of outside work.
5. *a*. who thinks logically.
   b. who is friendly.
6. *a*. who is well thought of by former teachers.
   b. who makes the classroom pleasant.
7. a. who has the teacher's interests in mind.
   *b*. who does his work thoroughly.

8. a. who likes the teacher.

    *b.* who knows a large number of facts.

9. *a.* who thinks logically.

    b. who is grown up.

10. a. who is friendly.

    *b.* who is well thought of by former teachers.

RELIABILITY AND VALIDITY: A split-half reliability coefficient of .91 was obtained using sixty-one junior high school teachers. Using the same teachers, a test-retest reliability coefficient of .63 was obtained. No validity data exist except construct validity indicators. The fact that mean scores of teachers increase as the teachers at successively higher levels in the educational system are tested is suggestive of validity, since college teachers are presumably much more cognitive in their orientation than elementary teachers.

BIBLIOGRAPHY:

Krumboltz, J. D., and Farquhar, W. W. "The Effect of Three Teaching Methods on Achievement and Motivational Outcomes on a New Study Course." *Psychological Monographs General and Applied*, 1957, *71*, 1-26.

Nelson, C. C. "Affective and Cognitive Attitudes of Junior High School Teachers and Pupils." *Journal of Educational Research*, 1964, *58*, 81-83.

Schmidt, L. J. "An Investigation of Attitude Change in Special Education Teachers After Classroom Experience." Unpublished doctoral dissertation. University of Southern California, Los Angeles, 1968.

Schmidt, L. J., and Nelson, C. C. "The Affective/Cognitive Attitude Dimension of Teachers of Educable Mentally Retarded Minors." *Exceptional Children*, 1969, *35*, 695-701.

Sigler, G. R., and others. *A Study of Sex Differences in the Attitudes of Male and Female Teachers of the TMR*. Washington, D.C.: Bureau of Education for the Handicapped, Office of Education, Department of Health, Education and Welfare, 1973. ERIC document no. 085 948.

---

# PRIMARY CHILDREN'S ATTITUDE SCALES

AUTHOR: Joan C. Barker-Lunn

AGE: 9 to 11 years

VARIABLE: Children's attitudes

TYPE OF MEASURE: Guttman and factor scales

SOURCE FROM WHICH MEASURE MAY BE OBTAINED: Guidance and Assessment

Service, National Foundation for Educational Research for England and Wales, The Mere, Upton Park, Slough, Bucks, England.

DESCRIPTION OF MEASURE: The scales were developed in 1966 for a study investigating the effects of streaming and nonstreaming in junior schools in England. They were derived empirically; the items were based on statements actually made by children during group discussions. Each scale is made up of six to ten items selected after factor analyses and scalogram analyses. For each scale the aim is to achieve homogeneity of content and where possible a cumulative structure. The questionnaire contains sixty-four items and covers ten attitude areas. These scales offer a means of measuring and describing important attitudinal differences among groups of children in junior schools. All scales differentiate between boys and girls and between able and less-able children at highly statistically significant levels. Likewise scales C, G, H, J differentiate between upper and lower social-class groups (Barker-Lunn, 1972).

As examples, one item from each of the ten attitude scales, along with its letter designation, are given below:

A. *Attitude to school:* I would leave school tomorrow if I could. (Yes, Not sure, No)
B. *Interest in school work:* I enjoy most school work. (Yes, Not sure, No)
C. *Importance of doing well:* I work and try very hard in school. (Always, Most of the time, Sometimes)
D. *Attitude to class:* I'd rather be in my class than in the others for my age. (Yes, Not sure, No)
E. *"Other" image of class:* Other children think we're clever in this class. (Yes, true; Not sure; False)
F. *Conforming versus nonconforming:* I like children who get me into mischief. (Yes, Not sure, No)
G. *Relationship with teacher:* Teacher is nice to me. (Most of the time, Sometimes, Hardly ever)
H. *Anxiety in the classroom situation:* I'm scared to ask my teacher for help. (Yes, often; Sometimes; Never)
I. *Social adjustment:* I have no one to play with me at playtime. (Often true, Sometimes, Never)
J. *Academic self-image:* My teacher thinks I'm clever. (Yes, Not sure, No)

RELIABILITY AND VALIDITY: The stages involved in the development of the scales were (1) group discussions, (2) selection of a pool of items, (3) administration of scale development questionnaire, (4) structuring and clarification of the data by factor analysis, (5) scale construction, and (6) a second stage of field work to refine the scales. The original questionnaire (stage 3), providing information for stages 4 and 5, involved 355 children aged 9 to 11. The revised questionnaire (stage 6) was administered to 2,300 children; the final scales were developed on the basis of the responses of 400 children selected at random from the total sample. For the Guttman scales, coefficients of reproducibility were calculated; all exceeded a value of .90. The internal consistency of all the scales, whether derived by Guttman or factor criteria, was determined by Cronbach's *alpha* coefficient (Barker-Lunn, 1969). Support for the validity of the children's attitude scales comes from three sources: the internal structure of the instruments, discussed above; the correlation of the different scales with other measures with which they would be presumed to be related; and testing expected group differences—those predicted on theoretical grounds or on the basis of other researchers' findings (Barker-Lunn, 1969, 1972). These scales were adapted for use in the United States by Berk, Rose, and Stewart (1970).

BIBLIOGRAPHY:

Barker-Lunn, J. C. "The Development of Scales to Measure Junior School Children's Attitudes." *British Journal of Educational Psychology*, 1969, *39*, 64-71.

Barker-Lunn, J. C. *Streaming in the Primary School.* Slough, England: National Foundation for Educational Research for England and Wales, 1970.

Barker-Lunn, J. C. *Social Class, Attitudes and Achievement.* Slough, England: National Foundation for Educational Research for England and Wales, 1971.

Barker-Lunn, J. C. "The Influence of Sex, Achievement Level and Social Class on Junior School Children's Attitudes." *British Journal of Educational Psychology*, 1972, *42*, 71-74.

Barker-Lunn, J. C. "Manual of Instructions for Use of Primary Children's Attitude Scales." Mimeographed. Slough, England: National Foundation for Educational Research for England and Wales, n.d.

Berk, L., Rose, M., and Stewart, D. "Attitudes of English and American Children Toward Their School Experience." *Journal of Educational Psychology*, 1970, *61*, 33-40.

---

# PRIMARY PUPIL READING ATTITUDE INVENTORY

AUTHOR: Eunice N. Askov

AGE: Primary grades

VARIABLE: Attitudes toward reading

TYPE OF MEASURE: Forced-choice picture test

SOURCE FROM WHICH MEASURE MAY BE OBTAINED: Kendall/Hunt Publishing Company, 2460 Kerper Boulevard, Dubuque, Iowa 52001. Cost: $2.98.

DESCRIPTION OF MEASURE: The paired comparisons format is used to pair a picture of a child reading with a picture of a child engaged in recreational activities. *S* is asked to mark the picture of the activity that he would prefer to do in his spare time. To determine the recreational activities preferred by primary pupils, twenty second- and third-grade children balanced for sex and reading ability were asked to name their favorite activities after school and on weekends. The nine most frequently named activities (excluding reading) were then depicted by an artist. Two pictures involving reading were also drawn. Separate versions for boys and girls were devised because it was believed that pictures of like-sexed children would facilitate identification of the subject with the child in the picture. Most of the activities were the same for both sexes except for four of the nonreading activities. The measure in its revised form includes eighteen items involving choice between reading and other activities, and twelve distractor items involving choice between two nonreading activities. Eighteen is the highest obtainable score in the revised version, and 0 the lowest. The sequence of the items is random.

RELIABILITY AND VALIDITY: A study of the reliability of the revised version was made through item analysis, using the Generalized Item Analysis Program (Baker, 1969). The reliabilities ranged from .77 for first-grade girls to .87 for third-grade boys. Because the number of items in the revised version had been reduced by one-third (eighteen items as opposed to twenty-seven in the original version), the drop in reliability coefficients was not considered significant. The Primary Pupil Reading Attitude Inventory was first administered with the teachers absent from the room to ninety-four second- and third-grade children in three classrooms. The three classroom teachers, who did not know the attitude inventory scores of the children in their rooms, were then asked to select in their classrooms the five students highest and the five lowest in leisure-time reading interest. A $t$ test ($t$ = 3.36) indicated that the means of the Primary Pupil Reading Attitude Inventory scores of the two groups, identified by their teachers, were different at the .01 level of significance. The mean of the total group of students tested ($N$ = 94) was 8.21.

BIBLIOGRAPHY:

Baker, F. B. *FORTAP: A FORTRAN Test Analysis Package.* Laboratory of Experimental Design. Department of Educational Psychology, University of Wisconsin, Madison, 1969.

*Improving Reading Instruction: An Inventory of Reading Attitude.* Monograph no. 4. San Diego, California: Superintendent of Schools, Department of Education, 1961.

MacDonald, J. B., Harris, T. L., and Rarick, G. L. "An Experimental Study of the Group Versus the One-to-One Instructional Relationship in First Grade Basal Reading Programs." Mimeographed. U.S. Office of Education Cooperative Research Project no. 2674, 1966.

Schotanus, H. D. *The Relationship Between Difficulty of Reading Material and Attitude Toward Reading.* Wisconsin Research and Development Center for Cognitive Learning, Technical Report no. 29, 1967.

*Prepared by Eunice N. Askov and Orval G. Johnson*

# PUPIL ATTITUDE QUESTIONNAIRE

AUTHOR: Henry Kolesar

AGE: High school

VARIABLE: Alienation

TYPE OF MEASURE: Questionnaire

SOURCE FROM WHICH MEASURE MAY BE OBTAINED: See Kolesar (1967a, 1967b). Technical report available from Henry Kolesar, Alberta Advanced Education, 11160 Jasper Avenue, Edmonton, Alberta, Canada T5K OL1.

DESCRIPTION OF MEASURE: The questionnaire is designed to measure the attitudes of pupils toward their school. An initial pool of 164 items that had previously been prepared and submitted to a panel of judges was administered to 163 pupils in grades 10 to 12 of a large urban high school. The initial item pool was reduced to sixty items using a discrimination analysis to select items discriminating between the quarter of the pupils with high and the quarter with low subscale totals, correlation of each item with the subscale total, and a factor analysis of the items remaining after the first two item selection procedures were completed. On the basis of the factor analysis, the following five factors were identified and items identified for these subscales: normlessness, powerlessness, isolation, self-estrangement, and meaninglessness.

RELIABILITY AND VALIDITY: The scale in its final form was administered to ninety-two high school pupils on two occasions separated by a one-week time interval. Coefficients of stability were calculated for each of the subscales and for the total scale by correlating subtotal and total scores from the first with those from the second responses of pupils. These coefficients are: powerlessness, .73; self-estrangement, .74; normlessness, .71; meaninglessness, .63; isolation, .66; and total scale, .79. A multiple correlational analysis of the predictive validity of combinations of items indicated that maximum validity was achieved for each subscale with four to six items. This number was increased to twelve items for three subscales, to ten for one subscale, and to fourteen for one subscale to improve scale reliability. Factorial validity was determined via several factor analyses as reported above. The Pupil Attitude Questionnaire was administered to ninety-seven pupils in one high school not included in the major study sample. The names of the ten with highest scores, ten with scores nearest the median, and ten with the lowest scores were given to five classroom teachers on the high school staff of the school. Teachers were directed to rank these pupils on a 3-point scale: high, medium, or low alienation from the school. Spearman's *rho*s were calculated between the ranking of pupils provided by the scale, the rankings given by each teacher, and the combination of the rankings of the five teachers. The lowest *rho*, .47, is significantly different from 0 at less than the .001 level, two-tailed. This test of construct validity indicated that there was an acceptable degree of correlation between the expressed attitudes of pupils and the attitudes of pupils as judged by their teachers.

BIBLIOGRAPHY:

Kolesar, H. "An Empirical Study of Client Alienation in the Bureaucratic Organization." Unpublished doctoral dissertation. University of Alberta, Edmonton, Canada, 1967.

Kolesar, H. "Pupil Attitude Questionnaire." Technical report. Department of Educational Administration, University of Alberta, Edmonton, Canada, 1967.

*Prepared by Orval G. Johnson*

---

## PUPIL BEHAVIOR CHECKLIST

AUTHOR: Fen Rhodes

AGE: Kindergarten to grade 6

VARIABLE: Attitude toward school and learning

TYPE OF MEASURE: Thurstone checklist

SOURCE FROM WHICH MEASURE MAY BE OBTAINED: Fen Rhodes, Psychology Department, California State University, Long Beach, California 90840.

DESCRIPTION OF MEASURE: The Pupil Behavior Checklist is a forty-five-item inventory of specific pupil behaviors judged to be reflective of individual attitude toward school and learning of children in kindergarten to grade 6. Emphasis is placed upon overt aspects of behavior that can be readily observed by teachers in the normal school setting. Each behavioral statement has an associated scale value indicating on a 9-point scale the degree of enthusiasm for school that the particular behavior represents. A pupil's attitude score is computed by averaging the scale values of those statements checked by his teacher as descriptive of his current general behavior. Higher scores represent more favorable attitudes. Complete details concerning construction of the checklist, including scaling procedures and criteria used in selecting statements, are reported by Rhodes (1971).

As examples, the first ten of the forty-five items of the checklist are given below.

1. Volunteers answers.
2. Dawdles and procrastinates.
3. Is discourteous to teachers.
4. Is willing to help others.
5. Hits school personnel.
6. Is unable to make friends easily.
7. Keeps desk and possessions neat.
8. Writes on the desk.
9. Remains seated during assigned work.
10. Is enthusiastic and eager to respond.

RELIABILITY AND VALIDITY: Internal evidence of validity is demonstrated by the high degree of agreement among twenty-seven teacher-judges with respect to categorization of behavioral statements during the scaling process. For the forty-five statements in the completed checklist, the average interquartile range of judgments was 1.3. In terms of external validity, it has been found that checklist attitude scores are relatively independent of pupil achievement as measured by the Wide Range Achievement Test ($r \leqslant$ .03, $N$ = 316).

BIBLIOGRAPHY:

Rhodes, F. "Team Teaching Compared with Traditional Instruction in Grades Kindergarten Through Six." *Journal of Educational Psychology,* 1971, *62,* 110-116.

---

# PUPIL CONTROL IDEOLOGY FORM

AUTHORS: Donald J. Willower, Terry L. Eidell, and Wayne K. Hoy

AGE: Educators

VARIABLE: Attitudes toward pupil control

TYPE OF MEASURE: Likert-type paper-and-pencil test

SOURCE FROM WHICH MEASURE MAY BE OBTAINED: Donald J. Willower, Rackley Building, Pennsylvania State University, University Park, Pennsylvania 16802.

DESCRIPTION OF MEASURE: The Pupil Control Ideology Form consists of twenty items on a 5-point scale ranging from "strongly agree" to "strongly disagree." Orientations toward pupil control are measured on a humanistic-custodial continuum. A humanistic ideology stresses an accepting, trustful view of pupils and optimism concerning their ability to be self-disciplining and responsible. A custodial ideology emphasizes the maintenance of order, distrust of pupils, and a moralistic stance toward deviance. The Pupil Control Ideology form has also been used to tap perceptions of the PCI of others. See Willower, Eidell, and Hoy (1973) and Packard and Willower (1972).
As examples, six of the twenty items of the form are given below.

4. Beginning teachers are not likely to maintain strict enough control over their pupils.
5. Teachers should consider revision of their teaching methods if these are criticized by their pupils.
6. The best principals give unquestioning support to teachers in disciplining pupils.
10. Being friendly with pupils often leads them to become too familiar.
13. Pupils can be trusted to work together without supervision.
20. Pupils often misbehave in order to make the teacher look bad.

RELIABILITY AND VALIDITY: Split-half reliabilities have ranged from .91 to .95 in a number of samples of public-school educators. The instrument has been shown to discriminate between teachers and schools judged to be humanistic or custodial.

BIBLIOGRAPHY:

Packard, J. S., and Willower, D. J. "Pluralistic Ignorance and Pupil Control Ideology." *Journal of Educational Administration,* 1972, *10,* 78-87.

Rexford, G., Willower, D. J., and Lynch, P. "Teachers' Pupil Control Ideology and Classroom Verbal Behavior." *Journal of Experimental Education,* 1971, *40,* 78-82.

Willower, D. J., Eidell, T. L., and Hoy, W. K. *The School and Pupil Control Ideology.* In *Pennsylvania State Studies* No. 24, 2nd edition. University Park: Pennsylvania State University Press, 1973.

---

## PUPIL'S PERCEPTION OF THE SCHOOL

AUTHOR: Douglas S. Finlayson

AGE: 12 to 18 years

VARIABLE: Perception of peer and teacher behavior

TYPE OF MEASURE: Questionnaire

SOURCE FROM WHICH MEASURE MAY BE OBTAINED: National Foundation for Educational Research for England and Wales, The Mere, Upton Park, Slough, Bucks, England SL1 2DQ.

DESCRIPTION OF MEASURE: Four scores are derived from the measure, two referring to peer behavior (task orientation and emotional tone) and two to teacher behavior (concern and social control). The thirty-four items in these four scales are factorially derived from responses according to a 5-point category system from "strongly agree" to "strongly disagree" about the appropriateness of the statement as a description of the situation in the school.

RELIABILITY AND VALIDITY: The items were administered to representative samples of pupils in twelve different secondary schools, selected for their size, socioeconomic status of the catchment area which they serve, allocation of teacher resources, and organizational structure. Evidence about validity is complex and is in the process of being written. The reliability of each scale, using the McKennel's *alpha* coefficient, is given below, following each sample item.
     Examples of items from each scale of the measure are given below.

*Pupil Behavior:*
     Task Orientation: Pupils work here only because they have to. (.77)
     Emotional Tone: Pupils feel very satisfied with this school. (.79)

*Teacher Behavior:*
  Concern: Teachers here go out of their way to help you. (.84)
  Social Control: Teachers soon lose their tempers here. (.82)

BIBLIOGRAPHY:

Finlayson, D. S. "Measuring School Climate." *Trends in Education,* 1973, *30,* 19-27.
Finlayson, D. S. *Pupil's Perception of the School Manual.* Bucks, England: National Foundation for Educational Research for England and Wales, n.d.

---

# QUESTIONNAIRE OF SCHOOL-RELATED
# ATTITUDES AND MOTIVATION

AUTHORS: Sar B. Khan; adapted from McGuire and others (1961) and Child, Frank, and Storm (1956)

AGE: Junior high school

VARIABLE: (1) Attitudes toward education; (2) attitudes toward teacher, study habits, achievement motivation, need achievement, achievement anxiety

TYPE OF MEASURE: Likert scale

SOURCE FROM WHICH MEASURE MAY BE OBTAINED: See Khan (1966).

DESCRIPTION OF MEASURE: This scale consists of 122 items designed to measure the above variables. Each respondent is asked to indicate if a statement is rarely, sometimes, frequently, generally, or almost always true for him. The scale includes both positive and negative statements. A factor analysis of the item responses yielded eight factors for both males and females; however, only six factors could be psychologically interpreted for males and five factors for females.
     As examples, two selected items from each of the seven factors are given below.

*Factor 1: Attitude toward education in general*
1. I feel that I would study harder if I were given more freedom to choose subjects that I like.
7. I think that football coaches do more for school life than do the teachers.
*Factor 2: Attitude toward teachers*
2. My dislike for certain teachers causes me to neglect my school work.
4. I feel that teachers do not allow their likes or dislikes for students to influence their grading too much.
*Factor 3: Study habits and test-taking techniques*
 8. I have troubles with the rules for writing correct themes and reports.
12. I keep all my work on each subject together, carefully arranged in some planned order.

*Factor 4: Academic motivation*

1. Whether I like a subject or not, I still work hard to make a good grade.

7. I am unable to study well because I get restless, moody, have the blues.

*Factor 5: Interest in academic work*

1. I lose interest in my studies after the first few days each year.

8. Having many other things to do causes me to get behind in my school work.

*Factor 6: Need achievement*

1. I feel that my grades really show what I can really do.

5. I'd rather live a quiet and modest life than keep striving for advancement.

*Factor 7: Achievement anxiety*

1. I get nervous and confused when taking a test and fail to answer questions as well as I could.

3. I would be annoyed at myself if I let some minor failure upset me.


RELIABILITY AND VALIDITY: An index of internal consistency was obtained for each hypothetical factor. These correlations ranged from .85 to .95 for males and from .84 to .95 for females. The instrument was administered to 509 males and 529 females in grade 8, and their subsequent performance on six subtests (reading, language, arithmetic computation, problem solving, social studies, science) of the Metropolitan Achievement Test Series (MAT) in grade 9, and on four subtests (English, social studies, natural sciences, mathematics) of an especially designed test in grade 12 was predicted. The initial samples were subdivided for cross-validation of the factor-analytic results. The multiple correlations for the initial male sample ($N$ = 211) ranged from .45 to .55, and for the cross-validation sample ($N$ = 217) they ranged from .41 to .61. For females, the multiple correlations for the initial sample ($N$ = 231) ranged from .57 to .67, and for the cross-validation sample ($N$ = 225) they ranged from .58 to .67. Canonical correlations of .69 and .76 were obtained between the composites of affective and achievement variables for males and females respectively. Multiple correlations for the grade 12 male sample ($N$ = 142) ranged from .51 to .59, and for the female sample ($N$ = 152) they ranged from .50 to .62. Canonical correlations of .62 and .66 were obtained for males and females, respectively, between affective variables and achievement at the grade 12 level.

BIBLIOGRAPHY:

Child, T. L., Frank, K. F., and Storm, T. "Self-Rating and TAT: Their Relation to Each Other and Childhood Background." *Journal of Personality,* 1956, *25,* 96-114.

Khan, S. B. "The Contribution of Attitudinal Factors to the Prediction of Academic Achievement in Secondary School." Unpublished doctoral dissertation. Florida State University, Tallahassee, 1966.

Khan, S. B. "The Factorial Invariance of Academic Attitudes and Interests." *Ontario Journal of Educational Research,* 1967-1968, *10,* 117-124.

Khan, S. B. "Affective Correlates of Academic Achievement." *Journal of Educational Psychology,* 1969, *60,* 216-221.

Khan, S. B. "Affective Correlates of Academic Achievement: A Longitudinal Study." *Measurement and Evaluation in Guidance,* 1970, *3,* 76-80.

McGuire, C., Hindsman, E., King, F. J., and Jennings, E. "Dimensions of Talented Behavior." *Educational and Psychological Measurement,* 1961, *21,* 3-38.

# SCALE OF READING ATTITUDE BASED ON BEHAVIOR

AUTHOR: C. Glennon Rowell

AGE: Elementary and middle school

VARIABLE: Attitudes toward reading instruction, reading for pleasure, and reading in content areas

TYPE OF MEASURE: Rating scale

SOURCE FROM WHICH MEASURE MAY BE OBTAINED: C. Glennon Rowell, Language Department, Florida State University, Tallahassee, Florida 32306.

DESCRIPTION OF MEASURE: The scale is designed to be used by an observer for the purpose of recording how students react to a variety of reading situations. Sixteen items are included. For each item, five possible responses are provided ranging from "always occurs" to "never occurs." The scale was specifically designed to determine reading attitude where children have problems in reading; hence the reason for an observer.

As examples, five selected items from the sixteen-item measure are given below.

1. The student exhibits a strong desire to come to the reading circle or to have reading instruction take place.
3. The student asks permission or raises his hand to read orally.
6. Contributions in the way of voluntary discussions are made by the student in the reading class.
8. The student makes an effort to read printed materials on bulletin boards, charts, or other displays having writing on them.
10. The student expresses genuine interest in going to the school's library.

RELIABILITY AND VALIDITY: Validity was determined by having each of four upper-grade teachers who were supervising student teachers place each child in her classroom in one of five categories ranging from "best" to "poorest" attitude toward reading. Each student teacher completed the reading attitude scale on the children in her respective classroom. Correlations were computed between the category ratings given by the supervising teachers and the attitude scale ratings made by the student teachers. Coefficients ranged from .52 to .84, with an average of .70. Interrater reliability of the scale was determined by having each supervising teacher complete the attitude scale on every third student in her classroom. These were then correlated with the ratings given by the student teachers for the same children. Coefficients ranged from .76 to .95, with an average of .88.

BIBLIOGRAPHY:

Rowell, C. G. "Change in Attitude Toward Reading and Its Relationship to Certain Variables Among Children with Reading Difficulties." Unpublished doctoral dissertation. George Peabody College for Teachers, Nashville, Tennessee, 1967.
Rowell, C. G. "An Attitude Scale for Reading." *The Reading Teacher,* 1972, *25,* 442-447.

Rowell, C. G. "An Investigation of Factors Related to Change in Attitude Toward Reading." *Journal of Reading Behavior,* 1972-1973, *5,* 266-272.

---

# SCHOOL ATTITUDE RESEARCH INSTRUMENT (SARI)

AUTHOR: Thomas A. Ringness

AGE: Junior and senior high school

VARIABLE: Identification and achievement values

TYPE OF MEASURE: Likert-type scale

SOURCE FROM WHICH MEASURE MAY BE OBTAINED: Thomas A. Ringness, School of Education, Department of Educational Psychology, 1025 West Johnson Street, Madison, Wisconsin 53706.

DESCRIPTION OF MEASURE: The SARI consists of fifty-nine items of which five each are concerned with identification of S with mother, with father, with teachers, and with peers; five items each are concerned with S's estimate of academic achievement values of mother, father, teachers, and peers, and S's own values; five items concern characteristics of popular peers; five items concern perceived teacher characterization of model pupil behavior; and four items concern peer attitudes toward scholars. In scoring the SARI, "strongly agree" is weighted at 5, "agree" at 4, "neutral" at 3, "disagree" at 2, and "strongly disagree" at 1. Thus for identification and achievement values, scores may range from a high of 25 for the sum of five items to a low of 5. Other items are scored singly.

As examples, the first ten of the fifty-nine items are given below.

1. My mother values education highly.
2. Teachers seem to like creative students best.
3. I value my close friends' advice.
4. Most students here work as hard as possible.
5. My close friends study hard.
6. I admire my father.
7. I feel close to my father.
8. I study hard.
9. I appreciate the values of school.
10. My mother insists upon regular study habits.

RELIABILITY AND VALIDITY: A pilot study showed that for thirty-two Ss one-week test-retest reliability ranged from .999 (Spearman-Brown formula) for peer identification to .69 for own values, with reliability of seven of the nine scales above .94. Validity rests on the opinions of judges who were either advanced graduate students and staff members in school psychology or active school pupil personnel workers.

BIBLIOGRAPHY:

Ringness, T. A. "Identifying Figures, Their Achievement Values, and Children's Values as Related to Actual and Predicted Achievement." *Journal of Educational Psychology,* 1970, *61,* 174-185.

---

# SCHOOL ATTITUDE SURVEY

AUTHOR: Harold F. Burks

AGE: Elementary school

VARIABLE: Feelings of children in academic studies

TYPE OF MEASURE: Questionnaire

SOURCE FROM WHICH MEASURE MAY BE OBTAINED: Arden Press, 8331 Alvarado Drive, Huntington Beach, California 92646.

DESCRIPTION OF MEASURE: The purpose of this measure is to assess children's feelings in the school setting. The instrument is deliberately designed to avoid posing questions to children concerning their home environment, their parents, their church, or their community activities. The author originally constructed an item pool of 123 items that were administered to 104 elementary-school children. Twenty-one public-school teachers judged the appropriateness of the items based on understandability to elementary-aged pupils, pertinence of the items to school activities, relationship to some school condition or situation that could be changed, nonduplication of items, and absence of potential to embarrass the child. The jury selected forty-six items out of the original 123, and these were cut down further to the final thirty-six. The items are grouped into four areas: about the things we learn, about the teacher and me, about the other children and me, and about me and my classroom.

As examples, three items from the section of the measure entitled About the Teacher and Me are given below.

15. *About the Teacher Helping Me*

| [ ] | [ ] | [ ] |
|---|---|---|
| The teacher helps me enough. | Sometimes I wish the teacher would help me more. | Often I wish the teacher would help me more. |

16. *About the Teacher Calling on Me for Answers*

| [ ] | [ ] | [ ] |
|---|---|---|
| The teacher calls on me as much as I want her to. | Sometimes I think the teacher calls on me too much or not enough. | Often I think the teacher calls on me too much or not enough. |

17. *About Things That Bother Me*

| [ ] | [ ] | [ ] |
|---|---|---|
| I can talk to the teacher as much as I want to about things that bother me. | Sometimes I wish I could talk to the teacher about things that bother me. | Often I wish I could talk to the teacher about things that bother me. |

RELIABILITY AND VALIDITY: Regarding reliability, the manual for the measure simply states that most items were found to be reliable. The author found that educable mentally retarded children showed significantly more dissatisfaction with school life than did normal class pupils. The same was true with educationally handicapped children. The author found that the relationship between reported inner feelings (as measured by the School Attitude Survey) and rated outward conduct (measured by teacher ratings) for forty-seven children was significant at the .01 level ($chi$-square = 7.53).

BIBLIOGRAPHY: None reported.

*Prepared by Orval G. Johnson*

---

# SCHOOL MORALE SCALE

AUTHORS: Lawrence S. Wrightsman, Maria Taranto, and Ronald H. Nelson

AGE: 9 years and up

VARIABLE: Children's attitudes about school

TYPE OF MEASURE: Questionnaire

SOURCE FROM WHICH MEASURE MAY BE OBTAINED: Packet of materials including monograph, scale, score sheet, and reliability information available from L. S. Wrightsman, Box 512, Psychology Department, Peabody College, Nashville, Tennessee 37203. Cost: $3.00.

DESCRIPTION OF MEASURE: This measure is composed of eighty-four statements to which children mark "agree" or "disagree." Twelve items each on the following subscales deal with attitudes toward: school plant; instruction; administration, regulations, and staff; community support of schools; other students; teacher-student relations; and general school feelings. For group administration at the junior high level or above, the test takes about 30 minutes. Younger children may be tested in small groups by the examiner reading each statement aloud; time is about 45 minutes. Norms are available in the monograph by Wrightsman, Nelson, and Taranto (1968). The School Morale Scale is designed particularly for use in evaluation of ESEA programs and other educational interventions.

As examples, the first ten of the eighty-four statements on the scale are given below.

1. Compared to most school buildings I've seen, this building is nicer.
2. There are many more audio-visual materials available at this school than at the average school.
3. There are too many rules and regulations at this school.
4. The people in this community want the schools to try out new educational methods and materials.
5. If there were more clubs here, this school would be a lot friendlier place.
6. All my teachers know me by name.
7. I look forward to Friday afternoons because I won't have to go to school for two days.
8. My school building is too large; it is too far to walk from one class to another.
9. Our library is not a very friendly place.
10. The principal of this school is very fair.

RELIABILITY AND VALIDITY: For 127 fifth graders, Cronbach *alpha* reliabilities of subscales range from .42 to .78; there are equivalent reliabilities for seventh and ninth graders. Validity is demonstrated by comparing responses of children at different schools differing in such areas as plant facilities and innovative programs.

BIBLIOGRAPHY:

Wrightsman, L. S., Nelson, R. H., and Taranto, M. "The Construction and Validation of a Scale to Measure Children's School Morale." Unpublished monograph. George Peabody College for Teachers, Nashville, Tennessee, 1968.

---

## SCHOOL SENTIMENT INDEX (SSI)

AUTHOR: Instructional Objectives Exchange

AGE: Kindergarten to grade 12

VARIABLE: Attitude toward school

TYPE OF MEASURE: Self-report inventory

SOURCE FROM WHICH MEASURE MAY BE OBTAINED: Instructional Objectives Exchange, Box 24095, Los Angeles, California 90024. The SSI is contained in an Instructional Objectives Exchange collection entitled *Attitude Toward School K-12* (1972). Cost: Total collection, $8.00.

DESCRIPTION OF MEASURE: This instrument is designed to measure five aspects of attitude toward school: teacher, school subjects, school social structure and climate, peer, and general. There are separate forms for the primary level (thirty-seven items), intermediate level (eighty-one items), and secondary level (seventy-two items). The entire set of items for each test may be administered and a single score obtained, yielding a global estimate of attitude toward school. Items representing each subscale may be scored separately, yielding information on the attainment of each dimension.

As examples, the first seven of the thirty-seven items of the SSI, primary level, are given below. Questions are read orally and answered "yes" or "no" by marking the appropriate response boxes. For children unable to identify numerals for each question, pictures (see left-hand column) are provided.

(face)      1. Is your teacher interested in the things you do at home?
(star)      2. When you are trying to do your schoolwork, do the other children bother you?
(bell)      3. Does your teacher care about you?
(phone)    4. Do other children get you into trouble at school?
(flower)    5. Do you like being at school?
(clown)    6. Would you be happier if you didn't have to go to school?
(house)    7. Does it bother you because your teacher doesn't give you enough time to finish your work?

RELIABILITY AND VALIDITY:

| | Internal Consistency Index | | Test-Retest Stability Index | |
|---|---|---|---|---|
| | n | r | n | r |
| *Primary* | | | | |
| *SSI–Total* | 108 | .72 | 151 | .87 |
| Teacher | 128 | .62 | 163 | .61 |
| Peer | 124 | .42 | 161 | .35 |
| Subjects | 128 | .49 | 164 | .68 |
| Social Structure and Climate | 123 | .48 | 161 | .55 |
| General | 122 | .70 | 158 | .85 |
| *Intermediate* | | | | |
| *SSI–Total* | 54 | .80 | 129 | .83 |
| *Teacher: Instruction* | 67 | .76 | 141 | .70 |
| *Teacher: Authority* | 66 | .71 | 141 | .77 |
| *Teacher: Peers* | 67 | .65 | 139 | .81 |
| Peers | 60 | .54 | 135 | .73 |
| Learning | 81 | .71 | 137 | .63 |
| Social Structure and Climate | 63 | .47 | 137 | .70 |
| General | 67 | .73 | 138 | .90 |
| *Secondary* | | | | |
| *SSI–Total* | 47 | .88 | 80 | .49 |
| *Teacher: Instruction* | 74 | .73 | 101 | .68 |
| *Teacher: Authority* | 75 | .71 | 107 | .65 |
| *Teacher: Peers* | 76 | .76 | 104 | .81 |
| Social Structure and Climate | 78 | .77 | 105 | .64 |
| Learning | 74 | .68 | 104 | .62 |
| Peer | 73 | .71 | 100 | .71 |
| General | 72 | .79 | 111 | .68 |

BIBLIOGRAPHY:

Instructional Objectives Exchange, *Attitude Toward School K-12,* 1972.

*Prepared by Diane Narikawa*

---

# SECONDARY SCHOOL INVENTORY

AUTHOR: Val R. Christensen

AGE: Junior and senior high school

VARIABLE: Attitudes toward school

TYPE OF MEASURE: Likert-type scale

SOURCE FROM WHICH MEASURE MAY BE OBTAINED: Val R. Christensen, Utah State University, Logan, Utah 84322.

DESCRIPTION OF MEASURE: The Secondary School Inventory consists of ninety-five questions. It tests student attitudes in three main areas: attitude toward the school situation, attitude toward peers, and attitude toward the teacher. The scale is specifically designed to compare random-grouped vs. ability-grouped students in these three areas.

Examples of items from each variable are given below. The student responds by circling "yes," "no," or "?."

*School:*   Do you think your school requires too much homework?
*Teacher:* Does your teacher really care whether you learn something in this class?
*Peer:*     Are the students in this school fair in their play?

RELIABILITY AND VALIDITY: An original list of 109 items was given to 130 sixth-grade students. An item analysis was made based upon the highest 27 percent of the papers and lowest 27 percent. Only those items that clearly differentiated between these two extreme groups were included in the final form of the inventory. The corrected odd-even coefficient of reliability for the inventory is .94. The corrected split-half reliability coefficient for the attitude toward teacher subtest is .95, and for the school and peer subtests, .91 and .82, respectively. The correlation of school attitude score with peer attitude score is .54; of teacher attitude with peer attitude, .46; and of teacher attitude with school attitude, .57.

BIBLIOGRAPHY:

Christensen, V. R. "Pupil Attitudes Toward School, Peers, and Teachers Under Ability-Grouped and Random-Grouped Systems in Weber and Ogden School Districts." Unpublished master's thesis. Utah State University, Logan, 1964.

## SEMANTIC DIFFERENTIAL:
## ACHIEVEMENT-RELATED CONCEPTS

AUTHORS: Helen H. Davidson and Judith W. Greenberg

AGE: 8 to 16 years

VARIABLE: Meanings attached to, or attitudes toward, achievement-related concepts

TYPE OF MEASURE: Semantic differential scale

SOURCE FROM WHICH MEASURE MAY BE OBTAINED: Judith W. Greenberg, City College of the City University of New York, Convent Avenue and 138th Street, New York, New York 10031.

DESCRIPTION OF MEASURE: This Semantic Differential Scale, following Osgood's method, is designed to measure meanings children attach to certain significant concepts and persons that may be related to their school achievement. It consists of six concepts (mother, father, teacher, me, reading, and school work), each of which is rated on twelve 5-point bipolar adjective scales. There are four scales on each of the three main dimensions identified by Osgood: evaluative (e.g., good-bad), potency (e.g., hard-soft), and activity (e.g., fast-slow). The scale is administered to groups of children and contains a practice item with which the examiner can explain the rating procedure. Each concept appears on a separate sheet followed by the twelve rating scales. In scoring, the rating for each scale is assigned a value ranging from 1 to 5. A value of 5 is given to the end of the scale representing the most positive, most powerful, or most active pole. Subscores may be obtained for each concept on each of the three dimensions of meaning. Response-set controls consist of varying direction of the scales. An index of "caution" has also been obtained by scoring the number of times the child marks the middle or neutral position.

RELIABILITY AND VALIDITY: None reported.

BIBLIOGRAPHY:

Davidson, H. H., and Greenberg, J. W. *School Achievers from a Deprived Background.* New York: Associated Educational Services, 1967.

*Prepared by Judith W. Greenberg*

## STUDENT ATTITUDE SURVEY

AUTHOR: Grant H. Hendrickson

AGE: High school

VARIABLE: Student morale

TYPE OF MEASURE: Equal-appearing interval scale

SOURCE FROM WHICH MEASURE MAY BE OBTAINED: Bureau of School Service, University of Washington, Seattle, Washington 98195.

DESCRIPTION OF MEASURE: The scale purports to measure high school student morale (individual and group) as defined by the tenets of humanistic psychology. It assumes that students with feelings of positive self-image, a high degree of self-actualization, good relationships with others in the school environment, and a sense of self-direction in the educational process will have a high level of morale. Traditional measures of student morale (winning athletic teams, "school spirit," facilities, and so forth) are not included in the scale. The instrument is suitable for administering to large groups of students. Computerized norms are available with respondents grouped by grade levels and sex. Norms are based on usage of the instrument in the state of Washington and involve approximately ten thousand students.

As examples, the first five of the twenty-items on the scale are given below. The respondent answers "agree" or "disagree."

1. Adults in this school are more interested in controlling kids than they are in helping them to become successful human beings.
2. Teachers around here seem willing to give up their own free time to help students.
3. Education in this school is boring.
4. Very few people in this school really care what happens to the problem students.
5. The student in this school learns because he feels it is important for himself—because he wants to learn.

RELIABILITY AND VALIDITY: Validity tests were inconclusive, although predicted scores of students made by a group of school psychologists familiar with the concepts upon which the scale is based correlated .85 with the actual scores of a group of students.

BIBLIOGRAPHY:

Hendrickson, G. H. "The Development of an Instrument to Measure Student Morale as Defined by Third Force Psychology." Unpublished doctoral dissertation. University of Washington, Seattle, 1971.
Hendrickson, G. H. "High School Morale and Humanistic Psychology." *Journal of Humanistic Psychology,* 1973, *13,* 69-75.

## STUDENT OPINION INSTRUMENT

AUTHOR: Stephen H. Davidoff

AGE: 7 to 12 years

VARIABLE: Student opinion of teacher behavior

TYPE OF MEASURE: Paired-comparison questionnaire

SOURCE FROM WHICH MEASURE MAY BE OBTAINED: Stephen H. Davidoff, 7 Underwood Road, Wyncote, Pennsylvania 19095. Cost: $2.50 for entire report and sample instrument.

DESCRIPTION OF MEASURE: The Student Opinion Instrument is a paired-comparison device designed to obtain student assessments of teacher behavior. The teacher behaviors selected for the construction of items were definable, observable, recordable, and empirically related to student gain in other major investigations. Three forms of the instrument were constructed by randomizing the order of items in each form. The effect of item order is thus controlled. A pilot study was conducted to test the readability and stability of the instrument. Items that fluctuated significantly ($p < .10$) over a forty-eight-hour period were deleted from further consideration,

As examples, four selected items from Form A of the instrument are given below. The student selects one statement from each pair.

1. A—When we start new work this teacher helps us to see why the work is important to all of us.
   B—This teacher allows us enough time to develop our thoughts and ideas.
3. E—This teacher uses many examples to help us learn.
   A—When we start new work this teacher helps us to see why the work is important to all of us.
4. C—This teacher is friendly.
   B—This teacher allows us enough time to develop our thoughts and ideas.
7. B—This teacher allows us enough time to develop our thoughts and ideas.
   D—The way this teacher organizes the lesson helps me to understand the ideas.

RELIABILITY AND VALIDITY: The subjects were ninth- and tenth-grade public-school children ($N = 550$) enrolled in Green Version Biology (*Biological Sciences,* 1973). One intact class from each of the twenty-one instructors' rosters was selected using a random-numbers table. Each teacher devoted approximately 2,400 minutes of instruction to the selected chapters. Two equivalent forms of the Biological Sciences Curriculum Studies Third Quarter Achievement Test were available for pre- and post-testing. The designation of a form as either pre- or posttest was randomized. The student-opinion instrument was administered twice during the course of the unit. The days on which the classes reacted to the instrument were randomized. Three equivalent forms of the instrument were constructed and were administered twice. The *tau* coefficients were .94 for the entire instrument and .86 for each scale. No consistent relationship was found between student opinion and student gain.

BIBLIOGRAPHY:

Davidoff, S. H. "The Development of an Instrument Designed to Secure Student Assessment of Teacher Behaviors That Correlate with Objective Measures of Student Achievement." 1973. ERIC document no. ED 039 170.

*Biological Sciences: An Ecological Approach.* (2nd ed.) Chicago: Rand McNally, 1973.

---

## STUDENT OPINION POLL II

AUTHORS: P. W. Jackson and J. W. Getzels (original); R. J. Spillman (first revision); and Henriette M. Lahaderne (revision).

AGE: Grade 5 through high school

VARIABLE: Attitude toward school

TYPE OF MEASURE: Multiple-choice test

SOURCE FROM WHICH MEASURE MAY BE OBTAINED: Henriette M. Lahaderne, Chula Vista City School District, 84 East "J" Street, P.O. Box 907, Chula Vista, California 92012.

DESCRIPTION OF MEASURE: The Student Opinion Poll II is a revision of a sixty-item test developed by Jackson and Getzels (1959). The forty-nine questions concern four aspects of school life: the teacher, the curriculum, peers, and the school. The test is scored by giving 1 point each time the student chooses the response indicating the highest degree of satisfaction with the aspect of school life under question. One item is repeated three times—each time with the responses listed in different order—to check students' consistency of responses. A point is assigned to the item if the three responses are consistent.

As examples, four of the forty-nine items on the revised test are given below.

1. This school listens to parents' opinions
    a. too much.
    b. just enough.
    c. too little.
3. Although teachers differ in this school, most are
    a. very good.
    b. good.
    c. fair.
    d. poor.
12. Students in this school are
    a. too smart—it is difficult to keep up with them.
    b. just smart enough—we are all about the same.
    c. not smart enough—they are so slow I get bored.

16. When teachers "go too fast," students do not know what is going on. In this school, most teachers teach

a. too slowly.

b. about right.

c. too fast.

RELIABILITY AND VALIDITY: The Student Opinion Poll II was administered to 293 sixth-grade pupils in a predominantly white, working-class suburb. The reliability of the instrument was estimated by using Kuder-Richardson formula 20. The coefficient was .86 for the total sample, .85 for boys ($N$ = 148), and .86 for girls ($N$ = 145). In a subsequent study of 125 sixth-grade pupils the reliability coefficient, based on the Kuder-Richardson formula, was .89 for boys ($N$ = 62) and .84 for girls ($N$ = 63).

BIBLIOGRAPHY:

Diederich, R. "Teacher Perceptions as Related to Teacher Student Similarity and Student Satisfaction with School." Unpublished doctoral dissertation. University of Chicago, Illinois, 1965.

Jackson, P. W., and Getzels, J. W. "Psychological Health and Classroom Functioning: A Study of Dissatisfaction with School Among Adolescents." *Journal of Educational Psychology,* 1959, *50, 295-300.*

Jackson, P. W., and Lahaderne, H. M. "Scholastic Success and Attitude Toward School in a Population of Sixth Graders." *Journal of Educational Psychology,* 1967, *58,* 15-18.

Lahaderne, H. M. "Attitudinal and Intellectual Correlates of Attention: A Study of Four Sixth-Grade Classrooms." *Journal of Educational Psychology,* 1968, *59,* 320-324.

Lahaderne, H. M., Jackson, P. W., and Happel, L. C. "Visibility of Discontent: An Analysis of Teachers' Perceptions of Students' Attitudes." *Proceedings of the American Psychological Association,* 1966, *74,* 267-268.

Spillman, R. J. "Psychological and Scholastic Correlates of Dissatisfaction with School Among Adolescents." Unpublished master's thesis. University of Chicago, Illinois, 1959.

*Prepared by Henriette M. Lahaderne*

---

# STUDENT REACTION INVENTORY

AUTHORS: Cyril J. Hoyt and Paul R. Grim

AGE: Grades 7 to 12

VARIABLE: Pupils' reactions to teachers' classroom behavior

TYPE OF MEASURE: Questionnaire

SOURCE FROM WHICH MEASURE MAY BE OBTAINED: Minnesota Test Publishers, 1323 Keston Street, St. Paul, Minnesota 55108.

DESCRIPTION OF MEASURE: The Student Reaction Inventory consists of 200 statements selected from remarks that students have been known to make about their experiences in particular classes. The items are in the form of statements of feelings of the individual toward some aspect of the instructional environment. Each item is scored on one of these seven areas: quality of classroom government—cooperative vs. other; clarity of objective (as viewed by pupils); cooperative group work; incentive quality; motivational intensity level; provision for students' psychological needs; and individualization of instruction. Several forms of the inventory have been developed, including one for evaluating student teachers.

As examples, the first ten of the two hundred items on student teacher Form B of the inventory are given below. The respondent answers "agree," "uncertain," or "disagree."

This student teacher
1. is easy to talk to.
2. makes me feel a part of things.
3. has helped me to find the answers to some questions that have been bothering me.
4. seems to welcome our suggestions.
5. is good at answering questions.
6. knows how to handle anyone who causes a disturbance.
7. makes sure we understand important concepts.
8. changes his mind too often.
9. is very understanding.
10. easily spots the difficulty and gets me back on the track when I get confused about something.

RELIABILITY AND VALIDITY: Henjum (1966) reported reliability and correlations of average scores (of pupils in class) with personality test scores of teachers and other teacher characteristics.

BIBLIOGRAPHY:

Grim, R. L., and Hoyt, C. J. "Excerpts from Two Instruments for Appraising Teacher Competency." *Journal of Educational Research,* 1953, *46,* 705-710.

Henjum, A. E. "The Relationships Between Certain Personality Characteristics of Student Teachers and Success in Student Teaching." Unpublished doctoral dissertation. University of Minnesota, Minneapolis, 1966.

Henjum, A. E. "A Study of the Significance of Student Teachers' Personality Characteristics." *Journal of Teacher Education,* 1969, *20,* 143-147.

# SURVEY OF SCHOOL-RELATED ATTITUDES

AUTHOR: Sar B. Khan

AGE: 8 years and up

VARIABLE: Attitudes toward school, teacher, self; independence

TYPE OF MEASURE: Likert scale

SOURCE FROM WHICH MEASURE MAY BE OBTAINED: Sar B. Khan, Ontario Institute for Studies in Education, 252 Bloor Street West, Toronto, 181 Ontario, Canada.

DESCRIPTION OF MEASURE: The scale was developed for use with 8-year-old school children in Toronto in a study of the open-learning environment. The questionnaire consists of seventy-eight items, and the child responds to whether each statement is true for him, he is not sure, or it is not true for him. "Attitude toward school" consists of twenty items; "attitude toward teacher," twenty-one items; "attitude toward self," twenty-one items; and "independence," sixteen items.

As examples, three selected items from each of the four subscales of the survey are given below.

*Attitude Toward School*
  3. Each morning I look forward to coming to school.
  6. I would like to go to school all year long.
19. My school is like a jail.
*Attitude Toward Teacher*
  3. Teachers try to be fair with students.
11. I want to be a teacher.
14. Teachers talk too much.
*Attitude Toward Self*
1. My parents like me.
6. I am a happy person.
7. I get nervous when talking to teachers.
*Independence*
1. I return my library books on time.
3. I stand up for my rights with other children.
4. I decide which clothes I will wear to school every day.

RELIABILITY AND VALIDITY: The internal consistency reliability coefficients are .84, .74, .70, and .25, respectively, for the four subscales. These correlations are based on responses of 387 8-year-old children. The correlations between the four subscale scores and performance on three subtests of a standardized test of basic skills are as follows: language (.33, .26, .33, .11); work study (.23, .15, .30, .08); and arithmetic (.22, .17, .27, .08). The multiple correlations of the four attitude subscales with achievement in the above three areas are .41, .35, .31, and .32, respectively.

BIBLIOGRAPHY: None reported.

# TEACHER ATTITUDE SCALE

AUTHOR: Paul Hurewitz

AGE: High school and college

VARIABLE: The perception of learning and the educative process, the children, and the teacher

TYPE OF MEASURE: Questionnaire

SOURCE FROM WHICH MEASURE MAY BE OBTAINED: Paul Hurewitz, Herbert H. Lehman College, Beford Park Boulevard, West, Bronx, New York 10468. Send large self-addressed envelope and $.50 for handling.

DESCRIPTION OF MEASURE: This measure consists of sixty items that are answered on a 3-point scale, "agree," "no opinion," or "disagree." There are three subscales comprising twenty items each, dealing with perception of learning and the educative process (Scale 1), perception of children (Scale 2), and perception of the teacher's role (Scale 3). There is also a ten-item Lie Scale. IBM scoring sheets may be used, and there is a computerized program kit. Norms for the three subscales are available for college-age students.

As examples, the first four items from each of the three subscales are given below.

*Perception of the Learning Process*
1. The learning that occurs in kindergarten and first grade is not as important as what one learns in high school.
2. The school, rather than the family, is the prime contributor in helping the child to develop proper attitudes toward learning.
3. Children in the early grades are usually not ready to help choose what they should learn.
4. A classroom cannot be organized along truly democratic lines as the teacher has to usually act as the judge and the jury and cannot delegate this responsibility to young children.

*Perception of Children*
21. Children can learn some basic rules about getting along with others when they play during free time.
22. Children usually have to be pressured to want to learn.
23. IQ is a good measure of native intelligence.
24. The child who cannot sit still must be taught self-control.

*Perception of the Teacher's Role*
41. The teacher's values are usually not very different from the values of lower-class children.
42. The teacher's main responsibility is to teach the majority in the classroom.
43. The technique a teacher uses may reflect the kind of values he or she has.
44. The teacher's main job is to teach children, and they should not be expected to handle children's emotional problems. Children should be sent to a guidance counselor if they need help.

RELIABILITY AND VALIDITY: Test-retest reliabilities for the measure, with a two-week interval, were: Scale 1 (perception of the learning process), .80; Scale 2 (perception of children), .82; Scale 3 (perception of the teacher's role), .80; and total scale, .86. Intercorrelation of the subscales ranged from .40 to .51.

BIBLIOGRAPHY: None reported.

---

# THINKING ABOUT MY SCHOOL (TAMS)

AUTHOR: Joanne R. Whitmore

AGE: 8 to 14 years

VARIABLE: Perception of the school environment or attitude toward school

TYPE OF MEASURE: Questionnaire

SOURCE FROM WHICH MEASURE MAY BE OBTAINED: See Whitmore (1974).

DESCRIPTION OF MEASURE: TAMS is a forty-seven-item Likert-type questionnaire constructed for immediate use with pupils in grades 4, 5, and 6 in a low-SES, predominantly black community. TAMS items were derived from statements about school made by students in the population for which data were being collected. Items were clustered to form five theoretical scales: power, social (peer relations), work, teachers, and liking for school. TAMS can be administered to groups of any size in about 30 minutes. With careful administration the questionnaire can be given to students with weak test-taking skills. The teacher should be absent when the instrument is administered for research purposes, and confidentiality should be guaranteed. TAMS is easily hand-scored. TAMS has three types of uses: (1) as a measure of pupil perceptions and attitudes for research purposes, (2) as a tool for providing teachers with objective information on pupil perceptions and attitudes, and (3) as a source of information to students providing leadership to improve the school.

As examples, the first ten of the forty-seven items on the questionnaire are given below. The respondent answers on a 4-point frequency scale ranging from "not at all" to "all the time."

1. My school is a friendly place.
2. I look forward to going to school.
3. Teachers at Brentwood like kids.
4. Kids are happy most of the time at our school.
5. Grownups at school listen to the ideas of kids.
6. Some days there is so much noise I can't work in class.
7. Kids are proud to say they go to Brentwood.
8. Kids think most of the grownups at school are their good friends.

9. The kids help decide what should be done in the school.

10. Sometimes I feel no one at Brentwood likes me.

RELIABILITY AND VALIDITY: Reliability and validity data are present to date only for a population sample of about 215 students in a low-SES black community. The author's objective in constructing TAMS was to produce a reliable instrument for students with low reading skills, low power of concentration for test taking, and a low level of task motivation. The *alpha* coefficient of internal consistency for total responses on TAMS was .92. The fall-winter correlation ($N = 163$) was .52 for total scores (.61 for females and .40 for males). Since the data were obtained during a period of intervention, they are not very informative. Reliability over a shorter period of time needs to be tested. TAMS scale scores and total scores were useful in discriminating groups of subjects who have been identified informally by teachers and researchers as differing in their attitudes toward school. Inconsistent findings regarding construct and criterion validity may be due to the nature of the sample. In the research study for which TAMS was constructed, it was found to have moderate reliability and validity comparable to that obtained on other self-report measures.

BIBLIOGRAPHY:

Crist, J. L., Marx, R. W., Whitmore, J. R., and Sears, P. S. "Effective Reinforcement for Achievement Behaviors in Minority Children: The Second and Third Years." Technical report, Stanford Center for Research and Development in Teaching. Stanford University, Palo Alto, California, 1975.

Whitmore, J. R. "The Modification of Undesirable Attitudes and Classroom Behavior Through Constructive Use of Social Power in the School Peer Culture." Technical report no. 36, Stanford Center for Research and Development in Teaching. Stanford University, Palo Alto, California, 1973. ERIC document no. ED 084 489.

Whitmore, J. R. "Student Leadership: Guidelines for Developing Programs in Distressed Low-Income Elementary School." Memorandum no. 113, Stanford Center for Research and Development in Teaching. Stanford University, Palo Alto, California, 1973. ERIC document no. ED 083 348.

Whitmore, J. R., Crist, J. L., and Marx, R. W. "An Experimental In-Service Teacher Education Program for Distressed Elementary Schools." Memorandum no. 117, Stanford Center for Research and Development in Teaching. Stanford University, Palo Alto, California, 1974. ERIC document no. ED 087 777.

Whitmore, J. R. "Thinking About My School (TAMS): The Development of an Inventory to Measure Pupil Perception of the Elementary School Environment." Memorandum no. 125, Stanford Center for Research and Development in Teaching. Stanford University, Palo Alto, California, 1974.

# WHAT I DO IN SCHOOL (WIDIS)

AUTHORS: N. J. Entwistle, G. Long, and Barbara E. Wade

AGE: 9 to 11 years

VARIABLE: Classroom behavior and attitudes

TYPE OF MEASURE: Questionnaire

SOURCE FROM WHICH MEASURE MAY BE OBTAINED: Department of Educational Research, Cartmel College, University of Lancaster, Bailrigg, Lancaster, England.

DESCRIPTION OF MEASURE: These scales were designed for use in a project on teaching styles to measure dimensions that could form the basis of a pupil typology, which was then used to examine the effects of a range of classroom environments on behavior and attainment. The dimensions measured include contentiousness, sociability/extraversion, attitudes to school, fidgeting/restlessness/distractability, positive self-evaluation, fear of getting into trouble, evaluation anxiety, fear of peers, fear of not being liked, competition, novelty/creativity, need achievement, school affect, and need affiliation. The sixty items on each of the two forms of the measure refer specifically to classroom behavior and attitudes. The dimensions were formed from principal-component analyses of three separate pilot studies, each of which used a sample of approximately three hundred 9- to 11-year-old children. The original item bank, drawn from interviews with teachers and children as well as discussions and observation, consisted of approximately 350 items.

As examples, the first ten of the sixty items on Form A of the questionnaire are given below. The respondent answers on a 5-point frequency scale ranging from "hardly ever" to "very often."

 1. Does your mind wander during lessons?
 2. Does it bother you if you get your work wrong?
 3. Do you mess about in class?
 4. Do you enjoy school?
 5. When you tell other children your ideas do they agree with them?
 6. Are you just a little scared of getting into fights?
 7. Do you laugh and joke a lot with other children in class?
 8. Do you try to be top of the class?
 9. Do you like doing new things even if they are difficult?
10. Have you had things taken from you by the teacher?

RELIABILITY AND VALIDITY: Test-retest reliabilities of the fifteen dimension subscales ranged from .52 to .80 (two-week interval) and .45 to .68 (eight-month interval). Validity studies are at present in the process of analysis.

BIBLIOGRAPHY: None reported.

*Prepared by G. Long, N. J. Entwistle, and Barbara Wade*

# WRITTEN SCHOOL ATTITUDE TEST

AUTHOR: Earl McCallon

AGE: 10 to 14 years

VARIABLE: Attitude toward school

TYPE OF MEASURE: Test

SOURCE FROM WHICH MEASURE MAY BE OBTAINED: Learning Concepts, Inc., 2501 North Lamar, Austin, Texas, 78705.

DESCRIPTION OF MEASURE: This test consists of forty-six items that measure three dimensions of attitude toward school: interpersonal relations (nine items), student-instruction interaction (twenty-six items), and general school factor (eleven items). Designed for group administration for students in grades 4 to 6, it is available in both English and Spanish, and it can be administered and scored by the classroom teacher.

As examples, five selected items from the forty-six item test are given below.

1. I like my school friends.
5. My teachers help us to be friends again after a fight.
9. My teachers punish the whole class for something one of the pupils did.
13. In learning our lessons in class, we do most of the talking.
17. My principal likes children.

RELIABILITY AND VALIDITY: Content and concurrent validity data are available. Several reliability studies are reported in the manual (McCallon, 1973). Test-retest reliabilities in these studies have ranged between .72 and .85.

BIBLIOGRAPHY:

McCallon, E. *School Attitude Test Manual.* Austin, Texas: Learning Research, Inc., 1973.

# Group 8-b

# Miscellaneous Attitudes
and Interests

## ADOLESCENT-MIDDLESCENT ATTITUDE SCALE (AMAS)

AUTHOR: Barbara N. Armstrong

AGE: 13 to 65 years

VARIABLE: Life attitudes

TYPE OF MEASURE: Semantic differential

SOURCE FROM WHICH MEASURE MAY BE OBTAINED: Barbara N. Armstrong, 215 Schrank Hall, University of Akron, Akron, Ohio 44325.

DESCRIPTION OF MEASURE: This thirty-six-item scale utilizes twelve major concepts to measure basic attitudes of adolescent and middlescent individuals. Concepts included in the instrument are: children, health, marriage, leisure, future, daily tasks, self, parents, school, community, friends, and church. The wording of items is designed to avoid emotionally loaded terms. The concepts are noncontroversial and are deemed useful in measuring basic attitudes. The relative adjustment of the individual is inferred from the direction and intensity of attitude scores. Scores near the middle, or neutral, point of the attitude continuum are interpreted as representing psychological conflict or marginal adjustment. Far judgments (those varying away from neutral) are interpreted as representing better than marginal adjustment. The farther away from neutral the score, the better the inferred adjustment. Each of the twelve concepts included on the AMAS appears three times for a total of thirty-six items, each of which the respondent rates on a 5-point continuum (4-0). The most intense positive response for each item is given a rating of 4 and the most negative rating a 0, with a neutral rating 2. The moderately positive response is rated 3 and the moderately negative response is rated 1. Thus, the highest possible score for each of the thirty-six items is 4, for each basic concept the highest possible score is 12, and for the entire instrument the highest possible score is 144.

As examples, fifteen of the thirty-six items are given below, each to be rated from 0 to 4.

| | | |
|---|---|---|
| 1. *Children:* | considerate | inconsiderate |
| 2. *Health:* | excellent | poor |
| 3. *Marriage:* | happy | unhappy |
| 4. *Leisure:* | challenging | unchallenging |
| 5. *Future:* | bright | dull |
| 6. *Community:* | desirable | undesirable |
| 7. *Friends:* | cooperative | uncooperative |
| 8. *School:* | valuable | worthless |
| 9. *Parents:* | consistent | inconsistent |
| 10. *Church:* | important | unimportant |
| 11. *Daily Tasks:* | pleasant | unpleasant |
| 12. *Self:* | successful | unsuccessful |
| 13. *Health:* | improving | declining |
| 14. *Marriage:* | creative | routine |
| 15. *Friends:* | accepting | rejecting |

RELIABILITY AND VALIDITY: The test-retest reliability coefficient for the AMAS with a one-week interval between administrations to seventy-one ninth-grade adolescents was .87. Validation was established by comparing scores on the instrument with mean attitude scores derived by two independent raters of tapes of the participants responding to open-ended questions pertaining to the concepts included on the AMAS. The Spearman rank correlation was .91 ($p = .01$).

BIBLIOGRAPHY:

Armstrong, B. N. "A Comparison of the Attitudes and Adjustments of Middlescent Mothers and Their Ninth and Tenth Grade Adolescents." Unpublished doctoral dissertation. Ohio State University, Columbus, 1970.

Armstrong, B. N., and Scotzin, M. M. "Intergenerational Comparison of Attitudes Toward Basic Life Concepts." *Journal of Psychology*, 1974, *87*, 293-304.

Armstrong, B. N., and Taylor, C. M. "Attitudes and Adjustment of Adolescents and Their Middlescent Mothers." *Journal of Psychology*, 1972, *81*, 105-115.

---

## ADOLESCENT VALUE-ORIENTATIONS PROFILE

AUTHOR: Richard O. Ulin

AGE: 12 to 20 years

VARIABLE: Adolescent values

TYPE OF MEASURE: Questionnaire

SOURCE FROM WHICH MEASURE MAY BE OBTAINED: Richard O. Ulin, School of Education, University of Massachusetts, Amherst, Massachusetts 01002.

DESCRIPTION OF MEASURE: Forty-two "either-or" situations are set up in which subjects can envision themselves being involved. Each situation poses a choice between two of seven values: peer group, family, athletics, sex, financial security, upward mobility, and academic achievement. Each value is matched against every other value twice. The strength of an individual's (or group's) adherence to a given value can be measured by the total number of times he (or the group) chooses to follow that value in the twelve situations in which it is involved. Maximum potential adherence to a given value is 12, minimum potential 0. In the degree to which an individual shows the strength of an attachment to certain values, a complementary weakness of attachment to other values necessarily reveals itself. Thus through an examination of a subject's (or group's) pattern of choices, one can plot a subject's or a group's hierarchy of values.

As examples, three of the forty-two items on the questionnaire are given below.

2. Milton is both a good student and an excellent pianist. He is urged to become a con-

cert pianist, but if he chooses to do so, he will have to devote all his time to his music. This means he will have to give up school.
a. He should quit school for his music.
b. He should not quit school for his music.
4. Pete has two job opportunities which are alike in most respects. However, one is a steady position for life at a fair salary. The other, though it offers no security, gives him a chance to work his way to the top.
a. Pete should take the steady job.
b. Pete should take the job which gives him a chance to get to the top.
5. Fred has a busy schedule. He is in the college course and works after school and on weekends. He'd like to play on the school basketball team, but if he does, he won't have any time left for seeing girls, for dates and parties.
a. He should give up basketball.
b. He should give up dates and parties.

RELIABILITY AND VALIDITY: None reported.

BIBLIOGRAPHY:

Ulin, R. O. "Ethnicity and School Performance: An Analysis of Variables." *California Journal of Educational Research*, 1968, *19*, 190-197.

---

# AGE INDEPENDENCE SCALE, FORM II (PRESCHOOL)

AUTHORS: Robert Allen Keith, Margaret A. Blair, and Gordon S. Markie

AGE: Parents of preschool children

VARIABLE: Attitudes toward independence

TYPE OF MEASURE: Rating scale

SOURCE FROM WHICH MEASURE MAY BE OBTAINED: Robert Allen Keith, Department of Psychology, Claremont Graduate School, Claremont, California 91711.

DESCRIPTION OF MEASURE: The Preschool Form of this scale consists of seventy-five items of specific behavior. Parents (or others assessing a child) go through the items twice: first to check those items they believe the child is able to do currently, and second to give an age at which they believe the child will be able to perform independently. The scale has been used principally by comparing parents' ratings of the child with those of professionals working with the child. For handicapped children there is often a division between a reasonably realistic appraisal of present functioning with an unrealistic projection of future functioning.

As examples, the first twenty of the seventy-five items are given below.

 1. Sit unsupported for at least 1 minute.
 2. Crawl for a distance of 10 feet.
 3. Drink from a cup.
 4. Say a few words like "mama" or "dada."
 5. Stand without support.
 6. Walk a few steps.
 7. Eat with a spoon.
 8. Occupy himself for periods of 15 minutes.
 9. Talk in simple sentences.
10. Point to his eyes, ears, and nose.
11. Know the difference between a boy and a girl.
12. Play by himself in the yard.
13. Look at picture books by himself.
14. Tell the difference between a cow and a horse.
15. Use crayons.
16. Build a six-block tower.
17. Turn on TV if asked.
18. Ride a tricycle.
19. Use "I" rather than "me."
20. Know how old he is.

RELIABILITY AND VALIDITY: No reliability data. In Keith and Markie (1969) the scale was given to both parents of the handicapped child. Nursery school teacher, occupational therapist, physical therapist, and pediatrician also completed scales for a total of seventeen children with cerebral palsy. There were significant differences between parents and staff but also between various staff members. Differences between parents and staff became wider the lower the developmental quotient of the child.

BIBLIOGRAPHY:

Blair, A. "Child Rearing Attitudes: A Comparative Study of Hospital Staff and Mothers of Orthopedically Handicapped Children." Unpublished master's thesis. Claremont Graduate School, Claremont, California, 1963.

Keith, R. A., and Markie, G. S. "Parental and Professional Assessment of Functioning in Cerebral Palsy." *Developmental Medicine and Child Neurology,* 1969, *11,* 735-742.

---

# AGE INDEPENDENCE SCALE, ELEMENTARY SCHOOL FORM

AUTHORS: Audrey W. Gray and Robert Allen Keith

AGE: Parents of elementary-school children

VARIABLE: Attitude toward independence

TYPE OF MEASURE: Rating scale

SOURCE FROM WHICH MEASURE MAY BE OBTAINED: Robert Allen Keith, Department of Psychology, Claremont Graduate School, Claremont, California 91711.

DESCRIPTION OF MEASURE: The Elementary School Form of this scale is designed to elicit parental age norms for independent behavior for both boys and girls. The respondent gives ages at which the average child should be able to perform 100 activities, first for boys and then for girls. There are six subscales: self-care, cognitive facility, physical skills, social responsibility, autonomy, and wide experience.

As examples, the first twenty items of the 100-item scale are given below.

1. Dress self completely (zippers, buttons, shoes).
2. Comb hair.
3. Pour milk from a half-gallon milk carton.
4. Make a peanut butter sandwich.
5. Play simple table games (checkers, fish, etc.).
6. Name the days of the week in order.
7. Count to 100.
8. Skip.
9. Jump rope.
10. Pound a nail straight into a board.
11. Go about close neighborhood unattended.
12. Cross a busy street with no traffic signal.
13. Cross a residential street to play.
14. Stand up for rights with other children.
15. Play without guidance for 2-3 hours.
16. Walk five or six blocks to school.
17. Plan how to spend a Saturday afternoon.
18. Come home at a certain time.
19. Tell the truth about a misdeed.
20. Know that it is wrong to break a promise.

RELIABILITY AND VALIDITY: The scale was administered to fifty parents with an interval of one to four weeks between administrations. Median Pearson $r$ was .66 for boys and .68 for girls. On the thirty-eight items with social-class differences in mothers, middle-class mothers consistently had earlier age expectations than lower-class mothers. On the eighteen items separating middle-class mothers and fathers, mothers again had lower age expectations. In a study of parents of achieving and unachieving elementary-school boys, the parents of achieving boys expected earlier independence mastery.

BIBLIOGRAPHY:

Gray, W. "Independence Concepts of Parents Concerning Elementary School Children." Unpublished doctoral dissertation. Claremont Graduate School, Claremont, California, 1968.

Whiting, A. "Independence Concepts Held by Parents of Successful and Unsuccessful Elementary School Boys." Unpublished doctoral dissertation. Claremont Graduate School, Claremont, California, 1969.

*Prepared by Robert Allen Keith*

# AGE INDEPENDENCE SCALE, FORM III (ADOLESCENCE)

AUTHORS: Robert Allen Keith, Katherine K. Heinz, and Erlinda G. Barranda

AGE: Parents and adolescents

VARIABLE: Attitude toward independence

TYPE OF MEASURE: Rating scale

SOURCE FROM WHICH MEASURE MAY BE OBTAINED: Robert Allen Keith, Department of Psychology, Claremont Graduate School, Claremont, California 91711.

DESCRIPTION OF MEASURE: The Adolescence Form of this scale has seventy-five items with four subscales: economic, social, institutional (academic, religious and civic activities), and caretaking. It is designed to find at what age adults and young people believe youth should be able to complete various tasks and make suitable decisions and judgments.

As examples, twenty-five selected items of the seventy-five-item scale are given below. The respondent indicates the appropriate age at which he believes a young person should be able to handle the task or activity without help.

1. Order a meal in a restaurant.
2. Drink alcoholic drinks.
3. Decide whether or not to smoke.
4. Know how much father earns.
8. Open a savings account.
9. Rent an apartment.
15. Leave or quit school.
19. Learn how to dance.
24. Go steady.
27. Wear lipstick. (girl)
28. Own and use a razor. (boy)
29. Decide how long to stay out on a date. (girl)
30. Decide how long to stay out on a date. (boy)
36. Have children and support them.
39. Get up for school without being called.
40. Name the three branches of national or federal government.
41. Know the name of the governor of one's state or province.
42. Vote in a public election.
47. Decide whether or not to attend church.
50. Picket in a legal demonstration.
52. Decide what college or university to attend.
60. Make and care for a home garden.
62. Learn to swim.
67. Travel alone by train.
68. Travel alone by ship.

RELIABILITY AND VALIDITY: In the Heinz (1969) study, age norms of high school students were compared with their parents. Parents held higher ages for independent behavior than did their children. In a cross-cultural study (Keith and Barranda, 1969), 17- to 18-year-old American high school students' age norms were compared to those of comparable-age Filipino college students from an urban and a rural college. The norms for rural and urban Filipinos were very similar. The ages at which American high school students expected to engage in various independent behaviors were markedly lower than those for Filipino students.

BIBLIOGRAPHY:

Heinz, K. "A Comparison of Student and Parent Attitudes Toward Age Norms for Independent Behavior." Unpublished master's thesis. Claremont Graduate School, Claremont, California, 1969.
Keith, A., and Barranda, G. "Age Independence Norms in American and Filipino Adolescents." *Journal of Social Psychology*, 1969, *78*, 285-286.

---

## ALLEN SCALE OF BELIEFS

AUTHOR: B. J. Allen, Jr.

AGE: 13 years to adult

VARIABLE: Attitudes toward American sociopolitical values

TYPE OF MEASURE: Attitude scale

SOURCE FROM WHICH MEASURE MAY BE OBTAINED: See Allen (1972). Please cite credit and source.

DESCRIPTION OF MEASURE: The Scale of Beliefs is a Likert-type instrument designed to measure the extent of commitment to American sociopolitical values. Scoring is accomplished by weighting each item in the direction of the American value position, some of which are stated negatively and others positively. Responses can be analyzed for each item by computing item means or for the whole scale by computing cumulative score means. The utility of the instrument is greatest as a diagnostic tool for assessing students' belief systems about the spectrum of American values. It can also be used to determine the effect of selected moderator variables on the belief system, for example, comparing group means according to some socioeconomic background criteria.

As examples, the first twenty of the forty-six items, scored on a 5-point scale (strongly agree to strongly disagree), are given below.

1. Citizens should be allowed to criticize government officials and policies freely, even if it is embarrassing to government.

2. Profit making is exploitation and should be eliminated.
3. The men who control the industrial and agricultural wealth of a nation should have more influence on government policies than others.
4. During peacetime, members of extremist groups should be allowed to speak on radio and television.
5. We should make it our business to find out with whom the people in our neighborhood associate.
6. The administration of justice should be based on whatever is best for the nation.
7. In some cases a warrant should not be necessary in order for police to search a person or his home.
8. Since we are all Americans, having only one political party in operation would better represent the totality of American interests.
9. Private groups, such as civic and veterans' organizations, should not be allowed to participate in political campaigns.
10. Citizens should have the same general belief about the role of government in the economy.
11. Political parties should carefully screen all persons who want to join the party.
12. Teachers should be carefully restricted in what they teach in schools.
13. To insure future participation in politics, all young people should be required to join a political youth group.
14. Laws should be designed to serve the interest of the state.
15. The right to vote should be granted to all qualified persons, even those having radically different ideas.
16. In some criminal cases a trial by jury should not be allowed.
17. Appointed officials, such as police, should be given the authority to censor certain books and movies.
18. Any person or group should be allowed to circulate a petition without governmental approval.
19. Only persons with high ability should be provided a free education at the high school level.
20. Public opinion should not be a major concern of political leaders in writing party platforms, but only what is best for the people.

RELIABILITY AND VALIDITY: Using the split-half method with 312 students, the reliability coefficient was .83. Content validity is based on reactions from a small group of social scientists and on a review of the relevant literature. Concurrent validity was determined by administering four criterion scales to the original sample during the administration of the Scale of Beliefs. Each criterion measure has been used to measure closely related attitudes, and the obtained correlation between the scale and each criterion measure is significant at the .01 level. A jury of experts consisting of sixty-six justices from thirty-two state supreme courts were administered the scale as a means for validating the weighting directions determined for each scale item.

BIBLIOGRAPHY:

Allen, B. J., Jr. "The Construction of an Instrument to Measure American Sociopolitical Values." *Journal of Social Psychology*, 1972, *87*, 45-49.

# ATTITUDE BEHAVIOR SCALE:
# MENTALLY RETARDED (ABS-MR)

AUTHOR: John E. Jordan

AGE: Adults

VARIABLES: Attitude behavior in relation to the mentally retarded

TYPE OF MEASURE: Guttman-Jordan scale

SOURCE FROM WHICH MEASURE MAY BE OBTAINED: John E. Jordan, Director, International Rehabilitation-Special Education Center, 444 Erickson Hall, College of Education, Michigan State University, East Lansing, Michigan 48824.

DESCRIPTION OF MEASURE: The ABS-MR is an instrument designed to assess attitudes and behaviors in relation to the mentally retarded. The instrument is based on Guttman (1959) facet theory. A number of ABS-type instruments have been developed toward various attitude objects; common to all of these is the six-level subscale structure that measures degree of subject-object interaction. The scale contains 140 items divided into sections covering the following: what other people believe the mentally retarded ought to do and not to do, what the respondent believes is right or wrong for the mentally retarded to do, what the respondent would do for the mentally retarded, how the respondent actually feels about the mentally retarded or the handicapped, experiences the respondent may have had with the mentally retarded or the handicapped, and personal data about the respondent.

The instrument is self-administered. Scoring is done by summarizing the response categories. Six separate scores are obtained that are not additive into a total score and that can be used independently or in any combination thereof. Normative data have been gathered from eight nations and on five groups: parents of retarded, parents of nonretarded, teachers of retarded, teachers of nonretarded, and employers of retarded (Harrelson, Jordan, and Horn, 1972; Jordan, 1971). The scale was constructed and the content of the items were determined by the a priori facet theory method proposed by Guttman (1959, 1968) and Jordan (1968). From a theory of content and structure six levels or subscales of strength of interpersonal interaction were constructed with twenty items at each level, yielding 120 attitude items from the total of 140 items in the instrument. A measure of intensity was also obtained for each item. All items are scored such that a higher score means favorableness (or overfavorableness) toward the mentally retarded.

As examples, the first twelve items of the scale are given below, with directions for answering the forty items of Section I.

In the statements that follow you are to circle the number that indicates *how other people* compare *mentally retarded persons* to those who are not mentally retarded, and then to state how sure you felt about your answer. Usually people are sure of their answers to some questions, and not sure of their answers to other questions. *It is important to answer all questions, even though you may have to guess at the answers to some of them.* (Items read from left to right.)

Other people generally believe the following things about the mentally retarded as compared to those who are not retarded:

1. Energy and vitality:
   a. Less energetic.
   b. About the same.
   c. More energetic.

2. How sure are you of this answer?
   a. Not sure.
   b. Fairly sure.
   c. Sure

3. Ability to do school work:
   a. Less ability.
   b. About the same.
   c. More ability.

4. How sure are you of this answer?
   a. Not sure.
   b. Fairly sure.
   c. Sure.

5. Memory:
   a. Not as good.
   b. Same.
   c. Better.

6. How sure are you of this answer?
   a. Not sure.
   b. Fairly sure.
   c. Sure.

7. Interested in unusual sex practices:
   a. More interested.
   b. About the same.
   c. Less interested.

8. How sure are you of this answer?
   a. Not sure.
   b. Fairly sure.
   c. Sure.

9. Can maintain a good marriage:
   a. Less able.
   b. About the same.
   c. More able.

10. How sure are you of this answer?
    a. Not sure.
    b. Fairly sure.
    c. Sure.

11. Will have too many children:
    a. More than most.
    b. About the same.
    c. Less than most.

12. How sure are you of this answer?
    a. Not sure.
    b. Fairly sure.
    c. Sure.

RELIABILITY AND VALIDITY: Construct, content, and face validity have been determined (Jordan, 1971). Predictive validity was determined via the known-group method (Jordan, 1971). Reliability coefficients ranged from .60 to .90 for the six subscales, considered separately (Harrelson, Jordan, and Horn, 1972). Estimates have been obtained for groups varying in age, education, and amount of contact with the mentally retarded and across national and cultural groups (Jordan, 1970a).

BIBLIOGRAPHY:

Guttman, L. A. "A Structural Theory for Intergroup Beliefs and Action." *American Sociological Review,* 1959, *24,* 318-328.

Guttman, L. A. "A General Nonmetric Technique for Finding the Smallest Coordinate Space for a Configuration of Points." *Psychometrika,* 1968, *33,* 469-506.

Harrelson, L. E., Jordan, J. E., and Horn, H. "An Application of Guttman Facet Theory to the Study of Attitudes Toward the Mentally Retarded in Germany." *Journal of Psychology,* 1972, *80,* 323-335.

Jordan, J. E. *Attitudes Toward Education and Physically Disabled Persons in Eleven Nations.* East Lansing, Michigan: Latin American Studies Center, Michigan State University, 1968.

Jordan, J. E. *Attitude-Behaviors Toward Mentally Retarded Persons: A Cross-Cultural Analysis.* Final Report, U.S. Office of Education, Grant no. OEG-0-8-00126-0197, Project no. 7-E-126. Washington, D.C., 1970a.

Jordan, J. E. "Attitude-Behavior Research on Physical-Mental-Social Disability and Racial-Ethnic Differences." *Psychological Aspects of Disability*, 1970b, *18*, 5-26.

Jordan, J. E. "Construction of a Guttman Facet Designed Cross-Cultural Attitude Behavior Scale Toward Mental Retardation." *American Journal of Mental Deficiency*, 1971, *76*, 201-219.

---

## ATTITUDE MEASURE OF SEXUAL BEHAVIORS

AUTHOR: Bruce R. Fretz

AGE: 15 years and up

VARIABLE: Attitudes toward sexual behaviors

TYPE OF MEASURE: Semantic differential rating scale

SOURCE FROM WHICH MEASURE MAY BE OBTAINED: See Fretz (1975). A copy of the measure and the reference may be obtained by sending $3.00 to: *The Counseling Psychologist*, Washington University, Box 1180, St. Louis, Missouri 63130.

DESCRIPTION OF MEASURE: The measure includes twelve concepts regarding sexually related behaviors, each rated on seven bipolar dimensions. This measure was derived factor analytically from an initial measure of thirty concepts, each rated on seventeen bipolar dimensions. Administration time averages 20 to 30 minutes. Ratings can serve as process or outcome measures, as well as a stimulus variable, for instructional and counseling programs concerning sexual development.

As examples, the first five of the twelve items are given below. The respondent makes a check along a 7-interval scale between each of the seven adjective pairs. The same seven adjective pairs are used for all the items.

1. A homosexual.
   good        bad
   valuable        worthless
   kind        cruel
   active        passive
   fast        slow
   understandable        mysterious
   familiar        strange
2. An unmarried woman who takes birth control pills.
3. A woman who masturbates.
4. A child who writes "obscene" words on a wall.
5. An engaged person who has premarital intercourse.

RELIABILITY AND VALIDITY: Test-retest reliability over a period of one week ranges from .52 to .72 for college age $S$s; the measure's validity is mostly evidenced by changes in ratings obtained from parents, students, nurses, and teachers after being exposed to sex education workshops and courses.

BIBLIOGRAPHY:

Fretz, B. R. "Assessing Attitudes Toward Sexual Behaviors." *The Counseling Psychologist,* 1975, *5,* 100-106.

---

# ATTITUDE TOWARD UNDERPRIVILEGED CHILDREN AND YOUTH

AUTHOR: T. Bentley Edwards

AGE: Adult

VARIABLE: Attitude toward the underprivileged

TYPE OF MEASURE: Likert-type scale

SOURCE FROM WHICH MEASURE MAY BE OBTAINED: See Edwards (1966).

DESCRIPTION OF MEASURE: This is a Likert-type scale consisting of seventy-two items to which subjects respond on a 6-point scale from "strongly agree" to "strongly disagree." The items were constructed by panels of teachers based upon the following six dimensions, postulated by the staff of the research project for which the measure was constructed: compassionate, punitive, austere-rigid, flexible, knowing school, and sentimental. Factor loadings suggested twenty-five different factor characteristics. These were grouped under the following headings: authority for decisions, acceptance of underprivilege, a liking for simple solutions, the teaching art, and a miscellaneous category.

Some examples (answered on the 6-point scale mentioned above) are given below.

1. The so-called "scientific" studies of juvenile delinquency are run by those who favor a "soft" approach.
3. Enforcement of the laws against homosexuality should be more stringent.
8. The goal of the high schools must be 100 percent graduation.
11. Homogeneous grouping is one of the best ways to take care of individual differences.
14. I can't stand the sight of a child with a runny nose.
20. Students ought to share in making curriculum plans.

23. Those who attempt to abolish capital punishment are guilty of soft thinking.
37. The chief cause of delinquency is a lack of parental discipline.
40. It's normal for children to test limits and break rules from time to time.
46. Literature for adolescents must be censored.

RELIABILITY AND VALIDITY: Coefficients of reproducibility varying between .91 and .95 were obtained for the six scales.

BIBLIOGRAPHY:

Edwards, T. B. "Teacher Attitudes and Cultural Differentiation." *Journal of Experimental Education,* 1966, *35* (2), 80-86.
Edwards, T. B., and Wilson, A. B. "The Development of Scales of Attitudinal Dimensions." *Journal of Experimental Education,* 1959, *28* (1), 3-36.

*Prepared by Orval G. Johnson*

---

# ATTITUDES TOWARD THE RETARDED

AUTHORS: Rosalyn E. Efron and Herman Y. Efron

AGE: 14 years and up

VARIABLE: Attitudes toward the retarded

TYPE OF MEASURE: Questionnaire

SOURCE FROM WHICH MEASURE MAY BE OBTAINED: Herman Y. Efron, Veterans Administration, 810 Vermont Avenue N.W., Washington, D.C. 20420.

DESCRIPTION OF MEASURE: Attitudes Toward the Retarded consists of seventy statements followed by a 6-point agree/disagree continuum. Six factors that provide the most psychologically meaningful dimensions underlying the questionnaire items are: segregation via institutionalization, cultural deprivation, noncondemnatory etiology, personal exclusion, authoritarianism, and hopelessness. Embedded among the items (and also cast in the Likert format) is a 9-item scale measuring factual knowledge concerning retardation.

As examples, seven of the seventy items on the questionnaire are given below.

1. With the current trend in industrial technology, there are going to be fewer jobs that retardates can fill.
2. Retardates are responsible for more crimes than their proportion in the population.
3. Any perfectly normal parents may have a retarded child.
4. It's unfair to the retardate to put him in a classroom with normal children.
5. Beautiful children are seldom retarded.

6. Every person should have complete faith in some supernatural power whose decisions he obeys without question.

7. The most important principle in teaching retardates is to protect them against experiencing failure.

RELIABILITY AND VALIDITY: The questionnaire was administered to 245 subjects. Single and married persons were equally represented, and females outnumbered males by about two to one. Reliability coefficients were as follows: Factor I, .79; Factor II, .63; Factor III, .57; Factor IV, .73; Factor V, .69; and Factor VI, .59. As a measure of construct validity the six factor scores of different occupational groups were compared. Occupation was classified into the following categories: teachers of mentally retarded, teachers or students not in any branch of special education, students (both graduate and undergraduate) in retardation, and persons employed in a field other than education. Groups differed significantly on all factors except noncondemnatory etiology (III). Students and teachers in mental retardation did not differ from each other on any factor, nor did the people in general education ever differ from those in noneducation occupations. Except for Factors III and IV, the teachers of retarded always differed from the people in general education (in the favorable direction). Similarly the students in retardation always differed from the general education group except for Factors III and IV. It is felt that the ability of the factors to differentiate between occupational groups attests to the meaningfulness of the dimensions revealed by the attitude questionnaire.

BIBLIOGRAPHY:

Efron, R. E., and Efron, H. Y. "Measurement of Attitudes Toward the Retarded and an Application with Educators." *American Journal of Mental Deficiency,* 1967, *72,* 100-108.

Kephart, A. "Home Economics Teachers' Attitudes Toward Mentally Retarded Students." Unpublished master's thesis. Indiana University of Pennsylvania, Indiana, Pennsylvania, 1975.

Overbeck, D. "Attitude Sampling of Institutional Charge Attendant Personnel: Cues for Intervention." *Mental Retardation,* 1971, *9* (4), 8-10.

*Prepared by Herman Y. Efron*

---

# BERG-WOLLEAT MODIFIED SEMANTIC DIFFERENTIAL

AUTHORS: Marlowe Berg and Patricia Wolleat

AGE: Elementary-school children

VARIABLE: Children's attitudes toward other national groups

TYPE OF MEASURE: Semantic differential scales

SOURCE FROM WHICH MEASURE MAY BE OBTAINED: Marlowe Berg, School of Education, San Diego State University, San Diego, California 92115.

DESCRIPTION OF MEASURE: The Berg-Wolleat Modified Semantic Differential is based on Osgood's measuring device but utilizes pictures as stimuli to probe children's affective orientations toward other national groups. The stimuli consist of pictures of Brazilians, Germans, Japanese, and South Africans, as well as Americans, obtained from the *National Geographic* (Abercrombie, 1970; Graves and Dale, 1967; Grosvenor, 1970; Jones and Allard, 1967; Ross, 1962; Shor and Luanois, 1960; White and Parks, 1962). Subjects' reactions to the picture sets, or national concepts, are recorded on eight scales, each of which includes four steps along a continuum between two diametric adjectives, for example, good to bad. Each scale is scored from 1 to 4, 4 being the most negative position on the continuum, with the possibility of scoring 32 points for each national concept.

RELIABILITY AND VALIDITY: A factor analysis was done to determine whether the eight scales clustered into factors that measured similar semantic connotations. The factor analysis indicated two factors. Seven scales drawn from Osgood's evaluative factor all loaded highly into one factor. The second factor was composed of the single-similarity or "like us" scale. Further reliability of the semantic differential was determined by Hoyt's analysis-of-variance method. The reliability coefficient for all four national concepts was estimated to be .89 on all eight scales, .83 on Factor I, and .48 on Factor II. Evidence for the validity of the semantic differential was based on its extensive use by other researchers as an attitude measure and on the concurrent validity that had been found to exist between the semantic differential and other attitude scales.

BIBLIOGRAPHY:

Abercrombie, T. J. "Kansai: Japan's Historic Heartland." *National Geographic,* 1970 (3), 295-339.

Berg, M. and Wolleat, P. "A Comparison of the Effects of Information and the Effects of Contact on Children's Attitudes toward Other National Groups." *California Journal of Educational Research,* 1973, *24,* 200-208.

Graves, P. and Dale, B. "The Rhine: Europe's River of Legend." *National Geographic,* 1967, *132* (4), 449-499.

Grosvenor, M. B. "Vacationland U.S.A." *National Geographic,* 1970 (5), 734-740.

Jones, S. E. and Allard, W. A. "Houston, Prairie Dynamo." *National Geographic,* 1967 (3), 338-377.

Ross, K. "South Africa Close-up." *National Geographic,* 1962 (5), 640-681.

Shor, F. and Luanois, J. "Japan, the Exquisite Enigma." *National Geographic,* 1960 (6), 733-778.

White, P. T. and Parks, W. "Brazil, Ôba!" *National Geographic,* 1962, *122,* 299-353.

# BRIEF CRIMINAL ATTITUDE SCALE (CATS)

AUTHOR: A. J. W. Taylor

AGE: 13 years to adult

VARIABLE: Differences in criminal attitudes

TYPE OF MEASURE: Checklist

SOURCE FROM WHICH MEASURE MAY BE OBTAINED: See Taylor (1968).

DESCRIPTION OF MEASURE: The CATS consists of fifteen attitudes that were frequently expressed by criminals to the author, and the attitudes were arranged in such a way as to avoid a response set by the subjects. The latter were asked to signify their agreement or disagreement with each of the fifteen attitudes. Different forms of the CATS were also prepared to enable different groups of offenders to respond from their different probation, borstal, prison, or noncriminal backgrounds without changing the essence of the scale.

As examples, the first five items of the fifteen-item scale are given below. The subject responds to one of the two portions of the item, depending on which portion is applicable.

1. I deserved my sentence/criminals deserve their sentence.                    (−)
2. I did not want the police to catch me/criminals do not want
   the police to catch them.                                    (+ for females only)
3. There are bigger criminals outside prison than inside it.
4. The Judge or Magistrate sentences you/criminals, not the Probation Officer.                                                      (−)
5. The police hound you if you have a criminal record.                      (+)

RELIABILITY AND VALIDITY: The test reliability with samples of noncriminal males and females was sufficiently high to be acceptable ($r$ for males = .86; $r$ for females = .65). The CATS separated all three groups of female offenders from female nonoffenders, but for the males the discrimination was between the persistent criminals, senior borstal trainees, and all four other groups together. Female prisoners, borstal trainees, and probationer groups differed significantly from the noncriminal group at the .01 level, but not from one another. The prisoners also differed significantly at the .05 level from the mean score of the probationers. Male persistent criminals and senior borstal trainees were discriminated at the .05 level from the four other groups and from one another. These results were also true at the .01 level except that the senior borstal trainees were not significantly different from the probationers and noncriminal controls. Initially the CATS was found to have some reliability and internal validity when compared with the response of three comparable groups of borstal girls and with other tests and scales that were used as a part of the same test battery. Tetrachoric correlations between factors on various psychological tests and rating scales showed that those with high scores on the CATS were inclined to be depressive, outgoing, radical, and toughminded with little concern for their personal standards of hygiene. The same subjects also had a tendency toward paranoia, excitability, and insensitivity with little interest in their own rehabilitation and much psychopathic deviation.

BIBLIOGRAPHY:

Taylor, A. J. W. "An Evaluation of Group Psychotherapy in a Girls' Borstal." *International Journal of Group Psychotherapy*, 1967, *17*, 168-177.

Taylor, A. J. W. "A Brief Criminal Attitude Scale." *Journal of Criminal Law, Criminology and Police Science*, 1968, *59*, 37-40.

## CHASEN DIAGNOSTIC SEX-ROLE BIAS SCALE

AUTHORS: Barbara Chasen and Sharon Weinberg

AGE: Adults (clinicians, teachers, and administrators)

VARIABLE: Mental-health diagnoses of active and passive girls

TYPE OF MEASURE: Case-history rating scale

SOURCE FROM WHICH MEASURE MAY BE OBTAINED: Barbara Chasen, 160 West End Avenue, New York, New York 10023. Cost: $3.00.

DESCRIPTION OF MEASURE: The Chasen Diagnostic Sex-Role Bias Scale is designed to measure whether clinicians and others have sex-role stereotypic standards of mental health for girls and boys. If expectations of others influence behavior, often as a self-fulfilling prophecy, do clinicians perpetuate or create sex bias by having differential expectations and diagnoses for activity and passivity in girls and boys? The scale consists of eight case histories equated along the "somewhat unhealthy" dimensions of activity and passivity, plus two "noise" cases along the active dimension. Activity is defined as aggression or independence; passivity as nonaggression or dependence. From the construction of case histories with the same severity of pathology, the only apparent differences between pairs of case histories is the sex of the child, as determined by her or his name. Resulting differences in diagnoses would be due to differential expectations due to sex. The construct of diagnostic sex-role bias is made up of a combination of interrelated biases. Male-role bias ascribes activity (independence and aggression) to the male; female-role bias ascribes passivity (dependence and nonaggression) to the female. Within-sex-male-role-bias judges active boys healthier than passive boys. Within-sex-female-role-bias judges passive girls healthier than active girls. Across-sex-role-bias judges active boys healthier than active girls, and passive girls healthier than passive boys. Obtained scores can be in a stereotypic, counterstereotypic, or equal direction. Stereotypic diagnostic sex-role bias is operating if a combination of scores for the active boy plus passive girl is lower (healthier) than the combination of scores for the active girl plus passive boy, resulting in a minus score. Counterstereotypic diagnostic sex-role bias is operating if the active boy plus passive girl score is higher (unhealthier) than the combination of scores for the active girl plus passive boy, resulting in a plus score.

As an example, the first item of the scale is given below.

1. Frieda, 8 years old, is so independent she never needs others. She never accepts the teacher's suggestions, even when she knows they are appropriate. She is stubborn and resistant. She goes out of her way to disregard the advice or help of others. She is dominant and needs to be in charge all the time. She calls out and interrupts, often just to assert herself. She has to be a leader, regardless of the resentment often engendered. Her over-confidence borders on selfishness. She has no hesitation in making decisions.

   a. Assessment of health/pathology:
      1. Extremely unhealthy.
      2. Very unhealthy.
      3. Moderately unhealthy.
      4. In some ways healthy, in some ways unhealthy.
      5. Moderately healthy.
      6. Very healthy.
      7. Extremely healthy.
   b. Assessment of the priority of the referral:
      1. Do not see any problem here.
      2. Slight problem; not serious enough for referral.
      3. Possible referral; conference with school staff.
      4. Refer to school psychologist; low priority.
      5. Refer to school psychologist; medium priority.
      6. Refer to school psychologist; high priority.
      7. Refer to school psychologist; urgent.
   c. Treatment recommended:
      1. None.
      2. Parent or teacher advisement.
      3. Environmental manipulation.
      4. Short-term counseling.
      5. Long-term counseling.
      6. Psychotherapy.
      7. Extensive psychotherapy.
   d. With no treatment, what is your prognosis for this child, as an adolescent?
      1. Extremely unhealthy.
      2. Very unhealthy.
      3. Moderately unhealthy.
      4. In some ways healthy, in some ways unhealthy.
      5. Moderately healthy.
      6. Very healthy.
      7. Extremely healthy.

RELIABILITY AND VALIDITY: Content validity was obtained by ten expert school psychologists who rated each case, sex-unspecified, in terms of mental health or illness, on a 9-point scale. A Hotelling one-sample $T^2$ test was performed on the eight cases to determine if they differed from one another by more than chance. The means on the eight cases ranged from 5.9 to 6.8, equivalent to a "somewhat unhealthy" rating. An *F* of 2.20 was obtained with 8 and 2 degrees of freedom, which is nonsignificant at even the .25 level. It can be inferred that the paired cases, the two pairs within each category, and the active/passive dimensions are similar in severity. Further, when asked to label the cases as independent, dependent, aggressive, or nonaggressive, the experts correctly assigned the cases to proper categories with 100-percent accuracy. Discriminative validity was obtained using three criterion groups: female school psychology students, male medical students, and male accounting students; all three means fell in the expected direction. A test-retest reliability coefficient of .71 was obtained.

BIBLIOGRAPHY:

Chasen, B. "Diagnostic Sex-Role Bias and Its Relation to Authoritarianism, Sex-Role Attitudes and Sex of the School Psychologist." Unpublished doctoral dissertation. New York University, New York, 1974.
Chasen, B. "Diagnostic Sex-Role Bias and Its Relation to Authoritarianism, Sex-Role Attitudes, and Sex of the School Psychologist." *Sex Roles: A Journal of Research* (in press).
Chasen, B., and Weinberg, S. "Diagnostic Sex-Role Bias—How Can We Measure It?" *Journal of Personality Assessment*, 1975, *39*, 620-629.

# CHASEN EARLY CHILDHOOD TEACHER
# SEX-ROLE ATTITUDE SCALE

AUTHOR: Barbara Chasen

AGE: 3 to 8 years

VARIABLE: Teacher beliefs, observations, and action regarding sex-role stereotyping in early childhood classes

TYPE OF MEASURE: Rating scale and questionnaire

SOURCE FROM WHICH MEASURE MAY BE OBTAINED: Barbara Chasen, 160 West End Avenue, New York, New York 10023. Cost: $.50.

DESCRIPTION OF MEASURE: This eighty-two-item scale focuses on both overt and subtle ways in which sex-role stereotyping can occur in early childhood classes. The scale is divided into three sections: teacher observations (nineteen items), teacher practices in the classroom (thirty-nine items), and open-ended questions of beliefs and practices (twenty-four items).

As examples, the first ten of the eighty-two items on the scale are given below. The respondent is asked to check one of three possible answers for each item: "boys," "girls," or "equal."

*In general, who*
1. is more physically afraid?
2. plays more often in doll house area?
3. is better behaved?
4. plays with blocks more often?
5. is smarter?
6. has better verbal ability?
7. cleans up more readily?
8. is more prone to volunteer for table setting, giving out straws, etc.?
9. is natively more aggressive?
10. is natively more passive?

RELIABILITY AND VALIDITY: None reported.

BIBLIOGRAPHY:

Chasen, B. "Sex-Role Stereotyping and Prekindergarten Teachers." *Elementary School Journal,* 1974, *74,* 220-235.

---

# CHILDREN'S ATTITUDES TOWARD PHYSICAL ACTIVITY (CATPA)

AUTHORS: Julie A. Simon and Frank L. Smoll

AGE: Grades 4 to 6

VARIABLE: Attitudes toward physical activity

TYPE OF MEASURE: Semantic differential

SOURCE FROM WHICH MEASURE MAY BE OBTAINED: A copy of the CATPA instrument and description of group-testing procedures for its administration have been deposited with the National Auxiliary Publications Service (NAPS document no. 02297). Order from ASIS/NAPS, c/o Microfiche Publications, 440 Park Avenue South, New York, New York 10017. Cost: $3.00 for microfiche, $6.50 for photocopies. Make checks payable to Microfiche Publication.

DESCRIPTION OF MEASURE: The Children's Attitudes Toward Physical Activity (CATPA) Scale evolved from the work of Kenyon (1968a, 1968b, 1968c), who formulated a conceptual model for physical activity. The physical-activity domain was classified into six subsets. The six dimensions identified were: physical activity as a social experience, as health and fitness, as the pursuit of vertigo, as an aesthetic experience, as catharsis, and as an ascetic experience. Both a Likert and a semantic differential scale were then developed to assess attitudes toward each of these dimensions among adolescents and adults. In order to examine the attitudinal dispositions of children, a children's version of the semantic differential scale was constructed incorporating similar subdomain descriptions and adjective terms as in the test used by Kenyon (1968b). Explanations of subdomains are presented in simple one- or two-sentence-phrase combinations. Eight pairs of polar terms appear below each subdomain explanation; subjects respond to each set of adjectives along a 7-point continuum. Each individual will have six scores—a total for each of the subdomains. A single combined score for each subject across all subdomains *is not* calculated, as it is the purpose of the instrument to examine attitudes toward each of the separate components or subdomains of physical activity.

A sample page from the instrument is given below. Questions 2, 3, 4, and 7 are scored from 1 to 7 with the low (negative) end of the scale being on the left side and the high (positive) end on the right. Questions 1, 5, 6, and 8 are scored in a reversed procedure from 7 to 1 with the high end of the scale situated at the left side and the low end on the right.

What does the idea in the box mean to you?

> Physical Activity as a Social Experience
> Physical activities which give you a chance to meet new people and be with your friends.

Always think about the idea in the box:

| | | | | | | | | |
|---|---|---|---|---|---|---|---|---|
| 1. good | 1 | 2 | 3 | 4 | 5 | 6 | 7 | bad |
| 2. of no use | 1 | 2 | 3 | 4 | 5 | 6 | 7 | useful |
| 3. not pleasant | 1 | 2 | 3 | 4 | 5 | 6 | 7 | pleasant |
| 4. bitter | 1 | 2 | 3 | 4 | 5 | 6 | 7 | sweet |
| 5. nice | 1 | 2 | 3 | 4 | 5 | 6 | 7 | awful |
| 6. happy | 1 | 2 | 3 | 4 | 5 | 6 | 7 | sad |
| 7. dirty | 1 | 2 | 3 | 4 | 5 | 6 | 7 | clean |
| 8. steady | 1 | 2 | 3 | 4 | 5 | 6 | 7 | nervous |

RELIABILITY AND VALIDITY: The internal consistency of the instrument has been examined through calculation of Hoyt (1941) reliabilities for each subdomain. The coefficients ranged from .80 for the social and health and fitness dimensions to .89 for the aesthetic subdomain (Simon and Smoll, 1974). These data are based on group testing of 992 fourth- through sixth-grade children.

BIBLIOGRAPHY:

Hoyt, C. "Test Reliability Estimated by Analysis of Variance." *Psychometrika*, 1941, *6*, 153-160.
Kenyon, G. S. "A Conceptual Model for Characterizing Physical Activity." *Research Quarterly*, 1968a, *39*, 96-105.
Kenyon, G. S. "Six Scales for Assessing Attitudes Toward Physical Activity." *Research Quarterly*, 1968b, *39*, 566-574.
Kenyon, G. S. *Values Held for Physical Activity by Selected Urban Secondary School Students in Canada, Australia, England, and the United States.* Washington, D.C.: U.S. Office of Education, 1968c.

Simon, J. A. "Assessing Children's Attitudes Toward Physical Activity: Development of an Instrument." Unpublished master's thesis. University of Washington, Seattle, 1973.

Simon, J. A., and Smoll, F. L. "An Instrument for Assessing Children's Attitudes Toward Physical Activity." *Research Quarterly,* 1974, *45,* 407-415.

---

## CHILDREN'S QUESTIONNAIRE ABOUT SMOKING

AUTHORS: Frank W. Schneider and Loretta A. Vanmastrigt

AGE: 7 to 14 years

VARIABLE: Attitudes and beliefs about smoking

TYPE OF MEASURE: Questionnaire

SOURCE FROM WHICH MEASURE MAY BE OBTAINED: Frank W. Schneider, Department of Psychology, University of Windsor, Windsor, Ontario, Canada N9B 3P4.

DESCRIPTION OF MEASURE: This forty-three-item questionnaire is designed to elicit information about children's smoking experiences and their attitudes and beliefs about smoking. It is also intended to provide information about children's perceptions of the experiences, attitudes, and beliefs of significant others. When administering the questionnaire to young children (7 to 8 years old) it is advisable for the administrator to read each question aloud twice. The children should read silently with the investigator before checking their answers.

As examples, four of the forty-three items on the questionnaire are given below.

3. Do you think that you will smoke when you grow up?
   a. Definitely yes.
   b. Probably yes.
   c. Probably no.
   d. Definitely no.
   e. I don't know.
4. When you become a parent, how do you think you will feel about your children smoking?
   a. I will definitely want my children to smoke.
   b. I will probably want my children to smoke.
   c. I will probably *not* want my children to smoke.
   d. I will definitely *not* want my children to smoke.
   e. I don't know how I will feel.
3. If you smoked cigarettes, how do you think your mother would feel about it?
   a. My mother would be very happy.

b. My mother would like it.

c. My mother would not like it.

d. My mother would be very mad.

e. I don't know how my mother would feel.

4. If someone were to tell you not to smoke, who would you most likely obey?

a. Father.

b. Mother.

c. Teacher.

d. Brother.

e. Sister.

f. Best friend.

RELIABILITY AND VALIDITY: None reported.

BIBLIOGRAPHY:

Schneider, F. W., and Vanmastrigt, L. A. "Adolescent-Preadolescent Differences in Beliefs and Attitudes About Cigarette Smoking." *Journal of Psychology,* 1974, *87,* 71-81.

---

# CHILDREN'S SCALE OF SOCIAL ATTITUDES

AUTHORS: Paul M. Insel and Glenn D. Wilson

VARIABLE: Social attitudes

AGE: 8 to 14 years

TYPE OF MEASURE: Questionnaire

SOURCE FROM WHICH MEASURE MAY BE OBTAINED: Paul M. Insel, Stanford Research Institute, 333 Ravenswood Avenue, Menlo Park, California 94025.

DESCRIPTION OF MEASURE: The fifty-item Children's Scale of Social Attitudes was based directly on the adult Conservatism Scale (Wilson and Patterson, 1968, 1970); the aim was to provide an equivalent scale suitable for children. It was constructed by modifying the adult items where possible so as to make them more appropriate for children. This was usually achieved by making the items more concrete without changing their sense; for example, "Sabbath observance" was changed to "Sunday school." A few items did not need to be changed, and a few that seemed applicable only to adults had to be replaced altogether. Compared with the adult scale, it was difficult to find items concerned with attitudes on politics and science. The exact wording of the items finally selected was arrived at following interviews with children between 8 and 12 years; this procedure helped to insure that the items would be understood by children of this age group. The final fifty items are seen as covering the majority of issues on which children might be expected to express attitudes. These items may be summarized as relating to the following "adult" areas: religious beliefs; ethnocentrism or intolerance of minority groups; preference for conventional art, clothing, and institutions; respect for authority and insistence on strict rules and punishments; and anti-hedonistic outlook and a strict sexual morality. Each of these areas is represented by at least five items. The same layout for the scale was used as for the adult version, including alternating pattern of hypothesized conservative and liberal items.

Most children are able to complete the scale comfortably within about 10 minutes. Gaining and maintaining rapport with the subjects is no problem; children seem to enjoy taking the test. Nias (1972) administered the children's scale to 217 boys and 224 girls, aged 11 and 12 years, at an English comprehensive school for children from a wide cross-section of social backgrounds. A principal-components analysis was performed on the intercorrelations obtained among the fifty items. The results were very similar for boys and girls, but unlike the case with adults, a general factor did not emerge clearly. The first component, while accounting for a relatively large amount of variance compared with the second component, appeared to represent a broad dimension of religiosity rather than a general factor of conservatism. Rotation toward oblique simple structure using the promax method yielded four clearly defined factors, which have been given the abbreviated labels religion, ethnocentrism, punitiveness, and sex. These factors are, of course, rather broader than these brief labels might seem to imply. The measure may be either hand- or machine-scored.

The fifty items of the measure are given below. *S* responds either "yes," "?," or "no."

| | | |
|---|---|---|
| 1. Hanging thieves | 18. Kissing | 35. Church |
| 2. Space travel | 19. Strapping bad boys | 36. Chinese food |
| 3. School uniforms | 20. Swearing | 37. Politeness |
| 4. Bikinis | 21. Servants | 38. Telling fibs |
| 5. Sunday school | 22. Miniskirts | 39. Whipping criminals |
| 6. Bearded men | 23. Saving money | 40. The Germans |
| 7. Saluting the flag | 24. Playing pranks | 41. Strict rules |
| 8. Modern art | 25. Policemen | 42. The Beatles |
| 9. Obedience | 26. Computers | 43. Killing enemies |
| 10. Comics | 27. Saying prayers | 44. Laughing in class |
| 11. Miracles | 28. Going barefoot | 45. Fox hunting |
| 12. Dancing | 29. The Queen | 46. Divorce |
| 13. Army drill | 30. Women doctors | 47. Confessing sins |
| 14. Mixed schools | 31. Hard work | 48. Colored people |
| 15. The Ten Commandments | 32. Drinking beer | 49. Bible reading |
| 16. The Russians | 33. Atomic bombs | 50. Playing doctors |
| 17. Whites only | 34. Nude swimming | |

RELIABILITY AND VALIDITY: The internal consistency of the scales was checked by correlating the C-score obtained on the first twenty-five items with that obtained on the second twenty-five and applying the Spearman-Brown correction for test length. The split-half reliability coefficients thus obtained were .89 for the children's scale and .84 for the adult scale. In order to investigate the concurrent validity of the children's scale, Insel and Wilson (1971) administered it along with the adult version to 185 girls, aged 12 to 16 years, from two different schools. The correlation between the C-scores obtained from the two scales was .86; this figure may be regarded as evidence of satisfactory concurrent validity. In other words, the two scales, when scored for conservatism, may be regarded as approximately equivalent for pupils around the borderline age group. Insel and Wilson (1971) also demonstrated the discriminative validity of the scale by comparing the mean C-scores obtained from the two different schools. One was a Catholic convent school and the other was a state secondary school situated in the same area. It was hypothesized that the Catholic children would obtain higher C-scores. Results consistent with this hypothesis were obtained with both the children's scale and the adult scale.

BIBLIOGRAPHY:

Insel, P. M. "Family Similarities in Personality, Intelligence and Social Attitudes." Unpublished doctoral dissertation. University of London, 1971.

Insel, P. M., and Wilson, G. D. "Measuring Social Attitudes in Children." *British Journal of Social and Clinical Psychology,* 1971, *10,* 84-86.

Nias, D. K. "The Structuring of Social Attitudes in Children." *Child Development,* 1972, *43,* 211-219.

Wilson, G. D., and others. *The Coloured Progressive Matrices.* London: Academic Press, 1973.

Wilson, G. D., Nias, D. K., and Insel, P. M. *Manual for the Children's Scale of Social Attitudes.* London: Children's Studies Limited, 1972.

Wilson, G. D., and Nias, D. K. "Measurement of Social Attitudes: A New Approach." *Perceptual and Motor Skills,* 1972, *35,* 827-834.

Wilson, G. D., and Patterson, J. R. "A New Measure of Conservatism." *British Journal of Social and Clinical Psychology,* 1968, *7,* 264-269.

Wilson, G. D., and Patterson, J. R. *Manual for the Conservatism Scale.* Windsor, England: National Foundation for Educational Research, 1970.

*Prepared by Orval G. Johnson*

---

# CHILDREN'S SMOKING QUESTIONNAIRE

AUTHORS: J. M. Bynner and A. C. McKennell

AGE: 11 to 15 years

VARIABLE: Variable attitudes to smoking; smoking behavior and related attitudinal, personality and behavioral characteristics

TYPE OF MEASURE: Battery of self-administered questionnaires

SOURCE FROM WHICH MEASURE MAY BE OBTAINED: See Bynner (1969).

DESCRIPTION OF MEASURE: The questionnaire contains biographical questions concerning personal and family background characteristics, smoking experience and a number of attitude, personality, and behavior inventories including a semantic differential measuring perceptions of four images—the smoker, the nonsmoker, the ideal self, and the self. Variables constructed from the questionnaire are of three types: single question, composite scales derived from factor analysis and constructed to have *alpha* reliability values above a minimum level (McKennell, 1970), and factor scales obtained directly from the factor analysis of the semantic differential data.

As examples, fifteen items from one section of the questionnaire are given below. Statements are responded to on a 5-point scale from "strongly agree" to "strongly disagree." Other sections cover general background; attitudes not on smoking; attitudes toward smoking for nonsmokers, "triers," and smokers; and a vocabulary test.

1. Smoking is only dangerous to older people.
2. Smoking is a dirty habit.
3. Smoking makes you feel on top of the world.
4. Smoking is bad for you.
5. Smoking is only dangerous if you have been smoking for many years.
6. Smoking gives your breath a bad smell.
7. Smoking helps you to feel more at ease in a group.
8. Smoking is very enjoyable.
9. Smoking helps you to feel more at ease.
10. Smoking stains your teeth.
11. There is nothing wrong with smoking.
12. Smoking can help people when they feel nervous or embarrassed.
13. All cigarette slot machines should be taken away.
14. Boys who are caught smoking should be punished much more than they are.
15. Smoking is only dangerous if you smoke a *lot*.

RELIABILITY AND VALIDITY: *Alpha* reliability values for the composite scales are shown in Bynner (1969). The scales were constructed to meet a minimum *alpha* reliability criterion of .50 in a pilot survey that preceded the main investigation. Scales for which a reliability of .50 was replicated in the pilot investigation were retained for analysis in the main investigation. Both pilot and main investigation reliability values are shown in Bynner (1969), and they range from .53 (frustration scale) to .79 (disapproval of smoking scale). The pilot survey sample size was 1,180 boys and girls aged 11 to 15. The main survey sample was 5,601 boys aged 11 to 15, a representative sample of boys in this age group in England and Wales.

BIBLIOGRAPHY:

Bynner, J. M. *The Young Smoker.* London: HMSO, 1969.

Bynner, J. M. "Behavioral Research into Children's Smoking: Some Implications for Antismoking Strategy." *Royal Society of Health Journal,* 1970, *3,* 159-163.

McKennell, A. C., and Bynner, J. M. "Self-Images and Smoking Behavior Among Schoolboys." *British Journal of Educational Psychology,* 1969, *39,* 27-39.

McKennell, A. C. "Attitude Measurement: Use of Coefficient *Alpha* With Cluster or Factor Analysis." *Sociology,* 1970, *4,* 227-245.

*Prepared by J. M. Bynner and A. C. McKennell*

## CHILDREN'S SOCIAL ATTITUDE AND VALUE SCALES

AUTHORS: Daniel Solomon, Arthur J. Kendall, and Mark I. Oberlander

AGE: 8 to 15 years

VARIABLE: Various social values and attitudes

TYPE OF MEASURE: Questionnaire

SOURCE FROM WHICH MEASURE MAY BE OBTAINED: Daniel Solomon, Psychological Services Section, Montgomery County Public Schools, 850 Hungerford Drive, Rockville, Maryland 20850. No charge, but only one copy per request.

DESCRIPTION OF MEASURE: Seven scales are included in this set, one (democratic values) with four subscales. Subjects respond on a 6-point scale from "strongly disagree" to "strongly agree." Following are their names, descriptive information (where it seems necessary), and an example of one item from each scale. *Task self-direction vs. authority-reliance* (6 items): "When you want to make something, it is best to start with some help or advice from a teacher." *Democratic values* (16 items). This measure is composed of four subscales, each with four items: Assertion (the responsibility to state one's position, even if unpopular):—"Your family is planning an outing. You already know that everyone else except you wants to go to a museum. You should not say what you want to do." Compromise: "Two friends are playing Wizard of Oz and both want to be the scarecrow. The one who thought up the game should get to be the scarecrow. If you disagreed, write in what you think they should do." Equality of representation: "When the kids in a class at school are voting on something, the kids who are always making noise should not be allowed to vote." Equality of participation: "When kids are playing games, the ones who don't know how to play should get to play as much as anyone." *Attitude toward group activities* (12 items): "It is more fun to do scientific experiments with groups of kids than by yourself." *Cooperation vs. competition* (9 items): "You learn more when you try to do better than other kids in school than when you try to help other kids in school." *Value on decision-making autonomy* (10 items): "Kids should be the ones to decide if they need to do homework." *Value on heterogeneity (tolerance for differences)* (4 items): "Only kids who have the same ideas and interests can be good friends." *Concern for others* (9 items): "It would be a big waste of time if you jumped to help people whenever they had problems."

RELIABILITY AND VALIDITY: Early versions of these measures were revised on the basis of pilot-study results. Internal reliability (*alpha*) coefficients in that pilot study were: task self-direction, .18; democratic values (total), .49; attitude toward group activities, .54; cooperation vs. competition, .07; decision-making autonomy, .73; value on heterogeneity (−.24). Reliability coefficients obtained in a later study, with 1,250 children (fourth grade) each filling out the same instruments in September-October and May of the 1973-1974 school year, were as follows:

|                        | Fall Coefficients | Spring Coefficients |
|------------------------|-------------------|---------------------|
| Task self-direction*   | .38               | .42                 |
| Democratic values (tot)* | .69             | .74                 |

|                                  | *Fall Coefficients* | *Spring Coefficients* |
|----------------------------------|---------------------|-----------------------|
| Attitude toward group activities | .68                 | .74                   |
| Cooperation vs. competition*     | .38                 | .46                   |
| Decision-making autonomy         | .77                 | .79                   |
| Value on heterogeneity           | .61                 | .62                   |
| Concern for others               | .47                 | .58                   |

*One item was eliminated from each of these scales to improve reliability.

BIBLIOGRAPHY:

Crandall, V. C., Crandall, V. J., and Katovsky, W. "A Children's Social Desirability Questionnaire." *Journal of Consulting Psychology,* 1965, *29,* 27-36.

Solomon, D., Ali, F. A., Kfir, D., Houlihan, K. A., and Yaeger, J. "The Development of Democratic Values and Behavior Among Mexican-American Children." *Child Development,* 1972, *43,* 625-638.

Solomon, D., and Kendall, A. J. "Individual Characteristics and Children's Performance in Varied Educational Settings." Progress report, Spencer Foundation Project. Montgomery County Public Schools, Rockville, Maryland, August 1974.

Solomon, D., and Kendall, A. J. *Individual Characteristics and Children's Performance in Varied Educational Settings.* Final report, Spencer Foundation Project. Montgomery County Public Schools, Rockville, Maryland, Fall 1975.

---

# COLOR MEANING TEST (CMT)

AUTHOR: John E. Williams

AGE: 3 to 9 years

VARIABLE: Evaluative responses to the colors white and black

TYPE OF MEASURE: Picture-story interview

SOURCE FROM WHICH MEASURE MAY BE OBTAINED: John E. Williams, Department of Psychology, Box 7775, Wake Forest University, Winston-Salem, North Carolina 27109.

DESCRIPTION OF MEASURE: The Color Meaning Test (CMT) assesses the attitudes of preliterate children toward the colors white and black by means of the child's response to simple evaluative adjectives contained in the stories he is told. The original version of the procedure—CMT I—is described by Williams and Roberson (1967). The lengthened and revised version—CMT II—is described by Williams, Boswell, and Best (1975). The CMT II test materials consist of twelve 8 × 10-inch colored photographs and twenty-four associated stories. Each photograph depicts a drawing of two animals that are identical except that one is colored white and the other is colored black. The animals depicted are: horses, dogs, kittens, rabbits, cows, bears, ducks, pigs, chicks, mice, sheep, and squirrels. The twelve stimulus pictures are used in the order indicated for stories one to twelve and then are used again in the same order for stories thirteen to twenty-four.

CMT II is scored by counting 1 point for the selection of the white animal in response to a positive adjective and 1 point for the selection of the black animal in response to a negative adjective. The score range is 0-24 with high scores indicative of a prowhite/antiblack attitude (W+/B−), low scores indicative of a problack/antiwhite attitude (B+/W−), and mid-range scores (around 12) indicative of no consistent color attitude. The basic standardization group for CMT II consists of 320 preschool children from Winston-Salem, North Carolina, who were tested in 1972 and 1973. The children ranged in age from 40 months to 91 months, with a mean age of 61 months. Half of the children were Euro-American and half were Afro-American, with each race group composed of equal number of males and females. Half of each race-sex group were examined by female Euro examiners and half by female Afro examiners.

As examples, the first six of the twelve items of Series A are given below. Series B consists of items thirteen to twenty-four.

1. Here are two horses. One of them is a kind horse. He lets Billy pet him and give him apples. Which is the kind horse?
2. Mr. Jones has two pigs. One of them is an ugly pig. He is so ugly that Mr. Jones doesn't want anybody to see it. Which is the ugly pig?
3. Sammy has two bears. One of them is a friendly bear. He likes to play with all Sammy's friends. Which is the friendly bear?
4. Here are two ducks. One of them is a wrong duck. He went swimming right after dinner, even though his mommy told him not to. Which is the wrong duck?
5. Joey has two mice. One of them is a nice mouse and likes to play with Joey. Which is the nice mouse?
6. Here are two cats. One of them is a bad cat and scratches on the furniture. Which is the bad cat?

RELIABILITY AND VALIDITY: The internal consistency of the test at the preschool level is .63. The high correlation between scores on the first twelve items and second twelve items, and the virtually identical means and standard deviations, indicate that the two halves can be considered as equivalent twelve-item short forms of CMT II. The construct validity of CMT II rests on the fact that the procedure is a downward extension of the evaluation factor of the semantic differential, which has been shown to be an effective way of assessing attitudes among older children and young adults. The use of the evaluation factor rationale at the preschool level is supported by a series of studies that have demonstrated the existence of the evaluation factor in the semantic space of the 5-year-old child (Edwards and Williams, 1970; Gordon and Williams, 1973; and McMurtry and Williams, 1972).

BIBLIOGRAPHY:

Boswell, D. A. "An Empirical Investigation of Some Theoretical Components of Racial Bias in Young Children." Unpublished master's thesis. Wake Forest University, Winston-Salem, North Carolina, 1974.

Edwards, C. D., and Williams, J. E. "Generalizations Between Evaluative Words Associated with Racial Figures in Preschool Children." *Journal of Experimental Research in Personality*, 1970, *4*, 144-155.

Figura, A. L. "The Effect of Peer Interaction on the Self-Concept of Negro Children." Unpublished master's thesis. DePaul University, Chicago, 1971.

Gordon, L. H., and Williams, J. E. "Secondary Factors in the Affective Meaning System of the Preschool Child." *Developmental Psychology,* 1973, *8,* 25-34.

McAdoo, J. L. "An Exploratory Study of Racial Attitude Change in Black Preschool Children Using Differential Treatments." Unpublished doctoral dissertation. University of Michigan, Ann Arbor, 1970.

McMurtry, C. A., and Williams, J. E. "The Evaluation Dimension of the Affective Meaning System of the Preschool Child." *Developmental Psychology,* 1972, *6,* 238-246.

Parish, T. S. "Changing Anti-Negro Attitudes in Caucasian Children Through Mediated Stimulus Generalization." Unpublished doctoral dissertation. University of Illinois, Urbana, 1972.

Renninger, C. A., and Williams, J. E. "Black-White Color Connotations and Race Awareness in Preschool Children." *Perceptual and Motor Skills,* 1966, *22,* 771-785.

Shanahan, J. K. "The Effects of Modifying Black-White Concept Attitudes of Black and White First Grade Subjects upon Two Measures of Racial Attitudes." Unpublished doctoral dissertation. University of Washington, Seattle, 1972.

Skinto, S. M. "Racial Awareness in Negro and Caucasian Elementary School Children." Unpublished master's thesis. West Virginia University, Morgantown, 1969.

Traynham, R. M. "The Effects of Modifying Color Meaning Concepts on Racial Concept Attitudes in Five- and Eight-Year Old Children." Unpublished master's thesis. University of Arkansas, Fayetteville, 1974.

Vocke, J. M. "Measuring Racial Attitudes in Preschool Negro Children." Unpublished master's thesis. University of South Carolina, Columbia, 1971.

Williams, J. E. *Color Meaning Test II (CMT II): General Information and Manual of Directions.* Department of Psychology, Wake Forest University, Winston-Salem, North Carolina, 1972.

Williams, J. E., Boswell, D. A., and Best, D. L. "Evaluative Responses of Preschool Children to the Colors White and Black." *Child Development,* 1975, *46,* 501-508.

Williams, J. E., and Edwards, C. D. "An Exploratory Study of the Modification of Color Concepts and Racial Attitudes in Preschool Children." *Child Development,* 1969, *40,* 737-750.

Williams, J. E., and Roberson, J. K. "A Method of Assessing Racial Attitudes in Preschool Children." *Educational and Psychological Measurement,* 1967, *27,* 671-689.

Williams, J. E., and Rousseau, C. A. "Evaluation and Identification Responses of Negro Preschoolers to the Colors Black and White." *Perceptual and Motor Skills,* 1971, *33,* 587-599.

# CONTRADICTION INVENTORY

AUTHOR: Sally M. Anthony

AGE: Secondary School

VARIABLE: Inconsistent value systems

TYPE OF MEASURE: Questionnaire

SOURCE FROM WHICH MEASURE MAY BE OBTAINED: See Anthony (1965).

DESCRIPTION OF MEASURE: The purpose of this 102-item questionnaire is to measure contradictory beliefs in the following controversial areas: sex, courtship and marriage; economics; prejudice; nationalism and patriotism; social class; and religion and morality. The questionnaire contains statements that represent common American beliefs. The 102 statements are actually fifty-one pairs of contradictory statements. Respondents are asked to agree, disagree, or express no opinion. Agreement with both statements in a pair constitutes a contradiction. The statements were culled from sociological literature. The definitions and rationale for the controversial areas used may be found in Hunt and Metcalf (1955).

As examples, the first twenty of the 102 items are given below.

1. Males and females should follow the same rules of moral conduct.
2. Morality is the responsibility of both sexes.
3. The subject of sex is perfectly normal and should be treated as normal.
4. Sexually attractive females usually have larger male followings than do less attractive women, despite personality differences.
5. Sexual virtue before marriage is important to the success of the marriage.
6. Books about sex should be made readily available to teenagers.
7. In general, people have a better understanding of sex than they did fifty years ago.
8. Modesty is a quality which men look for in women.
9. Pictures of naked women should not be allowed on television programs.
10. High school girls are old enough to be allowed to date anyone they choose.
11. A social climber does not make a good friend.
12. There will always be social classes in the U.S. as long as there are men with differences in intelligence and industry.
13. Success is largely a matter of intelligence and hard work.
14. Almost anyone can succeed in the U.S. if he really tries.
15. Parents should want to make the road to success smoother for their children than it was for themselves.
16. Children of lower social classes are more likely to smoke, drink, date, and be wild at an earlier age.
17. Students should be taught to love and honor our form of government, our heritage, and our flag.
18. It is treason to undermine the sovereignty of the U.S.
19. The U.S. should not become so entangled in treaties with other countries that it becomes impossible to act without asking our allies first.
20. We should do everything possible to prevent nuclear war.

RELIABILITY AND VALIDITY: Judges passed on the contradictory nature of the pairs of statements. All five judges agreed on the fifty-one pairs retained. A second set of judges were given the 102 statements and asked to pair them as contradictions. Eighty-six percent agreement was received on the fifty-one pairs retained. Another set of judges were asked to determine whether the pairs fitted into the six controversial subject areas. Ninety-percent agreement was received on the pairs retained. Two hundred and one ninth- and twelfth-grade students were tested and retested within a fourteen-day period. The coefficient of stability was $r = .75$, significant beyond the .001 level of confidence.

BIBLIOGRAPHY:

Anthony, S. M. "Contradictions in Beliefs Among Ninth and Twelfth Grade Students." Unpublished doctoral dissertation. Rutgers, State University, New Brunswick, New Jersey, 1965.

Anthony, S. M., and Barnard, H. B. "Consistency—An Aspect Neglected in Critical Thinking." *Education,* 1968, *88,* 326-330.

Hunt, M., and Metcalf, L. *Teaching High School Social Studies.* New York: Harper & Row, 1955.

# DEAN'S ALIENATION SCALE

AUTHOR: Dwight G. Dean

AGE: College youth and adults

VARIABLE: Three subcomponents of alienation: powerlessness, normlessness, and social isolation

TYPE OF MEASURE: Likert-type scale

SOURCE FROM WHICH MEASURE MAY BE OBTAINED: Dwight G. Dean, Department of Sociology, Iowa State University, Ames, Iowa 50010. Keyed copy at no cost. Request reprint or abstract.

DESCRIPTION OF MEASURE: A total of 139 items presumably measuring alienation (which had been gleaned from the literature, from more than seventy interviews, or specially constructed) were typed on 3 X 5-inch cards and judged by seven experts (instructors and assistants in the Department of Sociology at Ohio State University), who were requested to judge each statement as to its applicability or nonapplicability, first, to the component of powerlessness (using a one-page description as the criterion). When this part of the task was finished, each expert received a second set of cards to judge, again, as to whether each of the 139 items specifically and only referred to normlessness. Finally, a third set of cards was presented for judging of items as they might relate to social isolation. For retention of an item, agreement of at least five of the seven judges was required, with no judge placing the item in more than one category. This measure thus contains a nine-item powerlessness scale, a six-item normlessness scale, and a nine-item social isolation scale. Scores are usually reported separately.

As examples, ten of the twenty-four items on the scale are given below. The respondent answers on a 5-point scale ranging from "strongly agree" to "strongly disagree."

I   1. Sometimes I feel all alone in the world.
P   2. I worry about the future facing today's children.
I   3. I don't get invited out by friends as often as I'd really like.
N   4. The end often justifies the means.
I   5. Most people today seldom feel lonely.
P   6. Sometimes I have the feeling that other people are using me.
N   7. People's ideas change so much that I wonder if we'll ever have anything to depend on.
I   8. Real friends are as easy as ever to find.
P   9. It is frightening to be responsible for the development of a little child.
N  10. Everything is relative, and there just aren't any definite rules to live by.

RELIABILITY AND VALIDITY: Validity was determined by presenting 139 proposed items to seven instructors and assistants at Ohio State University with a request for them independently to judge each statement as to its applicability or nonapplicability to the component of powerlessness. Second and third sets were presented with similar instructions for normlessness and social isolation. Reliability when corrected by the Spearman-Brown prophecy formula was .78 for powerlessness, .73 for normlessness, and .84 for social isolation.

BIBLIOGRAPHY:

Blane, H. T., Hill, M. T., and Brown, E. "Alienation, Self-Esteem, and Attitudes Toward Drinking in High School Students." *Quarterly Journal of Studies on Alcohol,* 1968, *29,* 350-354.
Dean, D. G. "Alienation: Its Meaning and Measurement." *American Sociological Review,* 1961, *26,* 753-758.
Dodder, R. A. "Factor Analysis of Dean's Alienation Scale." *Social Forces,* 1969, *48,* 252-255.
Warner, R. W., Jr., and Hansen, J. C. "The Relationship Between Alienation and Other Demographic Variables Among High School Students." *High School Journal,* 1970, *54,* 202-210.

# DISABILITY SOCIAL DISTANCE SCALE (DSDS)

AUTHOR: John L. Tringo

AGE: 12 years through adult

VARIABLE: Attitudes toward disability groups (social distance)

TYPE OF MEASURE: Social distance scale

SOURCE FROM WHICH MEASURE MAY BE OBTAINED: See Tringo (1970).

DESCRIPTION OF MEASURE: The Disability Social Distance Scale (DSDS) is an instrument designed to measure the degree of social distance from various disability groups perceived by students, professionals, and other disabled and nondisabled subjects. The primary purpose of the instrument is to assess attitudes toward specific disability groups by establishing a hierarchy of preference with respect to these groups. The DSDS is a 9-point scale applied to twenty-one groups with these disabilities: alcoholism, amputee, arthritis, asthma, blindness, cancer, cerebral palsy, deafness, diabetes, dwarf, epilepsy, exconvict, heart disease, hunchback, mental illness, mental retardation, old age, paraplegic, stroke, tuberculosis, and ulcer. The subject is asked to rate each of the twenty-one disabilities on a 9-point scale of closeness from "would marry" to "would put to death." The extent and hierarchy of social distance felt toward disability groups and the relationship to age, sex, and education can be determined. The instrument can be administered to a group. The procedure takes 15 to 30 minutes. Normative data for college and high school students are available in Tringo (1970).

RELIABILITY AND VALIDITY: Results indicate high reliability, but specific reliability data are not reported.

BIBLIOGRAPHY:

Tringo, J. L. "The Hierarchy of Preference Toward Disability Groups." *Journal of Special Education,* 1970, *4,* 295-306.

---

# ENVIRONMENTAL PREFERENCE SCALES (EPS)

AUTHOR: John N. McCall

AGE: 12 years to adult

VARIABLE: Preferences for comfortable, exciting, natural, sociable, and urban surroundings

TYPE OF MEASURE: Self-report questionnaire

SOURCE FROM WHICH MEASURE MAY BE OBTAINED: John N. McCall, Psychology Department, Southern Illinois University, Edwardsville, Illinois 62025.

DESCRIPTION OF MEASURE: The EPS consists of seventy-five item-pairs in a forced-choice format. Responses are scored for five preferences that concern surroundings at home, work, or when one is relaxing. Items representing each preference type are paired equally often, or fifteen times, with every other type. Thus, raw scores range from 0 to 15. Norms for different age, sex, or population groups are advisable. T-score norms have been prepared for college males and females. The preferences associated with each subscale are described as *comfortable:* manmade physically comfortable surroundings; *exciting:* rapid change, strong stimulation, or novelty; *natural:* contact with natural landscapes and wildlife; *sociable:* close human contact, stimulation, or support; and *urban:* metropolitan attractions or services such as stores, restaurants, and museums.

RELIABILITY AND VALIDITY: Over five hundred persons, aged 15 to 65, rated 150 Likert scale items singly. These were factor analyzed for simple factor structure, with the resulting five factors. Items were selected to represent each factor independently, and those paired in the forced-choice format were equated for popularity. Test-retest coefficients of reliability, based on responses of college freshmen thirty days apart, ranged from a low of .61 for sociable to .83 for natural. Concurrent validity for college students is suggested by moderate correlations of the exciting scale with Zuckerman's Stimulus Seeking Scale and Eyseneck's Extraversion Scale; only the sociable scale correlated moderately with the Femininity Scale of the California Personality Inventory. Other CPI correlations suggest some tendency for psychologically healthier persons to prefer natural rather than comfortable surroundings, and vice versa. The highest intercorrelations between subscales concerns the natural scale, which is correlated negatively with comfortable and urban.

BIBLIOGRAPHY:

Weaver, D. A. "Selected Personality and Demographic Correlates of Environmental Preference." Unpublished master's thesis. Southern Illinois University, Edwardsville, 1974.

---

# FEELEY INTEREST INVENTORY

AUTHOR: Joan T. Feeley

AGE: 9 to 12 years

VARIABLE: Content interest patterns and media preferences

TYPE OF MEASURE: Inventory with Likert-type scale

SOURCE FROM WHICH MEASURE MAY BE OBTAINED: See Feeley (1972).

DESCRIPTION OF MEASURE: This inventory consists of fifty-four (four are "truth" items not to be analyzed) fictitious, annotated titles of content that may be found in print or on television. Children are first asked to indicate their interest in a title on a 4-point weighted scale (a). Next they indicate media preference by circling *Read, Watch,* (or both), or *Do Nothing* (b). Interest, read, and watch scores may be computed for clusters of items developed by the investigator via factor analyses, or researchers may develop their own clusters from data generated by the weighted-interest scores. Cluster scores may be rank-ordered to describe patterns or interests and preferences.

As examples, the first three of the fifty-four descriptions making up the inventory are given below. The child circles one choice only in line (a); he or she may circle more than one choice in line (b).

*Let's Experiment with Rockets and Jets*
Discover how rocket and jets work, how man travels in space.

| (a) Yes | Maybe Yes | Probably Not | No |
|---------|-----------|--------------|-----|
| (b)   Read |   Watch |   Do Nothing | |

*Dating Days*
Chuck gets jealous when he sees girl friend Sally out with his best friend Hank and decides to get even.

| (a) Yes | Maybe Yes | Probably Not | No |
|---------|-----------|--------------|-----|
| (b)   Read |   Watch |   Do Nothing | |

*Do Your Own Thing*
About coin collecting, stamp collecting, model assembly, and other hobbies.

| (a) Yes | Maybe Yes | Probably Not | No |
|---------|-----------|--------------|-----|
| (b)   Read |   Watch |   Do Nothing | |

RELIABILITY AND VALIDITY: To group the fifty variables (inventory items minus "truth" items) into statistically valid clusters based on simultaneous intercorrelations of the items, the interest responses of 250 boys and 282 girls in grades 4 and 5 were separately subjected to principal-components factor analyses with varimax rotations. The responses of the boys and girls were treated separately because most previous research has shown that sex accounts for the major differences in the interests of middle-grade children. Only variables with loadings of .30 or over on at least one factor were included in the clusters that are described—nine for the boys and ten for the girls. Reliability coefficients, based on Nunnally's (1967) domain sampling model, were computed on the clusters and ranged from .73 to .92. These coefficients, referred to as $r_{tt}$, are the correlations of scores of a collection of items with true scores. Content validity was established by submitting the items to a panel of experts in the fields of teaching reading, children's literature, and children's television. Any items they questioned or that loaded on more than one factor or on only a nonsignificant factor were excluded from the inventory. Before the inventory was used in the above study, it was pilot-tested on a sample of 196 fourth and fifth graders to test the suitability of the format and to establish preliminary data on the validity and reliability of the emerging clusters. The $r_{tt}$ coefficients of these clusters ran from .77 to .95.

BIBLIOGRAPHY:

Feeley, J. T. "Interest Patterns and Media Preferences of Boys and Girls in Grades Four and Five." Unpublished doctoral dissertation. New York University, New York, 1972. Ann Arbor, Michigan: University Microfilms, 1972, no. 72-20, 628.

Feeley, J. T. "Sex Influences Children's Interests." *New Jersey Educational Association Review,* 1973, *46,* 54.

Feeley, J. T. "Children's Content Interests: A Factor-Analytic Study." ERIC/RCS, abstracted in *Research in Education,* Dec. 1974.

Feeley, J. T. "Content That Captures Today's Kids." *Senior Scholastic* (Scholastic Teacher Edition), 1974, *83,* 16-18.

Feeley, J. T. "Interest Patterns and Media Preferences of Middle-Grade Children." *Reading World,* 1974, *13,* 224-237. Excerpted in J. Porter (Ed.), "Research Reports." *Elementary English,* 1974, *51,* 1006-1008.

Feeley, J. T. "Television and Reading in the Seventies." Paper presented at the annual meeting of the International Reading Association. New Orleans, Louisiana, May 1974. ERIC document no. ED 089 258.

Nunnally, J. C. *Psychometric Theory.* New York: McGraw-Hill, 1967.

---

# FLEXIBILITY OF MORAL JUDGMENT INDEX

AUTHOR: Morton P. Birnbaum

AGE: 11 to 15 years

VARIABLE: Rigidity or flexibility of moral judgment

TYPE OF MEASURE: Questionnaire

SOURCE FROM WHICH MEASURE MAY BE OBTAINED: See Birnbaum (1968).

DESCRIPTION OF MEASURE: A flexible moral judgment reflects the subject's view that rules must be used in the service of humanistic ends and that when the rule conflicts with such ends, it may be permissible to violate that rule. This index consists of eight items, seven of which present stories in which the main character, under clearly extenuating circumstances, violates or adheres to a moral rule conflicting with those circumstances. Two items are based on Kohlberg's (1958) work and one on Lenrow (1965). The items can be easily administered to groups of children with sixth-grade reading ability. Subjects are scored from 0 to 5 on each item, based on their judgments, statements of their own likely behavior in the situations, and their acknowledgments of being tempted to break the rule, according to the following scheme: 5 points = flexible judgment and action (temptation implied). 4 points = flexible judgment, rigid action, but would be tempted to be flexible. 3 points = flexible judgment, rigid action, and no temptation. 2 points = rigid judgment, but flexible action (temptation implied). 1 point = rigid judgment, rigid action, but would be tempted to be flexible. 0 points = rigid judgment, rigid action, and no temptation. Item means ranged from 1.61 to 2.83 and standard deviations from 1.8 to 2.3.

As an example, the third "story" and its question are given below.

A man was caught breaking into a gas station. He got scared, hit a policeman, and ran away to hide. Johnny saw the whole thing, and he heard the other policemen say they would shoot the robber as soon as they found him. Johnny knew where the robber was hiding, but when the police asked, Johnny said he did not know where the robber went.

1. Do you think Johnny was right or wrong to do that? (Right/Wrong) Why do you think that?
2. If you were in Johnny's place, would you tell the police where the robber was hiding? (Yes/No)
3. If you circled "Yes" above, would you be tempted not to tell? (Yes/No) Why or why not?

RELIABILITY AND VALIDITY: Evidence for validity comes in two main forms. First, flexibility scores for almost every item (one was not pretested for developmental changes) increase as one moves from sixth-grade to seventh- and eighth-grade children (based on a pretest sample of forty-six junior high school youngsters). This finding is concurrent with a previous consensus of theory and research on a child's development from an earlier, rigid moral judgment position to a later, more flexible one. Second, in a fuller sample of ninety-nine seventh-grade girls and eighty-eight seventh-grade boys, girls were found to be significantly more rigid and dependent upon adult rules than their male counterparts. Such greater masculine moral autonomy is consistent with a considerable body of previous data. Data on reliability are not available.

BIBLIOGRAPHY:

Birnbaum, M. P. "Anxiety and Moral Judgment in Early Adolescence." Unpublished doctoral dissertation. University of Michigan, Ann Arbor, 1968.

Birnbaum, M. P. "Anxiety and Moral Judgment in Early Adolescence." *Journal of Genetic Psychology,* 1972, *120,* 13-26.

Kohlberg, L. "The Development of Modes of Moral Thinking and Choice in the Years Ten to Sixteen." Unpublished doctoral dissertation. University of Chicago, Illinois, 1958.

Lenrow, P. "Studies of Sympathy." In S. Tomking, and C. Izard (Eds.), *Affect, Cognitive and Personality.* New York: Springer, 1965.

---

# FORBES INTERRACIAL PICTURE FRUSTRATION TEST

AUTHOR: Gordon B. Forbes

AGE: Grade 6 to adult

VARIABLE: Responses to interracial frustration

TYPE OF MEASURE: Semiprojective

SOURCE FROM WHICH MEASURE MAY BE OBTAINED: Gordon B. Forbes, Department of Psychology, Millikin University, Decatur, Illinois 62522.

DESCRIPTION OF MEASURE: The Forbes Interracial Picture Frustration Test is an objectively scored, semiprojective test of reactions to interracial frustration. Test materials depict ten faceless figures in situations that might be interpreted as frustrating. However, direct pictorial cues of frustration are minimized to facilitate projection. Five pictures are used and each picture is presented in two conditions. In one condition (WB) the race of the frustrator is white and the race of the "victim" of the frustration is black. The respective races of the two figures are reversed in the second condition (BW). Below each picture are 9-point scales used to measure the subject's attribution of blame, feelings of anger, and direction of anger. Scores in condition WB are compared with scores in condition BW to yield a measure of racial effects on the three dimensions measured by the instrument. An example of a picture is as follows: Ted (W) is wheeling his bicycle through a mudpuddle, and Bill (B) is likely to be splashed. The child is given three sentence stems for each picture: (1) What is happening in this picture is ("clearly Ted's fault" to "clearly Bill's fault"); (2) This picture makes me ("very mad" to "not at all mad"); and (3) If I were Bill, I would ("be mad at Ted" to "be mad at myself").

RELIABILITY AND VALIDITY: Formal reliability and validity data are not available. However, analyses of the direction-of-anger scale are rarely significant, and it appears that the structure of this scale is ambiguous and the scores unreliable.

BIBLIOGRAPHY:

Forbes, G. B., and Mitchell, S. "Attribution of Blame, Feelings of Anger, and Direction of Aggression in Response to Interracial Frustration Among Poverty-Level Female Negro Adults." *Journal of Social Psychology*, 1971, *83*, 73-78.

---

# HOME INTERVIEW SCHEDULE (HIS)

AUTHORS: Perry A. Zirkel and John F. Greene

AGE: Parents of Spanish-speaking students

VARIABLE: Parental perceptions and attitudes

TYPE OF MEASURE: Individual interview instrument

SOURCE FROM WHICH MEASURE MAY BE OBTAINED: See Greene and Zirkel (1973) and Zirkel (1972, 1973).

DESCRIPTION OF MEASURE: The Home Interview Schedule (HIS) is a survey instrument designed to be individually administered to Spanish-speaking parents by a bilingual interviewer. It is available in Spanish and English forms. It includes modified versions of

Hoffman's (1934) Bilingual Scale and Mosely's (1969) Attitude Toward Bilingualism Scale. The HIS covers the following categories of parental attitudes and perceptions relating to the education of Spanish-speaking students: educational and occupational levels, geographic origin and orientation, language proficiency and dominance, attitude toward bilingualism and bilingual/bicultural education, interest in education, and evaluation of child's progress.

As examples of the total sixty-two items, given below are five of the questions to be answered on a 5-point scale from "never" to "always," followed by ten items to be responded to on a 5-point scale from "no, of course not" to "yes, of course."

20. Do the following read any books in Spanish?
    a. Father.
    b. Mother.
    c. Child.
21. Do the following write any letters in Spanish?
    a. Father.
    b. Mother.
    c. Child.
22. Are letters written in Spanish received in your home?
23. Do the following watch television in Spanish?
    a. Father.
    b. Mother.
    c. Child.
26. Does (child) think in Spanish?
30. Being bilingual (being able to understand or speak two languages) has more advantages than disadvantages.
31. Both Puerto Ricans and Anglo-Americans should be bilingual.
32. Puerto Rican children should try to forget Spanish so they can improve their English.
33. Being able to converse in two languages is a satisfying experience.
34. If properly educated, Puerto Rican children have an unusual opportunity to become truly bilingual.
35. A good school will encourage the learning of Spanish and the learning of English on the part of all pupils attending.
36. Learning to speak two languages takes more time than it is worth.
37. Being bilingual is a source of pride.
38. Bilinguals are happier than those who speak only one language.
39. Bilingualism is so important in Connecticut that all Connecticut schools should try very hard to teach both English and Spanish to every child.

RELIABILITY AND VALIDITY: The instrument was administered to 208 Puerto Rican parents in two large Connecticut cities after being reviewed for face validity. In a separate study, Greene and Zirkel (1972) found a split-half reliability coefficient corrected for length of .76 and .57 for the attitude toward bilingualism subtest with Anglo and Puerto Rican subjects, respectively.

BIBLIOGRAPHY:

Greene, J. F., and Zirkel, P. A. "Revising the Attitude Toward Bilingualism Scale for Use in the Northeast." *Journal of Comparative Cultures*, 1972, *1*, 71-76.

Greene, J. F., and Zirkel, P. A. *The Family Background of Puerto Rican Students.* Bridgeport, Connecticut: Bridgeport Model Cities, 1973.

Hoffman, M. H. N. *The Measurement of Bilingual Background.* New York: Teachers College Press, Columbia University, 1934.

Mosley, R. T. "Development and Application of a Spanish-English Bilingualism Attitude Scale." Unpublished doctoral dissertation. Texas A and M University, College Station, 1969.

Zirkel, P. S. *An Evaluation of the Effectiveness of Selected Experimental Bilingual Progress in Connecticut.* West Hartford, Connecticut: Connecticut Migratory Children's Program, 1972. ERIC document no. ED 070 325.

Zirkel, P. A. *Puerto Rican Parents and Mainland Schools.* Hartford, Connecticut: Hartford Model Cities, 1973.

Zirkel, P. A. "A Sociolinguistic Survey of Puerto Rican Parents." Paper presented at the annual meeting of the American Orthopsychiatric Association. New York, May 1973. ERIC document no. ED 074 191.

---

# INDIVIDUAL MODERNITY

AUTHOR: Michael Armer

AGE: 15 years and older

VARIABLE: Attitudinal modernity

TYPE OF MEASURE: Structured interview

SOURCE FROM WHICH MEASURE MAY BE OBTAINED: Michael Armer, Department of Sociology, Indiana University, Bloomington, Indiana 47401.

DESCRIPTION OF MEASURE: This is a measure of a syndrome of values and beliefs. The concepts of empiricism or belief in science, secularism, and receptivity to change, all of which capture the notion of rationalism, are drawn from the writings of Weber, Parsons, Becker, and Inkeles in particular. The dimensions of trust, futurism, independence from family, and mastery stem largely from the work of Kluckhohn and Strodtbeck, and Kahl. Dimensions of openness to new ideas, women's equality, and ethnic tolerance are suggested by others. Questionnaire items tapping these ten value orientations were constructed or borrowed from Inkeles, Kahl, and others. The internal consistency of items within each of the postulated dimensions was analyzed separately by means of factor analysis, and items were eliminated if their loadings on the principal axis of the unrotated matrix were less than .30. Factor analysis of just the successful items was used as a basis for developing principal-axis factor-weighted composite scores of each dimension. The dimension scores themselves were then factor analyzed in order to ascertain the extent to which they formed a single syndrome of modern value orientations. Six of the original ten dimensions were found to have loadings above .30 on the principal axis, and factor-weighted composite measure was constructed from these six dimensions. The resulting individual modernity scale consists of twenty-two items weighted by the product of their dimension loadings and their item loadings within each dimension.

As examples, the first five of the twenty-two items of the scale are given below.

1. When looking for a place for one's own family to live, a man ought to find a place located in the same neighborhood as his parents, even if that means losing a better place elsewhere.
   1. Disagree very much.
   2. Disagree a little.
   3. Agree a little.
   4. Agree very much.
   0. dk/na/other.*
2. If a man has the chance to hire an assistant in his work, do you think it is better to hire a relative than a stranger even if the relative is less qualified than the stranger?
   1. Yes.
   2. No.
   0. dk/na/other.*
3. Do you greatly prefer, slightly prefer, or dislike work that is easy?
   1. Greatly prefer.
   2. Slightly prefer.
   3. dk/na/neither.
   4. Dislike.
4. A person should be taught to protect the welfare of his own people and let other groups look out for themselves.
   1. Disagree very much.
   2. Disagree a little.
   3. Agree a little.
   4. Agree very much.
   0. dk/na/other.*
5. Associating and making friends with persons of other (ethnic) groups is risky, if not impossible.
   1. Disagree very much.
   2. Disagree a little.
   3. Agree a little.
   4. Agree very much.
   0. dk/na/other.*

*dk/na/other: = don't know/not answered/other response (specify): _____. The answer is not read by the interviewer.

RELIABILITY AND VALIDITY: Kuder-Richardson formula 20 reliability of the scale for a probability area sample of 591 young men (aged 17 years old) from Kano, Nigeria, was .88 for the twenty-two items and .90 for the six dimensions included in the measure. The inferred average interitem correlation is .25. A separate factor analysis of the final set of twenty-two items produced a unitary factor structure controlling 34 percent of the variance. Cronbach's *alpha* reliability of an English version of the scale among a sample of 156 white married males from the uptown area of Chicago in

1970 was .56 for the twenty-two items. Test-retest reliability after a two-month interval for 109 of the uptown sample respondents was .66. Correlations with Smith and Inkeles' OM-6 Modernity Scale, Kohl's Modernity I, and Schnaiberg's Emancipation Scale were .57, .64, and .41, respectively. The average correlation with these three alternative measures of individual modernity was .54, which was slightly higher than the average intercorrelation of any of the other three scales in this set. In a test of discriminant validity, the average correlation of .54 was higher than correlations with Srole's Anomia Scale ($r = -.52$), Middleton's Alienation Scale ($r = -.39$), and a composite measure of socioeconomic status ($r = .39$). All three of the other modernity scales failed to discriminate validity on one or more of these tests. A full analysis of reliability and validity of the modernity scales is reported in Armer and Schnaiberg (1972).

BIBLIOGRAPHY:

Armer, M. "Formal Education and Psychological Malaise in an African Society." *Sociology of Education,* 1970, *43,* 143-158.
Armer, M., and Schnaiberg, A. "Measuring Individual Modernity: A Near Myth." *American Sociological Review,* 1972, *37,* 301-316.
Armer, M., and Schnaiberg, A. "Individual Modernization, Alienation and Socioeconomic Status: A Replication in Costa Rica." Paper presented to the Eighth World Congress of Sociology. Toronto, Canada, 1974.
Armer, M., and Youtz, R. "Formal Education and Individual Modernity in an African Society." *American Journal of Sociology,* 1971, *76,* 604-626.

---

## INTEREST OF STUDENTS IN PARTICIPATION IN ADULT CIVIC ACTIVITIES

AUTHOR: William G. Trenfield

AGE: Senior high school

VARIABLE: Anticipated civic participation

SOURCE FROM WHICH MEASURE MAY BE OBTAINED: William Trenfield, 1915 West Purdue Avenue, Muncie, Indiana 47304.

DESCRIPTION OF MEASURE: The measure consists of thirty activities centered around participation in community affairs. The student responds on a 5-point scale (0 to 4) from "never" to "regularly" as to how frequently he expects to participate in those activities as an adult. Mean-score norms are provided for each item, based on results from 300 high school students.

As examples, the first six of the thirty activities on the scale are given below.

1. Listen to political speeches on radio or television.
2. Vote in national elections for Senators and Representatives.
3. Discuss political or civic problems with a house guest.
4. Vote in elections for school board members.
5. Read a weekly news magazine thoroughly.
6. Visit a public school.

RELIABILITY AND VALIDITY: The odd-even reliability coefficient was .81, adjusted to .90 by the Spearman-Brown formula. Students' scores and their homeroom teachers' estimates of their probable participation correlated .40.

BIBLIOGRAPHY:

Trenfield, W. G. "Analysis of Relationship to Civic Interests of High School Students." *Journal of Educational Research*, 1965, *58*, 460-462.

---

# JUNIOR SCALE OF ANOMIE

AUTHOR: Thomas M. Elmore

AGE: Approximately grades 3 to 7

VARIABLE: General anomie, plus five aspects of anomie

TYPE OF MEASURE: Likert-type scale

SOURCE FROM WHICH MEASURE MAY BE OBTAINED: Thomas M. Elmore, Department of Education, Wake Forest University, Winston-Salem, North Carolina 27109.

DESCRIPTION OF MEASURE: The Junior Scale of Anomie (called "The How I Feel Sentences" in booklet form) consists of forty-one items based closely on the Elmore Scale of Anomie, the longer adult form (Elmore, 1962) but adapted in word usage and instructions for use with younger children. The subject responds to the items on a 5-point scale ranging from "agree a lot" to "disagree a lot." Scoring is done by summating the scores of the six scales; high scores indicate highly anomic individuals. The test measures five aspects of anomie along with general anomie (meaninglessness), namely, valuelessness, hopelessness, powerlessness, aloneness, and closedmindedness.

As examples, six selected statements from the forty-one-item scale are given below. The anomie (A) items are scored from 5 to 1 and the nomie (N) items are scored from 1 to 5.

1. The people who are running our country are making it a place where all people are treated fairly. (N)

 5. Sometimes a man may have to do bad things to make money for his family. (A)
 9. My life doesn't mean anything. (A)
13. People can understand each other better now that we have television, telephones, and other means of communication. (N)
15. Most of the unhappy things in my life have been caused by bad luck. (A)

RELIABILITY AND VALIDITY: In a test-retest reliability study (Elmore and Aldret, 1972) with 100 third graders, a coefficient of .70 was obtained on the general anomie (meaninglessness) scale, and coefficients ranging from .56 to .72 were obtained on the subscales.

BIBLIOGRAPHY:

Adams, S. P. "A Study of Social Values, Relationships, Psychological Anomie and Behavioral Restraints Among Eighth Grade Students." Unpublished master's degree research report. Wake Forest University, Winston-Salem, North Carolina, 1975.

Coover, C. D. "A Study of Self-Concept and Psychological Anomie with Fifth Grade Students." Unpublished master's degree research report. Wake Forest University, Winston-Salem, North Carolina, 1974.

Elmore, T. M. "Development of a Scale to Measure Psychological Anomie." Unpublished doctoral dissertation. Ohio State University, Columbus, 1962.

Elmore, T. M., and Aldret, J. "A Study of Psychological Anomie Among Elementary Children." Unpublished research study. Wake Forest University, Winston-Salem, North Carolina, 1972.

Heussenstamm, F. K. "Creativity and Alienation: An Exploration of Their Relationship in Adolescence." *California Journal of Educational Research,* 1970, *21,* 140-146.

*Prepared by Thomas M. Elmore and Orval G. Johnson*

---

# JUVENILE PROBATIONER'S BEHAVIOR AND ATTITUDE RATING SCALE

AUTHOR: Charles R. Horejsi

AGE: Adolescents

VARIABLE: Parents' perceptions of changes in probationer's behavior and attitudes

TYPE OF MEASURE: Rating scale

SOURCE FROM WHICH MEASURE MAY BE OBTAINED: Charles R. Horejsi, Department of Social Work, University of Montana, Missoula, Montana 59801. Cost: $1.00.

DESCRIPTION OF MEASURE: The scale is designed for use with the parents or parent-surrogates of youngsters on probation. Thirty-seven items relating to the youngster's behavior and attitudes measure the parents' assessment of position or negative changes resulting from a one-to-one, court-volunteer/probationer relationship. Only those changes attributed to the volunteer's influence are considered in the scoring procedure. A high positive score results when parents report many improvements and attribute these to volunteer intervention. Low positive scores result when parents report few improvements or when improvements are counterbalanced by undesirable changes. Negative scores result when parents believe that volunteer intervention does more harm than good. The interview schedule consists of three orientation items, ten items dealing with parent characteristics, thirty-seven items focusing primarily on the attitudes and behavior of probationers, and one open-ended question for eliciting parents' comments. Following are the scoring system and possible scores for each test item: (A) improved, (B) remained the same, (C) gotten worse. (If either improved or worse): In your opinion, to what extent did the volunteer have something to do with this change? (1) Volunteer had a great deal to do with the change. (2) Volunteer had quite a bit to do with the change. (3) Volunteer had only a little bit to do with the change. (4) Volunteer had nothing to do with the change. Possible scores: A–1 = +10; A–2 = +6; A–3 = +2; A–4 = 0; B = 0; C–1 = –10; C–2 = –6; C–3 = –2; C–4 = 0.

As examples, five of the thirty-seven questions are given below.

14. Since _____ first began meeting with the volunteer, has _____'s general physical health improved, remained the same, or gotten worse?
18. In your opinion, has _____'s *general attitude toward school* improved, remained the same, or gotten worse?
22. How about _____'s *choice of friends*? Has this improved, remained the same, or gotten worse since _____ first began meeting with the volunteer?
26. What about the amount of *respect that* _____ *shows for the rights and feelings* of other people? Would you say this has improved, remained the same, or gotten worse?
30. How about _____'s *willingness to pitch in and do necessary work around home*? Has this improved, remained the same, or gotten worse?

RELIABILITY AND VALIDITY: The instrument appears to meet basic criteria for content validity. Split-half reliability was obtained by summing and then correlating the odd- and even-numbered items. Using the Spearman rank correlation coefficient, split-half reliability was found to be .88.

BIBLIOGRAPHY:

Horejsi, C. R. "Parent's Perceptions of the Effect of Volunteers on Juvenile Probationers." Unpublished doctoral dissertation. University of Denver, Colorado, 1971.

Horejsi, C. R. "Attitude of Parents Toward Juvenile Court Volunteers." *Federal Probation*, 1972, *36*, 13-18.

Horejsi, C. R. "Unhappy Experiences with Court Volunteers: A Source of Learning." *Volunteer Administration*, 1972, *6*, 18-22.

# KATZ-ZALK OPINION QUESTIONNAIRE

AUTHORS: Phyllis A. Katz and Sue Rosenberg Zalk

AGE: Grades 1 to 6

VARIABLE: Racial attitudes in children

TYPE OF MEASURE: Questionnaire

SOURCE FROM WHICH MEASURE MAY BE OBTAINED: Phyllis A. Katz, City University of New York, Graduate Center, 33 West 42nd Street, New York, New York 10036. Cost: $30.00, set of test slides; $1.00 per test booklet (reductions for larger orders).

DESCRIPTION OF MEASURE: The Katz-Zalk Opinion Questionnaire may be administered in a group setting. Children view slides of two or four children interacting and are asked to select the child who was credited with either a positive or negative act or attribute. A sketch of the slide is included in the answer booklet so the child merely has to put an "X" in the box under the child selected. Of the fifty-five items, thirty-eight are race-related questions and seventeen are buffer items (same-race, other-sex, or same-sex). The race items are divided into two subtest scores, one for items depicting positive events (seventeen items) and one for negative events (twenty-one items). Conceptually, the slides depicting negative actions have been more typical of prejudicial responses (e.g., who broke the window), whereas the responses to more positive items (e.g., getting an award) might be more indicative of racial pride. These are added together to obtain the total p-score. Positive scores can be further differentiated into: leadership, academic achievement, athletic achievement, and achievement in nonathletic games. Subtest scores for the negative portion of the instrument can be derived in the following areas: initiation of aggression, immoral behavior, nonacceptance by peers, and negative evaluations by adults. Each race item on the test receives a score of either 0 or 1, and the total score can range from 0 to 38. Children are given 1 point each time they attribute a negative characteristic to an other-race child or a positive characteristic to a same-race child. The reverse selections receive a score of 0. The test booklet has a code to facilitate scoring.

RELIABILITY AND VALIDITY: The test was standardized on 587 children in grades 1 through 5 from a lower-middle-class urban community in New York City. The standardization sample was approximately 56-percent black and 44-percent white. Spanish-surnamed children were not included in the sample. An additional 1,800 children in second through sixth grades from a northeastern suburban community were tested to provide a comparison sample. The ethnic makeup of these school children was approximately 35-percent black and 65-percent white. Economically the community ranged from lower class to upper class, with the majority representing the middle class. Analyses of variance on the standardization sample revealed that the scores varied as a function of the child's age and race and the race of the examiner administering the test. The scores of the second- and fifth-grade children from the two locations were compared. Second and fifth grades were used because the race of the examiner was only controlled for these two grades in the suburban sample. The scores differed for these two locations as a function of the age and race of the child and the race of the examiner. Split-half reliability for the total urban standardization group, corrected by the Spearman-Brown formula, was .81. The reliabilities for the white and black children were .76 and .83, respectively. The first, second, third, fourth, and fifth grades had reliabilities of .86, .79, .86, and .71, respectively. Split-half reliabilities for the suburban comparison group were similar to those of the urban sample.

BIBLIOGRAPHY:

Katz, P. A., Sohn, M., and Zalk, S. R. "Perceptual Concomitants of Racial Attitudes in Urban Grade-School Children." *Child Development,* 1975, *11,* 135-144.

---

## KENYON'S ATPA (ATTITUDE TOWARD PHYSICAL ACTIVITY) SCALES

AUTHOR: Gerald S. Kenyon

AGE: Adolescents and adults

VARIABLE: Attitude toward physical activity and sport

TYPE OF MEASURE: Likert-type scales; semantic differential scales

SOURCE FROM WHICH MEASURE MAY BE OBTAINED: Gerald S. Kenyon, Faculty of Human Kinetics and Leisure Studies, University of Waterloo, Ontario, Canada N2L 3G1. ED 019 709 available from ERIC Document Reproduction Service, Drawer O, Bethesda, Maryland 20014. Cost: Microfiche, $.65; hard copy, $13.16.

DESCRIPTION OF MEASURE: The scales were developed within the context of a model characterizing physical activity on six dimensions based on the "perceived instrumentality" of each dimension—specifically, physical activity perceived as a social experience, health and fitness, the pursuit of vertigo, an aesthetic experience, catharsis, and an ascetic experience. A seventh dimension, physical activity perceived as chance, was later added in the inventory employing the semantic differential scales. *Likert-type scales:* Alternative, Likert-type attitude statements representative of each of the six dimensions were developed for two separate inventories, one for males (Form DM: fifty-nine items) and one for females (Form DW: fifty-four items). Items are weighted in accordance with discrimination of each of five response categories: strongly agree, agree, undecided, disagree, and strongly disagree. Examples of items from Form DM for each variable are given below.

*Social experience:* I enjoy sports mostly because they give me a chance to meet new people.
*Health and fitness:* Of all physical activities, my first choice would be those whose purpose is primarily to develop and maintain physical fitness.

*Pursuit of vertigo:* Physical activities having a strong element of daring or requiring one to take chances are highly desirable.

*Aesthetic experience:* Among the best forms of physical activity are those which use the body as an instrument of expression.

*Catharsis:* Watching athletes becoming completely absorbed in their sport nearly always provides me with a welcome escape from the many demands of present-day life.

*Ascetic experience:* I would get by far the most satisfaction from games requiring long and careful preparation and involving stiff competition against a strong opposition.

*Semantic differential scales:* In the Semantic Differential Scales of ATPA, a seventh dimension was added—physical activity perceived as chance—to the six dimensions of the original model. Definitions were provided for each of the seven dimensions and required judgment against eight descriptive scales: good/bad, worthless/worthwhile, pleasant/unpleasant, and so forth. The a priori weights for each scale were 1 through 7, or 7 through 1, depending upon the direction of evaluation. Using the entire sample ($N$ = 3,198) in the cross-national study (Kenyon, 1968c), the scales were reweighted for each concept using a reciprocating-averages procedure to maximize internal consistency. The new weights were used to generate a total score for each subject in each of the seven dimensions.

RELIABILITY AND VALIDITY: *Likert-type scales:* The validity of each scale was inferred by using preferred type of activity—through direct or vicarious participation—as a criterion. It was found that scale scores differentiated between strong and weak preference groups in the predicted direction for all scales except catharsis. Hoyt reliabilities for each of the six scales ranged from .68 to .89. An oblique rotation of the first six factors following an incomplete image analysis yielded clusters of items clearly corresponding to each of the six postulated subdomains. No two factors shared more than 32 percent of the variance, and usually much less. *Semantic differential scales:* For the total sample ($N$ = 3,198) in the cross-national study (Kenyon, 1968c) Hoyt reliability coefficients ranged from .76 for physical activity as a social experience to .87 for physical activity as chance when a priori weights were employed in the analysis. Hoyt reliabilities using the maximized weights yielded slightly higher *r*s, ranging from .78 to .87.

BIBLIOGRAPHY:

Kenyon, G. S. "A Multidimensional Scaling Approach to Validation of an A Priori Model for Characterizing Values Held for Physical Activity." Paper presented to the annual meeting of the American Association for Health, Physical Education, and Recreation. Dallas, Texas, March 1965.

Kenyon, G. S. "Values Held for Physical Activity: A Cross-Cultural Approach." Unpublished report, 1965.

Kenyon, G. S. *The Assessment of Attitude Toward Physical Activity.* Final progress report, National Institute of Mental Health, 1966.

Kenyon, G. S. "Attitude Toward Vertiginous Physical Activity as a Function of Self- and Body-Esteem." Paper presented at the annual meeting of the American Association for Health, Physical Education, and Recreation. Las Vegas, Nevada, March 1967.

Kenyon, G. S. "A Conceptual Model for Characterizing Physical Activity." *Research Quarterly,* 1968a, *39,* 96-105.

Kenyon, G. S. "Six Scales for Assessing Attitude Toward Physical Activity." *Research Quarterly*, 1968b, *39*, 566-574.

Kenyon, G. S. *Values Held for Physical Activity by Selected Urban Secondary School Students in Canada, Australia, England and the United States.* Washington, D.C.: U.S. Office of Education, 1968c. ERIC document no. ED 019 709.

Kenyon, G. S. "Attitude Toward Sport and Physical Activity Among Adolescents from Four English-Speaking Countries." In G. Luschen (Ed.), *Cross-Cultural Analysis of Sports and Games.* Champaign, Illinois: Stipes, 1970.

Kenyon, G. S., Loy, J. W., and Isaacman, B. S. "Values Held for Physical Activity as a Function of Social Class Background." Paper presented to the annual meeting of the American Association for Health, Physical Education, and Recreation. Chicago, March 1966.

*Prepared by Lorraine Molloy*

---

# KNOWLEDGE AND ATTITUDE SURVEY
## CONCERNING EPILEPSY

AUTHOR: Jane W. Martin

AGE: Adults

VARIABLE: Knowledge of and attitude toward epileptics

TYPE OF MEASURE: Questionnaire

SOURCE FROM WHICH MEASURE MAY BE OBTAINED: Please send self-addressed stamped envelope to Jane Martin, 131 Mesilla NE, Albuquerque, New Mexico 87108.

DESCRIPTION OF MEASURE: This ten-item questionnaire was sent to over five hundred high school counselors and teachers in Buffalo, New York to determine their familiarity with epilepsy and their attitudes toward persons having epilepsy. The results of the study are reported in Martin (1974). The questionnaire can be used to compare knowledge and attitudes between two groups, such as teachers vs. general public or teachers vs. special teachers. It can also be used to measure the attitudes and knowledge of any group, such as PTAs, parents, or service organizations.

The ten items of the questionnaire are given below. The respondent replies "yes," "no," or "no answer."

1. Do you know what epilepsy is?
2. Have you ever known a person who had epilepsy?
3. Epilepsy is inherited.
4. Have you ever witnessed an epileptic seizure?
5. When a seizure is in progress, an object should be placed between the patient's teeth.

6. When a seizure is in progress, an ambulance should be called immediately.

7. Would you be nervous if you knew the person next to you had epilepsy?

8. During a seizure, most epileptics are dangerous to others.

9. It is possible to swallow your tongue while having a seizure.

10. Epilepsy is contagious.

RELIABILITY AND VALIDITY: None reported.

BIBLIOGRAPHY:

Force, D. G. "A Descriptive Study of the Incidence of Seizures and Teachers' Attitudes Toward Children with Epilepsy in the Minneapolis, Minnesota, Public Schools." Mimeographed. Minneapolis: Minnesota Epilepsy League, 1965.

Martin, J. W. "Attitudes Toward Epileptic Students in a City High School System." *Journal of School Health,* 1974, *44,* 144-146.

Peters, E. L. "Attitudes Toward Epileptics in Public Elementary and Secondary Schools as Reflected by Administrators." Unpublished doctoral dissertation. University of Denver, Colorado, 1967.

# LIBERAL-CONSERVATIVE RELIGIOUS ATTITUDE SCALE

AUTHOR: Robert D. Coursey

AGE: 14 years and up

VARIABLE: Liberal-conservative religious attitudes

TYPE OF MEASURE: Likert-type attitude scale

SOURCE FROM WHICH MEASURE MAY BE OBTAINED: Robert D. Coursey, Department of Psychology, University of Maryland, College Park, Maryland 20742.

DESCRIPTION OF MEASURE: Liberal (L) is defined simply as someone who seeks changes in religious practices and beliefs, while conservative (C) is seeking to maintain traditional approaches. The forty-item scale was developed for the average Catholic. A 4-point, forced-choice, Likert format is used (strongly agree-strongly disagree), with L items reverse-keyed. For each item, 1 = most liberal choice, 5 = most conservative; 3 is not used except where the testee fails to respond. Response style is controlled by an equal number of L and C items. All items are summed for a summary score. Subscale 1 unites traditional piety with authoritarian submission. Subscale 2 reflects ecumenical attitudes. Subscale 3 emphasizes the right to follow one's conscience, especially on issues related to marriage and birth control. Subscale 4 measures the desire to change or retain church regulations, subscale 5 measures attitudes toward public worship and changes in the liturgy, while subscale 6 deals with the church's involvement in social rights.

As examples, the first ten of the forty items, together with their subscale numbers, are given below.

*Subscale Item*

|   |   |
|---|---|
| 1 | 1. A good Catholic should say the Rosary often. (C) |
| 6 | 2. Catholics should help disadvantaged groups to secure equal rights. (L) |
| 5 | 3. Many popular hymns lack the majesty which is fitting for Mass. (C) |
| 4 | 4. Nuns should wear modern dress. (L) |
| 6 | 5. A priest should run his parish and not get involved in political issues. (C) |
| 1 | 6. Sunday Mass should remain obligatory. (C) |
| 3 | 7. Disobedience to Church authority leads to chaos and anarchy. (C) |
| 1 | 8. It is a Catholic's duty to defend the Church when someone criticizes it. (C) |
| 2 | 9. Catholic children should not be exposed to non-Catholic ways. (C) |
| 2 | 10. Protestant hymns and prayers should be avoided in Catholic services. (C) |

RELIABILITY AND VALIDITY: Test construction, face validity, and content validity are reported in Coursey (1971, 1974). The scale was administered to 486 ninth- and twelfth-grade boys and girls in four coeducational Catholic high schools. For the thirty-eight-item high school version, overall M = 108.83, SD = 15.28; the most liberal school M = 102.94; most conservative, 116.47. M for females = 107.16, for males = 111.15. M for ninth grade = 112.86; for twelfth grade, M = 105.45. Analysis of variance showed significant differences among schools, grades, and sexes. Summary score correlated $-.22$ with Otis IQ; $-.36$ with SAT, verbal; $-.29$ with SAT, math; and $-.59$ with teacher's measure of motivation in religious class, all $p < .01$. Internal consistency reliability based on interitem correlations was .84. Partial correlations showed the L-C summary score unrelated to parent's socioeconomic level, amount of parents' education, or their Catholic education. The scale was administered to 275 parishioners at a conservative parish and 403 at a liberal parish, and it significantly differentiated the two parishes on thirty-five of the items, all but one item in the predicted direction. Factor analysis using the principal-components method and orthogonal rotation established the six factor subscales. Factor reliability across samples was established by factor analyzing the parishes separately; factor reliability across time was established by three further factor analyses one year later. L-C summary score correlated .32 with age, .29 with occupational level, and $-.40$ with education. The forty-item scale was cross-validated on a sample of subscribers who read and endorsed either a liberal or a conservative journal. Ninety-eight pairs were individually matched on sex, age, income, education, and vocational status. Every item of the scale differentiated the two groups with $p < .001$. Ms and SDs are reported in Coursey (1971, 1974). Split-half reliabilities for the summary score ranged from .89 to .97, while those for the subscales ranged from .65 to .88. A multiple-regression analysis using 1532 $Ss$ found that the L-C scale accounted for almost 60 percent of the variance of a criterion variable of reader agreement with the editorial policies of six liberal and conservative Catholic journals.

BIBLIOGRAPHY:

Coursey, R. "The L-C Scale Measuring Liberal-Conservative Religious Attitudes Among Roman Catholics." Unpublished doctoral dissertation. University of Rochester, New York, 1971.
Coursey, R. "Consulting and the Catholic Crisis." *Journal of Consulting and Clinical Psychology,* 1974, *42,* 519-528.

## LIFESTYLE ORIENTATION

AUTHOR: Frank Friedlander

AGE: 14 years and up; eighth-grade education

VARIABLE: Values, preferences, and beliefs of three lifestyles

TYPE OF MEASURE: Questionnaire

SOURCE FROM WHICH MEASURE MAY BE OBTAINED: Frank Friedlander, Department of Organizational Behavior, School of Management, Case Western Reserve University, Cleveland, Ohio 44106.

DESCRIPTION OF MEASURE: The Lifestyle Orientation is a measure of three contrasting sets of beliefs and preferences: (1) the formalistic lifestyle, in which a person places a heavy reliance on higher authority, law and order, precedent, and advancement as a criterion of success. The formalistic is older, higher in men than women, typical of sales, business, and technical occupations, and greatest in the Protestant religions. (2) The sociocentric lifestyle, in which a person looks to close intimate relationships for guidance and direction. The sociocentric shows a drop with age until 25 years and then a rise, is most typical of the social service and science occupations, and is higher in women than men. (3) The personalistic lifestyle, in which a person looks to himself for guidance and direction and places a high value on his personal freedom to decide how he wants to live and act. The personalistic declines steadily from the teens to the mid-50s, is typical of those in the arts, entertainment, cultural and student occupations, is higher in women than men, and is characteristic of Jews and agnostics. Norms by age, occupation, sex, and religion are available.

As examples, the first six of the twelve items of the questionnaire are given below. The respondent answers the question "To what extent does the statement represent your own attitude?" using a 5-point scale ranging from "completely" to "not at all."

1. In deciding how I want to live and act, I am most satisfied if
   a. I am completely free to make this decision by myself.
   b. I have some close friends or colleagues who will help me reach this decision.
2. I believe that my life will be most satisfying to me if
   a. there are some clear pathways for advancing and being rewarded.
   b. I am completely free to choose how I want to live.
3. I place a great deal of faith in
   a. what my close friends say.
   b. law and order.
4. I can only get the really important things in life by
   a. doing what I want to do.
   b. working closely with friends and colleagues.
5. What is important is that I
   a. have a secure job and a comfortable house.
   b. experiment and discover who and what I am.
6. I will do what is right when I am guided by
   a. the close relationships I have made with others.
   b. the precedents and policies that have been established over the years.

RELIABILITY AND VALIDITY: The three lifestyle scales were derived through a factor analysis of a 78-item questionnaire administered to over eleven hundred people of different ages, religions, countries, and occupations. Kuder-Richardson reliabilities are .78, .72, and .70, respectively. In addition to the biographic and demographic correlates noted above, the scales have been noted to differentiate among preferred organization, group, and classroom structures—in terms of how conflict, decision-making, communication, and leadership issues are handled.

BIBLIOGRAPHY:

DiMarco, N. "Life Style, Learning Structure, Congruence, and Student Attitudes." *American Education Research Journal,* 1974, *11,* 203-209.

DiMarco, N. "Supervisor-Subordinate Life Style Compatability and Interpersonal Need Complementarity as Determinants of Attitudes Towards the Supervisor." *Academy of Management Journal,* 1974, *17,* 575-578.

DiMarco, N. "Life Style, Work Group Structure, Compatability, and Job Satisfaction." *Academy of Management Journal,* 1975, *18,* 313-322.

DiMarco, N., and Kapnick, P. L. "Relationship of Life Style and Interpersonal Need Orientation." *Journal of Psychology,* 1974, *86,* 13-15.

DiMarco, N., and Norton, S. "Life Style, Organization Structure, Congruity, and Job Satisfaction." *Personnel Psychology,* 1975, *28* (in press).

Friedlander, F. "Emergent and Contemporary Life Styles: An Intergenerational Issue." *Human Relations,* 1975, *28,* 329-347.

Vinton, J. C. "The Relationship Between Student Life Styles and University Classroom Structures." *College Student Journal,* 1974, *8,* 47-54.

# MALPASS AND SYMOND'S VALUE PREFERENCE MEASURE

AUTHORS: Roy S. Malpass and John D. Symonds

AGE: 16 years and up

VARIABLE: Personal values

TYPE OF MEASURE: Rating scale of preference-for-value statements

SOURCE FROM WHICH MEASURE MAY BE OBTAINED: Roy S. Malpass, State University of New York, Faculty of Social Sciences, Plattsburgh, New York 12901.

DESCRIPTION OF MEASURE: The measure contains ninety-three value statements that were collected from a number of cross-cultural studies of values. Factor analysis of responses from ten groups of high school students, college students, and other young adults yielded five value composites, subsuming fifteen of the ninety-three items. These composites were labeled: the good life, pleasant working companions, balance and adjustment, artistic creativity, and religiousness. Because the samples were diverse in ethnic background and reading-comprehension level, the value items were "decentered" to widely understood forms of English usage. Four black undergraduates who had direct and extensive experience with ghetto life rewrote each item into a form they felt would be appropriately comprehended by the subject population. Each "translator" worked separately, and their translations were compared. A large degree of agreement was found about which items would cause problems, and there was considerable similarity in the translations offered. In a few cases where there were differences, the four arrived at a consensual translation. Some representative translations were as follows: (1) "To be able to integrate action, enjoyment and reflection" became "to be able to mix together action, fun and thought in life." (2) "Being initiating" became "Being able to start things off and make changes in things." (3) "Being conservative" became "Wanting to keep old habits and ways of doing things."

As examples, the first twenty of the ninety-three items from the "decentered" form of the test are given below. The Roman numerals following certain of the items indicate the value composite from Malpass and Symonds (1974) to which the item belongs: I = the good life, II = pleasant working companions, III = balance and adjustment, IV = artistic creativity, V = religiousness.

1. Being wise (having good judgment). (III)
2. A job with white people and where you like the people you are working with. (II)
3. Accepting other people's ideas most of the time (not insisting on your own views).
4. Being skillful (good at doing things with your hands).
5. Being famous (like some great person in the past).
6. Being very smart (bright).
7. Being able to get along well with people and with nature.
8. Being honest (never lie, cheat).
9. To be able to mix together fun, action, and thought in life.
10. Being able to start things off or make changes in things.
11. Not being worried all the time or always having a guilty conscience.
12. Being loving (warm, cuddly).

13. To have good health.
14. Being well taken care of (by others).
15. To have an active life with many friends and doing many things with them.
16. Having no worldly desires (not wanting physical pleasures, like cars, good clothes, lots of food, etc.).
17. To go to heaven after death.
18. A job that has excitement and adventure.
19. Doing something for the good of world peace.
20. Being able to get people to work together well.

RELIABILITY AND VALIDITY: The value scale was given to a group of 142 high school students and to a group of 264 students and young adults. The responses of these groups were separately intercorrelated and submitted to factor analysis. From these analyses, the results of which were very similar, the five value composites noted above were constructed. Since these composites appeared in factor analyses for two separate samples, they can be considered cross-validated composites. Twenty-five percent of the items were repeated in each of four forms of the questionnaire, thus giving reliability data on each item for about one hundred respondents. Only one item ("To have enough to eat") had a reliability coefficient less than .50.

BIBLIOGRAPHY:

Malpass, R. S., and Symonds, J. D. "Value Preferences Associated with Social Class, Sex and Race." *Journal of Cross-Cultural Psychology,* 1974, *5,* 282-300.

---

# MARIJUANA ATTITUDE SCALE

AUTHOR: Daniel J. Baer

AGE: High school and older

VARIABLE: Attitudes about marijuana

TYPE OF MEASURE: Thurstone scale

SOURCE FROM WHICH MEASURE MAY BE OBTAINED: Daniel J. Baer, Psychology Department, McGuinn Hall, Boston College, Chestnut Hill, Massachusetts 02167.

DESCRIPTION OF MEASURE: There are two forms of this measure, each of them consisting of twenty-two items. The forms may be used individually or in combination. *S*s are asked to indicate either agreement with, disagreement with, or doubtfulness to the statements.

As examples, the twenty-two items of Form A are given below.

1. Marijuana gives more pleasure than pain.

2. Marijuana is harmful to health.
3. Marijuana should be legalized.
4. Using marijuana is a revolting vice.
5. Marijuana helps you cope with problems.
6. Marijuana dulls your mind.
7. Marijuana increases a person's creativity.
8. Marijuana corrupts morals.
9. Marijuana is better than alcohol.
10. People should not use marijuana.
11. Marijuana is one of life's greatest pleasures.
12. Marijuana users should be severely punished.
13. Marijuana is a popular fad.
14. Marijuana is a harmful drug.
15. No one should be allowed to use marijuana.
16. Marijuana helps you understand yourself.
17. Marijuana is a stepping stone to drug addiction.
18. Penalties are too severe for those who use marijuana.
19. Marijuana induces passivity.
20. Our national morality is safeguarded by the present laws regarding marijuana.
21. Marijuana users are misunderstood.
22. Those who use marijuana are searching for security.

RELIABILITY AND VALIDITY: The correlation between Forms A and B is reported as .83. Baer (1973) found that conservatives agreed more often than liberal nonusers of marijuana that users and sellers should be severely punished, and the conservatives were less likely to agree that the penalty for users was too severe. For the $S$s who had used marijuana, however, there was no significant relationship between political beliefs and attitudes toward punishment toward users and sellers.

BIBLIOGRAPHY:

Baer, D. J. "Attitudes About Marijuana and Political Views." *Psychological Reports,* 1973, *32,* 1051-1054.
Baer, D. J., and Ordway, D. "Alcoholics Anonymous Members' Attitudes Towards Marihuana and Its Users." *Psychological Reports,* 1973, *32,* 950.

*Prepared by Orval G. Johnson*

---

# MEXICAN-AMERICAN FAMILY ATTITUDE SCALE

AUTHOR: Manuel Ramirez III

AGE: Junior high, high school, and college

VARIABLE: Traditional Mexican-American attitudes and family values

TYPE OF MEASURE: Likert-type scale

SOURCE FROM WHICH MEASURE MAY BE OBTAINED: Manuel Ramirez III, Social Sciences Building #25, University of California, Santa Cruz, California 95064.

DESCRIPTION OF MEASURE: The Mexican-American Family Attitude Scale consists of twenty-nine items designed to differentiate between traditional Mexican Americans and non-Mexican Americans. The pool of items from which the final set was selected was drawn from a scale of Mexican family values developed by Diaz-Guerrero (1955), the Traditional Family Ideology Scale (Levinson and Huffman, 1962), and items developed by the author. The items include factors of traditional Mexican-American family values and attitudes such as separation of sex roles, strictness of child rearing, importance of extended family, father's authority, and self-abnegation of the mother.

As examples, the first five of the twenty-nine items of the measure are given below. The respondent answers on a 6-point scale ranging from "I agree very much" to "I disagree very much."

1. The stricter the parents the better the child.
2. It is all right to have a good time even when there is work to be done.
3. All adults should be respected.
4. More parents should teach their children to be loyal to the family.
5. Girls should not be allowed to play with boys' toys such as soldiers and footballs.

RELIABILITY AND VALIDITY: The original pool of items was administered to Mexican-American and non-Mexican-American (Caucasian monolingual English-speaking) junior high, high school, and college students. Items showing the greatest discriminatory power were retained for the final version of the scale. The final scale has been used to distinguish between Mexican-Americans who are well identified with traditional Mexican-American culture and those who are participating more extensively in mainstream American culture.

BIBLIOGRAPHY:

Diaz-Guerrero, R. "Neurosis and the Mexican Family Structure." *American Journal of Psychiatry,* 1955, *112,* 411-417.

Kaplan, R. M., and Goldman, R. D. "Interracial Perception Among Black, White, and Mexican-American High School Students." *Journal of Personality and Social Psychology,* 1973, *28,* 383-389.

Levinson, D. J., and Huffman, P. E. "Traditional Family Ideology and Its Relation to Personality." *Journal of Personality,* 1962, *23,* 251-273.

Ramirez, M. "Identification with Mexican-American Values and Psychological Adjustment in Mexican-American Adolescents." *International Journal of Social Psychiatry,* 1961, *15,* 151-156.

Ramirez, M. "Identification with Mexican Family Values and Authoritarianism in Mexican-Americans." *Journal of Social Psychology,* 1967, *73,* 3-11.

Ramirez, M. *Potential Contributions by the Behavioral Sciences to Effective Preparation Programs for Teachers of Mexican-American Children.* New Mexico State University, Las Cruces: Clearing House for Rural Education and Small Schools, 1969.

# MORAL DILEMMA EXPERIMENT

AUTHORS: Urie Bronfenbrenner, Ed C. Devereux, Jr., G. J. Suci, and R. R. Rodgers

AGE: 10 to 14 years

VARIABLE: Response to adult-vs.-peer pressure in moral conflict

TYPE OF MEASURE: Experiment and questionnaire

SOURCE FROM WHICH MEASURE MAY BE OBTAINED: Elizabeth Kiely, Martha Van NG 29, Cornell University, Ithaca, New York 14580. Cost: $1.00.

DESCRIPTION OF MEASURE: There are thirty-six items in the dilemma experiment, of which thirty are an overall measure of the child's degree of conformity to adult standards, with the remaining six items a measure of informing on one's peers. Evidence to date indicates that the informing items are factorially independent of the thirty conformity items. Children are asked to respond to a series of conflict situations under three different conditions: (a) a *base* condition, in which they are told that no one will see their responses except the investigators conducting the research; (b) an *adult* condition, in which they are informed that the responses of everyone in the class will be posted on a chart and shown to parents at a special meeting scheduled for the following week; and (3) a *peer* condition, in which the children are notified that the chart will be prepared and shown a week later to the class itself. Each response is scored on a scale from $-2.5$ to $+2.5$, a negative value being assigned to the behavior urged by age-mates. To control for a positional response set, scale direction was reversed in half of the items. The situations were divided into three alternate forms of twelve items each, with a different form used for each experimental condition. Thus, under any one condition a child can obtain a conformity score ranging from $-25$ to $+25$ and an informing score ranging from $-5$ to $+5$, with 0 representing equal division between behavior urged by peers and adults.

As an example, one complete three-part dilemma situation is given below. All responses are made on a 6-point scale as shown under (a).

### The Lost Test

(a) You and your friends accidentally find a sheet of paper which the teacher must have lost. On this sheet are the questions and answers for a quiz that you are going to have tomorrow. Some of the kids suggest that you not say anything to the teacher about it, so that all of you can get better marks. What would you *really* do?

|              Tell them they have to              |            Let each one            |
|            tell the teacher about it.            |          decide for himself.          |

:_____:_____:_____:  :_____:_____:_____:

| absolutely | fairly | I guess | I guess | fairly | absolutely |
| certain | certain | so | so | certain | certain |

(b) Suppose your friends decide to go ahead. Would you go along with them, or refuse?

|            Refuse to go along            |          Go along with          |
|            with my friends.            |          my friends.          |

(c) The next morning the teacher speaks to you in private. She asks if you saw the lost sheet of paper. After you answer, she asks you to name the kids who saw the paper. What would you *really* do?

RELIABILITY AND VALIDITY: Split-half reliabilities for the ten-item forms (based on American samples only) ranged from .75 to .86 under different experimental conditions; the reliability of the total score (in other words, sum across all three conditions) was .94. For the informing items, split-half reliabilities ranged from .79 to .87 under the three conditions; the reliability of the total score was .92. The measure has a high degree of construct validity. Peer-oriented children report spending more time with friends and less time with parents than do adult-oriented children. In addition, peer-oriented children report having a greater number of friends, at least outside of class. Finally, on a listing of personal characteristics, the peer-oriented children see themselves, and are seen by their friends and teachers, as being more peer-conforming than their adult-oriented classmates (Condry and Siman, 1974).

BIBLIOGRAPHY:

Beloff, H., and Patton, X. "Bronfenbrenner's Moral Dilemmas in Britain: Children, Their Peers and Their Parents." *International Journal of Psychology*, 1970, *1*, 27-32.

Bronfenbrenner, U. "Response to Pressure from Peers Versus Adults Among Soviet and American School Children." *International Journal of Psychology*, 1967, *2*, 199-207.

Bronfenbrenner, U. "Reactions to Social Pressure from Adults Versus Peers Among Soviet Day School and Boarding School Pupils in the Perspective of an American Sample." *Journal of Personality and Social Psychology*, 1970, *15* (3), 179-189.

Bronfenbrenner, U. *Two Worlds of Childhood: U.S. and U.S.S.R.* New York: Russell Sage Foundation, 1970.

Condry, J., and Siman, M. "Characteristics of Peer- and Adult-Oriented Children." *Journal of Marriage and the Family*, 1974, *36*, 543-554.

Devereux, E. C. "The Role of the Peer-Group Experience in Moral Development." In J. P. Hill (Ed.), *Minnesota Symposia on Child Psychology*. Vol. 4. Minneapolis: University of Minnesota Press, 1970.

Devereux, E. C. "Authority and Moral Development Among German and American Children: A Cross-Cultural Pilot Experiment." *Journal of Comparative Family Studies*, 1972, *3*, 99-124.

Garbarino, J., and Bronfenbrenner, U. "The Socialization of Moral Judgment and Behavior in Cross-Cultural Perspective." In T. Lickona (Ed.), *Morality: A Handbook of Moral Development and Behavior*. New York: Holt, Rinehart and Winston (in press).

Lüscher, K. "Dreizehnjahrige Schweizer Zwischen Peers und Erwachsenen im Interkulturellen Vergleich." ("Thirteen-Year-Old Swiss Children Between Peers and Adults in Cross-Cultural Comparison.") *Schweizerische Zeitschrift fur Psychologie und Ihre Anwendungen Revue Suisse de Psychologie Pure et Appliquée*, 1971, Separatabzuq aus 30, Nr. 3, 219-229.

Rim, Y., and Seidoenross, H. "Personality and Response to Pressure from Peers vs. Adults." *Personality*, 1971, *2*, 35-43.

Shouval, R., Bronfenbrenner, U., Kav-Venaki, S., Devereux, E. C., and Kiely, E. "The Anomalous Reactions to Social Pressure of Israeli and Soviet Children

Raised in Family vs. Collective Settings." *Journal of Personality and Social Psychology* (in press).

Simon, M. A. "Peer Group Influence During Adolescence: A Study of Forty-one Naturally Existing Friendship Groups." Unpublished doctoral dissertation. Cornell University, Ithaca, New York, 1973.

Smart, R., and Smart, M. "New Zealand Preadolescents' Parent-Peer Orientation: Parent Perceptions Compared with English and American." *Journal of Marriage and the Family,* 1973, *35,* 142-149.

---

## MORALITY TEST FOR CHILDREN (MOTEC)

AUTHOR: Avner Ziv

AGE: 7 to 13 years

VARIABLE: Five aspects of moral judgments: resistance to temptation, stage of moral judgment, fear and guilt associated with transgression, readiness to confess, and severity of punishment after transgression

TYPE OF MEASURE: Test

SOURCE FROM WHICH MEASURE MAY BE OBTAINED: Avner Ziv, School of Education, Tel Aviv University, Tel Aviv, Israel.

DESCRIPTION OF MEASURE: The MOTEC presents seven pictures of situations in which a child finds himself in a moral dilemma. The subject has to answer how the child in the picture will behave. The answers for the situations are scored according to norms calculated from 1,000 children's answers and give the score for the first variable of the test: resistance to temptation. For each situation the subject is asked to give the reason for the child's behavior by choosing from four possibilities. The four alternatives reflect the stages of moral judgment according to Bull (1969), and the subject's answers are calculated and express his level of moral judgment. The other three aspects measured by the test are: feeling of guilt or shame after transgression, readiness to confess, and severity of punishment following transgression. There are two test forms, one for boys and one for girls. The situations are identical but in the drawings there are boys in the boys' test or girls in the girls' test. The scoring uses norms that take into consideration the percentage of children who transgress in different situations. Although there is no doubt that it is easier to transgress in some situations than in others, generally tests of moral judgment do not take this well-documented fact into consideration.

As an example, one of the seven episodes is given below.

6. In the picture in front of you there are children your age who are preparing for a class campfire. One of the boys who is not succeeding in collecting enough firewood

for the fire goes across to the children's playground; the playground is surrounded by a fence made of boards. In one corner a few boards collapsed. Nobody is around.

a. Give the picture a name: _____

b. Will the boy take the boards for the campfire? Put a circle around the answer that is most acceptable to you. Yes   No   If you answered yes, turn to the pink page. If you answered no, turn to the blue page.

(*Pink page*)

Before you there are four statements. Choose from them only one sentence that best explains according to your opinion why the boy will take the boards from the fence. Underline the statement you choose.

1. Because he promised his friends that he would gather wood.
2. Because nobody sees him.
3. Because he likes campfires very much.
4. Because the fence was broken anyway.

(*Blue page*)

Before you there are four statements. Choose from them only one statement that best explains according to your opinion why he does not take the boards from the fence. Underline the statement that you choose.

1. Because he is likely to get bruised.
2. Because his friends are likely to be punished because of him.
3. Because he will ruin something that belongs to somebody else.
4. Because he's afraid he will get a severe punishment.

(*Following page*)

Let's suppose that the boy in the picture took the boards from the fence for the campfire.

1. How do you think he will feel? Put a line under the *one* word that best describes the way the boy in the picture feels.
   Happy      Afraid      Guilty      Satisfied
2. What will he do afterwards? Put a line under *one* of the two answers below.
   a. He will tell this to somebody.
   b. He will keep this to himself and not tell anybody.
3. Which punishment does he deserve? Put a line under *one* of the four answers.
   A very severe punishment, a severe punishment, not too severe a punishment, no punishment at all.

RELIABILITY AND VALIDITY: Reliability was calculated by test-retest after a one-month interval. The correlations obtained varied from .52 to .71 on the five subscores. Split-half procedure was also used on 500 tests, and the correlations for each variable (after Spearman-Brown correction) varied from .43 to .70. All correlations obtained were significant at $p < .001$. Validity was examined in several ways. (1) In six class-rooms sociometric tests were conducted in which children were asked how each child in the classroom would react in a moral situation (e.g., giving back change received unjustly). For each child a score obtained from the sociometric test was compared with his score on transgression obtained on MOTEC. Correlations ranged from .81 to .30. The children obtaining scores in the highest 25 percent were compared with those scores obtained in the lowest 25 percent on their MOTEC scores; *t*-tests were significant at $p < .05$. (2) The stages of moral judgment were longitudinally validated. The correlation between stage scores and chronological age for 500 children was .32 ($p < .001$). On a cross-validation using an additional 500 children the correlation was .39.

(3) Intercorrelations between the subtests were computed and a Guttman smallest-space analysis was conducted. The results are in accordance with the theoretical assumptions relating the variables (Aronfreed, 1968; Wright, 1971). (4) Validity with behavior was calculated using cheating situations from Hartshorne and May. Correlations between cheating in situations and transgression on MOTEC were significant at $p < .001$.

BIBLIOGRAPHY:

Aronfreed, J. *Conduct and Conscience.* New York: Academic Press, 1968.
Bull, N. J. *Moral Education.* London: Routledge & Kegan Paul, 1969.
Wright, D. *The Psychology of Moral Behavior.* London: Penguin, 1971.
Ziv, A., and Shulman, S. "The Influence of Televised Modeling on Children's Moral Judgment." *Journal of Moral Education* (in press).

---

## MORLAND PICTURE INTERVIEW (MPI)

AUTHOR: J. Kenneth Morland

AGE: 3 to 9 years

VARIABLE: Racial acceptance, preference, self-identification, and classification ability

TYPE OF MEASURE: Structured interview with pictures

SOURCE FROM WHICH MEASURE MAY BE OBTAINED: J. Kenneth Morland, Box 301, Randolph-Macon Women's College, Lynchburg, Virginia 24504. Rental fee: $10.00.

DESCRIPTION OF MEASURE: The MPI involves the use of six color photographs about which questions are asked. The first picture is of six children, three boys and three girls, of the respondent's race and approximate age. The second picture is just like the first one, taken in exactly the same setting, but the children are of another race. The third picture shows six men, three of one race and three of the other, and the fourth picture shows six women, three of each of the two races. The fifth picture is of six girls, three of each of the two races, and the final picture is of six boys, three of one race and three of the other. The pictures were made by professional photographers, and nonracial characteristics of the models, such as dress and facial expressions, were kept as similar as possible. There are two versions of the MPI, one with Afro and Euro-American models and the other with Chinese and European models. In the American version Afro-American models include those of light, medium, and dark shades of skin color and different hair styles; Euro-American models include blonds and brunettes. A comparable variety of models is also found in the Chinese-European version. In the standard MPI administration, the child is first asked questions relating to racial acceptance, preference, and self-identification, in that order. Following this, race is mentioned for the first time when the child is asked questions to determine his ability to classify other persons and himself using common racial designations.

RELIABILITY AND VALIDITY: The measure has been checked only for racial classification ability. Reliability by the split-half method was .98; validity by comparing scores on photographs with the ability to indicate the race of the interviewer showed 98.7 percent of those scoring "high" who give the correct identity of the race of the interviewer in contrast to only 30 percent of those who scored "low" (Morland, 1958).

BIBLIOGRAPHY:

Floyd, J. A. "Self-Concept Development in Black Children." Unpublished senior thesis. Princeton University, Princeton, New Jersey, 1969.

Morland, J. K. "Racial Recognition by Nursery School Children." *Social Forces*, 1958, *36*, 132-137.

Morland, J. K. "Racial Self-Identification: A Study of Nursery School Children." *American Catholic Sociological Review*, 1963, *24*, 231-242.

Morland, J. K. "A Comparison of Race Awareness in Northern and Southern Children." *American Journal of Orthopsychiatry*, 1966, *36*, 22-31. In M. L. Goldschmidt (Ed.), *Black Americans and White Racism*. New York: Holt, Rinehart and Winston, 1970.

Morland, J. K. "Race Awareness Among American and Hong Kong Chinese Children." *American Journal of Sociology*, 1969, *75*, 360-375. Reprinted in S. S. Guterman, *Black Psyche: Modal Personality Patterns of Black Americans*. Berkeley, California: Glendessary Press, 1972.

Morland, J. K. "Racial Acceptance and Preference of Nursery School Children in a Southern City." *Merrill-Palmer Quarterly*, 1962, *8*, 271-280. Reprinted in J. C. Brigham and T. A. Wissbach (Eds.), *Racial Attitudes in America: Analyses and Findings of Social Psychology*. New York: Harper & Row, 1972.

Morland, J. K. "Racial Attitudes in School Children: Kindergarten Through High School." Multilithed. Washington, D.C.: U.S. Office of Education, 1972.

## OPINION OF TEACHERS IN JUNIOR SCHOOLS

AUTHOR: Joan Barker-Lunn

AGE: Teachers of all ages of children

VARIABLE: Attitude of teachers to six specific aspects of teaching

TYPE OF MEASURE: Guttman-type scales

SOURCE FROM WHICH MEASURE MAY BE OBTAINED: Principal Research Officer,

Guidance and Assessment Service, National Foundation for Educational Research, The Mere, Upton Park, Slough, England. Approximate cost: Questionnaire, £4.80 per 100 copies; manual, 19 pence per copy.

DESCRIPTION OF MEASURE: The instrument has seven scales, each scale consisting of a number of statements to which the respondent is asked to indicate his degree of agreement or disagreement on a 5-point scale. There are forty items, and they have been randomized so as not to indicate to the respondent that there are a number of scales. In scoring, a number of the response categories have been combined in order to produce the closest possible approximation to a perfect Guttman-type scale. Consequently the majority of items have been reduced to dichotomies.
    Examples of items under each scale are given below.

*Permissive-Nonpermissive*
I cannot stand children fidgeting in class.
*Attitude to Physical Punishment*
Physical punishment is out of the question and completely unnecessary.
*11+ section*
The 11+ can prevent slackness in Junior Schools and this is a good thing.
*Noise in the Classroom*
I don't mind a reasonably high working noise in my class.
*Streaming*
Streaming makes slow children inferior.
*A-Stream*
The atmosphere in A-streams is too competitive.
*Attitude to Backward Child*
I would enjoy the challenge of teaching less able children.

RELIABILITY AND VALIDITY: The original statements were collected during interviews with a sample of teachers stratified with respect to age, sex, and teaching in A-, B-, or C-streams or in nonstreamed classes. These were tried on two random samples of 100 teachers each and the responses were factor analyzed. Seven attitude areas were further investigated, and all except the attitude towards backward children were subject to Guttman's method of scalogram analysis. The coefficients of reproducibility were as follows: permissive-nonpermissive (5 items), .94; attitude to physical punishment (6 items), .95; attitude to 11+ selection (5 items), .95; attitude to noise in the classroom (5 items), .93; attitude to streaming (7 items), .95; attitude to A-stream (5 items), .94; attitude to backward child (6 items), .70. Factor scale: Internal consistency calculated by Cronbach's *alpha* coefficient.

BIBLIOGRAPHY:

Barker-Lunn, J. C. *Streaming in the Primary School.* Windsor, England: National Foundation for Educational Research in England and Wales, 1970.

Tappen, C. J. "A Study of the Expressed Attitude of Junior School Teachers Toward Aspects of Teaching Using a Guttman Scaling Method." Unpublished master's thesis. University of London, 1965.

# PARENT-ATTITUDE SURVEY

AUTHOR: Carl F. Hereford

AGE: Adults (parents)

VARIABLE: Parental attitudes

TYPE OF MEASURE: Likert-type scale

SOURCE FROM WHICH MEASURE MAY BE OBTAINED: See Hereford (1963).

DESCRIPTION OF MEASURE: This seventy-seven-item instrument is used to measure parental attitudes in five areas: confidence, causation, acceptance, understanding, and trust. The five scales representing these areas contain fifteen items each. The first two items of the survey are used to break any response set, one being a statement with which nearly all parents would agree and the other a statement with which nearly all parents would disagree. The parent answers all items on a 5-point scale, with choices ranging from "strongly agree" to "strongly disagree." The items in the first scale, confidence, that have the highest item-scale correlations are those concerned with the parent's feeling that he has more problems than most parents and feelings concerned with an attitude of uncertainty and unsureness as to what to do about these problems. Also high in the order of discriminatory power are items that either say or imply that being a parent requires suffering and sacrifice. Causation, the second scale, measures the dimension of natural or inherent causation as contrasted to environmental or parental influence. The third scale, acceptance, is less clearly defined than the others. Some of the items carry the idea of "pushing" the child, that is, of not accepting childhood behavior. But present, too, are statements that indicate parental reluctance to accept normal developmental changes in the child. The fourth scale, understanding, is heavily weighted with items dealing with communication between parents and children—including freedom of expression, talking out problems, and joint participation in decision making. The items that define trust, the fifth scale, are mainly those that deny the individuality of the child. In these items children are seen merely as extensions of the parent, not as individuals in their own right.

As examples, ten items from the seventy-seven of the five scales of the survey are given below.

*Confidence*
38. I feel I am faced with more problems than most parents.
23. It's hard to know what to do when a child is afraid of something that won't hurt him.
*Causation*
74. Some children are just naturally bad.
64. If a child is born bad there's not much you can do about it.
*Acceptance*
 5. The earlier a child is weaned from its emotional ties to its parents the better it will handle its own problems.
40. A child who misbehaves should be made to feel guilty and ashamed of himself.

*Understanding*

31. Family life would be happier if parents made children feel they were free to say what they think about anything.

71. Talking with a child about his fears most often makes the fear look more important than it is.

*Trust*

67. Children who are not watched will get in trouble.

32. Children must be told exactly what to do and how to do it or they will make mistakes.

RELIABILITY AND VALIDITY: The split-half reliabilities computed for the five attitude scales ranged from .68 to .86. Interscale correlation coefficients ranged from .33 to .62.

BIBLIOGRAPHY:

Hereford, C. F. *Changing Parental Attitudes Through Group Discussion.* Austin, Texas: University of Texas Press, 1963.

*Prepared by Carl F. Hereford and Orval G. Johnson*

---

# PARENT OF RETARDED CHILD ATTITUDE SURVEY

AUTHORS: Edward J. Gumz and Jaber F. Gubrium

AGE: Parents of retarded children

VARIABLE: Attitudes toward a retarded child

TYPE OF MEASURE: Likert-type questionnaire

SOURCE FROM WHICH MEASURE MAY BE OBTAINED: Jaber F. Gubrium, Marquette University, Department of Sociology, Milwaukee, Wisconsin 53201.

DESCRIPTION OF MEASURE: The survey consists of thirty-two Likert-type items designed to obtain the attitudes of parents toward the crisis of having a mentally retarded child, the child in extrafamilial roles, and the child in future roles. Both expressive and instrumental aspects of these three dimensions are tapped.

As examples, the first five of the thirty-two items of the survey are given below. The parent responds on a 4-point scale ranging from "strongly agree" to "strongly disagree."

1. When I think of having a handicapped child I am most concerned about the added expense of providing help for him/her.

2. I think that having a handicapped child has caused everyone in our family to adjust in our daily routine.

3. It is important to me that my handicapped child obtains a high school diploma.

4. The handicapped child takes a lot of additional time and I worry about neglecting my other children.

5. It really doesn't make too much difference what kind of grades my child eventually will get in school, as long as he/she gets along well with other children.

RELIABILITY AND VALIDITY: None reported.

BIBLIOGRAPHY:

Gumz, E. J., and Gubrium, J. F. "Comparative Parental Perceptions of a Mentally Retarded Child." *American Journal of Mental Deficiency*, 1972, 77, 175-180.

*Prepared by Jaber F. Gubrium*

---

# PARENTAL ATTITUDE SCALE (PAS)

AUTHORS: Ruth Doris Sinay, Alvin Yusin, and Kazuo Nihira

AGE: Mothers of adolescent youngsters

VARIABLE: Parent's present-day attitudes about their adolescent's behavior

TYPE OF MEASURE: Rating scale

SOURCE FROM WHICH MEASURE MAY BE OBTAINED: Ruth Sinay, Child/Adolescent Psychological Services and Training Programs, Los Angeles County USC Medical Center, 1934 Hospital Place, Los Angeles, California 90033.

DESCRIPTION OF MEASURE: The Parental Attitude Scale (PAS) analyzes parents' present-day attitudes about the adolescent's behaviors in social, familial, and educational interactions. It is made up of forty statements derived from sentences that reflect common concerns parents have in dealing with their adolescents. Parents indicate the extent to which the statements on the PAS scale best fit the way their adolescent acts, thinks, and feels. Choices range from "never" to "always" on a 5-point scale. The items are grouped into ten subscales by face validity, as follows: positive parent-child communication, depreciatory behaviors, positive affectional expression, negative affectional expression, externally disciplined behaviors, self-disciplined behaviors, prosocial behaviors, antisocial behaviors, sexual behaviors, and drug-taking behaviors.

As examples, the first ten of the forty scale items are given below.

1. My child talks with me about all his (her) feelings.

2. My child says nice things about me to other people.
3. My child is affectionate with me.
4. My child thinks I'm old-fashioned.
5. My child hates me.
6. My child loves me.
7. My child does what I tell him (her).
8. My child is satisfied with me as a parent.
9. My child enjoys talking with me.
10. My child helps me around the house.

RELIABILITY AND VALIDITY: The ten subscale classifications of the PAS were confirmed by a correlational analysis of the PAS items and by checking reliability with regard to internal consistency. Internal consistency reliabilities of subscales, estimated by the Spearman-Brown formula, ranged from .83 to .46 with a mean of .69. In addition, a factor analysis of the subscales was performed. In the analysis, the first three factors were rotated orthogonally to the varimax criterion. The bipolar factors extracted are: the gratifying adolescent vs. the nongratifying adolescent, the loving adolescent vs. the rebellious adolescent, and the nondelinquent, self-controlled adolescent vs. the prodelinquent, impulse-ridden delinquent.

BIBLIOGRAPHY:

Sinay, R., Nihira, K., and Yusin, A. "Crisis in Adolescence: Parental Attitudes of Children's Behavior." Paper presented at the annual meeting of the Orthopsychiatry Association. San Francisco, April 1974.

---

## PARENTAL ATTITUDES TOWARD
## MENTALLY RETARDED CHILDREN SCALE

AUTHOR: Harold D. Love

AGE: 18 to 65 years

VARIABLE: Attitudes toward mentally retarded children

TYPE OF MEASURE: Rating scale

SOURCE FROM WHICH MEASURE MAY BE OBTAINED: Harold D. Love, Special Education Department, University of Central Arkansas, Conway, Arkansas 72032. Cost: $1.00 per copy.

DESCRIPTION OF MEASURE: The instrument consists of a list of thirty statements about mentally retarded children. The parent indicates with a checkmark whether he strongly agrees, agrees, disagrees, or strongly disagrees with the statement, or if he is undecided. The higher the score the more positive attitude toward mentally retarded children. The possible range of scores is from 30 to 150.

As examples, the first five of the thirty items on the scale are given below.

1. Mentally retarded children are usually better off in mental institutions.
2. I would not mind if my child sat by a mentally retarded child in the classroom.
3. If I were an employer, I would hire a mentally retarded person.
4. There is a high relationship between immorality and mental retardation.
5. Mentally retarded adults tend to lower the standard of living of their neighbors.

RELIABILITY AND VALIDITY: Split-half reliabilities corrected with the Spearman-Brown formula were computed for two groups. The coefficient of reliability is .91, using the scores of sixty-two parents in Greeley, Colorado, and .92 when using the scores of 200 parents in southern Louisiana.

BIBLIOGRAPHY:

Love, H. D. "Characteristics of Parents Having Mentally Retarded Children as Compared with Parents Not Having Mentally Retarded Children." *Digest of the Mentally Retarded,* 1967-1968, *4,* 103-106.
Love, H. D. *Parental Attitudes Toward Exceptional Children.* Springfield, Illinois: C. C Thomas, 1970.

---

# PEOPLE TEST

AUTHORS: Sandra C. Koslin, Bertram L. Koslin, and Richard Pargament

AGE: Grades 2 to 12

VARIABLE: Students' racial attitudes

TYPE OF MEASURE: Nonverbal social-distance scale

SOURCE FROM WHICH MEASURE MAY BE OBTAINED: Riverside Research Institute, 80 West End Avenue, New York, New York 10023. Limited supplies in inventory; prices available upon request. Scoring services available at additional cost.

DESCRIPTION OF MEASURE: The People Test is a quasi-disguised and quasi-structured method for representing in geometric distance the cognitive and affective social distances that exist between children as a function of race and sex. The cognitive and affective distinctions that a student makes between people are inferred from how close together he clusters drawings of those people when instructed to cluster as a function of similarity. The technique is derived principally from judgment theory and extends the logic of the work of Bogardus with social distance. Students are asked to make two sets of proximity judgments concerning pairs of social stimuli. One set of judgments involves making distinctions between generalized others, and the second set involves making distinctions between oneself and others. Children are presented with a set of age-appropriate figures who vary by race and by sex. A raceless, sexless self-figure is also introduced. All possible pairs of these figures are constituted and presented to students in a format where one figure of each pair is fixed and the other figure is movable. The subject's task is to place the movable figure of the pair somewhere along the available response scale to reflect the degree to which the figures are alike. Test items are scored by measuring the distance between target figures; a centimeter scale printed on the test page facilitates the scoring. Data are typically reduced using analysis of variance to compare the distances placed between various pairs of figures as a function of student race, sex, age, and so forth, and as a function of the type of school racial composition the student has been exposed to. One important empirical application of the measure is in assessing attitudinal outcomes associated with alternative racial balance policies.

RELIABILITY AND VALIDITY: Individual item test-retest reliabilities for a fifth-grade population on an earlier version of the test ranged from $.65 \leqslant r \leqslant .75$ for distance judgments involving the self and $.32 \leqslant r \leqslant .50$ for distance judgments not involving the self. Since these correlations are based on individual test items, they are considered acceptably high. Reliability data for the current test forms are not available but should be higher than for earlier forms because the latest format was designed to help students anchor their judgmental scales more rapidly. Several types of evidence indicate the People Test's validity. Developmental changes shown by students in racial and sexual distances on the People Test correspond to developmental changes in racial and sexual attitudes well established in the literature. There is strong intersubject agreement concerning the normative (socially standardized) distances between the races and the sexes. Multidimensional scaling analysis has recovered the dimensions built into the stimulus figures. It has been demonstrated that students with extreme prowhite attitudes place significantly less distance between self and white target figures than students with extreme problack attitudes. Those with extreme problack attitudes place less distance between self and black figures than do students with prowhite attitudes.

BIBLIOGRAPHY:

Koslin, S. C. "The Measurement of Schoolchildren's Racial Attitudes: A Validation Study." Paper presented at the meetings of the Eastern Psychological Association. Philadelphia, Pennsylvania, April 1969.

Koslin, S. C., Amarel, M., and Ames, N. "A Distance Measure of Racial Attitudes in Primary Grade Children: An Exploratory Study." *Psychology in the Schools,* 1969, *6,* 382-385.

Koslin, S. C., Koslin, B. L., and Pargament, R. "Relationships Between Educational Integration Policies and Students' Racial Attitudes." Paper presented at the meetings of the American Educational Research Association. New York, February 1971.

Koslin, S. C., Koslin, B. L., and Pargament, R. "Efficacy of School Integration Policies in Reducing Racial Polarization." Paper presented at the meetings of the American Psychological Association. Honolulu, Hawaii, September 1972.

Koslin, S. C., Koslin, B. L., Pargament, R., and Bird, H. *The Development of Norma-*

*tive Racial and Sexual Social Distance Beliefs.* New York: Riverside Research Institute, 1971.

Koslin, S. C., Koslin, B. L., Pargament, R., and Waxman, H. "Classroom Racial Balance and Students' Interracial Attitudes." *Sociology of Education,* 1972, *45,* 386-407.

---

# PICK-A-CLASS TEST

AUTHORS: Sandra C. Koslin, Bertram L. Koslin, and Richard Pargament

AGE: Primary to early intermediate grades

VARIABLE: Students' racial attitudes

TYPE OF MEASURE: Nonverbal preference scale

SOURCE FROM WHICH MEASURE MAY BE OBTAINED: Riverside Research Institute, 80 West End Avenue, New York, New York 10023. Limited supplies in inventory; prices available upon request. Scoring services available at additional cost.

DESCRIPTION OF MEASURE: The Pick-a-Class Test employs the method of paired comparisons to measure, in a nonverbal, semidisguised form, student preferences for black or white teachers and black, white, or racially mixed classmates. Sketches portray classes engaged in three different activities, and the racial composition of each class is varied in six different ways to complete all possible combinations of teacher-race and class-racial composition. The eighteen sketches resulting from these race-by-activity combinations are arranged in a series of paired comparisons, and students are asked to select which class of each pair they would prefer to be in. In some comparisons teacher race is varied while peer race is held constant; in other comparisons peer race is varied while teacher race is held constant. Classroom activity is varied in all comparisons. Because the different racial compositions are embedded within different class activities on each page, it is difficult for the student to infer which aspect(s) of the stimuli are important to the tester. Hence the purpose of the preference task is somewhat disguised. No child is ever confronted with having to choose between two pictures varying only in racial composition. Students' preference scores are based on their pattern (consistency) of responses with regard to the racial composition of the stimuli. Scores are computed separately for teacher preference, for peer preference when a white teacher is portrayed, and for peer preference when a black teacher is portrayed.

RELIABILITY AND VALIDITY: In a test-retest reliability study of 200 third graders, 70 percent of the students had identical pretest and posttest scores for racial preferences for teachers, and 55 percent and 58 percent had identical pretest and posttest scores for classmate preferences where teachers were white and black, respectively.

Nearly all remaining students had highly similar posttest-pretest scores. Only 2 percent reversed their racial preferences from the pretest to the posttest. Using Guttman's procedure for estimating the reliability of nominal data, reliability boundaries for the teacher-preference subtest were estimated as $.57 \leqslant p \leqslant .75$; for classmate preferences with a black teacher, $.45 \leqslant p \leqslant .68$; and for classmate preferences with a white teacher, $.41 \leqslant p \leqslant .64$. Evidence for test validity may be inferred from the fact that when the test is administered, white students tend overwhelmingly to choose white classmates and teachers, whereas black students strongly prefer black teachers and classmates. Scores on the test have also been found to be sensitive to school racial balance policies; less polarization of racial preferences on the Pick-a-Class Test has been observed under conditions of greater classroom racial balance, where other attitude measures also had indicated reduced racial polarization.

BIBLIOGRAPHY:

Koslin, S. "The Measurement of Schoolchildren's Racial Attitudes: A Validation Study." Paper presented at the meetings of the Eastern Psychological Association. Philadelphia, Pennsylvania, April 1969.
Koslin, S., Amarel, M., and Ames, H. "The Effect of Race on Peer Evaluation and Preference in Primary Grade Children: An Exploratory Study." *Journal of Negro Education,* 1970, *39,* 346-350.
Koslin, S., Koslin, B. L., and Pargament, R. "Relationships Between Educational Integration Policies and Students' Racial Attitudes." Paper presented at the meetings of the American Educational Research Association. New York, February 1971.
Koslin, S., Koslin, B. L., and Pargament, R. "Efficacy of School Integration Policies in Reducing Racial Polarization." Paper presented at the meetings of the American Psychological Association. Honolulu, Hawaii, September 1972.
Koslin, S., Koslin, B. L., Pargament, R., and Waxman, H. "Classroom Racial Balance and Students' Interracial Attitudes." *Sociology of Education,* 1972, *45,* 386-407.

# PRESCHOOL RACIAL ATTITUDE MEASURE (PRAM)

AUTHOR: John E. Williams

AGE: 3 to 9 years

VARIABLE: Evaluative responses to Euro- and Afro-American persons

TYPE OF MEASURE: Picture-story interview

SOURCE FROM WHICH MEASURE MAY BE OBTAINED: John E. Williams, Department of Psychology, Box 775, Wake Forest University, Winston-Salem, North Carolina

27109. Cost: Manual, no cost; 36 8 X 10-inch color photos, purchase $125.00 or rental $25.00.

DESCRIPTION OF MEASURE: The Preschool Racial Attitude Measure (PRAM) assesses the attitudes of preliterate children toward Euro-American and Afro-American persons. PRAM is a picture-story technique in which attitudes are assessed by means of the child's response to simple evaluative adjectives contained in the stories he is told. The original version of the procedure—PRAM I—is described by Williams and Roberson (1967). The lengthened and revised version—PRAM II—is described by Williams, Best, Boswell, Mattson, and Graves (1975). The PRAM II test materials consist of thirty-six colored photographs and thirty-six associated stories. Twenty-four of the pictures and stories are used in the assessment of racial attitude, while the remaining twelve are used to obtain the control sex-role awareness score. The twenty-four racial-attitude pictures each depict drawings of two dark-haired human figures that are identical in all respects except that one has a pinkish-tan skin color (Euro-American) while the other has a medium-brown skin color (Afro-American). The twelve pictures used for the sex-role items each display a male and female figure of the same general age and of the same race, with half of the pictures representing Euro-Americans and half Afro-Americans.

The PRAM II racial-attitude responses and sex-role responses are scored in the following manner. The racial-attitude score is determined by counting 1 point for the selection of the light-skinned figure in response to a positive adjective and 1 point for the selection of a dark-skinned figure in response to a negative adjective. The racial-attitude total score based on all twenty-four items thus has a range of 0 to 24, with high scores indicating a pro-Euro/anti-Afro bias, low scores indicating a pro-Afro/anti-Euro bias, and mid-range scores (around 12) indicating no bias. The twelve sex-role items are scored by giving 1 point for each sex-appropriate response, yielding a possible score range of 0 to 12.

The basic standardization group for PRAM II consists of 272 preschool children from Winston-Salem, North Carolina, who were tested in 1970-1972. The children ranged in age from 37 months to 85 months, with a mean age of 65 months (SD = 7.64). Half of the children were Euro-American and half were Afro-American, with each race group composed of equal numbers of males and females. Half of each race-sex group were tested by female Euro examiners and half by female Afro examiners. Standardization data are also available for 458 elementary-school-age children in grades 1 through 4 (Williams, Best, and Boswell, 1975).

As examples, the first five of the thirty-six items of the measure are given below.

1. *SR—Euro girl—Euro boy sitting*
   Here are two children. One of these children has four dolls with which they like to have tea parties. Which child likes to play with dolls?
2. *RA—Afro little boy—Euro little boy—walking*
   Here are two little boys. One of them is a kind little boy. Once he saw a kitten fall into a lake and he picked up the kitten to save it from drowning. Which is the kind little boy?
3. *RA—Euro little girl—Afro little girl—standing*
   Here are two little girls. One of them is an ugly little girl. People do not like to look at her. Which is the ugly little girl?

4. *SR—Afro teenage boy—Afro teenage girl—sitting*
   Here are two children. They are thinking about what they want to be when they grow up. One of them wants to be a policeman. Which one wants to be a policeman?
5. *RA—Euro teenage boy—Afro teenage boy—standing*
   Here are two boys. One of them is a friendly boy. He has a lot of friends. Which one is the friendly boy?

RELIABILITY AND VALIDITY: The internal consistency of the test at the preschool level is .80, and the test-retest reliability, from age 4 to age 5, is .55. The high correlation between scores on the first twelve items and second twelve items (.71), and the virtually identical means (A = 8.20; B = 8.24) and standard deviations (A = 2.74; B = 2.79), indicate that the two halves can be considered as equivalent twelve-item short forms of PRAM II. The construct validity of PRAM II rests on the fact that the procedure is a downward extension of the evaluation factor of the semantic differential, which has shown to be an effective way of assessing attitudes among older children and young adults. The use of the evaluation-factor rationale at the preschool level is supported by a series of studies that have demonstrated the existence of the evaluation factor in the semantic space of the 5-year-old child (Edwards and Williams, 1970; Gordon and Williams, 1973; McMurtry and Williams, 1972). In a study of concurrent validity, Mabe (1974) demonstrated that PRAM II scores correlated .52 with frequency of sociometric choice of Euro-American classmates among second-grade children in an integrated public school.

BIBLIOGRAPHY:

Best, D. L. "Race of Examiner Effects on the Racial Attitude Responses of Preschool Children." Unpublished master's thesis. Wake Forest University, Winston-Salem, North Carolina, 1972.

Best, D. L., Smith, S. C., Graves, D. J., and Williams, J. E. "The Modification of Racial Bias in Preschool Children." *Journal of Experimental Child Psychology*, 1975, *20*, 193-205.

Edwards, C. D., and Williams, J. E. "Generalizations Between Evaluative Words Associated with Racial Figures in Preschool Children." *Journal of Experimental Research in Personality*, 1970, *4*, 144-155.

Gordon, L. H., and Williams, J. E. "Secondary Factors in the Affective Meaning System of the Preschool Child." *Developmental Psychology*, 1973, *8*, 25-34.

Mabe III, P. A. "The Correlation of Racial Attitudes as Measured by the Preschool Racial Attitude Measure and Sociometric Choices for Second-Grade Children." Unpublished master's thesis. East Carolina University, Greenville, North Carolina, 1974.

McMurtry, C. A., and Williams, J. E. "The Evaluation Dimension of the Affective Meaning System of the Preschool Child." *Developmental Psychology*, 1972, *6*, 238-246.

Williams, J. E. *Preschool Racial Attitude Measure II (PRAM II): General Information and Manual of Directions*. Department of Psychology, Wake Forest University, Winston-Salem, North Carolina, 1971.

Williams, J. E., Best, D. L., and Boswell, D. A. "The Measurement of Children's Racial Attitudes in the Early School Years." *Child Development*, 1975, *46*, 494-500.

Williams, J. E., Best, D. L., Boswell, D. A., Mattson, L. A., and Graves, D. J. "Preschool Racial Attitude Measure II." *Educational and Psychological Measurement,* 1975, *35,* 3-18.

Williams, J. E., Boswell, D. A., and Best, D. L. "Evaluative Responses of Preschool Children to the Colors White and Black." *Child Development,* 1975, *46,* 501-508.

Williams, J. E., and Edwards, C. D. "An Exploratory Study of the Modification of Color Concepts and Racial Attitudes in Preschool Children." *Child Development,* 1969, *40,* 737-750.

Williams, J. E., and Roberson, J. K. "A Method of Assessing Racial Attitudes in Preschool Children." *Educational and Psychological Measurement,* 1967, *27,* 671-689.

Williams, K. H., Williams, J. E., and Beck, R. C. "Assessing Children's Racial Attitudes via a Signal Detection Model." *Perceptual and Motor Skills,* 1973, *36,* 587-598.

---

## RATING SCALE OF CHILDREN'S ATTITUDES TOWARD THE PHYSICALLY HANDICAPPED

AUTHORS: Jacqueline Rapier, Ruth Adelson, Richard Carey, and Katherine Croke

AGE: 8 to 12 years

VARIABLE: Attitudes towards the physically handicapped

TYPE OF MEASURE: Rating scale

SOURCE FROM WHICH MEASURE MAY BE OBTAINED: Jacqueline Rapier, 110 Webster Street, Palo Alto, California 94301.

DESCRIPTION OF MEASURE: The Rating Scale of Children's Attitudes Toward the Physically Handicapped is a group-administered instrument loosely based on the semantic-differential technique. The measure consists of twenty pairs of polar adjectives describing children's characteristics, arranged on a 3-point scale. Children are asked to respond to one of three verbal categories. This rating scale was developed for research purposes only, and it is not intended for individual or classroom use.

As examples, the first five of the twenty items of the scale are given below.

| | | |
|---|---|---|
| 1. need help | don't need help | need lots of help |
| 2. are friendly | are unfriendly | are very unfriendly |
| 3. are happy | are unhappy | are very unhappy |
| 4. want attention | want little or no attention | want lots of attention |
| 5. work fast | work slow | do not work |

RELIABILITY AND VALIDITY: None reported.

BIBLIOGRAPHY:

Rapier, J., Adelson, R., Carey, R., and Croke, K. "Changes in Children's Attitudes Toward the Physically Handicapped." *Exceptional Children,* 1972, *39,* 219-223.

---

## REED SCIENCE ACTIVITY INVENTORY

AUTHOR: Horace B. Reed

AGE: Upper elementary, junior, and senior high school

VARIABLE: Science interest

TYPE OF MEASURE: Rating scale

SOURCE FROM WHICH MEASURE MAY BE OBTAINED: Horace B. Reed, School of Education, University of Massachusetts, Amherst, Massachusetts 01002.

DESCRIPTION OF MEASURE: The instrument uses manifest interests or actual activities, rather than statements of preferences or wishes. There are seventy items with a 6-point frequency scale for each item. It is aimed at grades 7 to 10 but may be adapted to other levels. The score range is 0-350, and the test requires about 15 minutes to complete. Items that tap both male and female activities are included. Factor analysis of the seventy items suggests four main subcomponents of science interests: a general science dimension, "woodsy, birdsy" factor, science tinkerer, and "thinking about" science concepts.

As examples, the first ten of the seventy items of the inventory are given below. The respondent replies to how often he has done these things voluntarily, because he was interested, during the current school year by circling one answer on the 6-point scale ranging from "never" to "very often."

1. Read newspaper articles concerning scientific things, because I like to.
2. Visited the pet section of stores to watch birds, fish, etc.
3. Spent my own money for scientific things.
4. Built or repaired radio sets or other electronic equipment, because I am interested.
5. Tried to predict the weather from clouds, temperature, and other things.
6. Made extra drawings of animals or plants.
7. Used a home chemistry set.
8. Listened to scientific talks on the radio, because I am interested.
9. Worked on my rock collection or tried to figure out reasons for local land formations.
10. Made extra drawings of scientific equipment.

RELIABILITY AND VALIDITY: Split-half reliability computed from responses of 1,945 ninth-grade pupils, when corrected by the Spearman-Brown formula, was .97. Logical validity is based on the idea of establishing greater predictability of interest by using actual participation, rather than statements of likes and dislikes.

BIBLIOGRAPHY:

Cooley, W., and Reed, H. B. "The Measurement of Science Interests: An Operational and Multidimensional Approach." *Science Education,* 1961, *45,* 320-326.
Cooley, W., and Reed, H. B. "Implications for Science Education of a Teacher Competence Research." *Science Education,* 1962, *46,* 473-486.
Reed, H. B. "Teacher Variables of Warmth, Demand, and Utilization of Intrinsic Motivation Related to Pupils' Science Interests." *Journal of Experimental Education,* 1961, *29,* 205-229.

## RELIGIOUS BELIEF QUESTIONNAIRE

AUTHORS: Walter J. Smith and Max Apfeldorf

AGE: 12 years and up

VARIABLE: Religious beliefs and attitudes

TYPE OF MEASURE: Likert-type questionnaire

SOURCE FROM WHICH MEASURE MAY BE OBTAINED: Max Apfeldorf, Veterans Administration Center, Martinsburg, West Virginia 25401.

DESCRIPTION OF MEASURE: This was constructed as a multidenominational religious belief questionnaire designed to be relevant to all individuals in the Judaeo-Christian tradition. There are two alternative forms, each containing sixty-four items and yielding a range of scores from 64 to 320. The categories of belief and attitude and the number of items for each are: God's existence and control of the universe (20), prayer (9), the Bible (4), good and evil consequences (11), organized religion (7), religious practices (6), and duties of daily living (7). The pool of items from which the two forms were derived consisted of 338 statements. The original 338-item scale was administered to all chaplains in the Veterans Administration hospital system. Approximately 57 percent of the chaplains returned completed questionnaires. Means and standard deviations on all items were obtained. In order to check on the validity of assignment of each item to its category, ninety theological students (thirty from each major faith group) were asked to sort the items into the nine categories. Items assigned to their original categories by 75 percent or more of the judges were retained. Of the remaining items, all with a standard deviation of more than 1 were discarded. The items remaining were separated into two parallel forms; the sixty-four items were matched item for item by mean value.

As examples, the first item from each of the seven categories is given below.

1. I am sometimes very conscious of the presence of God.
21. I feel spiritually better after prayer.
30. I believe that the Bible is the word of God.
34. Our good actions are rewarded only by the praise and thanks of people we are good to.
45. The church (synagogue) works to have peace and good will take the place of hate and fighting in the world.
52. I believe in keeping the Sabbath.
58. We should visit the sick when the visit is welcomed by the patient.

RELIABILITY AND VALIDITY: Interform reliability (Form A vs. Form B) was .95 based on a population of fifty-three VA medical and surgical patients. Split-half, odd-even reliability for the same population was .95 for Form A and .96 for Form B. Both forms correlated .69 with the Religious Scale of the Study of Values (Waldrop version). The score of Form A of the Religious Belief Questionnaire correlated .72 with the Religious Scale of the Study of Values (Waldrop version) for fifty-four high school boys. A correlation of .53 was obtained between the two scales for sixty-eight school girls. The Religious Belief Questionnaire correlated .62 with the Religious Behavior Questionnaire in the population of fifty-three VA medical and surgical patients. A correlation of .48 between the Religious Belief Questionnaire and the Religious Behavior Checklist was found in the same population of medical surgical patients.

BIBLIOGRAPHY:

Apfeldorf, M. "Multidenominational Instruments for the Measurement of Religious Belief and Behavior." *PIRI Newsletter,* 1973, *23* (11), 4-6.
Apfeldorf, M., Smith, W. J., and Nagley, R. "Religious Beliefs and Other Values of High School Students." *Psychological Reports,* 1974, *35,* 811-816.
Smith, W. J. "Difficulties in Constructing Instruments to Measure Religious Belief and Behavior." *PIRI Newsletter,* 1974, *24* (8), 4-5.
Smith, W. J., and Apfeldorf, M. "Multidenominational Instruments for the Assessment of Religious Belief and Behavior." Paper presented at the twentieth annual meeting of the Society for the Scientific Study of Religion. Boston, Massachusetts, October 1969.

*Prepared by W. J. Smith and M. Apfeldorf*

---

# ROKEACH VALUE SURVEY

AUTHOR: Milton Rokeach

AGE: 11 to 90 years

VARIABLE: Human values

TYPE OF MEASURE: Ranking measure

SOURCE FROM WHICH MEASURE MAY BE OBTAINED: Halgren Tests, 873 Persimmon Avenue, Sunnyvale, California 94087.

DESCRIPTION OF MEASURE: The Rokeach Value Survey provides a simple method for measuring human values. It consists of eighteen terminal values—end-states of existence —and eighteen instrumental values—modes of behavior. The respondent ranks each set of eighteen values in order of their importance. The average adult requires about 15 minutes to complete the rankings. Form D of the Value Survey, which employs a gummed-label technique of ranking, has been successfully used with respondents from 11 to 90 years of age.

RELIABILITY AND VALIDITY: Test-retest reliabilities were obtained for each of the values considered separately for time intervals ranging from three to seven weeks. For terminal values, the reliabilities range from .51 for a sense of accomplishment to .88 for salvation. For instrumental values, individual reliabilities range from .45 for responsible to .70 for ambitious. For additional information, see Rokeach (1971b). Reliability of total value system was obtained for each subject by correlating the rankings obtained from test and retest data. The table below shows the median reliabilities obtained for three samples of college students:

| N | Sample | Time between Test-Retest | Terminal Value Scale | Instrumental Value Scale |
|---|--------|--------------------------|----------------------|--------------------------|
| 26 | Seventh grade | 3 weeks | .62 | .53 |
| 26 | Ninth grade | 3 weeks | .63 | .61 |
| 26 | Eleventh grade | 3 weeks | .74 | .71 |
| 117 | College | 3 weeks | .78 | .72 |
| 36 | College | 4.5 weeks | .80 | .70 |
| 100 | College | 7 weeks | .78 | .71 |
| 108 | College | 3-5 months | .73 | — |
| 103 | College | 15-17 months | .65 | — |
| 32 | Adults | 12 weeks | .74 | — |

BIBLIOGRAPHY:

Beech, R. P., and Schoeppe, A. "Development of Value Systems in Adolescents." *Developmental Psychology*, 1974, *10*, 644-656.

Cochrane, R., and Rokeach, M. "Rokeach's Value Survey: A Methodological Note." *Journal of Experimental Research in Personality*, 1970, *4*, 159-161.

Feather, N. T. "Educational Choice and Student Attitudes in Relation to Terminal and Instrumental Values." *Australian Journal of Psychology*, 1970, *22*, 127-144.

Feather, N. T. "Value Systems in State and Church Schools." *Australian Journal of Psychology*, 1970, *22*, 299-313.

Feather, N. T. "Similarity of Value Systems as a Determinant of Educational Choice at University Level." *Australian Journal of Psychology*, 1971, *23*, 201-211.

Homant, R. "Semantic Differential Ratings and the Rank-Ordering of Values." *Educational and Psychological Measurement*, 1969, *29*, 885-889.

Homant, R. "Denotative Meaning of Values." *Personality*, 1970, *1*, 213-219.

Homant, R., and Rokeach, M. "Value for Honesty and Cheating Behavior." *Personality*, 1970, *1*, 153-162.

Penner, L., Homant, R., and Rokeach, M. "Comparison of Rank-Order and Paired-Comparison Methods for Measuring Value Systems." *Perceptual and Motor Skills,* 1968, *27,* 417-418.

Raymond, B., Damino, J., and Kandel, N. "Sex Stereotyping in Values: A Comparison of Three Generations and Two Sexes." *Perceptual and Motor Skills,* 1974, *39,* 163-166.

Rim, Y. "Values and Attitudes." *Personality,* 1970, *1,* 243-250.

Rokeach, M. *Beliefs, Attitudes, and Values.* San Francisco: Jossey-Bass, 1968.

Rokeach, M. "A Theory of Organization and Change Within Value-Attitude Systems." *Journal of Social Issues,* 1968, *24,* 13-33.

Rokeach, M. "The Role of Values in Public Opinion Research." *Public Opinion Quarterly,* 1968-1969, *32,* 547-559.

Rokeach, M. "Religious Values and Social Compassion." *Review of Religious Research,* 1969, *11,* 24-38.

Rokeach, M. "Value Systems and Religion." *Review of Religious Research,* 1969, *11,* 2-23.

Rokeach, M. "Faith, Hope, and Bigotry." *Psychology Today,* 1970, *3,* 33-37, 58.

Rokeach, M. "Long-Range Modification of Values, Attitudes, and Behavior." *American Psychologist,* 1971a, *26,* 453-459.

Rokeach, M. "The Measurement of Values and Value Systems." In G. Abcarian and J. W. Soule (Eds.), *Social Psychology and Political Behavior.* Columbus, Ohio: Merrill, 1971b.

Rokeach, M. *The Nature of Human Values.* New York: Macmillan, 1973.

Rokeach, M., Homant, R., and Penner, L. "A Value Analysis of the Disputed Federalist Papers." *Journal of Personality and Social Psychology,* 1970, *16,* 245-250.

Rokeach, M., Miller, M. G., and Snyder, J. A. "The Value Gap Between Police and Policed." *Journal of Social Issues,* 1971, *27,* 155-171.

Rokeach, M., and Parker, S. "Values as Social Indicators of Poverty and Race Relations in America." *Annals of the American Academy of Political and Social Science,* March 1970.

Shotland, R. L., and Berger, W. G. "Behavioral Validation of Several Values from the Rokeach Value Scale as an Index of Honesty." *Journal of Applied Psychology,* 1970, *54,* 433-435.

---

## RUBRIC FOR EXPRESSED VALUES (REV III)

AUTHORS: Prudence Dyer and Richard Brooks

AGE: 6 years and older

VARIABLE: Cultural values expressed in oral and written communication

TYPE OF MEASURE: Content-analysis system

SOURCE FROM WHICH MEASURE MAY BE OBTAINED: Prudence Dyer or Richard Brooks, Drake University, Des Moines, Iowa 50311. Cost: $2.50.

DESCRIPTION OF MEASURE: The Rubric for Expressed Values (REV III) is an instrument used to judge cultural values expressed in written or oral communication. The scale is based upon the theories of Spindler (1955) that the values of any culture may be described in four categories and that the values in any culture are in movement between traditional and emergent positions, with the emergent positions of one generation becoming the traditional values of the next. His categories, which describe the values of any culture, are those relating to an ethical code, concepts of success, concepts of self and others, and an orientation to time. REV III is an instrument that identifies a number of subcategories in each of Spindler's major divisions and describes how these are expressed throughout a continuum from extremely conservative to extremely liberal positions. Each of the five positions identified on the scale is descriptive but not exhaustive of the values frequently and characteristically expressed by persons espousing one of these points of view: refluent (reactionary), traditional, transitional, integrative, and transformative. REV III is used as a summary guide by trained observers; interscorer reliability may be established in several short practice sessions. Students or other subjects of the research do not see or use it. Values expressed by individuals in open-ended compositions, in printed documents, in group discussion, or in small-group situations may be recorded by the use of tally marks directly on the scale or in an open grid corresponding to the scale.

As an example, one of the twenty "cells" (four value categories X five points of view) is given below. It describes the concept of self/others from the traditional point of view.

*Individualism*
—Believes self is basis for success.
—Values rights and freedoms for those "like me."
—Admires, respects elders, family.
—Demands respect for authority, age.
—Forms friendships with families "like mine."
—Admires those of higher status.
—Believes others "like me" can succeed.
—Supports successful aesthetic pursuits.

RELIABILITY AND VALIDITY: The scale was developed through established procedures of identification of a range of values expressed in contemporary literature, the mass media, or from other public forums. One set of judges sorted these into positions in the matrix of the rubric; another set of judges generated statements characteristic of values expressed by known groups. Comparisons and refinements produced the current scale. Validation data and interscorer reliability data have been reported. The interscorer reliability coefficient was found to be .94.

BIBLIOGRAPHY:

Dyer, P. "An Encounter: Humanities and Values." *Bulletin of Research in Humanities Education*, 1970, *1*, 11-12.

Dyer, P. "Expressed Values of Students and Schools." *Delta Kappa Gamma Bulletin*, 1970, *36*, 27-37.

Dyer, P. "Changing Values of Students." *Elementary English,* 1972, *49,* 697-705.

Dyer, P. "Youth in Contemporary Greece: An Exploratory Study of the Expressed Values of Selected Greek Youth." Mimeographed. Drake University, Des Moines, Iowa; and the National Centre for Social Research, Athens, Greece, 1973.

Spindler, G. D. "Education in a Transforming American Culture." *Harvard Educational Review,* 1955, *35,* 145-156.

*Prepared by Prudence Dyer and Richard Brooks*

---

# SEAMAN'S ATTITUDE INVENTORY

AUTHOR: Janet A. Seaman

AGE: Grade 6 reading level and up

VARIABLE: Attitudes of the handicapped toward physical education

TYPE OF MEASURE: Likert-type scale

SOURCE FROM WHICH MEASURE MAY BE OBTAINED: Educational Studies Center for Adapted Physical Education, Department of Physical Education, California State University, 5151 State University Drive, Los Angeles, California 90032. Cost: $5.00 for inventory, scoring plate, clustered items.

DESCRIPTION OF MEASURE: The Seaman Attitude Inventory consists of forty items that assess attitudes of the handicapped toward physical education. The items were rated by twenty-two judges as to their favorability or unfavorability toward physical education. Favorable items or ones judged to be in support of physical education are scored 5 points for a "strongly agree" response; a score of 1 point is given for a "strongly disagree" response to the same item. Four categories into which the items clustered were judged by a panel of experts to be: social development, psychological effects, administration, and physical effects.

As examples, selected items from each of the four categories of the inventory are given below.

*Social Development*
1. Physical education provides leadership opportunities for everyone.
2. Learning to play in a group is a major contribution of physical education to one's personality.

*Psychological Effects*
1. It is not possible for everyone to be good at every game, but it is fun to try.
2. Physical education helps to work off emotional tensions.

*Administration*
1. Teachers of physical education take into consideration the physical needs of the students.

2. In a physical education class everyone should be allowed to participate.
*Physical Effects*
1. One who participates in physical education looks healthy.
2. I do not want to be in good physical condition.

RELIABILITY AND VALIDITY: The reliability of the attitude inventory, as determined by the coefficient of internal consistency, was .96 when corrected by the Spearman-Brown formula. The external validity of the inventory was determined by correlating the responses on the inventory with responses on a 5-point self-rating scale. Forty-one orthopedically and neurologically handicapped subjects in remedial physical education classes and thirty-two similar subjects in regular physical education classes responded to both instruments. Coefficients of validity for the two groups were .76 and .71, respectively. Each correlation was statistically different from 0 at the .01 level.

BIBLIOGRAPHY:

Seaman, J. A. "Attitudes of Physically Handicapped Children Toward Physical Education." *Research Quarterly*, 1970, *41*, 439-445.

---

## SEMANTIC DIFFERENTIAL SCALES, ELEMENTARY AND SECONDARY

AUTHOR: Russell N. Cassel

AGE: Elementary, 10 to 14 years; secondary, 14 years and up

VARIABLE: Attitude toward select phenomena

TYPE OF MEASURE: Rating scale

SOURCE FROM WHICH MEASURE MAY BE OBTAINED: See Benfield (1971) and Ludwig (1972) (elementary form); Cassel (1970) (secondary form); or write Project Innovation, 1362 Santa Cruz Court, Chula Vista, California 92010.

DESCRIPTION OF MEASURE: This measure consists of three semantic differentials: thirty adjective-antonyms for the elementary form, thirty-five adjective-antonyms for the secondary form, and another instrument for primary grades using boxes and squares for establishing the ordinal scale value on a Likert-type basis. Five concepts are used in the elementary form: my home and family, rules and law, me as a person, people and friends, and school and learning. The secondary form uses semantic scales that are related to effectiveness in learning, at both the secondary and the college levels. The three important concepts used in the validation of this SD are: teacher, learning, and student. Any number of other pertinent concepts may be used with the same thirty and thirty-five pairs of adjectives. An ordinal scale with five different positions is used for the assessment of the elementary scale. It is scored in Likert fashion. The semantic scales have been reversed in part to eliminate the bias of the rater and to insure that it is not a scale position rating but rather a semantic rating based on the paired adjectives.

As examples, given below are the thirty pairs of adjectives of elementary form used to measure the following concepts: my home and family, rules of law, me as a person, people and friends, and school and learning. Responses are made on a 5-point scale.

| | | |
|---|---|---|
| 1. pleasant/unpleasant | 11. clean/dirty | 21. cruel/kind |
| 2. ugly/beautiful | 12. busy/lazy | 22. colorless/colorful |
| 3. fast/slow | 13. quick/slow | 23. familiar/strange |
| 4. good/bad | 14. new/old | 24. cold/warm |
| 5. weak/strong | 15. wise/foolish | 25. timid/bold |
| 6. dull/sharp | 16. sad/happy | 26. selfish/unselfish |
| 7. deep/shallow | 17. valuable/worthless | 27. clear/confusing |
| 8. heavy/light | 18. hard/soft | 28. easy/difficult |
| 9. dark/bright | 19. interesting/boring | 29. talkative/quiet |
| 10. large/small | 20. excited/calm | 30. neat/messy |

RELIABILITY AND VALIDITY: The reliability score based on internal consistency for 150 items where four separate concept ratings were added was $r = .96$ based on the Kuder-Richardson formula (Benfield, 1971; Ludwig, 1972).

BIBLIOGRAPHY:

Benfield, K. "Comparing Fifth Grade Pupils' Attitude and Ego Development Ratings with Teacher Performance Ratings." Unpublished master's thesis. University of Wisconsin, Milwaukee, 1971.

Cassel, R..N. "Development of a Semantic Differential to Assess the Attitude of Secondary School and College Students." *Journal of Experimental Education,* 1970, *39,* 10-14.

Ludwig, J. "Comparison of Attitudes and Ego-Development of Fifth Grade Pupils for Two Grouping Methods." Unpublished master's thesis. University of Wisconsin, Milwaukee, 1972.

---

# SEMANTIC DIFFERENTIAL VALUE SCALE

AUTHORS: Richard L. Gorsuch and Ruth Arbitman-Smith

AGE: Grades 4 to 6

VARIABLE: Development of basic social values

TYPE OF MEASURE: Questionnaire

SOURCE FROM WHICH MEASURE MAY BE OBTAINED: See Gorsuch (1971).

DESCRIPTION OF MEASURE: Following Scott's (1965) approach to values, the items for the scale were generated by asking children open-ended questions concerning the norms they saw people (parents, teacher, peers, and themselves) holding for them. Analyses of a large number of such items given to a new sample suggested that there was one general factor appearing in lower- and middle-class black and white children. The items in the scale were those that correlated significantly with that general factor in each of the eight samples formed by crossing lower- and middle-class with black and white with boy and girl (and thus were unlikely to reflect, for example, only middle-class norms). On the basis of item content and comparison with another study at the college level, the general factor was labeled *basic value socialization* and appears to reflect the process of learning how to fit into a society. Basic value socialization appears to be a task of the upper-elementary school years, which is normally completed by the sixth grade. Semantic Differential Value Scale can be used with elementary-school children only if the examiner is well trained and has prior experience in administering SD scales to this age level. They are not self-administering and cannot be used successfully by the classroom teacher without training. The scale takes approximately 10 to 15 minutes to administer.

RELIABILITY AND VALIDITY: Separate reliabilities were computed for each of the eight groups formed by crossing social class, race, and sex. Analyses also indicate the scale functions equally well in the fourth and sixth grades. The reliabilities were at the same level (.7 to .8) for each of the groups in the original sample and upon cross-validation. The scale has been found to be predictive of teachers' evaluations of children as personality or behavior problems, of the child's involvement in negatively evaluated value-laden classroom incidents, and of grades.

BIBLIOGRAPHY:

Gorsuch, R. L. *Value Conflict in the School Setting.* Final report, project no. 9-0427, U.S. Office of Education, Department of Health, Education and Welfare. George Peabody College for Teachers, Washington, D.C., 1971. ERIC document no. 057 410.

Scott, W. A. *Values and Organizations.* Chicago: Rand McNally, 1965.

---

# SEX BIAS QUESTIONNAIRE

AUTHOR: Myra Sadker

AGE: Teachers and school administrators

VARIABLE: Sex bias

TYPE OF MEASURE: Questionnaire

SOURCE FROM WHICH MEASURE MAY BE OBTAINED: Myra Sadker, School of Education, The American University, Washington, D.C. 20016. Cost: $10.00.

DESCRIPTION OF MEASURE: This questionnaire provides a gross assessment of the degree of sex bias existing in a school or school system. The instrument also serves to generate a fundamental awareness of the various dimensions of sexism. There are two forms, one for teachers and one for administrators, each composed of ten items.

As examples, the first five items from each ten-item checklist are given below. All questions are to be answered "yes" or "no."

*Teachers*

1. Do you expect girls to do well in spelling, reading, and language arts and boys to excel in math, science, and mechanical skills?
2. Do you ever use sex as a basis for separating students for classroom activity (asking boys to line up on one side of the room and girls on the other; organizing girls against boys in academic competition)?
3. Do you discuss sex-typing with your students—its causes and possible effects?
4. When students help with school chores, do you usually expect boys to run projectors and move books from room to room, and girls to keep attendance and banking records?
5. When report cards are processed, do girls usually receive the highest scores? (Do these grades truly reflect academic achievement or are they a reward for more submissive and controllable behavior?)

*Administrators*

1. When you interview new teachers for your school staff, would you rather hire a competent male than a competent female teacher?
2. Are all courses and activities in your school open to both males and females?
3. If your school has segregated sports programs, are more money, facilities, and attention given to the boys' physical education program than the girls'?
4. When students are brought to you for disciplinary action, do you discipline males more severely than females—even when both are guilty of the same or equivalent misdemeanors?
5. Does your school have a policy which forces female employees to leave at some officially designated time during pregnancy?

RELIABILITY AND VALIDITY: None reported.

BIBLIOGRAPHY:

Frazier, N., and Sadker, M. *Sexism in School and Society.* New York: Harper & Row, 1973.

Sadker, M., and Sadker, D. *Sexism in Education.* Three tape series for Behavioral Sciences Tape Library. Leonia, New Jersey, 1974.

Sadker, D., Sadker, M., and Cooper, J. M. "Elementary School Through Children's Eyes." *Elementary School Journal,* 1973, *73,* 289-296.

# SEXUAL ATTITUDE AND BEHAVIOR SURVEY (SABS)

AUTHORS: Dean G. Kilpatrick and Alma Dell Smith

AGE: Late adolescence and up

VARIABLE: Reported liberality of sexual attitudes and behavior

TYPE OF MEASURE: Rating scale

SOURCE FROM WHICH MEASURE MAY BE OBTAINED: Dean G. Kilpatrick, Medical University of South Carolina, Department of Psychiatry, 80 Barre Street, Charleston, South Carolina 29401.

DESCRIPTION OF MEASURE: The 112-item Sexual Attitude and Behavior Survey (SABS) is an objective measure of reported liberality of sexual attitudes and behavior. It consists of an attitude section and a behavior section. In the Attitude Section, $S$s are asked to indicate under which circumstances a series of sexual activities are permissible. The activities include kissing, petting, heavy petting, sexual intercourse, anal intercourse, oral-genital relations, group sexual activities, and homosexual activity. Each $S$ is also asked to select the circumstances under which it is permissible to think about indulging in the above-mentioned activities. Each thought and activity item is responded to in three ways: permissible for males, permissible for females, and permissible personally. On the basis of these responses, six attitude scores are constructed: male behavior score (MBS), male fantasy score (MFS), female behavior score (FBS), female fantasy score (FFS), personal behavior score (PBS), and personal fantasy score (PFS). Scores on each scale may range from 0 to 23, with a high score reflecting liberality of reported attitudes. In the behavior section of the SABS, $S$s are asked to indicate the frequency with which they have (1) thought about indulging in each sexual activity and (2) actually indulged in the activity.

As examples, four selected items of the 112 on the survey are given below. The first two are from the "permissible for males" section, and the second two from the "permissable for females" section. Each of the items is to be responded to as indicated, except item 51 omits "only if partners are married."

24. Petting with a woman is permissible
    a. only if partners are married.
    b. only if there is strong affection between partners.
    c. if the only emotional relationship between partners is sexual attraction.
    d. never.
26. Heavy petting with a woman resulting in orgasm of one or both partners is permissible . . .
45. Having sexual intercourse with a man is permissible . . .
51. Engaging in sexual activities with more than one person at the same time is permissible . . .

RELIABILITY AND VALIDITY: None reported.

BIBLIOGRAPHY:

Marcotte, D. B., Kilpatrick, D. G., Geyer, P. R., and Smith, A. D. "The Effect of a
    Spaces Sex Education Course on Medical Students' Sexual Knowledge and Atti-
    tudes." *British Journal of Medical Education* (in press).
Smith, A. D., Kilpatrick, D. G., and Sutker, P. B. "Male Student Professionals: Their
    Attitudes Toward Women, Sex, and Change." Paper presented at the Eighty-
    third annual meeting of the American Psychological Association. Chicago,
    August 1975.

---

## SEXUAL ATTITUDE SURVEY (SAS)

AUTHORS: Dean G. Kilpatrick and L. F. Quattlebaum

AGE: Late adolescence and up

VARIABLE: Reported liberality of sexual attitudes and behavior

TYPE OF MEASURE: Rating scale

SOURCE FROM WHICH MEASURE MAY BE OBTAINED: Dean G. Kilpatrick, Medical University of South Carolina, Department of Psychiatry, 80 Barre Street, Charleston, South Carolina 29401.

DESCRIPTION OF MEASURE: The Sexual Attitude Survey (SAS) is designed to measure reported liberality of sexual attitudes and behavior. The present form of the SAS
consists of twenty biographical questions and twelve multiple-choice items tapping liberality of reported sexual attitudes and behavior. Each item is to be responded to
according to the subject's own views, as well as according to what he or she thinks
most of the opposite sex will answer and what he or she thinks most of the same sex
will answer. The SAS was primarily designed for use with college-student populations,
although its use has not been limited to such subjects. Two scores may be obtained
from the SAS. Sexual liberality score $A$ (SLSA) is equivalent to the sexual liberality
score (SLS) previously reported (Kilpatrick and Cauthen, 1969; Kilpatrick and others,
1968). An examination of the items in SLSA will show it to reflect reported liberality
of sexual behavior as well as liberality of sexual attitudes.
    The second scoring yields sexual liberality scale $A'$ (SLSA'; SLSA prime) from
which are omitted items concerning reported sexual behavior. SLSA' is a purely attitudinal measure. Both SLSA and SLSA' are unidimensional scales, and on both high
scores are indicative of liberality of sexual attitudes and/or behavior.
    As examples, the first two multiple-choice items of the survey are given below.

1. Restriction on sexual behavior should apply to
    a. girls only.

b. girls more than boys.

c. both sexes equally.

d. boys more than girls.

e. boys only.

2. Who is primarily at fault regarding premarital pregnancy?

a. The girl only.

b. The girl more than the boy.

c. Both equally.

d. The boy more than the girl.

e. The boy only.

RELIABILITY AND VALIDITY: Test-retest reliability coefficients of .46 for SLSA and .86 for SLSA' were obtained in a sample of 120 freshmen medical students with three months separating administrations of the test. Not surprisingly, the purely attitudinal measure—SLSA'--is the more reliable. The SAS appears to have both face validity and construct validity. An examination of the items contained in the scale reveals item content to be obviously related to sexual attitudes and behavior, thus demonstrating the face validity of the scale. Previous research has shown sexual attitudes and behavior as measured by the SAS to be related in a predictable fashion to such variables as gender, dogmatism, religious preference, strength of religious conviction, and race. Such information suggests that the attitudes and behavior measured by the SAS have at least a certain amount of construct validity. The authors request that they be informed of the results of any research using the SAS.

BIBLIOGRAPHY:

Kilpatrick, D. G., and Cauthen, N. R. "The Relationship of Ordinal Position, Dogmatism, and Personal Sexual Attitudes." *Journal of Psychology,* 1969, *72,* 115-120.

Kilpatrick, D. G., Cauthen, N. R., Sandman, C. A., and Quattlebaum, L. F. "Dogmatism and Personal Sexual Attitudes." *Psychological Reports,* 1968, *23,* 1105-1106.

Sutker, P. B., and Gilliard, R. S. "Personal Sexual Attitudes and Behavior in Blacks and Whites." *Psychological Reports,* 1970, *27,* 753-754.

Sutker, P. B., and Kilpatrick, D. G. "Personality, Biographical and Racial Correlates of Sexual Attitudes and Behavior." *Proceedings of the 81st Annual Convention of the American Psychological Association,* 1973, *8,* 261-262.

Sutker, P. B., Sutker, L. W., and Kilpatrick, D. G. "Religious Preference, Practice, and Personal Sexual Attitudes and Behavior." *Psychological Reports,* 1970, *26,* 835-841.

## SOCIAL INTERACTION TEST

AUTHOR: June Moss Handler

AGE: 4 to 7 years

VARIABLE: Children's verbal attitudes toward black and white children

TYPE OF MEASURE: Structured interview with projective test

SOURCE FROM WHICH MEASURE MAY BE OBTAINED: See Handler (1966).

DESCRIPTION OF MEASURE: This measure, based on Trager and Yarrow's Social Episodes Test (1952), is designed to be used with kindergarten children in integrated suburban schools, to determine their verbal social perception of white and black children after particular intervening experiences. Specific areas analyzed are: children's racial choice for measures of "nicer," "nicer looking," and "cleaner"; and reasons for selection of race. Children are given 8X10-inch photographs of black and white children in typical but ambiguous kindergarten situations. Photographs are posed. In each picture the children are interacting in a way that might be considered negative or positive. The child makes general statements about the picture and is then asked specific questions as the interview progresses. Neutral pictures are used first and at intervals to stimulate story telling and put the child at ease. The pictures depict humorous animal scenes or children in pleasant surroundings. The number of neutral pictures depend upon the reactions of the child. Comments are written down while the children play with plasticine. Raw data are transformed into scales for measurement according to standards suggested by Selltiz and others (1960) using analysis of variance. The means of white, black, operational, and comparison groups are obtained and the internal variations measured.

RELIABILITY AND VALIDITY: Black children were tested by a black interviewer and white children by a white examiner. Items were checked on written forms during tests and then put into specific categories per child, per class, per pre- and posttests. Analysis of data was done by means of contingency tables. The amount of internal agreement was calculated using *chi*-square tests. An examination of the comparison between the researcher and a checker showed no significant difference.

BIBLIOGRAPHY:

Handler, J. M. "An Attempt to Change Kindergarten Children's Attitudes of Prejudice Toward the Negro." Unpublished doctoral dissertation. Teachers College, Columbia University, New York, 1966.

Selltiz, C., and others. *Research Methods in Social Relations.* (Rev. ed.) New York: Holt, Rinehart and Winston, 1960.

Trager, H. G., and Yarrow, M. R. *They Learn What They Live: Prejudice in Young Children.* New York: Harper & Row, 1952.

# SOCIAL JUSTICE STORY MEASURE

AUTHORS: D. Michelle Irwin, Shirley G. Moore, and Sueann R. Ambron

AGE: 3 to 7 years

VARIABLE: Social justice

TYPE OF MEASURE: Modified interview

SOURCE FROM WHICH MEASURE MAY BE OBTAINED: D. Michelle Irwin, Department of Psychology, Stanford University, Stanford, California 91305.

DESCRIPTION OF MEASURE: The Social Justice Story Measure consists of twenty-four illustrated stories designed to assess young children's understanding of blameworthiness, restitution, apology, and intentionality. In the restitution and intentionality categories, half of the stories involve equal amounts of damage done by both of the story characters, and half involve one character doing more damage than the other character. In addition, in half the stories both characters do the damage by accident, and in the other half one character does the damage accidentally while the other does it intentionally. After the illustrated story is read to the child, the examiner asks which character in the story is the naughtiest and why. The child is then given a choice between punishments for the character selected as naughty based on expiatory and restitutive justice.

Examples of a moral judgment story and follow-up interview question are given below.

Karen and Sue were putting puzzles together. Karen finished her puzzle first. Sue got mad and grabbed it and threw it on the floor, spilling all the pieces.

Another girl named Jane was running by and accidentally bumped the table knocking Karen's other puzzle off and spilling all the pieces.

Point to the girl that Karen should be most angry at for spilling her puzzle. Why did you pick her? Now, what do you think should be done to (Jane, Sue) for spilling Karen's puzzle? That sounds good, but suppose the teacher didn't think of that? Which of these punishments would be most fair; telling (Jane, Sue) to help Karen put the puzzle together or making her stand in the corner?

Responses are scored as 2 points for an appropriate choice and rationale, 1 point for an appropriate choice only, and 0 points for an inappropriate choice and rationale. *S*s who select punishments based on restitutive justice are given 1 point and those who select punishments based on expiative justice are scored 0.

RELIABILITY AND VALIDITY: The stories have content validity, and the test-retest reliability is .80.

BIBLIOGRAPHY:

Ambron, S. R., and Irwin, D. M. "The Relation Between Role-Taking and Moral Judgment in Five- and Seven-Year-Olds." *Developmental Psychology*, 1975, *11*, 102.

Irwin, D. M., and Ambron, S. R. "Moral Judgment and Role-Taking in 5- and 7-Year-old Children." Paper presented at biennial meeting of the Society for Research in Child Development. Philadelphia, Pennsylvania, March 1973.

Irwin, D. M., and Moore, S. G. "The Young Child's Understanding of Social Justice." *Developmental Psychology*, 1971, *5,* 406-410.

---

# STRUCTURED PARENTAL INTERVIEW

AUTHORS: Robert C. Warren, Anna M. Jackson, Judith Nugaris, and Gordon K. Farley

AGE: Parents of children in treatment

VARIABLE: Attitudes toward psychotherapy

TYPE OF MEASURE: Structured interview

SOURCE FROM WHICH MEASURE MAY BE OBTAINED: Anna M. Jackson, 4200 East Ninth Avenue, #2581, Denver, Colorado 80220.

DESCRIPTION OF MEASURE: The Structured Parental Interview consists of 140 questions extended over two schedules—Schedule A and Schedule B. The 114 items on Schedule A are subsumed under eight categories: perceived attitude of the therapist toward the patient, perceived attitude of others in the clinic toward the patient, perceived helpfulness of therapy, expectations of therapy (reasons for seeking help), perceived resistances toward therapy, special problems related to having a white therapist, perceived psychological mindedness, and fantasy expressions toward the therapist. Interview Schedule B is designed for black parents and includes twenty-six items. Questions are geared to special problems black patients might encounter with white therapists. Responses to items are scored either 0 for "no," 1 for "yes," or 2 for "not applicable." These numbers are entered into the squares at the right-hand side of the scales. Separate scores are obtained for each parent for all the items. Overall composite scores are derived by adding all of the responses given by both parents. Individual or composite scores can be obtained for each of the eight categories on Schedule A as well.

    As an example, the first item on each of the eight scales is given below. The interviewer scores both mother and father for their answers.

  I. *Therapist's Attitude Toward the Patient*                  *Mother*   *Father*
       1. Do you think your therapist liked you?
  II. *Attitude of Other People in the Clinic*
      21. Do you remember seeing Negro patients in the Clinic?
  III. *Helpfulness of Therapy*
      34. Do you feel that seeing a therapist helped you in handling the problems for which you came to the Clinic?

IV. *Expectations of Therapy and Reasons for Seeking Help*
    51. When you initially came to the Clinic did you think that people would tell you how to solve your problem?
V. *Resistances*
    73. How often were you late for therapy sessions?
VI. (a) *Special Problems Around Having a White Therapist*
    86. Would you have preferred to have had a Negro therapist?
VII. *Psychological Mindedness*
    98. Before you came to the Clinic, did you have some fairly definite idea about what your problems were?
VIII. *Fantasy Expression*
    107. Did you sometimes wish for a more social personal type of relationship with your therapist?

RELIABILITY AND VALIDITY: None reported.

BIBLIOGRAPHY:

Jackson, A. M., Warren, R. C., Nugaris, J., and Farley, G. K. "Differential Attitudes of Black and White Patients Toward Treatment in a Child Guidance Clinic." *American Journal of Orthopsychiatry*, 1973, *43*, 384-393.
Sattler, J. "Racial Experimenter Effects in Experimentation, Testing, Interviewing and Psychotherapy." *Psychology Bulletin*, 1970, *73*, 137-160.

*Prepared by Anna M. Jackson*

---

# TANNENBAUM'S MEASURE OF ATTITUDES TOWARD ACADEMIC BRILLIANCE

AUTHOR: Abraham J. Tannenbaum

AGE: 16 years to adult

VARIABLE: Verbal stereotypes associated with academic brilliance

TYPE OF MEASURE: Checklist

SOURCE FROM WHICH MEASURE MAY BE OBTAINED: Abraham J. Tannenbaum, Box 232, Teachers College, Columbia University, New York, New York 10027.

DESCRIPTION OF MEASURE: The instrument consists of eight imaginary high school students, each described on a separate page and followed by an identical list of fifty-four traits, some desirable, others undesirable, and still others neutral, as determined by the independent judgments of 200 high school students. Every one of the eight imaginary characters is presented in three sentences. The first sentence refers to the character's academic ability (brilliant or average), the second to effort at school (studious or nonstudious), and the third to sportsmindedness (athletic or nonathletic). These three dichotomized personal qualities appear in every possible combination, thus creating the description of the eight characters: brilliant-nonstudious-athletic, brilliant-nonstudious-nonathletic, average-nonstudious-athletic, average-nonstudious-nonathletic, average-studious-athletic, average-studious-nonathletic, brilliant-studious-athletic, and brilliant-studious-nonathletic. Since every "brilliant" stereotype has an "average" counterpart with identical characteristics denoting effort and sportsmindedness, it is possible to compare the two types of characters while holding their other characteristics constant. It is also possible to determine attitudes toward brilliance (vs. average ability) in the context of the other characteristics (effort and sportsmindedness). The respondent checks "yes" or "no" for each of the fifty-four traits separately for every one of the eight characters to indicate whether or not he thinks the trait typifies that particular character. A "yes" for a desirable trait or a "no" for an undesirable trait is converted to a rating of +1, while a "no" for a desirable trait or a "yes" for an undesirable trait yields a −1 rating. These ratings are summed separately for the eight characters, giving each a total score by the respondent. Finally, there is space for the respondent to indicate whether he or she thinks the character is male, female, or could be either.

As examples, the first twenty trait-items for Pupil A (brilliant-studious-athletic) are given below. There are identical lists for the seven other stereotypes described above.

*Pupil A is:*   1. A good sport.
2. A perfectionist.
3. A teacher's pet.
4. A brain.
5. A walking dictionary.
6. A good school citizen.
7. A bookworm.
8. A creep.
9. A good conversationalist.
10. A good leader.

11. Spoiled.
12. Serious.
13. Nervous.
14. Competitive.
15. Proud of his (her) school work.
16. Conscientious.
17. Dull.
18. Mature.
19. Cheerful.
20. Shy.

RELIABILITY AND VALIDITY: The following table reports the split-half reliability coefficients on separate scores for desirable and undesirable traits ascribed to the eight characters by a random sample of sixty-five respondents drawn from the junior class of a large, comprehensive urban high school.

| Stimulus Characters | Desirable Traits | Undesirable Traits |
|---|---|---|
| Brilliant-Nonstudious-Athletic | .86 | .82 |
| Average-Nonstudious-Athletic | .92 | .85 |
| Average-Studious-Athletic | .90 | .88 |
| Brilliant-Studious-Athletic | .94 | .87 |
| Brilliant-Nonstudious-Nonathletic | .88 | .92 |
| Average-Nonstudious-Nonathletic | .89 | .91 |
| Average-Studious-Nonathletic | .89 | .88 |
| Brilliant-Studious-Nonathletic | .91 | .80 |

Content validity was substantiated in several ways. First, the trait list contained items that were synonymous with some information given in the character descriptions, and the response followed the predicted pattern. Secondly, final scoring for the eight characters showed that finely differentiated responses had been made, and that was confirmed by the per-trait comparisons across the eight characters.

BIBLIOGRAPHY:

Tannenbaum, A. J. *Adolescent Attitudes Toward Academic Brilliance.* New York: Teachers College Press, Columbia University, 1962.

---

# TEENAGE SELF-TEST: CIGARETTE SMOKING

AUTHORS: Ann M. Milne and Joseph G. Colmen

AGE: 13 to 18 years

VARIABLE: Psychosocial forces affecting decision to smoke

TYPE OF MEASURE: Likert-type questionnaire

SOURCE FROM WHICH MEASURE MAY BE OBTAINED: Bureau of Health Education, Center for Disease Control, 1600 Clifton Road, Atlanta, Georgia 30333.

DESCRIPTION OF MEASURE: This instrument is self-administered, self-scored, and self-interpreted. It consists of eight scales: (1) health concern: cost; (2) nonsmokers' rights; (3) positive smokers' attributes; (4) direct effects: benefit, (5) negative smoker attributes; (6) parental control: authority; (7) destiny control: independence; and (8) rationalization. Norms for the Teenage Self-Test are based on a national probability sample of public schools, including participation by some six thousand teenagers in grades 7 to 12.

As examples, the first twelve of the twenty-nine items are given below, to be answered on a 5-point scale from "strongly agree" to "strongly disagree." There are also fourteen additional "survey" items.

1. Smoking cigarettes gives you a good feeling.
2. I often do things even when I know inside myself that they are not the right thing to do.
3. Teenagers who smoke cigarettes are more likely to be troublemakers than those who don't.
4. I can control the kind of person I will become.
5. Smoking cigarettes can help you enjoy life more.
6. It annoys me that my parents have so much control over things I want to do.
7. A person who smokes is more of a follower than one who doesn't smoke.
8. I do not want to be just one of the crowd.
9. People who smoke seem to be more at ease with others.
10. I wish I were older than I am now.

11. Kids who smoke are show-offs.

12. I don't want to get hooked on anything, including cigarettes.

RELIABILITY AND VALIDITY: Reliabilities for the eight scales (Kuder-Richardson formula 20) range from .83 for Scale 1 to .50 for Scale 8. The validity is based on differential responses between smokers and nonsmokers.

BIBLIOGRAPHY:

Caramancia, V. P., Feiler, E. G., and Olsen, L. K. "Evaluation of the Effects of Performance Based Teacher Knowledge of the Health Knowledge and Attitude of Fifth Graders." *Journal of School Health,* 1974, *44,* 449-454.

*Teenage Self Test.* Department of Health, Education and Welfare. Publication no. (HSM)-73-8723. Washington, D.C.: Public Health Service, 1973.

Williams, T. M. *Summary and Implications of Review of Literature Related to Adolescent Smoking.* Bethesda, Maryland: National Clearinghouse for Smoking and Health, Department of Health, Education and Welfare, 1972.

*Prepared by Joseph G. Colmen*

---

# TENTATIVE DRUG USE SCALE (TDUS)

AUTHORS: John J. Horan and John M. Williams

AGE: Adolescents and adults

VARIABLE: Tentative or probable drug use

TYPE OF MEASURE: Questionnaire

SOURCE FROM WHICH MEASURE MAY BE OBTAINED: See Horan and Williams (1975).

DESCRIPTION OF MEASURE: The Tentative Drug Use Scale (TDUS) was designed in response to difficulties involved with assessing the effects of drug-prevention programming (see Horan, 1974; Horan and Williams, 1975). It consists of nine "yes" or "no" questions emanating from a common stem: "If given the opportunity would you try: Marijuana (pot)? Hashish (hash)? Bindro? Hallucinogens (LSD, peyote)? Stimulants (uppers)? Depressants (downers)? Cocaine? Curare (coolies)? Heroin (smack)?" Items may be added, deleted, grouped, or weighted to suit the experimenter's intentions. For example, legal drugs such as cigarettes and alcohol could also be included. Furthermore, instead of obtaining a total-drug-use score by summing the number of "yes" responses, it might be preferable to derive separate scores for "socially acceptable" illegal drugs (e.g., marijuana and hashish) and hard illegal drugs. Finally, some experimenters might choose to weight each drug's contribution to the total score based on factors such as potentiality for addiction or tissue damage.

RELIABILITY AND VALIDITY: A test-retest reliability coefficient of .96 was found on a sample of twenty-two college upperclassmen over a one-week period. Concurrent validity coefficients ranging from .96 for hashish to .63 for hallucinogens were found when forty-four similar subjects completed both the TDUS and the Personal Drug-Use Scale of the Pennsylvania State University Drug Education Evaluation Scales (Horan and Swisher, 1973). It should be pointed out that the items on the TDUS are relatively nonincriminating. For example, responding "yes" to "Would you try marijuana?" is a much easier admission than indicating in writing how much marijuana one smoked in the previous week.

BIBLIOGRAPHY:

Horan, J. J. "Outcome Difficulties in Drug Education." *Review of Educational Research,* 1974, *44,* 203-211.

Horan, J. J., and Swisher, J. D. "The Pennsylvania State University Drug Education Evaluation Scales." In L. A. Abrams, E. F. Garfield, and J. D. Swisher (Eds.), *Accountability in Drug Education: A Model for Evaluation.* Washington, D.C.: Drug Abuse Council, 1973.

Horan, J. J., Westcott, T. B., Vetovich, C., and Swisher, J. D. "Drug Usage: An Experimental Comparison of Three Assessment Procedures." *Psychological Reports,* 1974, *35,* 211-215.

Horan, J. J., and Williams, J. M. "The Tentative Drug Use Scale: A Quick and Relatively Problem-Free Outcome Measure for Drug Abuse Prevention Projects." Unpublished manuscript. The Pennsylvania State University, University Park, 1975.

---

## TEST OF ATTITUDES TOWARD THE GIFTED

AUTHOR: Jon C. Jacobs

AGE: Adults working with gifted children

VARIABLE: Attitude of school personnel toward the gifted

TYPE OF MEASURE: Error-choice questionnaire

SOURCE FROM WHICH MEASURE MAY BE OBTAINED: Jon C. Jacobs, Special Services Division, Plymouth Community Schools, Plymouth, Michigan 48170.

DESCRIPTION OF MEASURE: This device is designed to measure adults' attitudes toward gifted children and to classify those attitudes as positive or negative. In an attempt to decrease the subject's awareness that attitudes are being measured, an error-choice design (with factual questions having two equally wrong answer choices) is used, and the measure is presented as a test of information. Form I, a sentence-completion form, is presented first, as it apparently measures attitudes. While this provides excellent information concerning adult feelings about gifted children, it is not used in dichotomizing attitudes. After Form I is completed, Form II is presented as a test of factual information. Of the eighteen questions, five serve simply as fillers and the thirteen are used to determine attitudes.

As examples, the first five of the fifteen items of Form I (structured sentence-completion questionnaire) are given below.

1. A gifted child should feel proud when . . .
2. In class, a gifted child is . . .
3. A gifted child's greatest problem . . .
4. A gifted child . . .
5. Parents of a gifted child should . . .

The first five of the eighteen items of Form II (test of information—gifted children) are:

1. In 1955 (a) 18 percent (b) 38 percent of the highest-ranking tenth of the nation's high school graduates did not enter college.
2. Mozart composed music when he was (a) 3½ (b) 4½.
3. (a) 25 percent (b) 75 percent of gifted children learn to read before they enter school.
4. Gifted children have (a) more (b) fewer adjustment problems than average children.
5. Gifted children are usually thought of as having IQs of (a) 115 (b) 130 or higher (filler item).

RELIABILITY AND VALIDITY: The test-retest reliability correlation at a three-week interval was .74. Validity: The test was administered to teachers at a private school for the gifted, with positive attitudes toward the gifted assumed. Their scores ranged from 8 to 11 positive responses; mean positive responses, 9.43, SD = .91. When administered to a group of high school dropouts with negative attitudes toward the gifted assumed, scores ranged from 1 to 7 positive responses; mean positive responses, 4.76, SD = 1.60.

BIBLIOGRAPHY:

Jacobs, J. C. "Teacher Attitude Toward Gifted Children." *Gifted Child Quarterly,* 1972, *16,* 23-26.

---

## TOBACCO USE QUESTIONNAIRE

AUTHORS: Herbert S. Rabinowitz and William H. Zimmerli

AGE: Grade 7 to 9—students, parents, teachers

VARIABLE: Attitudes toward tobacco use, knowledge of health hazards in smoking, actual tobacco consumption (cigarettes)

TYPE OF MEASURE: Likert-type scale

SOURCE FROM WHICH MEASURE MAY BE OBTAINED: Herbert S. Rabinowitz, Community Services Group, United Way of Buffalo and Erie County, 742 Delaware Avenue, Buffalo, New York 10209.

DESCRIPTION OF MEASURE: The Tobacco Use Questionnaire consists of fifty-eight items that cover attitudes toward smoking (ten items), knowledge about health hazards in smoking (forty-five items), and smoking behavior (three items). Items are scored in varying ways, including an "agree-disagree" continuum, multiple-choice, and true-false. Higher scores were associated with: (attitudes) greater acceptance of personal responsibility for the consequences of tobacco use and (tobacco consumption) higher level of cigarette use.

As examples, seven of the fifty-eight items on the questionnaire are given below. The respondent answers Part A by "true" or "false"; Part B is multiple-choice among five answers; Part C is a 5-point Likert scale ranging from "the statement and the proposed reason are both true and related in cause and effect" to "the statement and the proposed reason are both false." Part D is a 5-point Likert scale ranging from "strongly agree" to "strongly disagree"; and Part E is yes/no and choice of six answers in response.

*Part A*
1. Many young people who do not really enjoy cigarettes feel that they will be left out of things if they do not "go along."
2. Habits can be substituted for one another if they are about equal in satisfying the same need.
3. Cigarette ads seem to have more of an impact on teenagers than on older or younger people.
4. Experience shows that informing the people about the health risks in smoking has had almost no lasting effect on their cigarette habits.

*Part B*
12. The reaction time of a person is
    a. unaffected by smoking.
    b. slowed down when one smokes.
    c. speeded up when one smokes.
    d. varied with the amount of inhaling.
    e. affected only in beginning smokers.

*Part C*
37. More cancer of the throat is caused by drinking coffee than by smoking cigarettes *because* heat can cause cancer.

*Part D*
46. Smoking cigarettes is harmful for health.

RELIABILITY AND VALIDITY: An original battery of 300 items derived by deductive methods was administered to a randomly selected group of 133 junior high school students and was reduced to fifty-eight final form items using conventional measures of item difficulty, item-response functioning, and item-discrimination index. Validity was determined by having a panel of thirty-five master's-level health-education teachers sort out the 160 of 300 items that adequately met the above criteria. Only those items recommended for inclusion by 80 percent or more of the teachers were included in the final fifty-eight-item version. Kuder-Richardson formula 20 reliability was .84.

BIBLIOGRAPHY:

Rabinowitz, H. S., and Zimmerli, W. H. "Effects of a Health Education Program on Junior High School Students' Knowledge, Attitudes, and Behavior Concerning Tobacco Use." *Journal of School Health,* 1974, *44,* 324-330.

---

# TRADITIONAL FAMILY IDEOLOGY (TFI) SCALE

AUTHORS: Daniel J. Levinson and Phyllis Huffman Courtney

AGE: Parents

VARIABLE: Authoritarian attitudes toward family

TYPE OF MEASURE: Likert-type scale

SOURCE FROM WHICH MEASURE MAY BE OBTAINED: Daniel J. Levinson, Department of Psychiatry, Yale University, 34 Park Street, New Haven, Connecticut 06519.

DESCRIPTION OF MEASURE: The TFI Scale differentiates between authoritarian and egalitarian attitudes with respect to various aspects of family relationships: the role of the male; the role of the female; husband-wife relationships; parent-child relationships; values with respect to sex, aggression, and status. The major psychological variables are conventionalism, authoritarian submission, exaggerated masculinity and femininity, emphasis on discipline, and moralistic rejection of impulse life. The initial form of the scale is comprised of forty items. An abbreviated form containing twelve items is also available.

As examples, the first five of the twelve items on the abbreviated scale are given below. The respondent answers on a 6-point scale ranging from "strong agreement" to "strong disagreement."

1. Some equality in marriage is a good thing, but by and large the husband ought to have the main say-so in family matters.
2. If children are told much about sex, they are likely to go too far in experimenting with it.
3. Women who want to remove the word *obey* from the marriage service don't understand what it means to be a wife.
4. The most important qualities of a real man are determination and driving ambition.
5. A child should never be allowed to talk back to his parents or else he will lose respect for them.

RELIABILITY AND VALIDITY: The original scale was administered to 109 subjects, members of adult evening classes in Cleveland College, heterogeneous with respect to age, religion, occupation, and marital status. Split-half reliability, corrected by the Spearman-Brown formula, was .84. The initial results support the general theory, in that the categories that differentiate the high and low scorers reflect the genotypic variables on which the TFI Scale was originally constructed. This scale correlates on the order of .7 to .8 with Adorno's F Scale, a measure of general authoritarianism.

BIBLIOGRAPHY:

Dreyer, A. S., and Rigler, D. "Cognitive Performance in Montessori and Nursery School Children." *Journal of Educational Research,* 1969, *62,* 411-416.

Levinson, D. J., and Huffman, P. E. "Traditional Family Ideology and Its Relation to Personality." *Journal of Personality,* 1955, *13,* 251-273.

*Prepared by Phyllis Huffman Courtney and Daniel J. Levinson*

---

# TRICULTURAL ATTITUDE SCALE

AUTHOR: Perry A. Zirkel

AGE: 6 to 14 years

VARIABLE: Attitudes and knowledge: Puerto Rican, Anglo-American, and black American cultures

TYPE OF MEASURE: Pictorial scale

SOURCE FROM WHICH MEASURE MAY BE OBTAINED: Learning Concepts, 2501 North Lamar, Austin, Texas 78705. Cost: Test manual and set of six face cards, $3.95; each ethnic module (sold separately), $.40; score sheet (twenty-five pupils per sheet), $.05 each.

DESCRIPTION OF MEASURE: The Tricultural Attitude Scale is a modularized measure to indicate attitudes and knowledge regarding the Puerto Rican, Anglo-American, and black American cultures, respectively. Despite similarities in form and content, the three modules are independent measures. They are designed for the evaluation of programs that propose to enhance ethnic identity or cross-cultural understanding among any one or more of these three target groups. Orally reinforced pictorial stimuli and response options were selected to obviate necessity for reading ability. Responses to a series of five faces on a happy-sad continuum yield a cultural-attitude index. Responses to an alternate facial option yield a cultural-knowledge index. The early childhood version (ages 6 to 9) contains three faces. The intermediate version contains six faces.

RELIABILITY AND VALIDITY: The scale was developed within a culturally pluralistic framework. Members of each cultural group served to establish an item pool, illustrate and screen the items, and provide item-analysis data for their respective module.

Reliability studies based on a multiethnic sample of 330 elementary-school pupils yield split-half reliability coefficients, corrected by the Spearman-Brown formula, ranging from .68 to .77 and test-retest reliability coefficients ranging from .52 to .61. Content validity was reflected in the pooling and screening procedures. Construct validity was reflected by the general tendency of higher knowledge scores for each succeeding grade level and of higher attitude and knowledge scores for the cultural group represented by the module compared to the other two cultural groups. Criterion validity was indicated by studies revealing significant relationships between the instrument's cultural-attitude index scores and teacher ratings, sociogram data analyzed according to ethnic group, and a verbal cultural-attitude measure.

BIBLIOGRAPHY:

Zirkel, P. A. "Self-Concept and the 'Disadvantage' of Ethnic Group Membership." *Review of Educational Research*, 1971, *41*, 211-225.

Zirkel, P. A. "A Sociolinguistic Survey of Puerto Rican Parents." Paper presented at the annual meeting of the American Orthopsychiatric Association. New York, May 1973. ERIC document no. ED 074 191.

Zirkel, P. A., and Green, J. F. "The Measurement of Self-Concept of Disadvantaged Students." Paper presented at the annual meeting of the National Council on Measurement in Education. New York, 1971.

---

# TWO HOUSES TECHNIQUE (2HT)

AUTHOR: Victor Szyrynski

AGE: 5 to 17 years

VARIABLE: Attitudes toward different family members and perception of the dynamic family structure

TYPE OF MEASURE: Structured-play interview

SOURCE FROM WHICH MEASURE MAY BE OBTAINED: The mimeographed manual in English may be obtained from Victor Szyrynski, Department of Psychiatry, Faculty of Medicine, University of Ottawa, Ontario Canada K1N 9A9; and in French from Rene Lefebvre, Department of Education, University of Sherbrooke, Quebec, Canada. For Polish translation, see Sypniewska (1973).

DESCRIPTION OF MEASURE: The Two-Houses Technique facilitates analysis of intrafamilial dynamics in a very quick, convenient, and relatively simple manner. With an ordinary pencil and a standard sheet of paper, and with the child sitting on his left side, the examiner draws the family members of the child and then in the middle of the paper the two equal houses between which the family members are divided according to the directions of the child. In the following stages of the test, the family members, including the child, are moved from one house to the other, and the order of different moves and the emotional reactions of the child in different phases of the game are carefully noted. Feelings of isolation, rejection, hostility, insecurity, weakening of the family ties, and various compensatory reactions (e.g., excessive attachment to domestic animals) are easily observed. It is essential that all the drawing be done by the examiner himself and that all the minute details of the test application given in the manual be precisely followed. In spite of its apparent simplicity, the technique requires great precision in its application and a good knowledge of psychodynamics for its interpretation.

RELIABILITY AND VALIDITY: During the initial evaluation of the technique with eighty-six children, in 73 percent of the cases the result obtained with the 2HT corresponded very closely to the findings on family dynamics and the child's attitudes obtained with the assistance of lengthy interviews and more complicated tests. In the remaining 27 percent, the test was either rejected or the results were not fully compatible with other findings from different clinical techniques. With improved skill in application of the test, the results of the findings improved still further and the cases of rejection diminished. The technique contains this built-in verifying aspect: The initial order in the family ("parents-dominated," "children-dominated," "dominated by a particular sibling") is usually repeated at the subsequent stages of the "game." At the end of the testing, two opposite statements are introduced by suggesting to the child that he prefers to play with the sibling rejected during the previous stages of the game or prefers spending time with the less-acceptable parent. The intensity of denial verifies previous impressions of the examiner. Further research suggested the particular value of the technique in determining the severity of various psychoneurotic, psychosomatic, and psychotic disorders as well as other forms of maladjustments in children and adolescents. Domestic and scholastic adjustment was studied by some investigators; transcultural research was carried out by others.

BIBLIOGRAPHY:

Lefebvre, R. "La Technique des Deux Maisons '2HT.'" *Bulletin de la Société de Psychologie Midi-Pyrenees.* 1973, Numéro spécial, 65-82. Université de Toulouse-Le Mirail, 31076 Toulouse, Cedex, France.

Lefebvre, R. *Mode d'Application de la Technique des Deux Maisons,* "2HT." 31076 Toulouse, Cedex, France: Université de Toulouse-Le Mirail, 1974.

Sypniewska, J. "Technika (Test) Dwóch Domków Domkow W. Szyrynskiego (The Two Houses Technique—2HT)." *Zdrowie Psychiczne (Mental Health),* 1973, *14,* 101-121 (Poland).

Szyrynski, V. "A New Technique to Investigate Family Dynamics in Child Psychiatry." *Canadian Psychiatric Association Journal,* 1963, *8,* 94-103.

Szyrynski, V. "Pattern Analysis of the 'Two Houses Technique' in Child Psychiatry." *Atti II Congresso Europeo di Pedopsychiatria,* 1963, *2,* 1082-1093 (Rome).

Szyrynski, V. "La Tecnica delle due case." *Panorama Medico,* 1967, November, *1,* 18-19 (Milano, Gennaio-Febbraio).

Szyrynski, V. "The International Use of the 2HT in the Decade 1962-1972." Paper presented at a meeting of the Athenian Institute of Anthropos. Athens, Greece, June 1972.

# VALUE-ORIENTATION SCALE

AUTHOR: Audrey Schwartz (modified by John W. Friesen)

AGE: 10 years to adult

VARIABLE: Value preferences

TYPE OF MEASURE: Rating scale

SOURCE FROM WHICH MEASURE MAY BE OBTAINED: (As modified) John W. Friesen, Department of Educational Foundations, University of Calgary, Calgary, Alberta, Canada T2N 1N4.

DESCRIPTION OF MEASURE: The Value-Orientation Scale (as modified) seeks information according to twelve classifications with two to four items on each, making a total of forty items. The twelve classifications are: faith in human nature; formal school compliance; futuristic orientation; independence from peers; instrumental orientation scale; orientation to family authority scale; occupational values: reward orientation scale; occupational values: social orientation scale; expressive orientation scale; index of autonomy; index of idealized school goals; and index of self-esteem. In the Friesen (1974) study, the administration of the questionnaires was carried out by teachers; Indian parents were interviewed by an Indian parent. Part Two of the instrument is titled Value Orientation re. Indian Culture and is an attempt to get at some insights regarding Indian culture among Canadians of unspecified age.

   As examples, six selected items from the forty-item scale are given below, to be responded to with "agree," "slightly agree," or "disagree."

   1. In general, people can be trusted.
   4. Even when they punish the whole class, I feel that teachers are usually right.
  10. I wouldn't mind being thought of as an "odd ball."
  13. If I disagree with what the group decides, I would never say so.
  20. Children should obey all the rules their parents make for them.
  25. A job should let me work with people more than with things.

RELIABILITY AND VALIDITY: In comparing Indian pupils, Friesen (1974) found that they scored lower on the following subscales: faith in human nature, interest in future planning and life expectations, education as instrumental to later success, and self-esteem. They scored higher on these items: independence from peers, respect for family authority, and faith in occupational rewards. Indian pupils indicated less faith in human nature and less self-esteem than did either parents or teachers. However, they showed more confidence in the future and in eventual occupational rewards than either their parents or teachers.

BIBLIOGRAPHY:

Friesen, J. W. "Education and Values in an Indian Community." *Alberta Journal of Educational Research,* 1974, *20,* 146-155.

*Prepared by John W. Friesen*

# VALUE SCALE, ESTABLISHED NORMATIVE PATTERN SCALE, AND EMERGENT NORMATIVE PATTERN SCALE

AUTHORS: Stuart H. Traub and Richard A. Dodder

AGE: Junior high school to adult

VARIABLE: Degree of agreement with dominant American value orientations and corresponding normative patterns

TYPE OF MEASURE: Questionnaire

SOURCE FROM WHICH MEASURE MAY BE OBTAINED: See Traub and Dodder (1974a).

DESCRIPTION OF MEASURE: The Value Scale consists of ten items, conceptualized to identify generally accepted dominant American values. Each item is accompanied by a conventional 5-point strongly agree-strongly disagree response continuum and scaled by the summated ratings method. All items are reverse-weighted in determining scale scores. The total possible sum for strong agreement with all items making up the Value Scale is 50, with the total-scale sum for an indifference score being 30 (3 points for each item falling in the indifference range). The higher the score, the greater the degree of value acceptance. The Established Normative Pattern and Emergent Normative Pattern Scales each consist of eighteen items. Both scales were constructed and used with the idea that adult (established) norms are relatively more structured than youth (emergent) norms. Both normative pattern scales correspond to behavior patterns utilized in the actualization of specified values. For each item in the Value Scale, two items to identify corresponding established norms and two items to identify corresponding emergent norms were developed. These items are not presented in the questionnaire as separate scales but are randomly ordered in a single section. The subject responds on a conventional 5-point strongly agree-strongly disagree response continuum, and the items are scaled by the summated-ratings method. All items in both scales are reverse-weighted in determining scale score. The total possible sum for strong agreement with all items making up *each* scale is 90, with the total-scale sum for an indifference score being 54 (3 points for each item falling in the indifference range). The higher the score for an individual/group on either normative pattern scale, the greater the degree of acceptance of those normative patterns. The scales are easily administered by questionnaire. Approximate time required to complete the items is 10 minutes. The population best suited for completing the questionnaire is junior and senior high school students, college students, and adults. The questionnaire was originally given to college students and their parents.

The Value Scale measures degree of acceptance of dominant American values. The two Normative Pattern Scales operationally discriminate between divergent types of normative patterns predominantly accepted and utilized for value actualization by youth and adults. The development of these scales is based on a theoretical orientation that views behavioral dissimilarity between youth and adults as a result of the acceptance and utilization of divergent conduct norms rather than value discontinuity. Thus, in employing divergent means in attempting to actualize similarly accepted values, normative dissensus would then appear as a primary factor related to a generation gap between youth and adult behavioral patterns.

As examples, five items from each of the three scales are given below.

*Value Scale*
1. Pursuit of productive activity which provides you with a satisfying experience. (work)
2. Some type of spiritual experience. (religion)
3. Establishment of your own family. (family)
4. Enjoyment of sexual relations. (sex)
5. Concern for others who are less fortunate or who need assistance. (humanitarianism)

*Established Normative Pattern Scale*
1. In order to be successful in life, as much school as possible is needed. (education)
2. In order to aid people who are in need of help one should contribute time, effort, or money to public assistance organizations. (humanitarianism)
3. It is better to stick by what we have than to be looking for new ways of doing things that we really don't know about. (change)
4. One should be actively engaged in some kind of disciplined productive activity. (work)
5. In their actions, people should attempt to stay within the boundaries of social rules. (individualism)

*Emergent Normative Pattern Scale*
1. If a couple finds getting along with each other a struggle, they should not feel obligated to remain married. (family)
2. In order to help others in need, one should get personally involved with them. (humanitarianism)
3. Since nothing lasts forever, people should accept ways of thinking and doing which meet the needs of immediate situations. (change)
4. Men and women should find out if they are sexually suited before marriage. (sex)
5. It is important to incorporate all people on an equal basis into our society, no matter how different their beliefs or what groups they are members of. (equality)

RELIABILITY AND VALIDITY: Pearson correlation coefficients between each item of a scale and the totals of the scale, scale means, *sigmas,* and an *alpha* coefficient of internal consistency (in terms of overlapping variances) among the various items making up each scale were computed. All items making up each final scale correlated beyond the .001 level of significance. The *alpha* coefficients for each scale are: Value Scale, .73; Established Normative Pattern Scale, .82; and Emergent Normative Pattern Scale, .81. These *alpha* values represent a high degree of internal consistency of the items making up each scale.

BIBLIOGRAPHY:

Traub, S. H., and Dodder, R. A. *The Construction of an Instrument to Measure Normative Dissensus Between Youth and Adults.* NAPS document 02304. New York: Microfiche Publications, 1974a.
Traub, S. H., and Dodder, R. A. "An Instrument to Measure Normative Dissensus Between Youth and Adults." *Journal of Social Psychology,* 1974b, *93,* 149-150.

*Prepared by Stuart H. Traub and Orval G. Johnson*

# VALUE SOCIALIZATION SCALE

AUTHORS: Richard L. Gorsuch and Ruth Arbitman-Smith

AGE: Grades 4 to 6

VARIABLE: Development of basic social values

TYPE OF MEASURE: Questionnaire

SOURCE FROM WHICH MEASURE MAY BE OBTAINED: See Gorsuch (1971).

DESCRIPTION OF MEASURE: Following Scott's (1965) approach to values, the items for the scales were generated by asking children open-ended questions concerning the norms they saw people (parents, teachers, peers, and themselves) holding for them. Analyses of a large number of such items given to a new sample suggested that there was one general factor appearing in lower-class and middle-class black and white children. The items in the scale were those that correlated significantly with that general factor in *each* one of the eight samples formed by crossing lower- and middle-class black and white with boy and girl (and thus were unlikely to reflect, for example, only middle-class norms). On the basis of item content and comparison with another study at the college level, the general factor was labeled basic value socialization and appears to reflect the process of learning how to fit into a society. Basic value socialization appears to be a task of the upper-elementary school years, which is normally completed by the sixth grade. (It appears that one learns the values by which he selects the society he would like to fit into at a later age.)

The ten items of the scale (first item is not scored) are given below, to be responded to with "I always admire," "I sometimes admire," or "I always dislike." Reverse items are indicated.

1. A child's helping everybody who needs help.
2. A child's doing what he wants instead of what his parents ask.
3. A child's doing the best he can. (R)
4. A child's getting by in school with little work.
5. A child's giving wrong answers on a test.
6. A child's doing what the teacher wants. (R)
7. A child's talking back to his parents.
8. A child's being kind to others. (R)
9. A child's talking back to the teacher.
10. A child's going to the store for somebody. (R)

RELIABILITY AND VALIDITY: Separate reliabilities were computed in each of the eight groups formed by crossing social class, race, and sex. Analyses also indicated the scale functions equally well at the fourth and sixth grades. The reliabilities were at the same level for each of the groups (.7 to .8) in the original sample and upon cross-validation. The scale has been found to be predictive of teachers' evaluations of children as personality or behavior problems, of the child's involvement in negatively evaluated, value-laden classroom incidents, and of grades.

BIBLIOGRAPHY:

Gorsuch, R. L. *Value Conflict in the School Setting.* Final report, George Peabody College for Teachers, Project no. 9-0427, U.S. Office of Education, Department of Health, Education and Welfare. Nashville, Tennessee, 1971. ERIC document no. ED 057 410.

Scott, W. *Values and Organizations.* Chicago: Rand McNally, 1965.

---

# YOUTH RESEARCH SURVEY

AUTHOR: Merton P. Strommen

AGE: 14 to 19 years

VARIABLE: Concerns, beliefs, values, and perceptions of youth

TYPE OF MEASURE: Questionnaire

SOURCE FROM WHICH MEASURE MAY BE OBTAINED: Youth Research Center, 122 West Franklin Avenue, Minneapolis, Minnesota 55404. Costs vary according to number of answer sheets processed.

DESCRIPTION OF MEASURE: The Youth Research Survey is a self-report instrument of 420 items that form twenty-five scales. A standardization sample of 7,050 youths (drawn randomly from major denominations) was used to form the scales, to weight responses, and to establish the norms. A full description of how items were selected, scales developed using multivariate analyses, responses weighted by means of reciprocal averages, and survey scales standardized for use among major denominational groups is given in Strommen and Gupta (1971c). The survey is printed in two books. Book One, entitled "Myself and My View of the World," deals with concerns and attitudes that are important to counselors and teachers in parochial and public schools and to clergymen in congregations. Its 220 items give measures on twelve dimensions or scales. They also provide biographical and sociological information important for describing a group. Book Two, entitled "My Values and Beliefs," is designed primarily for use in a religious institution. Though half of its 200 items reflect Christian concepts, an alternate form gives comparable measures for youth of the Jewish faith. It gives assessments on thirteen dimensions or scales in addition to other information useful in describing the values and beliefs of youth. A profile in the form of a bar graph presents the scores resulting from the twenty-five measures of Books One and Two.

As examples, ten items from the concerns section of Book One are given below. The respondent answers by choosing one of six answers: N—never bothered, NL—no longer bothered, V—very much bothered, Q—quite a bit bothered, S—somewhat bothered, and L—very little bothered.

*I am bothered by the fact that . . .*
21. we are not close as members of a family.
22. my parents seem to have forgotten how it feels to be young.
23. I am easily carried away by my emotions.
24. I become discouraged rather easily.
25. I have little interest in school studies.
26. some teachers act as though a teenager knows practically nothing.
27. classmates at school could be more friendly.
28. our national government often seems unresponsive to the needs of people.
29. I do not feel I help others enough.
30. pollution of our air and water threatens to destroy all human life.

RELIABILITY AND VALIDITY: Two methods of assessing reliability have been used. Hoyt's method of determining homogeneity of scales yields a median reliability of .86 for the ten concern scales, a median reliability of .75 for the eleven values and beliefs scales, and a median reliability of .79 for the three perception scales. A test-retest assessment of reliability on eighty-eight high school juniors showed relatively high reliability over a seven-month period for nine scales (.70-.80), medium reliability for eight scales (.60-.69), and low reliability for eight others (.48-.59). The rationale that served as a guide in the construction and use of the instrument also provides the conceptual framework for establishing construct validity. Seventy null hypotheses based on the rationale for the ten concern scales are all confirmed empirically in the predicted or hypothesized direction. With respect to the values and beliefs scales, ten of the eleven scales are provided validity-supporting evidence from tests of an additional seventy null hypotheses. A final group of three perception scales are confirmed by evidence (.01 level) on forty-two tests of validity. A comparison of responses to items found both in the Lie Scales of the MMPI and in the Youth Survey shows a higher degree of candor and frankness among respondents in the sample of 7,050.

BIBLIOGRAPHY:

Strommen, M. P. *Five Cries of Youth.* New York: Harper & Row, 1974.
Strommen, M. P., and Gupta, R. K. *Youth Research Survey Manual: Section 1. How the Survey Is Used.* Minneapolis, Minnesota: Youth Research Center, 1971a.
Strommen, M. P., and Gupta, R. K. *Youth Research Survey Manual: Section 3. How the Survey Is Interpreted.* Minneapolis, Minnesota: Youth Research Center, 1971b.
Strommen, M. P., and Gupta, R. K. *Youth Research Survey Manual: Section 4. How the Survey Was Developed.* Minneapolis, Minnesota: Youth Research Center, 1971c.
Williams, D. L. *Becoming the Gift.* Minneapolis, Minnesota: Youth Research Center, 1975.

# Category 9

Social Behavior

*This category includes measures of interaction, particularly between children and the adults in their environment. Measures of aggressive behavior are included here because aggression is usually defined as involving others; thus in that sense it is social behavior. Several of the measures are frames of reference for observing social behavior.*

## AGGRESSION INVENTORY (AI)

AUTHOR: Guy T. Doyal

AGE: Kindergarten to grade 12

VARIABLE: Manifest aggression in school

TYPE OF MEASURE: Self-report inventory

SOURCE FROM WHICH MEASURE MAY BE OBTAINED: Guy T. Doyal, Department of Educational and Clinical Psychology, Wayne State University, Detroit, Michigan 48202.

DESCRIPTION OF MEASURE: The Aggression Inventory (AI) was constructed to measure the ways in which a child describes his responses to common aggressive or hostile behavior. The AI consists of seventeen questions dealing with common school and home situations that can provoke counteraggressive responses from a child. The child is given four possible responses from which to describe how he would react. Possible scores for each question range from 1 for a low aggressive response to 4 for a high aggressive response. A total manifest aggression score is obtained by summing the individual question scores. A low total score indicates an $S$ who reacts to an aggressive act with less counteraggression than does an $S$ who obtains a higher score.

As examples, six items of the inventory are given below, with their aggression value indicated.

1. A boy is walking down the aisle to the teacher's desk and a girl stuck out her foot and tripped him. If you were the boy, would you
   a. stick your tongue out at her? (2)
   b. hit her back as hard as possible? (4)
   c. scream, "Don't do that again"? (3)
   d. ignore it and walk away? (1)
2. Someone threw a wet spitball at the back of your head when the teacher wasn't looking. Would you
   a. throw one back at who you think did it? (3)
   b. yell, "Someone threw a spitball at me"? (2)
   c. tell the teacher? (1)
   d. kick the one you think did it as you walk past his desk? (4)
3. The teacher is out of the room. You are all working on a test assignment. The person in front of you turned around and scribbled on your test paper. Would you
   a. scribble back on his paper? (3)
   b. hit him? (4)
   c. wait and tell the teacher when he comes back? (2)
   d. erase the marks and finish your test? (1)
12. You bring a friend home from school to play. While playing, your friend accidently breaks something belonging to your mother. Should you
   a. tell your clumsy friend to go home because you're going to catch heck from your mother? (4)
   b. clean up the mess and hide it so you won't get in trouble? (2)

c. holler for mother and tell her in front of your friend that you had nothing to do with it? (3)

d. after your friend leaves try to explain to mother it was an accident? (1)

14. Your parents punish you for coming home late. Should you

a. go to your room and draw angry pictures while playing your record player loud-ly? (1)

b. pout the rest of the evening? (2)

c. take it out on your little brother or sister? (4)

d. complain about dinner? (3)

15. You are mad because mother is calling you to come in to do a chore you did not finish while you are having fun playing outdoors with your friends. Would you

a. pretend you didn't hear her? (4)

b. go in, finish the chore quickly and return outdoors to play with your friends? (1)

c. yell back to mother, "Can't we finish this game first, it's my turn to be up soon"? (3)

d. try to get your brother to do it so you won't have to leave the game? (2)

RELIABILITY AND VALIDITY: None reported.

BIBLIOGRAPHY:

Doyal, G. T., Ferguson, J., and Rockwood, I. "A Group Method for Modifying In-appropriate Aggressive Behavior in the Elementary School." *American Journal of Orthopsychiatry*, 1971, *41*, 311-312.

---

# ANGER SELF-REPORT (ASR)

AUTHORS: Martin L. Zelin, Gerald Adler, and Paul Myerson

AGE: 13 years to geriatrics

VARIABLE: Awareness and expression of anger, guilt, mistrust

TYPE OF MEASURE: Likert-type questionnaire

SOURCE FROM WHICH MEASURE MAY BE OBTAINED: For reprint write Martin L. Zelin, 260 Tremont Street, Seventh Floor, Boston, Massachusetts 02166.

DESCRIPTION OF MEASURE: The items and scores of existing aggression inventories confound the awareness of angry feelings with the expression of hostility and anger in behavior. Separation of these factors is crucial for psychodynamic formulations of aggression and for related psychotherapies. The Anger Self-Report (ASR) differentiates between the awareness and expression of aggression. The ASR is a sixty-four-item

Likert-type questionnaire yielding separate scores for awareness of anger; expression of anger (subscales for general, physical, and verbal expression); guilt; condemnation of anger; and mistrust. The reliabilities of the eight ASR scales and their intercorrelations indicate sufficient independent, reliable variance so that an anger profile based on the eight ASR scores can be validly employed for predictions about individuals. For example, Ss high on Awareness and low on Expression can be differentiated from Ss who are high on both scales.

Sample items from each scale are given below. The number of items in each scale appears in parenthesis. The respondent answers on a 6-point scale ranging from "strong agreement" to "strong disagreement."

*Awareness of Anger* (13)
Sometimes I feel that I could injure someone.
*General Expression of Aggression* (7)
If I am mad, I really let people know it.
*Physical Aggression* (5)
I can think of no good reason for ever hitting anyone.
*Verbal Aggression* (11)
I will criticize someone to his face if he deserves it.
*Guilt* (9)
I blame myself if anything goes wrong.
*Condemnation of Anger* (7)
It's useless to get angry.
*Mistrust or Suspicion* (12)
People will hurt you if you don't watch out.

RELIABILITY AND VALIDITY: Validation studies were done on samples of eighty-two psychiatric patients and sixty-seven college students. In the patient sample, ASR scores were correlated with psychiatrists' ratings on the sixteen most relevant Problem Appraisal Scales (PAS) developed by Endicott and Spitzer (1972). A multitrait, multimethod of analysis of these correlations yielded substantial convergent and discriminant validities for the ASR scales. For example, the highest correlation (.41) for the physical expression scale is with ratings of assaultive acts on the PAS. The largest correlations for verbal expression were $-.36$ with dependency and $-.31$ with anger, belligerence, negativism. Verbal expression also correlated .28 with antisocial attitudes and acts. The total expression scale, obtained by summing the expression subscales, correlated even more saliently than the subscales. Awareness of anger correlated .24 with antisocial attitudes and acts and $-.37$ with ratings of obsessions and compulsions. Furthermore, awareness lacked sufficient correlations with PAS scales reflecting the expression of anger, thereby demonstrating its discriminant validity. The highest correlations of the ASR guilt scale was .48 with suicidal thoughts and .33 with depression—inferiority. Finally, the highest correlation for the ASR mistrust scale was with ratings of mistrust—suspicion (.33). (All above $r$s are significant beyond the .05 level and some beyond the .01 level.)

BIBLIOGRAPHY:

Endicott, J., and Spitzer, R. L. "What! Another Rating Scale? The Psychiatric Evaluation Form." *Journal of Nervous and Mental Disease,* 1972, *154,* 88-104.

Zelin, M. L., Adler, G., and Myerson, P. G. "The Anger Self-Report: An Objective Questionnaire for the Measurement of Aggression." *Journal of Consulting and Clinical Psychology,* 1972, *39,* 340.

---

# APPLE OBSERVATION SYSTEM

AUTHORS: Nadine M. Lambert, Carolyn S. Hartsough, and Barbara C. Moore

AGE: School-age children

VARIABLE: Noncognitive classroom behavior

TYPE OF MEASURE: Observation system

SOURCE FROM WHICH MEASURE MAY BE OBTAINED: Nadine M. Lambert, School of Education, University of California, Berkeley, California 94720.

DESCRIPTION OF MEASURE: Events in the APPLE Observation System are sentences describing the behavior of a child in the classroom. They focus on what the child is observed to do, the antecedent conditions producing the observed behavior, the teacher response to the child (if any), and the learning context of the observed behavior. An observation is composed of the information that normally accompanies different kinds of school events.

The observer reports (1) pupil behavior, (2) the pupil activity (curriculum content), (3) the context of interaction (teacher-class, teacher-individual pupil, pupil-pupil, and so on), (4) the teacher activity, and (5) the teacher response to the pupil behavior. These mandatory sets of information make the APPLE analogous to the multiple-category rather than to the single-category observation systems used and recommended by other investigators. The five were those considered critical for the interpretation of a pupil's events.

Following the designation of the mandatory information, the observer reports the event in natural English language, avoiding inferential statements unless they are marked "observer inference" or "observer judgment" in the observation report. At the end of a period of observation, the observation report forms contain a series of descriptions of classroom behavior along with the applicable mandatory information, and without further editing, they are ready for coding and formating, keypunching and entry into a computer system.

The *Lexicon for Observation in the Schools* (Lambert and Hartsough, 1971) contains the names used to label observational events. Derived empirically from an analysis of over 20,000 school observations, the names defined represent a comprehensive collection of the total possible observable behaviors of children in school, pupil activities, context, teacher activities, and teacher responses.

The main categories of pupil event names have been defined as (1) academic performance, abilities, and interests; (2) personality traits and attitudes; (3) physical characteristics and activity; (4) health and illness; (5) family status and characteristics; (6) orientation to instruction; (7) affective behavior; (8) social interactions; and (9) administrative actions and judgments. Subheadings further define the content of each of these categories.

RELIABILITY AND VALIDITY: The authors (1971) had six observers record the behavior of twenty-four children divided among grades 1, 4, and 6 with the following results: (1) When no instructions are given, and the children to be observed are selected and agreed upon by the observers, the relative frequency of observations per child is fairly reliable ($r = .8$). (2) Multiple observers record relatively similar behaviors and the proportions of observations of different types in an observation sample do not differ from the proportions in a record of 7,590 observations. (3) When two judges coded each observation according to the *Lexicon* instructions, they were in general agreement as to the assignment of event names. Disagreements resulted from multiple behaviors within a single observation and such situations are now specified with an alternate event name option at the time the observation is coded for entry to the APPLE information system. The validity of the system for defining teacher performance related to pupil learning was established in the *Beginning Teacher Evaluation Study* (Lambert and Hartsough, 1975a).

BIBLIOGRAPHY:

Lambert, N. M. and Hartsough, C. S. *Lexison for Observation in the Schools.* Berkeley: University of California, 1971.

Lambert, N. M. and Hartsough, C. S. "APPLE Observation Variables and Their Relation to Reading and Mathematics Achievement," in *Beginning Teacher Evaluation Study,* Vol. 3. Princeton, N.J.: Educational Testing Service, 1975a.

Lambert, N. M. and Hartsough, C. S. *Lexicon for APPLE Observations.* Berkeley: University of California, 1975b.

Lambert, N. M. and Hartsough, C. S. *Manual for APPLE Observers.* Berkeley: University of California 1975c.

Lambert, N. M., Hartsough, C. S., and Moore, B. C. *Manual for Observation in the Schools.* Berkeley: University of California, 1971.

---

# BEHAVIOR-OBSERVATION FORMAT FOR CHILDREN INTERACTING IN A CLASSROOM

AUTHORS: John S. Wodarski, Robert L. Hamblin, David R. Buckholdt, and Daniel E. Ferritor

AGE: 6 to 12 years

VARIABLE: Peer tutoring, studying, nonstudying, and disruptive behaviors

TYPE OF MEASURE: Behavioral rating scale

SOURCE FROM WHICH MEASURE MAY BE OBTAINED: For copy of measure and/ or permission to reproduce: John S. Wodarski, University of Tennesee, School of Social Work, Knoxville Branch, Box 8820 University Station, Knoxville, Tennessee 37916.

DESCRIPTION OF MEASURE: This behavior-observation procedure measures peer tutoring, studying, nonstudying, and disruptive behavior of children interacting in classroom contexts. Peer-tutoring behavior is recorded whenever any of the following occur: (1) A pupil hands another pupil a material object such as a pencil, paper, or eraser that the other needs to continue working on his assignment. (2) One pupil asks the teacher to help another pupil with his assignment. The teacher follows up the request by going to the pupil. In order for this to be designated as peer tutoring, the teacher must go to the child and help with a problem. (3) One pupil clarifies the teacher's instructions for another pupil. The pupil who had the instructions clarified now begins to work on the assignment. (4) One pupil gives the meaning of a word in the assignment to another pupil. After the pupil gives the meaning of the word, he begins to work on his assignment. (5) Two pupils ask the teacher together for help on a problem or for an answer to a problem. The teacher assists them with the problem or gives them the answer. (6) Two pupils work on the same problem. For example, one pupil shows the other pupil the mechanics of "carrying." The other three basic categories of interaction (studying, nonstudying, and disruptive) are similarly spelled out.

RELIABILITY AND VALIDITY: Reliability was established through simultaneous ratings of pupils in a fourth-grade classroom and videotapes illustrating classroom interaction of children between the ages of 6 and 12. The tapes included numerous instances of peer tutoring, studying, nonstudying, and disruptive behavior. After 8 hours of training wherein conceptual categories were clarified and observers became accustomed to the behavioral checklist, reliability consistently averaged at the 96-percent-agreement level.

BIBLIOGRAPHY:

Wodarski, J. S., Hamblin, R. L., Buckholdt, D. R., and Ferritor, D. E. "Individual Consequences Versus Different Shared Consequences Contingent upon the Performance of Low Achieving Group Members." *Journal of Applied Social Psychology,* 1973, *3,* 276-290.

Wodarski, J. S., Hamblin, R., and Hathaway, C. "Group Contingencies, Peer Tutoring, and Accelerating Academic Achievement." In E. A. Ramp and B. L. Hopkins (Eds.), *A New Direction for Education: Behavior Analysis.* Lawrence: University of Kansas Press, 1971.

# BEHAVIOR PROBLEMS CHECKLIST

AUTHORS: John F. Feldhusen and John R. Thurston

AGE: Elementary, junior high, and senior high school students

VARIABLE: Socially approved and aggressive-disruptive classroom behavior

TYPE OF MEASURE: Checklist

SOURCE FROM WHICH MEASURE MAY BE OBTAINED: John F. Feldhusen, Educational Psychology Section, Purdue University SCC-G, West Lafayette, Indiana 47906.

DESCRIPTION OF MEASURE: The Behavior Problems Checklist was designed to help teachers designate children whose behaviors would be considered socially disapproved. It was used in obtaining samples of children whose behavior was judged either socially approved or socially disapproved for evaluation in the Eau Claire County Youth Study research on disruptive school children. Each teacher participating in the study was asked to indicate on the checklist which of eighteen behavior traits were characteristic of each child nominated. These behavior traits are: "is quarrelsome," "is sullen," "is rude," "is defiant," "is resentful," "steals," "lies," "is destructive," "disrupts class," "is a bully," "has temper tantrums," "is tardy or absent without excuse," "uses profanity or obscenity," "fights with other pupils," "is deceptive," "is overly dominant," "is cruel," and "talks back." The Behavior Checklist takes 15 minutes to complete.

RELIABILITY AND VALIDITY: The reliability was checked and found satisfactory through interteacher and intrateacher renominations at two-week and one-year intervals. Information on validity may be obtained from articles emanating from the Eau Claire County Youth Study (see Thurston, Feldhusen, and Benning, 1964).

BIBLIOGRAPHY:

Benning, J. J., Feldhusen, J. F., and Thurston, J. R. "A Study of Children Who Display Aggressive Behavior in the Classroom." *Wisconsin Journal for Curriculum Leadership,* 1964-65, *2,* 19-22.

Feldhusen, J. F., Thurston, J. R., and Ager, E. G. "Delinquency Proneness of Urban and Rural Youth." *Journal of Research in Crime and Delinquency,* 1965, *2,* 32-44.

Feldhusen, J. F., Thurston, J. R., and Benning, J. J. "Sentence Completion Responses and Classroom Social Behavior." *Personnel and Guidance Journal,* 1966, *45,* 165-170.

Feldhusen, J. F., Thurston, J. R., and Benning, J. J. "Classroom Behavior, Intelligence, and Achievement." *Journal of Experimental Education,* 1967, *36,* 82-87.

Thurston, J. R., Benning, J. J., and Feldhusen, J. F. "Delinquency Proneness and Classroom Behavior." *Criminologica,* 1967, *4,* 36-43.

Thurston, J. R., Feldhusen, J. F., and Benning, J. J. *Classroom Behavior: Background Factors and Psycho-Social Correlates.* Madison, Wisconsin: State Department of Public Welfare, 1964.

*Prepared by John R. Thurston*

## BEHAVIOR RATINGS AND ANALYSIS OF
## COMMUNICATION IN EDUCATION (BRACE)

AUTHORS: Garda W. Bowman and Rochelle Selbert Mayer

AGE: Kindergarten to grade 6

VARIABLE: Adult/child verbal communication and behavior; characteristics of educational settings

TYPE OF MEASURE: Systematic classroom observation, behavior ratings, and activity sampling

SOURCE FROM WHICH MEASURE MAY BE OBTAINED: Hyman Wolotsky, Bank Street College of Education, 610 West 112th Street, New York, New York 10025. The cost of the printed instrument and training package varies with the combination of components purchased. Information is available upon request.

DESCRIPTION OF MEASURE: The BRACE system of observation and analysis of child/adult interaction in educational settings is a merging of two instruments: the ACE (Analysis of Verbal Communication in Education) and the BORIS (Behavioral Observation Ratings in Settings). The combination of these two instruments makes it possible to correlate child/adult patterns of communication and behavior with the components and climate of the learning environment. The system yields an objective, quantifiable, and comprehensive picture of a classroom and the quality of learning that is taking place therein. BRACE can be and has been used (1) as a staff development instrument, to sensitize teachers and paraprofessionals to their own patterns of communication and classroom management (a short form has been devised for this purpose); (2) as a diagnostic tool, to assess individual children's language and behavior; (3) as a process-evaluation instrument, to assess the learning environment and the quality of interaction within it in relation to specific educational objectives; and (4) as a program evaluation instrument, to measure the impact of a given type of intervention upon the language, behavior, and activities of children. In 1974 a training package was prepared that includes the printed instrument, a manual, training films with coded transcripts of same, and a computer program for data processing.

RELIABILITY AND VALIDITY: ACE was developed for Bank Street's Follow-Through Program in 1970 and has been refined through the years. In 1972 a rigid reliability test was applied when seventy-seven classrooms in the Career Opportunities Program (COP) were observed by teams of two, coding the same subject at the same time in each classroom. Reliability scores for the various categories tested ranged from 71.6 percent to 94 percent. BORIS has been used in comparing several Follow-Through sponsors in a study conducted for Harvard University. Reliability scores for the various categories tested ranged from 82 percent to 96 percent. The instrument was utilized in the combined form in seventeen communities across the nation in 1974-1975. At least 80 percent agreement has been required before observers were qualified to start data collection in these studies and in all summative research. Validity was established by reference to an advisory committee of educators and also by the fact that the instrument measured statistically significant differences between the Bank Street Laboratory

School, the Follow-Through classrooms, the COP-aided classrooms, and comparison groups in the regular school system. The consistency of these differences, as measured by *chi*-square, suggests that the instrument provides valid indexes of goal fulfillment. The most positive scores consistently occurred in the Laboratory School where there were optimum conditions for goal fulfillment, and the least positive scores consistently occurred in the regular school system where there were no innovative programs designed to help children develop autonomy, motivation, self-confidence, productivity, and the ability to reason and to think creatively or to interact cooperatively.

BIBLIOGRAPHY:

Bowman, G. W. "Team Training in Systematic Observation of Early Childhood Education in the Career Opportunities Program." *Journal of Research and Development in Education,* 1973, *5,* 106-148.
Boyer, E. G., Simon, A., and Karafin, G. (Eds.) *Measures of Maturation: An Anthology of Early Childhood Observation Instruments.* Philadelphia, Pennsylvania: Research for Better Schools, 1973.
Mayer, R. S. "Describing Children's Experiences in Theoretically Different Classrooms: An Observational Assessment of Four Early Education Curriculum Models." Unpublished manuscript. Cambridge, Massachusetts: Harvard University, 1973.

*Prepared by Garda W. Bowman and Rochelle Selbert Mayer*

---

# BEHAVIORAL-OBSERVATION CHECKLIST FOR CHILDREN AND THERAPIST INTERACTING IN A GROUP

AUTHORS: John S. Wodarski and Ronald A. Feldman

AGE: 8 to 16 years

VARIABLE: Various behaviors of children and therapist

TYPE OF MEASURE: Behavioral-observation checklist

SOURCE FROM WHICH MEASURE MAY BE OBTAINED: John S. Wodarski, University of Tennessee, School of Social Work, Knoxville Branch, Box 8820 University Station, Knoxville, Tennessee 37916.

DESCRIPTION OF MEASURE: This behavioral rating scale measures prosocial, non-social, and antisocial behavior of children interacting in groups. In addition it measures the following therapist behaviors: individual or group interventions, directions, physical contact, praise, positive attention, holding, criticism, threats, negative attention, and time-out.

    As an example, the section of the checklist concerned with prosocial behavior is given below.

1. Mark "1" if the child exhibits any of the following prosocial behaviors:
   a. One child hands another child a material object, such as a basketball or hockey stick, which the latter child needs to continue participating in the group activity.
   b. One child asks the group leader or another child to help someone in the activity.
   a. Two children work on the same activity together. For example, one child shows the other, or helps the other overcome difficulties so that they may execute the activity.
   d. One child helps another participate in the discussion of some topic by making a comment that elicits continued verbal behavior. Example: One child is talking about drugs and the other says "good point," "please continue," "elaborate more," "tell us more," and so forth.
   e. A child is engaged in the group activity.
   f. A child asks the worker about the group activity.
   g. A child engages in the decision-making process verbally or nonverbally, e.g., nods his head, pats another child for engaging in the process, smiles, is listening or sitting, has eye contact with the worker or another child.
   h. A child makes an appropriate comment.
   i. A child tries to help someone, shares something with another child, stops other children from arguing or fighting, helps children be friends with one another, or tries to do something nice even though nobody expected it.
   j. A child says nice things to another child, such as "I like you."
   k. A child helps other group members to straighten up their belongings, solve a problem, or fix something that was broken.
   l. A child helps the group leader by paying attention to him, cooperating with him, or carrying out reasonable instructions.

RELIABILITY AND VALIDITY: Checklist reliability was established through simultaneous ratings of behavior recorded on videotapes illustrating the small-group behavior of prosocial and antisocial children. The tapes include numerous instances of prosocial, nonsocial, and antisocial behavior. The tapes illustrate children interacting in various types of situations, such as discussing difficulties at school or with parents, painting, playing ball, building a campfire, situations involving drugs and sexual relationships, and so forth. After 20 hours of training wherein conceptual categories were clarified and observers became accustomed to the behavioral checklist, reliability on the checklist measuring children's prosocial, nonsocial, and antisocial behaviors consistently averaged above 92 percent. Reliability for the therapists' behavior part of the checklist was established in the same manner as described for the children's part of the checklist. After 20 hours of training with considerations for clarification of conceptual categories and becoming accustomed to the scale, reliability for this aspect of the behavioral scale was 85 percent. This criterion is considered adequate since there are eighteen categories into which the various behaviors can be scored.

BIBLIOGRAPHY:

Feldman, R. A., Wodarski, J. S., and Flax, N. "Anti-Social Children in a Summer Camp Environment: A Time Sampling Study." *Community Mental Health Journal,* 1975, *11,* 10-18.

Wodarski, J. S., Feldman, R. A., and Flax, N. "Group Integration and Behavioral Change: Pro-Social and Anti-Social Children at Summer Camp." *Social Work,* 1973, *18,* 26-37.

Wodarski, J. S., Rubeiz, G., and Feldman, R. A. "Social Group Work with Anti-Social Children: An Empirical Investigation of the Relevance of Programming." *American Journal of Orthopsychiatry*, 1973, *43*, 250-251.

---

# BRIEF MEASURES OF EXPLORATIONS
# OF PREFERENCES AND BEHAVIOR

AUTHOR: Daniel W. Edwards

AGE: Grade 8 to adult

VARIABLE: Social exploration behavior

TYPE OF MEASURE: Questionnaire and frequency scales

SOURCE FROM WHICH MEASURE MAY BE OBTAINED: Daniel W. Edwards, University of California–Davis, Sacramento Medical Center, 4430 "V" Street, Sacramento, California 95817.

DESCRIPTION OF MEASURE: These measures were created as part of a longitudinal study of the social and emotional development of high school students (Edwards, 1971). Their major use was in a validity study of a measure of exploration preferences, to insure that preference and not behavior was the major variable assessed.
    Examples are given below.

*Social Exploration Behavior*
How many times in the last seven days "I looked for new people to meet" (responses from 0 to 13+).
*Classroom Exploration Behavior*
How many times in the last seven days "I looked for a new way of doing something in class" (responses from 0 to 13+).
*Social Exploration Preferences*
"How often would you prefer to look for new people to meet?" (7-point scale from "never," 1, to "always," 7).
*Classroom Exploration Preferences*
"How often would you prefer to look for a new way of doing something in class?" (7-point scale from "never," 1, to "always," 7).

RELIABILITY AND VALIDITY: Coefficient *alpha* (internal consistency) for the two behavior subscales is .88 (social) and .87 (classroom). The two behavior scales correlate less than .60 with the preference scales. The behavior scales correlate .31 and .28 with an alternative measure of exploration preferences, while the preference scales correlate .67 and .57 with the alternative measure of exploration preferences. The scales have low correlations with the Marlowe-Crowne Social Desirability Scale ($r = .31$).

BIBLIOGRAPHY:

Edwards, D. W. "Exploration and the High School Experience: A Study of Tenth Grade Boys' Perceptions of Themselves, Their Peers, and Their Schools." Unpublished doctoral dissertation. University of Michigan, Ann Arbor, 1971.

---

## CHECKLIST FOR EARLY RECOGNITION
## OF PROBLEMS IN CLASSROOMS

AUTHOR: Jay Schleichkorn

AGE: Elementary school

VARIABLE: Deviant behavior

TYPE OF MEASURE: Checklist

SOURCE FROM WHICH MEASURE MAY BE OBTAINED: School of Allied Health Professionals, State University of New York at Stony Brook, Stony Brook, New York 11794.

DESCRIPTION OF MEASURE: The checklist is simply to be used to help determine if an apparent problem should be further checked by medical and educational personnel. By itself, the checklist can assist the teacher to recognize any early developing problems, but it should not be the final word on labeling the child.

As examples, twenty-eight items of the checklist are given below. Other categories include behavior, responses (aural), communication (verbal), conceptual ability, and perception.

*Coordination and Motor Activities*
1. Has difficulty in walking up stairs.
2. Cannot skip.
3. Holds a pencil or pen in a weak or clumsy grasp.
4. Has difficulty in using scissors.
5. Has jerky movements.
6. Trips often.
7. Bumps into objects.
8. Cannot tie knots, zip zippers, button buttons.
9. Turns head from side to side in a rhythmic pattern.
10. Demonstrates poor balance.
11. Touches other children all the time.
12. Startles easily.
13. Appears hyperactive.
14. Fatigues easily.

15. Can't manage two subjects.
16. Is clumsy in general.
17. Can't catch a ball.
18. Has sloppy eating habits.
19. Has difficulty in walking a straight line.
20. Cannot balance objects.
21. Cannot stay neat for any length of time.
22. Drools.
23. Displays weakness in an extremity.
24. Walks with feet turned inward.
25. Walks on toes.
26. Favors one extremity.
27. Drags a foot.
28. Shuffles feet.

RELIABILITY AND VALIDITY: None reported.

BIBLIOGRAPHY: None reported.

---

# CHILDREN'S PATHOLOGY INDEX (CPI)

AUTHORS: Harvey R. Alderton and B. A. Hoddinott

AGE: 6 to 12 years

VARIABLE: Four factors described below

TYPE OF MEASURE: Rating scale

SOURCE FROM WHICH MEASURE MAY BE OBTAINED: Harvey R. Alderton, Department of Psychiatry, Faculty of Medicine, University of Toronto, Toronto, Canada.

DESCRIPTION OF MEASURE: The CPI (copyrighted) consists of twenty-five categories of disturbed behavior, relationship, attitude, or emotional response. There are five statements within each category, ranging from normal to increasing disturbance. Factor analysis showed twenty-five categories that loaded most strongly on four factors: (I) disturbed behavior toward adults (ten categories), (II) neurotic construction (five categories), (III) destructive behavior (five categories), and (IV) disturbed self-perception (five categories). The rater selects one item from each category as best representing the child's current status. Selections are made in the order in which the categories are printed on the form. Scores for each category range from 5 for the most normal to 1 for the most abnormal functioning. Ratings are made by four staff familiar with the child and the results pooled to give scoring ranges for factor I of 40-200 and factors II, III, and IV, each 20-100.

As examples, two of the twenty-five categories of the index are given below. The rater chooses the statement from each category that best describes the child.

1. *Affection and Staff*
   a. Actively rejects affection from anyone.
   b. Indifferent when affection shown by anyone.
   c. Seeks excessive affection from most of the staff.
   d. Seeks excessive affection from a few favorite staff only.
   e. Seeks normal affection from favorite staff.
2. *Hostility–General*
   a. Extremely hostile most of the time towards everyone, often with physical violence.
   b. Very hostile much of the time, sullen, bitter, or resentful.
   c. Very hostile part of the time but can be cooperative and friendly.
   d. Occasional outbursts of hostility without a sufficient cause.
   e. Not hostile but normally assertive and active.

RELIABILITY AND VALIDITY: Test-retest reliability for ratings made forty-two days apart ($N = 26$) ranged from .72 to .88. A significant test-retest relationship was found in twenty-three subjects up to thirty weeks between ratings, but it expectedly falls with time. Interrater reliability using randomly assigned raters (for $N = 42$ children) gave $W$ (coefficient of concordance) values of .69, .67, .70, and .62. With $N = 14$, $W$ values were .71, .74, .73, and .69, all significant at the .001 level. Face validity is evident for all four factors. Construct validity was demonstrated for Factor I, through a significant correlation between time-sample observed aggression to adults and the Factor I scores in forty subjects. A biserial correlation of .82 between Factor I scores and the psychiatric estimate of prognosis demonstrated concurrent validity. Predictive validity was shown for Factors I, III, and IV (at the $< .005$, $< .05$, and $< .025$ levels, respectively) in forty children followed up eighteen months after discharge from treatment. Another study found a significant relationship between Factor I ratings at discharge and antisocial symptoms (.003) at follow-up, and between the discharge Factor III score and antisocial symptoms ($< .01$).

BIBLIOGRAPHY:

Alderton, H. R. "The Children's Pathology Index as a Predictor of Follow-up Adjustment." *Canadian Psychiatric Association Journal,* 1970, *15,* 289-294.
Alderton, H. R. "A Comparison of the Residential Treatment Response of Children's Aid Society Wards and Nonwards." *Canadian Psychiatric Association Journal,* 1972, *17,* 291-293.
Alderton, H. R. "The Residential Treatment Response of Disturbed Children Using Serial Ratings of Adjustment." *Canadian Psychiatric Association Journal,* 1972, *17,* 294-298.
Alderton, H. R. "A Comparison of Two Residential Treatment Units for Children." In D. S. Sankar (Ed.), *Mental Health in Children.* Vol. 3. New York: P. J. D. Publishers, 1975.
Alderton, H. R., and Hoddinott, B. A. "The Children's Pathology Index." *Canadian Psychiatric Association Journal,* 1968, *13,* 353-361.

# CLASSROOM SOCIO-OBSERVATION

AUTHORS: Jo Lynn Cunningham and R. F. Reyes

AGE: 2 to 6 years

VARIABLE: Peer proximity, thematic proximity

TYPE OF MEASURE: Classroom observation

SOURCE FROM WHICH MEASURE MAY BE OBTAINED: Institute for Family and Child Study, Home Management Unit #2, Michigan State University, East Lansing, Michigan 48824.

DESCRIPTION OF MEASURE: This classroom socio-observation technique is a point-time sampling procedure to be used in a classroom setting during a free-play session. The observer notes the spatial relationship of children, adults, and materials in the classroom making two observations each day, both during indoor free-play times. The observational protocol is a drawing of the classroom with major furnishings and activity areas placed on the drawing. The observer places the children's code letters (first-name initials) on the drawing to correspond to their placement in the classroom, along with a rating of their level of social participation. The primary variable derived from repeated daily or weekly observations is the mean level of social behavior that comes from the rating of the child according to the following format: 1 = unoccupied behavior, 2 = solitary play, 3 = onlooker behavior, 4 = parallel play, 5 = associative play, 6 = cooperative play. These are extensively described for the observer's use. Variables derived from repeated daily or weekly observations include mean level of social behavior, mean number of children in proximity, heterogeneity of peer proximity, and adult dependence. Depending on the purposes for implementing the procedure, other behaviors can be noted. For example, sex-role behaviors can be observed by noting the sex typing of the play materials and the type of peers the subjects are involved with.

RELIABILITY AND VALIDITY: None reported.

BIBLIOGRAPHY:

Cunningham, J. L., and Reyes, R. F. "The Sociometry of Preschool Children." Unpublished paper. Michigan State University, East Lansing, 1969.
Parten, M. "Social Participation Among Preschool Children." *Journal of Abnormal and Social Psychology*, 1932, *22*, 243-269.

*Prepared by Robert P. Boger*

## COMPLIANT, AGGRESSIVE, DETACHED (CAD) INTERPERSONAL INVENTORY

AUTHOR: Joel B. Cohen

AGE: Adolescence and up

VARIABLE: Compliant, aggressive, detached interpersonal orientations

TYPE OF MEASURE: Likert-type instrument

SOURCE FROM WHICH MEASURE MAY BE OBTAINED: See Cohen (1967).

DESCRIPTION OF MEASURE: The thirty-five-item CAD instrument was developed to assess Horney's (1945) categorization of people's predominant modes of response to others: moving toward others (compliant), moving against others (aggressive), and moving away from others (detached). Compliant and aggressive people desire to be with others; however, the compliant individual wishes to be loved, wanted, and valued as a companion. Compliant-oriented people tend to be oversensitive to others' needs, overgenerous, and overconsiderate, and to avoid interpersonal conflict. The compliant person seeks to manipulate others by being weak and dependent and relying on others to help him achieve his goals. Aggressive-oriented individuals want to excel, to achieve prestige and admiration from others. Other people are viewed both as competitors and as means to achieving desired ends. The aggressive person seeks to manipulate others by achieving power over them. Detached-oriented people want to put emotional distance between themselves and others. Freedom from obligation, independence, self-sufficiency, and withdrawal from situations involving interpersonal influence are desired. People are conceptualized as differing on the relative strength of each orientation, ranging from a "balanced" personality to one more strongly tied to one or two of the orientations. The CAD instrument assesses the relative strength of all three orientations. No norms (means and standard deviations) have been established for the three scales; females tend to score higher on C, males on A. Average scores for groups of college-aged men and women on the ten-item C scale range from 40 to 44, on the fifteen-item A scale from 46 to 51, and on the ten-item D scale from 28 to 30. Most people require about 10 minutes to complete the instrument.

As examples, the first ten of the thirty-five items on the instrument are given below. The respondent answers on a 6-point scale ranging from "extremely undesirable" to "extremely desirable."

1. Being free of emotional ties with others is . . .
2. Giving comfort to those in need of friends is . . .
3. The knowledge that most people would be fond of me at all times would be . . .
4. To refuse to give in to others in an argument seems . . .
5. Enjoying a good movie by myself is . . .
6. For me to pay little attention to what others think of me seems . . .
7. For me to be able to own an item before most of my friends are able to buy it would be . . .
8. Knowing that others are somewhat envious of me is . . .
9. To feel that I like everyone I know would be . . .
10. To be able to work hard while others are elsewhere having fun is . . .

RELIABILITY AND VALIDITY: First, high interjudge agreement that each item reflected the appropriate interpersonal orientation was established. Consistent predicted relationships between CAD and appropriate FIRO-B scales were found for fifty college students. Significant correlations were observed between CAD scales and scales developed to assess occupational preferences (differing in interpersonal characteristics) for seventy-eight college students. As predicted, college students studying in the graduate school of social welfare were found to be significantly higher on C, students working on master's degrees in business administration were higher on A, and students studying geology were higher on D. Response to personal influence was also studied. One study using thirty adults found that face-to-face group discussion produced the most opinion change among compliant people and the least change among aggressive people. In another study looking at the impact of social influence on college students' product evaluations, compliant people rated the product closest to the modal value, aggressive people furthest from the modal value, and detached people intermediate. A number of consumer-behavior applications have revealed weak to moderate predicted relationships with product preference and choice and response to persuasive communications. A CAD interpersonal anxiety measure has been developed by Tinkham (1973) to assess anxiety associated with each dimension. Test-retest reliability coefficients for the three scales over a one-month interval are: C = .75, A = .89, and D = .81. Because the CAD instrument was not designed to measure narrowly conceived traits but more multidimensional orientations, emphasis was not placed on internal consistency reliability in scale construction. Kuder-Richardson formula 20 coefficients for the three scales have been developed by both Kernan and Cohen. Kernan (1971) reports that C = .74, A = .71, and D = .72. Cohen (1966) reports that C = .82, A = .69, and D = .66.

BIBLIOGRAPHY:

Cohen, J. B. "Interpersonal Response Traits and Consumer Behavior." Unpublished doctoral dissertation. University of California, Los Angeles, 1966.

Cohen, J. B. "An Interpersonal Orientation to the Study of Consumer Behavior." *Journal of Marketing Research,* 1967, *4,* 270-278.

Cohen, J. B. "Toward an Interpersonal Theory of Consumer Behavior." *California Management Review,* 1968, *10,* 73-80.

Cohen, J. B., and Golden, E. "Informational Social Influence and Product Evaluation." *Journal of Applied Psychology,* 1972, *56,* 54-59.

Horney, K. *Our Inner Conflicts.* New York: Norton, 1945.

Kernan, J. B. "The CAD Instrument in Behavioral Diagnosis." In D. M. Gardner (Ed.), *Proceedings, Second Annual Conference of the Association for Consumer Research.* College Park, Maryland: Association for Consumer Research, 1971.

Kernan, J. B. "Her Mother's Daughter? The Case of Clothing and Cosmetic Fashions." *Adolescence,* 1973, *8,* 343-350.

Munson, J. M. "A Typological Investigation of Self-Concept Congruity and Brand Preferences: Toward a Predictive Model." Unpublished doctoral dissertation. University of Illinois, Urbana-Champaign, 1973.

Tinkham, S. F. "Interpersonal Traits, Interpersonal Anxiety and Response to Need-Oriented Communication." Unpublished doctoral dissertation. University of Illinois, Urbana-Champaign, 1973.

## COOPERATION-AGGRESSION BEHAVIOR SCALES

AUTHOR: Donald B. Keat III

AGE: Teachers of elementary-school children

VARIABLE: Cooperative vs. aggressive behaviors

TYPE OF MEASURE: Rating scale

SOURCE FROM WHICH MEASURE MAY BE OBTAINED: Donald B. Keat III, Department of Counselor Education, Pennsylvania State University, University Park, Pennsylvania 16802.

DESCRIPTION OF MEASURE: This instrument is essentially a short rating scale that can be quickly completed by teachers to help indicate the extent of a child's cooperativeness or aggressiveness. Extreme scores on the twenty-item scale can give a sense of whether or not specific help should be given. It is primarily useful as an "observation checklist" kind of aid.

As examples, the first five of the twenty items are given below, to be answered on a 5-point scale from "never" to "very frequently."

1. Does what is asked of him.
2. Gets along well with adults.
3. Follows directions, instructions, or rules.
4. Puts things away when finished or is asked to stop.
5. Plays well with other children.

RELIABILITY AND VALIDITY: None reported.

BIBLIOGRAPHY: None reported.

*Prepared by R. Judah*

---

## DELINQUENCY CHECKLIST (DCL)

AUTHORS: Kenneth B. Stein, Theodore R. Sarbin, and James A. Kulik

AGE: Adolescent males

VARIABLE: Delinquency

TYPE OF MEASURE: 5-point Likert scale

SOURCE FROM WHICH MEASURE MAY BE OBTAINED: Kenneth B. Stein, 517 Moraga Avenue, Piedmont, California 94611.

DESCRIPTION OF MEASURE: The scale consists of a self-report list of fifty-two types of antisocial behavior, and the subject indicates the category that reflects the frequency of having committed each act. The total score is the sum of the frequency categories endorsed. These items cover a wide spectrum of acts ranging from the very mild to very serious criminal behavior. An analysis of the internal structure of the test disclosed four oblique dimensions: delinquent role, drug usage, parental defiance, and assaultiveness.

As examples, the first fifteen even-numbered items are given below, to be answered from 0 to 4 ("never" to "very often").

To what extent have you broken the following rules and regulations since beginning grade school?
2. Defied your parents' authority (to their face)?
4. Cursed at your mother or father?
6. Come to school late in the morning?
8. Cheated on any class test?
10. "Run away" from home?
12. Been out past midnight when you were not accompanied by an adult?
14. "Beaten up" on a kid who hadn't done anything to you?
16. Bought or drank beer, wine, or liquor? (Include drinking at home.)
18. Drunk beer or liquor in a bar?
20. Stopped someone on the street, and asked for money?
22. Snuck into some place of entertainment (movie theater, ball game) without paying admission?
24. Carried a switchblade or other weapon?
26. Drunk so much that you could not remember afterwards some of the things you had done?
28. Gone for a ride in a car someone had stolen?
30. Taken things of medium value (between $2 and $50) that did not belong to you?

RELIABILITY AND VALIDITY: The internal reliabilities of the four dimensions in the order enumerated above are .95, .92, .78, and .88. The stability of these clusters was demonstrated in a replication on two other samples. Each dimension was found to be significant when the mean differences of delinquents and nondelinquents were compared. An inverse factoring produced seven patterned types of delinquents based on the four dimensions. These types were related to such variables as race, intactness of the home, socioeconomic status, slang knowledge, IQ, and anxiety. A comparison of the DCL administered under anonymous and nonanonymous conditions disclosed relatively small absolute change in scores and very high correlations between conditions.

BIBLIOGRAPHY:

Kulik, J. A., Stein, K. B., and Sarbin, T. R. "Dimensions and Patterns of Adolescent Antisocial Behavior." *Journal of Consulting and Clinical Psychology*, 1968, *32,* 375-382.
Kulik, J. A., Stein, K. B., and Sarbin, T. R. "Disclosure of Delinquent Behavior Under Conditions of Anonymity and Nonanonymity." *Journal of Consulting and Clinical Psychology,* 1968, *32,* 506-509.

# ECOLOGICAL ASSESSMENT OF CHILD PROBLEM BEHAVIOR

AUTHORS: Robert G. Wahler, A. E. House, and E. E. Stambaugh

AGE: 4 to 14 years

VARIABLE: Child behavior, peer behavior, caretaker behavior

TYPE OF MEASURE: Structured observation

SOURCE FROM WHICH MEASURE MAY BE OBTAINED: Robert G. Wahler, Child Behavior Institute, University of Tennessee, Knoxville, Tennessee 37916.

DESCRIPTION OF MEASURE: This is a structured observation procedure for use in home and school, comprised of six social-event (stimulus) categories and nineteen child-behavior (response) categories. Two of the social-event categories sample a grouping of adult behaviors that appear to be significant antecedents of child problem behaviors. These adult behaviors (nonaversive and aversive instructions) are common precursors of deviant child actions. Four other social-event categories describe frequent consequences of deviant and normal child behavior. These include nonaversive and aversive attention provided by adults and peers. The nineteen child-behavior categories are described in groupings that refer to general classes of behavior. Child behavior in home and school settings is segmented into five classes of behavior: compliance-opposition, autistic, play, work, and social. The category names are as follows:

*Response categories*

| | |
|---|---|
| Compliance | Self stimulation |
| Opposition | Object play |
| Aversive opposition | Self talk |
| Compliant | Sustained noninteraction |
| Sustained school work | Mand adult |
| Sustained toy play | Mand child |
| Sustained work | Social approach adult |
| Sustained attending | Social approach child |
| | Social interaction adult |
| | Social interaction child |

    Slash

*Stimulus categories*
    Instruction adult, nonaversive
    Instruction adult, aversive
    Social attention adult, nonaversive
    Social attention adult, aversive
    Social attention child, nonaversive
    Social attention child, aversive

*Procedural category*
    Obstruct

The manual provides detailed scoring examples and guidelines for the training of observers.

RELIABILITY AND VALIDITY: The authors recommend retraining of observers when interobserver reliability falls below 80 percent. Median percentage agreements between pairs of observers over all school observation sessions were found by the authors to be predominantly in the 80s. Reliability of the home observations was somewhat lower.

BIBLIOGRAPHY:

Wahler, R. G. "Setting Generality and General Effects of Child Behavior Therapy." *Journal of Applied Behavior Analysis,* 1969, *2,* 239-246.
Wahler, R. G., and Cormier, W. H. "The Ecological Interview: A First Step in Out-Patient Child Behavior Therapy." *Journal of Behavior Therapy and Experimental Psychiatry,* 1970, *1,* 279-289.

*Prepared by Orval G. Johnson*

---

# FAMILY INTERACTION SCALES (FIS)

AUTHORS: Jules Riskin and Elaine Faunce

AGE: 5 years to old age, in family groups

VARIABLE: Family interaction

TYPE OF MEASURE: Rating scale

SOURCE FROM WHICH MEASURE MAY BE OBTAINED: Coding manual available from Jules Riskin, 555 Middlefield, Palo Alto, California 94301. Cost: $5.00.

DESCRIPTION OF MEASURE: The FIS utilizes the author's *microanalytic* technique (that is, analyzing family interchange speech-by-speech) but has recently been modified for *macroscopic* or global ratings (that is, analyzing a family vocal interchange as a whole). The instrument assesses the following dimensions: clarity (verbal and tonal) of interaction; topic continuity vs. topic change; commitment vs. avoidance of commitment; agreement vs. disagreement; affective relationships (friendly, mutual, or attacking); intensity of affect (increased, normal, or decreased affect); who speaks and to whom; interruptions. All speech is scored on all variables.

RELIABILITY AND VALIDITY: See Riskin (1964) and Riskin and Faunce (1972).

BIBLIOGRAPHY:

Riskin, J. "Family Interaction Scales." *Archives of General Psychiatry,* 1964, *11,* 484-494.
Riskin, J., and Faunce, E. *Family Interaction Scales and Scoring Manual.* Published privately. 1968.

Riskin, J., and Faunce, E. "An Evaluative Review of Family Interaction Research." *Family Process,* 1972, *11,* 365-455.

Titchener, J. L., Vanderheide, C., and Woods, E. "Profiles of Family Interaction Systems." *Journal of Nervous and Mental Disease,* 1966, *143,* 473-480.

---

# HO-AG BIOGRAPHICAL INDEX

AUTHOR: Robert T. Green

AGE: 16 years and up

VARIABLE: Hostility-aggression

TYPE OF MEASURE: Edwards-type questionnaire

SOURCE FROM WHICH MEASURE MAY BE OBTAINED: Specimens of the revised scales are obtainable from R. T. Green, 15 Clifton Gardens, London, NW 11, England.

DESCRIPTION OF MEASURE: There are two equal forms of the index, A and B, with sixty items per scale plus eleven additional items per scale intended to measure introjected hostility and aggression. For these twenty-two items there are no data on validity, reliability, or norms. Some normative data are provided.

As examples, the first ten item pairs from Form A are given below.

| | |
|---|---|
| 1. I hardly ever chew gum. | I often chew gum. |
| 2. Most people are quite bright. | Most people are fairly stupid. |
| 3. When someone goes to the front of a queue out of turn I do something about it. | When someone goes to the front of the queue out of turn I let it pass. |
| 4. It is usually possible to avoid the kind of person who likes to push other people around. | Anyone who tries to push me around is asking for trouble. |
| 5. Power is important to most people. | Most people are not particularly interested in power. |
| 6. I go to see horror films at the cinema. | I do not go to see horror films at the cinema. |
| 7. If someone does me a bad turn I do not feel obliged to pay them back. | If someone does me a bad turn I feel I have to pay them back as a matter of principle. |
| 8. Sometimes I will take a risk just for the fun of it. | I avoid taking any unnecessary risks. |
| 9. Most people seem to be less patient than I am. | Most people seem to be more patient than I am. |

| 10. It is best to forget about it when some-<br>one does you a bad turn. | It pays to remember anyone who does<br>you a bad turn. |
|---|---|

RELIABILITY AND VALIDITY: The equivalent-form reliability coefficient was .79. On the average, men score about 1.7 higher than women. Age correlates —.16; that is, there is a tendency for older people to score lower. A later validation study using peer ratings produced 181 pairs of judgments from 181 respondents, each of whom selected two people, one of whom was judged to be more hostile/aggressive than the other. When these judgments were compared with actual scores on the scales, the null hypothesis was rejected well beyond the .001 level on a two-tailed test.

BIBLIOGRAPHY:

Green, R. T., and Stacey, B. G. "The Development of a Questionnaire Measure of Hostility and Aggression." *Acta Psychologica,* 1967, *26,* 265-285.

---

## INFANT ADAPTATION SCALES

AUTHORS: William Fowler and James Sutherland

AGE: 9 to 30 months

VARIABLE: Adaptation of infants to physical environments and persons

TYPE OF MEASURE: Rating scale

SOURCE FROM WHICH MEASURE MAY BE OBTAINED: William Fowler, Department of Applied Psychology, Ontario Institute for Studies in Education, 252 Bloor Street West, Toronto, Ontario, Canada.

DESCRIPTION OF MEASURE: There are three categories of 5-point scales, one each on which the infant is rated from low adaptation (1) to unregulated adaptation (5), the center point (3) of each scale representing optimal or ideal functioning. The three sets of scales and the order in which they are administered are:

A. Constructiveness of response to unfamiliar physical environment
B. Adaptation to unfamiliar person
C. Quality of attachment relations with a familiar adult
    1. Physical contact
    2. Verbal interaction
    3. Tension level
    4. Recovery from trauma (if child reacts emotionally to test situation)
    5. Dependence-independence
    6. Complexity-diversity

As an example, the rating scale for constructiveness of response to unfamiliar physical environment is given below.

*Low*   1 No adaptation    No movement away from caretaker into room, clings to caretaker, remains tense and/or anxious, emotional reaction, may whimper or cry.

       2 Some adaptation   After prolonged hesitation and anxious visual scanning (several minutes) child moves into room remaining short time, returns, little exploration, leaves caretaker no more than twice probably with a substantial interval between the departures.

*Ideal*  3 Ideal adaptation   After initial hesitation, leaves caretaker quickly and moves into room; may visually scan room; calm, wary at first; makes use of new environment (note quality of exploration); continues exploration and/or becomes well engaged in play (with objects) for several minutes or more before returning; if returns earlier it is to share interest briefly with caretaker; focus remains centered on toy whether child returns to room or stays near caretaker.

       4 Overreacts       Very little hesitation, no anxiousness or scanning; leaves caretaker quickly, returns to caretaker only once briefly; outgoing, no hesitation.

*High*   5 Reckless        Leaves caretaker immediately, no hesitation or scanning to adjust to room, runs ahead, doesn't return to caretaker, ignores caretaker, no fear or even minimal hesitation at any time, uninhibited, no reflectiveness.

RELIABILITY AND VALIDITY: The original scales were administered in a research investigation on infant day care, comparing the adaptation responses of day-care to home-reared infants ($N = 18$, mean age 19 months for each group). Interrater reliability between two raters with four children was .90 ($X$ transformation).

BIBLIOGRAPHY:

Fowler, W. "A Developmental Learning Approach to Infant Care in a Group Setting." *Merrill-Palmer Quarterly*, 1972, *18*, 145-175.

---

# KOHN SOCIAL COMPETENCE SCALE

AUTHOR: Martin Kohn

AGE: 3 to 6 years

VARIABLE: Social-emotional functioning

TYPE OF MEASURE: Rating scale

SOURCE FROM WHICH MEASURE MAY BE OBTAINED: Martin Kohn, William Alanson White Institute, 20 West 74th Street, New York, New York. Cost: $5.00.

DESCRIPTION OF MEASURE: The Kohn Social Competence Scale is a teacher rating instrument designed to assess the child's mastery of a kindergarten or preschool setting. There are two forms of the scale: a seventy-three-item version for full-day programs and a sixty-four-item version for half-day programs. The scale measures two bipolar dimensions of children's social-emotional functioning: interest-participation vs. apathy-withdrawal and cooperation-compliance vs. anger-defiance.

Examples of items are given below. Each item is rated on a 7-point scale.

*Interest-participation*
1. Child gets others interested in what he is doing.
*Apathy-withdrawal*
1. Child has difficulty getting the attention of the group.
2. Child is at a loss without other children directing him or organizing activities for him.
*Cooperation-compliance*
1. Child cooperates with rules and regulations.
*Anger-defiance*
1. Child disrupts activities of others.
2. Child expresses open defiance against teacher's rules and regulations.

The scale was developed through a factor analysis applied to teacher ratings (completed by pairs of full-time teachers) of 407 children in public day-care centers. The pool of items on which the children were rated contained various categories of high and low socially competent behavior. Only the first two of six rotated factors were retained since they accounted for 74 percent of the communal variance. The two factor dimensions are relatively independent of each other ($r$ = .33). The instrument requires about 15 minutes per child for completion. Scoring is greatly facilitated through a scoring key and requires approximately 3 minutes per child. A rating and scoring manual is available from the author.

RELIABILITY AND VALIDITY: Interrater reliability (Spearman-Brown corrected) was found to be .77 for the interest-participation vs. apathy-withdrawal dimension and .80 for the cooperation-compliance vs. anger-defiance dimension. The scales have been shown to measure relatively enduring personality predisposition; that is, children are stable across situations and over a time interval (from preschool to early elementary years) on the two dimensions of the scale. One dimension of the scale is related to children's cognitive functioning and school achievement—the higher the child on apathy-withdrawal during the preschool period, the more impaired his preschool cognitive functioning and the lower his scholastic attainment during his elementary school attendance. Anger-defiance, on the other hand, is unrelated to cognitive functioning during the preschool period and to scholastic attainment during the first two years of elementary school. The scales differentiate between normal and emotionally disturbed children. Children with varying levels of disturbance but enrolled in normal preschool settings can be differentiated from one another as well as from more severely disturbed children with known psychiatric diagnoses in therapeutic day nurseries and mental hospitals. Further evidence of validity was shown by comparing the peer interactions of children high in apathy-withdrawal with those high in anger-defiance. A study of the early mother-child relationship (Kohn and Rosman, 1971) suggests that children high on apathy-withdrawal have had a very different kind of maternal experience from children high on anger-defiance. The mothers of the former were primarily controlling and overprotective, while the mothers of the latter were rejecting and provided discontinuous care. In a program of therapeutic intervention it was found that children high on apathy-withdrawal responded quite differently from children high on anger-defiance. The differential response of the children was in line with their early experience in the mother-child relationship.

BIBLIOGRAPHY:

Kohn, M. "The Social Systems Meaning of the Two-Factor Model of Social-Emotional Competence." Paper presented at the meeting of the American Educational Research Association. Washington, D.C., April 1975.

Kohn, M., and Cohen, J. "Emotional Impairment and Achievement Deficit in Disadvantaged Children—Fact or Myth?" *Genetic Psychology Monographs*, 1975, *92*, 57-78.

Kohn, M., and Parnes, B. "Social Interaction in the Classroom—A Comparison of Apathetic-Withdrawn and Angry-Defiant Children." *Journal of Genetic Psychology*, 1974, *125*, 165-175.

Kohn, M., and Rosman, B. L. "Therapeutic Intervention with Disturbed Children in Day Care: Implications of the Deprivation Hypothesis." *Child Care Quarterly*, 1971, *1*, 21-46.

Kohn, M., and Rosman, B. L. "Relationship of Preschool Social-Emotional Functioning to Later Intellectual Achievement." *Developmental Psychology*, 1972, *6*, 445-452.

Kohn, M., and Rosman, B. L. "A Social Competence Scale and Symptom Checklist for the Preschool Child: Factor Dimensions, Their Cross-Instrument Generality, and Longitudinal Persistence." *Developmental Psychology*, 1972, *6*, 430-444.

Kohn, M., and Rosman, B. L. "Cognitive Functioning in Five-Year-Old Boys as Related to Social-Emotional and Background-Demographic Variables." *Developmental Psychology*, 1973, *8*, 277-294.

Kohn, M., and Rosman, B. L. "Cross-Situational and Longitudinal Stability of Social-Emotional Functioning in Young Children." *Child Development*, 1973, *44*, 721-727.

Kohn, M., and Rosman, B. L. "A Two-Factor Model of Emotional Disturbance in the Young Child: Validity and Screening Efficiency." *Journal of Child Psychology and Psychiatry*, 1973, *14*, 31-56.

Kohn, M., and Rosman, B. L. "Social-Emotional, Cognitive, and Demographic Determinants of Poor School Achievement: Implications for a Strategy of Intervention." *Journal of Educational Psychology*, 1974, *66*, 267-276.

## MULTIDIMENSIONAL AGGRESSION SCALE AND SCORING SYSTEM FOR THE STRUCTURED DOLL-PLAY INTERVIEW

AUTHORS: Paul R. Abramson, Linda M. Abramson, Paul Wohlford, and Stephen Berger

AGE: 2 to 10 years

VARIABLE: Aggression

TYPE OF MEASURE: Structured interview and play

SOURCE FROM WHICH MEASURE MAY BE OBTAINED: Paul R. Abramson, Department of Psychology, U-20, University of Connecticut, Storrs, Connecticut 06268.

DESCRIPTION OF MEASURᴇ: The present authors contend that categorizing the aggressive responses a child gives to the structured doll-play interview along the dimensions of intensity, agent, and directionality allows for a more precise specification of the relationships among the variables that produce aggressive behavior. With this system the child uses three dolls (an adult male, an adult female, and a child doll representing the same sex, age, and race of the subject) and is presented with twelve doll-play response situations (e.g., "The boy is playing. The girl comes up and hits the boy. What does he do?"). The intensity of the aggressive responses to these twelve situations is rated from 0 to 3. Scoring is: 0—nonaggressive response, one in which there is an absence of any retaliatory behavior; 1—assertive response, one in which the $S$ states positively to maintain or defend his rights without an overt physical response; 2—aggressive response, one in which there is behavior intended to hurt or injure another individual or animal; and 3—violent response, one in which the actual killing of another human being or animal is present. In addition to intensity, each response is scored for the dimensions of agent and directionality. For agent, the responses are scored for the instigator of aggressive behavior. The instigator may be either self, environment, mother, father, or other. For directionality, the object of the scored response is noted; aggression may be directed toward self, environment, mother, father, or other.

RELIABILITY AND VALIDITY: A Spearman-Brown rank-order correlation of .92 was obtained between a previous scoring system and aggression as scored with the present system. Interscorer reliability $r$ ranged from .84 to 1.0. The intercorrelations of the scales are presented in Abramson and others (1974). A factor-analytic study (Abramson and Abramson, 1974) supported the present authors' contention that aggression can be conceptualized dimensionally. Other studies (Abramson, 1973; Abramson and others, 1972) have exhibited its potential validity.

BIBLIOGRAPHY:

Abramson, P. R. "Familial Variables Related to the Expression of Violent Aggression in Preschool-Age Children." *Journal of Genetic Psychology,* 1973, *122,* 345-346.
Abramson, P. R. "The Holtzman Inkblot Test, Violent Aggression in Fantasy, and Black Preschool-Age Children." *Journal of Community Psychology,* 1974, *2,* 139-140.

Abramson, P. R., and Abramson, S. D. "A Factorial Study of a Multidimensional Approach to Aggressive Behavior in Black Preschool-Age Children." *Journal of Genetic Psychology,* 1974, *125,* 31-36.

Abramson, P. R., Abramson, L. M., Wohlford, P., and Berger, S. "Maternal Influences on the Development of Aggression in Black Preschool Age Children." In Paul Wohlford (Ed.), *Changing Parental Attitudes and Behavior Through Participant Group Methods.* Washington, D.C.: Office of Research and Evaluation, Office of Economic Opportunity, 1972. U.S. Department of Health, Education and Welfare.

Abramson, P. R., Abramson, L. M., Wohlford, P., and Berger, S. E. "The Multidimensional Aggression Scale for the Structured Doll-Play Interview." *Journal of Personality Assessment,* 1974, *38,* 436-440.

# NONVERBAL MEASURE OF
# CHILDREN'S FRUSTRATION RESPONSE

AUTHOR: Fred W. Vondracek

AGE: 3½ to 7 years

VARIABLE: Responses to frustrating situations

TYPE OF MEASURE: Picture sequences

SOURCE FROM WHICH MEASURE MAY BE OBTAINED: Fred W. Vondracek, Beecher House, Pennsylvania State University, University Park, Pennsylvania 16802. Cost: Duplication plus postage.

DESCRIPTION OF MEASURE: The Nonverbal Measure of Children's Frustration Response consists of eighteen sets of pictures: two pictures in each stimulus set and three pictures in each corresponding response set. There are two parallel forms: one for girls in which girls are portrayed as protagonists, and one for boys in which boys are shown as the protagonists. The subjects' task, essentially, is to look at the stimulus pictures that depict a "frustrating" situation and then to identify among the three response pictures the response most likely to be emitted by the protagonist. For each set the three choices consist of an "aggressive" response choice, a "prosocial" response choice, and an "avoidance" response choice. The number of aggressive, prosocial, and avoidance choices made by each subject represents the subject's test score. Administration time is about 10 to 15 minutes. The pictures are presented with brief commentaries that have been printed on the bottom of the picture cards.

RELIABILITY AND VALIDITY: Internal reliability coefficients for a sample of preschool boys ($N = 70$) and girls ($N = 70$) were as follows (girl's coefficients presented in parentheses): aggression, .63 (.51); prosocial, .80 (.60); avoidance, .47 (.37). Some evidence for the validity of the measure has been obtained in three different ways. Correlations between children's aggressive and prosocial choices on the present measure and extensive behavior observations in a nursery school yielded significant positive correlations for observed physical aggression, verbal aggression, interpersonal aggression, object aggression, and serious aggression, and significant negative correlations for observed verbal, interpersonal, and serious aggression—the former with aggressive choices and the latter with prosocial choices involving adults as the depicted frustrating agents. Other validity evidence includes significant correlations between aggressive choices and preferring aggressive TV programs, significant positive correlations between mental age and prosocial choices, and significant negative correlations between mental age and aggressive and avoidance choices.

BIBLIOGRAPHY:

Vondracek, F. W., Stein, A. H., and Friedrich, L. K. "A Nonverbal Technique for Assessing Frustration Response in Preschool Children." *Journal of Personality Assessment,* 1973, *37,* 355-362.

---

# NORMATIVE INTEGRATION

AUTHOR: Ronald A. Feldman

AGE: 9 to 16 years

VARIABLE: Normative integration of small groups and of individual members

TYPE OF MEASURE: Likert-type scale

SOURCE FROM WHICH MEASURE MAY BE OBTAINED: Ronald A. Feldman, Center for the Study of Youth Development, 8401 West Dodge Road, Omaha, Nebraska 68114.

DESCRIPTION OF MEASURE: Normative integration is defined as the degree of consensus among group members concerning group-relevant behaviors. In order to measure normative integration within groups of adolescents, a questionnaire consisting of twenty items was designed. The items refer to normative behaviors within a group living situation, such as a summer camp. It is possible, however, to construct similar items relevant to other social situations. Identical questions are administered for populations of both boys and girls except for references to gender. For each normative item, respondents are instructed to select one of five scale positions. The average score for each of the twenty items is calculated for each separate group. The extent to which the individual group members vary from the group average for each item is determined and the member's total deviation, summed for all twenty items, is figured. The total deviation for each member is then divided by twenty, the total number of items, in order to ascertain his average normative deviation. This figure is then subtracted from 4.00, since responses are coded from 0 to 4, so that higher scores reflect higher normative integration into the group. The resultant score can be considered to represent an individual's "normative integration into the group." The "normative integration of the group" is then determined by calculating the average of the individual normative integration scores for each group. Groups with high scores are considered to have greater normative integration than groups with low scores.

As examples, the first five of the twenty items on the questionnaire are given below.

1. Should it be alright for the guys in this cabin to smoke cigarettes? (Possible answers: definitely alright; usually alright; at times it is alright; not alright; definitely not alright.)
2. Should people go to religious services? (Possible answers: definitely yes; probably yes; undecided; probably not; definitely not.)
3. What do you think about the guys in your cabin telling dirty stories or jokes? (Possible answers: it is never alright; it is usually not alright; it is alright sometimes; it is usually alright; there is nothing wrong with it.)
4. How often should the guys in this cabin swear? (Possible answers: never; not very often; fairly often; often; very often; if they want to.)
5. Is it bad to have fist fights with persons in your cabin? (Possible answers: not bad at all; not very bad; undecided; bad; very bad.)

RELIABILITY AND VALIDITY: From a pre-test series of 120 questionnaire items, 20 were chosen for inclusion in the final questionnaire; selection was based upon the ability of the items to discriminate separate normative orientations from one another.

BIBLIOGRAPHY:

Feldman, R. A. "Interrelationships Among Three Bases of Group Integration." *Sociometry,* 1968, *31,* 30-46.
Feldman, R. A. "Group Integration and Intense Interpersonal Disliking." *Human Relations,* 1969, *22,* 405-414.
Feldman, R. A. "Group Integration, Intense Interpersonal Dislike, and Social Group Work Intervention." *Social Work,* 1969, *14,* 30-39.
Feldman, R. A. "Social Attributes of the Intensely Disliked Position in Children's Groups." *Adolescence,* 1969, *4,* 181-198.
Feldman, R. A. "Normative Integration, Alienation, and Conformity in Adolescent Groups." *Adolescence,* 1972, *7,* 327-342.
Feldman, R. A. "Power Distribution, Integration and Conformity in Small Groups." *American Journal of Sociology,* 1973, *79,* 639-664.

## OBSERVATION OF SOCIALIZATION BEHAVIOR (OSB)

AUTHORS: Jo Lynn Cunningham and Robert P. Boger

AGE: 3 to 8 years

VARIABLE: Peer-group interaction

TYPE OF MEASURE: Observation rating procedure

SOURCE FROM WHICH MEASURE MAY BE OBTAINED: Institute for Family and Child Study, Home Management House Unit No. 2, Michigan State University, East Lansing, Michigan 48824.

DESCRIPTION OF MEASURE: Two forms of the OSB are available. Form 1 is designed for use in videotaped controlled setting interaction situations, while Form 2 is an abbreviated version appropriate for direct observation in the classroom. Both forms are designed for use in unstructured (free-play) situations. Behaviors of interest are quantity and quality of verbal and nonverbal communication, individual and group interaction, social involvement, and situational tone. Time and event sampling techniques are employed to secure a representative sample of the children's frequently occurring behaviors while also capturing less frequently occurring behaviors of interest. The system readily lends itself to quantitative analysis without losing its qualitative dimensions, especially those related to sequence of events and context of activities. The scoring categories and the number of interaction behavior classes under each are: emotional tone (5), social behavior (6), nonverbal behavior—physical behavior (5), nonverbal behavior—play context (5), verbalization (15), involvement (12), peer interaction (2), group interaction (1), adult interaction (1), and inferred motivation (14).

RELIABILITY AND VALIDITY: The authors suggest a minimum of 85-percent agreement among observers in using the measure. Behavioral constructs are based on theoretical contributions of social and developmental psychology, and many scales have been adapted from previously validated instruments.

BIBLIOGRAPHY:

Boger, R. P., and Cunningham, J. L. *Observation of Socialization Behavior.* Unpublished manuscript. Head Start Research Center, Michigan State University, East Lansing, 1969.

Cunningham, J. L., and Boger, R. P. *Development of an Observational Rating Schedule for Preschool Children's Peer-Group Behavior.* East Lansing: Institute for Family and Child Research, Michigan State University, 1971. ERIC document no. ED 056 055.

*Prepared by Robert P. Boger*

# OREGON PRESCHOOL TEST OF
# INTERPERSONAL COOPERATION (OPTIC)

AUTHOR: F. Leon Paulson

AGE: 3 to 5 years

VARIABLE: Cooperation

TYPE OF MEASURE: Situational test

SOURCE FROM WHICH MEASURE MAY BE OBTAINED: See Paulson (1974).

DESCRIPTION OF MEASURE: The Oregon Preschool Test of Interpersonal Cooperation (OPTIC) consists of seven problem-solving situations and an observational protocol. Preschool children tested in pairs are scored on whether or not they cooperate
when solving the problems. Provision is made for videotaping. A score on cooperation
is obtained by summing across the seven situations. Although tested in pairs, scores for
individual children are obtainable by testing each child with a different partner across
situations. While scoring is binary (the children do not cooperate), the observation
protocol permits recording of seven levels of behavior. They are: full cooperation, pre-
cooperation, active interaction, parallel play, watching, minimal interaction, and
obstructive interaction.

An example is given below.

*Truck and Blocks*
*Materials:* 1. Twelve wooden blocks and one toy truck. The truck is ten inches long
and dimensions of the blocks vary from two inches to ten inches. 2. A small card
table.
*Arrangement:* The truck is given to one child, the blocks are piled on the table in
front of the second child.
*Directions:* "Here is a truck for you . . . and here are some blocks for you." (Examiner
distributes materials.) "Play with these things on the table. Don't put them on the
floor and try not to get in each other's way." (If either truck or blocks is removed
from the table top the examiner reminds them to play on the table.)
*Duration:* 2 minutes.
*Special Scoring Instructions:* If the children build any kind of a structure for the truck
to go into, or on (for example, a road, a bridge, a garage) then *modeling* is scored.
*Cooperation* is scored if they take turns with the materials, or if they combine forces
to build one thing with the blocks.

RELIABILITY AND VALIDITY: An early version of OPTIC (employing a 5-point
scale rather than binary scoring) demonstrated interrater correlations of from .35 to
.87 on two test situations. Agreement of raters viewing live and on television is comparable to agreement of raters using the same medium. Interrater agreement on the
revised version (all seven situations using binary scoring) varies between 89 and 100
percent. While formal validity studies have not been conducted, the test has a high degree of face validity by virtue of being a situational test. OPTIC was used in a study of
the impact of television programs designed to teach children cooperation (Paulson,

McDonald, and Whittemore, 1973). Children who viewed the programs scored significantly higher on OPTIC than children who did not view.

BIBLIOGRAPHY:

Paulson, F. L. "Live Versus Televised Observations of Social Behavior in Preschool Children." *Proceedings, 80th Annual Convention, American Psychological Association,* 1972. ERIC document no. ED 071 735.

Paulson, F. L. "Teaching Cooperation on Television: An Evaluation of Sesame Street Social Goals Program." *Audio-Visual Communications Review,* 1974, *22,* 229-246.

Paulson, F. L., McDonald, D. L., and Whittemore, S. L. *An Evaluation of Sesame Street Programming to Teach Cooperation.* Monmouth, Oregon: Teaching Research, 1973.

---

## PARTEN SCALE

AUTHOR: Mildred B. Parten

AGE: Preschool to 10 years

VARIABLE: Social behavior

TYPE OF MEASURE: Observation frame of reference

SOURCE FROM WHICH MEASURE MAY BE OBTAINED: See Parten (1932) and Wintre and Webster (1974).

DESCRIPTION OF MEASURE: There are six categories or degrees of social participation in the Parten Scale. The categories as described by Parten (1932) are as follows: unoccupied behavior, solitary independent play, onlooker, parallel activity, associative play, and cooperative or organized play. Wintre and Webster (1974) added a seventh category as follows: adult-directed behavior—any behavior toward an adult. This includes such activities as playing with the therapist (coders), looking at the therapist (coders), and touching the therapist (coders). Parten observed each nursery school child for 1 minute daily.

RELIABILITY AND VALIDITY: Parten observed nineteen children over a twenty-day period and correlated the behavior of children on the ten odd days vs. the ten even days. Using the rank difference method, she found a coefficient of .76. When twenty odd-even day observations were weighted, scored, ranked, and correlated, the coefficient was .90. Parten further found 89 percent agreement between herself and three assistants. Wintre and Webster (1974) found 85.9 percent agreement between two coders. Correlations of Parten Scale scores of thirty-four preschoolers with ratings by five teachers ranged from .59 to .79. The Parten scores correlated .26 with IQ, .97 with a leadership measure score, and .61 with age.

BIBLIOGRAPHY:

Parten, M. B. "Social Participation Among Preschool Children." *Journal of Abnormal and Social Psychology,* 1932, *27,* 243-269.

Wintre, M. G., and Webster, C. D. "A Brief Report on Using a Traditional Social Behavior Scale with Disturbed Children." *Journal of Applied Behavior Analysis,* 1974, *7,* 345-348.

*Prepared by Orval G. Johnson*

---

# PERSONAL OPINION STUDY

AUTHORS: Herbert C. Quay and Donald R. Peterson

AGE: Reading ability near sixth grade

VARIABLE: Delinquency-related behavior categories

TYPE OF MEASURE: Questionnaire

SOURCE FROM WHICH MEASURE MAY BE OBTAINED: See Quay and Parsons (1971).

DESCRIPTION OF MEASURE: The Personal Opinion Study is a 100-item true-false questionnaire. It is composed of factorially homogeneous scales measuring three behavior categories: neurotic-disturbed, unsocialized-psychopathic, and socialized-subcultural. The test was developed out of a series of factor-analytic studies of the responses of both delinquents and normals to a large pool of items related to attitudes, beliefs, feelings, and behavior (Peterson, Quay, and Cameron, 1959; Peterson, Quay, and Tiffany, 1961; Quay, Peterson, and Consalvi, 1960). The test can be taken by anyone whose reading ability is near sixth grade. It can also be administered orally or by tape recorder to nonreaders. The items are generally straightforward, and many are couched in the language of delinquent youth. Administration of the test should be done individually or in small groups under the supervision of a psychologist or psychometrist. The development of the measure is described in Quay and Parsons (1971). It is one of three instruments designed to measure ten delinquency-related behavior categories.

RELIABILITY AND VALIDITY: Test-retest reliability was established on a sample of sixty-five institutionalized delinquents over an interval of approximately ninety days. Stability coefficients were .76 for neuroticism, .75 for psychopathy, and .61 for the subcultural scale. These values are about average for this type of instrument when stability is assessed on a delinquent sample. Kuder-Richardson formula 20 reliability coefficients ($N = 1,075$) for the three scales were: psychopathic, .92; neurotic, .87; and subcultural, .62. The scales are factorially independent and the obtained scores are reasonably empirically independent in new (particularly delinquent) samples. The subcultural scale clearly provided the best validity for concurrent discrimination. Ninety percent of both normal samples ($N = 156$ and 125) obtained a score of 13 or less while 89 percent of each of the three delinquent samples ($N = 116, 65$, and 122) exceeded this score. It should be noted, however, that the two public school samples are probably significantly higher in socioeconomic status than the delinquent groups. At the same time previous work has shown that multifactor "delinquency" scales are not highly related to socioeconomic status per se (Peterson, Quay, and Anderson, 1959). The neuroticism and subcultural scales appear to be independent of intelligence. There is a significant negative relationship between both achievement and Otis IQ and the psychopathy scale. Further details on validity can be found in Quay and Parsons (1971).

BIBLIOGRAPHY:

Peterson, D. R., Quay, H. C., and Anderson, A. D. "Extending the Construct Validity of a Socialization Scale." *Journal of Consulting Psychology*, 1959, *23*, 182.
Peterson, D. R., Quay, H. C., and Cameron, G. R. "Personality and Background Factors in Juvenile Delinquency as Inferred from Questionnaire Responses." *Journal of Consulting Psychology*, 1959, *23*, 392-399.
Peterson, D. R., Quay, H. C., and Tiffany, T. C. "Personality Factors Related to Juvenile Delinquency." *Child Development*, 1961, *32*, 355-372.
Quay, H. C., and Parsons, L. B. *The Differential Behavioral Classification of the Juvenile Offender.* (2nd ed.) Washington, D.C.: Robert F. Kennedy Youth Center, Bureau of Prisons, U.S. Department of Justice, 1971.
Quay, H. C., Peterson, D. R., and Consalvi, C. "The Interpretation of Three Personality Factors in Juvenile Delinquency." *Journal of Consulting Psychology*, 1960, *24*, 555.

*Prepared by Orval G. Johnson*

# PERSONAL SKILLS INVENTORY (PSI)

AUTHOR: William Vogel

AGE: Retarded persons

VARIABLE: Adaptive behaviors

TYPE OF MEASURE: Rating scale

SOURCE FROM WHICH MEASURE MAY BE OBTAINED: William Vogel, Department of Psychology, Worcester State Hospital, Worcester, Massachusetts 01613.

DESCRIPTION OF MEASURE: The PSI is a research device, not designed for clinical use. The fifteen-item measure is used in conjunction with the Social and Emotional Behavior Inventory (see pp. 1213-1214) to provide a quantified scoring system that permits raters to objectively assess the degree of adaptive behavior of which a retarded person is capable. The device is designed to be applied to institutional records rather than to "live" behavior. A nonprofessional person (e.g., a research assistant) can become skilled in the use of the device after only several hours of training and practice.

As examples, the first three of the fifteen items of the PSI are given below, to be scored as follows: a = 1, b = 2, c = 3, d = 4, e = 5.

1. Bowel training:
   a. Untrained.
   b. Partially day-trained (does not soil during the day if given assistance by the staff; e.g., must be taken or told to go to the toilet after meals).
   d. Fully day-trained (requires no assistance from the staff); not night-trained (e.g., soils in his sleep).
   e. Completely bowel trained; needs no assistance whatever.
2. Bladder training:
   a. Untrained.
   b. Partially day-trained.
   d. Fully day-trained; not night-trained.
   e. Completely bladder trained; requires no assistance whatever.
3. Dining behavior:
   a. Must be fed and is resistive.
   b. Must be fed, but is cooperative.
   c. Feeds self with fingers using no utensils at all.
   d. Uses cup for self-feeding, but no other utensils.
   e. Uses cup and other utensils to feed self.

RELIABILITY AND VALIDITY: Reliability, when used in conjunction with the Social and Emotional Behavior Inventory, was .90. A factor analysis of ratings on 132 institutionalized retardates supports inclusion of all of the items in this scale. Scores relate significantly to EEG, institutional release and prognosis, intellectual functioning, and adaptive behavior.

BIBLIOGRAPHY:

Vogel, W., Kun, K. J., and Meshorer, E. "Changes in Adaptive Behavior in Institutionalized Retardates in Response to Environmental Enrichment or Deprivation." *Journal of Consulting and Clinical Psychology*, 1968, *32*, 76-82.

Vogel, W., Kun, K. J., and Meshorer, E. "The Behavioral Significance of EEG Abnormality in Mental Defectives." *American Journal of Mental Deficiency*, 1969, *74*, 62-68.

Vogel, W., Kun, K. J., and Meshorer, E. "Determinants of Institutional Release and Prognosis in Mental Retardates." *Journal of Abnormal Psychology*, 1969, *74*, 685-692.

# PLAY REPORT

AUTHOR: May V. Seagoe

AGE: 5 to 11 years

VARIABLE: Social development

TYPE OF MEASURE: Interview and questionnaire

SOURCE FROM WHICH MEASURE MAY BE OBTAINED: May V. Seagoe, 15-410 Brownwood Place, Los Angeles, California 90024. Cost: Under $5.00 for duplication and postage.

DESCRIPTION OF MEASURE: The Play Report consists of the following five questions, with two responses requested for each question: (1) "What do you spend most of your time playing at school?" (2) "What do you spend most of your time playing at home?" (3) "What do you spend most of your time playing at other places?" (4) "What do you like to play most?" (5) "What do you like to play least?" As a cross-check for categorizing responses the child indicates for each response whether he usually plays "by myself," "with grownups," "with friends," or "on a team." Each response is categorized as: informal-individual play, adult-oriented play, informal-social play, or individual-competitive play, and weights are assigned according to the social context indicated (Seagoe, 1970). Norms were derived from approximately equal numbers of girls and boys aged 5 to 11. Norms are based on responses for 620 boys and 625 girls, and separate norms proved essential because of acceleration in the development of boys aged 6 to 8. The Play Report has been used chiefly to compare differences between cultures and subcultures, though it has distinct merit in identifying individual play styles in young children for aid in psychological diagnosis, quite apart from cultural milieu.

RELIABILITY AND VALIDITY: The reliability of rating by two independent psychologists for age and sex groups varied from .84 to .99 for boys and from .76 to .99 for girls. The validity of the instrument was based on the theoretical construct (Sullivan's developmental patterns) and on the assumption that since developmental stages were concerned the scores would relate to chronological age. Such correlations were .75 for boys and .64 for girls in the preliminary sample and .63 for boys and .55 for girls in the larger standardization group.

BIBLIOGRAPHY:

Seagoe, M. V. "Children's Play as an Indicator of Cross-Cultural and Intra-Cultural Differences." *Journal of Educational Sociology*, 1962, *35*, 278-283.

Seagoe, M. V. "An Instrument for the Analysis of Children's Play as an Index of Degree of Socialization." *Journal of School Psychology*, 1970, *8*, 139-144.

Seagoe, M. V. "Children's Play in Three American Subcultures." *Journal of School Psychology*, 1971, *9*, 167-172.

Seagoe, M. V. "A Comparison of Children's Play in Six Modern Cultures." *Journal of School Psychology*, 1971, *9*, 61-72.

Seagoe, M. V., and Murakami, K. "A Comparative Study of Children's Play in America and Japan." *California Journal of Educational Research*, 1961, *11*, 124-130.

---

## POSITIVE SOCIAL REINFORCEMENT OBSERVATION INSTRUMENT

AUTHORS: Rosalind Charlesworth and Willard W. Hartup

AGE: 2½ to 5½ years

VARIABLE: Positive social reinforcement in the nursery social peer group

TYPE OF MEASURE: Classroom observation method

SOURCE FROM WHICH MEASURE MAY BE OBTAINED: Observation and Coding Manual, Document no. 9617, ADI Auxiliary Publications Project, Photoduplication Service, Library of Congress, Washington, D.C. 20540. Cost: Photoprints, $2.50; 35 mm microfilm, $1.75.

DESCRIPTION OF MEASURE: This is an observational method for obtaining normative information on the amount and kinds of positive social reinforcement dispensed by preschool-age children to one another during school free-play periods. Positive social reinforcement is defined under Skinner's rubric "generalized reinforcer." Skinner's conceptualization is used as a guide for defining the observational categories of attention and approval, affection and personal acceptance, submission, and token giving. The information obtained was found to be predictive of other child behaviors. (Hartup and Coates, 1967; Hartup, Glazer, and Charlesworth, 1967).

   As examples, Category II and its definitions for observation are given below. The other three categories are: giving positive attention and approval, submission, and giving tokens.

*II: Giving Affection and Personal Acceptance*
1. Offering physical affection and acceptance: (hugging, kissing, handholding, patting, arm around shoulders, sitting close to).
2. Offering verbal affection, attention, and acceptance—status giving: Verbal statements such as "I like you," "You are my friend," "We are both cowboys"; inviting another to play or join an activity; giving reassurance: offering sympathy, comfort, or consolation; giving protection: verbally or physically defending another; greeting another warmly; giving another a status name (chief, boss, king, father); asking for an opinion or for a rule ("Can M _____ play with us, too?"); asking for help; asking a question.

RELIABILITY AND VALIDITY: A comparison of the number of codable incidents recorded by each of two observers showed that one observer recorded 16 percent more

codable incidents than did the other. The observations were coded by one of the observers and a naive coder in order to obtain information on reliability of the coding
procedure. Two ratios of agreement/agreement + disagreement were computed. There
was a .77 ratio of agreement that reinforcement was present. A ratio of .64 was found
when agreement was defined as the presence of a particular category of reinforcement.

BIBLIOGRAPHY:

Charlesworth, R., and Hartup, W. "Positive Social Reinforcement in the Nursery School
    Peer Group." *Child Development,* 1967, *38,* 993-1002.
Hartup, W., and Coates, B. "Imitation of a Peer as a Function of Reinforcement of the
    Peer Group and Rewardingness of the Model." *Child Development,* 1967, *38,*
    1003-1016.
Hartup, W., Glazer, J., and Charlesworth, R. "Peer Reinforcement and Sociometric
    Status." *Child Development,* 1967, *38,* 1017-1024.

---

# A PROCEDURE FOR PATTERNING RESPONSES
# OF ADULTS AND CHILDREN (APPROACH)

AUTHORS: Bettye M. Caldwell and Alice S. Honig

AGE: Infancy through adulthood

VARIABLE: Human interactions

TYPE OF MEASURE: Observation

SOURCE FROM WHICH MEASURE MAY BE OBTAINED: See Caldwell and Honig
(1971). Journal Supplement Abstract Service, American Psychological Association,
1200 Seventeenth Street, N.W., Washington, D.C. 20036. Cost: $2.00.

DESCRIPTION OF MEASURE: APPROACH is a technique for coding observations
and behavior sequences and the settings in which they occur. The code is applied to a
behavior record obtained by stationing an observer near the subject to be observed and
having the observer whisper into a tape recorder every change of behavior noted in the
subject and every response directed toward the subject or emitted within his social
range. Coding is being as efficiently done directed from the tape as it was previously
from a typescript of the behavior record. Ongoing behaviors are recorded every 5 seconds. Simultaneous or complex behaviors are recorded consecutively or by means of a
modifying clause, for example, "Mother shows Jim the picture book while smiling at
him." Emitted behaviors are coded by breaking up the narrative description into behavioral clauses, each of which contains four basic components: the subject of the clause
(who or what does something), the predicate (what is done), the object (toward whom
or what the action is directed), and some qualifier (adverbial descriptions of the

action). Each of these four components is then translated into a numerical code and grouped into a five-digit statement (two digits being required for the predicates) that summarizes the subject-predicate-object-adverb involved in a single behavior unit. The complete chain of numerical statements is then key-punched for computer analysis. Behavior settings are also converted to numerical statements describing the type of activity taking place in the observational environment, the geographic region in which the behavior occurs, and the dramatis personae of the total social scene.

RELIABILITY AND VALIDITY: The average level of interobserver reliability achieved so far (and computed as number of agreements/average number of scores for both observers) is .92 for the subject, .87 for the object, and .77 for the predicate. To obtain these reliabilities, one senior observer was paired with each of two observers gathering data on six different children. It has been found advisable to monitor the proficiency of coders every few months as a precaution against the interpretive "drift" that sometimes occurs when observational data is coded over a long period of time.

BIBLIOGRAPHY:

Caldwell, B. M. "A New 'Approach' to Behavioral Ecology." In J. P. Hill (Ed.), *Minnesota Symposia on Child Psychology*. Vol. 2. Minneapolis: University of Minnesota Press, 1969.

Caldwell, B. M., and Honig, A. S. *APPROACH—A Procedure for Patterning Responses of Adults and Children*. Washington, D.C.: American Psychological Association Journal Supplement Abstract Service. Abstracted in *Catalog of Selected Documents in Psychology*, 1971, *1*, 1-2.

Honig, A. S., Caldwell, B. M., and Tannenbaum, J. "Patterns of Information Processing Used By and With Young Children in a Nursery School Setting." *Child Development*, 1970, *41*, 1045-1065.

Honig, A. S., Tannenbaum, J., and Caldwell, B. M. "Maternal Behavior in Verbal Report and in Laboratory Observation: A Methodological Study." *Child Psychiatry and Human Development*, 1973, *3*, 216-230.

*Prepared by Alice S. Honig*

---

# PROGRESS ASSESSMENT CHART OF SOCIAL AND PERSONAL DEVELOPMENT (P-A-C); PROGRESS EVALUATION INDEX OF SOCIAL DEVELOPMENT (P-E-I)

AUTHOR: H. C. Gunzburg

AGE: 2 years to adult

VARIABLE: Social (and personal) development of mentally retarded people

TYPE OF MEASURE: Checklist/rating scale and diagrammatic analysis

SOURCE FROM WHICH MEASURE MAY BE OBTAINED: In U.S.A.: Aux Chan-delles, P-A-C Department, P.O. Box 398, Bristol, Indiana 46507. In Canada: ASH/ Deerhome, P-A-C Department, P.O. Box 5002, Red Deer, Alberta T4N 541.

DESCRIPTION OF MEASURE: The five versions of the P-A-C and P-E-I forms and folders serve several purposes: (1) diagnosis of specific weaknesses in social develop-ment, (2) assessment of progress, (3) evaluation of backwardness in relation to other mentally handicapped children and adults of the same age, (4) provision of a program of teaching essential social skills, (5) comparison of social functioning and personal assets. The social skills listed in the inventories are arranged in order of normal devel-opment in the diagrams of the P-P-A-C and the P-A-C 1 and in relation to usage and difficulty in the P-A-C 2. In the M/P-A-C 1, skills have been arranged in order of difficulty for mongol children, and the skills in the P-A-C 1A are positioned according to difficulty experienced by different levels of intellectual functioning. The diagram-matic presentation of weaknesses and assets in social functioning reflects visually the *quality* of social achievement, and the norms contained in the P-E-I folders provide information relating to the *quantity* of that achievement compared with other mentally handicapped people. The Social Competence Index (SCI) indicates the degree of devia-tion from this norm.

As examples, twenty of the 120 items of this form are given below. (Numbers correspond to the diagram, not shown here.)

*Table Habits*
1. Uses spoon when eating without requiring help.
2. Drinks without spilling, holding glass in one hand.
18. Uses fork without difficulty (food may be cut and prepared).
19. Capable of helping himself to a drink.
34. Serves himself and eats without requiring much help.
51. Uses table knife for spreading butter, jam, etc.
69. Uses table knife for cutting without much difficulty.
92. Uses knife and fork correctly and without difficulty.
93. Pours liquids (e.g., coffee, milk).
109. Uses knife for peeling fruit or slicing bread.

*Mobility*
3. Walks upstairs, both feet together on each step.
4. Walks downstairs, both feet together on each step.
20. Uses play vehicle of some kind.
35. Walks upstairs, one foot per step, without supporting himself.
36. Walks downstairs, one foot per step, without supporting himself.
52. Goes to neighbors and places nearby.
70. Requires little supervision playing outside house, absent for one hour or more.
71. Roams about without need for much supervision.
94. Goes about neighborhood unsupervised, but does not cross streets.
110. Goes about neighborhood unsupervised, crosses streets.

RELIABILITY AND VALIDITY: The average achievement levels of young mentally handicapped children aged 2 to 7 were obtained on a sample of 156 children (P-P-A-C), of children aged 6 to 16 on a sample of 337 children (P-A-C 1). Two hundred mongol children provided the information for the M/P-A-C 1 form, and 144 adults for the P-A-C 2. Full information on scientific work with the P-A-C and P-E-I is contained in the P-A-C Manual (third edition).

BIBLIOGRAPHY:

Gunzburg, H. C. "The Assessment and Evaluation of Social Development in the Mentally Handicapped Child." In *Proceedings of the First Congress of the International Association of Scientific Study of Mental Deficiency.* Reigate, England: Michael Jackson, 1968.

Gunzburg, H. C. *Social Competence and Mental Handicap: An Introduction to Social Education.* Baltimore, Maryland: Williams & Wilkins, 1973.

Gunzburg, H. C. *Experiments in the Rehabilitation of the Mentally Handicapped.* London: Butterworth's, 1974.

---

## PUPIL PERCEPTIONS TEST OF CHILD AND ADULT SEX-TYPED ROLES AT SCHOOL AND HOME

AUTHOR: Edward E. Gotts

AGE: 5 to 12 years

VARIABLE: (1) Sex-role identity (M-F) and (2) maturity of perception of sex-role stereotypes

TYPE OF MEASURE: Test (Cattell's *T*-type data)

SOURCE FROM WHICH MEASURE MAY BE OBTAINED: Edward E. Gotts, Appalachia Educational Laboratory, Inc., Box 1348, Charleston, West Virginia 25325. Please send a copy of any reports of research with the instrument.

DESCRIPTION OF MEASURE: The first twenty items (school) and second twenty items (home) provide entirely parallel descriptions of an instrumental and/or expressive interaction between a child and an adult. Contrasts of the two halves of the test provide a third measure or index: the differential applicability of the stereotypes of masculinity and femininity to school (public) and home (private) settings. No norms are available for the sex-role identity component, derived from a representative sample of fifth-grade children from a metropolitan school system. Unit-weight-item scoring directions for the second scale, maturity of stereotype, are available, based on a less representative age cross-section of elementary-school pupils. Details for group administration are available. Instructions, materials, and answer forms are designed to permit responses by children of differing racial background (as in original sample). See references below for details of theoretical rationale of Scale 1.

As examples, the first ten of the forty items are given below.

1. The teacher is sorry that the child has not minded.
   a. Do you think the child is a girl or a boy?
   b. Do you think the teacher is a man or a woman?
2. The teacher is scolding the child for misbehaving on the school grounds.
   a. Do you think the child is a boy or a girl?
   b. Do you think the teacher is a woman or a man?
3. The teacher is helping the child to find a place to sit down.
   a. Do you think the child is a girl or a boy?
   b. Do you think the teacher is a man or a woman?
4. The child is telling the teacher about being unhappy in school.
   a. Do you think the child is a boy or a girl?
   b. Do you think the teacher is a woman or a man?
5. The child is whispering to the teacher about something that someone has done.
   a. Do you think the child is a girl or a boy?
   b. Do you think the teacher is a man or a woman?
6. The child is asking the teacher how to hold the baseball bat.
   a. Do you think the child is a boy or a girl?
   b. Do you think the teacher is a woman or a man?
7. The child is promising the teacher to behave so the teacher will not send a bad report home.
   a. Do you think the child is a girl or a boy?
   b. Do you think the teacher is a man or a woman?
8. The child is inviting the teacher to attend a birthday party.
   a. Do you think the child is a boy or a girl?
   b. Do you think the teacher is a woman or a man?
9. The child is asking the teacher for help with a school problem.
   a. Do you think the child is a girl or a boy?
   b. Do you think the teacher is a man or a woman?
10. The teacher is questioning the child about someone who was hurt on the way to school.
    a. Do you think the child is a boy or a girl?
    b. Do you think the teacher is a woman or a man?

RELIABILITY AND VALIDITY: Reliability is not available for Scale 1 (M-F). Boys' and girls' responses were differentiated by the discriminant root, *chi*-square 62.94 with 14 *df* for a probability of less than .001. The root was derived from a socially and ethnically diverse sample. Boys and girls were equally differentiated within each applicable social and ethnic group (e.g., black, Spanish-surname, white). Less masculine boys were more anxious ($r = .44$), whereas among girls M-F was unrelated to anxiety ($r = -.04$), as predicted from the relevant literature. Compared to teacher-supplied behavioral data, more masculine boys are more aggressive ($r = .3$), blunt ($r = .46$), competitive ($r = .38$), and exploitative ($r = .44$), whereas these relations are all of the order of 0 for girls. For the second scale, maturity of stereotype, internal consistency reliability (Cronbach's *alpha*) was .85 for children aged 5 to 10 years. This is a normally distributed variable. The stereotype becomes stronger with increasing age. This index of maturity relates positively to other developmental indexes over this age range (e.g., conservation of number, mass, and volume). An index has been derived for comparing applicability of the stereotype to home vs. school. The stereotype is stronger in the public (school) setting. No additional data have been analyzed in this regard.

BIBLIOGRAPHY:

Gotts, E. E. "Pupil Perceptions of Child and Adult Roles." Unpublished pilot study, 1965.

Gotts, E. E. "Developmental Trends in Responding to the Pupil Perceptions Test (PPT)." Unpublished technical note, 1968.

Gotts, E. E. "Scoring and Interpretation of the Pupil Perceptions Test (PPT)." Unpublished technical note, 1968.

Gotts, E. E. "Developmental Scoring of the Pupil Perceptions Test (PPT)." Unpublished technical note, 1971.

Gotts, E. E., and Phillips, B. N. "The Relation Between Psychometric Measures of Anxiety and M-F." *Journal of School Psychology,* 1968, *6,* 123-130.

---

## SCORING SYSTEM FOR HOME AND SCHOOL

AUTHORS: M. E. Bernal and J. A. North

AGE: 4 to 10 years

VARIABLE: Behavior in home or school classroom

TYPE OF MEASURE: Behavioral coding system

SOURCE FROM WHICH MEASURE MAY BE OBTAINED: M. E. Bernal, Department of Psychology, University of Denver, Colorado 80210. Cost: $2.75.

DESCRIPTION OF MEASURE: This scoring system includes codes suitable for identification of children who are low in compliance and high in acting out disruptive behaviors. It yields information regarding the consequences produced by the child's acceptable and unacceptable behaviors. It was designed to reflect therapeutic interventions consisting of changes in parental management patterns, particularly the use of social reinforcement and time out. The system permits easy retrieval and summarization of data via computer programs. There are four major behavior categories for the target child: compliance-noncompliance, annoying, deviant, and desirable behavior. The two major behavior categories for adults and peers are commands and attention. In general, the compliance, annoying, deviant, and desirable categories require the scoring of chains of behaviors. For instance, whenever a command is given, the observer scores repetitions of the commands, whether or not the child complies, the nature of the attention given him (when he finally does or does not comply) by adults and peers. Likewise, if the child is scored as annoying, attention by teacher, peers, or parents is scored. In this manner, the consequence of a sample of child behavior are recorded.

    As an example, the last item in the annoying behavior category is given below. (Verbal abuse, whining, nonverbal abuse, and motor behavior are the other behaviors examined in this category.)

*Inappropriate Task Behavior: IT*
*School only:* Child is working on the wrong material when he has been told to do something else, or there is some clear indication that there is something else he should be doing. Inappropriate use of materials is also scored IT.
*Examples of IT:* C is told to put his work away, and he continues working, or he is working, but not on the material designated by the teacher. Using an object in an inappropriate manner, such as pounding chalk eraser on table or chalkboard, coloring on book cover.

RELIABILITY AND VALIDITY: Interobserver agreement is 78 percent or better. School data have been analyzed, and an absence of a sequence main effect ($F = .40$, $df = 6, 1,086$, $p < .25$) has been demonstrated for observations for a large sample; that is, over four to six observations there is no effect of repeated testing. A nonsignificant main effect of sequence ($F = .65$, $df = 5,576$) was found over six baseline observations in the home for child behavior rates. Correlations were significant for child behavior between the first and last two baseline observations and between the first three and the last three. Negative correlations between acceptable and unacceptable behaviors and positive correlations within acceptable and unacceptable types of behavior have been demonstrated. Significant differences have been found on these measures between parent-referred discipline problems and nondiscipline-problem boys.

BIBLIOGRAPHY:

Bernal, M. E., Delfini, L. F., North, J. A., and Kreutzer, S. L. "Comparison of Boys' Behaviors in Homes and Classrooms." Paper presented at the Sixth Banff International Conference on Behavior Modification. Alberta, Canada, 1974. In L. A. Hamerlynck, L. C. Handy, and E. J. Mash (Eds.), *Behavior Modification and Families.* New York: Brunner/Mazel, 1976.

Bernal, M. E., Dreutzer, S. L., North, J. A., and Pelc, R. E. "Scoring System for Home and School: Rationale, Use, Reliability and Validity." Paper presented at the meeting of the American Psychological Association. Montreal, Quebec, Canada, 1973.

Bernal, M. E., and North, J. A. *Scoring System for Home and School: Manual.* Mimeographed. 1973.

Delfini, L. F., Bernal, M. E., and Rosen, P. M. "Comparison of Deviant and Normal Boys in Home Settings." Paper presented at the Sixth Banff International Conference on Behavior Modification. Alberta, Canada, 1974. In L. A. Hamerlynck, L. C. Handy, and E. J. Handy (Eds.), *Behavior Modification and Families.* New York: Brunner/Mazel, 1976.

Johnson, S. M., and Bolstad, O. D. "Methodological Issues in Naturalistic Observation: Some Problems and Solutions for Field Research." In F. W. Clark and L. A. Hamerlynck (Eds.), *Critical Issues in Research and Practice: Proceedings of the Fourth Banff International Conference on Behavior Modification.* Champaign, Illinois: Research Press, 1973.

Kreutzer, S. L., Bernal, M. E., North, J. A., and Pelc, R. E. "Observer Reactivity to Agreement Checks in Field Research." Paper presented at the meeting of the Western Psychological Association. San Francisco, April 1974.

*Prepared by J. North*

# SENTENCE COMPLETION FORM (SCF)

AUTHORS: John F. Feldhusen, John R. Thurston, and James J. Benning

AGE: Elementary and junior high school

VARIABLE: Socially approved and aggressive-disruptive classroom behavior

TYPE OF MEASURE: Incomplete sentences

SOURCE FROM WHICH MEASURE MAY BE OBTAINED: John F. Feldhusen, Department of Educational Psychology, Purdue University, SCC-G, West Lafayette, Indiana 47906.

DESCRIPTION OF MEASURE: The Sentence Completion Form (SCF) is designed to measure socially approved vs. aggressive-disruptive behavior tendencies in third-, sixth-, and ninth-grade school children. The SCF consists of twenty incomplete sentences to be completed by the subjects. Some sample items are: "I like . . . ," "Other kids . . . ," "I can't . . . ," "What bothers me most . . . ." For very young children the SCF is administered in an interview; for older children it is self-administering. There is no time limit imposed. The SCF was quantified empirically, evaluating the completions of 192 children divided into two groups exhibiting socially approved and aggressive-disruptive behavior. Intensive study and comparison were used to identify characteristic completion patterns of the groups. A similar sample of children were used for cross-validation purposes. In the scoring, completions characterizing the socially approved group are given a score of 1, those completions characteristic of the socially disapproved group are given a score of 3, and those not characteristic of either group are given a score of 2.

RELIABILITY AND VALIDITY: The scores differentiated the criterion groups in the cross-validation sample at the .01 level. Interscorer reliability among three members of the research team scoring according to a prepared manual was considered satisfactory (rs were .70, .77, and .79).

BIBLIOGRAPHY:

Feldhusen, H. F., Thurston, J. R., and Benning, J. J. "Sentence Completion Responses and Classroom Social Behavior." *Personnel and Guidance Journal,* 1966, *45,* 165-170.
Soh, K. C. "Sentence Completion Form: A Validation Study." *Psychology in the Schools,* 1973, *10,* 316-319.

*Prepared by John R. Thurston*

# SITUATION EXERCISES

AUTHORS: John F. Feldhusen, John R. Thurston, and James J. Benning

AGE: Elementary and junior high school

VARIABLE: Socially approved and aggressive-disruptive classroom behavior

TYPE OF MEASURE: Projective

SOURCE FROM WHICH MEASURE MAY BE OBTAINED: John F. Feldhusen, Department of Educational Psychology, Purdue University, SCC-G, West Lafayette, Indiana 47906.

DESCRIPTION OF MEASURE: The Situation Exercises are designed to appraise responses to certain frustrations often encountered by children of several age groups. Four different personally frustrating experiences are described in short paragraphs: being accused of cheating in school, being threatened with punishment for an unavoidable mistake, receiving a social rejection, and not being allowed to make a simple decision over clothing selection. Subjects are asked after reading about a situation to write down all the things that could be said or done in response to the dilemma. The exercises are differentiated for adaptation to sex and age differences. The instrument is administered individually by a trained social worker or psychologist and has an imposed time limit of 4 minutes per situation. Two scores are drawn from the exercises, an adaptive score and a second score comprising a qualitative measure of abasement, dependence, and aggression. The qualitative measures were established through content analysis of each situation separately according to overall scoring principles.

As examples, the four situation exercises used for boys at the sixth-grade level are given below.

*Situation I*
Tommy's teacher called his mother to tell her that Tommy was caught copying from another pupil during a test. Tommy knows the teacher called his mother. Write all the things you can think of that Tommy might do or say about this.
*Situation II*
Bobby's father scolded him for coming home late from visiting a friend. The reason Bobby was late was because the bus was late. His father says he does not want to hear any excuses. Write all the things you can think of that Bobby might say or do to anyone about this.
*Situation III*
John met a group of kids who were going to walk home together from school. John said that he wanted to walk with them. The kids said they didn't want John to walk home with them. Write all the things you can think of that John might do or say to anyone about this.
*Situation IV*
Jim picked out a sweater in a store. He wanted to buy it with money which he had saved from his allowance. Jim's mother would not let him buy it because she said it was not a good color and it would not look nice on Jim. Write all the things you can think of that Jim might say or do to anyone about this.

RELIABILITY AND VALIDITY: The adaptive scoring system was derived empirically, consisting of those responses that differentiated two groups: socially approved ($N = 96$) and aggressive-disruptive ($N = 96$). This scoring system was cross-validated on a new, independent sample of the same number and composition. These groups were differentiated at the .01 level. Interscorer reliability was tested by comparing scores arrived at independently by two of the authors. The Pearson product-moment correlation coefficient for the two score sets ranged from .86 to .96 over the four situations.

BIBLIOGRAPHY:

Feldhusen, J. F., Thurston, J. R., and Benning, J. J. "Studying Aggressive Children Through Responses to Frustrating Situations." *Child Study Journal,* 1970, *2*, 1-17.

*Prepared by John R. Thurston*

---

## SITUATIONAL PREFERENCE INVENTORY (SPI)

AUTHOR: Carl N. Edwards

AGE: Junior high school to adult

VARIABLE: Styles of social interaction and adaptation

TYPE OF MEASURE: Forced ranking scales

SOURCE FROM WHICH MEASURE MAY BE OBTAINED: See Edwards (1973). Copies of the monograph may be obtained at a cost of $2.00 by addressing requests to Carl N. Edwards, P.O. Box 86, Village Station, Medway, Massachusetts 02053. Copies of the SPI Inventory and scoring are also available at cost from the author.

DESCRIPTION OF MEASURE: The Situational Preference Inventory (SPI) has been developed as a brief, self-administering, paper-and-pencil questionnaire designed to assess individual styles of social interaction. The SPI consists of twenty-two sets of statements. Each set contains three statements, each representing a different style of interaction: cooperational, instrumental, or analytic. Subjects are asked to indicate which of the three statements they agree with most and which they agree with least. Average administration time is approximately 10 to 15 minutes. Scale measures are described as follows: Cooperational interaction is characterized by receptivity to and understanding of the needs of others and resolution of social conflicts through personal sacrifice. Instrumental interaction reflects a preference for dealing with situations by structuring them and through close reliance upon lines of authority, similarity of interest, and adherence to tradition and custom. Analytic interaction is characteristically represented by a tendency to deal with people and situations through an understanding of situational and interpersonal cues and through exploration of other than existing or normative courses of action.

As examples, the first three of the twenty-two items of the inventory are given below. The respondent circles the answer "plus" for the statement he agrees with most or is most true for him and "minus" for the statement that is least true for him. The third statement in each item is left unmarked.

1. Most of the world's problems could be solved through
   a. better analysis and understanding of their causes.
   b. cooperation and mutual understanding.
   c. compliance with the appropriate policies and regulations.
2. Of the following I prefer
   a. sociology.
   b. economics.
   c. literature.
3. I prefer to attend parties or gatherings with
   a. close friends.
   b. people in my occupation or profession.
   c. interesting people, whether friends or strangers.

RELIABILITY: The Situational Preference Inventory has been administered to 1,421 males and 962 females from fourteen populations. Populations included high school students, college students, working adults, t-group members, psychiatrists, musicians, medical patients, American Indians, nurses, clergymen, and prisoners. In addition, the scale has been used in numerous other studies and translated into languages other than English. Six-week test-retest reliabilities are as follows: cooperational, .74; instrumental, .82; and analytic, .80. Internal consistency was determined through factor analysis. Evidence of validity is provided by research based on a wide range of empirical and conceptual designs and is presented in Edwards (1973).

BIBLIOGRAPHY:

Edwards, C. N. "Interactive Styles and Social Adaptation." *Genetic Psychology Monographs*, 1973, *87*, 123-174.

---

# SMITH INVENTORY

AUTHOR: John E. Smith

AGE: Grade 7

VARIABLE: Dropout proneness

TYPE OF MEASURE: Fixed-alternative questionnaire

SOURCE FROM WHICH MEASURE MAY BE OBTAINED: Office of Research and

Development, Appalachian Center, West Virginia University, Morgantown, West Virginia 26505, for Research Series 3 [Series 68 Number 9-13 4M (June 1968)].

DESCRIPTION OF MEASURE: The Smith Inventory is a self-rating scale that can be easily administered and quickly scored. The scale was constructed for use with seventh graders and is simple in language (fifth-grade reading level) and format. Items were selected from among those characteristics identified by research as being highly correlated with dropping out of school. Of the thirty-eight items, the first thirty-four consist of questions that can be answered by the student checking one of from three to five alternatives. The last four items attempt to assess the attitude of the student by requiring him to make value judgments on four important educational issues. The items fall into three main classes: a pattern of failure or a failure syndrome, involvement in extracurricular activities, and home life or background.

As examples, seven selected items from the scale are given below.

1. How old were you in the 7th grade? _____13 or under _____14-15 _____over 15
3. How much time did you spend reading a day? _____very much _____much _____little _____very little
5. Have you ever failed a grade before the seventh grade? _____none _____one _____two or more
7. Did you like your school work? _____yes _____usually _____seldom _____no
9. Did you like other students in your class? _____almost all _____most of them _____a few of them _____almost no one
11. Did you attend the school ball games, dances, or parties? _____never _____seldom _____often _____very often
13. How well did you like your teacher? _____very much _____much _____little _____very little

RELIABILITY AND VALIDITY: (1) In order to test the ability of the Smith Inventory items to differentiate between dropouts and nondropouts, a study was conducted involving 123 dropouts (sixty-one males and sixty-two females) and 207 nondropouts (114 males and ninety-three females). The nondropouts were high school seniors at the time of the study, 1966-1967. The items were analyzed by *chi*-square tests computed on each item for (a) total dropouts and total nondropouts, (b) male dropouts and male nondropouts, and (c) female dropouts and female nondropouts. Of the thirty-eight items, twenty were significant for the total groups of dropouts and nondropouts, fifteen for males, and sixteen for females. (2) In a 1971 study using 113 pairs of subjects matched by age and IQ, the null hypothesis that no significant difference would exist between the selections made by the seniors and the dropouts was tested by *chi-square*. The null hypothesis was rejected for eighteen of the thirty-four items used.

BIBLIOGRAPHY:

Mink, O. G., and Barker, L. W. *Dropout Proneness in Appalachia, Research Series 3.* Office of Research and Development, West Virginia University, Morgantown, 1968.

Smith, J. E., Tseng, M. S., and Mink, O. G. "Prediction of School Dropouts in Appalachia: Validation of a Dropout Scale." *Measurement and Evaluation in Guidance,* 1971, *4,* 31-37.

*Prepared by Oscar G. Mink*

## SOCIAL ACTIVITIES SCALE

AUTHORS: James W. Bush and others

AGE: All ages (social activities will vary according to social role)

VARIABLE: Performance measure of social activities

TYPE OF MEASURE: Structured interview, rating scale

SOURCE FROM WHICH MEASURE MAY BE OBTAINED: See Patrick, Bush, and Chen (1973). Also available through the Division of Health Policy and Management, Muir 2-D, Room 2346, Department of Community Medicine, School of Medicine, University of California, La Jolla, California 92037.

DESCRIPTION OF MEASURE: The Social Activities Scale is used in conjunction with measures of mobility and physical activity to determine function level for a health-status index. The Social Activities Scale is the basic component of the function status measurement, and it deals in terms of *performance* rather than *capacity*. Deviations from the "normal" or "usual" performance of social activities are measured according to age and social role. Social activities include three types: major, other, and self-care. The specific social activity scales for two age groups are:

> *Social Activity—Below Age 6*
> 5. Played and did other activities.
> 4. Played but limited in other activities.
> 3. Limited in amount or kind of play.
> 2. Performed self-care as usual for age, but did not play.
> 1. Needed more help with self-care than usual for age.
> *Social Activity—6 to 17 Years*
> 5. Did school work and other activities.
> 4. Did school work but limited in other activities.
> 3. Limited in amount or kind of school work.
> 2. Performed self-care as usual for age, but not school work.
> 1. Needed more help with self-care than usual for age.

RELIABILITY AND VALIDITY: None reported.

BIBLIOGRAPHY:

(All but the last item are unpublished papers, available from Division of Health Policy and Management, University of California, La Jolla 92037.)

Bush, J. W. "Description of the Health Index Project."
Bush, J. W. "Health Indices, Outcomes, and Quality Care."
Bush, J. W. "A Health-Status Index and Its Application to Health Services Outcomes."
Bush, J. W. "Maintaining Health in a Defined Population Using a Health Status Index."
Bush, J. W. "Measuring Levels of Well-Being for a Health Status Index."
Bush, J. W. "Social Indicators for Health Based on Function Status and Prognosis."
Bush, J. W. "Sources of Items for the Definition and Classification of Function Status."

Bush, J. W. "A Successive Intervals Analysis of Social Preference Measures for a Health Status Index."

Bush, J. W. "Toward an Operational Definition of Health."

Patrick, D. L., Bush, J. W., and Chen, M. M. "Toward an Operational Definition of Health." *Journal of Health and Social Behavior,* 1973, *14,* 6-23.

*Prepared by Carolyn André*

---

# SOCIAL BEHAVIOR TEST (SBT)

AUTHORS: Carol K. Whalen and Barbara A. Henker

AGE: Retarded and severely disturbed children and adolescents

VARIABLE: Social, imitative, and communicative skills

TYPE OF MEASURE: Structured behavioral inventory

SOURCE FROM WHICH MEASURE MAY BE OBTAINED: Carol K. Whalen, Program in Social Ecology, University of California, Irvine, California 92664.

DESCRIPTION OF MEASURE: The SBT is intended as a system for structured observation of target social behaviors. It consists of 142 items in five basic skill areas: nonverbal imitation (thirty items), vocal imitation (twelve items), verbal imitation (forty-two items), language comprehension–nonverbal response (twenty-eight items), and language comprehension–verbal response (thirty items). The test is designed for use with children and adolescents who have severely limited repertoires of social and communicative skills. The examiner attempts to maximize the child's performance by using multisensory cues, providing social and material rewards for attention and cooperation (but not for correct responses), and presenting each item twice if necessary. The SBT is administered in two sessions to minimize fatigue and boredom. Two types of responses are given scoring credit: correct and incorrect. Items are scored correct if the child executes the entire action demonstrated or requested. Approximations or responses correct for previous items are scored incorrect. Only task-oriented responses receive credit; stereotyped and other atavistic or disruptive behaviors are not scored. It is important to note that an increase in incorrect responses—even without significant gains in correct responses—can index improvements in social and communicative behavior patterns. In a behavior modification program using the SBT (Whalen and Henker, 1971b), correct and incorrect responses were summed to yield a measure of total responsivity.

As examples, fifteen selected items from five basic skill areas are given below. Each item is presented to the child twice, if necessary.

*I. Test of Nonverbal Imitation*
  1. Hammer pegboard.

2. Dial telephone.
3. Squeeze sound toy.
4. Throw ball.
*II. Test of Vocal Imitation*
1. Cluck.
2. Indian call.
*III. Test of Verbal Imitation*
1. Baby.
2. Zebra.
3. Sink.
*IV. Test of Language Comprehension–Nonverbal Response*
1. Draw a line.
2. Stamp your feet.
3. Touch your eyes.
*V. Test of Language Comprehension– Verbal Response*
A. What is this?
   1. Cookie.
   2. Doll.
   3. Shoe.

RELIABILITY AND VALIDITY: The SBT was initially used in a pyramid therapy program for retarded children. The scale was administered to ten children before and after two phases of a behavior modification program in which older, retarded patients served as therapists. Two independent raters agreed on 95 percent of the items scored correct and on 84 percent of the items scored incorrect. The inventory was found to provide a functional assessment of basic social skills and of changes in these skills over time. Children participating in the pyramid therapy program showed gains in both correct and incorrect responses, indicating they were acquiring a precise imitative repertoire as well as improving in attention and cooperation. In contrast, children in the attention-control groups showed gains in incorrect responding, again indicating improved attention and cooperation but no increases in correct responding. Within populations of severely retarded youngsters, SBT scores are uncorrelated with standardized intelligence measures. The test should be most useful in research or clinical situations for either assessment of present repertoire or measurement of behavioral improvement.

BIBLIOGRAPHY:

Henker, B. A., and Whalen, C. K. "Pyramid Therapy in a Hospital for the Retarded." In the *Proceedings of the 77th Annual Convention,* American Psychological Association, 1969.

Whalen, C. K., and Henker, B. A. "Play Therapy Conducted by Mentally Retarded Inpatients." *Psychotherapy: Theory, Research and Practice,* 1971a, *8,* 236-245.

Whalen, C. K., and Henker, B. A. "Pyramid Therapy in a Hospital for the Retarded: Methods, Program Evaluation and Long-Term Effects." *American Journal of Mental Deficiency,* 1971b, *75,* 414-434.

*Prepared by Carol K. Whalen and Barbara A. Henker*

# SOCIAL AND EMOTIONAL BEHAVIOR INVENTORY (SEBI)

AUTHOR: William Vogel

AGE: Retarded persons

VARIABLE: Social and emotional behaviors

TYPE OF MEASURE: Rating scale

SOURCE FROM WHICH MEASURE MAY BE OBTAINED: William Vogel, Department of Psychology, Worcester State Hospital, Worcester, Massachusetts 01613.

DESCRIPTION OF MEASURE: The SEBI is a research device, not designed for clinical use. The fifteen-item measure is used in conjunction with the Personal Skills Inventory (see pp. 1194-1195) to provide a quantified scoring system permitting raters to assess objectively the social and emotional behaviors that characterize retarded people. The device is designed to apply to institutional records rather than to live behavior. A nonprofessional employee (e.g., a research assistant) can become skilled in the use of the device after only several hours of training and practice.

As examples, the first two of the fifteen items of the SEBI are given below, to be scored as follows: a = 1, b = 2, c = 3, d = 4, e = 5.

1. *Control of Aggression*
   a. Is self-abusive (bangs head, tears clothing, etc.).
   b. Not ordinarily self-abusive, but is spontaneously physically aggressive toward others (combative, assaultive).
   c. Not ordinarily physically aggressive, but is spontaneously verbally abusive (customarily shouts, curses, or threatens).
   d. Ordinarily controls spontaneous displays of verbal and physical aggression, but is easily provoked.
   e. Controls aggression well; does not allow self to become easily provoked.
2. *Social Interaction*
   a. Takes no notice of others, or of attempts to interact with him.
   b. Takes notice of others' attempts to interact, but responds by being unfriendly or withdrawn.
   c. Friendly, if approached, but never makes advances to others.
   d. Friendly, occasionally makes advances.
   e. Outgoing, gregarious, socially aggressive.

RELIABILITY AND VALIDITY: Reliability, when used in conjunction with the Personal Skills Scale, was .90. A factor analysis of ratings on 132 institutionalized retardates supports inclusion of all but one of the items in this scale. Scores relate significantly to EEG, institutional release and prognosis, intellectual functioning, and adaptive behavior.

BIBLIOGRAPHY:

Vogel, W., Kun, K. J., and Meshorer, E. "Changes in Adaptive Behavior in Institutionalized Retardates in Response to Environmental Enrichment or Deprivation." *Journal of Consulting and Clinical Psychology*, 1968, *32*, 76-82.

Vogel, W., Kun, K. J., and Meshorer, E. "The Behavioral Significance of EEG Abnormality in Mental Defectives." *American Journal of Mental Deficiency,* 1969, *74,* 62-68.

Vogel, W., Kun, K. J., and Meshorer, E. "Determinants of Institutional Release and Prognosis in Mental Retardates." *Journal of Abnormal Psychology,* 1969, *74,* 685-692.

# STANFORD RESEARCH INSTITUTE (SRI)
# CLASSROOM OBSERVATION INSTRUMENT

AUTHOR: Jane Stallings

AGE: 3 to 12 years

VARIABLE: Classroom instructional processes and child behaviors

TYPE OF MEASURE: Interaction observation; checklist; inventory

SOURCE FROM WHICH MEASURE MAY BE OBTAINED: Education Research Department, Classroom Processes Group, Stanford Research Institute, 333 Ravenswood Avenue, Menlo Park, California 94025. Cost available upon request.

DESCRIPTION OF MEASURE: There are three major sections of the SRI Classroom Observation Instrument. The first one, the Physical Environment Information, assesses the physical environment and records classroom summary information. The second section, the Classroom Checklist (CCL), is known as the "snapshot." The CCL attempts to record a series of relatively static pictures (four times an hour) of the distribution of adults and children to activities. Essentially, the CCL assesses: activities occurring, materials used within activities, grouping patterns, teacher and aide responsibilities, and child independence. The third part of the observation, the Five-Minute Observation (FMO), is also recorded four times an hour following each CCL. The FMO, an interaction observation, uses four types of categories: "Who does the action?" "To whom is it done?" "How is it done?" and "What is done?" When strung into a kind of "sentence," these categories code a piece of interaction. A subsequent sentence codes a response, if any, or, in a one-way communication (such as a teacher lecturing or a child manipulating materials) continues to describe the primary action. This sentence-structure format, which uses interchangeable "parts of speech" or components, was patterned after Flanders' (1967) interaction-analysis strategy. Since very young mobile children are being observed, it was necessary to devise components in this instrument that could record movement, nonverbal behavior, and child-to-child interaction.

RELIABILITY AND VALIDITY: Four dimensions of reliability have been examined in Stallings and Kaskowitz (1974): day-to-day stability of classroom processes, observer reliability, confusability of the operational definitions of the observation codes, and anomalies in the data collected. Any codes found to be unreliable were omitted from further study (see Stallings and Giesen, 1974). Anomalies in the data were deleted where warranted; for example, if the teacher went home sick in the middle of the morning, that day's observation was deleted. Classrooms were found to be acceptably stable on observed variables from one day to another.

BIBLIOGRAPHY:

Boyer, E. G., Simon, A., and Karafin, G. R. *Measures of Maturation.* Philadelphia, Pennsylvania: Research for Better Schools, 1973.

Flanders, N. A. "Interaction Analysis in the Classroom: A Manual for Observers." In A. Simon and E. G. Boyer (Eds.), *Mirrors for Behavior.* Vol. 3, no. 2. Philadelphia, Pennsylvania: Research for Better Schools, 1967.

Stallings, J. "An Implementation Study of Seven Follow-Through Models for Education." Paper presented to the American Educational Research Association annual meeting, Chicago, Illinois, April 1974.

Stallings, J. "Is Compensatory Education Working?" Paper presented to Elementary, Kindergarten, Nursery School Education (E/K/N/E) Research Committee Conference, Menlo Park, California, January 1974.

Stallings, J. "What Teachers Do Does Make a Difference—A Study of Seven Follow-Through Educational Models." Paper presented to the Early Child Conference on Evaluation, Menlo Park, California, August 1974.

Stallings, J., and Giesen, P. *A Study of Reliability in Observational Data.* Menlo Park, California: Stanford Research Institute, 1974.

Stallings, J., and Kaskowitz, D. *Follow-Through Classroom Observation Evaluation, 1972-1973.* Menlo Park, California: Stanford Research Institute, 1974.

---

## STARKWEATHER SOCIAL CONFORMITY TEST FOR PRESCHOOL CHILDREN

AUTHOR: Elizabeth K. Starkweather

AGE: 3 to 7 years

VARIABLE: Social conformity and nonconformity

TYPE OF MEASURE: Preference test with visual aids

SOURCE FROM WHICH MEASURE MAY BE OBTAINED: Materials needed for the test can be obtained in the researcher's local community. Further information about the test can be obtained from E. K. Starkweather, Family Relations and Child Development Department, Oklahoma State University, Stillwater, Oklahoma 74074.

DESCRIPTION OF MEASURE: The Starkweather Social Conformity Test is a research instrument designed to measure conforming behavior by providing the young child with opportunities to make choices in a situation in which he can follow a model or respond freely according to his own preferences. The test discriminates between children who are compulsive conformists or nonconformists and children who are free to use either conforming or nonconforming behavior. The design of the social conformity test meets the following criteria: (1) The compulsive quality and the conforming quality of a child's behavior must be measured independently. The child who is a compulsive nonconformist is just as rigid as the child who is a compulsive conformist. (2) The test must be adjustable in order that the opportunity to conform be of similar potency for all children. Conforming behavior is common when a child has an opportunity to conform to persons he likes, whereas the reverse is true in the case of persons he dislikes. Similarly, conforming behavior is to be expected when it involves the choice of a preferred object. The social conformity test is based on color preferences and is adjusted to the actual preferences of individual children. A pretest provides an opportunity for each child to indicate his color preferences. Then in the test proper, each child is given opportunities to conform as he constructs a picture booklet, page by page, identical to or different from booklets constructed for other persons (e.g., parents or peers).

RELIABILITY AND VALIDITY: The reliability of the method of determining color preferences was tested by administering the pretest twice to a group of twenty-nine children and analyzing their responses for consistency of color preferences. The colors that were high ranking and low ranking during the first session did retain their relative positions during the second session (*chi-square* = 29.27; $p < .001$). The internal consistency of the social conformity test was determined by a split-half analysis of the responses of the children when they had an opportunity to conform to parents. The Spearman-Brown formula yielded a correlation coefficient of .78 ($p < .01$). The validity of the social conformity test was determined by a comparison of the responses of children in experimental control groups. For the child in the experimental group, the test provided an opportunity for conformity to parents. For the children in the control group, there was no opportunity for conforming behavior. The test scores for children in these two groups were significantly different (*chi-square* = 8.219; $p < .01$), indicating that the children in the experimental group were influenced by the opportunity to conform.

BIBLIOGRAPHY:

Starkweather, E. K. *Conformity and Nonconformity as Indicators of Creativity in Preschool Children.* Cooperative Research Project no. 1967. Washington, D.C.: U.S. Office of Education, Department of Health, Education and Welfare, 1964.

Starkweather, E. K. "Studies of the Creative Potential of Young Children." In F. Williams (Ed.), *Creativity at Home and in School.* St. Paul, Minnesota: Macalester Creativity Project, 1968.

Starkweather, E. K. "Creativity Research Instruments Designed for Use with Preschool Children." *Journal of Creative Behavior,* 1971, *5,* 245-255.

Starkweather, E. K., and Cowling, F. G. "The Measurement of Conforming and Nonconforming Behavior in Preschool Children." In R. Mooney and T. Razik (Eds.), *Explorations in Creativity.* New York: Harper & Row, 1967. (Also in *Proceedings of the Oklahoma Academy of Science,* 1963, *44,* 168-180.)

## STARKWEATHER SOCIAL RELATIONS TEST
## FOR PRESCHOOL CHILDREN

AUTHOR: Elizabeth K. Starkweather

AGE: 3 to 7 years

VARIABLE: A child's social value within his own peer group

TYPE OF MEASURE: Picture interview technique

SOURCE FROM WHICH MEASURE MAY BE OBTAINED: Materials needed for the test can be obtained in the researcher's local community. Further information about the test can be obtained from E. K. Starkweather, Family Relations and Child Development Department, Oklahoma State University, Stillwater, Oklahoma 74074.

DESCRIPTION OF MEASURE: The Starkweather Social Relations Test is designed to measure a young child's social value within his own peer group. It is more than a test of popularity. It combines a picture interview technique with gift giving, and each child's value in his group is measured in terms of the extent to which his gift giving is reciprocated by the children whom he chooses. The assumption underlying the choice of gift giving as a technique for measuring social relations is that an individual wants to benefit someone he likes. The materials needed for the social relations test include the following: (1) A composite picture of the child in the group. A picture is needed to help each child remember the other children in his group and to permit him to indicate each choice by pointing to a picture or by naming a child. (2) Inexpensive toys, such as small plastic cars, marbles, balloons, and pictures. These toys are the gifts that are given by each child to the children he chooses. Gift giving as the technique for measuring social relations among young children is of particular value because the child makes his choice of other children in terms of specific criteria (the gifts) that he can understand, and the actual giving of a gift, as a consequence of the child's naming another child, emphasizes the importance of his choice and thereby increases the probability of the test results being valid. (3) Envelopes, prelabeled with the names of the children in the group. The use of these envelopes insures the privacy of the children's choices of other children by providing a method of distributing the gifts without identifying the giver. The scoring of the Social Relations Test is designed to show the relationship between the child's choice of other children and their choice of him.

RELIABILITY AND VALIDITY: The Social Relations Test is assumed to have face validity.

BIBLIOGRAPHY:

Starkweather, E. K. "A Comparison of Two Techniques for Measuring Sociometric Status Among Nursery School Children." *Proceedings of the Oklahoma Academy of Science,* 1961, *42,* 199-205.
Starkweather, E. K. "Potential Creative Ability and the Preschool Child." *First Seminar on Productive Thinking in Education.* Creativity Project, Macalester College, St. Paul, Minnesota, January 1966.

# ST. PAUL SCALE OF FAMILY FUNCTIONING

AUTHORS: Ludwig L. Geismar and Beverly Ayres

AGE: One- or two-parent families with one or more dependent children

VARIABLE: Social functioning of families

TYPE OF MEASURE: Narrative data rating scale

SOURCE FROM WHICH MEASURE MAY BE OBTAINED: See Geismar (1971).

DESCRIPTION OF MEASURE: A schedule composed of nine areas and twenty-five sub-categories serves as a basis for collecting narrative data on the social functioning of a family. These data, comprising interview, observation, and available materials (tests, official records, and so forth), are rated (with the aid of a seventeen-page guideline) on a 7-point scale ranging from inadequate (1) to marginal (4) to adequate (7) social functioning. Criteria of adequacy are based on the dimensions health and welfare and conformity-deviance. The quantified data have been subjected to Guttman scaling (Geismar, LaSorte, and Ayres, 1962) and factor analysis (Geismar, 1973). Populations sampled in various studies include stable and disorganized families, middle- and lower-class families, blacks, whites, and Puerto Ricans, Americans, Canadians, and three European societies.

As an example, one of the twenty-five subcategories of the schedule is given below. It is part of the economic practices area. The other eight areas of the scale are: family relationships and family unity, individual behavior and adjustment, care and training of children, social activities, home and household practices, health conditions and practices, relationship to social worker, and use of community resources.

3. *Use of Money*

| *Inadequate* | *Marginal* | *Adequate* |
|---|---|---|
| Severe conflict over control of income endangers children's welfare. Budgeting and money management are so poor that basic necessities are not provided. Excessive debt results in legal action. | Disagreement over control of income leads to conflict or dissatisfaction among family members. Family is unable to live within budget, money management is poor, luxuries take precedence over basic necessities, there is impulsive spending. (Above do not seriously endanger family's welfare.) | Money is spent on the basis of agreement that such is responsibility of one or more members of family. Family budgets income; money management is carried out with realistic regard to basic necessities. Debts are manageable and planned for in budget. |

RELIABILITY AND VALIDITY: Interrater reliability, based on the independent ratings of three and two coders, ranges from 65 to 87-percent agreement on items rated. Evidence of validity comes in two forms: (1) a comparison of the ratings of husbands' and wives' independent accounts of family functioning, which showed a mean validity ratio of .80 (SD = .067), and a subcategory range from .68 to .93; (2) a comparison of the results of measuring family change with the aid of the St. Paul Scale and those obtained by using the Hunt-Kogan Movement Scale (1966). The two types of measures applied to fifty-one families showed identical ratings for 40 percent of the cases and differences of one degree in an additional 40 percent of the cases (see Wallace, 1967).

BIBLIOGRAPHY:

Geismar, L. "Family Functioning as an Index of Need for Welfare Services." *Family Process,* 1964, *2,* 99-113.
Geismar, L. "The Results of Social Work Intervention: A Positive Case." *American Journal of Orthopsychiatry,* 1968, *38,* 444-456.
Geismar, L. *Family and Community Functioning.* Metuchen, New Jersey: Scarecrow Press, 1971.
Geismar, L. *555 Families.* New Brunswick, New Jersey: Transaction Books, 1973.
Geismar, L., and Gerhart, U. "Social Class, Ethnicity, and Family Functioning: Exploring Some Issues Raised by the Moynihan Report." *Journal of Marriage and the Family,* 1968, *30,* 480-487.
Geismar, L., and Krisberg, J. *The Forgotten Neighborhood.* Metuchen, New Jersey: Scarecrow Press, 1967.
Geismar, L., Lagay, B., Wolock, M., Gerhart, U., and Fink, H. *Early Supports for Family Life.* Metuchen, New Jersey: Scarecrow Press, 1972.
Geismar, L., and LaSorte, M. "Factors Associated with Family Disorganization." *Marriage and Family Living,* 1963, *25,* 479-481.
Geismar, L., and La Sorte, M. *Understanding the Multi-Problem Family.* New York: Association Press, 1964.
Geismar, L., La Sorte, M., and Ayres, B. "Measuring Family Disorganization." *Marriage and Family Living,* 1962, *24,* 51-56.
Kogan, L. S., and Shyne, A. W. "The CSS Movement Scale: A Methodological Review." In C. S. Chilman (Ed.), *Approaches to the Measurement of Family Change.* Washington, D.C.: U.S. Department of Health, Education, and Welfare, Welfare Administration, 1966.
Wallace, D. "The Chemung County Evaluation of Casework Service to Dependent Multi-Problem Families: Another Problem Outcome." *Social Service Review,* 1967, *41,* 379-389.

---

# TEACHER ATTENTION AND
# RETARDATE BEHAVIOR RECORD

AUTHORS: Barry S. Parsonson, Ann M. Baer, and Donald M. Baer

AGE: Retarded children 4 to 12 years

VARIABLE: Teacher attention to retardate behaviors

TYPE OF MEASURE: Behavior sampling

SOURCE FROM WHICH MEASURE MAY BE OBTAINED: Ann M. Baer, Psychology, Kansas Neurological Institute, 3107 West 21st Street, Topeka, Kansas 66604.

DESCRIPTION OF MEASURE: This is a sequential record of topography of teacher attention (positive and negative) to ten defined categories of child behavior (eight with both appropriate and inappropriate forms, and two having only inappropriate forms) representing all possible classes of child behavior within the observational context. Data are collected by recording five consecutive blocks of fifteen sequential teacher attentions identifiable as having been specifically directed at individual children, and they are used to provide feedback to the teacher (after each block of fifteen attentions) on the percentage of attention to appropriate and inappropriate behavior. The recording format may also be used to identify and measure behavior of individual retarded children in the preschool context.

As examples, the following abbreviated definitions of child behavior comprising the first four of the ten-category code are given below. (A detailed list of the definitions of child behaviors may be obtained from the first or third author.)

| Category of Child Behavior | Appropriate Form | Inappropriate Form |
|---|---|---|
| 1. Activity | Acceptable use of identifiable activity. | (1) Unoccupied. (2) Avoidance of positive activity. |
| 2. Bizarre | Not applicable. | (1) Autisms. (2) Self-destructive acts. (3) Habits. |
| 3. Compliance | Follows instructions, requests, etc., within 10 seconds. | Does not comply or approximate compliance within 10 seconds. |
| 4. Disruptive | Not applicable | (1) Disruptive (2) Destructive |

RELIABILITY AND VALIDITY: Interobserver reliability data were obtained, independently, for each category of child behavior and its classification as appropriate or inappropriate for both teachers (in a two-teacher classroom) at each phase of the study. Mean percentage interobserver agreement on these variables exceeded 80 percent for both teachers. As sequences of attending behavior were recorded, loss of sequence between observers was found to contribute to poor reliability. Sequence was maintained using a signaling procedure to cue occurrences of teacher attention. Observers alternated as signalers to reduce bias, and the nonsignaling observer used a code to note disagreements over occurrence of teacher attentions while retaining the signaler's sequence.

BIBLIOGRAPHY:

Parsonson, B. S., Baer, A. M., and Baer, D. M. "The Application of Generalized Correct Social Contingencies: An Evaluation of a Training Program." *Journal of Applied Behavior Analysis,* 1974, *7,* 427-437.

# TEACHER RECORD

AUTHOR: Deanne Boydell

AGE: Teachers of children 7 to 11 years

VARIABLE: Teacher-pupil interaction

TYPE OF MEASURE: Observational category system

SOURCE FROM WHICH MEASURE MAY BE OBTAINED: *The Teacher Record: A Manual for Observers* available from Deanne Boydell, School of Education, University of Leicester, Leicester, England LE1 7RH.

DESCRIPTION OF MEASURE: The Teacher Record is a multiple-coding technique that describes the teacher's interaction with pupils, with observations based on time signals emitted every 25 seconds into the observer's ear from a small portable cassette tape recorder. At each signal the observer indicates the type of conversation (or silence); the teacher's audience (class, group, or individual child); and one other selected feature of the contact (e.g., the activity of the child with whom the teacher is interacting). Each record sheet has space for fifteen signals, and the observer completes about eight sheets per hour. The Teacher Record must only be used in conjunction with *The Teacher Record: A Manual for Observers,* which explains the observation procedure in full and gives detailed category definitions.

RELIABILITY AND VALIDITY: Full information about the instrument's reliability is available in Appendix B of *The Teacher Record: A Manual for Observers.*

BIBLIOGRAPHY:

Boydell, D. "Teacher-Pupil Contact in Junior Classrooms." *British Journal of Educational Psychology,* 1974, *44,* 313-318.
*The Teacher Record: A Manual for Observers.* Duplicated. 1974.

---

# VIDEO-TAPE BEHAVIORAL CHECKLIST
## (FOR USE WITH STANDARDIZED PLAY INTERVIEWS)

AUTHORS: Mary R. Haworth and Frank J. Menolascino

AGE: 2 to 9 years

VARIABLE: Behavioral reactions in structured-play situations

TYPE OF MEASURE: Checklist

SOURCE FROM WHICH MEASURE MAY BE OBTAINED: Mary R. Haworth, Research Scientist Development Section, Division of Extramural Research Programs, National Institute of Mental Health, 5600 Fishers Lane, Rockville, Maryland 20852.

DESCRIPTION OF MEASURE: The checklist serves as a means of evaluating young children's reactions to a standardized play interview recorded on videotape. The sequence of tasks is designed to aid in differential diagnosis between young normal or retarded children and those with psychotic tendencies. Interview sequences are planned to allow for specific behavioral reactions such as free choice and use of toys, persistence, imitation, and reactions to frustration and gratification, as well as for increasing amounts of interaction with the examiner. The checklist describes major response patterns in segments of the play interview and includes behaviors generally assumed to represent adequate adjustment and behaviors considered to be pathological (such as withdrawal, inappropriate reactions, or outright refusal to respond). In accordance with this theoretical frame of reference, corresponding positive or negative valences are assigned to each behavioral description; for example, in ball play, *positive* items include catching and returning the ball and looking at *E* while doing so; *negative* ball play responses include not looking at *E* even though entering into the activity, throwing the ball away from *E,* or refusing to become involved. Final scoring of the checklist yields a positive or a negative score for each interview segment. The labels given to each dimension or segment of activity in the Behavioral Checklist are listed below, followed by the scoring instructions for free play (the positive and negative checks for each dimension are summed separately and reduced, if necessary, to conform to the maximums allowed as indicated): communication ($\pm1$), free play ($\pm3$), interference ($\pm1$), speech ($\pm3$), activity level ($\pm1$), general affect ($\pm2$), gratification ($\pm1$), imitation ($\pm1$), ball play ($\pm3$), phones ($\pm3$), hand games ($\pm1$), lap ($\pm2$), cookie-speech ($\pm1$), locked box ($\pm3$), goodbye ($\pm1$).

| *Positive Items* | *Negative Items* |
|---|---|
| Gets toy from reserve table. | Uses maximum of two toys. |
| Spontaneously hands toy to *E.* | Holds something in hand as uses other toys. |
| Appropriate combination of two toys. | Negative, pushes toys away. |
| | Inappropriate toy use. |
| (If no negative checks, start with minimum score of $\pm2$.) | No toy play, or just touches. |

An example of the interview sequence is given below, with explanations of *E*'s role in attempting to elicit specific types of behaviors.

On entering the room with the child, *E* engages in brief conversation to establish rapport, asks the child's name, age and sex, and then points to the toys and invites *S* to play with anything he wishes. *E* remains in the background for the next five minutes. (If *S* hesitates unduly or appears uneasy, *E* becomes more active and supportive as needed.) Then, while *S* is engaged in an activity, *E* offers a different toy, to determine whether *S* will shift or continue previous activity.

*Communication*

*Toy Choice*
*Free Play* (ability to function in unstructured situation)

*Interference* (frustration, tolerance)

RELIABILITY AND VALIDITY: When viewing tapes of eleven play interviews, two judges achieved 82-percent agreement on scores for each of the fifteen dimensions from each tape. Groups of normal children and those diagnosed as adjustment reactions of childhood and those diagnosed as retardates consistently scored in positive directions, while autistic children scored negatively in all areas. Childhood schizophrenics gave predominantly negative scores. Young normals and children with brain damage or sensory handicaps demonstrated varied patterns, with positive scores on some dimensions and negative scores on others.

BIBLIOGRAPHY:

Haworth, M. R., and Menolascino, F. J. "Videotape Observations of Disturbed Young Children." *Journal of Clinical Psychology,* 1967, *23,* 135-140.

---

## WAYS OF LOOKING AT PEOPLE (WLP) SCALE

AUTHOR: Janet P. Moursund

AGE: 13 years and up

VARIABLE: Social maturity

TYPE OF MEASURE: Test (Likert-type scale)

SOURCE FROM WHICH MEASURE MAY BE OBTAINED: Janet P. Moursund, The Lila Acheson Wallace School of Community Service and Public Affairs, University of Oregon, Eugene, Oregon 97403. Cost: Postage and handling.

DESCRIPTION OF MEASURE: The Ways of Looking at People (WLP) Scale attempts to determine the age group most similar to the testee in terms of stated attitudes about loyalty to friends, sharing of resources, the basic nature of people, and so forth. It consists of fifty-three item statements, each of which is to be responded to on a Likert-type scale. Forty of the items are grouped into eight subscales of five items each; the remaining thirteen items serve as fillers. The eight subscales used in evaluating the protocol are: (1) similarity to adults, containing relatively straightforward items relating to the degree to which the respondee feels himself to be "like" an adult; (2) giving and taking, dealing with a variable that might be characterized as selfishness-unselfishness—helping others at the expense of one's self, responsibility to others, and so forth; (3) pity and blame, concerned with a permissive, forgiving attitude as opposed to a strict eye-for-an-eye philosophy; (4) basic values, dealing not with the nature of the respondee's values but rather with the importance he places upon awareness of these values; (5) confidence, concerned with the respondee's estimation of himself and his capabilities; (6) liking others, dealing with general sociability and friendliness; (7) trust and mistrust, which elicits information about the respondee's opinion of others' trustworthiness; and (8) basic nature, which asks whether people in general are "good" or "bad." Of the forty scored items, twenty-two are worded in a reverse fashion; that is, high agreement reflects negative rather than positive attitudes. Scores may be tallied on a score sheet; a FORTRAN program for scoring individual protocols also exists. Norms should be updated and scoring revised appropriately.

As examples, the first ten of the fifty-three items on the scale are given below. The respondent answers on a 5-point scale ranging from "I agree very much" to "I disagree very much."

1. I believe in standing by a friend, no matter what.
2. When I get out into the world, I really think I will do well.
3. These days you just can't trust people.
4. Often criminals don't get punished enough for the bad things they do.
5. If you really trust people, they'll almost always come through for you.
6. The most important question a person can ask is, "Who am I?"
7. I guess I just plain like people.
8. Most people really try to do the right thing.
9. Things are either right or wrong—there's no in-between.
10. More than anything else, I want to do something worthwhile for the world.

RELIABILITY AND VALIDITY: Test-retest reliabilities on subscales range from .48 to .72. Median interitem $r = .26$. Seven out of eight subscales show score increase with increased age; four of these are statistically significant. Girls score significantly higher than boys. The middle socioeconomic range score is higher than that of the high socioeconomic range or low socioeconomic range.

BIBLIOGRAPHY:

Moursund, J. P. "Development of a Scale of Social Perception: The WLP." *Educational and Psychological Measurements,* 1967, *27,* 479-484.

# Category 10

---

# Vocational

---

*Included here are measures of vocational maturity and readiness, vocational aspirations and interests, and career knowledge.*

# CAREER DEVELOPMENT INVENTORY (CDI)

AUTHOR: Donald E. Super

AGE: High school form: grades 6 to 12; college form also available

VARIABLE: Vocational maturity

TYPE OF MEASURE: Inventory

SOURCE FROM WHICH MEASURE MAY BE OBTAINED: Donald E. Super, Department of Psychology, Teachers College, Columbia University, New York, New York 10027. The Career Development Inventory, high school form, is copyrighted but not yet published. Qualified persons wishing to use it experimentally upon agreeing to make resulting data available for use by the authors and to use the published version rather than their own reproduction once such becomes available will be authorized to reproduce the CDI for their own use. A mimeographed copy of the inventory will be sent to such potential users. Cost: $2.50 for specimen sets (manual and inventory).

DESCRIPTION OF MEASURE: The Career Development Inventory is an objective, multifactor, self-administering, paper-and-pencil inventory measuring the vocational maturity of adolescent boys and girls. It yields three scale scores, two of them attitudinal and one of them cognitive, plus a total score. The names of the scales are: (A) planning orientation (attitudinal), (B) resources for exploration (attitudinal), and (C) information and decision making (cognitive). The scales contain thirty-three, twenty-eight, and thirty items, respectively. The questions are appropriate for both boys and girls. The reading difficulty of the CDI makes its use appropriate at and above the sixth grade, and its vocabulary and content make it acceptable to junior and senior high school students in any grade. The average student takes no more than 30 minutes to complete the CDI, and all students easily complete it in one school period. It may be hand-scored or easily scored by computer. The three scales of the CDI represent the readily assessed important aspects of vocational maturity. Scale A represents the degree of the student's awareness of and inclination toward planning and choice, Scale B assesses a quality or soundness of individuality used and potential available resources, and Scale C samples the amount of the educational and occupational information that the student has acquired together with his mastery of the use of the information for sound decisions. Thus both attitudinal (self-rated and subjective) and cognitive (factual and objective) aspects of vocational development are tapped by the instrument. The Total Career Development Scale is an arbitrary combination of Scales A, B, and C. Norms are provided based on use of the instrument in Genessee County (Flint), Michigan.

RELIABILITY AND VALIDITY: Test-retest reliability coefficients obtained from eighty-two tenth graders after an interval of two to four weeks were as follows: Scale A, .85; Scale B, .82; Scale C, .71; total, .87. Stability coefficients for the scales, over six months using the tenth graders, were as follows: Scale A, .71; Scale B, .64; Scale C, .68; and total, .71. Significant differences were found between the mean scores of eighth, tenth, and twelfth graders on Scales A, B, and C and on the total scale. The CDI scales are virtually unrelated to the father's occupation and own vocational preference, measures of present and hoped-for socioeconomic levels. The attitudinal scales (A and B) are unrelated to verbal aptitude and GPA, while the cognitive scale (Scale C) is moderately related to these variables. Validation data involve increase with grade and correlations with Crites' CMI (1973), Westbrook's CVMT (1971, 1972), and Bribbons' and Lohnes' RVP scale (1968).

BIBLIOGRAPHY:

Crites, J. O. *Career Maturity Inventory.* New York: McGraw-Hill, 1973.

Forrest, D. J. "The Construction and Validation of an Objective Measure of Vocational Maturity for Adolescents." Unpublished doctoral dissertation. Teachers College, Columbia University, New York, 1971.

Gribbons, W. D., and Lohnes, P. R. *Emerging Careers.* New York: Teachers College Press, Columbia University, 1968.

Super, D. E., Bohn, M. J., Jr., Forrest, D. J., Jordaan, J. P., Lindeman, R. H., and Thompson, A. S. *The Career Inventory, Form I.* New York: Teachers College, Columbia University, 1971.

Super, D. E., and Overstreet, P. L. *The Vocational Maturity of Ninth Grade Boys.* New York: Teachers College Press, Columbia University, 1960.

Westbrook, B. W. "The Development of a Measure of Vocational Maturity." *Educational and Psychological Measurement,* 1971, *31,* 541-543.

Westbrook, B. W. "An Instrument to Measure Vocational Maturity." *Educational and Psychological Measurement,* 1972, *32,* 1131-1133.

*Prepared by Orval G. Johnson*

---

## COULD YOU EVER SCALE

AUTHOR: Philip R. Jones

AGE: 13 to 21 years

VARIABLE: Appropriateness of vocational outlook for educable retarded children

TYPE OF MEASURE: Test

SOURCE FROM WHICH MEASURE MAY BE OBTAINED: Philip R. Jones, Department of Education, Indiana University, Bloomington, Indiana 47401. Cost: Reproduction plus mailing and handling.

DESCRIPTION OF MEASURE: This instrument contains forty items requiring "yes" and "no" responses relating to whether or not the individual could perform a certain task or hold a certain type of job. Ten of the questions are divided so that boys and girls answer to different tasks or jobs. Twenty of the items are scored as appropriate responses, while twenty are considered inappropriate as vocational choices for mentally handicapped individuals. The measure was constructed for a study that investigated the relationship between vocational outlook of high school educable mentally handicapped students and the type of programs in which they were found (Jones, 1966).

As examples, the first twenty items of the scale are given below. $X$ denotes appropriate responses.

$X$   1. Could you ever have a garden?
$X$   2. Could you ever obtain a driver's license?
$X$   3. Could you ever take care of a pet dog or cat?
    4. Could you ever teach the class if the teacher got sick?
$X$   5. Could you ever learn to read a map?
    6. Could you ever
      G. be the best cook in the world?
      B. repair an auto engine?
$X$   7. Could you ever
      G. take care of a baby all day?
      B. make a sled?
    8. Could you ever go to college?
    9. Could you ever fly an airplane around the world?
    10. Could you ever run a hospital?
$X$   11. Could you ever save fifty dollars?
$X$   12. Could you ever save a baby from a burning house?
    13. Could you ever be a leader and make people do what you told them to do?
    14. Could you ever discover something that would save many people's lives?
    15. Could you ever be the most famous person in your state?
    16. Could you ever write a book with 300 pages?
$X$   17. Could you ever own a car?
$X$   18. Could you ever learn to drive a car?
    19. Could you ever be
      G. a librarian?
      B. a doctor?
$X$   20. Could you ever be a sales clerk in a store downtown?

RELIABILITY AND VALIDITY: None reported.

BIBLIOGRAPHY:

Jones, P. R. "The Relationship of Vocational Outlook and Special Educational Programs for Adolescent Educable Mentally Handicapped." Unpublished doctoral dissertation. ERIC document no. ED 018 883. University Microfilms Order no. 67-6640. University of Illinois, Urbana, 1966.

# JOB-READINESS EVALUATION CHECKLIST

AUTHOR: John W. Kidd

AGE: 16 years and up

VARIABLE: Job readiness

TYPE OF MEASURE: Rating scale

SOURCE FROM WHICH MEASURE MAY BE OBTAINED: Special School District of St. Louis County, 12110 Clayton Road, Town and Country, Missouri 63131; or see Kidd (1967).

DESCRIPTION OF MEASURE: This evaluation form incorporates items from the special-education literature, from a personal characteristics profile, and from the experiences of job-placement consultants. It consists of a number of characteristics that are rated on a 5-point scale from "well above average" to "well below average." Some of the characteristics are broken down into subbehaviors (see, for example, "dependability"). There are seventeen items rated in this way. Other items are concerned with hearing, vision, and motor limitations, and these are answered on a yes/no basis.

As examples, the first six items from the measure are given below.

1. Output (productivity).
2. Cooperation.
3. Effort.
4. Cautiousness—safety consciousness.
5. Accuracy and consistency in following directions.
6. Dependability.
   a. Attendance.
   b. Promptness.
   c. Independence.
   d. Awareness of time.

RELIABILITY AND VALIDITY: None reported.

BIBLIOGRAPHY:

Kidd, J. W. "A Job-Readiness Evaluation Checklist." *Exceptional Children*, 1967, *34*, 581-583.

*Prepared by Orval G. Johnson*

# KULDAU OCCUPATIONAL DEVELOPMENT INVENTORY (KODI)

AUTHORS: Von D. Kuldau and Janice E. Kuldau

AGE: Grades 4 to 6

VARIABLE: Attitudes toward work

TYPE OF MEASURE: Forced-choice inventory

SOURCE FROM WHICH MEASURE MAY BE OBTAINED: Information concerning the KODI may be obtained by writing Von D. Kuldau and Janice E. Kuldau, 1 White Birch Trail, Superior, Wisconsin 54880.

DESCRIPTION OF MEASURE: The Kuldau Occupational Developmental Inventory (KODI) was developed as a means of measuring attitudes children in grades 4, 5, and 6 have acquired toward the world of work. The instrument samples attitudes in the following six areas related to the adult world of work: money, working conditions, status and prestige, leadership, self-expression, and independence on the job. The forty-item instrument has a reading level of 4.75 as measured by the Dale-Chall Readability Test. To counteract any other reading disability that might occur, each item is printed on a transparency and shown using an overhead projector. The item is then read orally by the test administrator. A standardized answer sheet is used and children are instructed to answer "yes" if they agree with the item and "no" if they do not agree. An administrator's manual including scoring keys, scaled scores, and norms (based on results of administration of KODI to 1,606 children) has been developed.

As examples, six of the forty items of the test are given below.

1. A person seeking a job must be willing to learn the new skills that are needed to do that job.
2. The most important reason a person works is to make money.
3. I would like a job at which I could be famous and known all over the world.
4. I would like a chance to make important decisions on the job where I work.
5. Working just means carrying out someone else's ideas.
6. The boss should be someone who is well liked by other people.

RELIABILITY AND VALIDITY: Two procedures were followed to establish validity for the KODI. The first, which provided content validity, was based on the results of a panel of individuals from the areas of elementary education, counseling and guidance, English, psychology, and physical education. The second procedure provided empirical evidence of validity and included a factor analysis on the results of a study using 1,606 elementary-school children. Males and females in three grades (4, 5, and 6) and three socioeconomic levels (inner-city, working-blue-collar and professional-white-collar) made up the population. Information related to reliability is being established through current research.

BIBLIOGRAPHY:

Kuldau, J. E. "Occupational Development Among Upper-Elementary-School-Age Children." Unpublished doctoral dissertation. Ball State University, Muncie, Indiana, 1970.

Kuldau, J. E., and Hollis, J. W. "The Development of Attitudes Toward Work Among Upper-Elementary-School-Age Children." *Journal of Vocational Behavior,* 1971, *1,* 387-398.

*Prepared by Von D. Kuldau and Janice E. Kuldau*

---

## MATTHEWS STUDENT EVALUATION FORM (MSEF)

AUTHOR: Peter R. Matthews

AGE: Prevocational- and vocational-aged retarded students

VARIABLE: Students' performance at school and on the job

TYPE OF MEASURE: Rating scale

SOURCE FROM WHICH MEASURE MAY BE OBTAINED: *The Pointer,* P.O. Box 131, Syracuse, New York 13210.

DESCRIPTION OF MEASURE: This is a rating form, consisting of forty-two defined and weighted variables, that helps educators determine strengths and weaknesses in a student's performance at school and on the job as well as providing a general indication of performance. Each variable is scored on a 5-point scale from low (1) to high (5). Variables were established after twenty-nine people engaged in work programs for the mentally retarded from state, federal, and private agencies and schools were asked what determines the success of these students in employment. Their responses were compiled, and thirty-nine items resulted. Items were added or discarded to bring the total to forty-two. Each item was defined so that it would have the same meaning for everyone. Weighting the MSEF followed when thirteen employers of the unskilled and semiskilled were asked to rate on a scale from 1 to 10 each of the items on the MSEF in regard to importance to job success.

As examples, the first eight of the forty-two variables are given below, with their weighted values, to be scored from 1 to 5.

9.9 *Attendance*—Does the student come to school or work unless there is a reasonable excuse?

8.0 *General appearance*—Does the student look clean and neat?

8.2 *Appropriateness of dress*—Does the student wear clothes that are suited for the situation?

8.1 *Ability to communicate*—Is the student able to convey ideas and feelings to you?

7.7 *Maturity*—How does the student act in comparison to the other workers or pupils?

7.7 *Emotional stability*—Does the student possess an even temperament as opposed to being dominated by feelings?

7.5 *Can work calmly under stress*—Does the student get nervous when pressure is exerted or performance is demanded?

7.0 *Patience (calm, not easily excitable)*–Does the student refrain from complaining?

RELIABILITY AND VALIDITY: None reported.

BIBLIOGRAPHY:

Mathews, P. R. "The Matthews Student Evaluation Form." *The Pointer*, 1973, *18*, 116-120.

---

## OCCUPATIONAL ASPIRATION SCALE (OAS)

AUTHORS: Archibald O. Haller and Irwin W. Miller

AGE: Primarily male high school students

VARIABLE: Level of occupational goal

TYPE OF MEASURE: Questionnaire and rating scale

SOURCE FROM WHICH MEASURE MAY BE OBTAINED: Schenkman Publishing Co., Inc., 3 Mt. Auburn Place, Cambridge, Massachusetts 02138. Cost: $1.95. All requests for or permission to use the scale should be directed to the Schenkman Company with a copy sent to Archibald O. Haller, Rural Sociological Research Laboratory, WARF Office Building, Room 617, 610 Walnut Street, Madison, Wisconsin 53706.

DESCRIPTION OF MEASURE: The level of occupational aspiration has been determined to be at least a moderately successful predictor of levels of educational and occupational attainment. The OAS consists of eight multiple-choice questions, each listing ten different occupations of various prestige from which the respondent is to choose. There are four types of items dealing with which occupation the respondent would choose for an ideal short-term goal, a realistic short-term goal, an ideal long-term goal, and a realistic long-term goal. There are two questions (each composed of ten alternative responses) pertaining to each of the four item types, and the scores of alternative responses for each stimulus question range from 0 to 9. The sum of all eight question scores is taken as the individual's level of occupational aspiration as measured by the OAS. Little normative data on the OAS are available at this time, but for 442 boys residing in a Michigan county the scores range from 2 to 65, with a mean of 36.20 and a standard deviation of 12.99. The distribution of total OAS scores appears to be approximately normal in shape. The OAS can be given individually or in groups in about 20 minutes. Scoring is a very simple procedure and generally can be completed in a minute or two.

As examples, the first two of the eight questions of the scale are given below.

1. Of the jobs listed in this question, which is the *best one* you are *really sure you can get* when your *schooling is over*?

| Lawyer. | Night watchman. |
| Welfare worker for a city government. | Sociologist. |
| United States representative in Congress. | Policeman. |
| Corporal in the Army. | County agricultural agent. |
| United States Supreme Court Justice. | Filling station attendant. |

2. Of the jobs listed in this question, which *one* would you choose if you were *free to choose any* of them you wished when your *schooling is over*?

| Member of the board of directors of a large corporation. | Clothes presser in a laundry. |
| | Accountant for a large business. |
| Undertaker. | Railroad conductor. |
| Banker. | Railroad engineer. |
| Machine operator in a factory. | Singer in a night club. |
| Physician (doctor). | |

RELIABILITY AND VALIDITY: There are nineteen estimates of the reliability of the OAS, yielding figures ranging from .69 to .84, with a mean of .73. From the same data there are nineteen estimates of the standard error of measurement, which range from 4.75 to 5.70, with a mean of 5.43. The only available estimate for a coefficient of concurrent validity is a moderate value of .62 based on the OAS's correlation with the North-Hatt technique. Factor analysis shows the OAS to be essentially a one-factor test. An inter-technique factorial validity test shows the main OAS factor to be essentially the same as the main North-Hatt technique factor.

BIBLIOGRAPHY:

Haller, A. O. *The Occupational Aspiration Scale: Theory, Structure, and Correlates of an Instrument Designed to Measure Differential Levels of Occupational Aspiration.* Final report to the U.S. Office of Education. East Lansing: Michigan Agricultural Experiment Stations, 1961.

Haller, A. O. "On the Concept of Aspiration." *Rural Sociology,* 1968, *33,* 484-487.

Haller, A. O., and Miller, I. W. "A Measure of Level of Occupational Aspiration." In G. D. Demos (Ed.), *Vocational Guidance Readings.* Springfield, Illinois: C. C Thomas, 1965. (Reprinted from *Personnel and Guidance Journal,* 1964, *42,* 448-455.)

Haller, A. O., Otto, L. B., Meier, R. F., and Ohlendorf, G. W. "An Empirical Evaluation of a Scale to Measure Occupational Aspiration Level." *Journal of Vocational Behavior,* 1974, *4,* 1-11.

Haller, A. O., Otto, L. B., Meier, R. F., and Ohlendorf, G. W. "Level of Occupational Aspiration: An Empirical Analysis." *American Journal of Sociological Review,* 1974, *39,* 113-121.

*Prepared by Stephen J. Miller*

## OCCUPATIONAL CONSTRUCT INVENTORY (OCI)

AUTHOR: Julian L. Biggers

AGE: Grades 4 to 12

VARIABLE: Type of occupational information used by students in decision making

TYPE OF MEASURE: Picture-preference test

SOURCE FROM WHICH MEASURE MAY BE OBTAINED: Julian Biggers, College of Education, Texas Tech University, Box 4560, Lubbock, Texas 79409.

DESCRIPTION OF MEASURE: Kelly's Role Construct Repertory Test (1955) served as the model for the preparation of the Occupational Construct Inventory (OCI). The OCI requires that the participant decide between three occupations: In what way are two occupations alike and different from the third. The decision-making process requires that the participant use information known about the three occupations. The OCI was constructed using line drawings illustrating different occupations to eliminate potential reading problems in the younger members of the sample. Selection of occupations to illustrate was based upon the following considerations: occupations should be familiar to a wide age range, the occupations had to represent the range of occupational levels, and the occupations included should portray a range of information attributes. An initial pool of fifty pictures was reviewed by elementary-education and counselor-education specialists. A final pool of fifteen pictures was chosen as meeting the criteria for selection. The fifteen pictures were arranged in combinations of three, yielding fifteen triads. (It was unnecessary to arrange the pictures in all possible combinations because the purpose of the instrument was to find out how students decided between occupations, not to obtain a ranking of the fifteen occupations.) Responses are classified into the following categories: education or training, income, prestige-status, type of work, working conditions, skills or aptitudes, interests, concrete—subject uses some aspect of the picture detail as the reason, and unclassified.

RELIABILITY AND VALIDITY: Biggers (1971) found that increased age and experience did not result in any significant change in the magnitude, ordering, or number of informational categories used in decision making.

BIBLIOGRAPHY:

Biggers, J. L. "The Use of Information in Vocational Decision Making." *Vocational Guidance Quarterly,* 1971, *19,* 171-176.
Kelly, G. A. *The Psychology of Personal Constructs.* New York: Norton, 1955.

# ORIENTATION OF CAREER CONCEPTS SERIES

AUTHORS: Barbara Fulton and Robert Tolsma

AGE: 8 to 14 years

VARIABLE: Career knowledge

TYPE OF MEASURE: Test

SOURCE FROM WHICH MEASURE MAY BE OBTAINED: Evaluative Research Associates, 5431 Trailbend, St. Louis, Missouri 63033.

DESCRIPTION OF MEASURE: The quickly administered tests in this series are used to measure students' career knowledge. Each of the ten tests is aimed at one facet of a child's concept of careers. The individual tests of twenty items each are: work awareness, worker activities, vocational vocabulary, absurdities (a picture test), occupational similarities, occupational tools, work stories, working conditions, occupational training, and workers earnings.

As an example, the practice item for eight tests in the series is given below. Excluded are absurdities (a picture scale) and occupational training (subject estimates years of schooling needed to qualify for a particular job).

*Work Awareness*
Cindy and Scott help their Mother by dusting the tables, sweeping the floor, and making their beds. Of the jobs listed [below], which one is most like the work done by Cindy and Scott?
a. Room clerk.
b. Cook.
c. Window washer.
d. Maid.
e. Janitor.

*Worker Activities*
A teacher *does not* do which one of the following activities?
a. Grade papers.
b. Teach children reading, arithmetic, or other subjects.
c. Give shots to sick people.
d. Watch children during lunchroom or playground periods.
e. Write on the blackboard.

*Vocational Vocabulary*
The key word is *man*. Which one of the following words is the most different from the word *man*?
a. Male.
b. Boy.
c. He.
d. Woman.
e. Him.

*Occupational Similarities*
The key job is *baker*. Which one of the following occupations is most like the job of *baker*?

a. Plumber.

b. Teacher.

c. Chef.

d. Salesman.

e. Lifeguard.

*Occupational Tools*

A nurse uses a(n)

a. thermometer.

b. hammer.

c. mop.

d. egg beater.

e. vise.

*Work Stories*

Tommy is a very good student. His favorite subject is science. He really likes studying about his body. Tommy also likes people and doesn't like to see them hurt. Which one of these jobs do you think Tommy might like best?

a. Scientist.

b. Meat cutter.

c. Artist.

d. Doctor.

e. Policeman.

*Working Conditions*

In which one of the following jobs does the worker most often have to *stand or walk for long periods of time*?

a. Truck driver.

b. Personnel man.

c. Appliance repairman.

d. Farmer.

e. Waitress.

*Workers' Earnings*

Which one of the following workers generally makes the *most* money?

a. Taxi driver.

b. Waiter.

c. Doctor.

d. Barber.

e. Janitor.

RELIABILITY AND VALIDITY: None reported.

BIBLIOGRAPHY:

Fulton, B. J. "Vocational Development of Children." Unpublished doctoral dissertation. University of Missouri, Columbia, 1971.

# PROJECT TALENT INTEREST INVENTORY

AUTHORS: Project TALENT staff

AGE: Grades 4 to 12

VARIABLE: Interest in occupations and activities job or education related

TYPE OF MEASURE: Rating scale

SOURCE FROM WHICH MEASURE MAY BE OBTAINED: Project TALENT tests and inventories are available to researchers as Project TALENT Specimen Set from American Institutes for Research, P.O. Box 1113, Palo Alto, California 94302. Cost: $3.00. The Project TALENT battery is not to be used for nonresearch testing.

DESCRIPTION OF MEASURE: The Project TALENT Interest Inventory is composed of 205 items dealing with 122 occupations and eighty-three activities. The directions emphasize that the student should respond in terms of how well he would like or dislike a specific occupation or activity disregarding educational requirements, salary, social standing, or other factors. The item format is a 5-point rating from "I would like this very much" to "I would dislike this very much." The activities are directly job related (keep records for a store, hire a person), recreational (watch TV, play tennis), or involve attitudes that might be job related (become a millionaire, studying).

RELIABILITY AND VALIDITY: No reliability data are available. Predictive validity is extensively documented by Project TALENT's one-, five-, and eleven-year follow-up studies. The *Career Data Book* (Flanagan and others, 1973), based on the five-year study, provides profiles that include the Interest Inventory variables for each of 138 occupations. Concurrent validity is implied by positive correlations between scores on certain interest scales and related cognitive tests in the TALENT battery. For example, scores on the biological science and medicine interest scales are positively correlated with scores on the biological science information test.

BIBLIOGRAPHY:

Cooley, W. W. "Interactions Among Interests, Abilities, and Career Plans." *Journal of Applied Psychology Monograph,* 1967, *2* (whole number 640), 1-16.

Cooley, W. W., and Lohnes, P. R. "Predicting Development of Young Adults." Interim report 5 to the U.S. Office of Education, Cooperative Research Project no. 3051. Palo Alto, California: Project TALENT Office, American Institutes for Research and University of Pittsburgh, 1968.

Cureton, E. E. "A Factor Analysis of Project TALENT Tests and Four Other Test Batteries." Interim Report 4 to the U.S. Office of Education, Cooperative Research Project no. 3051. Palo Alto, California: Project TALENT Office, American Institutes for Research and University of Pittsburgh, 1968.

Flanagan, J. C., Tiedeman, D. V., Willis, M. B., and McLaughlin, C. H. *The Career Data Book: Results from Project TALENT's Five-Year Study.* Palo Alto, California: American Institutes for Research, 1973.

*Prepared by Wendy Yen*

# READINESS FOR CAREER PLANNING (RCP)

AUTHORS: Warren D. Gribbons and Paul R. Lohnes

AGE: Grades 8 to 9

VARIABLE: Vocational maturity

TYPE OF MEASURE: Structural interview

SOURCE FROM WHICH MEASURE MAY BE OBTAINED: Warren D. Gribbons, Department of Psychology, Regis College, Weston, Massachusetts 02193. Cost: $.50 to cover printing and postage.

DESCRIPTION OF MEASURE: Readiness for Career Planning is a shortened version of a measure of vocational maturity called Readiness for Vocational Planning (RVP). In RVP vocational maturity is treated as a syndrome of eight moderately correlated traits. Twenty-two of the original forty-five items of RVP were selected by factor analysis procedures, and the new univariate instrument is called Readiness for Career Planning (RCP). Preliminary findings indicate that RCP is not significantly correlated with sex or socio-economic status, and its correlation with intelligence is modest (.31).

As examples, five selected items from the twenty-two items of the measure are given below. The items are rated by the counselor on a 3-point scale reflecting the degree of maturity shown by the respondent's answer. Detailed scoring instructions are available.

1. At the ninth (or appropriate) grade students have to make a choice among several different curricula or programs for their high school years. Could you tell me what these programs are called?
2. Why have you decided to take the _____ curriculum?
3. Would you tell me why you decided not to take the other programs available to you?
4. Can you think of any advantages to taking the college preparatory program?
5. Can you tell me any disadvantages of taking the _____ program?
   Can you tell me any advantages of taking the _____ program?

RELIABILITY AND VALIDITY: None reported.

BIBLIOGRAPHY:

Gribbons, W. D. "Evaluation of an Eighth-Grade Group Guidance Program." *Personnel and Guidance Journal,* 1960, *38,* 740-745.
Gribbons, W. D. "Changes in Readiness for Vocational Planning from the Eighth to the Tenth Grade." *Personnel and Guidance Journal,* 1964, *41,* 908-913.
Gribbons, W. D., and Lohnes, P. R. "Relationships Among Measures of Readiness for Vocational Planning." *Journal of Counseling Psychology,* 1964, *11,* 13-19.
Gribbons, W. D., and Lohnes, P. R. "Validation of Vocational Planning Interview Scales." *Journal of Counseling Psychology,* 1964, *11,* 20-26.
Gribbons, W. D., and Lohnes, P. R. "Predicting Five Years' Development in Adolescents from Readiness for Vocational Planning Scales." *Journal of Educational Psychology,* 1965, *56,* 244-253.

Gribbons, W. D., and Lohnes, P. R. "Shifts in Adolescents' Vocational Values." *Personnel and Guidance Journal,* 1965, *44,* 248-252.

Gribbons, W. D., and Lohnes, P. R. "A Five-Year Study of Students' Educational Aspirations." *Vocational Guidance Quarterly,* 1966, *15,* 66-70.

Gribbons, W. D., and Lohnes, P. R. "Occupational Preferences and Measured Intelligence." *Vocational Guidance Quarterly,* 1966, *14,* 211-214.

Gribbons, W. D., and Lohnes, P. R. *Emerging Careers.* New York: Teachers College Press, Columbia University, 1968.

Gribbons, W. D., and Lohnes, P. R. *Career Development from Age 13 to 25.* Regis College, Weston, Massachusetts, 1969.

---

# TEST OF BOYS' ATTITUDES TOWARD CAREERS IN ENGINEERING

AUTHOR: Raymond Hume

AGE: Grammar and technical school boys from first to sixth forms

VARIABLE: Attitudes toward careers in engineering

TYPE OF MEASURE: Thurstone-type scale

SOURCE FROM WHICH MEASURE MAY BE OBTAINED: Raymond Hume, Department of Education, Sunderland Polytechnic, Chestor Road, Sunderland, Durham, England SR1 3SD.

DESCRIPTION OF MEASURE: The test consists of twenty-one statements each with a scale value calculated in accordance with the method described by Thurstone. The subject simply indicates agreement or disagreement with each statement by means of a checkmark or a cross. The test is easily administered and is best scored with the aid of a template bearing the scale value of each item.

As examples, the first ten of the twenty-one statements of the test, with scale value, are given below.

1. Engineers work in factories. (5.8)
2. I would rather be an engineer than anything else. (0.3)
3. Only those who cannot make the grade in science go in for engineering. (6.3)
4. Engineering offers a great future. (1.1)
5. If I took up engineering it would only be second place to science. (6.9)
6. The more I learn about engineering the more I am attracted to it. (1.4)
7. An engineer today knows nothing but his own special job. (7.2)
8. An engineer has little chance to use his imagination. (7.5)
9. I would be happy as an engineer. (2.0)
10. I would rather have a clean job than one in engineering. (8.1)

RELIABILITY AND VALIDITY: The first-draft questionnaire of twenty-three statements was given to 150 boys and an item analysis of the results conducted. This indicated
that two of the statements were being endorsed for implied reasons that may or may not
be connected with the attitude under consideration. Removal of these two statements
sharpened the scale considerably, with resulting clearer differentiation between shades of
opinion. The sensitivity of the final scale was revealed by a comparison of the scores of
boys majoring in arts and sciences. The arts side showed an expected bias away from
engineering with a mean of 6.5 and an SD of 1.9. The science side showed a mean of 3.4
and an SD of 1.1 (the smaller the score the more favorable the attitude). Results were
checked by the standard error of means and by student's $t$ and found to be statistically
highly significant.

BIBLIOGRAPHY:

Hume, R. "Effects of School Curriculum on Boys' Attitude Toward Careers in Engineering." Unpublished master's thesis. University of Newcastle-Upon-Tyne, England,
1967.
Hume, R. "Effects of School Curriculum on Boys' Attitudes Toward Engineering." *British Journal of Educational Psychology*, 1968, *38*, 322-323.

---

# TEST OF VOCATIONAL KNOWLEDGE

AUTHORS: Francis J. Reardon, James P. Lewis, Gregory A. Shannon, and John K. S.
Senier

AGE: Grades 5, 8, and 11

VARIABLE: Knowledge of occupations and associated traits

TYPE OF MEASURE: Test

SOURCE FROM WHICH MEASURE MAY BE OBTAINED: Division of Educational
Quality Assessment, Bureau of Planning and Evaluation, Pennsylvania Department of
Education, Box 911, Harrisburg, Pennsylvania 17126. A request for these instruments
should be accompanied by a statement of purpose, since their availability is restricted due
to test security considerations.

DESCRIPTION OF MEASURE: Separate measures of vocational knowledge were developed for grade levels 5, 8, and 11. These instruments are currently used in Pennsylvania's
Educational Quality Assessment program and are intended as survey measures providing
school-reliable data. The grades 5 and 8 tests are composed of thirty multiple-choice
items measuring awareness of duties, conditions, training, salary, and educational requirements for various occupations. The eleventh-grade test contains thirty-five items (twenty
multiple-choice, fifteen matching) that, in addition to the above, tap interest and temper-

ament characteristics associated with various kinds of occupations. One point is given for each correct response with no adjustment for guessing.

An example is given below.

1. A claims adjuster would most likely be working for
    *a. an insurance company.
    b. a hospital.
    c. a welfare office.
    d. a department store.

RELIABILITY AND VALIDITY: Instrument development followed a process of refinement through several field trials at each grade level with $N$s ranging from about 250 to 2,600. A panel of experts (vocational educators, guidance counselors, and staff from the Testing Services Section of Manpower Training Programs, Department of Labor and Industry) examined the original pool of items and judged that they possessed content validity. Statistical data gathered during the March 1974 statewide testing may be summarized as follows: Internal consistency reliability (Kuder-Richardson formula 20) based on a sample of approximately 3,300 cases at each grade level was found to be .71, .75, and .74, respectively, for grades 5, 8, and 11. Test-retest reliabilities were obtained for grades 8 and 11 ($N$s approximately 80) and found to be .76 and .82, respectively, for an interval of five weeks.

BIBLIOGRAPHY:

Reardon, F. J., Lewis, J. P., and Senier, J. K. "The Development and Evaluation of an Occupational Inventory." *Journal of Educational Measurement*, 1972, *9*, 151-153.
Russel, N. F. *Getting Inside the EQA Battery*. Technical manuals for each grade level. Pennsylvania Department of Education, Harrisburg, 1974.

*Prepared by Richard L. Kohr*

---

# THOMPSON-TSENG OCCUPATIONAL PRESTIGE SCALE

AUTHORS: Donald L. Thompson and Meng-Shu Tseng

AGE: 10 years and up

VARIABLE: Perception and knowledge of prestige hierarchy of occupations

TYPE OF MEASURE: Ranking scale

SOURCE FROM WHICH MEASURE MAY BE OBTAINED: See National Opinion Research Center (1947).

DESCRIPTION OF MEASURE: This occupational prestige rating scale consists of twenty occupations and takes the subject about 10 minutes to complete with very few errors or omissions. The twenty occupations were selected by drawing two representative occupations from each of the ten prestige levels consisting of nine occupations each on the original North-Hatt (1961) Scale. The relative rankings assigned to the occupations are taken from the original North-Hatt Scale. Although the North-Hatt study was done in 1947, several authors have verified in recent studies the continued validity of the original rankings. The instrument is scored using a deviation scoring method. The subject's ranking of the twenty occupations is compared to the ideal ranking, and in the case of each occupation, the lower ranking is subtracted from the higher ranking (e.g., accountants: subject's rank of 9 minus ideal rank of 7 equals 2). The twenty deviation scores are added, producing a total score. Thus, the higher the subject's score, the more inaccurate his perception of the occupational prestige hierarchy. Several studies indicate the usefulness of the instrument in educational settings. Scores on this instrument have been shown to be predictive of school grades, need for vocational counseling, socioeconomic status, need achievement, and fear of failure.

The twenty occupations (items) of the scale are given below. The respondent ranks all the items from 1 to 20. The rankings indicated in the left column are the ideal ranks used for scoring.

(7)  Accountant
(4)  Architect
(14) Auto mechanic
(12) Bookkeeper (including bookkeeping machine operator)
(15) Clerk in a store
(17) Coal miner
(9)  County agricultural agent
(3)  County judge
(10) Electrician
(18) Filling station attendant
(11) Insurance agent
(19) Janitor
(5)  Lawyer
(6)  Mining engineer
(1)  Physician (medical doctor)
(13) Policeman
(8)  Public school teacher
(2)  Scientist
(20) Shoe shiner
(16) Truck driver

RELIABILITY AND VALIDITY: A group of thirty-eight college seniors were tested and retested with the short-form instrument. There was a one-week interval between tests, and the results yielded a test-retest reliability coefficient of .69. Split-half reliability, corrected by the Spearman-Brown formula, using high school juniors and seniors as subjects ($N$ = 238) was .76. A concurrent validity study was conducted with the same thirty-eight subjects who were involved in the test-retest reliability study, comparing scores on the ninety-item North-Hatt Scale to scores obtained on the twenty-item short form. Correlation between the two sets of scores yielded a concurrent validity coefficient of .58. In a study using the short-form instrument, Tseng and Thompson (1968) found that high school students who had more accurate perception of occupational prestige were more likely to voluntarily seek vocational counseling. It would appear that the occupational prestige measure yielded by this instrument is a significant predictor of counseling-seeking behavior. In a follow-up study (Thompson and Tseng, 1970) it was found that counseling had a significant effect in increasing the accuracy of perception of occupational prestige. Another study by Tseng and Thompson (1969) found that the perception of occupational prestige was highly predictive of socioeconomic status of Appalachian high school students. Poor children tended to have a less accurate perception of the prestige hierarchy of occupations. It may be hypothesized, therefore, that children who do poorly on the scale come from environments with limited informational inputs. Using the twenty-item Occupational Prestige Scale, Tseng and Carter (1970) revealed the scale's predictive validity for the motive to approach success and the motive to avoid failure. Subjects in whom need for achievement exceeded fear of failure showed significantly more accurate perception of occupational prestige hierarchy than subjects in whom fear of failure exceeded need for achievement.

BIBLIOGRAPHY:

National Opinion Research Center. "Jobs and Occupations: A Popular Evaluation." *Opinion News,* 1947, *9,* 3-13.

North, C. C., and Hatt, P. K. "The NORC Scale." In A. J. Reiss, Jr., O. D. Duncan, P. K. Hatt, and C. C. North (Eds.), *Occupations and Social Status.* Glencoe, Illinois: Free Press, 1961.

Thompson, D. L., and Tseng, M. S. "Counseled vs. Noncounseled: One Year Later." Paper presented at the annual convention of the American Personnel and Guidance Association. New Orleans, Louisiana, 1970.

Thompson, D. L., and Tseng, M. S. "The Development of a Short Scale to Measure the Perception of Occupational Prestige." Paper presented at the annual meeting of the National Council on Measurement in Education, Chicago, Illinois, April 1972.

Tseng, M. S., and Carter, A. R. "Achievement Motivation and Fear of Failure as Determinants of Vocational Choice, Vocational Aspiration, and Perception of Vocational Prestige." *Journal of Counseling Psychology,* 1970, *17,* 150-156.

Tseng, M. S., and Thompson, D. L. "Differences Between Adolescents Who Seek Counseling and Those Who Do Not." *Personnel and Guidance Journal,* 1968, *47,* 333-336.

Tseng, M. S., and Thompson, D. L. "Need Achievement, Fear of Failure, Perception of Occupational Prestige, and Occupational Aspiration of Adolescents of Different Socioeconomic Groups." Paper presented at the annual meeting of the American Educational Research Association, Los Angeles, California, 1969.

## VOCATIONAL ADJUSTMENT RATING SCALE (VARS)

AUTHORS: R. H. Song and A. Y. Song

AGE: Adolescent to adult handicapped

VARIABLE: Vocational adjustment

TYPE OF MEASURE: Rating scale

SOURCE FROM WHICH MEASURE MAY BE OBTAINED: Ralph H. Song, Department of Psychology, Wisconsin State University, 800 West Main Street, Whitewater, Wisconsin 53190.

DESCRIPTION OF MEASURE: This instrument was developed to help fill the need for an instrument that will serve as a communication medium between vocational staffs and other staff members, especially in large vocational training centers and institutions. The Vocational Adjustment Rating Scale (VARS) has been developed to meet such a need. The primary purpose of the scale is to provide a quantitative estimate of vocational adjustment based on observable behavior. It is designed for use with functionally retarded adolescents and adults who are either mentally retarded, socially handicapped, mentally ill, or any combination of these. It consists of fifty-two items divided into five parts: (I) work ability, (II) work habits, (III) withdrawn behavior, (IV) aggressive behavior, and (V) bizarre behavior. The scale items are rated by the immediate work supervisors. Parts I and II are rated in terms of degree ("very poor" to "excellent," 5-point scale values from 0 to 4); and Parts III, IV, and V are rated in terms of frequency ("very often" to "never," 5-point scale values from 0 to 4). The reference point for rating is an average worker in a particular work setting. The raters are asked to check every item on the scale. The scores are simply the cumulative summation of all the scale values checked on the rows of the scale. The maximum obtainable raw scores for scale Parts I, II, III, IV, and V and for the total scale are 36, 56, 36, 40, 40, and 208, respectively. A work-efficiency score is derived from Parts I and II; a general-behavior score from Parts III, IV, and V. The instrument requires about 15 to 20 minutes to complete and is hand-scored.

As examples, the first two items of each of the five subsections are given below.

I. *Work Ability*
   1. Handling tools and materials.
   2. Following directions.
II. *Work Habits*
   1. Attendance.
   2. Punctuality.
III. *Withdrawn Behavior*
   1. Stays by himself.
   2. Shows no interest in anything.
IV. *Aggressive Behavior*
   1. Sassy, disrespectful of authority.
   2. Gets angry easily.
V. *Bizarre Behavior*
   1. Talks to himself.
   2. Smiles or laughs for no apparent reason.

RELIABILITY AND VALIDITY: The reliability of the scale was assessed by Pearson $r$s between the scores obtained from the first and second ratings. The time interval between the two ratings was about a week. The test-retest reliability coefficients for Parts I, II, III, IV, and V and the total scale were .90, .93, .78, .91, .75, and .92, respectively. The comparability of the halves of the scale was indicated by a high split-half reliability coefficient of .97.

BIBLIOGRAPHY:

Song, R. H., and Song, A. Y. "Development of a Vocational Adjustment Rating Scale for the Retarded." *Journal of Consulting Psychology,* 1971, *18,* 173-176.

---

## VOCATIONAL INTEREST INVENTORY (VII)

AUTHOR: Janice J. Lokan, based on work by Norman E. Freeberg

AGE: 13 to 17 years (low achievers)

VARIABLE: Vocational interests

TYPE OF MEASURE: Rating scale

SOURCE FROM WHICH MEASURE MAY BE OBTAINED: Research Center, Ottawa Board of Education, 330 Gilmour Street, Ottawa, Ontario, Canada K2P 0P9. Cost: Postage and handling charges. The VII is adapted from the *Vocational Interest* booklet. Copyright © by Educational Testing Service, 1968. All rights reserved. Adapted and reproduced by permission.

DESCRIPTION OF MEASURE: The VII, which is based on an inventory developed to aid in the assessment of disadvantaged adolescents (Freeberg, 1970), was prepared to help meet the needs of low-reading students in high school occupational training programs. The items illustrate and briefly describe job tasks relevant to such programs. Degree of interest in each task is rated on a 4-point scale, ranging from "pretty bad—I couldn't take doing it" to "this is great—just the kind of thing I would like to do." The items are the same in format as Freeberg's but many differ in content. Separate forms of the VII, containing thirty and twenty-eight items each, are available for boys and girls. The items in each form are grouped in four scales: clerical, technical, service, and low level/outdoor. The inventory can be administered orally to students reading as low as the grade-3 level and can be self-administering for students reading above the grade-5 level. The maximum administration time required is about 10 minutes.

      Each of the thirty items on the boys' form of the inventory has a drawing of a male figure performing the job described in the caption below the picture. The respondent has the same four options on each item: (1) pretty bad—I couldn't take doing it; (2) not too good—I might do this but I wouldn't like it; (3) this is OK—I wouldn't mind this too much; and (4) this is great—just the kind of thing I would like to do. As examples, the first three captions are given below.

1. Run an office machine that handles all kinds of paperwork.
2. Help take care of sick people in the hospital.
3. Fix leaky pipes and faucets.

Each of the twenty-eight items on the girls' form of the inventory has a drawing of a female figure performing the job described in the caption below the picture. The response format is the same as for the boys' form. The first three captions are given below.

1. Do hair styling.
2. Act a small part in a movie or a play.
3. Run a pressing machine.

RELIABILITY AND VALIDITY: The VII was administered to 400 boys and 240 girls aged 14 to 17 years who comprised the entering cohorts in two successive years in a special vocational high school. The allocation of items to the four scales for each sex was based on Freeberg's findings and on factor analyses of responses in each cohort, conducted separately by sex. Internal consistency reliabilities of the scales ranged from .68 to .91, and test-retest reliabilities after three weeks ranged from .73 to .79 for boys ($N = 57$) and from .50 to .87 for girls ($N = 22$). Stability indices after nine months ranged from .52 to .72 for boys ($N = 96$) and from .46 to .63 for girls ($N = 71$). Some evidence of criterion-related validity was obtained, inasmuch as scale scores contributed significantly, together with measures of aptitudes, to the prediction of grades in several shop course areas, and the prediction equations held up well on cross-validation.

BIBLIOGRAPHY:

Freeberg, N. E. "Assessment of Disadvantaged Adolescents: A Different Approach to Research and Evaluation Measures." *Journal of Educational Psychology,* 1970, *61,* 229-240.

Lokan, J. J. "The Development and Preliminary Evaluation of an Instrument to Measure the Vocational Interests of Low-Reading High School Students." Paper presented at the annual meeting of the National Council for Measurement in Education, New Orleans, Louisiana, 1973.

Lokan, J. J., and Halpern, G. "Differential Validities for Shop Courses." Paper presented at the annual meeting of the American Educational Research Association, Chicago, 1972.

---

## VOCATIONAL INTEREST INVENTORY (VII)

AUTHOR: Patricia W. Lunneborg

AGE: Grades 10 to 12

VARIABLE: Vocational interests

TYPE OF MEASURE: Forced-choice questionnaire

SOURCE FROM WHICH MEASURE MAY BE OBTAINED: Patricia Lunneborg, Department of Psychology, University of Washington, Seattle, Washington 98105.

DESCRIPTION OF MEASURE: The VII is based on Roe's classification of occupations into eight groups: service, business contact, organization, technology, outdoor, science, general cultural, and arts and entertainment. It consists of 112 forced-choice items divided into two sets of fifty-six items each, an occupations section and an activities section. Within each section each VII scale consists of twenty-eight items, fourteen from each of the two sections of the test. Items are given unit weight so that scores range from 0 to 28. The VII requires a minimal amount of administrator effort and takes a maximum of 25 minutes' testing time. Machine-scorable answer sheets are used, and clients receive a computer-printout profile of their standard scores and percentile equivalents. VII items are designed to keep sex differences at a minimum, and the scales are normed on several thousand Washington state high school juniors *not* separately for the sexes.

As examples, three selected items from occupations, ("Pick the one occupation from each pair that you prefer") and three from activities ("Which of the following pair of statements is more true for you?") are given below. The Roe classifications are indicated in parentheses.

11. (a) Construction laborer. (OUT)    (b) House-to-house salesperson. (BUS)
20. (a) Attorney at law. (CUL)         (b) Hospital administrator. (ORG)
29. (a) House parent. (SER)            (b) Greenhouse attendant. (OUT)
 5. I would rather watch a television interview with a university professor in (a) American literature. (CUL) (b) Nutritional research. (SCI)
11. At a family camp I would rather (a) direct a musical. (ART) (b) paint cabins. (TEC)
16. For my club I would rather be in charge of (a) finding new members. (BUS) (b) correspondence. (ORG)

RELIABILITY AND VALIDITY: Reliability: Occupations and activities sections *r*s for the eight scales range from .34 to .67. Split-half reliabilities for the occupations section subscales range from .25 to .71; for the activities subscales from .29 to .62. Three-week test-retest correlations based on total scores range from .75 to .88. Validity: Correlations between VII scores and Holland's Vocational Preference Inventory scores support the validity of the VII concurrently; for example, VII service and VPI social correlate .53, VII business contact and VPI enterprising, .55. VII profiles for students intending different college majors are in accord with prediction; for example, science scores were high for students majoring in science, with service also high among health science students but low among natural science students. Evidence of predictive validity is based on profiles of students who graduated from college in different majors, the VII having been taken in high school. Even within a broad area such as humanities, the VII differentiates specific majors; for example, art majors had high scores on ART and low ones on CUL (Roe classifications), with English majors scoring the reverse.

BIBLIOGRAPHY:

Lunneborg, C. E., and Lunneborg, P. W. "Factor Structure of the Vocational Models of Roe and Holland." *Journal of Vocational Behavior* (in press).

Lunneborg, P. W. "Interest Differentiation in High School and Vocational Indecision in College." *Journal of Vocational Behavior* (in press).

Lunneborg, P. W. *Manual for the Vocational Interest Inventory, Preliminary Draft.* Seattle: University of Washington, Educational Assessment Center, 1975.

Mitchell, S. K., Lunneborg, P. W., and Lunneborg, C. E. "Vocational Interest Inventory Based on Roe's Interest Areas." *Proceedings of the 79th Annual Convention of the American Psychological Association,* 1971, *6,* 569-570.

# Category 11

---

# Unclassified

---

*These measures could not be classified into any of the previous categories or groups.*

# CHILD SLEEP QUESTIONNAIRE: CHILD FORM

AUTHOR: Ronald P. Graef

AGE: 8 to 14 years

VARIABLE: Children's presleep and sleep experiences

TYPE OF MEASURE: Questionnaire

SOURCE FROM WHICH MEASURE MAY BE OBTAINED: Ronald Graef, Committee on Human Development, University of Chicago, Chicago, Illinois 60637. Cost: $.45 for xeroxing, $.20 for postage.

DESCRIPTION OF MEASURE: The Child Sleep Questionnaire: Child Form consists of seventy-two questions about children's presleep and sleep patterns. It was designed to provide self-report information about children's knowledge and perceptions of their own sleep-related experiences. The questionnaire was administered by teachers as a written task to groups of school children. However, it may also be administered individually as an oral task with an administrator recording the child's responses. The oral procedure will lower the age at which the questionnaire can be administered by a year or so. Graef (1974) provides scoring and coding procedures for the original questionnaire, which can be applied to the 1975 revision, and provides descriptive information (means, ranges, and standard deviations) for the total sample on most of the questionnaire items.

As examples, seven of the seventy-two items on the questionnaire are given below.

8. How many hours do you usually sleep at night?
16. Did you have trouble falling asleep last night?
   a. Yes.
   b. No.
20. How often are you afraid to go to bed at night?
   a. More than twice a week.
   b. Once or twice a week.
   c. One or two times a month.
   d. Less than once a month.
   e. Never.
30. What was the last thing you did last night after getting ready for bed but before going to bed?
36. How often do you give your parents a hard time when they want you to get ready for bed?
   a. More than twice a week.
   b. Once or twice a week.
   c. One or two times a month.
   d. Less than once a month.
   e. Never.
49. What do you dream about in your nightmares?
66. How rested do you usually feel when you wake up in the morning?
   a. Very rested.
   b. Kind of rested.

c. Not very rested.

d. Not rested at all.

RELIABILITY AND VALIDITY: The original questionnaires (1973) were administered to 425 children (grades 4 through 6) and their parents. The children filled out the questionnaire at school, and their parents filled out a similar questionnaire at home (see Child Sleep Questionnaire: Parent Form, pp. 1251-1252). Two hundred and eighty-three persons (66 percent) returned completed questionnaires. They and their children constitute the total sample. The parents' occupational status ranged from lower-middle to upper-middle levels. Validity of the questionnaires to measure children's sleep behaviors was determined by comparing parents' responses with children's responses to the most "objective" items: the time the child goes to bed at night and the time the child wakes in the morning. Pearson product-moment correlations between parents' and children's responses on these two items were .71 and .77. The ranges and means data for the objective items were also compared with previous studies on children's sleep patterns (see Graef, 1974, for complete details). There is no evidence available yet, however, on the reliability and validity of the questionnaires to measure the nature and extent of "disturbed sleep" in children.

BIBLIOGRAPHY:

Csikszentmihalyi, M., and Graef, R. "Socialization into Sleep: Exploratory Findings." *Merrill-Palmer Quarterly,* 1975, *21,* 3-18.

Graef, R. "A Preliminary Report on the Extent and Composition of Sleep Disturbing Behavior in Children." Unpublished master's thesis. University of Chicago, 1974.

---

# CHILD SLEEP QUESTIONNAIRE: PARENT FORM

AUTHOR: Ronald P. Graef

AGE: Parents or guardians

VARIABLE: Children's presleep and sleep experiences

TYPE OF MEASURE: Questionnaire

SOURCE FROM WHICH MEASURE MAY BE OBTAINED: Ronald Graef, Committee on Human Development, University of Chicago, Chicago, Illinois 60637. Cost: $.50 for xeroxing, $.20 for postage.

DESCRIPTION OF MEASURE: The Child Sleep Questionnaire: Parent Form consists of sixty-five questions about children's presleep and sleep patterns and twenty-one questions about parents' presleep and sleep patterns. It is designed to provide self-report information about parents' knowledge and perceptions of their children's sleep-related experiences. The questionnaires were administered as a written task to parents in their homes. Each student in the child sample took home a sealed envelope containing the parent form and a letter of explanation. Sixty-six percent (283 persons) returned completed questionnaires. Graef (1974) provides scoring and coding procedures for the original questionnaire, which can be applied to the 1975 revision, and provides descriptive information (means, ranges, and standard deviations) for the total sample on most of the questionnaire items.

As examples, six of the eighty-six items on the questionnaire are given below.

7. What time does your child usually get up in the morning?
23. Was your child afraid to go to bed last night?
   a. Yes.
   b. No.
43. After your child gets into bed, how often does he/she usually get up again before falling asleep?
   a. More than once a night.
   b. About once a night.
   c. Couple times a week.
   d. Couple times a month.
   e. Less than once a month.
45. How often does your child wake up during the night after falling asleep?
   a. More than once a night.
   b. About once a night.
   c. Couple times a week.
   d. Couple times a month.
   e. Less than once a month.
50. How often do you leave a light on for your child at night?
   a. More than twice a week.
   b. Once or twice a week.
   c. One or two times a month.
   d. Less than once a month.
   e. Never.
64. When was the last time your child wet the bed while sleeping?
   a. Last night.
   b. During the last week.
   c. Two or three weeks ago.
   d. Almost a month ago.
   e. Many months ago.
   f. Many years ago.

RELIABILITY AND VALIDITY: See Child Sleep Questionnaire: Child Form (pp. 1250-1251).

BIBLIOGRAPHY:

Csikszentmihalyi, M., and Graef, R. P. "Socialization into Sleep: Exploratory Findings." *Merrill-Palmer Quarterly,* 1975, *21,* 3-18.
Graef, R. P. "A Preliminary Report on the Extent and Composition of Sleep Disturbing Behavior in Children." Unpublished master's thesis. University of Chicago, 1974.

# CRISIS EVALUATION QUESTIONNAIRE (FOR ADOLESCENTS)

AUTHORS: Alvin S. Yusin, Ruth Sinay, and Kazuo Nihira

AGE: Adolescence

VARIABLE: Crisis behaviors and life situations

TYPE OF MEASURE: Checklist for structured interview

SOURCE FROM WHICH MEASURE MAY BE OBTAINED: See Yusin, Sinay, and Nihira (1972).

DESCRIPTION OF MEASURE: The Crisis Evaluation Questionnaire consists of a total of sixty-six questions covering eight general areas of the patient's life situations: thirteen questions related to the causes and the situations in which crisis behavior occurred, the patient's attitude toward the crisis behavior, and the reaction of parents to the crisis; eleven questions covering the patient's relationship to his parents; seventeen questions covering the patient's school performance and parental attitude toward schooling; seven questions in the area of peer relationships; and five questions concerning the patient's sexual adjustment. Some of the questions require only a "yes" or a "no" response, but the majority of the questions have multiple-response categories. Information necessary to complete the form is obtained from patients and their families.

As examples, three items from the crisis and family sections of the form are given below. The remaining sections are school, peers, drugs, medical, authorities, and sex.

*Crisis*

H. How does patient view the crisis behavior at time of interview with therapist?
   a. Behavior was irrational.
   b. Behavior was logical.
   c. Behavior was justified.
   d. Refuses to discuss behavior.
   e. Other: Specify _____

L. What did parents do about patient following crisis?
   a. Took patient to hospital.
   b. Called on authorities to handle patient.
   c. Called on relatives to handle patient.
   d. Called on friend to handle patient.
   e. Were not involved in crisis.
   f. Other: Specify _____

*Family*

D. Do parents feel they can talk to patient about his (her) problems or feelings? Yes _____ No _____
   1. What interferes with their talking to him (her) about them?
      a. Patient doesn't listen to what they say.
      b. Patient gets belligerent, angry and argumentative, closing communication.
      c. Parents believe that expressing their feelings will hurt patient.
      d. Parents feel patient is responsible for his (her) behavior and it is no concern of theirs.

e. Don't know what interferes.

f. Parents don't know how to approach patient.

g. Parents don't think patient's behavior will ever change.

h. Patient refuses to talk to parents.

i. Other: Specify _____

RELIABILITY AND VALIDITY: Analysis of variance indicates that the Crisis Evaluation Questionnaire can discriminate four adolescent groups on the basis of crisis behaviors: aggressive, suicidal, chronic psychotic, and acute psychotic secondary to drugs.

BIBLIOGRAPHY:

Sinay, R., Yusin, A., and Nihira, K. "Adolescents in Crisis." *Journal of Psychosynthesis,* 1973, *5,* 30-39.

Yusin, A., Sinay, R., and Nihira, K. "Adolescents in Crisis: Evaluation of a Questionnaire." *American Journal of Psychiatry,* 1972, *219* (5), 86-89.

*Prepared by Ruth Sinay*

---

# DREAM INTERVIEW (*See note, p. 60)

AUTHOR: Jean Piaget (adaptation and scoring by Lawrence Kohlberg)

AGE: Normal children 4 to 9 years

VARIABLE: Beliefs about dreams: awareness of subjective experience and causality, and immateriality

TYPE OF MEASURE: Structured interview

SOURCE FROM WHICH MEASURE MAY BE OBTAINED: See DeVries (1971).

DESCRIPTION OF MEASURE: The child is asked to recount a dream he has had, and then many issues are raised about the dream, including where it took place, whether some object was real, what the dream was made of, what made it happen, and so forth. Ss are scored on a 10-point Guttman scale from 0 to 9. Norms are available (on a 7-point scale) for sixty-four children 4 to 7 years of age (Kohlberg, 1963). Also, norms for the 10-point scale are available for 143 bright and average children chronologically aged 5 to 7 years and retarded children mentally aged 5 to 7 years, according to Stanford-Binet IQ (DeVries, 1971).

As examples, the introductory remarks and two of the ten sections of the interview are given below. The first two of the nine scoring positions on the Guttman scale appear after the items.

1. "You know what a dream is, don't you? Do you dream sometimes during the night?"

"Can you have a dream if you stay awake and don't go to sleep?" (If he says he does not dream, go on to 5; if he says he dreams, ask):

2. "What did you dream about last time: tell me a dream you had."

RELIABILITY AND VALIDITY: Interscorer agreement on 261 items for twenty randomly selected children was 75 percent. Kohlberg (1969, pp. 347-480) reports some cross-cultural research that validates the developmental sequence but indicates that this development can be arrested and regressed by the effect of cultural mores concerning dreams. The studies by Kohlberg and DeVries basically replicate the findings of Piaget.

BIBLIOGRAPHY:

DeVries, R. *Evaluation of Cognitive Development with Piaget-type Tests: Study of Young Bright, Average, and Retarded Children.* Final report to the Department of Program Development for Gifted Children, Illinois Office of Public Instruction, 1971. ERIC document no. ED 075 065.

DeVries, R. "Relationships Among Piagetian, IQ, and Achievement Assessments." *Child Development,* 1974, *45,* 746-756.

Kohlberg, L. "Stages in Children's Conceptions of Physical and Social Objects in the Years Four to Eight." Unpublished monograph, 1963.

Kohlberg, L. "Cognitive Stages and Preschool Education." *Human Development,* 1966, *9,* 5-17.

Kohlberg, L. "Stages and Sequence: The Cognitive-Development Approach to Socialization." In D. Golsin (Ed.), *Handbook of Socialization Theory and Research.* Chicago: Rand McNally, 1969.

Piaget, J. *The Child's Conception of the World.* Totowa, New Jersey: Littlefield, Adams, 1960 (originally published in French, 1938).

*Prepared by Rheta DeVries*

---

# EWALT-COHEN-HARMATZ CONTINUANCE PREDICTION SCALE

AUTHORS: Patricia L. Ewalt, Margrit Cohen, and Jerold S. Harmatz

AGE: Parents of children 4 to 17 years

VARIABLE: Treatment continuance

TYPE OF TEST: Structured interview

SOURCE FROM WHICH MEASURE MAY BE OBTAINED: See Ewalt, Cohen, and Harmatz (1972).

DESCRIPTION OF MEASURE: This scale identifies, by means of a telephone interview, those clients of a child-guidance agency who choose to continue with postdiagnostic therapeutic service of any type. The interviewer asks the parents or parent-surrogate five questions and scores each answer A or B. The first question is, "How old is (the child for whom application is made)?" If the child is less than 12, he checks column A; if 12 or above, he checks column B. The second question is, "How far did (the present mother or mother-surrogate) go in school?" If she is a high school graduate or above, the interviewer checks column A; otherwise, he checks column B. The third question is, "What worries you most about (the child's) problem?" If the parent's main worry is that someone in authority is making the problem worse by calling attention to it, the interviewer checks column B. If the parent's main worry is for any other reason, or if he says he is not worried, the interviewer checks column A. The fourth question is, "Do you feel that stubbornness is a major problem with (the child)?" If the parent definitely states that he feels stubbornness is a major problem with the child, the interviewer checks column A. If the parent does not feel that stubbornness is a major problem, or if he is uncertain, if he says "sometimes," or if he says others feel that way but he doesn't, the interviewer checks column B. The fifth question is, "What were you hoping the clinic might do to help?" (If the response is at first "I don't know," the interviewer may say, "I understand, but perhaps you had some idea how we might help." No explanations or suggestions should be offered by the interviewer.) If the parent answers that he himself wishes advice or understanding so that he may help the child with the problem, the interviewer checks column A. (The answer must include elements of the parent's belief that the child is now having a problem and the parent's emphasis on his desire to increase his own ability to be helpful in his ongoing interaction with the child at home.) If the parent's answer is any other than the above or is a continued "I don't know," the interviewer checks column B. One point is given for each check in column A, and the total score indicates the likelihood of continued participation of parents and/or the child in a regime of counseling, medication, or educational management following and resulting from psychiatric evaluation. Norms for the scale are available.

RELIABILITY AND VALIDITY: No reliability assessments have yet been made. Construct validity and internal consistency were established by sequential item analyses.

BIBLIOGRAPHY:

Ewalt, P. L. "Use of Child Guidance Services: Some Indicators of Changing Patterns." *Massachusetts Journal of Mental Health*, 1974, *4*, 13-26.

Ewalt, P. L., Cohen, M., and Harmatz, J. S. "Prediction of Treatment Acceptance by Child Guidance Clinic Applicants: An Easily Applied Instrument." *American Journal of Orthopsychiatry*, 1972, *42*, 857-864.

## EXPERIENTIAL INVENTORY

AUTHOR: Thomas J. Cottle

AGE: 10 years and up

VARIABLE: Orientation in time

TYPE OF MEASURE: Test

SOURCE FROM WHICH MEASURE MAY BE OBTAINED: See Cottle, Pleck, and Kakar (1968).

DESCRIPTION OF MEASURE: Respondents are instructed to list the ten most important experiences of their lives. These may be experiences they have had, are having, or expect to have. When they are done, they are instructed to consider five time zones: (1) distant past, (2) near past, (3) present, (4) near future, and (5) distant future. Then they are instructed to assign one number to each experience, thereby designating the time zone in which each experience falls. An experiential mean may then be computed by adding all the numbers and dividing by ten the number of experiences. The higher the score the more future-oriented the inventory. Simply categorizing people according to whether they list future experiences at all has been found to be a better way of scoring. So-called future avoiders are identified as those listing no future experiences.

RELIABILITIES AND VALIDITY: None reported.

BIBLIOGRAPHY:

Cottle, T. J. "The Location of Experience: A Manifest Time Orientation." *Acta Psychologica,* 1968, *28,* 129-149.
Cottle, T. J. "The Duration Inventory: Subjective Extensions of Temporal Zones." *Acta Psychologica,* 1969, *29,* 333-352.
Cottle, T. J., and Klineberg, S. L. *The Present of Things Future: Explorations of Time in Human Experience.* New York: Free Press, 1974.
Cottle, T. J., Pleck, J., and Kakar, S. "Time and Content of Significant Life Experiences." *Perceptual and Motor Skills,* 1968, *27,* 155-171.

---

## FUTURE EVENTS TEST (FET)

AUTHORS: Theodore R. Sarbin and James A. Kulik

AGE: Boys, 13 to 18 years

VARIABLE: Future-time perspective

TYPE OF MEASURE: Test

SOURCE FROM WHICH MEASURE MAY BE OBTAINED: Kenneth B. Stein, 517
Moraga Avenue, Piedmont, California 94611.

DESCRIPTION OF MEASURE: The FET consists of thirty-six events that could happen some time in the future. These events were selected from a tabulation of future
events given freely by a large group of adolescent delinquent and nondelinquent boys.
On the right there are two columns, one with the word "never" and the other with a
space in which the subject is asked to enter the future age at which time he guesses
the event will occur. If he thinks the event will never happen, he circles the word
"never." The future-time-perspective score is the mean of the future ages listed by the
subject. Future-time perspective is conceptualized as an outcome of the socialization
process and reflects the capacity for delay in contrast to impulsive behavior or short
tension tolerance.

As examples, ten of the thirty-six items are given below, to be answered
"never" or "if you think it will happen, guess age."

1. Finish college.
2. Visit a foreign country.
3. Have a new car.
4. Get a job you really want.
5. Get married.
6. Have an auto accident.
7. Die.
8. Buy a home.
9. Get a ticket for fast driving.
10. Move to another city.

RELIABILITY AND VALIDITY: One hundred nondelinquents (*ND*) and 100 delinquents (*D*) matched for age, social status, race, and intelligence were administered the
FET. The *ND*s achieved a significantly greater future-time perspective score than the
*D*s. These results were replicated on another sample of 100 *ND*s and 100 *D*s (Sarbin
and Stein, 1966). An item analysis indicated that the *ND*s endorsed more prosocial
items, were more homogeneous in item scores, and were more reality oriented with
regard to the future.

BIBLIOGRAPHY:

Sarbin, T. R., and Stein, K. B. "Self-Role Theory and Antisocial Conduct: A Progress
        Report." Bethesda, Maryland: National Institute of Mental Health, 1966.
Stein, K. B., Sarbin, T. R., and Kulik, J. A. "Future Time Perspective: Its Relation to
        the Socialization Process and the Delinquent Role." *Journal of Consulting and
        Clinical Psychology,* 1968, *32,* 257-264.

*Prepared by Kenneth B. Stein*

# INDEX OF STATUS CHARACTERISTICS (ISC)

AUTHORS: W. Lloyd Warner, Marchia Meeker, and Kenneth Eells

AGE: Unlimited

VARIABLE: Social-class position

TYPE OF MEASURE: Rating scale

SOURCE FROM WHICH MEASURE MAY BE OBTAINED: See Warner, Meeker, and Eells (1960).

DESCRIPTION OF MEASURE: The Index of Status Characteristics has been used and modified over the years since it was first developed. It is the basis for most of the more recent similar indexes. The four status characteristics rated are: occupation, source of income, house type, and dwelling area. Occupation is rated on a 7-point scale from "professionals and proprietors of large businesses" to "unskilled workers." Source of income is rated on a 7-point scale from "inherited wealth" to "public relief and nonrespectable income." A 7-point scale ranging from "large houses in good condition" to "all houses in very bad condition; dwellings in structures not intended originally for homes" (later revised to include as the extreme points, "excellent houses" and "very poor houses") is used to evaluate house type. Finally, the 7-point scale for dwelling area ranges from "very high; Gold Coast, North Shore, etc." to "very low; slum." The authors provide extensive descriptions of the rating categories to guide the rater. The ratings are weighted as follows: occupation, 4; source of income, 3; house type, 3; and dwelling area, 2. The weighted total of the ratings is derived by multiplying each of the four ratings by their respective weights and summing, which total score comprises the index.

RELIABILITY AND VALIDITY: Warner, Meeker, and Eells (1960) used the ISC to estimate the social-class placement of individuals or families, 208 "old Americans" and 93 "ethnics." They used five social-class systems (upper, upper-middle, lower-middle, upper-lower, and lower-lower); within each the individual or family is further classified as strong, solid, or weak. The criterion is social-class placement on the authors' Evaluated Participation (EP) measure, determined by an evaluation in the community of participation in status-significant activities. Both the EP and the ISC are 15-point scales. None of the "old Americans" scores on the two 15-point indices differed by more than 2 points. Of the "ethnics," 92.5 percent of the scores were within 2 points and 98.9 were within 3 points.

BIBLIOGRAPHY:

Warner, W. L., Meeker, M., and Eells, K. *Social Class in America.* New York: Harper & Row, 1960.

*Prepared by Orval G. Johnson*

# INDEX OF TEACHER'S PERCEPTIONS
# OF PARENTS AS DEVIANTS

AUTHOR: Timothy B. Dailey

AGE: Elementary-school teachers

VARIABLE: The extent to which parents who neglect children are seen as deviant by the child's teacher

TYPE OF MEASURE: Self-administered questionnaire

SOURCE FROM WHICH MEASURE MAY BE OBTAINED: Timothy B. Dailey, Department of Sociology, Ohio State University, Columbus, Ohio 43210; or see Dailey (1975).

DESCRIPTION OF MEASURE: The index is used to measure teachers' responses to several stories about neglect. However, it could be used for actual situations. The goal of the study for which this index was developed was to measure the extent to which different factors influenced perceptions of parents as deviant: quality of parental behavior, personal characteristics of teachers, and type of school the neglected child was attending. The items represent four dimensions derived from the "labeling theory" concept of deviance (Schur, 1971): whether the parental behavior is a departure from norms, is discrediting to the parent, is behavior about which some action should be taken, and, for this study, whether the child is viewed as a victim or himself as deviant. The original data did not permit separate scales to be constructed for each dimension. The thirty-eight items of the original index are scored in the reverse of actual numbering (4 becomes 1, and so forth) with the exception of item 5 of Part Two ("Take unusual care about supervision") and item 2 of Part Four ("Wait to see if the parents change their behavior toward the child"), which are phrased in the opposite direction from the others. Individual scores are summed to produce a "reaction score" for each respondent. The stronger the reaction, the more deviant is the parent.

As examples, the first eight items of the original thirty-eight-item index are given below. The starred items were omitted from the final index.

*This is the situation:*

Mr. M. is a strict disciplinarian, as he often tells his friends when they discuss children. He claims that the more serious the misbehavior, the more serious the punishment should be. Usually he uses physical kinds of punishment. For small problems he spanks his children, but for bigger problems he has a special strap. One child came to school recently with bruises on his arms because of this. In school, this child seems to do alright. But several children in the class have said some of their things were missing, and they accuse him of taking them. Other teachers say they have seen him in the room when he wasn't supposed to be, looking into desks.

*How do you react?* Remember that this child is in your classroom. Indicate your evaluation of these various aspects of the parents' behavior as reflected in the description above, by circling the appropriate number to the right of each item: 1—acceptable; 2—acceptable with reservations; 3—undecided; 4—unacceptable with reservations; or 5—unacceptable.

As the child's teacher, *how do you find the parents'* . . .

    1. efforts to provide necessary physical care for the child?

    2. method of controlling the child's behavior?

 *3. awareness of the emotional needs of the child?

    4. strength of concern for the safety of the child?

*What caused their behavior?* Indicate what you think is the relative applicability of each statement below to the parental behavior described above. Circle the appropriate number to the right of each item: 1—quite likely; 2—somewhat likely; 3—somewhat unlikely; or 4—quite unlikely. As the teacher, *did you think the parents behave this way because they* . . .

    1. are suffering from emotional disturbance?

    2. were probably brought up in a deprived and neglected way themselves?

 *3. have child-rearing values different from yours, but acceptable in some groups that you know about?

    4. are basically irresponsible people?

RELIABILITY AND VALIDITY: Item analysis was a process of discarding items with little or no variation in responses, correlating individual items to total-scale scores, and keeping items that correlated .30 or higher with the total. This left twenty items for the final index. Reliability was determined by use of Cronbach's *alpha,* a measure of internal consistency. The average *alpha* coefficient was .72 (since several stories were used, the set of responses to each was analyzed separately). Also, item analysis was conducted on two halves of the sample, and it was found that the same items were selected in each case. Validity was determined by comparing the rank ordering of the stories used to stimulate responses with an ordering produced by a panel of experts (teachers and social workers). Ordering of stories was determined by the mean reaction to each. The same order was produced by the experts and the respondents, with one minor exception. Criterion validity was established by the finding that teachers in schools with stronger policies about neglect cases had stronger reactions in the study, and teachers who had stronger reactions to parents in actual neglect situations (saw them as more deviant) also had stronger reactions to the stories in this study. The sample consisted of 516 elementary-school teachers from western Massachusetts. Scores on the index of perception of parents as deviant ranged from 20 (not deviant) to 83 (most deviant). The actual mean ranged from 51.85 to 68.82 for the several stories, the actual standard deviation ranged from 6.50 to 9.60, and the actual range of scores ranged from 30 to 49.

BIBLIOGRAPHY:

Dailey, T. B. "The Labeled Deviant as Victim or Culprit: The Case of Child Neglecters." Unpublished doctoral dissertation. University of Massachusetts, Amherst, 1975.

Schur, E. *Labeling Deviant Behavior.* New York: Harper & Row, 1971.

# INVENTORY OF DRAMATIC BEHAVIOR (IDB)

AUTHORS: Gilbert Lazier, Brian Sutton-Smith, Douglas A. Zahn, and E. Joseph Karioth

AGE: Unlimited; current use, 6 to 12 years

VARIABLE: Improvisational dramatic behavior

TYPE OF MEASURE: Content-analysis system for video samples

SOURCE FROM WHICH MEASURE MAY BE OBTAINED: Gilbert Lazier, School of Theatre, Florida State University, Tallahassee, Florida 32306.

DESCRIPTION OF MEASURE: Many video samples were analyzed to ascertain types of behavior most crucial to dramatic events and most sensitive to differences among subjects. Through the extended observation of the videotapes, a "developmental vocabulary" adequate to the data was created. This vocabulary was then reduced to an inventory of items, hereafter called the IDB (Inventory of Dramatic Behavior), scored for presence or absence and number of times phenomena recurred within categories. Such a scoring procedure avoids the usual evaluative ratings commonly employed to ascertain whether one subject is "better" than another at given tasks. The authors were concerned with the accurate recording of specific, observed behavior, thus minimizing value judgments of quality or appropriateness. Of the many dimensions of behavior subsequently created for the IDB, eight were tested as reliable: time taken per improvisation, amount of space traversed, number of stops made, number of dramatic incidents created, number of novel incidents, number of smaller acts within the incidents, number of repeated acts, and number of other characters created.

RELIABILITY AND VALIDITY: In studies using the IDB, each child performed three scenes. Each of the eight dimensions was measured in each scene. The reliability of the scoring procedure was investigated by having seven trained raters independently rate each of five randomly chosen children. For each of the twenty-four variables measured, the intraclass reliability coefficients were all large, with twenty of the twenty-four being between $r = .65$ and $r = 1.00$. The only dimension with rather low reliability coefficients was "number of other characters created."

BIBLIOGRAPHY:

Lazier, G., and Sutton-Smith, B. *Assessment of Role Induction and Role Involvement in Creative Drama.* 1970. ERIC document no. ED 039 254.

Lazier, G., Sutton-Smith, B., Karioth, E. J., and Zahn, D. A. *The Inventory of Dramatic Behavior: A Content Analysis Technique for Creative Dramatics.* Monograph published through HEW funds (1-D-063) for the ASSITEJ International Congress. Florida State University, Tallahassee, 1972.

Lazier, G., Sutton-Smith, B., and Zahn, D. A. "A Systematic Analysis of Developmental Differences in Dramatic Improvisational Behavior." *Speech Monographs,* 1971, *38,* 155-165.

Lazier, G., Zahn, D. A., and Karioth, E. J. "Dramatic Behavior Norms of Florida Children." *Empirical Research in Theatre,* 1973, *3,* 41-70.

Sutton-Smith, B., Lazier, G., and Zahn, D. A. "Developmental Stages in Dramatic Improvisation." *American Psychological Association Proceedings*, 1971, *79*, 421-423.

*Prepared by Gil Lazier and Douglas A. Zahn*

---

# LENGTH-COMPLEXITY INDEX (LCI)

AUTHOR: L. E. Miner

AGE: Unlimited

VARIABLE: Sentence length and complexity

TYPE OF MEASURE: Linguistic-numeric analysis system

SOURCE FROM WHICH MEASURE MAY BE OBTAINED: Miner (1969).

DESCRIPTION OF MEASURE: The Length-Complexity Index (LCI) measures sentence length and complexity according to a numeric weighting system. It is a measure of structural complexity, not grammatical accuracy; consequently, it is not dialect-bound. The LCI is applicable for analysis of any oral or written language sample for the purpose of describing linguistic performance and determining baseline performance. Norms and a standardized procedure for evoking oral language samples are available on 5-year-old children (Miner, 1970). Lists of frequently occurring syntactic structures are available.

RELIABILITY AND VALIDITY: Temporal reliability for LCI scores on kindergarten children equals .93 (intraclass correlation coefficient). Interexaminer and intraexaminer reliability scores from numerous studies exceed .95. The standard error of the mean for kindergarten children ($N = 300$) is .46. The standard error of the measure for kindergarten children is 1.24. Measures of distribution shape (skewness and kurtosis) suggest the LCI has its greatest discrimination power at the distribution extremes. Construct validity has been assessed by comparing psychological scale values derived from observer judgments to LCI values. Resulting correlations exceed .85.

BIBLIOGRAPHY:

Barlow, M. C., and Miner, L. E. "Temporal Reliability of the Length-Complexity Index." *Journal of Communication Disorders*, 1969, *2*, 241-251.

Griffith, J., and Miner, L. E. "LCI Reliability and Size of Language Sample." *Journal of Communication Disorders*, 1969, *2*, 264-267.

Hon, M. "Construct Validity of the Length-Complexity Index." Unpublished master's thesis. Eastern Illinois University, Charleston, 1970.

Miner, L. E. "Scoring Procedures for the Length-Complexity Index: A Preliminary Report." *Journal of Communication Disorders*, 1969, *2*, 224-240.

Miner, L. E. "A Normative Study of the Length-Complexity Index for Five Year Old Children." Unpublished doctoral dissertation. University of Illinois, Urbana, 1970.

---

## MOTORIC IDEATIONAL SENSORY TEST (MIST)

AUTHORS: Kenneth B. Stein and Peter Lenrow

AGE: Adolescent to adult

VARIABLE: Expressive orientation and expressive style

TYPE OF MEASURE: Likert scale

SOURCE FROM WHICH MEASURE MAY BE OBTAINED: Kenneth B. Stein, 517 Moraga Avenue, Piedmont, California 94611.

DESCRIPTION OF MEASURE: The scale consists of forty-five items distributed as follows: fifteen motoric, fifteen ideational, and fifteen sensory-perceptual. The item content consists of an everyday activity representing one of the three expressive areas. The scale construction relied upon the cluster-analytic technique, and the fifteen best items based on internal consistency were selected for each of the three areas. Items that were male-female related were eliminated. Total score for each dimension is a simple sum of the fifteen item scores in that dimension. The theory behind the construction of the scale is that these expressive dimensions are general orientations toward the world of objects as well as toward the self. They reflect individual variations in preferred general modes of organizing and interacting with the stimulus world. These dimensions and styles are worthy of measurement for the description and prediction of behavior.

As examples, the first ten of the forty-five items of Form MF of the test are given below. Each item is to be answered on a 5-point scale: "none," "some," "pretty much," "very much," "extremely much."

1. Playing tennis.
2. Seeing grass glistening with dew.
3. Smelling fresh cut hay.
4. Smelling the air after a heavy rain.
5. Fishing or hunting.
6. Doing carpentry or handicrafts.
7. Listening to a panel discussion of national problems.
8. Browsing in a library.
9. Playing softball.
10. Watching the play of light on the surface of moving water.

RELIABILITY AND VALIDITY: Internal reliability of each dimension is as follows: motoric, .86; ideational, .92; and sensory, .96. The intercorrelations of these dimensions are relatively low. Test-retest reliability with a one-month interval for college males ranged from .74 to .81 and for females from .87 to .88. Significant associations have been found between the three dimensions and a variety of demographic and personality variables, which contribute validation evidence for the scale. Pattern types across the three dimensions were discovered and validated.

BIBLIOGRAPHY:

Stein, K. B., Korchin, S. J., and Cooper, L. "Motoric, Ideational and Sensory Expressive Styles: Further Validation of the Stein and Lenrow Types." *Psychological Reports,* 1972, *31,* 335-338.
Stein, K. B., and Lenrow, P. "Expressive Styles and Their Measurement." *Journal of Personality and Social Psychology,* 1970, *16,* 656-664.

---

## NONVERBAL SEMANTIC DIFFERENTIAL

AUTHORS: Peter M. Bentler and Allan L. LaVoie

AGE: Estimated 4 years to adult

VARIABLE: Five dimensions of semantic (connotative) space: evaluation, potency, activity, density, and orderliness (EPADO)

TYPE OF MEASURE: Bipolar pictorial scales

SOURCE FROM WHICH MEASURE MAY BE OBTAINED: Peter M. Bentler, Department of Psychology, University of California, Los Angeles, California 90024; or Allan L. LaVoie, Department of Psychology, Davis and Elkins College, Elkins, West Virginia 26241.

DESCRIPTION OF MEASURE: The three well-known dimensions of connotative meaning (evaluation, potency, and activity—E, P, and A) were identified in the early fifties but attempts to expand semantic space failed until recently. Bentler and La Voie (1972a) identified and provided reliable measures for four further dimensions: density (D), orderliness, (O), reality (R), and familiarity (F). These were later shortened for rapid administration (LaVoie and Bentler, 1974). Attempts were also made to provide nonverbal, graphic equivalents for these seven EPADORF dimensions. It proved possible to measure reliably and validly only EPADO (five of the seven) dimensions (Bentler and LaVoie, 1972b; LaVoie, 1972). The measure consists of a series of bipolar figures (line drawings) matched with bipolar adjectives (e.g., good/bad). The subject is asked to choose the member of each pair that better describes a given concept. The Nonverbal Semantic Differential should prove useful in studies with children, with persons who have language deficits, and in cross-cultural settings, as well as in basic studies of verbal and visual semantic information processing and its development. As yet, normative data are not available. Preliminary studies suggest that the measure can be used to obtain meaningful and consistent data from children as young as 4 years, but this work has not been fully analyzed nor has it been published. Hence, careful attention should be given to instruction, method of presentation, and experimental design.

RELIABILITY AND VALIDITY: With a sample of 160 undergraduate students, Spearman-Brown corrected split-half internal consistencies were as follows: evaluation, .78; potency, .89; activity, .84; density, .90; and orderliness, .89. The mean absolute intercorrelation among the five scales was .2, verifying the relative independence of the five dimensions. Each nonverbal scale correlated highly with its more traditional verbal counterpart as follows: evaluation, .75; potency, .65; activity, .69; density, .59; and orderliness, .69. The mean verbal-nonverbal validity was thus .67. In contrast, the mean absolute correlation for verbal-nonverbal scales across different dimensions was .19, indicating that the graphic scales correspond closely to their adjectival counterparts.

BIBLIOGRAPHY:

Bentler, P. M., and LaVoie, A. L. "An Extension of Semantic Space." *Journal of Verbal Learning and Verbal Behavior,* 1972a, *11,* 174-182.
Bentler, P. M., and LaVoie, A. L. "A Nonverbal Semantic Differential." *Journal of Verbal Learning and Verbal Behavior,* 1972b, *11,* 491-496.
LaVoie, A. L. "Verbal and Nonverbal Measures of Old and New Semantic Dimensions." Paper presented at the convention of the Western Psychological Association, Portland, Oregon, April 1972.
LaVoie, A. L., and Bentler, P. M. "A Short-Form Measure of the Expanded Seven-Dimensional Semantic Space." *Journal of Educational Measurement,* 1974, *11,* 65-66.

*Prepared by Peter M. Bentler and Allan L. LaVoie*

---

# PEOPLE'S WANTS

AUTHOR: Douglas H. Bray

AGE: 12 to 16 years

VARIABLE: Future-time perspective

TYPE OF MEASURE: Attitude scales

SOURCE FROM WHICH MEASURE MAY BE OBTAINED: D. H. Bray, Education Department, Massey University, Palmerston North, New Zealand. Sample set containing response booklet, instruction copy, and group administration directions, air-mailed beyond New Zealand for $10.00 (US). Cost of printing response booklets in bulk (adapted to country of user outside New Zealand) would depend on quantity. For example,

$200.00 (US) for 500 copies on printer's 1975 quotation. Cost based on $1.00 (NZ) equals approximately $1.30 (US).

DESCRIPTION OF MEASURE: Respondents are asked to choose among distances in time of imagined realization of desired objects or happenings first for vaguely specified persons and second for themselves. Respondents also decide among choices of money, the amount of which increases according to delay. For rationale and for the response patterns of 434 New Zealand adolescents (mean age of 14 years 3 months) with boys and girls shown separately for both Maoris and those of European descent, see Bray (1970, 1971). Directions for group administration are obtainable from the author. For use outside New Zealand the two money-choice questions may need to be altered, for example, from "dollars" to "pounds"; also the designation of ethnic groups needs to be altered or omitted.

As examples, the first three of the forty-one items of the test and one of the two items dealing with money are given below.

1. Now think of somebody of a different age from you, either younger or older, and the sort of wants this person might have. Let's call this person Z. Put a line in the box to show whether Z is older or younger than you.
   a. Z is younger.
   b. Z is older.
2. There is something that Z *most wants* to happen. *How soon* is Z thinking of this as happening?
   a. In less than 1 week.
   b. In 1 to 4 weeks.
   c. In 1 to 6 months.
   d. In 6 months to 1 year.
   e. In 1 to 5 years.
   f. In 5 to 10 years.
   g. Longer than 10 years.
3. How does Z *feel about its going to happen*?
   a. Is sure it will happen.
   b. Thinks it probably will happen.
   c. Is doubtful but it could happen.
   d. Thinks it probably won't happen.
   e. Is sure it won't happen.
34. If you were given some money, which would you prefer?
   a. 10 dollars now.
   b. 14 dollars in one month.
   c. 18 dollars in three months.
   d. 22 dollars in six months.
   e. 28 dollars in one year.

RELIABILITY AND VALIDITY: For construct validity see Bray (1970, 1971) showing confirmation of the hypotheses of ethnic difference. A study by Havighurst (1973) supports validity by similar findings of anticipated contrasts as between Maoris and non-Maoris by the use of different measures of time perspective. Research by Webster (1972) also supports validity by showing factor loadings from an abbreviated form of the measure of .35 on his factor I (family adjustment) for boys and .28 on his factor V (attitude to school) for girls.

BIBLIOGRAPHY:

Bray, D. H. "Extent of Future-Time Orientation: A Cross-Ethnic Study Among New Zealand Adolescents." *British Journal of Educational Psychology,* 1970, *40,* 200-208.
Bray, D. H. "Maori Adolescent Temporal Values: Distance of Goals Perceived as Important and of Delayed Gratification, as Compared with Pakehas." *New Zealand Journal of Educational Studies,* 1971, *6,* 62-77.
Havighurst, R. J. *Future Time Perspectives and Attitudes of New Zealand Maori and Pakeha Adolescents.* Wellington: New Zealand Council of Educational Research, 1973.
Webster, A. C. "Structure and Relationships of Standard Environmental, Personality and Ability Factors in Secondary School Adolescents." Unpublished doctoral dissertation. Massey University, Palmerston North, New Zealand, 1972.

---

## RUCKER-GABLE EDUCATIONAL PROGRAMING SCALE (RGEPS)

AUTHORS: Chauncy N. Rucker and Robert K. Gable

AGE: Teachers and administrators

VARIABLE: Attitude toward and knowledge of appropriate program placements for handicapped children

TYPE OF MEASURE: Likert-type scale

SOURCE FROM WHICH MEASURE MAY BE OBTAINED: Rucker-Gable Associates, Rockridge, Box 201C, Storrs, Connecticut 06268. Cost: Specimen set, $3.50; test booklets, $.35 each; optical scanning response sheets, $.12 each.

DESCRIPTION OF MEASURE: The RGEPS consists of thirty descriptions of actual children referred for special-education services. Items describe the behaviors of children who are either mentally retarded, emotionally disturbed, or learning disabled. The descriptions range from very mild to relatively severe in terms of degree of disability and offer a good cross-section of various types and degrees of handicapping conditions. Respondents are asked to choose what they feel is the best educational setting for each child at the present time from a continuum of seven educational programs or services. Attitude scores are calculated directly from the respondents' placement choices on the 7-point scale ranging from "regular classroom" to "not for regular or special public education." A total-attitude score can be generated as well as attitude subscores for three clusters of items differentiated as to type of handicapping condition (mental retardation, emotional disturbance, and learning disabilities) and three clusters differentiated by the degree of their disability (mild, moderate, and severe). The RGEPS also provides measures of knowledge of appropriate placement of handicapped children. A respondent's placement choice of each item is compared to the average placement on that item by a group of experts in special education (thirty-five directors of university training programs in either mental retardation, emotional disturbance, or learning disabilities). As with attitude, there is a total-knowledge score as well as knowledge subscores for the three clusters of items differentiated as to type of handicapping condition and three clusters differentiated by the degree of their disability. The RGEPS has been effectively used to do the following: (1) plan and evaluate workshops introducing mainstreaming rationale to administrators, or training teachers to work with mildly handicapped children; (2) measure readiness of a teacher, administrator, or school to move mildly handicapped children closer to the mainstream; (3) evaluate effect of alternative programming approaches; (4) evaluate impact of university training programs; and (5) assess state or local needs.

Example items from mental retardation (MR), emotional disturbance (ED), and learning disabilities (LD) are given below.

MR    Dan is a 6-year-old who is extremely immature in all areas. He is not able to do any of the tasks that are expected of a kindergartener. His speech is primarily limited to one- or two-word utterances. He has a negative approach to school.

ED    Jerry is a 7-year-old who disrupts group tasks and refuses to go with his class to lunch or gym. At recess he plays with older children from other classes since his own classmates won't play with him. Although he seems to like his teacher and has above-average potential, he seldom completes his work in a satisfactory manner.

LD    Nancy is a third grader who has difficulty keeping her place during oral reading. Her handwriting is labored, the letters are very large and irregular, and she cannot write on the lines. Her work is disorganized. She gives up easily and needs a lot of personal attention.

RELIABILITY AND VALIDITY: Since the experts' profile of placement decisions is the criterion to which the respondent's knowledge scores are generated, the interrater reliability of the experts' placements must be substantial. Reliabilities range from .87 to .99 for the subscales; .99 for the total score. Thus one can be confident in employing the experts' placement decision as a reliable criterion in any of the RGEPS knowledge areas. Since a respondent's knowledge score is based upon his deviation from the experts' placements, *alpha* internal consistency reliabilities were generated using these deviation scores for the six scales and the total score. Reliabilities range from .68 to .90, with a median of .80, for the subscales; from .87 to .94 for the total score for four samples of respondents from the following areas: special-education graduate students, nonspecial-education undergraduates, principals, and regular classroom teachers. Split-half internal consistency reliabilities for respondents were generated using attitude raw scores for the six scales and the total score. The resulting split-half reliabilities ranged from .36 to .92, with a median of .77, for the subscales; and from .81 to .96 for the total score for the four samples identified in the previous section. The content validity of the RGEPS is supported in two ways. First, actual case descriptions were used that were judged by content experts to reflect the mental retardation, emotional disturbance, and learning disabilities areas. Following this, judgments of item appropriateness and actual item-placement responses were obtained from thirty-five directors of university training programs for each item. These responses were employed to select the final set of thirty items representing a continuum of disability across each of the three disability areas. The construct validity of the RGEPS score interpretations has been supported by examining known-group differences and group differences before and after training experiences. See Rucker and Gable (1974) for detailed descriptions of these studies.

BIBLIOGRAPHY:

Rucker, C. N., and Gable, R. K. *Rucker-Gable Educational Programing Scale Manual.* Storrs, Connecticut: Rucker-Gable Associates, 1974.

---

## SCHOOL PROGRAM BONANZA GAME

AUTHOR: David John Mullen

AGE: Parents and teachers of pupils in grades 4 to 12

VARIABLE: Program goal priorities

TYPE OF MEASURE: Priority evaluator—needs assessment

SOURCE FROM WHICH MEASURE MAY BE OBTAINED: David J. Mullen, Bureau of Field Studies, College of Education, University of Georgia, Athens, Georgia 30602. Cost: $100.00 per elementary school and $150.00 per middle or senior school.

DESCRIPTION OF MEASURE: The School Program Bonanza Game is a needs-assessment survey designed to determine what kind of education students, school personnel, parents, and boards of education feel should have top priority at school. Participants are given twenty $100 bills to spend as they think best on various areas of the school program. For example, in the area of social world, players must choose among three options: learn enough social studies to get along (no bills), learn basic facts about how men live together (two bills or $200), and use social studies to understand man's present and future situation (four bills or $400). The nine areas on which respondents decide are: the "3 R's," social studies, science, vocational training, the arts, health and physical development, making choices, relationships with others, and development of self.

RELIABILITY AND VALIDITY: Q-sort was used for developing program categories. Cartoon drawings and captions were field-tested with randomly selected parents, students, and school staff. Experiments were conducted wherein different films were used to randomize the pictures, assign dollar amounts, and rank the pictures from least to most importance. Final assignments of dollar amounts and ordering of pictures were based on data from these experiments. To determine reliability two administrations were given to the same group. A *t*-test was applied to the corresponding mean responses for each of the nine program areas. Each of the nine pairs had a very low significance index at the .01 level, indicating high reliability.

BIBLIOGRAPHY:

Mullen, D. J. "Goal Setting: Clips and Cartoons Turn into a Bonanza." *Nation's Schools,* 1973, *93,* 5.
Mullen, D. J., and Mullen, R. C. "A Principal's Handbook for Conducting a Needs Assessment Using the School Program Bonanza Game." In *Quarterly of the Georgia Association of Elementary School Principals,* 1974, *11* (1), entire issue. GAE and Bureau of Field Studies, University of Georgia, Athens.
Mullen, D. J., and Schnittjer, C. "School Program Bonanza Game: A Study of the Structure and Consistency of the Instrument." Unpublished paper. Bureau of Field Studies, College of Education, University of Georgia, Athens, 1974.

---

## SELF-DISCLOSURE INVENTORY FOR ADOLESCENTS

AUTHORS: Lloyd W. West and Harvey W. Zingle

AGE: 12 to 18 years

VARIABLE: Communication patterns

TYPE OF MEASURE: Likert-type scale

SOURCE FROM WHICH MEASURE MAY BE OBTAINED: Single copies may be obtained from Lloyd W. West, Department of Educational Psychology, University of Calgary, Alberta, Canada.

DESCRIPTION OF MEASURE: The SDIA is a self-report instrument designed to survey the communication patterns of adolescents. It provides measures of self-disclosure in six content areas: school concerns, money and status concerns, personal concerns, home and family relationships, health and physical development, and boy-girl relations. The subject is directed to indicate on an IBM-type answer sheet the frequency with which he has discussed each of several topics with selected confidants—mothers, fathers, friends of same sex, friends of opposite sex, and so forth.

As examples, eight of the forty-eight items on the inventory are given below. The respondent answers every item for each of the confidants on a 4-point frequency scale ranging from "never" to "often."

1. Which school subjects I like and which I dislike.
2. My appetite and food preferences.
3. The ways in which my parents annoy me.
4. Whether I am popular with girls/boys.
5. Whether I can afford to buy the things I need.
6. Whether my parents understand me.
7. How I get along with my teachers.
8. The price of some of the things I have.

RELIABILITY AND VALIDITY: Test-retest and split-half reliability coefficients of the order .80 to .98 have been reported by West and Zingle (1969). Validity coefficients of the order .55 have been reported by West (1971).

BIBLIOGRAPHY:

West, L. W. "Some Implications of Disclosure Studies for Group Counseling with Adolescents." *Canadian Counselor,* 1970, *4,* 1, 57-62.

West, L. W. "A Study of the Validity of the Self-Disclosure Inventory for Adolescents." *Perceptual and Motor Skills,* 1971, *33,* 91-100.

West, L. W. "Mapping the Communication Patterns of Adolescents." *Canadian Counselor,* 1974, *8,* 54-65.

West, L. W., and Zingle, H. W. "A Self-Disclosure Inventory for Adolescents." *Psychological Reports,* 1969, *24,* 439-445.

---

## SELF-DISCLOSURE QUESTIONNAIRE FOR CHILDREN

AUTHORS: Genevieve Skypek and Sidney Jourard

AGE: 6 to 12 years

VARIABLE: Amount of personal disclosure given and received

TYPE OF MEASURE: Questionnaire, structured interview

SOURCE FROM WHICH MEASURE MAY BE OBTAINED: Genevieve Skypek, 600 Arcadia Lakes Drive East, Columbia, South Carolina 29206. Send self-addressed stamped envelope.

DESCRIPTION OF MEASURE: The Children's Self-Disclosure Questionnaire is a twenty-five-item instrument adapted from a questionnaire for adults developed by Jourard (1964). To date, this questionnaire has only been used to study changes in self-disclosure given and self-disclosure received from best same-sexed friend in children aged 6 to 12. The most effective method of administration is the structured interview, especially for the younger children.

As examples, four selected items of the twenty-five on the questionnaire are given below.

1. *Spare time:* What kinds of things do you like to do in your spare time when you are by yourself; have you told your best friend about this; has he told you what he likes to do in his spare time when he is by himself?

9. *Parents:* What do you like about your parents; have you told your best friend this; has he told you what he likes about his?

14. *Ambition:* What do you want to be when you grow up; have you told your best friend this; has he told you what he wants to be?

18. *Appearance:* Like—what do you like about the way you look; have you told your best friend this; has he told you what he likes about the way he looks?

RELIABILITY AND VALIDITY: Children ($N$ = 98) ranging in age from 6 to 12 years were individually administered the Self-Disclosure Questionnaire. For each item the $S$s were to indicate both if they had given disclosure to their best same-sexed friend and if they had received disclosure from this same friend. Given-disclosure scores and received-disclosure scores were treated separately as two dependent variables in analysis-of-covariance designs. The results of the analyses led to the following conclusions: (1) The amount of personal disclosure reported given to one's best same-sexed friend increases as age increases, independently of the amount of disclosure reported received from that friend. (2) The amount of disclosure reported received is not dependent on age but is instead significantly related to the amount of disclosure given. (3) There were no significant sex differences in the amount of disclosure given or received. However, there was a slight tendency for females to disclose more and receive more than males. Finally, (4) $t$-tests revealed that the total amount of disclosure reported given was significantly greater than the total amount of disclosure reported received. The last two conclusions were inconsistent with adult findings.

BIBLIOGRAPHY:

Jourard, S. M. *The Transparent Self.* New York: Van Nostrand Reinhold, 1964.

Jourard, S. M. *Self-Disclosure: An Experimental Analysis of the Transparent Self.* New York: Wiley, 1971.

Skypek, G. "Self-Disclosure in Children Between the Ages of Six and Twelve." Unpublished master's thesis. University of Florida, Gainesville, 1969.

# SLEEP BEHAVIORS OF TWO-YEAR-OLD CHILDREN

AUTHORS: Naomi Ragins and Joseph Schachter

AGE: 18 to 30 years

VARIABLE: Sleep behaviors and parental concerns

TYPE OF MEASURE: Questionnaire

SOURCE FROM WHICH MEASURE MAY BE OBTAINED: Naomi Ragins, Pittsburgh Child Guidance Center, 201 De Soto Street, Pittsburgh, Pennsylvania 15213.

DESCRIPTION OF MEASURE: This measure is a twenty-nine-item, multiple-choice, self-administrable questionnaire designed to elicit information about: (1) a child's sleep on the previous night, during the preceding week, and during the preceding three months; (2) the child's earlier sleep behavior; (3) the presence (or absence) of maternal concern about the child's sleep at present and/or in the past; and (4) past or present maternal concern about other aspects of the child's development. It was administered to forty-eight mothers who had a "normal" child between 21 and 27 months of age. Almost half (46 percent) of the mothers reported worrying about the child's sleep at some time during the child's life; 27 percent were worried about the child's sleep at present; 19 percent had worried only in the past. Normative data obtained with respect to amount of sleep, prevalence of daytime napping, bedtime rituals, and problematic sleep behaviors resembled findings from other studies of this age group.

As examples, five selected items of the twenty-nine on the questionnaire are given below.

1. How many hours did the child sleep last night?
   a. 10 hours or less.
   b. 11 to 12 hours.
   c. 12 to 13 hours.
   d. 14 or more hours.
3. When was the child put to bed last night?
   a. When child seemed sleepy.
   b. When child asked to go to bed.
   c. At the time child is put to bed every night.
   d. Other.
4. Last night the child went to bed
   a. willingly.
   b. reluctantly.
   c. actively delayed and resisted going to bed.
7. This morning the
   a. child woke himself and cried.
   b. child woke himself and was cheerful.
   c. child cried when wakened.
   d. child was cheerful when wakened.
12. On the average, during *the past week,* how long did it take the child to fall asleep?
   a. Less than 10 minutes.
   b. 15-30 minutes.
   c. Less than 1 hour.
   d. More than 1 hour.
   e. Don't know.

RELIABILITY AND VALIDITY: Since the mothers' sleep concerns did not derive from any particular sleep characteristics isolated by the questionnaire, the questionnaire did not serve as a screening instrument to select 2-year-olds with "deviant" sleep patterns. However, ongoing concern about a 2-year-old's sleep behavior was significantly more frequent among the child-family situations rated high with respect to nascent pathology or potential for the development of childhood disorder. These mothers gave more deviant responses (response categories used by less than 9 percent of the mothers) on the questionnaire. Other concerns about the child's development did not significantly differentiate from the remainder of our sample the group of child-family situations judged clinically to be at risk.

BIBLIOGRAPHY:

Ragins, N., and Schachter, J. "A Study of Sleep Behavior in Two-Year-Old Children." *Journal of the American Academy of Child Psychiatry,* 1971, *10,* 464-480.

## STANFORD UNIVERSITY EVALUATION SCALES

AUTHORS: Emily F. Garfield and Richard H. Blum

AGE: Grades 2 to 12

VARIABLE: Drug-related experience

TYPE OF MEASURE: Questionnaire

SOURCE FROM WHICH MEASURE MAY BE OBTAINED: See Garfield and Blum (1973).

DESCRIPTION OF MEASURE: These scales are made up of two instruments: the Stanford University Drug Evaluation Questionnaire and the Stanford Drug Evaluation Interview for Young Children. The questionnaire is designed to assess reported individual drug-use patterns in several age groups. Comparisons of the test replies administered at different times are used as indicators of the impact of an ongoing drug-education program. The questionnaire was originally designed for use with 3,300 suburban school-aged children, grades 5 through 12, who were participants in a longitudinal drug-evaluation project. The majority of the elementary-school population comprised children from either white blue-collar or white upper-middle-class families. The high school population included ethnic minorities. This instrument may also be used to determine drug-availability and drug-use patterns at any time. The areas of inquiry are: availability or exposure to a given substance, actual use, and intentions to use. The questionnaire can be administered in about 40 minutes.

The companion measure to the Drug Evaluation Questionnaire is the individually administered Stanford Drug Evaluation Interview for children below fifth grade. The instrument was originally used in a longitudinal study involving 900 children in grades 2 through 4. The interview, which takes approximately 5 to 10 minutes per child, focuses on a total set of twenty-two color photographs. There are two photographs for each of eleven drug categories. The drug-category sequence begins with coffee and progresses through tobacco, beer, wine, liquor, marijuana, hallucinogens, amphetamines, barbiturates, inhalants, and heroin. The areas of inquiry are: recognition, availability, experience, and intentions. Garfield and Blum (1973) give complete instructions for preparing the photograph sets. In finished form, the Interview for Young Children is a series of 8½ X 11-inch color photographs, each inserted in a clear plastic page protector and placed in a looseleaf notebook; the set of two photographs for any given category should be on facing pages so that they are both visible.

As examples, the questions by age group for one of the eleven drugs are given below. Each of the other ten drugs has a series of questions presented in the same way.

V. *Marijuana*

   *Fifth/sixth grades*

    1. Marijuana (pot, weed, grass, hash) comes from

      a. a tree.

      b. a root.

      c. a plant.

      d. don't know.

2. Marijuana is usually
   a. smoked.
   b. chewed.
   c. sniffed.
   d. don't know.

*Seventh/eighth grades*

1. Compared with marijuana, hashish is
   a. much less strong.
   b. about as strong.
   c. much stronger.
   d. don't know.
2. In the past marijuana plants were used to make
   a. hay.
   b. alfalfa.
   c. rope.
   d. don't know.

*High school*

1. The suspected active chemical principle in marijuana is
   a. PCP.
   b. STP.
   c. THC.
   d. don't know.

RELIABILITY AND VALIDITY: The approach to reliability and validity involved corroboration of *S*'s responses through contact with those he considers friends, models, and examples. For details see Garfield and Blum (1973).

BIBLIOGRAPHY:

Garfield, E. F., and Blum, R. H. "Stanford University Evaluation Scales." In L. A. Abrams, E. F. Garfield, J. D. Swisher, and others (Eds.), *Accountability in Drug Education.* Washington, D.C.: The Drug Abuse Council, Inc., 1973.

---

## TIME REFERENCE INVENTORY (TRI)

AUTHOR: Philip Roos

AGE: 8 years to adult

VARIABLE: Temporal orientation

TYPE OF MEASURE: Paper-and-pencil questionnaire

SOURCE FROM WHICH MEASURE MAY BE OBTAINED: Philip Roos, National Association for Retarded Citizens, P.O. Box 6109, Arlington, Texas 76011.

DESCRIPTION OF MEASURE: The Time-Reference Inventory is a thirty-item paper-and-pencil test containing ten pleasant items, ten unpleasant items, and ten effectively neutral items. The subject indicates for each item whether it most appropriately refers to his past, present, or future, and he estimates his age at the time to which the item refers. Four additional open-ended questions are designed to furnish projective material related to the past and future dimensions. Objective scoring yields the following quantitative information: number of positive, negative, and neutral items selected to refer to the past, present, and future; average years projected into the future (future extension); average years projected into the past (past extension); and average age focus. A simplified twelve-item form is available for use with children and mentally retarded subjects.

As examples, the first eight of the thirty-four items on the inventory are given below.

1. The most important time of my life is probably in the . . .
2. I believe the happiest time of my life is in the . . .
3. The most productive period of my life is in the . . .
4. The most peaceful time of my life is in the . . .
5. I usually *prefer* talking about the . . .
6. The most crucial period of my life is probably in the . . .
7. The most satisfying time of my life is probably in the . . .
8. My period of greatest accomplishment is probably in the . . .

RELIABILITY AND VALIDITY: The test has been successful in differentiating normals from mentally retarded persons (Roos and Albers, 1965b); normals from alcoholic subjects (Roos and Albers, 1965a); among normal subjects, chronic schizophrenics, acute schizophrenics, alcoholics, and depressive subjects (Foulks and Webb, 1970); and between normal persons and prison recidivists (Black and Gregson, 1973). Significant relationships have been reported between the TRI variables and other test measures (Oliver, 1973). Test-retest reliabilities have been reported as generally high and significant (Foulks and Webb, 1970).

BIBLIOGRAPHY:

Black, W. A., and Gregson, R. A. "Time Perspective, Purpose in Life, Extraversion and Neuroticism in New Zealand Prisoners." *British Journal of Social and Clinical Psychology*, 1973, *12*, 50-601.
Foulks, J. D., and Webb, J. T. "Temporal Orientation of Diagnostic Groups." *Journal of Clinical Psychology*, 1970, *26*, 155-159.
Megargee, E. I., Price, A. C., Frohwirth, R., and Levine, R. "Time Orientation of Youthful Prison Inmates." *Journal of Counseling Psychology*, 1970, *17*, 8-14.
Oliver, R. "Alienation and Temporal Experience." Unpublished doctoral dissertation. City University of New York, 1973.
Roos, P. *Time Reference Inventory: Manual.* National Association for Retarded Citizens. Arlington, Texas, 1964.
Roos, P., and Albers, R. "Performance of Alcoholics and Normals on a Measure of Temporal Orientation." *Journal of Clinical Psychology*, 1965a, *21*, 34-36.
Roos, P., and Albers, R. "Performance of Retardates and Normals on a Measure of Temporal Orientation." *American Journal of Mental Deficiency*, 1965b, *69*, 835-838.

Webb, J. T., and Mayers, B. S. "Developmental Aspects of Temporal Orientation in Adolescents." *Journal of Clinical Psychology*, 1974, *30*, 504-507.

---

## TP EVENTS TEST

AUTHOR: Elise E. Lessing

AGE: 8 to 18 years

VARIABLE: Length of future time perspective

TYPE OF MEASURE: Questionnaire

SOURCE FROM WHICH MEASURE MAY BE OBTAINED: Elise E. Lessing, Institute for Juvenile Research, 1140 South Paulina, Chicago, Illinois 60612. No cost for sample, which user can duplicate.

DESCRIPTION OF MEASURE: The TP Events Test consists of a list of twenty events such as "Getting a car of my own" and "Having my first child." Subjects are instructed to: "Read through the whole list and choose eleven events which you would most like to think about or plan for now. . . . On the line beside each of the eleven events you have chosen, write the age you would be when the event would occur in your life." The items are of two types: "milestone" items, which have a culturally agreed-upon age of occurrence such as retirement at age 65, and "diffuse" items, for which there is no cultural consensus on time of occurrence and for which a short span of anticipation might be reasonable. A typical diffuse item is "Getting some new clothes." The instrument provides two scores: (1) length of future time perspective (FTP) score, consisting of the median difference between the age of the subject and the ages of the future events chosen, and (2) a foreshortening score, consisting of the median of the ages for the events. A protocol should be discarded as invalid if $S$ circles less than nine or more than thirteen events; gives ages lower than his own age for enough items that there are not nine ages the same or greater than his own age; or gives incongruous ages for more than one item, for example, getting married at less than fourteen years or buying a house at less than eighteen years of age. Scoring is based only on valid responses. Before scoring a protocol classifiable as valid, eliminate any invalid response such as age over 115, an age less than child's own age, an absurd age assignment, and so forth. The FTP score is the median age recorded for the nine to thirteen events minus the child's present age rounded to a whole number representing age at last birthday. (Since few children give anything other than a whole number for their age, this shortening score can be a decimal if, for example, the child lists ten ages and the fifth and sixth highest are consecutive numbers.)

As examples, five of the twenty items on the test are given below.

1. Getting some new clothes.
2. Getting married.

3. Studying for a test or exam.
4. Enjoying a hobby like reading, painting pictures, collecting stamps, racing model cars, etc.
5. Graduating from high school.

RELIABILITY AND VALIDITY: Reliability and validity data are not available for this revision of a previous version of the Events Test. The previous version yielded odd-even reliability coefficients (correct by the Spearman-Brown formula) of .94 for forty-four fifth graders and .89 for fifty-one eighth graders. Test-retest reliability coefficients of .59 ($N$ = 44) and .55 ($N$ = 46) were found for the same groups. The previous version yielded moderate evidence of convergent validity. In a sample of 619 fifth graders, eighth graders, and eleventh graders, a correlation of .37 ($p$ < .01) was obtained with time-perspective scores from the Incomplete Sentences Test. The revised version was administered to 168 girls aged 9 to 15 years in the summer of 1968. The pattern of subgroup means was similar for the TP Events Test and the Incomplete Sentences Test, so that again there appears to be at least indirect evidence of convergent validity.

BIBLIOGRAPHY:

Lessing, E. E. "Demographic, Developmental, and Personality Correlates of Length of Future Time Perspective (FTP)." *Journal of Personality,* 1968, *36,* 183-201.
Lessing, E. E. "Extension of Personal Future Time Perspective, Age, and Life Satisfaction of Children and Adolescents." *Developmental Psychology,* 1972, *6,* 457-468.

---

# VIVIDNESS OF VISUAL IMAGERY QUESTIONNAIRE (VVIQ)

AUTHOR: David F. Marks

AGE: 8 to 80 years

VARIABLE: Visual imagery vividness

TYPE OF MEASURE: Questionnaire

SOURCE FROM WHICH MEASURE MAY BE OBTAINED: David Marks, Department of Psychology, University of Otago, Box 56, Dunedin, New Zealand.

DESCRIPTION OF MEASURE: Although this questionnaire contains only sixteen items, it has proved a useful instrument for the assessment of an individual's visual imaging ability. The items may be rated first with the eyes open and then with the eyes closed, on a 5-point scale of vividness, so that a total score can be obtained from 32 to 160. With children younger than 12, the VVIQ is best administered to individuals. Group administration is possible with older children and adults.

As an example, given below is the second of the four images presented, a total of sixteen items. The rating scale from 1 to 5 is as follows: perfectly clear and as vivid as normal vision, 1; clear and reasonably vivid, 2; moderately clear and vivid, 3; vague and dim, 4; no image at all, you only "know" that you are thinking of the object, 5.

2. *Visualize a rising sun. Consider carefully the picture that comes before your mind's eye.*
   Item:
   5. The sun is rising above the horizon into a hazy sky.
   6. The sky clears and surrounds the sun with blueness.
   7. Clouds. A storm blows up, with flashes of lightning.
   8. A rainbow appears.

RELIABILITY AND VALIDITY: No evidence is available for children. The VVIQ has a test-retest reliability coefficient of .74 ($N$ = 68) for adults and a split-half reliability coefficient of .85 ($N$ = 150). Evidence of validity is available in a number of papers reporting significant performance differences between high and low scores on the VVIQ on a number of visual tasks. Marks (1973a) showed that subjects reporting vivid visual imagery were more accurate in their recall of pictures than subjects who reported poor visual imagery on the VVIQ. Marks (1973b) observed less eye-movement activity during the visual imagery of vivid imagers than of poor imagers. Gur and Hilgard (1975) showed that good imagers had faster reaction times in a visual-comparison task than did poor imagers.

BIBLIOGRAPHY:

Gur, R., and Hilgard, E. "Vividness of Imagery and the Discrimination of Differences Between Altered Pictures Simultaneously and Successively Presented." *British Journal of Psychology,* 1975, *66,* 341-345.
Marks, D. R. "Individual Differences in the Vividness of Visual Imagery and Their Effect on Function." In P. W. Sheehan (Ed.), *The Function and Nature of Imagery.* New York: Academic Press, 1972.
Marks, D. R. "Visual Imagery Difference in the Recall of Pictures." *British Journal of Psychology,* 1973a, *64,* 17-24.
Marks, D. R. "Visual Imagery Differences and Eye Movements in the Recall of Pictures." *Perception and Psychophysics,* 1973b, *14,* 407-412.

---

# VULNERABILITY INVENTORY

AUTHOR: Lois B. Murphy

AGE: Infancy to adult

VARIABLE: Vulnerability to problems

TYPE OF MEASURE: Checklist

SOURCE FROM WHICH MEASURE MAY BE OBTAINED: See Dittman (1968) or Murphy and Moriarty (in press).

DESCRIPTION OF MEASURE: The Vulnerability Inventory is a pilot instrument intended to stimulate workers with children to watch for individual deviations from norms—handicaps, sensitivities, poor coordination, autonomic variability, proneness to infection, gastro-intestinal disturbances, and so forth. These deviations cumulatively and interacting create difficulties within the child with which he must cope.

As an example, one segment of each of the four sections of the inventory is given below.

I. Primary tendencies (constitutional or acquired early in the first six months)
   C. Sensitivities
      1. To extremes (inadequate stimulus barrier, hyper-input proneness, hypo-input proneness)
      2. In specific zones
         a. Tactile (skin sensitivities contributing to complex, ambivalent, or anxious reactions to contact)
         b. Temperature
         c. Auditory (sensitivity to loud sounds or special qualities)
         d. Visual (unusually painful or pleasurable reactions to light, and so forth)
         e. Pain
      3. To specific qualities (for example, shiny surfaces, rough textures)
      4. To general stimuli (for example, new situations, strangeness, sudden change)
II. Emerging tendencies (reactions to birth and early infantile distress, developed during the period of patterning of perceptual-cognitive-affective functioning, and later)
   D. Fatiguability
      1. Low energy reserve
      2. Poor energy management
      3. Inability to alternate activity and rest
      4. Progression and regression
III. Secondary outcomes of total infantile experience (learned or evolved after the first six months)
   B. Persistent anxiety regarding
      1. Separation from mother
      2. Doctors, pain, body handling by strangers
      3. Other stimuli experienced in a traumatic context
IV. All of the aforementioned may result in expressions of vulnerability in one or more zones
   C. Perceptual
      1. Loss of perceptual clarity under stress (vagueness, confusion, perceptual distortion due to projection, displacement, and so forth)
      2. Narrowed range of perceptual response (withdrawal; turning away; loss of curiosity, interest, and response to environment)
      3. Loss of control of attention, capacity to select, and so forth

RELIABILITY AND VALIDITY: The original inventory was developed in an intensive study of thirty-one normal children. Significant negative correlations with coping adequacy provide a major evidence of validity. The data come from medical and psychological examinations and involve very little subjective judgment.

BIBLIOGRAPHY:

Dittman, L. (Ed.) *Early Child Care: The New Perspectives.* Chicago: Aldine, 1968.
Escalona, S., and Heider, G. *Prediction and Outcome.* New York: Basic Books, 1959.
Gardner, R., and Moriarty, A. E. *Personality Development at Preadolescence: Explorations of Structure Formation.* Seattle: University of Washington Press, 1968.
Murphy, L. B., and Moriarty, A. E. *Coping, Vulnerability, and Development.* New Haven, Connecticut: Yale University Press (in press).

---

# WHAT PEOPLE THINK

AUTHOR: Walter Emmerich

AGE: 8 to 17 years

VARIABLE: Differentiation of social norms and extremity of response choice

TYPE OF MEASURE: Questionnaire

SOURCE FROM WHICH MEASURE MAY BE OBTAINED: Walter Emmerich, Institute for Research in Human Development, Educational Testing Service, Princeton, New Jersey 08540.

DESCRIPTION OF MEASURE: This instrument is a paper-and-pencil questionnaire suitable for group administration. It consists of eighty normative statements for which the respondent chooses one of the following categories of agreement: "very often," "often," "sometimes," "never." The following four bases or facets of normative differentiation are assessed: sex of source (male/female); generation of source (parent/peer); sex of object; and generation of object. Considering all possible combinations of these four facets (2 X 2 X 2 X 2) derives sixteen normative statements which are applied to four social acts or contents ("agree with other," "help other," "seek help," "argue"). In addition, the self as source is considered in relation to the two object facets and four social contents. The comparison of difference scores on these facets tests possible bases for normative differentiation. Both main effects and interactions were analyzed as sources of variance in a factorial design.

As examples, the first six of the eighty items on the questionnaire are given below.

1. How often does your mother think you should help your father?
2. How often does your friend (a boy) think you should argue with your friend (a girl)?
3. How often do you think you should ask your friend (a boy) for help?
4. How often does your friend (a girl) think you should agree with your mother?
5. How often does your father think you should help him?
6. How often does your mother think you should argue with your friend (a girl)?

RELIABILITY AND VALIDITY: Differentiation of social contents across ages was significant, and their ordering (height of standard) had face validity. With increasing age, more children targeted in accurately on the normative meanings. Sex-role norms were strongly sex-typed during middle childhood, a pattern that decreased during later childhood and adolescence. The generation facets and their interactions entered into a number of sharp differentiations and developmental trends revealing the importance of age grading in normative development. Higher standards were attributed to parents than to peers, and this decreased somewhat with age. Results also suggested that more advanced cognitive processes represent an important ego structure facilitating sex-role development. In a separate analysis of extreme response choice, it was hypothesized that brighter children would select extreme response categories less frequently than less-bright children, and/or that the former would select these categories earlier in development than the latter. In neither sex, however, was the positive extreme ("very often") significantly influenced by cognitive level or by cognitive level by age interactions. But brighter $S$s of both sexes did select the negative extreme ("never") less often than their less-bright peers. Also, the cognitive level by linear age interaction for "never" was significant in girls, indicating more rapid development of attenuation of choice of "never" in bright than in less-bright girls.

BIBLIOGRAPHY:

Emmerich, W. "Cognitive Mediation of Developmental Trends in Extreme Response Choice." *Developmental Psychology*, 1971, *5*, 540.

Emmerich, W. *Cognitive Mediation of Developmental Trends in Extreme Response Choice.* Princeton, New Jersey: Educational Testing Service, n.d.

Emmerich, W., Goldman, K. S., and Shore, R. E. "Differentiation and Development of Social Norms." *Journal of Personality and Social Psychology*, 1971, *18*, 323-353.

---

# YOUNG CLIENTS' COUNSELING RATING SCALE

AUTHOR: Patricia Baker Mallars

AGE: 6 years and up

VARIABLE: Client reaction to counseling experience

TYPE OF MEASURE: Rating scale

SOURCE FROM WHICH MEASURE MAY BE OBTAINED: Patricia Baker Mallars, John Tyler Elementary School, 3830 Webster Avenue, Stockton, California 95204.

DESCRIPTION OF MEASURE: The Young Clients' Counseling Rating Scale is used as a means to obtain data comparing reactions of clients to the counseling experience between standard counseling (one counselor only) and team counseling (two counselors together). The twenty-five-item scale contains twenty-three statements concerning the client's feelings about the counselor(s) and two questions about his talks with the counselor(s). Each item is given a rating of "good," "fair," or "poor." An adult form of the scale (Counseling Rating Scale) is available.

As examples, the first ten of the twenty-five items on the scale are given below.

Area I: *I felt that the counselor(s)*
1. Seemed relaxed or at ease.
2. Helped me to feel relaxed or at ease.
3. Seemed really interested in me.
4. Could be trusted or depended upon.
5. Knew what he (she) was doing.
6. Was polite, used good manners.
7. Gave me enough time.
8. Seemed really interested in people.
9. Stayed on the subject.
10. Seemed patient, did not become bothered.

RELIABILITY AND VALIDITY: None reported.

BIBLIOGRAPHY:

Mallars, P. "Team and Standard Approaches to Counseling." Unpublished doctoral dissertation. University of the Pacific, Stockton, California, 1965.

# Appendix

# Journals Searched

Journals marked with asterisks were searched by sampling selected volumes. For current addresses of journals, see *Ulrich's International Periodicals Directory*, R. R. Bowker Company, 1180 Avenue of the Americas, New York, N.Y. 10036.

*Academic Therapy*
*Acta Paedopsychiatrica*
*Acta Psychologica*
*Adolescence*
*Alberta Journal of Educational Research*
*American Annals of the Deaf*
*American Educational Research Journal*
\**American Journal of Disease in Children*
*American Journal of Mental Deficiency*
\**American Journal of Occupational Therapy*
*American Journal of Orthopsychiatry*
*American Journal of Psychiatry*
*American Journal of Psychology*
*American Journal of Sociology*
*American Psychologist*
*Australian Journal of Psychology*

*Behavior Genetics*
*Behavior Research and Therapy*
*Behavior Research Methods and Instrumentation*
*Behavioral Science*
*British Journal of Educational Psychology*
*British Journal of Disorders of Communication*
*British Journal of Educational Studies*
*British Journal of Psychology*
*British Journal of Social and Clinical Psychology*
*California Journal of Educational Research*
*Canadian Journal of Behavioral Science*
*Canadian Journal of Psychology*

*Child Care Quarterly
Child Development
Child Psychiatry and Human Development
Child Study Journal
Childhood Education
Cognitive Psychology
Colorado Journal of Educational Research
Creative Behavior
Developmental Psychology
*Education
Education Canada
*Education and Training of the Mentally Retarded
Education of the Visually Handicapped
Educational and Psychological Measurement
Educational Research (British)
Elementary English
Elementary School Guidance and Counseling
Elementary School Journal
Exceptional Child Education Abstracts
Exceptional Children
Genetic Psychology Monographs
Gifted Child Quarterly
Harvard Educational Review
*High School Journal
Human Development
Indian Journal of Psychology
*Indian Journal of Social Work
International Journal of Mental Health
International Journal of Psychology
Japanese Psychological Research
Journal of Abnormal Child Psychology
Journal of Abnormal Psychology
*Journal of Aesthetic Education
Journal of Applied Behavior Analysis
*Journal of Applied Psychology
Journal of Autism and Childhood Schizophrenia
Journal of Behavior Therapy and Experimental Psychiatry
Journal of Child Psychology and Psychiatry and Allied Disciplines
Journal of Clinical Psychology
Journal of Communication Disorders
Journal of Community Psychology

Journal of Consulting and Clinical Psychology
Journal of Counseling Psychology
Journal of Creative Behavior
*Journal of Cross-Cultural Psychology
Journal of Education (Boston University)
Journal of Educational Measurement
Journal of Educational Psychology
Journal of Educational Research
*Journal of Emotional Education
*Journal of Experimental Analysis of Behavior
Journal of Experimental Child Psychology
Journal of Experimental Education
Journal of Experimental Psychology
Journal of General Psychology
Journal of Genetic Psychology
*Journal of Health and Social Behavior
*Journal of Humanistic Psychology
Journal of Individual Psychology
Journal of Learning Disabilities
Journal of Marriage and the Family
Journal of Mathematical Psychology
*Journal of Mental Deficiency Research
Journal of Negro Education
Journal of Nervous and Mental Disease
Journal of Personality
Journal of Personality and Social Psychology
Journal of Personality Assessment
Journal of Psycholinguistic Research
Journal of Psychology
Journal of Reading
Journal of Reading Behavior
Journal of Research and Development in Education (University of Georgia)
Journal of School Health
Journal of School Psychology
Journal of Secondary Education
Journal of Social Psychology
Journal of Special Education
Journal of Speech and Hearing Disorders
Journal of Speech and Hearing Research
*Journal of Teacher Education
Journal of Verbal Learning and Verbal Behavior
Language Learning
Measurement and Evaluation in Guidance

*Mental Health Digest*
*MH. (Mental Hygiene)*
*Mental Retardation*
*Merrill-Palmer Quarterly*
*\*Neuropsychologica*
*\*New Outlook for the Blind*
*Orton Society Bulletin*
*Peabody Journal of Education*
*\*Perception and Psychophysics*
*Perceptual and Motor Skills*
*Personality: An International Journal*
*Personnel and Guidance Journal*
*\*Proceedings of the American Psychological Association*
*Psychological Record*
*Psychological Reports*
*Psychological Review*
*Psychology in the Schools*
*Psychopharmacology Bulletin*

*Reading Improvement*
*Reading Research Quarterly*
*Reading Teacher*
*Reading World*
*\*Rehabilitation Literature*
*Research Quarterly*
*Review of Educational Research*
*School Review*
*Sight-Saving Review*
*Slow Learning Child*
*Society for Research in Child Development Monographs*
*Sociology of Education*
*\*Sociometry*
*\*Soviet Psychology*
*Training School Bulletin*
*Vocational Guidance Quarterly*
*Volta Review*
*\*Young Children*

# Index of Authors
# of Measures

Pages 1-674 are in Volume 1; pages 675-1284 are in Volume 2.

Pages 1-674 are in Volume 1; pages 675-1284 are in Volume 2.

# Index of Measures

## A

Aberdeen Academic Motivation Inventory, 454-455

About Me, 676

About Me and My School Work, 677-679

Academic Achievement Accountability (AAA) Scale, 652-653

Academic Readiness Scale, 32

Achievement Motivation Test for Children —*Prestatie Motivatie Test voor Kinderen* (PMT-K), 455-456

Achievement Motive Questionnaire, 457-458

Achievement-Related Affect Scale, 458-459

A–C (Performance) Test, 1, 31

Adapted Modified Role Repertory Test, 303-304

Adaptive Strategies Interview, 736

Adjective Inventory Diagnostic (AID), 399-400

Adolescent-Middlescent Attitude Scale (AMAS), 1048-1049

Adolescent Value-Orientations Profile, 1049-1050

Age Independence Scale, Elementary School Form, 1051-1052

Age Independence Scale, Form II (Preschool), 1050-1051

Age Independence Scale, Form III (Adolescence), 1053-1054

Aggression Inventory (AI), 1160-1161

Albert Einstein Scales of Sensorimotor Development: Object Permanence, 33-34

Albert Einstein Scales of Sensorimotor Development: Prehension, 34-35

Albert Einstein Scales of Sensorimotor Development: Spatial Relationships, 35-36

Allen Scale of Beliefs, 1054-1055

Alphabet Name Inventory/Printed Upper Case (ANI/PUC) and Alphabet Name Inventory/Printed Lower Case (ANI/PLC), 160

Ambidexterity Target Test, 853

Ambiguity Test, 161-162

A-M-L Behavior Rating Scale, 541-542

Analytic Scale for Measuring the Semantic Novelty of Poems, 162-163

Pages 1-674 are in Volume 1; pages 675-1284 are in Volume 2.

# Subject Index

## A

Abilities, developmental, 49

Academic achievement responsibility, 652-653, 664-666

Academic skills, 101-102

Acceptance: of child behavior, 1113-1114; of others, expressed, 687-689

Achievement: attitude toward, 1035; motivation for, 402-404, 423-424, 455-456, 457-459, 464-466, 652-653; parental reaction to, 825-827; school, 146-147; tendency toward personal, 463-464

Achievement competence, 402-404

Achievement orientation, 478-479

Acoustic production, ability to imitate, 875-876

Active-passive style, 574-576

Activity level, 412-413, 537-538

Adaptation, of infants to physical environments and persons, 1182-1183; styles of, 1207-1208

Adjustment, 551-552, 556-557, 560-561; school, 543-544, 544-545, 546, 556-557, 570-571, 572-573; behavioral, 542-543; vocational, 1244-1245

Adults, disturbed behavior toward, 1172-1173; trust of. See Trust

Affiliation, tendency toward, 466-467

Aggression, 484-485, 1186-1187; manifest, 1160-1161; versus cooperation, 1177

Aggression training, 832-833

Aggressiveness, 1175-1176

Alienation, 1022-1023, 1079-1080

Alphabet, knowledge of upper- and lowercase, 160

Ambidexterity, 853

Ambiguity: tolerance for, 534-535; types of, 161

American Alliance for Health, Physical Education, and Recreation, 20

Anger, awareness and expression of, 1161-1163

Anger-defiance, 506-507

Animism, 390-391

Anomie, 1091-1092

Pages 1-674 are in Volume 1; pages 675-1284 are in Volume 2.

1317

Anxiety, 455-456, 507-509, 585-586, 590-591, 599-600; about academic achievement, 580-581; in the blind, 586-587; aggressive, 581-583; compliant, 581-583; death, 583-584; detached, 581-583; manifest, 587-588; school, 588-589, 591-593, 595-597, 1018-1020, 1026-1027, 1045; separation, 593-595

Arithmetic, attitude toward, 969-970, 970-971, 971-972, 977-978, 994-995, 995-996, 1001-1002

Arithmetic skills, 167-168

Art design, knowledge of, 252-253

Articulation, 856-857, 861-862, 893-894, 916; and intelligibility, 857-858

Articulatory placement for consonants, ability to imitate, 875-876

Aspiration, level of, 723-725

Assaultiveness, 1177-1178

Attention, 655-656; auditory, 928-929; by teachers to retardate behaviors, 1219-1220

Auditory age, 904-905

Auditory association, 928-929

Auditory closure, 955-956

Auditory function, central, 940

Auditory memory, integrative, 926-927, 204-205

Auditory sequencing, 926-927

Auditory vigilance, 899-900

Auditory-visual rhythm perception, 897

Authoritarian attitudes, 1148-1149

Authoritarianism, 534-535, 742-743

Authority: conformity to, 573-574; hostility toward, 610-611

Authority figures, perception of, 603-604

Authors of tests, locating, 5-6

Autism, 401-402, 418-421, 445-447

Autonomic arousal, 590-591

Autonomy, 411-412

Awareness of character, 500-501

**B**

Behavior: achievement-related, 577-578; adaptive, 1194-1195; adjustment in, 542-543; aggressive-disruptive, 1166, 1205, 1206-1207; annoying, 1203-1204; antisocial, 567-568; characteristics of, 126-127; children's, causation of, 1113-1114; classroom, 554-555, 576-577, 1163-1164, desirable in, 1171-1172, noncognitive, 441-443; cri-

sis, 1253-1254; cross-sex-role, attitude toward, 817-818; delinquency-related, 1193-1194; desirable, 1203-1204; deviant, 559-560, 1203-1204; disorder in, 450-451; disruptive, 1164-1165; dramatic, improvisational, 1262-1263; in family setting, 820-822; language, 193-194; of Neonates, 103-104; normative patterns, 1153-1154; passive-aggressive, 512-513; pathological, 1221-1223; peer, perception of, 1025-1026; personal-social, 561-563; problem, 1179-1180; problems in, 116-117, 541-542; school, 70; sexual, attitudes toward, 1058-1059; sleep, parental concern about, 1273-1274; social, 574-576, 577-578, 1192-1193, level of, 1174; structured-play, 1221-1223; symptoms of, 538-539; traits of, 645-646

Beliefs, 1156-1157

Bilingualism, 184-185, 190-191, 193-194, 200-201; attitude toward, 186-1088

Biology, formal reasoning in, 304-306

Black English, 216-217

Blind. *See* Visually handicapped

Body image, 127, 605-606, 680-682, 691-692, 731-732

Body knowledge, 251, 258-260

Body- and self-image, 560-561

Brain injury, 885

Brain pathology, organic, 860-861

Brilliance, academic, attitudes toward, 1141-1143

Buoyancy versus depression, 500-501

**C**

Care, quality of, provided in residential setting, 845-846

Career knowledge, 1235-1236

Caregiver: attitudes and behavior toward, 848-849; behavior of, 739-740, 1179-1180; language of, 746-747; skills of, 793-794

Categorization, modes of, 387-388

Causality, 1254-1255

Caution, 384-385

Center for the Study of Evaluation, 19, 23

Cerebral dysfunction, 868-869, 888-889

Cheating, attitude toward, 978-979

Permanence, person, 105

Permissiveness, in socialization, 737-739

Personality, 551-552; characteristics, 406-407, 409-410, 430-431, 432; development, 417-418; dimensions of, 333-334; dynamics, 449-450; problem areas, 585-586; traits, 573-574; traits, job-related, 437-438

Personal-social skill, 98-100

Phonemic output, accuracy of, 228-229

Phonology, contrastive, 190-191

Physical activity: attitude toward, 1067-1069, 1095-1097; attraction to, 704-705

Physical anomalies, multiple and minor, 963-964

Physical condition, 567-568

Physical contact, affectionate, with parents, 834-835

Physical development, 89-90

Physical dimensions, concepts related to, 213-214

Physical education: attitude toward, 991-992, 1010; attitudes of the handicapped toward, 1130-1131

Physically handicapped, attitude toward the, 1123-1124

Piagetian measures, 33-36, 51-52, 53, 55, 58-61, 62-66, 71-72, 79-80, 94-95, 105, 120-121, 138-139, 142-143, 148-149, 151-153, 165-166, 168, 246-248, 268-269, 307-308, 317-319, 338-340, 1254-1255

Pitch location, 266

Play, parent understanding of, 829-831

Playfulness, 515-516

Poems, semantic novelty of, 162-163

Preference, for adults or children, 604-605

Pregnancy, emotional outcome of, 494-496

Prehension, 34

Prepositions: spatial, understanding of, 236; use of, 203-204

Prescriptive teaching, 43

Prevocational skills of the retarded, 274-275

Probationers, attitudes of, 1092-1093

Problems, behavior, 116-117, 541-542

Problem solving, 352-354, 366-367

Projective tests, 110-112

Prosocial behavior, 559-560, 567-568

Psychiatric diagnosis, 399-400

Psychopathology, 416-417, 560-561

Psychotherapy, attitudes toward, 1140-1141

Psychotic children, communicativeness of, 226-227

Pupil control, attitude toward, by educators, 1024-1025

## Q

Quantitative concepts, 212-213

Quantity matching, 207

Questions, causal, 323-324

## R

Racial acceptance, 1110-1111

Racial attitudes, 1094-1095, 1117-1123, 1138, 1149-1150

Racial self-identification, 1110-1111

Readiness, 42; academic, 32, 204-205; arithmetic, 165-166; concepts, 84-85; English language, 190-191; language, 84-85; memory, 84-85; number, 208; reading, 180-181; school, 106-108, 118, 119-120, 154-155; visual motor, 84-85

Reading: attitude toward, 989-990, 990-991, 994-995, 1020-1021, 1028-1029; comprehension, 205-206; critical, 332-333; difficulties, 180-181; interpretation and appreciation of, 205-206; linguistic tests of, 191-193; motivational practices in, 659-660; oral, 205-206

Reading interests, 659-660; sophistication of, 224-225

Reading skills, 300-301; perceptual, 205-206

Reasoning: class, 324-325; concrete, 363; conditional, 77-79, 143-144, 326-327; deductive, 358-359; formal, 304-306, 338-340, in literature, 349-350; inductive, 97-98; logical, 149-150; perceptual, 238-240; verbal, 68, 238-240

Reciprocity, encouragement versus discouragement of, 810-813

Reference group, peer versus adult, 636-638

Reflectivity, 346-347, 350-351

Reinforcement emission, 517-518; history, 743-745; positive, in nursery peer group, 1197-1198; preference, 471-473, 517-518, 521-523, 756

Religious attitudes, liberal-conservative, 1098-1100

Religious beliefs and attitudes, 1125-1126

Representational ability, 79-80